CW01011522

)

SACRA DOC'

Christian Theology for a Postmodern Age

www.ctrf.info

SACRA DOCTRINA

Christian Theology for a Postmodern Age

IN THE DAYS OF CAESAR

Pentecostalism and Political Theology

• •

THE CADBURY LECTURES 2009

Amos Yong

WILLIAM B. EERDMANS PUBLISHING COMPANY

GRAND RAPIDS, MICHIGAN / CAMBRIDGE, U.K.

Published 2010 by
Wm. B. Eerdmans Publishing Co.
2140 Oak Industrial Drive N.E., Grand Rapids, Michigan 49505 /
P.O. Box 163, Cambridge CB3 9PU U.K.
www.eerdmans.com

Library of Congress Cataloging-in-Publication Data

Yong, Amos.
In the days of Caesar: Pentecostalism and political theology: the
Cadbury lectures 2009 / Amos Yong.
p.   cm.
ISBN 978-0-8028-6406-2 (pbk.: alk. paper)

1. Pentecostal churches — Doctrines.
2. Political theology.   I. Title.

BX8762.Z5Y66   2010
261.7 — dc22

                                                        2010016208

To

Jamie Smith

Proverbs 18:24b

Contents

Part II
Pentecostal Intersections with Political Theology:
Enacting the Performance

Contents

Acknowledgments

The original idea behind this book came from the prodding of my good friend, James K. A. Smith, who kept asking me when I was going to deal with the uncritical nationalism, consumerism, and political quiescence in many pentecostal circles. Then, the opportunity to engage with these topics in some depth arose when, in the fall of 2007, I received the invitation to deliver the Edward Cadbury Lectures in Theology at the University of Birmingham. I resolved then to work on a pentecostal contribution to the contemporary discussions in political theology, broadly conceived. Thanks, Jamie, for pushing me on these matters. Although I am sure there will be things about which we will disagree in the following pages, it will at least give us much to discuss. In gratitude for our friendship and brotherhood in Christ and the Spirit, I dedicate this book to you.

My thanks also to Allan Anderson at the University of Birmingham, who not only suggested me as Cadbury Lecturer, but also defended the choice to the Department of Theology and Religion of inviting a pentecostal theologian to deliver these prestigious lectures. Members of the Department — including Martin Stringer, David Cheetham, Garnet Parris, Marius C. Felderhof, Sigvard von Sicard, and Werner Ustorf — were kind and hospitable during my two-week stay in March 2009. Those who went above and beyond the call of duty in their hospitality included Edmond Tang, Mark Cartledge, and Frances Young; doctoral students KunJae Yu and Wessly Lukose (and his wife, Joyce); and Raymond Pfister (who was present at each of the eight lectures). Each of these as well as many other students and attendees have contributed to this book, particularly during the engaging question-and-answer period following each lecture. I am grateful finally to Sue Bowen for working out the logistical details of my trip and stay.

Portions of this book and earlier versions of some of the chapters were previously presented in various venues and forums. Thanks to:

- Joel Halldorf and Jan-Åke Alvarsson — the former for his role in my being invited to be the Theological Faculty guest lecturer at the Forum for Advanced Studies in Arts, Languages and Theology, Uppsala University, Uppsala, Sweden, 27 March 2008, when I delivered a preliminary version of chapter 1 under the title, "The Politics of Global Pentecostalism: Serving God or Mammon?" and both for the hospitality shown to me during my stay in Uppsala
- Ogbu Kalu (unexpectedly deceased in January 2009), for the invitation as keynote lecturer for the Chicago Center for Global Ministries World Mission Institute, held at the Catholic Theological Union, Chicago, Illinois, 17-18 April 2008, where I presented "Many Tongues, Many Practices: Christian Mission Post-Christendom — From the Center to the Margins and In-Between," an earlier version of what is now parts of chapters 5 and 6 in this book
- Mark Gornik and Manuel Vasquez — the former for the invitation to lecture at the "Local and Global: The Changing Church" Conference on World Christianity at City Seminary, New York City, 8 November 2008, where I unveiled an earlier draft of chapter 7, "Theology and Global Market Fundamentalism: Pentecostal W(h)ealth, Catholic Social Teaching, and the Quest for Human Liberation," and the latter for his comments in response to my talk that spurred me to develop my thinking on the informal economy
- Paul F. Knitter and Serene Jones for their invitation to present my "Principalities, Powers, and Politics: Spiritual Warfare as Pentecostal Political Praxis" (as rough draft of chapter 4) at Union Theological Seminary, New York City, 20 November 2008.

In each case, there were also many insightful questions from members of these vastly disparate audiences that have shaped the final draft of this book.

I am also grateful to the following colleagues for their contributions to various aspects of the research for and writing and rewriting of this book:

- Birgit Meyer, for making accessible a few of her more difficult-to-obtain essays and for sharing some of her unpublished and forthcoming work with me
- Paul Eddy for his help with approaching, understanding, and engaging the complex work of N. T. Wright

- Bradford McCall, formerly a graduate assistant, for help on an earlier version of chapter 7
- John Sniegocki, for his help with section 7.2, especially my interpretation of the Catholic Social Teaching tradition
- Timothy Essenburg, for his thoughtful comments on the informal economy in 7.3.2
- Calvin L. Smith, for his careful reading and comments on a draft version of the entire manuscript
- John Johnson, for his thoughtful questions in response to a draft of the manuscript.

I also appreciate Michael Palmer, dean of the School of Divinity where I teach and work, for supporting my work and generously granting me a course release for the academic year 2008-2009, which gave me additional time to prepare for the Cadbury Lectures. Academic dean Donald Tucker also allowed me to teach a doctoral seminar on political theology (cross-listed at the master's level as a special-topics course on "Renewal and Politics") in the summer of 2009. I received invaluable feedback from my students, especially Mary Fast, Hunter Hanger, and Timothy Lim Teck Ngern. Tim has also served as my graduate assistant this past year and has helped out in numerous other ways, including preparing the indexes for the book. Patty Hughson and her interlibrary loan staff also deserve huge kudos for so efficiently handling the many requests I sent their way.

Alan Padgett was enthusiastic in accepting a draft of a proposal for publication in the Sacra Doctrina series, and was then also very helpful in comments on the first draft of the manuscript. I have long appreciated his work at the vanguard of evangelical (broadly considered) theological scholarship. Thanks also to Jon Pott, Holly Hoover, Linda Bieze, and Jenny Hoffman at Eerdmans for their respective roles in bringing this book through the publication process. I am also indebted to David Cottingham, whose careful work copyediting the volume saved me from many blunders.

Needless to say, none of the above individuals are to be blamed for the errors of fact or of judgment in these pages; these remain my sole responsibility.

Research for this book was also supported in part by a Lilly Theological Research Grant given to me during the summer of 2008 by the Association of Theological Schools. Thanks to Dr. Stephen Graham and his staff for this assistance.

I have lived with this topic for the last two years, at the expense of time with my family. My beautiful and incredibly understanding wife Alma, and my unbelievably wonderful teenagers Aizaiah, Alyssa, and Annalisa, are the household that make possible and enjoyable our life in the *polis*. A husband cannot be more blessed, nor a father be more proud, than I. As words of thanks cannot do justice, I can only marvel at the goodness of God to one so undeserving.

Chesapeake, Virginia
August 2009

Prologue

Authors often overestimate the importance of their work, and I am sure that this case is no exception. Yet perhaps I might be forgiven still for trying to defend my decision to have devoted the kind of time and effort to writing a relatively long book. For this, I will engage in a very pentecostal kind of thing: telling (briefly) my testimony.

I was born and raised as a preacher's kid to Assemblies of God ministers. When I was ten, my parents moved our family from Malaysia to Northern California. I grew up anticipating the rapture of the church, periodically worrying that I might be "left behind." At one point in 1988, after being disappointed that prophecies of Jesus' return had not come to pass,[1] I became disillusioned with some aspects of my pentecostal heritage. Yet I stayed "in," even as that began a long period — continuing to the present — of my sorting out what it meant to "be pentecostal."

One of the things I thought it meant was that being pentecostal and being political were contradictory. Thus, even long after I had begun teaching theology, I paid little attention to political matters and wasn't even aware that there was a field of political theology. But like many others, I was jolted out of my nicely divided world by the events of 11 September 2001. Of course, at that time, I still thought that there was a right way to be religiously political, and the "enemies" of the U.S. were going about it in the wrong way.

However, I began having conversations with my colleague Sam Zalanga, who was in the sociology department at Bethel where I was teaching. Sam,

---

1. I had drunk deeply from the wells of dispensationalism and, during the summer of 1988, had swallowed hook, line, and sinker, the "argument" of Edgar C. Whisenant, *The Rapture: Rosh Hash Ana, 1988, and 88 Reasons Why the Rapture Will Be in 1988* (self-published, 1988).

who was raised pentecostal in Nigeria, kept asking theological questions and I began to see that there was a political dimension to pentecostalism that I had not previously noted.[2] However, the politics of pentecostalism was not "politics as usual," even if at that time, I did not have either the theological or theoretical categories to comprehend this phenomenon, criticize it, or use it as a springboard to rethink either my theology or pentecostalism. This book is a result of my having worked through, over the last few years, issues at the intersection of pentecostalism and the political that I have long lived — for good or ill — but failed to understand.

Allow me to clarify how I understand the two major subjects of this book: *pentecostalism* and *political theology*. The former, pentecostalism, can be understood variously: biblically in terms of its relationship to what is described in the New Testament book of Acts narrative as the Day of Pentecost; sociologically in terms of its institutions and organizations; phenomenologically in terms of recognizable features, characteristics, and practices of the global movement; theologically in terms of its defining or distinctive doctrinal commitments and ideas, etc. In this book, I adopt a broad and generic definition — hence the uncapitalized "p" in pentecostalism and its derivatives — that includes any churches or movements that self-identify as pentecostal, as well as others that may not explicitly, but yet have adopted a charismatic spirituality that looks like, sounds like, and even speaks (doctrinally and theologically) like that which lays claim to that name.[3] I will, however, tend to privilege what sociologists call classical pentecostalism — churches and groups derived from the Azusa Street revival in Los Angeles during the first decade of the twentieth century — as being at least somewhat representative of the genus of pentecostalism, even if I will continually make reference to non-classical aspects of modern pentecostalism.[4] Last but not least, as we will see in the first chapter, my horizons are specifically

2. We eventually co-authored an essay together: Amos Yong and Samuel Zalanga, "What Empire, Which Multitude? Pentecostalism and Social Liberation in North America and Sub-Saharan Africa," in Bruce Ellis Benson and Peter Goodwin Heltzel, eds., *Evangelicals and Empire: Christian Alternatives to the Political Status Quo* (Grand Rapids: Brazos Press, 2008), pp. 237-51.

3. My broad definition is informed by that at work in Stanley M. Burgess and Eduard M. van der Maas, eds., *The New Dictionary of Pentecostal and Charismatic Movements*, rev. and expanded ed. (Grand Rapids: Zondervan, 2002), pp. xviii-xxi. I fill in the empirical details of my broad definition in chapter 1.

4. For a discussion of "classical pentecostalism" in global context, see Allan Anderson, *An Introduction to Pentecostalism: Global Charismatic Christianity* (Cambridge and New York: Cambridge University Press, 2004), chap. 3. All further references in this book to classical pentecostalism will denote the specifically North American versions connected to the early Azusa Street phenomenon.

global, even if most of the published material I have consulted derives from Anglo-American scholarship.

A global pentecostal perspective, as we shall see, means a more palpable political presence and activity as well. In this book, however, the political is not limited to the formal dimension of politics understood in terms of government or statecraft. To be sure, this narrower aspect of the political will be registered and discussed a great deal in what follows. But my scope is much broader, taking off from the Greek root *polis,* which refers not only to the ancient city-state but also to the ways in which social and cultural life was organized. The political thus refers in the following pages to human life in the public square, where the various dimensions of religion, culture, society, economics, and government converge and interface. In effect, then, this book is about pentecostalism and its public domains, the political understood in this expansive and comprehensive sense.

I hope to achieve three goals in this book. First, I want to correct stereotypes of pentecostalism — both the political and the theological — which follow even those who like me have grown up in the movement. Politically, whereas it has been previously assumed that pentecostalism is apolitical, I want to paint what I believe to be a truthful portrait of the political dimensions of pentecostalism. Theologically, whereas it has been assumed that pentecostalism is an experience, spirituality, or piety, I want to present an interpretation of pentecostalism that has normative implications for Christian faith in the public square. This leads, second, to my desire to provoke my fellow pentecostals to reflect theologically from out of the depths of their own pentecostalism rather than to merely adopt one or other framework for theological or political self-understanding. Finally, I hope also to show that a distinctively pentecostal form of theological reflection is not a parochial activity but has constructive potential to illuminate Christian belief and practice for the twenty-first century. In short, this is a book that I hope will be beneficial for the church ecumenical and to the broader theological academy as we think about the intersection of Christian faith and the political and public square in the present time.

Precisely because I intend to bring into discussion pentecostalism, politics, and Christian theology, the scope of this book is vast and its interconnections hitherto unexplored in detail. What follows might constitute a steep learning curve: for pentecostals who might not be accustomed to thinking politically or in terms of political theology (which itself is a rich tradition of theological discourse); for political theologians who might not know much about pentecostalism (the contemporary study of which is inter- and multi-disciplinary in nature); and for Christians who may want to know about how pentecostalism and political theology might shape Christian witness in the public square in the twenty-first century. Hence I do not apologize in advance for the massive documentation — the diversity of dialogue partners for such a project was completely unexpected when I began my research — which will enable those who want to follow up on any or all of these three intertwined trajectories to pursue various matters of interest. Yet I also think it's appropriate that a volume arguing a central thesis based on the many tongues of Pentecost would allow, even celebrate, the many voices at the interface of pentecostal studies and political theology.

Part I lays out the conceptual terrain via an overview of the politics of pentecostal Christianity (chapter 1) and the story of political theology (chapter 2), leading to the thesis (chapter 3) that the many tongues of pentecostal politics and the many types of political theologies can be brought together in a fruitful dialogue. Part II is an attempt at such a dialogue, with its details summarized in chapter 3. I return in the Epilogue to bring some preliminary closure to my personal testimony — unfinished above . . .

PART I

On Pentecostalism and Political Theology: Setting the Stage

CHAPTER 1

A Phenomenology of the Pentecostal Body Politic

Pentecostalism and the political — what does Azusa Street have to do with the state and national capitals of this world? Perhaps more than might be initially surmised. Narrowly defined, politics and the political have to do with government, whether that is at the local, national, or international level. Broadly understood, however, politics and the political are concerned with the structures, processes, and relationships constituting the *polis*, the public sphere. This broader understanding, operative in the pages to follow, leads to the fundamental topic of this book: the intersection between pentecostalism — its beliefs and practices — and the public square.

This opening chapter provides a descriptive overview of pentecostal politics. In keeping with the broader definition, the three sections that follow discuss pentecostalism and politics (properly understood), pentecostalism and its interface with economics, and pentecostalism in relationship to society. Given the pentecostal center of gravity in the global south,[1] most of the data to be presented here will derive from pentecostalism in Asia, Africa, and Latin America.

Three interrelated objectives shape the discussion in this chapter. First and foremost, we need a survey of the political, economic, and social realities of global pentecostalism to ground the theological reflections to come in this book. From this, second, our survey will reveal a diverse and pluralistic phenomenology of pentecostal political practices, and such an account will challenge mono-dimensional stereotypes of world pentecostalism. Finally, while staying at the level of phenomenology and ethnography, implicit in the

---

1. E.g., Philip Jenkins, *The Next Christendom: The Coming of Global Christianity* (New York: Oxford University Press, 2002).

subsequent pages is a range of pentecostal political theologies — these will inform the constructive and normative political theology that will be proposed in Part II of this book, both in terms of enabling the critical evaluation of existing ideas and in terms of inspiring the construction of a pentecostal political theology. Because of the expansive ground that needs to be covered, the discussion will move swiftly, although I will try to ensure that enough socio-historical cues are given so that the pentecostal politics, economics, and social presence and action presented here can be appreciated on their own terms.

1.1. The Politics of Pentecostalism

One way of telling the history of modern pentecostalism has been to identify the movement as by-and-large apolitical according to certain categories and definitions. Any similar assessment in the contemporary scene, however, can be sustained only on the narrowest of interpretations. In this section, I sketch in broad strokes pentecostal political postures, ranging from the more or less apolitical perspectives on the right to the more politically engaged approaches on the left.[2] Yet there is another option for pentecostal politics, which is neither right nor left as commonly defined; rather, this alternative pentecostal politics is discursively and rhetorically non-political, but yet structurally and practically counter-political, at least according to the political conventions of our time. The following discussion highlights these three basic postures across the pentecostal spectrum.

1.1.1. Apolitical Pentecostalism

In some ways, much of global pentecostalism remains apolitical if this notion is understood according to a number of rather strictly defined parameters. In the following, I explicate such pentecostal apoliticism along three lines.

First, pentecostalism, especially those versions influenced by the North American fundamentalist-modernist controversies in the first part of the

2. There are a few surveys of the politics of pentecostalism. The discussion by the sociologist David Martin, *Pentecostalism: The World Their Parish* (Oxford and Cambridge, MA: Blackwell, 2002), focuses as much on pentecostalism as a force for cultural change as it does on the politics of pentecostalism. Meanwhile, Paul Freston, *Evangelicals and Politics in Asia, Africa, and Latin America* (Cambridge: Cambridge University Press, 2001), as the title suggests, discusses pentecostalism only as a subset of the broader world of evangelicalism.

twentieth century, has been largely comprised of biblical literalists who have taken Jesus' sayings like "My kingdom is not of this world" (John 18:36, KJV) straightforwardly. Hence pentecostal focus has remained, in a real sense, on the coming kingdom. In many cases, this millennial emphasis has often been mediated by a dispensational interpretive framework,[3] which has in turn exacerbated pentecostal political vision in both the radical dichotomy between "secular" and "redemptive" history of dispensationalism and the dispensationalist conviction regarding the imminent destruction of the world. Within such an apocalyptic scenario, energies directed toward the political are misplaced; instead, they need to be channeled toward ministry to the souls of humankind, for "what shall it profit a man, if he shall gain the whole world, and lose his own soul?" (Mark 8:36, KJV; cf. Matt. 16:26).

Unsurprisingly, pentecostals who have been shaped by dispensationalist eschatology have emphasized missions and evangelism over political engagement. An apocalyptic mentality suggests that things are going to get worse before they get better, and they will only get better after the return of Jesus Christ, since only he can right the wrongs in the world. Thus, in response to the question, "Should pentecostals be engaged in politics?" one study reports: "One Pentecostal pastor felt that the church as an institution should not participate in political activity, but that its members who were immersed in the society could not avoid their involvement in political matters. A Pentecostal church board member said that the church could not speak from a party political platform, but that it should speak as the mouthpiece of God. It had the right to speak when there was injustice and oppression."[4] Hence on the one hand there is pessimism about political involvement: many pentecostals "remain wary of the governmental approach to solving social problems because they place little hope in institutional remedies . . . [and since] outside Jesus, there is no salvation."[5] On the other hand, there may even be a deep mistrust of governmental activities and agencies, as the growth of secular power in the "last days" may precipitate the one-world rule of the Antichrist and usher in the final conflagration. (We will return to this topic later — in 9.1.1.)

Second, pentecostal dispensational and hermeneutical literalism has of-

---

3. For an overview of what might be called "dispensationalist politics," see Helen Lee Turner and James L. Guth, "The Politics of Armageddon: Dispensationalism among Southern Baptist Ministers," in Ted G. Jelen, ed., *Religion and Political Behavior in the United States* (New York, London, and Westport, CT: Praeger, 1989), pp. 187-208.

4. Allan Anderson with Samuel Otwang, *Tumelo: The Faith of African Pentecostals in South Africa* (Pretoria: University of South Africa, 1993), p. 61.

5. Arlene M. Sánchez-Walsh, *Latino Pentecostal Identity: Evangelical Faith, Self, and Society* (New York: Columbia University Press, 2003), p. 126.

ten taken hold among the socially and culturally disenfranchised.[6] Among such pentecostal groups, socio-economic survival has been the priority, and thus there has been much less interest shown in voting, lobbying, statecraft, etc. This is in part a matter of life-and-death economics: the poor and downtrodden are often living from day to day, looking to make ends meet until the next payday, if there is one coming at all. Some of this might be related to the belief in the charismatic worldview that because sin brings about God's displeasure and ruins the nation, personal morality issues are far more important than political, structural, or economic matters. Hence economic crises need to be addressed via improvements in personal and public morality before turning attention to matters of public policy.[7] Yet others like Andrew Chesnut have also argued that the explosive growth of pentecostalism in the global south among the impoverished has been due in part to the various ways in which pentecostal spirituality and piety have enabled concrete coping with poverty.[8] Pentecostal successes, in this case, are linked neither with political platforms nor with socio-economic programs, but with the communal networks and ecclesial practices that sustain people who exist amidst challenging conditions.

In many other cases, however, being poor means being excluded from the realm of the political. Hence the lack of pentecostal interest in *Realpolitik* is related to the inaccessibility of the political. Language barriers, nonownership in the political system, and, especially among migrant populations, a lack of citizenship and political rights have all discouraged or prohib-

6. This argument, informed by data derived from various socio-historical contexts — e.g., Christian Lalive d'Epinay, *Haven of the Masses: A Study of the Pentecostal Movement in Chile*, trans. Marjorie Sandle (London: Lutterworth, 1969), and Robert Mapes Anderson, *Vision of the Disinherited: The Making of American Pentecostalism* (Oxford: Oxford University Press, 1979) — is subject to various criticisms. However, these criticisms do not overturn the fact that many pentecostals, historically and in the present, have derived from the lower classes, and it is that which is under discussion here.

7. See William Thompson, "Charismatic Politics: The Social and Political Impact of Renewal," in Stephen Hunt, Malcolm Hamilton, and Tony Walter, eds., *Charismatic Christianity: Sociological Perspectives* (London: Macmillan, and New York: St. Martin's Press, 1997), pp. 160-83, esp. p. 169; cf. Corwin Smidt, "'Praise the Lord' Politics: A Comparative Analysis of the Social Characteristics and Political Views of American Evangelical and Charismatic Christians," *Sociological Analysis* 50, no. 1 (1988): 53-72.

8. See R. Andrew Chesnut, *Born Again in Brazil: The Pentecostal Boom and the Pathogens of Poverty* (New Brunswick, NJ, and London: Rutgers University Press, 1997); cf. also Cecília Loreto Mariz, *Coping with Poverty: Pentecostals and Christian Base Communities in Brazil* (Philadelphia: Temple University Press, 1994), and, in the African scene, Ogbu U. Kalu, *Power, Poverty and Prayer: The Challenges of Poverty and Pluralism in African Christianity, 1960-1996* (1996; reprint, Trenton, NJ, and Asmara, Eritrea: Africa World Press, 2006).

ited political participation.[9] For these pentecostals, then, the domain of politics is one from which they find themselves barred, unwanted, and without means of entry. Socio-economic and political marginalization thus translates into political non-involvement.

Finally, perhaps most intriguing, is the research that has suggested how pentecostal spirituality and piety are somehow intrinsically connected to political quiescence.[10] In Guatemala, for example, longitudinal studies have correlated greater experiential intensity (e.g., more frequent tongues-speaking or manifestation of other charismatic phenomena) with lower frequencies of voting, community volunteerism, and social activism.[11] Interestingly, this applies across the charismatic spectrum, not only among pentecostals or evangelicals but also among Roman Catholic charismatic communities and mainline Protestant charismatic churches and movements as well. As Andrew Walker puts it in his study of the charismatic renewal movement, "Although, undoubtedly, hundreds of thousands of Christians had entered into new spiritual experiences, the institutional structure of the historical and mainstream churches remained unchanged. Pentecost may have changed lives, but it blew over the organizational structure leaving everything exactly as it was before."[12] So while Protestant groups are not monolithically conservative or apolitical, those who practice a more charismatic or pentecostalized form of spirituality appear to be, in general, more politically disengaged.

1.1.2. Political Pentecostalism

Yet apoliticism represents only one set of pentecostal attitudes toward the public domain. Increasingly, recent researchers are finding ways to study

9. Sánchez-Walsh, *Latino Pentecostal Identity*, p. 169.

10. Margaret M. Poloma, "Pentecostals and Politics in North and Central America," in Jeffrey K. Hadden and Anson D. Shupe, eds., *Prophetic Religions and Politics* (New York: Paragon House, 1986), pp. 329-52.

11. Timothy J. Steigenga, *The Politics of the Spirit: The Political Implications of Pentecostalized Religion in Costa Rica and Guatemala* (Lanham, MD: Lexington Books, 2001).

12. Andrew Walker, "Pentecostal Power: The 'Charismatic Renewal Movement' and the Politics of Pentecostal Experience," in Eileen Barker, ed., *Of Gods and Men: New Religious Movements in the West* (Macon, GA: Mercer University Press, 1983), pp. 89-108, quotation from p. 103. For confirmation of Walker's thesis — this time noting how in the African context some churches touched by charismatic renewal do engage in social activity but still there is little or no explicitly political engagement — see Cephas Narh Omenyo, *Pentecost Outside Pentecostalism: A Study of the Development of Charismatic Renewal in the Mainline Churches of Ghana,* Mission Series 32 (Zoetermeer, The Netherlands: Uitgeverij Boekencentrum, 2002), pp. 261-65.

more explicit forms of pentecostal engagement with the political. In this section, I briefly describe pentecostal approaches to electoral politics in Brazil, a form of pentecostal nationalism in Zambia, and a pentecostally informed politics in Nigeria.

In the nominally Roman Catholic nation of Brazil, pentecostalism has been exploding over the last generation, increasing to include perhaps up to 50 percent of the 170 million plus inhabitants.[13] Along the way, the pentecostal experience of upward social mobility has brought with it a greater degree of political engagement. This led, in March 1989, to an unprecedented meeting of 129 representatives from twenty-nine pentecostal churches from across Latin America at the Latin American Pentecostal Conference (EPLA), called to discuss issues of common social and political concerns. This was followed, in October 1991, by the formation of the Latin American Union of Evangelicals in Politics in Buenos Aires, and the Third Latin American Congress on Evangelization (CELADE III) in August 1992, which combined 1000 Protestant pastors, many from evangelical and pentecostal backgrounds.[14]

The result, at least in part, was that in the 1994 elections, thirty Protestants were elected to congress, of which nineteen were evangelicals/pentecostals (ten from the Brazil Assemblea de Dios and six from the Iglesia Universal del Reino de Dios). In 1998 and 2000, forty-nine and fifty-four evangelicals were elected to congress respectively, with two-thirds of these pentecostals, the majority from the Iglesia Universal.[15] Many of these ran on a platform that included, usually, combating corruption, supporting conservative family values (e.g., rejecting abortion),[16] defending religious liberty (especially for the purposes of evangelism), promoting material benefits for their own constituencies (fairly common among patronage-based societies), targeting the allevia-

---

13. See "Spirit and Power: A 10-Country Survey of Pentecostals" (Washington, DC: The Pew Forum on Religion and Public Life, 2006), pp. 74-75; see http://pewforum.org/newassets/surveys/pentecostal/pentecostals-08.pdf (last accessed 8 February 2009).

14. For discussion, see Brian H. Smith, *Religious Politics in Latin America: Pentecostal vs. Catholic* (Notre Dame: University of Notre Dame Press, 1998), p. 40. Note that in Latin America, "evangelical" is by and large synonymous with "pentecostal."

15. Paul Freston, *Protestant Political Parties: A Global Survey* (Aldershot, UK, and Burlington, VT: Ashgate, 2004), pp. 42-50.

16. This opposition toward "liberalism" reflects a longstanding impulse motivating pentecostal entry into politics. Thus did Lewi Pethrus, one of the leaders of pentecostalism in Sweden, found the Christian Democratic Union/Party in 1964 — to combat the secularization, communism, and relativism he felt was threatening the country. For discussion, Ivar Lundgren, "Lewi Pethrus and the Swedish Pentecostal Movement," in Paul Elbert, ed., *Essays on Apostolic Themes: Studies in Honor of Howard M. Ervin Presented to Him by Colleagues and Friends on His Sixty-Fifth Birthday* (Peabody, MA: Hendrickson, 1985), pp. 158-72, esp. pp. 167-71.

tion of poverty, and separating the institutional powers of religion and the state (not surprisingly, given the dominance of the Catholic Church in Latin America).[17] Rather than being limited to Brazil, however, such pentecostal entry into electoral politics is gaining momentum all over Latin America.[18]

The case of pentecostal nationalism in the "Christian Nation" of Zambia is a stark contrast to the pentecostal politicking in Brazil. After having a born-again experience while in prison for union activism in 1981, the charismatic (in both senses of the term) evangelical Frederick Chiluba was elected as president of the nation in 1991. Upon election, Chiluba had the State House "cleansed" of evil spirits — a rite aimed specifically at countering the legacy of his predecessor, Kenneth Kaunda, who purportedly was influenced by Eastern religions — and repented on behalf of the Zambian people from witchcraft, idolatry, and immorality. He then proclaimed: "I submit the government and the entire nation of Zambia to the lordship of Jesus Christ. I further declare that Zambia is a Christian nation that will seek to be governed by the righteous principles of the word of God. . . . Then we shall see the righteousness of God exalting Zambia."[19]

Chiluba served two terms (ten years) as president, with his second term scandalized by charges regarding corruption in his administration.[20] What is interesting, however, is the pentecostal response to the various twists and turns during Chiluba's presidency. Even while many were questioning his plans for political and economic reform, some pentecostals like televan-

17. Brenda Maribel Carranza Dávila, "Pentecostal Flames in Contemporary Brazil," in José Oscar Beozzo and Luiz Carlos Susin, eds., *Brazil: People and Church(es)*, trans. Paul Burns (London: SCM, 2002), pp. 93-101, esp. pp. 96-97. At the same time, as Brian Smith notes, "Newly elected Pentecostal politicians are not supportive of policies that favor large business or landed interests nor those of U.S. corporations; rather they favor modifying current economic policies to alleviate the sufferings of the poor" (*Religious Politics in Latin America*, p. 48).

18. E.g., Dennis A. Smith, "Coming of Age: A Reflection on Pentecostals, Politics, and Popular Religion in Guatemala," *PNEUMA: The Journal of the Society for Pentecostal Studies* 13, no. 2 (1991): 131-40; Rommie Nauta and Hans Snoek, "Pentecostal Churches and Nicaraguan Politics — An Awakening Love," *Exchange* 23, no. 1 (1994): 25-43.

19. Cited in Freston, *Evangelicals and Politics in Asia, Africa, and Latin America*, p. 84. The declaration was made initially in December 1991, but not formalized through a constitutional revision until 1995. For further discussion, see Paul Gifford, *African Christianity: Its Public Role* (Bloomington and Indianapolis: Indiana University Press, 1998), chap. 5, and Isabel Apawo Phiri, "President Frederick Chiluba and Zambia: Evangelicals and Democracy in a 'Christian Nation,'" in Terence O. Ranger, ed., *Evangelical Christianity and Democracy in Africa* (Oxford: Oxford University Press, 2008), pp. 95-129.

20. The criminal case against Chiluba continues in the Zambian court system at the time of writing; see "Zambia Seizes 'Chiluba Millions,'" *BBC World News* (9 May 2008), available at http://news.bbc.co.uk/2/hi/africa/7392911.stm (last accessed 2 September 2008).

gelist Nevers Mumba insisted the problem was not that of declaring Zambia a Christian nation, but that Chiluba's policies did not go far enough in Christianizing the country.[21] But by contrast, in response to a failed coup against Chiluba's government by opponents not willing to allow his alleged illegalities and corruption to go unchallenged, the general secretary of the Zambian Assemblies of God stated that "God cannot allow Zambia to be disturbed by selfish individuals because he is in total control of the Christian nation. . . . [T]hanks and praise should be given to God for enabling Zambian soldiers to crush the coup attempt."[22] In the end, the "Christian nation" rhetoric, the freedom to propagate evangelical faith, the Zionism guiding Zambia's international policies in defense of Israel, and the constitutional bulwarks erected against the expansion of Islam in Central Africa were sufficient to motivate a form of pentecostal nationalism amidst an otherwise questionable administration.[23]

The issue of Islamism remains acute in sub-Saharan Africa, and nowhere more so than in the West African nation of Nigeria.[24] In a country that is about half Christian and half Muslim, Christian-Muslim tensions have intensified, especially during the economic crisis in the early 1980s, and since the public became aware in 1986 that Nigeria's status had been upgraded from observer to full membership with the Organization of the Islamic Conference, a coalition limited to sovereign Muslim states. It is fair to say that in the Nigerian context, pentecostal politics is motivated primarily in response to the fear of Islamization, and many pentecostals have been engaged with the political process as mobilized by the Christian Association of Nigeria. There

21. Thus Mumba himself founded the National Christian Coalition in 1997 precisely in order to complete this task, and then later ran for (but lost) the presidency. Although he was then appointed as vice-president (from 2003 to 2004), many pentecostals questioned Mumba's agenda: "Some were opposed out of a basically apolitical stance, while others disliked his use of the Christian label. Still others were disappointed because . . . Mumba used to say that his calling was to be a prophet and this was higher than being president; why on earth was he now deigning to run for the lesser office?" (quoted in Freston, *Evangelicals and Politics in Asia, Africa, and Latin America*, p. 89).

22. From *Zambia Today*, 28 October 1997, cited in R. Drew Smith, "Missionaries, Church Movements, and the Shifting Religious Significance of the State in Zambia," *Journal of Church and State* 41 (1999): 525-50, quotation from pp. 539-40.

23. Paul Gifford, "The Complex Provenance of Some Elements of African Pentecostal Theology," in André Corten and Ruth Marshall-Fratani, eds., *Between Babel and Pentecost: Transnational Pentecostalism in Africa and Latin America* (Bloomington and Indianapolis: Indiana University Press, 2001), pp. 62-79.

24. I have elsewhere discussed the Christian-Muslim confrontation in Nigeria; for the details, including extensive documentation, see Yong, *Hospitality and the Other: Pentecost, Christian Practices, and the Neighbor* (Maryknoll, NY: Orbis, 2008), pp. 15-29.

is an increasing recognition that political engagement by pentecostals is not a waste of time but is imperative given the volatile situation.[25]

Yet pentecostal politics in Nigeria retains a distinctively pentecostal flavor and discourse. Two interrelated aspects of this pentecostal distinctiveness deserve mention. On the one hand, there is the demonization of Islam and a characterization of the political as a spiritual realm contested by the God of Jesus Christ and the Allah of Mohammed.[26] On the other hand, there is a parallel strategy of "winning Nigeria for Jesus," which includes the conversion of unbelievers (i.e., Muslims) and the replacement of one theocracy (symbolized by the Muslim Sharia law) with another (the biblical law of both Old and New Testaments). So while pentecostals are mobilizing votes for fellow Christian brothers and taking palpable steps to address the concrete political issues in Nigeria, they are also engaged in spiritual activities of "warfare prayer" to overthrow the principalities and powers "behind" the nation's political structures, and they have enacted practical strategies of mission and evangelism to claim Nigeria for Christ. Such rhetoric and practices "[place] Nigerian Pentecostalism at the heart of the global battle against Satan being fought by all Pentecostals throughout the world."[27]

1.1.3. Pentecostalism as an Alternative Civitas *and* Polis

At this point I wish to complicate the apolitical-political characterization of pentecostalism by calling attention to some of the ways in which pentecostals are indirectly political, but nonetheless political for all that. Hence I will briefly describe what I call the "prophetic politics" and "politics of youth" developing in some pentecostal circles. We will see how what may be considered pentecostal apolitical rhetoric actually serves as a prophetic critique of the existing political order, and also get a sense for how pentecostal ecclesial practices function performatively to engage the domain of the political.

---

25. Samuel Ekpa (of the Foursquare Gospel Church), "Politics and Diplomacy: The Role of Christians," in Rev. O. A. Olukolade, compiler, *Arise and Build: The Role of Christians in Nation-Building* (Lagos: Pentecostal Assembly Publishers, 1988), pp. 17-26.

26. See Ogbu Kalu, *African Pentecostalism: An Introduction* (Oxford: Oxford University Press, 2008), esp. chap. 12.

27. Ruth Marshall-Fratani, "Mediating the Global and Local in Nigerian Pentecostalism," in Corten and Marshall-Fratani, eds., *Between Babel and Pentecost*, pp. 80-105, quotation from p. 101; see also Ruth Marshall, "'God Is Not a Democrat': Pentecostalism and Democratisation in Nigeria," in Paul Gifford, ed., *The Christian Churches and the Democratisation of Africa*, Studies of Religion in Africa 12 (Leiden: E. J. Brill, 1995), pp. 239-60, esp. p. 258.

What is meant by the notion of "prophetic politics"? There are at least three levels of response to this question. First is the fairly literal understanding of how pentecostal prophetic discourse engages the public sphere. One example of this is provided by Mathews Ojo, who reports that after a mass of local and national prayer meetings held in anticipation of the 1999 elections in Nigeria, the ascendancy of the self-confessed born-again but yet controversial figure Olusegun Obasanjo to the presidency brought forth a prophecy by Reverend Tunde Bakare, the founding pastor of an independent charismatic church in Lagos, Latter Rain Assembly, that "Obasanjo is Agag, he is the ram kept for slaughter, he is not our messiah . . . ," and that his fall, as well as that of Nigeria's, would be inevitable as a result of God's judgment.[28] Herein is a prophetic utterance that functioned politically and mobilized Obasanjo supporters for an all-night prayer vigil before his inauguration.[29]

At a second level, prophetic politics refers to the antithetical political stances often characteristic of pentecostalism's public pronouncements. We have already seen that in regions with Muslim presences like Nigeria pentecostalism wields an anti-Islamic rhetoric, and that in regions with Roman Catholic majorities like across Latin America pentecostalism projects an anti-Catholic discourse. Besides anti-Islamism and anti-Catholicism, however, pentecostalism has also exhibited an outspoken anti-communist agenda, especially in areas and regions of the world where pentecostals have been mobilized to resist the communist threat.[30] My labeling of such antithetical political postures as "prophetic" is more an attempt to describe how pentecostal rhetoric functions in the public square in opposition to the perceived evils of the world than an endorsement of such politically charged language as normative for pentecostals, much less Christians. My point is to emphasize the boldness that sometimes characterizes pentecostal political discourse, even if we may disagree with such pronouncements.

28. Cited in Matthews A. Ojo, *The End-Time Army: Charismatic Movements in Modern Nigeria* (Trenton, NJ, and Asmara, Eritrea: Africa World Press, 2006), p. 184. Agag is a reference to the Amalekite king whose compromises corrupted Israel's allegiance to God (1 Sam. 15:7-33).

29. The jury is still out on the extent to which Rev. Bakare's prophecy is proven true. As of the time of writing, Obasanjo has served his maximum of two terms and is therefore no longer in office, but he remains under investigation for illegal use of public funds; see "Nigerian Deal Wasted Billions," *BBC World News*, 14 March 2008, available at http://news.bbc.co.uk/2/hi/africa/7296466.stm (last accessed 2 September 2008).

30. E.g., in parts of Central America like Nicaragua during the Sandinista-Contra war. See David Martin, *Tongues of Fire: The Explosion of Protestantism in Latin America* (1990; reprint, Oxford and Cambridge, MA: Blackwell, 1993), chap. 12, esp. p. 236; cf. Calvin L. Smith, "Revolutionaries and Revivalists: Pentecostal Eschatology, Politics, and the Nicaraguan Revolution," *PNEUMA: The Journal of the Society for Pentecostal Studies* 30, no. 1 (2008): 55-82.

At a third level, however, I suggest that the prophetic politics of pentecostalism is manifest in the kinds of counter-cultural and counter-conventional communities shaped by pentecostal spirituality and piety. For example, in his ethnographic study of pentecostalism in Argentina, Daniel Míguez shows how pentecostal churches provide companionship and solidarity in the form of "family" or "sisterhood" that is an alternative to existing neighborhood patronage networks and clientelism. Within this ecclesially constructive public sphere, pentecostal congregations allow "independent neighbourhood inhabitants to bypass the clientele networks that political parties establish, and [provide] free space to local organizations."[31] The result is that pentecostal communities function as alternative "cities" that either intentionally ignore the broader political realities or simply set out to provide forms of socio-political and economic solidarity for people who otherwise find themselves on the margins of the *polis* conventionally defined.

Such prophetic politics is also manifest among the demographically youthful pentecostalism in Malawi. The brief history of Malawi since it achieved independence from British rule in 1964 has featured both the revitalization of indigenous African traditions (resisting the colonial rule), the emergence of African independent and spirit-type churches (contesting the dominance of missionary Christianity in the country), and a gradual movement to transform its political structure from being a single-party state to a multiparty and more democratic form of government. In the meantime, the last three decades have also gradually seen the development of pentecostalism, in part growing out of the independent church phenomena, in part sparked by the return of Malawian migrant laborers who brought their pentecostal experiences back with them from surrounding regions, and in part due to forces of globalization and more recent pentecostal missionary efforts.[32]

What is interesting about Malawian neo-pentecostalism is not the fact that it is numerically dominated by young people and women (which is often the case in the increasingly pentecostal global south), but how these demographic dynamics have impacted the Malawian political order. The key here is to recognize that young pentecostal preachers have challenged "business as usual" assumptions operative in the Malawian gerontocratic context.[33] In

31. Daniel Míguez, *Spiritual Bonfires in Argentina: Confronting Current Theories with an Ethnographic Account of Pentecostal Growth in a Buenos Aires Suburb* (Amsterdam: CEDLA, 1998), p. 135.

32. Matthew Schoffeleers, *Pentecostalism and Neo-Traditionalism: The Religious Polarization of a Rural District in Southern Malawi* (Amsterdam: Free University Press, 1985).

33. Here I rely on Rijk van Dijk, "Fundamentalism and Its Moral Geography in Malawi: The Representation of the Diasporic and the Diabolical," *Critique of Anthropology* 15, no. 2

contrast to the leadership of elders prominent among rural tribes and urban politics, African traditional religions, and even many African independent churches, neo-pentecostalism has empowered the youth — some females but especially males — to speak into and act within the public sphere and gain a hearing and following. If political power has been traditionally understood as connected with the ancestral spirits and if the elders have often resorted — both allegedly and in fact — to witchcraft and other rituals designed to curry supernatural forces for political ends, pentecostal preachers have not only expressed skepticism about such beliefs and practices and subjected such traditions to public mockery but also blamed the practices of the elders for existing socio-economic problems. Such ridicule has had a serious side precisely in pentecostalism's explicit denunciation of witchcraft and its aims, and in the youthful leadership's performances of "anti-witchcraft" public acts whereby they have attempted to name, resist, and cleanse their communities of these evil or harmful influences. If the elders are thought to be adepts at dealing with the nocturnal or dark side of the world, pentecostal youth preachers have challenged this gerontocratic "rule" both indirectly through their laughter/skepticism and directly in their preaching, spiritual warfare prayer, and rites of exorcism. In these very palpable ways, pentecostalism has forged an alternative *civitas* in the midst of an existing political order.

Clearly, young Malawian pentecostal preachers are not political in any conventional sense. However, their actions are not simply apolitical or non-political, but are also an indirect yet prophetic challenge to the political status quo. Interestingly, when viewed in light of the preceding discussion as a whole, such a stance can be said to be apolitical in some respects, political in others, and suggestive for an alternative politics as well. Much more can be said about pentecostalism and politics, but the preceding provides a number of cues for thinking about the distinctive contributions to political theology from a pentecostal perspective.

(1995): 171-91; "Pentecostalism, Gerontocratic Rule and Democratization in Malawi: The Changing Position of the Young in Political Culture," in Jeff Haynes, ed., *Religion, Globalization and Political Culture in the Third World* (London: Macmillan, and New York: St. Martin's Press, 1999), pp. 164-88; and "Witchcraft and Scepticism by Proxy: Pentecostalism and Laughter in Urban Malawi," in Henrietta L. Moore and Todd Sanders, eds., *Magical Interpretations, Material Realities: Modernity, Witchcraft and the Occult in Postcolonial Africa* (London and New York: Routledge, 2001), pp. 97-117. These essays are expansions and elaborations of van Dijk's doctoral thesis, *Young Malawian Puritans: Young Born-again Preachers in a Present-day African Urban Environment* (Utrecht University, 1992).

1.2. The Economics of Pentecostalism

We have already had occasion to mention the origins of much of pentecostalism around the world in the lower classes as well as to observe the interconnections between politics, properly considered, and economics. In this section we will examine more specifically the interface of pentecostalism and economics and look more deeply into the dynamics of pentecostal upward social mobility.[34] One of the features of the latter is further illuminated when we examine the phenomenon of the prosperity gospel. Our discussion of this issue will raise questions about the role of pentecostalism in the global market and as a vendor of neoliberal capitalist values. We will conclude this discussion, however, by attending more intentionally to how pentecostalism functions as an alternative *economicus* amidst the other socio-economic options of this world.

1.2.1. Pentecostalism and Prosperity

Later on in this book we will revisit the origins of the prosperity gospel in pentecostalism. In the following, however, our goal is to survey the global face of what might be called "prosperity pentecostalism," and to do so we will look at the unfolding of this phenomenon in Africa, Asia, and Latin America. What will become clear is that prosperity is a central feature of the globalization of pentecostalism, and that the prosperity message is traveling in multiple directions — from the "north" to the "south," and back again.

To begin I want to look at prosperity pentecostalism in Zimbabwe. David Maxwell's account of the Zimbabwe Assemblies of God Africa (ZAOGA) is suggestive for understanding the transnational dynamics of the prosperity gospel.[35] The founder of ZAOGA, Ezekiel Guti, himself came from fairly humble beginnings. Early in his public ministry (in the late 1950s), he established the Ezekiel Guti Evangelistic Association (the forerunner to ZAOGA), which gained increasing respectability over the next decade. In 1971, Guti

---

34. Our discussion needs to proceed circumspectly as there simply is not much hard data analyzing the relationship between pentecostalism and economics. There is a great need for more empirical research on this topic. See Robert D. Woodberry, "Pentecostalism and Economic Development," in Jonathan B. Imber, ed., *Markets, Morals and Religion* (New Brunswick, NJ, and London: Transaction, 2008), pp. 157-77.

35. David Maxwell, *African Gifts of the Spirit: Pentecostalism and the Rise of a Zimbabwean Transnational Religious Movement* (Athens: Ohio University Press, Harare: Weaver Press, and London: James Currey, 2007).

traveled to the United States, eventually enrolling in the Christ for the Nations Institute (CFNI) in Dallas, Texas, where he completed a diploma in "Charismatic Oriented Biblical Studies." Guti returned to Zimbabwe, however, with much more than the "degree." Rather, his travel to the U.S. earned him an enormous amount of not only ecclesial but also social and political capital, so that the wheels transforming ZAOGA into a respectable bourgeois movement were set in motion. Equally important were the connections he made, the links he secured, and the networks he entered into, many of which were central to the gospel of prosperity in the U.S. during that time.

Guti worked hard to ensure that his American contacts invested their "missions" moneys into his ministry "back home," and over time grew the church numerically and in terms of visibility. The result was that by the 1980s and 1990s ZAOGA had expanded, professionalized, and even become a major player in local and national Zimbabwean politics. Although arguably driven by pragmatic goals, Guti shrewdly orchestrated the church's increasing role in the public sphere, to the point of even lending legitimacy to Robert Mugabe's re-election campaign for the national presidency in 1996. ZAOGA's success, however, was undoubtedly first and foremost established on its exemplifying the power of the prosperity gospel. Upward social mobility, a growing middle-class membership, and Guti's affluent lifestyle were convincing indicators that association with the church brought with it not only eternal salvation but also material blessings. While funding came from the West for specific missional and evangelistic ventures, Guti capitalized on such proceeds by using them to motivate local church fundraising efforts — e.g., as manifest in the annual "penny capitalism" projects and the periodic resisting the "spirit of poverty" initiatives — among his parishioners. More strategically, Guti also developed connections with African American churches and organizations, linking the rhetoric of these groups with the pan-Africanist ideology prevalent in postcolonial Africa, and from this articulated his own theology of black power, black pride, and black prosperity for the southern African context.[36] In short, Guti the pastor and teacher morphed over the decades into Guti the "apostle, prophet, culture-broker, and community leader,"[37] the "man of God" through whom the people would experience the material blessings promised by God.

36. For an overview of these various developments, see Ogbu U. Kalu, "Black Joseph: Early African American Charismatic and Pentecostal Linkages and Their Impact on Africa," in Amos Yong and Estrelda Y. Alexander, eds., *Afropentecostalism: The Changing Discourses of Black Pentecostal and Charismatic Christianity* (New York: New York University Press, forthcoming).

37. Maxwell, *African Gifts of the Spirit*, p. 218; cf. David Maxwell, "'Catch the Cockerel before Dawn': Pentecostalism and Politics in Post-Colonial Zimbabwe," *Africa* 70, no. 2 (2000): 249 77.

The massive downturn of the Zimbabwean economy in the last decade has effectively undermined ZAOGA's focus on prosperity. Elsewhere in Africa, however, the prosperity gospel is alive and well, involving not only belief in material blessings but also deliverance from evil spirits, healing of the body, and expectations of social uplift as a whole.[38] Prosperity pentecostalism in Africa is thus holistic in its application.

Rather than staying on African soil, however, I want to briefly look at the El Shaddai movement in the Philippines.[39] El Shaddai not only represents prosperity pentecostalism in Asia, but also reveals a specifically Roman Catholic charismatic manifestation of that message. Founded by Mariono Velarde — known affectionately to his followers as Brother Mike — El Shaddai features what might be called "prosperity accents" on traditional Catholic beliefs and practices. Thus orthodox Catholic sacramentality is now understood in materialistic terms (material blessings are the signs of divine presence in the lives of the faithful); the traditional doctrine of indulgences has been reinterpreted in terms of the paying one's tithe and planting monetary "seeds" of faith in the form of gifts to the church which are expected to bring exponentially multiplied returns; and prayers to or through the saints for blessings have been redirected toward the three divine persons. Otherwise, Velarde's prosperity message goes out much like those of other purveyors of that gospel: through radio and television channels, a website (through which collections are also made), large crusades, and other services offered by the church. Noteworthy is the successful growth (and "marketing") of the movement in a Filipino context in which up to 80 percent of the members (those who have responded to El Shaddai's message) live below the nation's poverty line.[40]

Before turning to an analysis of prosperity pentecostalism as a force in the global market economy, I want to look quickly at what might be called "reverse flow prosperity," specifically as illuminated by the aforementioned Iglesia Universal del Reino de Dios (IURD, or Universal Church of the Kingdom of God) based in Brazil. While there is an emphasis on social action alongside political engagement (as we have already seen), these elements are more preva-

38. E.g., Rosalind I. J. Hackett, "The Gospel of Prosperity in West Africa," in Richard H. Roberts, ed., *Religion and the Transformations of Capitalism: Comparative Approaches* (London and New York: Routledge, 1995), pp. 199-214; George O. Folarin, "Contemporary State of the Prosperity Gospel in Nigeria," *Asia Journal of Theology* 21, no. 1 (2007): 69-95; and Joe Maxwell and Isaac Phiri, "Gospel Riches: Africa's Rapid Embrace of Prosperity Pentecostalism Provokes Concern — and Hope," *Christianity Today* 51, no. 7 (2007): 22-29.

39. Katharine L. Wiegele, *Investing in Miracles: El Shaddai and the Transformation of Popular Catholicism in the Philippines* (Honolulu: University of Hawaii Press, 2005).

40. Wiegele, *Investing in Miracles*, p. 81.

lent in Brazil than elsewhere, and even there, they serve the wider "ministry" of the church's economic vision. Adopting an entrepreneurial mentality, using up-to-date media, and deploying sophisticated forms of marketing techniques, the church has made the prosperity message central to its mission and evangelistic agenda.[41] Hence it has become a transnational organization (even business!) with churches (offices) set up in North America, Europe, and Africa, and even in parts of Asia. In these various domains, the IURD has very intentionally contextualized its Brazilian version of the prosperity gospel so as to emphasize healing in one location (across Latin America or in Asia), exorcism in another (e.g., in Africa), and internal or mental spirituality and strength in a third place (e.g., in Europe or North America). Whereas the global south had once been the "target" of missionaries from the north, there is now a reversal of mission movements and IURD missionaries are leading the way in a re-evangelization of the secularized north.

What is constant in the IURD agenda, however, is the theme of prosperity. The church is said to be "an enormous money machine."[42] To those in the lower classes the focus is on economic survival, while to those in the middle and upper classes the emphasis is on economic success. For all, the key is tithing and giving to the church. Yet the call to give is made within a broader framework emphasizing the giver's spiritual relations with God. Thus, congregations are led "to believe not that a miracle will occur in their pockets, but rather that the element of reciprocity in the giving relationship will change their lives"; hence, "in the discourse of the faithful, the 'gift' can mean personal empowerment and the capacity . . . to grow. . . . By giving she is entering into a set of obligations, a community of *dizimistas,* of the 'elect', symbolized by habits of dress and an aura of separateness and partaking of the *santa ceia,* who by committing themselves to the relationship, hope to create new opportunities in their lives."[43] In short, IURD has adopted a theological

41. See Ari Pedro Oro and Pablo Séman, "Brazilian Pentecostalism Crosses National Borders," and Paul Freston, "The Transnationalisation of Brazilian Pentecostalism," both in Corten and Marshall-Fratani, eds., *Between Babel and Pentecost,* pp. 181-95 and 196-215, respectively; cf. Manuel Silva, "A Brazilian Church Comes to New York," *PNEUMA: The Journal of the Society for Pentecostal Studies* 13, no. 2 (1991): 161-65.

42. Berge Furre, "Crossing Boundaries: The 'Universal Church' and the Spirit of Globalization," in Sturla J. Stålsett, ed., *Spirits of Globalization: The Growth of Pentecostalism and Experiential Spiritualities in a Global Age* (London: SCM, 2006), pp. 39-51, quote from p. 46.

43. David Lehmann, *Struggle for the Spirit: Religious Transformation and Popular Culture in Brazil and Latin America* (Cambridge, UK: Polity Press, and Cambridge, MA: Blackwell, 1996), pp. 205 and 206-7.

Thus, "Contrary to the 'promises' made by the Catholics, when the believer *pays* for what he or she received, the Pentecostal offering is an anticipation of God's response"; but more than

justification for its prosperity practices and succeeded in inserting its adherents into the global economy of migration.

1.2.2. Prosperity Pentecostalism, the Global Market, and the Neoliberal Economy

In this section, I discuss the suggestion, made by some observers, that pentecostalism not only enables its members to participate in the global market but is also ideologically compatible if not correlative with the fundamental axioms of the neoliberal capitalism that dominates the world economic system. There are two sides to this claim: the fact of accommodation to the market and the economic structures within which such accommodations are negotiated and accomplished. I discuss each in turn.

First, prosperity pentecostalism has promoted what might be called, from a phenomenological rather than theological perspective, a "sanctified consumerism" and a "holy materialism." Whereas the onset of classical pentecostal missions to the global south brought warnings against greed and consumption, the missionaries also discouraged local production and encouraged the embrace of Western dress, culture, and ideas. Hence this provided for a smooth transition in the last few decades when southern pentecostals embraced not just prosperity teachings from the West but also the global market economy (rather than the local village or peasant economies) and its products. The big difference was that whereas the asceticism of earlier missionaries put the focus on lifestyle simplicity, the hedonism of contemporary market liberalism emphasizes consumption instead.[44] Thus successful and victorious Christian living is now measured by Western economic standards: luxury clothes; fancy cars; household items "made in America" (or elsewhere in the world); Christian trinkets (e.g., miniature mangers, crosses, mustard-seed jewelry); books, cassettes (formerly), videos, CDs, and DVDs produced

---

this, "The believers are not necessarily 'buying' something (the logic of the marketplace), but 'giving,' participating in a cause. According to their reasoning, this changes everything. . . . The sacred values have priority. The main thing 'is that giving, instead of buying, is a gesture of "waste," a "luxury," . . . imagining that one is consuming.' And this act of generosity creates in the one that gives a style of life superior to the unfaithful; it gives them an image of moral greatness." See Richard Shaull and Waldo Cesar, *Pentecostalism and the Future of the Christian Churches: Promises, Limitations, Challenges* (Grand Rapids and Cambridge, UK: Eerdmans, 2000), p. 30, italics original.

44. Birgit Meyer, "Commodities and the Power of Prayer: Pentecostalist Attitudes towards Consumption in Ghana," *Development and Change* 29 (1998): 751-76.

by prosperity ministries from around the world; the latest video camera equipment and public announcement systems in the churches; professionalized worship services including song genres imported from the West, etc. The result, however, is that "Rather than merely enabling people to buy commodities, Christianity itself was produced through consumption."[45]

The existential question becomes: How one can accumulate and maintain one's level of consumption even when there is an economic downturn? On the one hand, consume we must, so protecting one's consumption practices is a high priority, and this is done through spiritual disciplines such as prayer — e.g., dedicating homes and automobiles, and purifying other commodities to make them safe for Christian use. On the other hand, since most pentecostals do not understand how the "invisible hand" of the market economy works (nor do many economists, for that matter), the goods and commodities desired are either inaccessible or mysteriously beyond local control. Consumption now becomes problematic in itself, not only fraught with spiritual dangers the devil uses to entrap believers, but also embedded within an unstable economy that leaves the faithful always on the brink of financial disaster. Pentecostalism provides adherents with the spiritual tools to fend off the evil one and access their God-given promises of prosperity. In fact, "Economic downturns . . . point to the urgency of evangelism for the sake of the nation and demand disciplined obedience, prayer, and evangelism on the part of the individual believer."[46] Thus, prosperity pentecostalism "claims to connect people with a global community of 'born again' Christians whose form of worship follows more or less the same pattern . . . and to offer true revelations about the state of the world. Local circumstances are understood in light of this knowledge. Pentecostalist churches thus clearly offer people a scope of identification far beyond local culture" and its "adherents can claim that a pentecostal religion is needed in order to profit from, rather than fall victim to, globalization."[47]

Yet while pentecostals emphasize the spiritual dimensions of prosperity within the global economy, it is also arguable that the dominant features of market neoliberalism are conducive to pentecostal sensibilities. The neoliberal framework features, especially in the global south, a diminished public sector, private enterprise, professional service provision, street vendors, domestic work, and the increase of export-production. Financial instability is

45. Meyer, "Commodities and the Power of Prayer," p. 757.

46. Isabelle V. Barker, "Charismatic Economies: Pentecostalism, Economic Restructuring, and Social Reproduction," *New Political Science* 29, no. 4 (2007): 407-27, quote from p. 421.

47. Meyer, "Commodities and the Power of Prayer," pp. 773-74.

almost normative as the "invisible" hand of the market results in the fluctuation and devaluation of currencies, rapid cycles of labor sector expansion and contraction in various areas, urbanization and industrialization, nuclear family–related transitions and labor migration including a larger number of women and youth in low-skilled manufacturing jobs, unemployment and poverty during recession, and greater personal insecurity for those on the edge of the market economy. Further, the globalization of markets brings in foreign investment but subjects local supply and demand to global factors. The common denominators are "minimal state regulation and increased vulnerability to bankruptcy, chronic poverty, or both. . . . In disembedding the market from society and disregarding social impacts, liberal economic policy-makers set in motion forces of dislocation — leading to the double movement of society's quest for self-protection from the volatility of the self-regulated global economy and the need to create new modes of governance by which to re-embed economic activities into social life."[48]

In this global context, the argument is that pentecostalism has become the religion of choice in part because it promotes values that enable transition into and survival within the market economy. I will explicate this claim at two levels: that of the logic of the market and that of the structures of the market.

First, the logic of the global market economy presumes pluralism, choice, and competition. Each of these registers favors pentecostal religiosity, particularly in light of its aggressive approach to mission and evangelism.[49] Further, these features of the global economy are supported by religious options that inculcate some kind of work ethic. In the case of Latin America, pentecostalism contests the former Roman Catholic hegemony by bringing with it a revised Protestant ethic that emphasizes a frugal lifestyle, disciplined habits of consumption, and honesty in relationship to one's employers.[50] Last but not least along these lines, competition fosters creativity and entrepreneurship. Pentecostalism as an egalitarian movement nurtures individual initiative, builds self-confidence, and thereby encourages risk-taking in business ventures — so long as that is discerned to be in line with the will of God (in fact, when pentecostal entrepreneurs opt for self-employment, they have a

48. Barker, "Charismatic Economies," p. 412. See also Peter L. Berger, "'You Can Do It!' Two Cheers for the Prosperity Gospel," *Books and Culture* 14, no. 5 (2008), available online at http://www.ctlibrary.com/bc/2008/sepoct/10.14.html (last accessed 24 January 2009).

49. This thesis is argued at length in R. Andrew Chesnut, *Competitive Spirits: Latin America's New Religious Economy* (Oxford: Oxford University Press, 2003).

50. Smith, *Religious Politics in Latin America,* chap. 2; cf. Henri Gooren, *Rich among the Poor: Church, Firm, and Household among Small-Scale Entrepreneurs in Guatemala City* (Amsterdam: Thela Thesis, 1999).

greater flexibility in their work schedules to incorporate regular if not added church-attendance and participation into their daily routines) — and empowers boldness in the sphere of public relations. As David Martin notes,

> The new urbanites have to make their way in the deregulated flexible labor markets of the post-industrial, service-based economy. The new Protestants are not typically part of a manufacturing "proletariat" but workers in the service sector, frequently in the informal economy, within a high-tech, information-based global capitalism. In such a world the ability to be punctual, regimented, and obedient, so crucial in the (Fordist) factory system, is less relevant than the capacity to be self-motivating, to control the work process without direct supervision, to be reflective and self-monitoring, and to manage interpersonal encounters skillfully. . . . This new labor market calls not for deference and hierarchy but for independence, initiative, high-octane energy, a willingness to ride the time and work rhythms of the 24-hour economy and above all, a refusal to accept failure.[51]

The result is seen in, among other economic manifestations, the wide range of pentecostal commercialism, its hybridity (contextual borrowings — some say "syncretisms") representing and enabling competition in the global, public, and postmodern sphere, and its creative networking through various sophisticated media forms.[52]

Second, the structures of neoliberal capitalism emphasize decentralization, privatization, and local enterprise, albeit conducted on the terms established by global markets. Ideologically, these presumptions correlate with pentecostal sensibilities. Not coincidentally, the expansion of prosperity pentecostalism in the global south in the last few decades has been most prominent in nations and regions of the world that have been seeking points of entry into the global market. The case of Ghana has been most extensively covered from an economic perspective,[53] although many other southern nations are grappling with similar issues. Structural adjustment programs requiring the government to turn over services to the private sector have left

51. Martin, *Pentecostalism,* p. 79.

52. Jean-Pierre Bastian, "Pentecostalism, Market Logic and Religious Transnationalisation in Costa Rica," in Corten and Marshall-Fratani, eds., *Between Babel and Pentecost,* pp. 161-80.

53. Paul Gifford, *Ghana's New Christianity: Pentecostalism in a Globalizing African Economy* (Bloomington and Indianapolis: Indiana University Press, 2004); cf. Akosua K. Darkwah, "Aid or Hindrance? Faith Gospel Theology and Ghana's Incorporation into the Global Economy," *Ghana Studies* 4 (2001): 7-29.

many struggling to survive against the forces of globalization. At the same time, this has opened up economic space for creative projects, encouraged local initiatives, and invited new religious and theological motivations to contribute to the transition. Ghanaian prosperity preachers have emerged to fill in the gaps left by indigenous explanations tied in with witchcraft rituals and other forms of premodern spirituality and piety even while, through providing ecclesial training on the management of finances, they have motivated their congregants to be more economically responsible and entrepreneurial.[54]

The suggestion is that pentecostalism may fit hand-in-glove with the neoliberal system within which social welfare and production is deregulated to a large extent. It empowers the exercise of individual initiative in an era of privatization and decreased government interventionism; it provides a meta-explanation for economic evils like unemployment and poverty through an all-encompassing moral and theological system, even while this system promotes a work ethic fit for the neoliberal market; and its "expect a miracle" mentality fosters hope amidst the unknowns of the free market. But how exactly is such an economic orientation and posture nurtured in pentecostalism?

1.2.3. Pentecostalism as an Alternative Economics

One answer to the preceding question is to observe how pentecostalism creates communities that provide new networks of social and economic services for uprooted populations. So while in the preceding I have commented on the interface of pentecostalism and the global economy as mediated by the prosperity message, here I want to focus on the concrete realities of pentecostal community that enable more modest forms of "prosperity" to be experienced, but that are no less radical and alternative. There are three levels of approaches to this issue.

First, pentecostalism functions as an alternative system of economics by restructuring kinship relations and moving people through conversion from their biological families and previous communities to being brothers and sisters within the church as a new family of God. This has significance not only for local socio-economic relations, but also for immigrant situations wherein older commitments are replaced by new ones. On the one hand, pentecostal believers are connected to new social and economic support networks; on the other hand, their conversion in effect separates them from previous socio-economic obligations tied in with their (often extended clan or village) fami-

---

54. We will return to a further discussion of the Ghanaian scene later (5.3.2 and 7.1.3).

lies. As Rijk van Dijk notes, "Pentecostalism reformulates the hierarchical and obligatory gift-giving system upon which kinship relations are based. It subjects reciprocity to moral supervision while making it thoroughly multi-local. This is of particular significance in the diaspora where many migrants see themselves faced with the obligation to send money to relatives living at home and elsewhere."[55] Conversion rituals that emphasize being "born again" (and hence being severed from past loyalties) secure the freedom to establish new familial relations, to develop new practices (e.g., prayer, fasting, and other congregational liturgies) directed toward prosperity and success, and to secure new modes of spiritual access to material wealth and social capital.

In other words, pentecostal churches function as alternative social and economic networks, with congregations providing local apprenticeship systems for members, especially in terms of knitting together people into communities with "mutual obligations and shared concerns."[56] Members are initiated into training programs focused on "developing self-esteem within the impoverished, by providing them hope and by arming them with skills applicable to the larger social system."[57] Some are enrolled in substance abuse programs and inserted into rehabilitation processes, others are provided with basic financial education, and all find themselves as members of a new community. In short, pentecostal congregations can be said to have become "alternative institutions" with "revolutionary potential" for developing further into the future as socio-economic and political agencies.[58]

Another angle on this phenomenon is to examine how an alternative economics emerges out of the new moral and theological values wrought by conversion. The work of Elizabeth Brusco exploring the impact of pentecostal conversion on the dynamics of family life in Latin America in general (her research was conducted in Colombia) is especially illuminating in this regard.[59] Focusing on the economic dimensions helps us to see how conversion redirects the husband's attention back toward the home and this in turn

---

55. Rijk van Dijk, "Religion, Reciprocity and Restructuring Family Responsibility in the Ghanaian Pentecostal Diaspora," in Deborah Bryceson and Ulla Vuorela, eds., *The Transnational Family: New European Frontiers and Global Networks* (New York and Oxford: Berg/Oxford International, 2002), pp. 173-96, quote from pp. 174-75.

56. Douglas Petersen, "Latin American Pentecostalism: Social Capital, Networks, and Politics," *PNEUMA: The Journal of the Society for Pentecostal Studies* 26, no. 2 (2004): 293-306, quote from p. 299.

57. Petersen, "Latin American Pentecostalism," p. 305.

58. Petersen, "Latin American Pentecostalism," pp. 304-6.

59. Elizabeth E. Brusco, *The Reformation of Machismo: Evangelical Conversion and Gender in Colombia* (Austin: University of Texas Press, 1995).

channels monies otherwise squandered on drinking, gambling, and prostitution back to the family. Over time, such wages kept within the household result in nicer clothes for the wife and children, an upgraded automobile, a larger home in a more upscale neighborhood, etc. — in short, an increasing affluence and a more clearly recognizable set of consumption patterns when measured by local community and ecclesial standards in the global south.

On the other side, pentecostal conversion transforms wives from being sexual objects to being partners, homemakers, and even ministers of various sorts in the ecclesial context. While clearly remaining subordinate to the "headship" of the husband in the home, the upward socio-economic mobility of the family nevertheless results in an elevated social and ecclesial status for wives and mothers. So if in the domestic sphere *machismo* and patriarchalism have been tempered, in the public (socio-economic) sphere women have been empowered and pentecostal families are transitioned into the market economy. The moral and theological transformations mediated by pentecostal conversion can thus be seen to have socio-economic results.

Besides economic and moral/theological analyses of pentecostalism as an alternative economics, however, there is also the more conventional sociological assessment of how pentecostalism provides unconventional social and economic options, especially for the poor. Here Chilean pentecostal scholar Juan Sepúlveda is insightful in his discussion of the masses of pentecostalism as a *bajo pueblo* (people from the underside of society).[60] In the Chilean context, pentecostalism emerged in the context of the struggle of the mestizo and indigenous underclasses, and forged their own socio-economic and political networks over and against the dominant local aristocracy on the one hand and the major religious options on the other. The result, to use classical sociological rhetoric, was the formation of a pentecostal sectarianism featuring its own economy of exchange. As already noted, such a pentecostal economy included its own forms of social and ecclesial patronage, systems of training and apprenticeship, and networks for business and entrepreneurs.

André Corten discusses such pentecostal sectarianism as the "anti-politics of the poor."[61] According to Corten, "anti-politics" is to be understood as being "neither apolitical nor opposed to the political system. It is because it is anti-political . . . that the sect . . . contributes to the 'discursive construction of the reality' . . . of the poor, [and] is a force of transformation."[62]

60. Juan Sepúlveda, "Reinterpreting Chilean Pentecostalism," *Social Compass* 43, no. 3 (1996): 299-318.

61. André Corten, *Pentecostalism in Brazil: Emotion of the Poor and Theological Romanticism,* trans. Arianne Dorval (London: Macmillan, and New York: St. Martin's Press, 1999), chap. 7.

62. Corten, *Pentecostalism in Brazil,* p. 145.

Thus the congregation's praises, singing, tongues, and liturgies carve out a distinctive socio-political space, enabling a new identity to emerge over time. Part of this sectarian confession is the liturgical declaration that "Jesus does not like poverty!"[63] The result is a theology of prosperity that provides the emerging pentecostal middle classes "with a means to identify themselves, notably *vis-à-vis* classes which are better established and have already developed their own network[s]."[64] In these ways, the church maintains itself over and against other institutions and social forces, rebelling against the economic structures of the world on the one hand, while forming alternatives to such systems on the other hand.

So on one end of the spectrum is prosperity pentecostalism, while on the other end of the spectrum is a pentecostalism of the *bajo pueblo*. This gives rise, as we have seen, to a wide range of economic modalities across the pentecostal world. In many instances, global pentecostalism is compatible with, if not itself supportive of, the neoliberal market economy. In other cases, pentecostalism remain sectarian, being opposed — sometimes radically so — to the dominant social, economic, and political structures within which it finds itself.[65] This raises the question: Is pentecostalism socially accommodative or counter-culturally resistant?

1.3. Pentecostalism, Society, and Culture

The answer to the preceding question will need to be just as nuanced here as when considering the relationship between pentecostalism and politics and between pentecostalism and economics. If before we have seen pentecostalism as being apolitical, political, and providing for an alternative *polis*, in different respects — and we have observed pentecostal economics across the prosperity-poverty spectrum as well — here we will also identify a diversity of pentecostal responses and postures toward socio-cultural engagement in general. I will discuss three types — pentecostal sectarianism, pentecostal conservatism, and pentecostal progressivism — in broad strokes. Some overlap between this section and the foregoing is unavoidable given the overlap between politics, economics, and society; however, I have chosen to have a separate discussion on pentecostal responses to society and culture because

---

63. Corten, *Pentecostalism in Brazil,* p. 148.
64. Corten, *Pentecostalism in Brazil,* pp. 112-13.
65. This general observation fits with the analysis of Robert D. Woodberry, "The Economic Consequences of Pentecostal Belief," *Society* 44, no. 1 (2006): 29-35, who suggests that pentecostal beliefs work differently in different contexts.

this puts into more stark relief the specifically theological issues at stake when we turn in Part II to the constructive argument of this book.

1.3.1. Pentecostal Sectarianism

We have already introduced pentecostal sectarianism in our earlier discussion of how alternative systems of business and exchange have emerged in pentecostal communities on the socio-economic margins of society. In what follows, I want to develop the phenomenology of pentecostal sectarianism with greater attention to diachronic factors. To do so, we will look at historic holiness-pentecostal sectarianism in the West, contemporary Chinese pentecostal house church movements, and sectarianism in the Afropentecostal diaspora. We will see that pentecostal sectarianism is not all of one stripe, and varies according to the broader social and cultural factors that are present.

The early pentecostal movement in North America was by and large of the sectarian type when viewed through sociological lenses. By this I am intending not to be pejorative, but to call attention to the following features of pentecostalism as a sectarian phenomenon:

- come-outism and separatism — involving mass migration from established churches toward (denominationally) independent churches; this was especially prevalent during the first two decades of the pentecostal movement in North America
- primitivism and restorationism — involving the rejection of historical and contemporary religious life in favor of a pragmatic retrieval and reappropriation of "the" biblical way of life;[66] this has remained as a central feature of new "waves" of pentecostal renewal, such as in the Latter Rain revival in the mid-twentieth century as well as the Third Wave movement in the 1970s and 1980s
- holiness and perfectionism — involving opposition to "liberal" trends in the mainline churches and the dominant culture in favor of a rigorous code of moral and ethical standards; this was a marked feature of some traditions of pentecostalism in the American South, which ex-

---

66. See Grant Wacker, "Searching for Eden with a Satellite Dish: Primitivism, Pragmatism, and the Pentecostal Character," in Richard T. Hughes, ed., *The Primitive Church in the Modern World* (Urbana: University of Illinois Press, 1995), pp. 139-66, and Edith L. Blumhofer, "Restoration as Revival: Early American Pentecostalism," in Edith L. Blumhofer and Randall Balmer, eds., *Modern Christian Revivals* (Urbana: University of Illinois Press, 1993), pp. 145-60.

tended the "higher Christian life" emphasis of Keswickian pentecostalism so that the two blessings of salvation and baptism in the Holy Spirit (for power to witness) became three works of grace: salvation, sanctification (or perfection), and Spirit-baptism[67]

- apocalypticism and millennialism — involving resistance to cultural accommodation in favor of emphasis on the world to come; the imminent end of the world meant, of course, that energies needed to be directed to global evangelism in order to both save the lost and hasten the return of Christ[68]
- biblicism and literalism — involving the denunciation of creedal Christianity in favor of "what the Bible says"; this was most prevalent among Oneness and Apostolic pentecostal groups that preferred the biblical rhetoric of the oneness of God over classical trinitarian formulations among other doctrinal revisions.

In some respects, the Oneness (the preferred nomenclature among white non-trinitarian) and Apostolic (the usual self-designation among African American and Latino non-trinitarian) pentecostals have maintained their sectarian posture most persistently over the course of pentecostalism's first century.[69] Oneness and Apostolic churches remain markedly distinctive due to their social codes of dress (women wear long dresses, do not wear makeup or jewelry, and do not cut their hair according to the Pauline injunction in 1 Cor. 11:6), holiness (resisting alcohol, tobacco, and other social "sins"), and lifestyle (rejecting television, the movies, social dancing, etc.). They have maintained these standards of world-denying and culture-resisting holiness rather than capitulate to what they see as forces of accommodation to contemporary sensibilities and values.

67. The standard discussion of pentecostal-holiness churches is Vinson Synan, *The Holiness-Pentecostal Movement in the United States* (Grand Rapids: Eerdmans, 1971). See also Richard T. Hughes, "Christian Primitivism as Perfectionism: From Anabaptists to Pentecostals," in Stanley M. Burgess, ed., *Reaching Beyond: Chapters in the History of Perfectionism* (Peabody, MA: Hendrickson, 1986), pp. 213-55; cf. 5.1.1. below.

68. E.g., as described by D. William Faupel, *The Everlasting Gospel: The Significance of Eschatology in the Development of Pentecostal Thought* (Sheffield: Sheffield Academic Press, 1996); see chap. 9.1.

69. E.g., James C. Richardson Jr., *With Water and Spirit: A History of Black Apostolic Denominations in the U.S.* (Washington, DC: Spirit Press, 1980); Kenneth D. Gill, *Toward a Contextualized Theology for the Third World: The Emergence and Development of Jesus' Name Pentecostalism in Mexico* (Frankfurt am Main and New York: Peter Lang, 1994); and Talmadge L. French, *Our God Is One: The Story of the Oneness Pentecostals* (Indianapolis: Voice and Vision Publications, 1999)

The most radically sectarian are pentecostals who not only believe in the centrality of Jesus' name but also in the scriptural injunction to handle serpents and the concomitant divine promise to protect such handlers.[70] Appalachian snake-handlers persist as a pentecostal subculture because they view the biblical text — "these signs shall follow them that believe; In my name shall they cast out devils; they shall speak with new tongues, they shall take up serpents; and if they drink any deadly thing, it shall not hurt them; they shall lay hands on the sick, and they shall recover" (Mark 16:17-18, KJV) — as commanding rather than merely allowing the handling of snakes. Thus they remain on the fringes not only of mainstream pentecostalism but even of the Oneness pentecostal tradition as a whole.

If the tradition of sectarian holiness and Oneness pentecostalism in North America was forged amidst the fundamentalist-modernist controversy at the turn of the twentieth century, contemporary sectarian pentecostalism in China has been shaped by the politics of Maoism and the Three-Self Patriotic Movement (TSPM). Since the formation of the TSPM in 1951, organized Christianity in China, especially its Protestant forms, has functioned through registration in the TSPM. The explosion of pentecostalism in China at the end of the twentieth century, however, has taken place largely outside the formal structures of the TSPM.[71] Growth has come in house church movements in the cities and, especially, the countryside, and often enough precipitated by persecution of its leaders and members. Within this historical and political context, Chinese pentecostal sectarianism is defined by its indigenousness (oftentimes developing quite apart from Western or missionary pentecostal or Christian influences) and marginality (intentionally in opposition to the religious center of the nation, as represented by the TSPM).[72]

Yet there are also some differences between sectarian pentecostalism in China when compared with its North American counterparts. The primitiv-

70. Ralph W. Hood and W. Paul Williamson, *Them That Believe: The Power and Meaning of the Christian Serpent-Handling Tradition* (Berkeley: University of California Press, 2008).

71. Luke Wesley, *The Church in China: Persecuted, Pentecostal, and Powerful*, Asian Journal of Pentecostal Studies Series 2 (Baguio, Philippines: AJPS Books, 2004).

72. What is happening in China is confirmed elsewhere — as in the Brazilian context where more sectarian pentecostals tend to be more radical in their approach to the political and public spheres, in contrast to "church-types" who are more apt to maintain the status quo; see Rowan Ireland, "Pentecostalism, Conversions, and Politics in Brazil," in Edward L. Cleary and Hannah W. Stewart-Gambino, eds., *Power, Politics, and Pentecostals in Latin America* (Boulder, CO: Westview, 1997), pp. 123-37; for the book-length argument, see Ireland, *Kingdoms Come: Religion and Politics in Brazil* (Pittsburgh: University of Pittsburgh Press, 1991).

ist, restorationist, perfectionist, and millenarian elements of pentecostal sectarianism are contextually tinged and flavored with similar motifs found in Chinese religious traditions.[73] Yet the staunch biblicistic literalism remains, such that cultural beliefs and practices are transformed in light of Scripture. The result is that Chinese pentecostal sectarianism says "yes" and "no" simultaneously: "yes" to the possibility of an authentically indigenous form of charismatic spirituality and piety, but "no" to any conscious efforts to articulate an intentionally accommodating or syncretistic form of belief and practice in light either of Chinese religions or even of mainline Protestant forms of Christian faith.

As should now be clear, pentecostal sectarianism in its diverse manifestations is shaped by its various socio-historical contexts. Hermione Harris's historical and cross-cultural study of an independent charismatic church in the African diaspora — the Nigerian-based and Yoruba-constituted Cherubim and Seraphim (C&S) Church — suggests how the sectarian self-understanding is differentiated over space and time.[74] Shifts in the C&S's self-perception in the United Kingdom, as studied over almost four decades (since the late 1960s), can be traced in response to at least the following three factors: 1) dynamics "back home" that are transforming African indigenous churches; 2) competition from other pentecostal churches in the United Kingdom, which requires maintaining sufficient continuity with others so as to be a "market" or ecclesial option on the one hand, but yet also being different enough so as to be able to offer something distinctive on the other hand; and 3) the general processes of secularization, which call into question certain pentecostal beliefs and practices even while providing the opportunity for churches such as the C&S to showcase its own counter-cultural religiosity and values.[75] Hence diaspora and immigrant churches like the C&S in the United Kingdom are sectarian according to register (3) in its resisting of modernity, but not according to register (1), which sees migrant communities as already

73. A historical perspective on these matters is Feiya Tao, "Pentecostalism and the Christian Utopia in China: Jing Dianying and the Jesus Family Movement, 1921-1952," in Ogbu U. Kalu and Alaine M. Low, eds., *Interpreting Contemporary Christianity: Global Processes and Local Identities* (Grand Rapids and Cambridge, UK: Eerdmans, 2008), pp. 238-52.

74. Hermione Harris, *Yoruba in Diaspora: An African Church in London* (New York: Palgrave Macmillan, 2006).

75. A similar study focused on cross-cultural analyses of Puerto Rican pentecostalism as transplanted to North America also reveals similar tensions; see Samuel Cruz, *Masked Africanisms: Puerto Rican Pentecostalisms* (Dubuque, IA: Kendall/Hunt, 2005). Cf. also André Droogers, Cornelis van der Laan, and Wout van Laar, eds., *Fruitful in the Land: Pluralism, Dialogue and Healing in Migrant Pentecostalism* (Zoetermeer, The Netherlands: Uitgeverij Boekencentrum, and Geneva: WCC, 2006).

compromised by social and cultural adaptations. More intriguingly, the C&S is sectarian in some respects but not according to register (2), since it is both more or less culturally accommodating when compared to other churches and communities across the British pentecostal spectrum.

In short, pentecostal sectarianism is complex and defies simplistic generalizations. Pentecostals cannot be said to be otherworldly or even against this world without qualification. Pentecostals worldwide hold their primitivism, millennialism, perfectionism, etc., with varying degrees of intensity, and this is certainly the case when measured over any significant span of time. Yet such a sociological and phenomenological assessment requires deeper theological analysis.

1.3.2. *Pentecostal Conservatism*

In some respects, what I am calling conservatism is similar to sectarianism, with the exception that the latter denotes more conscious counter-cultural as well as counter-ideological stances than does the former. More particularly, in this section the focus is on moral and cultural conservatism in world pentecostalism, even if such is inseparable from social and political conservatism in the final analysis. Our survey proceeds from pentecostal conservatism in East Asia and then explores the interface between pentecostal missions and indigenous moral and cultural traditions.

In some respects, pentecostalism in South Korea is as much a middle-class phenomenon as pentecostalism in North America. The Yoido Full Gospel Church in Seoul pastored by Rev. David Yonggi Cho, for example, has over 700,000 members and is the largest single and, arguably, the most affluent congregation in the world.[76] A recent discussion of the church by Ig-Jin Kim provides a glimpse into the South Korean pentecostal movement's overall conservative posture vis-à-vis Korean culture and society.[77] In contrast to South Korea's Minjung (liberation) theology, which focuses on achieving socio-structural changes, the Yoido approach is to indirectly engage with culture through relief activities, social welfare initiatives, and the use of mass

76. For discussion of various aspects of the ministries of Yoido, see Wonsuk Ma and William W. Menzies, *David Yonggi Cho: A Close Look at His Theology and Ministry* (Baguio City, Philippines: APTS Press, 2004). We will return to a more in-depth discussion of Cho's theology of mission later (6.1.2).

77. Ig-Jin Kim, *History and Theology of Korean Pentecostalism: Sunbogeum (Pure Gospel) Pentecostalism*, Mission Series 35 (Zoetermeer, The Netherlands: Uitgeverij Boekencentrum, 2003).

media, with the hopes of thereby shaping public opinion. The goal of influencing public opinion is not only to enable evangelism but also to ward off secularizing forces in the wider culture. The concern is basically to preserve a conservative — understood as "biblical" — morality: rejection of abortion, homosexuality, gambling, alcohol consumption, etc.

Not surprisingly, as in North America, the moral and cultural conservatism of South Korean pentecostalism is understood within a Lutheran Two Kingdoms model (see 2.2.2), which sees the church as being called to cooperate with and, in certain respects, be subordinate under the government. More precisely, the Spirit-filled Christian "is not involved in protest movements against dictatorships as long as the latter do not hinder the activities (evangelization and worship) of the church."[78] From here it is but a short step to a patriotic nationalism in which ideas of church growth, power evangelism, and South Korea as a chosen nation are all interwoven.[79] Thus "national pride and a deep sense of divine calling and responsibility for the salvation of the world are inextricably intertwined in most Korean missionary thought."[80] And such a Two Kingdoms framework also brings together material and spiritual concerns, both this-worldly and otherworldly commitments, so that economic prosperity and political power "are nothing but God's blessing as a means to world missions."[81]

In contrast to the middle-class moral and cultural conservatism of South Korean pentecostalism, there is also what might be called the radical cultural conservatism manifest among some Native American pentecostal communities. By use of the qualifier "radical," I am calling attention to the culture-denying rhetoric and culture-rejecting practices of Native American pentecostals,[82] especially those who have been influenced by classical or sectarian holiness pentecostal missions conducted under the colonial model.

---

78. Kim, *History and Theology of Korean Pentecostalism,* p. 273.

79. Kim, *History and Theology of Korean Pentecostalism,* chap. 14.

80. Kim, *History and Theology of Korean Pentecostalism,* p. 283, quoting Leo Oosterom, "Contemporary Missionary Thought in the Republic of Korea: Three Case-Studies on the Missionary Thought of Presbyterian Churches in Korea" (Ph.D. diss., Utrecht-Leiden University, 1990), p. 82.

81. Kim, *History and Theology of Korean Pentecostalism,* p. 284. For more on Cho's and Yoido's Threefold Blessings — in the spiritual, physical, and material domains — see Hyeon Sung Bae, "Full Gospel Theology and a Korean Pentecostal Identity," in Allan Anderson and Edmond Tang, eds., *Asian and Pentecostal: The Charismatic Face of Christianity in Asia* (Oxford, UK: Regnum, and Baguio City, Philippines: APTS Press, 2005), pp. 527-49, esp. pp. 537-38.

82. Thus note the title of Kirk Dombrowski's *Against Culture: Development, Politics, and Religion in Indian Alaska* (Lincoln, NE, and London: University of Nebraska Press, 2001), which is a study of Native American pentecostalism in the Southeastern Alaska region.

Conversion, in the understanding of these communities, involves a turning away from one's former way of life and a wholehearted turning toward Jesus Christ. In this scheme of things, it is not just that one is against Native culture, but that all culture represents the relative, fallen, and sinful order and Christian conversion is the means of redemption, and the key to the achievement of full humanization.[83]

The challenge for such Native American pentecostals is that of distinguishing their subsistence way of life from the cultural forms that conversion is supposed to have left behind. In other words, are there certain "cultural" ways of the seasonal fishing, hunting, trapping, or planting/harvesting that need to be abandoned in favor of authentically Christian ways of going about accomplishing the same objectives? Are certain ritual practices directed to conservation of the environment "Native," or can there be Christian approaches to these activities? Can one preserve certain traditional artifacts — e.g., heirlooms and other symbolic cultural products — as a Spirit-filled believer?[84] So while some pentecostals acknowledge the parallel of being drunk with alcohol and being "drunk" with the Spirit (affirming the latter), others reject the parallel between Native dancing and dancing in the Spirit (thus resisting the latter).[85] The most radical insist on a sanctified morality that attempts to cleanse Christian lives from the cultural accretions of Native traditions, sometimes taking the form of conducting bonfires to purify the community.[86]

The last example of moral-cultural conservatism I will present is what might also be called either a millennial or a postcolonial form of pentecostal conservatism. Here I have in mind pentecostalism as found among the

83. For further explication of how these pentecostals view culture in relativistic terms when compared to the universalism and absolutism of the gospel, see Dombrowski, *Against Culture*, p. 178.

84. For these and other questions debated among Native American pentecostals, see Dombrowski, *Against Culture*, chap. 4.

85. Dombrowski, *Against Culture*, p. 176.

86. Dombrowski, *Against Culture*, pp. 172-73; the model here is the Ephesian believers who burned their magic books and paraphernalia (Acts 19:19). While granting that pentecostal missionaries have contributed to the destruction of indigenous culture, they have also "played a critical role in promoting literacy, education, and other services that have translated into political resources among indigenous peoples. As is often the case, the interactions between religious and indigenous politics defy simply characterizations and linear explanations"; see Edward L. Cleary and Timothy J. Steigenga, "Resurgent Voices: Indians, Politics, and Religions in Latin America," in Edward L. Cleary and Timothy J. Steigenga, eds., *Resurgent Voices in Latin America: Indigenous Peoples, Political Mobilization, and Religious Change* (New Brunswick, NJ, and London: Rutgers University Press, 2004), pp. 1-24, quote from p. 13.

Urapmin tribes of Papua New Guinea.[87] The stark moral conservatism of the Urapmin can be analyzed from both a millennial and a postcolonial angle. The former illuminates how the message of the missionaries about the holiness required in order to be saved on the coming "Day of the Lord" was translated into a moralistic and legalistic set of norms guiding the formation of a new Christianized cultural reality. The latter reveals the Urapmin as active theologians and practitioners in their own way who adopted and adapted pentecostalism in response to the colonial administration's concerns about how to civilize the "pagan" Urapmin.

When put together, what emerged has been a form of pentecostal moral and cultural conservatism with both millennial undertones and postcolonial features. Thus, "The conviction of sinfulness, impending judgment, and the need for repentance that came upon people in the early days of the revival picked up and transformed the concern with lawlessness that the colonial administration's legalistic rhetoric had already bequeathed to them."[88] In short, as Joel Robbins argues, becoming Christian and pentecostal for the Urapmin involved becoming self-aware and self-conscious not about their heathen or pagan condition (as the colonial regime sought to inculcate), but about their being sinners (as proclaimed by the pentecostal missionaries). This was an essential "first step" for the conversion of the Urapmin so that they could be ready for the imminent return of Christ.

1.3.3. Pentecostal Progressivism

In this final part of the chapter, I wish to move us from pentecostal sectarianism and conservatism to a more progressive form of cultural and social engagement. Pentecostal progressivism, I suggest, can be seen in the activism of Afropentecostalism, in the liberationism of certain aspects of Latin American pentecostalism, and in the wide variety of social engagement projects that have emerged in pentecostalism in the global south.

In earlier work, I have highlighted what I have called the prophetic tradition of Afropentecostalism — short for pentecostalism in Africa and the African diaspora from the Caribbean to North America to Europe and the United Kingdom.[89] In the following, I want to expand specifically on the pro-

87. Joel Robbins, *Becoming Sinners: Christianity and Moral Torment in a Papua New Guinea Society* (Berkeley: University of California Press, 2004).

88. Robbins, *Becoming Sinners*, p. 131.

89. See Yong, "Justice Deprived, Justice Demanded: Afropentecostalisms and the Task of World Pentecostal Theology Today," *Journal of Pentecostal Theology* 15, no. 1 (2006): 127-47.

phetic activism of Afropentecostal churches such as those found in the Four Corners neighborhood in Boston, Massachusetts.[90] While some of the holiness pentecostal churches in this area have persisted with a sectarian stance in identifying the "streets" in terms of the "evil other," Rev. Eugene Rivers and the Azusa Christian Community along with other Afropentecostal congregations in the area like Holy Road and Jude Church have insisted on engaging the streets "as a point of contact with persons in need."[91] Following the example of Jesus and his mission as announced in Luke 4:18 — "The Spirit of the Lord is upon me, because he has anointed me to bring good news to the poor. He has sent me to proclaim release to the captives and recovery of sight to the blind, to let the oppressed go free" — results in seeing the streets as either mission grounds or arenas of social service. Hence the Azusa Christian Community and other affiliated congregations are more prophetic and "have some focus on nonmembers and aim to attack social problems, such as poverty, violence, and economic underdevelopment."[92] The goal is to develop holistic soteriologies focused on saving the "whole person," on linking conversion to community building, and on not dichotomizing spiritual from social transformation.

Other forms of progressive pentecostal projects are also emerging in Latin America. Influenced in part by the prominence of liberation theology in that region, some pentecostal churches have begun to think, even before the Azusa Christian Community was established, in terms of socio-structural transformation as intimately connected to pentecostal spirituality. In Chile, for example, pentecostal theologian Juan Sepúlveda has suggested the compatibility of pentecostalism and liberation theology.[93] He has been a longstanding member of the Misión Iglesia Pentecostal which from its beginnings in the early 1950s has nurtured a theological, social, and ecumenical vision, to the point of becoming one of the first pentecostal churches to apply for and be granted membership in the World Council of Churches in 1961.[94] In

90. Omar M. McRoberts, *Streets of Glory: Church and Community in a Black Urban Neighborhood* (Chicago and London: University of Chicago Press, 2003).

91. McRoberts, *Streets of Glory*, pp. 91-96, quotation from p. 94.

92. McRoberts, *Streets of Glory*, p. 101.

93. Juan Sepúlveda, "Pentecostal Theology in the Context of the Struggle for Life," in Dow Kirkpatrick, ed., *Faith Born in the Struggle for Life: A Rereading of Protestant Faith in Latin America Today* (Grand Rapids: Eerdmans, 1988), pp. 298-318, and "Pentecostalism and Liberation Theology: Two Manifestations of the Work of the Holy Spirit for the Renewal of the Church," in Harold D. Hunter and Peter D. Hocken, eds., *All Together in One Place: Theological Papers from the Brighton Conference on World Evangelization* (Sheffield: Sheffield Academic Press, 1993), pp. 51-64.

94. The history of Misión Iglesia Pentecostal is interwoven with that of other pentecostal

Sepúlveda's formulation, the distinctively Chilean pentecostal and liberation theology finds its origins among the poor — the *bajo pueblo* which we have already mentioned — but is at the same time centered on a conversion experience, popular Bible reading, and an understanding of the church as community.[95] Pentecostalism provides one avenue for the liberation of the poor, although such uplift involves at its core a Christian conversion, biblical spirituality, and charismatic piety.

While most Latin American pentecostals do not adopt the rhetoric and analyses of liberation theology, others are no less socially engaged. Latin American Childcare (LAC) can be characterized as an alternative voluntary organization directed at changing communities.[96] Its leadership has sought to distinguish authentic pentecostal social action from political engagement. In reacting against the premillennialist and otherworldly mentality, LAC focuses on concrete social conditions and the needs of families in community. Drawing inspiration from the biblical vision of the impending kingdom of God, her theologians have understood the key to social transformation as connected to the empowerment of the Spirit to bear witness to the gospel to a needy world in palpable ways.[97] There is thus a clear acknowledgment of the hermeneutical circle between concrete situation/praxis, social analysis/criticism, normative biblical and theological reflection, and pastoral action in LAC's approach. Pentecostal social action and criticism are derivative from pentecostal spirituality and piety and informed by pentecostal Bible reading that is shaped by pastoral action, etc.

Organizations like LAC are part of a growing number of socially concerned and active pentecostals in the global south. In their book *Global Pentecostalism: The New Face of Christian Social Engagement*, Donald E.

---

churches in Frans H. Kamsteeg, *Prophetic Pentecostalism in Chile: A Case Study on Religion and Development Policy*, Studies in Evangelicalism 15 (Lanham, MD, and London: Scarecrow Press, 1998).

95. Others who have begun to explore the correlations between pentecostalism and liberation theology include Miroslav Volf, "Materiality of Salvation: An Investigation in the Soteriologies of Liberation and Pentecostal Theologies," *Journal of Ecumenical Studies* 26, no. 3 (1989): 447-67; Veronica Melander, "'New' Pentecostalism Challenges 'Old' Liberation Theology?" *Swedish Missiological Themes* 87, no. 3 (1999): 341-57; Andréa Damacena Martins and Lucia Pedrosa de Pádua, "The Option for the Poor and Pentecostalism in Brazil," *Exchange* 31, no. 2 (2002): 136-56; and Michael Wilkinson and Steven M. Studebaker, "A Liberating Spirit: Liberation Theology and the Pentecostal Movement," *The Ecumenist: A Journal of Theology, Culture, and Society* 45, no. 4 (2008): 1-7.

96. Douglas Petersen, *Not By Might, Nor By Power: A Pentecostal Theology of Social Concern in Latin America* (Oxford: Regnum, 1996).

97. Petersen, *Not By Might, Nor By Power*, pp. 202-8 and 224-26.

Miller and Tetsunao Yamamori provide a kaleidoscopic account of the variety of socially engaged pentecostalisms across the southern hemisphere.[98] They document pentecostal churches and ministries in Asia, Africa, and Latin America that have provided various types of services (social, educational, counseling, medical, etc.) to the needy, worked with non-governmental organizations on social and economic projects, and, in a very few cases, engaged in a wide spectrum of political tasks intended to address systemic and structural issues. More intriguing is the finding that in response to the authors' call for nominations for the fastest-growing, most socially active, and most indigenous and self-supporting congregations in the developing world, over 85 percent of the churches and ministries nominated were pentecostal or charismatic.[99] In addition to this, about 15 percent of all pentecostal churches are socially engaged, focused on humanitarian ministries (clothing and feeding people in the community, not just in the church) and on personal crises (e.g., divorce, depression, drug and alcohol addiction), although some also are intentional about working for social transformation and community development (e.g., with regard to education, policy changes, and economic development).[100] To be sure, pentecostals remain less likely to want to confront the government, to use violence, or to engage in acts of radical civil disobedience: "Their operative strategy is to 'grow' a new crop of civic, business, and educational leaders from the ground up with the hope that they will infiltrate these institutions and inspire a higher level of moral engagement."[101] This is certainly the case in developing nations where pentecostalism has emerged as a viable religious option that itself becomes a marker for social change in that people can now choose their religion rather than just inherit it. Against secularization, rational choice, or deprivation theories, then, pentecostalism in the global south not only appears to be here to stay, but also to be much more this-worldly focused and engaged than its forebears.

In this chapter we have surveyed global pentecostalism in terms of its politics, economics, and socio-cultural stance. We have discovered a pluralism of pentecostalisms: apolitical, political, and alternatively political with regard to the sphere of statecraft; prosperity driven, neoliberal compatible, and alternatively economic with regard to the global market; and sectarian, con-

98. Donald E. Miller and Tetsunao Yamamori, *Global Pentecostalism: The New Face of Christian Social Engagement* (Berkeley: University of California Press, 2007).

99. Miller and Yamamori, *Global Pentecostalism*, p. 6.

100. Donald E. Miller, "2006 SSSR Presidential Address — Progressive Pentecostals: The New Face of Christian Social Engagement," *Journal for the Scientific Study of Religion* 46, no. 4 (2007): 435-45, esp. pp. 439-40.

101. Miller, "2006 SSSR Presidential Address," p. 441.

servative, and progressive in terms of socio-cultural posture and activity.[102] Many of the descriptions in the preceding will be qualified and elaborated upon in Part II of this volume. For the moment, however, our phenomenology of the pentecostal body politic leads me to suggest the following provisional thesis, to be explored in the remainder of this book: that pentecostalism invites not one but many forms of political, economic, and social postures and practices.[103] One of the major questions in exploring the viability of this thesis will be whether it is motivated purely phenomenologically and thereby functions as a descriptive claim for pentecostalism in relationship to politics, or whether there are theological reasons for defending such a pluralistic political theology. The attempt to answer this question will take up the remainder of this book.

102. Hence I confirm the findings of Günter Remmert, "Spiritual Movements and Political Praxis," in Christian Duquoc and Casiono Floristán, eds., *Spiritual Revivals* (New York: Herder & Herder, 1973), pp. 85-97, who suggests there are various political postures adopted by renewal movements, depending on political circumstances, social status, attitudes toward competition or cooperation, education, political-economic interests, etc.

103. Here I build on the work of Eric Patterson, *Latin America's Neo-Reformation: Religion's Influence on Contemporary Politics* (New York and London: Routledge, 2005), whose thesis is that in the Latin American context that includes Catholicism, (pentecostal) Protestantism, and indigenous movements, there are "different religions and different politics." My claim is that political diversity exists even within pentecostalism, even as I suspect that to be true within these other religious traditions.

CHAPTER 2

Political Theology: Surveying the Field

If many different political postures and practices can be identified within global pentecostalism as a renewal movement with origins at the beginning of the twentieth century, no doubt an even greater pluralism of beliefs and practices has existed within the Christian tradition stretching back over twenty centuries. In this chapter I provide a historical overview — in very quick succession — of Christian thinking about the political. The three sections begin with the biblical and patristic traditions, cover the mainstreams of medieval, Reformation, and modern developments, and then explore contemporary discussions in political theology. The major goal is to clarify the historical and theological issues with which pentecostalism will be engaging in developing its own theology of the political.

We should note that the concept of "political theology" is itself a twentieth-century formulation, first introduced by the jurist and political theorist Carl Schmitt.[1] We will return below to discuss the work of Schmitt in more detail (see 2.3.1 and 4.2.1). Meanwhile, however, it is worth noting that since its appearance, political theology has emerged as a discursive lens through which to revisit earlier Christian attitudes toward, doctrines about, and interfaces with especially the state.[2] Hence we will proceed to talk about

---

1. See Schmitt's *Politische Theologie: Vier Kapitel zur Lehre von der Souveränität* (München und Leipzig: Duncker & Humblot, 1922), trans. George Schwab, *Political Theology: Four Chapters on the Concept of Sovereignty* (Cambridge, MA, and London: MIT Press, 1985).

2. E.g., Lester L. Field Jr., *Liberty, Dominion, and the Two Swords: On the Origins of Western Political Theology (180-398)* (Notre Dame: University of Notre Dame Press, 1998), and Peter Scott and William T. Cavanaugh, eds., *The Blackwell Companion to Political Theology* (2004; paperback ed., Malden, MA: Blackwell, 2007), which includes chapters on Old and New Testaments as well as major Christian theologians on the political.

the Christian tradition of political theology, although we should be aware that the notion as we understand it today did not emerge until the modern period — during which the separation of church and state was formalized — and that its primary conceptual framework remains indebted to recent discussions.

One final caveat should be registered before proceeding. Although we began in the first chapter with a focus on pentecostal political practices, our historical survey here will remain primarily at the level of theory and doctrine, with the underlying Christian practices more implicitly than explicitly articulated. This is not because we are uninterested in historic Christian practices. However, the constructive work in Part II to follow will be focused on formulating a viable pentecostal political theology; hence, while we will certainly need to take into account pentecostal practices for such a constructive project, our primary dialogue partners will be the tradition of Christian political theology. So this will *not* be a case of comparing pentecostal practices with traditional Christian beliefs about the political; rather, it will be a triangulation of pentecostal practices, Christian beliefs, and the pentecostal or pneumatological imagination (to be further discussed in the following chapter), toward a pentecostal contribution to political theology.

2.1. Politics and Theology: Biblical and Early Christian Thinking

We begin our overview with the biblical traditions, of the Old and New Testaments, and then look toward patristic reflections on the political, especially as culminating in the thought of St. Augustine. Our focus will be on the major themes of political theology, particularly those that remain viable in contemporary theological discussions. What will emerge is that while the biblical and patristic traditions do not bequeath to us a normative political theological stance, what is consistent is the counter-ideological (or counter-political or counter-economic) orientation repeatedly observable in each of these periods.

2.1.1. Political Theology in Ancient Israel

At one level, the formation of ancient Israel as a theocracy would seem to put an end to all discussions of political theology — what else might be considered other than the reign of YHWH? At another level, however, as J. G. McConville reminds us,[3] there are a multitude of other themes within the

---

3. J. G. McConville, *God and Earthly Power — An Old Testament Political Theology:*

overarching framework of YHWH's rule that merit attention even within the Deuteronomic history. This is especially the case when we examine the politics of Israel against the broader context of the ancient Near East. In this framework, what emerges is the monotheism of Israel over and against the polytheism of her neighbors; the holiness, righteousness, and shalom symbolized by Israel as opposed to the violence of her adversaries; and Israel's culture of resistance against both Egypt's culture of oppression and the later Assyrian and Babylonian monopolistic claims. These distinctives are encapsulated in Israel's experience of worship, enabled in part through the covenant, and enacted in the people's acts of obedience in response to YHWH's beneficence.

McConville's survey from Genesis through Kings highlights the pluralism of political forms and doctrines in ancient Israel.[4] Genesis reveals the vocation of Israel as embedded in the order of creation itself, so that there is no dualism between nature and culture, between creation and the *polis*, as all exist under God as judge of the earth. The remaining Pentateuchal books highlight the movement of God's people from tyranny to freedom, God's opposition to the oppressive regimes of this world, and how God's covenant structures and organizes human life in community. If Joshua dramatizes the conflict with Chaos in the political domain — thus re-enacting the confrontation with Pharaoh in Egypt — then Judges shows how Chaos perennially threatens the *polis* of the people of God. Samuel and Kings reveal the ambivalence regarding the monarchy, even while they also show how the "sovereignty of God in human affairs is set against the fickleness of human rule, its tendency to tyranny, its self-deluding pretentiousness."[5] McConville concludes:

> Israel, in its laws and in its self-understanding according to its own literature, testifies to what it might mean to be a people that lives in obedience to norms of justice-righteousness that transcend its own life and become universal. . . . The Old Testament's story from creation to politics differs from the ancient Near East precisely in this respect, that its interpretation of origins is at the service neither of the idea of one nation's intrinsic right to predominate, nor of a given political *status quo*. There was a posi-

---

Genesis-Kings, Library of Hebrew Bible/Old Testament Studies 454 (London and New York: T. & T. Clark, 2006).

4. See also the pluralism of issues discussed in Henning Graf Reventlow, Yair Hoffman, and Benjamin Uffenheimer, eds., *Politics and Theopolitics in the Bible and Postbiblical Literature*, Journal for the Study of the Old Testament Supplement Series 171 (Sheffield: Sheffield Academic Press, 1994).

5. McConville, *God and Earthly Power*, p. 166.

tive side to the story in that it illustrated Yahweh's readiness to allow his rule to find correspondences in a variety of actual political forms.[6]

Moving into the remainder of the Hebrew Bible, we find the wisdom and prophetic literature. In his survey of this material, Walter Brueggemann also observes the emergence of Israel as a "contrast society" vis-à-vis her neighbors.[7] Besides the theme of covenant (requiring obedience, dialogue, and improvisation), there are also the neighborly and shalomic practices symbolized by Sabbath and Jubilee, the experiences of pain (in the exile, especially) that in turn produce the songs and laments of the nation, and the prophetic pronouncements against the injustices even amidst YHWH's generous economy of abundance (rather than scarcity). Given the imperial dynasties of the ancient Near Eastern world, Israel's story, song, and prophetic writings are "inescapably a *theological politics* in which the defining presence of YHWH, the God of Israel, impinges upon every facet of the political; or conversely, the God of Israel is intensely engaged with questions of power and with policies and practices that variously concern the distribution of goods and access."[8]

From sociological and political economy perspectives, scholarship in the last generation has also begun to clarify how the social and economic conditions of ancient Israel further shaped her religious experience. Norman Gottwald's opus, while disputable in terms of its application of Marxist methodology and its historical revisionism, ably calls attention to the stratified socio-economic and political system that the "tribes of Israel" revolted against (his preferred model) or supplanted.[9] This Israelite "socio-economic revolution" was egalitarian rather than hierarchical, and focused on invigo-

---

6. McConville, *God and Earthly Power*, pp. 170, 174. McConville's conclusions are compatible with those of Norman Gottwald, *The Politics of Ancient Israel* (Louisville: Westminster/John Knox Press, 2001), who argues that what is distinctive about ancient Israel is not its politics — which in terms of its structures and strategies were rather similar to those of its neighbors — but its literature and religion; and Gottwald's allowing for the role of religion to influence ancient Israelite politics, as he does, results (I proffer) in the political pluralism McConville observes.

7. Walter Brueggemann, "Scripture: Old Testament," in Peter Scott and William T. Cavanaugh, eds., *The Blackwell Companion to Political Theology* (2004; paperback ed., Malden, MA: Blackwell, 2007), pp. 7-20, from p. 10.

8. Brueggemann, "Scripture: Old Testament," p. 9; italics Brueggemann's. For case studies of the political dimension of various genres of the Hebrew Bible, see Richard Bauckham, *The Bible and Politics: How to Read the Bible Politically* (Louisville: Westminster/John Knox Press, and London: SCM, 1989).

9. See Norman K. Gottwald, *The Tribes of Yahweh: A Sociology of the Religion of Liberated Israel, 1250-1050 B C E* (Maryknoll, NY: Orbis, 1979).

rating an agrarian culture in response to the imperial class and feudal system of the pre-existing Canaanite society.[10] Although Gottwald's economic scenario may be inextricable from his overall social-scientific approach and historical reconstruction and thereby questioned on those grounds, his proposal highlights the social and economic aspects of the biblical text that have otherwise been neglected.[11]

The establishment of the monarchy slowly brought with it a more centralized and integrated Israelite economy.[12] Along with this came the development of industry, configuration of more extensive transport routes, growth of markets for production factors like commercial loans, slavery, land consolidation, specialized diets, and luxury consumption, and formation of income distribution strategies — even while each of these factors boosted the nation's social and political power, and further secured the prestige of her kings in the eyes of her neighbors. But by the eighth century, there is evidence to show that the prosperity of the royal courts, aided by all of these developments, had come at the expense of local farmers, landholders, and traders.[13]

This led to the emergence of a class of prophets calling for social justice, a central feature of the Old Testament witness. Morris Silver goes beyond observing the prophetic concern for the poor and proposes a controversial thesis that the prophets of the eighth and seventh centuries, while speaking out against the affluence of the nation and on behalf of the oppressed, were part of the ruling classes and that it was precisely because of this that their calls for socio-economic reforms were implemented; as a result, the economy took a downturn that allowed, in the end, for the conquest of Israel by her adversaries.[14] Silver's thesis can be contested along any number of lines — e.g., at the

---

10. Gottwald, *The Tribes of Yahweh*, chap. 46.

11. One of the results of Gottwald's Marxist approach is that few conservative scholars have been invited to engage his work so that, e.g., Roland Boer, *Tracking the Tribes of Yahweh: On the Trail of a Classic*, Journal for the Study of the Old Testament Supplement Series 351 (Sheffield: Sheffield Academic Press, 2002), by and large avoids the specifically *historical* issues, focusing instead on the ideological, sociological, hermeneutical, theological, and ecclesial dimensions of his hypothesis.

12. David Hopkins, "Bare Bones: Putting Flesh on the Economics of Ancient Israel," in Volkmar Fritz and Philip R. Davies, eds., *The Origins of the Ancient Israelite States*, Journal for the Study of the Old Testament Supplement Series 228 (Sheffield: Sheffield Academic Press, 1996), pp. 121-39, esp. pp. 132-38.

13. Marvin L. Chaney, "Bitter Bounty: The Dynamics of Political Economy Critiqued by the Eighth-Century Prophets," in Robert L. Stivers, ed., *Reformed Faith and Economics* (Lanham, MD: University Press of America, 1989), pp. 15-30.

14. Morris Silver, *Prophets and Markets: The Political Economy of Ancient Israel* (Boston, The Hague, London: Kluwer-Nijhoff, 1983).

level of the claim regarding the prophets as members of the ruling classes, or at the level that their economic recommendations were the "cause" of Israel's economic downturns — but my interest is less the details of his proposal than it is in the possible interconnections between prophecy in ancient Israel and political economy in general and political theology in particular. Silver at least calls us to attend to the class location of Israel's prophets as well as to socio-economic and political results of economic reforms and policies. These are essential factors to keep in mind when formulating a political theology today.

2.1.2. Jesus and Paul in the Context of Empire

By the first century c.e., the region of Palestine had experienced imperial domination successively under the Babylonians, the Medo-Persians, and the Greco-Romans. Warren Carter thus notes that the Roman Empire is not in the background to Christianity but the foreground, since it never goes away and is always present, even when not explicitly mentioned in the various New Testament texts.[15] The reality of empire is that 95 percent of the masses are lorded over by 5 percent of the religious, social, economic, military, and political elite; that the 95 percent are slaves, day laborers, artisans, and peasants, all of whom provide cheap labor and produce goods for consumption by the elite besides paying exorbitant taxes, tributes, and rents to them; and that there is therefore an extensive and multi-leveled network of patronage, with clients at each level surviving at the cost of loyalties incurred to their generous but yet calculating patrons (who in turn have to negotiate loyalties with those above them, and so on). If read in light of these socio-political realities, the New Testament turns out to be a very political document, and the Christian relationship to the Roman Empire becomes much more complex than if one remained on the surface of the text.

It is thus not surprising if we see a wide range of Christian evaluations of empire in the pages of the New Testament, as well as various strategies of response.[16] There are texts of resistance — e.g., the Apocalypse — that view the empire as controlled by the devil and thus being under imminent divine

---

15. Warren Carter, *The Roman Empire and the New Testament: An Essential Guide* (Nashville: Abingdon, 2006). An accessible overview is Richard A. Horsley, "The Imperial Situation of Palestinian Jewish Society," in Norman K. Gottwald and Richard A. Horsley, eds., *The Bible and Liberation: Political and Social Hermeneutics*, rev. ed. (Maryknoll, NY: Orbis, 1993), pp. 395-407.

16. A nice summary is provided by Carter, *The Roman Empire and the New Testament*, chap. 2; see also Richard J. Cassidy, *Christians and Roman Rule in the New Testament: New Perspectives* (New York: Crossroad, 2001), esp. pp. 127-32.

judgment,[17] even as there are recommendations to adopt a posture of quiet submission and prayer (reflecting strategies of survival and perhaps accommodation).[18] Still others advocate a more missional (even apostolic) approach, seeking to transform aspects of empire, even as there are also efforts to establish alternative communities and forms of life.

Read variously, each of these responses can be attributed to Jesus himself. A few interpreters understand him as standing on the margins, if not the center, of a long line of (messianic) revolutionary movements, except that even if Jesus is not seeking a violent political displacement of the Roman Empire with the kingdom of God, he is certainly interested in undermining entirely the existing social system of domination and oppression.[19] Still others suggest a less explicitly thematized political agenda for Jesus, observing instead from a more socio-economic perspective his solidarity with the poor (the masses of the empire), his egalitarianism regarding women, children, and outsiders like Samaritans and gentiles, and his counter-cultural meal practices that included the despised, outcast, and marginalized[20] — all of which combine to illuminate his vision of a new

17. E.g., Harry O. Maier, *Apocalypse Recalled: The Book of Revelation after Christendom* (Minneapolis: Fortress Press, 2002), and Elisabeth Schüssler Fiorenza, *The Power of the Word: Scripture and the Rhetoric of Empire* (Minneapolis: Fortress, 2007), chaps. 4 and 6.

18. Most famously, the controversial Romans 13 passage, to which we will return later in this book; however, there are many other New Testament texts urging quiet and peaceful lives, often in the face of persecution — e.g., 1 Pet. 2:13-17; 1 Thess. 4:10-12; and 1 Tim. 2:1-3.

19. For more on the insurrectionists in the decades before and after Jesus, see Richard A. Horsley and John S. Hanson, *Bandits, Prophets, and Messiahs: Popular Movements in the Time of Jesus* (Minneapolis: Seabury/Winston, 1985). The topic of Jesus against empire has been a burgeoning one in the last decade — e.g., Richard A. Horsley, *Jesus and Empire: The Kingdom of God and the New World Disorder* (Minneapolis: Fortress, 2003), and John Dominic Crossan, *God and Empire: Jesus against Rome, Then and Now* (New York: HarperSanFrancisco, 2007). My main gripe with these approaches is that scholars like Horsley and Crossan too quickly move from exegesis to "application," usually equating Roman Empire with contemporary American empire and therefore utilizing Jesus' life and teachings as a means to challenge American imperialism. To be sure, the latter needs to be critically questioned, so that strategy in itself is not completely out of place — except when Horsley, Crossan, et al. frame their interpretive commitments as being obviously motivated by the contemporary situation. For a more balanced approach to reading American empire vis-à-vis that of ancient Rome, see Christopher Bryan, *Render to Caesar: Jesus, the Early Church, and the Roman Superpower* (Oxford: Oxford University Press, 2005).

20. Bruce Chilton notes the centrality of meals to Jesus' vision of the kingdom; see Bruce Chilton, *Pure Kingdom: Jesus' Vision of God* (Grand Rapids: Eerdmans, and London: SPCK, 1996), p. 126. For socio-economic readings of Jesus' mission, I have found the work of Douglas Oakman helpful — e.g., Douglas E. Oakman, *Jesus and the Economic Questions of His Day,* Studies in the Bible and Early Christianity 8 (Lewiston, NY: Edwin Mellen Press, 1986); K. C. Hanson and

social order. In contrast, more traditional interpretations would see the political as being accidental to Jesus' ministry and emphasize instead that his teachings regarding the state, citizenship, and taxation, etc., need to be understood within the overall framework of the kingdom as a spiritual reality that is superimposed upon but does not seek to overthrow the existing political order. Jesus' mission is hence only indirectly political, and more intentionally focused on establishing a new people of God — the church — as a remnant within the wider *polis*.[21]

My own understanding of Jesus and the political has been deeply influenced by the work of N. T. Wright.[22] The basic thrust of Wright's retelling of the Jesus story highlights the Jewish expectations of the messiah as accomplishing the renewal of Israel from exile, and Jesus' understanding of God's acting in his own life and even death as inaugurating the restoration of the coming kingdom. Jesus' healings and exorcisms announce that the impure, imperfect, and unclean are being prepared for inclusion in the restored Israel, and his teachings are intended to mobilize new forms of community governed by Sabbath and Jubilee principles characterizing life in the kingdom. Jesus gets into trouble religiously because of his belief that God's offer of the forgiveness of sins, essential for the restoration of Israel, was no longer dependent on the sacrificial system of the Temple, and because he claimed in his own life to have fulfilled all of the lawful conditions required for Israel's return from exile. He then gets in trouble politically because he symbolically enacts the return of Israel's king to Zion in his journey to and arrival in Jerusalem, which coupled with his proclamation about the kingdom of God and the large numbers of followers responding to his call for a new familial community with primary allegiances not to Caesar but to YHWH, threatens the existing Roman imperial order.

Yet what may have separated Jesus from other messianic figures was not only that he advocated a non-violent response to Roman imperialism, but

---

Douglas E. Oakman, *Palestine in the Time of Jesus: Social Structures and Social Conflicts* (Minneapolis: Fortress, 1998); and Douglas E. Oakman, *Jesus and the Peasants* (Eugene, OR: Cascade, 2008) — and will return to this matter in 7.3.1.

21. See Alan Storkey, *Jesus and Politics: Confronting the Powers* (Grand Rapids: Baker Academic, 2005), whose reading of Jesus is solidly in the tradition of John Howard Yoder, *The Politics of Jesus* (Grand Rapids: Eerdmans, 1972).

22. Wright's hypothesis is being argued extensively in a series — titled *Christian Origins and the Question of God* — of five long volumes, only the first three of which have been published so far: *The New Testament and the People of God, Jesus and the Victory of God,* and *The Resurrection of the Son of God* (Minneapolis: Fortress, 1992, 1996, and 2003, respectively). For a compact overview of his argument, see N. T. Wright, *The Original Jesus: The Life and Vision of a Revolutionary* (Grand Rapids: Eerdmans, 1996).

that he warned specifically about how rejection of the messianic way of non-violence and a continued insistence on a militant Jewish nationalism would incur the wrath of the imperium and bring about the destruction of Jerusalem. Thus he called his followers to trust in his words and to follow his example in embracing the marginalized, to turn the other cheek to and love one's enemies, and to live self-sacrificially for others and even for the sake of the world. Against this backdrop, Jesus' death is a political event in at least three respects: 1) his condemnation and crucifixion occurred at the hands of the political forces governing the empire; 2) it manifests Jesus' conviction that the resistance toward empire is best demonstrated and then accomplished not by taking up the sword but by a path of non-violent resistance; and 3) the resulting resurrection served as a vindication, for him and his followers, that God was truly at work in Jesus messianically to restore Israel and establish the kingdom.

It is impossible to do justice to Wright's argument in this context, and there are certainly many unanswered questions about its details.[23] The most important ones, for our purposes, have to do with the relationship between Jesus' mission and what transpired later in the emergence of the church. While this is the subject of thus far unpublished volumes in Wright's project, the main issue is summarized in Alfred Loisy's observation that "Jesus proclaimed the kingdom of God, but it was the church which came."[24]

One way to address this set of issues is to focus on St. Paul's understanding of the political. As with Jesus, so also with Paul: we can discern a similar range of readings of Paul as a citizen of imperial Rome,[25] on the one hand resisting empire, on the other hand being content with the political status quo so long as followers of Jesus as the messiah are free to propagate their faith. The former approach is defensible especially when due attention is paid to what Paul did as an apostle and missionary: establish local congregations

23. Critical evaluations of the first two volumes of Wright's project are collected in Carey C. Newman, ed., *Jesus and the Restoration of Israel: A Critical Assessment of N. T. Wright's Jesus and the Victory of God* (Downers Grove, IL: InterVarsity, 1999). I will return later (in 3.2) to further discuss specific aspects of Wright's thesis in the context of Luke's Gospel.

24. Richard Bauckham, "Kingdom and Church according to Jesus and Paul," *Horizons in Biblical Theology* 18, no. 1 (1996): 1-26, quote on 1, from Loisy, *L'Évangile et l'Église* (Paris: Picard, 1902), p. 255.

25. Leading the way here again are Richard A. Horsley, ed., *Paul and Empire: Religion and Power in Roman Imperial Society* (Harrisburg, PA: Trinity Press International, 1997), and John Dominic Crossan and Jonathan L. Reed, *In Search of Paul: How Jesus' Apostle Opposed Rome's Empire with God's Kingdom* (New York: HarperSanFrancisco, 2004). I find Horsley's and Crossan's readings of Paul less fueled by an anti-American agenda and more committed to a closer reading of the Pauline texts than their interpretations of Jesus and the Gospels.

(ekklesia) that embodied and lived out the way of Jesus as messiah. In this framework, the Pauline emphasis on counter-ideological, christocentric, and cruciform praxis comes to the fore. Romans 13, for example, would be non-revolutionary in not advocating political violence, but would be radically revolutionary precisely in urging the Roman followers of the messiah to faithful anticipation of the restoration of divine justice through their believing in the God before whom even pagan rulers are finally accountable.[26] Hence Paul becomes "an ambassador for a king-in-waiting, establishing cells of people loyal to this new king, and ordering their lives according to his story, his symbols, and his praxis, and their minds according to his truth."[27]

Understood as such, the Pauline message of Jesus as savior through the cross and resurrection is not only scandalous to Jewish ears but an anti-imperial threat in its announcement of the end of the age and of the power structures of this world.[28] Here the work of Neil Elliott can be fruitfully brought into dialogue with that of Wright's since Elliott rightly notes how until his own encounter with the risen Christ, Saul would have thought the messianic belief in and proclamation about Jesus was misguided and would provoke the wrath of Rome.[29] But upon meeting Jesus on the Damascus Road, Paul came to see that although Jesus did not overthrow the gentile political power, God was accomplishing in Jesus' mission not only the eschatological redemption of Israel but also the renewal and salvation of the gentiles as well. On the one hand, the gentiles are saved through Israel, but on the

26. See N. T. Wright, "Paul and Caesar: A New Reading of Romans," in Craig Bartholomew, Jonathan Chaplin, Robert Song, and Al Walters, eds., *A Royal Priesthood? The Use of the Bible Ethically and Politically — A Dialogue with Oliver O'Donovan*, Scripture and Hermeneutics Series 3 (Carlisle: Paternoster, 2002), pp. 173-93, esp. p. 190. As Dieter Georgi notes in *Theocracy in Paul's Praxis and Theology*, trans. David E. Green (Minneapolis: Fortress, 1991), p. 83, "By using such loaded terms as *euangelion, pistis, dikaiosynē*, and *eirēnē* as central concepts in Romans, he evokes their associations to Roman political theology. Monuments of this theology were familiar to his contemporaries throughout the Empire, both east and west, and everyone carried the flyers of this ideology about in the form of Roman coins."

27. N. T. Wright, "Paul's Gospel and Caesar's Empire," in Richard A. Horsley, ed., *Paul and Politics: Ecclesia, Israel, Imperium, Interpretation — Essays in Honor of Krister Stendahl* (Harrisburg, PA: Trinity Press International, 2000), pp. 160-83, esp. pp. 161-62. The essay here and the one cited in the previous note give us a glimpse of what is forthcoming in the final two volumes of Wright's *Christian Origins and the Question of God*.

28. Neil Elliott, "The Anti-imperial Message of the Cross," in Horsley, ed., *Paul and Empire*, pp. 167-83, esp. p. 176; cf. Elliott, "The Apostle Paul's Self-presentation as Anti-imperial Performance," in Richard A. Horsley, ed., *Paul and the Roman Imperial Order* (Harrisburg, PA: Trinity Press International, 2004), pp. 67-88.

29. Neil Elliott, *Liberating Paul: The Justice of God and the Politics of the Apostle* (Maryknoll, NY: Orbis, 1994), esp. chap. 5.

other Israel also will be saved through the gentiles. Thus is the messianic community called to live out the true eschatological body politic around the resurrected messiah. For that reason, Paul formed communities of discernment, of resistance, of solidarity with the crucified, of those who opposed the ideologies of the privileged, and who would confront the ideologies of the oppressive systems of this world. As Horsley suggests, "Paul had come to believe that in an age of patrons and clients, of power and exploitation, of status and possessions, only continual acts of radical self-sacrifice, modeled on the crucified figure of Jesus Christ, could renew and redeem the world."[30] In sum, Paul's theology of the political emphasized the crucified lordship of Jesus over all the powers of the earth even while Paul's political praxis focused on building counter-ideological and egalitarian (rather than hierarchical) communities of love, mutuality, and friendship.

2.1.3. The Patristic Period and St. Augustine: Early Christian Theologies of the Political and the Polis

The major shift during the patristic centuries was that which catapulted Christianity from being a minority religion (which justified the persecution of Christians) to being the dominant religion after the ascension of Constantine to power. The former period (180-312) has been called the "church of the martyrs," with its central feature, from the political theology perspective, being the church's insistence upon and expression of its freedom to live and even die for her convictions.[31] The freedom of the church, and her members, was understood theologically and eschatologically — in contrast to "secular" notions of freedom — as freedom from sin and death, and it was the responsibility of the church's leaders, especially her bishops during times of persecution, to enable her members to courageously embrace her fate at the hands of the imperial sword.[32]

The post-Nicene period, on the other hand, saw the convergence of the

---

30. Richard A. Horsley and Neil Asher Silberman, *The Message and the Kingdom: How Jesus and Paul Ignited a Revolution and Transformed the Ancient World* (New York: Grosset/Putnam, 1997), p. 183.

31. Field, *Liberty, Dominion, and the Two Swords,* part 1.

32. While the sword wielded by the civil magistrates was, for Origen, "a purely secular good established by God essentially for the sake of non-Christians [or for all who were not of the people of God]," it could also become corrupt and when so, turned into being "an instrument of the Devil"; see Gerard E. Caspary, *Politics and Exegesis: Origen and the Two Swords* (Berkeley: University of California Press, 1979), p. 189.

episcopacy and the imperial rule. The hagiographic treatment of Constantine by the church historian Eusebius emphasized the emperor as the chosen instrument of God to bring what was begun during the time of Augustus Caesar — the formation of one Roman Empire — under the rule and reign of one (the true) God, and thereby to enable the advance of the gospel and of true worship across the world.[33] Thus also did Eusebius hold "that the beginning of the Roman empire coincided with the Christ-event as a sign of the rout of demons. The plurality of national governments was an aspect of polytheism, [but] the creation of a single empire a fulfillment of the prophecies which pointed to a universal reign of God."[34] Insofar as Constantine saw himself as an earthly monarch representing the High God, to that same degree he no doubt found in Eusebius someone who confirmed this self-understanding. Perhaps for similar reasons, many of the fourth-century emperors were partial to Arianism given that its strict and uncompromised monotheism (the Son as being *homoiousios* or only *like* the Father rather than *homoousios* or essentially identical with the Father) provided theological justification for the imperial order.[35]

But when the church catholic contested (with imperial backing) the Donatist churches in North Africa, the latter turned to define Christian liberty in terms of freedom from the emperor even while, in an ironic twist, they portrayed the state-sponsored church as being in league with the devil.[36] Donatism thus may be understood both as a protest against the "Constantinization" of the church and as a radically sectarian movement. Similarly, the convergence of church and state after Constantine may be understood either as an accommodation to the "secular" — a variation of the Donatist perspective — or in terms of the church's opportunistic efforts to fulfill her mission. Any rejection of the latter, "Christendom" view might assume that the "political authorities [are] incapable of evangelical obedience," but to "deny political authority obedience to Christ is implicitly to deny that obedience to society, too."[37] Yet at the same time, the Donatist commitments also lie squarely

33. See Eusebius's *Life of Constantine*, in *Nicene and Post-Nicene Fathers*, vol. 1, ed. Philip Schaff and Henry Wace (1890; reprint, Peabody, MA: Hendrickson, 1994), esp. I.24, II.28, 42, 57-59.

34. Oliver O'Donovan, *The Desire of the Nations: Rediscovering the Roots of Political Theology* (Cambridge: Cambridge University Press, 1996), p. 198.

35. I return to this point below (2.3.1) in my discussion of Erik Peterson's response to Carl Schmitt.

36. E.g., W. H. C. Frend, *The Donatist Church: A Movement of Protest in Roman North Africa* (Oxford: Clarendon Press, 1952), pp. 316 and 326.

37. O'Donovan, *The Desire of the Nations*, p. 246.

in the pre-Nicene church's tradition of martyrdom, with the concomitant emphasis on the counter-ideological and counter-conventional freedom of the followers of the messiah.

What then is true freedom when asked from a political point of view? Plato responded principally, understanding freedom in light of the good, the true, and the beautiful.[38] In addition, and more controversially, he further insisted that the desires of the masses would generally stray, in the course of any decentralized process of socialization, away from these ideals in pursuit of self-seeking and hedonistic pleasure. Hence, as Martha Nussbaum notes, "Once we grant to Plato that the bad desires are not altogether inevitable or natural, but are at least in part created by laws, norms, and social institutions, we must grant him, as well, that the damage they do is damage for which we should hold society responsible."[39] But what kind of politics would accomplish this task? Plato's *Republic* proposes what basically amounts to an elitist political philosophy emphasizing the responsibility of parents, teachers, and especially the philosopher-statesman to educate the young and to mold their minds toward the good, the true, and the beautiful.[40] Such a political arrangement would work most smoothly within a patriarchal society that included a hierarchical division of labor (with philosopher-kings at the top, the aristocracy in the middle, and the masses below).

Aristotle agreed with his teacher that the ideal *polis* needed to be shaped teleologically, but he focused more concretely on identifying individual happiness as the norm for assessing how the good, the true, and the beautiful are realized in human life.[41] How is such happiness to be achieved? Through cultivation of friendships, voluntary associations, and partnerships, since the happiness of each one is relationally intertwined with the happiness of others, and through development of those virtues that make such relationships meaningful. All of these occur most naturally in the *polis*, the structures and processes of which are directed toward our quest for the

38. Albert Keith Whitaker, *A Journey into Platonic Politics: Plato's Laws* (Lanham, MD: University Press of America, 2004), demonstrates how Plato's *Laws* remain beneficial for contemporary political philosophers precisely because these dialogues recognize the limits of reason and thus the need for friendship, the value in the different ideas/practices that others (including strangers in faraway lands) have, and the centrality of divine or transcendent law, goodness, beauty, truth, etc., for the political ordering of human life and society.

39. Martha Nussbaum, *Plato's Republic: The Good Society and the Deformation of Desire* (Washington, DC: Library of Congress, 1998), p. 21.

40. Plato, *Republic*, trans. Robin Waterfield (Oxford and New York: Oxford University Press, 1993).

41. For a comparative discussion, see Ernest Barker, *The Political Thought of Plato and Aristotle* (New York: Russell & Russell, 1959), esp. chap. 6 on happiness in Aristotle.

good life.[42] So if Plato emphasized the means of law, promulgated by the elite, as the most efficient means of achieving and regulating the ideal *polis,* Aristotle insisted on the formation of character in individual lives, and on the relational processes in and through which such are nurtured, so that virtuous citizens could contribute to the good life for each other.[43] Hence Aristotle concluded that *homo sapiens* is also "by nature a political animal."[44]

We now turn to Augustine, who is so important for various reasons. Not only is he the culmination of the tradition of political theology in the patristic period, but he also remains (as we shall see later in this book) a live conversation partner for a wide range of contemporary projects in political theology. Yet at the same time, it is anachronistic to talk about Augustine as a political theologian not merely because such a nomenclature and notion was as yet undeveloped in his time but also because he never wrote a treatise on politics,[45] and, as R. A. Markus rightly comments, after 400, "Augustine continued to think, with Cicero, that man was a social animal by nature, but that he came to reject the [Aristotelian] view that he was also naturally a political animal."[46] On this note, it is apt to note that the Platonism that dominated Augustine's theology as a whole also shaped his thinking about the political.

The fastest way into Augustine's ideas about the political is through his *City of God (CG).*[47] Here it is essential to remember that the motivation for this long book was the fall of Rome and the need to provide a response to pagans who blamed that disaster on the ancient city's turning away from its former deities to worship the Christian God. In that sense, *CG* is an apologetic against paganism and, especially, polytheism, and a theodicy against other competitor metanarratives (in the sense of providing a theological explanation for why God would allow for Rome's defeat at the hands of heathen — e.g., 5.15-16). Books 1-5 are specifically on paganism; 6-10 on Varro, Platonism,

42. Aristotle, *Politics,* trans. Ernest Barker (1995; reprint, Oxford and New York: Oxford University Press, 1998), book 1.

43. See Robert Mayhew, *Aristotle's Criticism of Plato's Republic* (Lanham, MD: Rowman & Littlefield, 1997), esp. chap. 5.

44. Aristotle, *Politics,* 10 (Book I, chap. 2, 1253a2).

45. In fact, Augustine's *Political Writings,* eds. E. M. Atkins and R. J. Dodaro (Cambridge: Cambridge University Press, 2001), consists of letters and sermons rather than any "book" on politics.

46. R. A. Markus, *Saeculum: History and Society in the Theology of St Augustine* (Cambridge: Cambridge University Press, 1970), p. 104.

47. St. Augustine, *City of God,* trans. Henry Bettenson, with a new intro. by G. R. Evans (1972; reprint, London and New York: Penguin, 2003); all references to the *City of God* will be made parenthetically in the text by book and chapter number.

and demonology; 11-14 on creation and the fall; 15-18 on a history of the two cities — of humankind and of God; and 19-22 on the dual final-destination possibilities for humankind: that of eternal bliss in the presence of God and that of eternal destruction in the rebellious city of fallen humanity.

Four major themes of this book stand out for our purposes. First is Augustine's discussion of Varro's *theologia fabulare, theologia naturale,* and *theologia civilis,* which translates into mythical (or mythological), natural (or philosophical), and civil (or political) theology, respectively (6.5-12).[48] Whereas mythical theology was that propounded by the poets and natural theology by the philosophers, civil theology for Varro "is that which the citizens in the cities, especially the priests, ought to know and administer. It includes which gods each person ought to worship officially . . . , and what should be done and offered in sacrifice."[49] So if poetical theology is inadequate for the masses and philosophical theology is too demanding, then political theology, which is performed in the public domain — e.g., in festivals or cultic ceremonies — mobilizes (sometimes coerces, through legal mandates) the citizens of the *polis* around a common deity or set of deities. Augustine's polemical response is registered at three levels: a) that if poetical theology is implicitly fraudulent given the Platonic view of the nature of poetic discourse, political theology is explicitly deceitful since it is instrumental to socio-political ends rather than being about things divine (6.7; 4.27); b) that Varro's political theology had already been thoroughly refuted by other pagans like Seneca (6.10); and c) that the gods of political theology can give neither temporal blessings nor eternal life (6.12). In short, if Varro condoned political theology for pragmatic reasons related to binding the *polis* together in common cause, Augustine ultimately rejected (Varro's) political theology for explicitly theological reasons.

Second, and perhaps unexpected in any contemporary project in politi-

48. Marcus Terentius Varro (116-27 B.C.E.) was a Roman scholar, philosopher, and writer. H. D. Jocelyn, "Varro's *Antiquitates rerum diuinarum* and Religious Affairs in the Late Roman Republic," *Bulletin of the John Rylands University Library of Manchester* 65, no. 1 (1982): 148-205, and Jörg Rüpke, "Varro's *Tria Genera Theologiae*: Religious Thinking in the Late Republic," *Ordia Prima* 4 (2005): 107-29, both locate Varro's accomplishments in the first century B.C.E. context. For more on Augustine's interpretation of Varro in the *CG,* see Burkhart Cardauns's "Varro" in chapter 6 of Harold Hagendahl, *Augustine and the Latin Classics,* Studia Graeca et Latina Gothoburgensia XX:1 (Stockholm: Acta Universitatis Gothoburgensis, 1967), pp. 589-630, esp. pp. 610-17.

49. From Varro's *Antiquitatum rerum divinarum Libri,* quoted in Michael J. Hollerich, "Augustine as a Civil Theologian," in Joseph T. Lienhard, Earl C. Muller, and Roland J. Teske, eds., *Augustine: Presbyter Factus Sum* (New York: Peter Lang, 1993), pp. 57-69, esp. p. 58; cf. *City of God* 6.5.

cal theology, is Augustine's discussion of demonology and angelology.[50] Demons have rational souls and airy bodies (8.14-15), are summoned through the practice of the magical arts (8.19), are incapable of assisting human beings to attain happiness or fellowship with God (9.2), are completely driven by their misguided passions (9.6), are malignant and deceitful (9.18), and have knowledge without charity (9.20). Most brazen of Augustine's claims for late modern minds is that the gods of the nations are no more or less than demons (1.29, 7.33), fallen angels who were created good but have defected, and thus cast out of their heavenly abode, because of deformed pride, defective wills, and distorted desires (12.6-9).[51] At one level, Augustine's demonology also provides his metaphysical, ontological, and theological "explanation" for the presence of evil in the world.[52] At another level, his discussion of the demonic sets up his central vision of the two cities: life lived in pursuit of the self and its lusts is demonic and characteristic of the earthly city; life lived in the worship of the true God succeeds in being touched by the good, guided by the true, and illuminated by the beautiful.

Third, the two cities are refracted through an ecclesiological rather than a political lens. The earthly city follows in the lineage of the fallen angels and of Cain, is characterized by fleshliness, pride, and selfishness, and is condemned to death and the judgment of God. The heavenly city, on the other hand, is preserved in the lineage of Abel (with its apex in Christ as the second Adam), is characterized by righteousness, peace, and love, and will receive the promise of eternal life in the presence of God. The church, a type of the heavenly city, is the vehicle through which the good, the true, and the beautiful are realized, however fragmentarily, for fallen humanity. More precisely, the church is the site of God's redemption of fallen creatures, even as the state and the political order are God's "secular" means of keeping human disorders in check, canceling out the effects of sin, restraining violence, and punishing crime.[53] Yet — and herein

50. Augustine discusses angels and demons throughout the *City of God,* but especially in books 8-9 and 11-12; see also J. Patout Burns, "Augustine on the Origin and Progress of Evil," *Journal of Religious Ethics* 16, no. 1 (1988): 9-27, esp. pp. 16-21.

51. Eugene Ignatius van Antwerp, *St. Augustine: The Divination of Demons and Care for the Dead,* Catholic University of America Studies in Sacred Theology 2:86 (Washington, DC: Catholic University of America Press, 1955), p. 6, reminds us that "Never does Augustine challenge the real existence of these pagan deities; he accepts it as a fact, and accepts too the reality of their powers."

52. For a contemporary discussion of Augustine's demonology vis-à-vis the problem of evil, see Jean Bethke Elshtain, *Augustine and the Limits of Politics* (Notre Dame: University of Notre Dame Press, 1995), chap. 5.

53. Thus, it is implied throughout Augustine's discussion of the prelapsarian state (*City of God,* book 14) that there is no need for the political and its constraints.

lies the complexity of Augustine's thought — the heavenly city should not be simply equated with the church or the earthly city with the state (or civil society). Against such a dualistic construal of church and world/society (as advocated by the Donatists), Augustine understood the parable of the wheat and the tares to indicate that the "world" is to be found "in" the church and vice versa (18.49). Wherein then the lines of demarcation between the two cities?

This leads, finally, to the distinction of the two cities as reflecting two foci of human desire: one oriented toward God (for those inhabiting the heavenly city), and the other ordered toward the fallen self (for those persisting in the earthly city; cf. 5.19-22). Here, Augustine presumes Plato's idea about the desire as being central to human political existence (14.7), and responds at length about how to reorient our desires, loves, and lives toward that which is finally and truly worthwhile. He summarizes: "The two cities were created by two kinds of love: the earthly city was created by self-love reaching the point of contempt for God, the Heavenly City by the love of God carried as far as contempt of self" (14.28). In effect, one way to read the *City of God* is as a pedagogical and pastoral tool designed to transform the loves of its readers so as to produce an ultimately just and peaceful society.[54] In short, Augustine's concern with the political is but a byproduct of his concern to diagnose the various structures and loves that hijack our desire for God.

Some of these central Augustinian themes will reappear in the constructive portion of this book. Suffice to say for now that there is no template in Augustine for any specific political structure or form. Instead, for Augustine, all social and political projects are "intrinsically provisional."[55] More to the point, the political inevitably usurps our lives, loves, and allegiances, so that what is needed is a method of resistance.[56] That is precisely what the gospel is, so that, ultimately, "the *City of God* strips imperial rhetoric of its divine pretensions."[57] The goal is neither the reformation of the *polis* nor the con-

54. Thomas W. Smith, "The Glory and Tragedy of Politics," in John Doody, Kevin L. Hughes, and Kim Paffenroth, eds., *Augustine and Politics* (Lanham, MD: Lexington Books, 2005), pp. 187-213.

55. Eugene TeSelle, *Living in Two Cities: Augustinian Trajectories in Political Thought* (Scranton, PA: University of Scranton Press, 1998), p. xii. TeSelle's is a valiant effort to articulate a more affirmative political posture drawing from Augustine than traditionally attempted.

56. Thus Augustine is less a political theologian than a pastoral theologian, concerned that the lives of church members in the world are not *of* the world; see Peter Dennis Bathory, *Political Theory as Public Confession: The Social and Political Thought of St. Augustine of Hippo* (New Brunswick, NJ, and London: Transaction, 1981).

57. Anthony J. Chvala-Smith, "Augustine of Hippo (354-430)," in Kwok Pui-lan, Don H. Compier, and Joerg Rieger, eds., *Empire and the Christian Tradition: New Readings of Classical Theologians* (Minneapolis: Fortress, 2007), pp. 79-93, esp. p. 91.

struction of a better form of statecraft but the strengthening of the church's critical resolve against the status quo and the nurturing of the ecclesia and even the household as alternative political sites.[58] In both of these domains, our loves and desires can be formed, reformed, and transformed, whereas in the *polis*, the expressions and manifestations of our distorted loves and desires can only be managed, controlled, and, if needed, remediated through punishment.

2.2. Theology and the Political: Mainstreams in the Christian Tradition

The preceding discussion reveals no one normative political structure (in ancient Israel), a counter-ideological and alternative *polis* set of approaches (in the early church), an anti-political posture (among the church of the martyrs and the Donatists), and an ecclesiological "politics" (Augustine). Yet Augustine's age was not too far removed from that of Constantine's, and even his emphasis on the centrality of the church for political existence could not stem the tide of Christendom and its intermixture of church and state. In this section, we explore the unfolding of the story of Christendom during the medieval period and then look particularly at how the Lutheran and Reformed traditions of political theology have responded since the sixteenth century. We will observe that, in spite of the emergence of Christendom in the Latin West, there nevertheless were a variety of relationships between the church and the state from the medieval through the Reformation and modern eras.

2.2.1. Christendom: Medieval Developments in Political Theology

If after Augustine's debate with the Donatists the church could not simply define its relationship to the state in dualistic terms, this set the stage for the major debate in political theology during the medieval period: What precisely was the relationship between the church and the state?[59] Pope Gelasius I

58. See Kevin L. Hughes, "Local Politics: The Political Place of the Household in Augustine's *City of God*," in Doody, Hughes, and Paffenroth, eds., *Augustine and Politics*, pp. 145-64.

59. A still dependable account of the debate is Luigi Sturzo, *Church and State*, 2 vols., trans. Barbara Barclay Carter (Notre Dame: University of Notre Dame Press, 1962). See also Brian Tierney, *The Crisis of Church and State, 1050-1300* (Englewood Cliffs, NJ: Prentice-Hall, 1964); Ernst H. Kantorowicz, *The King's Two Bodies: A Study in Mediaeval Political Theology* (1957; reprint, Princeton: Princeton University Press, 1997); Cary J. Nederman and Kate

(d. 496) argued that since only Christ combined the offices of priest and king in his one person, these offices should be separate, although mutually informing. This led to his distinction between the "two powers" of the church, as manifest in the authority of her bishops, and the state *(regalis potestas)*. Yet if Gelasius clearly stated that "the secular power cannot 'bind and loose' a pontiff,"[60] he was unclear if the emperor ruled in any other way over the church. To answer this question, Justinian the Great, emperor over the Eastern Roman Empire from 527 until his death in 565, enacted a *modus operandi* in which the emperor "has jurisdiction over ecclesiastical estates . . . , but not unfettered discretion."[61] To be sure, Justinian also publicly echoed the Gelasian view of mutuality between the church and the state,[62] but the legacy he left was one in which the will of the emperor was understood as having the force of law across the empire.[63]

Partly in the wake of Justinian, Pope Gregory the Great (540-604) argued that all rule is God-given, and even the rule of the wicked is meant by God for the punishment of a wayward community.[64] Although often cited as an authority advocating non-resistance to absolutists and tyrants, Gregory's more important contribution was to bequeath a model of kingship based on ecclesial authority so that earthly lords imitated episcopal leaders who served self-sacrificially following in the footsteps of Jesus, the heavenly king. In a by-and-large Christianized Latin West,[65] Christian teaching defined public service to be ministerial in character, shaped by "christological virtues of humility, obedi-

Langdon Forhan, eds., *Medieval Political Theology — A Reader: The Quest for the Body Politic, 1100-1400* (London and New York: Routledge, 1993); R. W. Dyson, *Normative Theories of Society and Government in Five Medieval Thinkers,* Mediaeval Studies 21 (Lewiston, NY: Edwin Mellen Press, 2003); and Michael Hoelzl and Graham Ward, eds., *Religion and Political Thought* (London and New York: Continuum, 2006). My account draws heavily from Oliver O'Donovan and Joan Lockwood O'Donovan, eds., *From Irenaeus to Grotius: A Sourcebook in Christian Political Thought 100-1625* (Grand Rapids and Cambridge, UK: Eerdmans, 1999), hereafter cited as *Sourcebook.*

60. Gelasius I, "The Bond of Anathema," in *Sourcebook,* p. 179.

61. *Sourcebook,* p. 190.

62. See the preamble to Justinian's regulations titled "On the Selection of Bishops," in *Sourcebook,* p. 194.

63. See Justinian, *Institutes,* 1.2.6; cf. *Sourcebook,* p. 233, and John W. Barker, *Justinian and the Later Roman Empire* (1966; reprint, Madison: University of Wisconsin Press, 1977), esp. pp. 261-66.

64. Gregory the Great, *Regula pastoralis* (or *Pastoral Rule*), part 2, and *Magna moralia,* 25.34-38 (exposition of Job), both in *Sourcebook,* pp. 197-203.

65. R. A. Markus, "Gregory the Great on Kings: Rulers and Preachers in the *Commentary on 1 Kings,*" in Diana Wood, ed., *The Church and Sovereignty c. 590-1918: Essays in Honour of Michael Wilks* (Malden, MA: The Ecclesiastical History Society and Basil Blackwell, 1991), pp. 7-21.

ence, self-sacrificial care of others, patience with human moral frailty, and compassion for the poor and defenseless."[66] All of this came to full fruition in Pope Leo III's crowning of Charlemagne in 800; here the "theocratic king-priest . . . , endowed with episcopal powers, was responsible for the temporal and eternal welfare of his subjects. Regenerated by baptism, supernaturally equipped by royal anointing, the new Moses (or David, or Solomon, or Melchizedek), vicar of God or of Christ, superintended his imperial church, mediating the divine will by teaching and enforcing Christian doctrine and morality."[67]

The High Middle Ages featured efforts on both sides of the church/papacy and state/emperor divide to wrest control of Christendom. The confrontation between Pope Gregory VII (1020/25-1085) and the German king Henry IV (1050-1106) exemplifies the issues at stake.[68] Whereas Gelasius had distinguished the "two powers" or authorities of the church and the state, albeit urging for their complementarity, Gregory emphasized the "divine power" of the papacy in spiritual matters (which sometimes had implications for the temporal realm) while Henry insisted on the "divine right" of kings in temporal matters (which oftentimes required intervention in ecclesial affairs). For Gregory, the church is the supremely established divine institution with oversight over the spiritual domain (which includes within it the affairs of the temporal world, as subordinate to the spiritual); and thus the pope, as head of the church, has supreme authority on earth (and, by extension, over the temporal affairs of the world, especially when these are intertwined with the spiritual matters of the church).[69] For Henry, on the other hand, the authority of the pope was limited to the sphere of the church and the domain of the spiritual life, whereas the authority of the king (or emperor) by divine appointment extended over all other temporal matters.

The next few centuries would see apologists on both sides dispute the issue. Gregory's position was defended by a number of leading popes (unsurprisingly), including Innocent III (1161-1216), who championed the notion that the spiritual domain and authority of the papacy included all things temporal given that the latter was included in the former,[70] and Boniface VII

66. *Sourcebook*, p. 173.

67. *Sourcebook*, p. 174.

68. See Brian Tierney, *Crisis of Church and State*, pp. 53-73; cf. Brian Tierney, Donald Kagan, and L. Pearce Williams, eds., *Gregory VII — Church Reformer or World Monarch?* (New York: Random House, 1967), chap. 4.

69. For a sympathetic treatment of Gregory's papacy as resisting the subservience of the church to the state, see Agnes Bernard Cavanagh, *Pope Gregory VII and the Theocratic State* (Washington, DC: Catholic University of America Press, 1934).

70. See Kenneth Pennington, "Pope Innocent III's Views on the Church and State: A

(1235-1303), whose papal bull *Unam Sanctum* (issued 18 November 1302) represented the height of Roman hierocratism and imperialism in its declaration that "it is absolutely necessary for salvation that every human creature be subject to the Roman Pontiff."[71] Boniface found support in the theologians Giles of Rome (1243-1316), who authored multiple volumes defending the lawful, just, and rightful rulership of the pope as Christ's vicar on earth over all temporal realities,[72] and James of Viterbo (d. 1308), who insisted that royal edicts based on natural laws had to be informed or completed by ecclesial directive, given the centrality of the church and the supreme authority (both pontifical and royal) of the vicar of Christ.[73]

Giles's arguments actually were an extension of his teacher's, St. Thomas Aquinas (1225?-74), whose corpus of work rehabilitated the notion, following Aristotle, of *homo sapiens* as *homo politicus*, which was delegitimized by Augustine.[74] However, on the question of the relationship between the two powers, Aquinas affirmed the authority of the priesthood and the papacy over all temporal authority, particularly with regard to spiritual matters.[75] More specifically, in his *De regimine principum* (ca. 1265-67), he writes:

> Thus, in order that spiritual things might be distinguished from earthly things, the ministry of this kingdom has been entrusted not to earthly kings but to priests, and most of all to the chief priest, the successor of St.

Gloss to *Per Venerabilem*," in Kenneth Pennington and Robert Somerville, eds., *Law, Church, and Society: Essays in Honor of Stephan Kuttner* (Philadelphia: University of Pennsylvania Press, 1977), pp. 49-67; for further discussion of the complexity of interpretations of Innocent, see James M. Powell, ed., *Innocent III: Vicar of Christ or Lord of the World?* 2nd ed. (Washington, DC: Catholic University of America Press, 1994).

71. See http://www.fordham.edu/halsall/source/b8-unam.html (last accessed 27 September 2008). Thus did *Unam Sanctum* demand "the most absolute subjection of the secular authority to the papal" (see Sturzo, *Church and State*, vol. 1, p. 118).

72. See especially Giles's *De renunciation papali* (1292), defending Pope Celestine V, and *De ecclesiastica potestate* (ca. 1301), written as an apologetic for Boniface VIII against Philip IV of France.

73. Viterbo wrote *De regimine christiano*, probably in 1302; see R. W. Dyson, ed., *James of Viterbo on Christian Government: De Regimine Christiano* (Woodbridge, UK: Boydell Press, 1995).

74. See Paul E. Sigmund, "Law and Politics," in Norman Kretzmann and Eleonore Stump, eds., *The Cambridge Companion to Aquinas* (Cambridge and New York: Cambridge University Press, 1993), pp. 217-31.

75. Thomas Aquinas, *Summa Theologica*, IIaIIas60.6, reply obj. 3; cf. Saint Thomas Aquinas, *On Law, Morality, and Politics*, eds. William P. Baumgarth and Richard J. Regan, SJ (Indianapolis: Hackett, 1988), p. 259.

Peter, the Vicar of Christ, the Roman Pontiff. To him all the kings of the Christian People are to be subject as to our Lord Jesus Christ Himself. For those to whom pertains the care of intermediate ends should be subject to him to whom pertains the care of the ultimate end, and be directed by his rule. . . . Consequently, in the law of Christ, kings must be subject to priests.[76]

Yet Aquinas's position raised questions about how to distinguish spiritual from temporal matters, and also if there could be temporal matters completely unrelated to the spiritual domain.

It was in part the concern that the spiritual would swallow up the temporal that Henry and those in his train resisted the claims regarding papal authority.[77] Perhaps in response to Boniface's *Unam Sanctum,* John Quidort of Paris (1250-1306) defended the royalist cause against the papal claims by insisting on communal election and representation, by understanding political office in terms of public stewardship, and by viewing political acts as subordinate to rather than generative of the law.[78] Other apologists in this vein included the poet/philosopher Dante Alighieri (1265-1321), who argued in the context of the disordered states of Italy and Germany and the papal captivity in France for a genuine duality, or diarchy, of imperial and papal authority (thus the authority of the emperor was not mediated through that of the pope but rather derived directly from God);[79] the scholar Marsilius of Padua (1275/80-1342/43), who presented not only the royalist defense against papal

76. Thomas Aquinas, *De Regno,* trans. Gerald B. Phelan, and I. Th. Eschmann, ed. Joseph Kenny (Toronto: Pontifical Institute of Mediaeval Studies, 1949), pp. 110-11. Leonard E. Boyle, "The *De Regno* and the Two Powers," in J. Reginald O'Donnell, ed., *Essays in Honour of Anton Charles Pegis* (Toronto: Pontifical Institute of Mediaeval Studies, 1974), pp. 237-47, emphasizes that Aquinas actually toes a more middle-of-the-road position in that temporal authorities are subject to the pope only with regard to spiritual matters. Even if so, the questions raised next in the text are not thereby resolved.

77. At one level, as Wm. D. McCready shows in "Papalists and Antipapalists: Aspects of the Church/State Controversy in the Later Middle Ages," *Viator* 6 (1975): 241-73, theorists on both sides agreed that the authority of the pope was first and foremost spiritual; the debate concerned the limits of such spiritual authority especially when that interfaced with temporal issues such as clerical or regal appointments, tithes and taxation, and church property rights and legal jurisdiction issues.

78. See John's *De postestate regio et papali (On Royal and Papal Power),* published in probably the same year as *Unam Sanctum* (1302); see Janet Coleman, "The Dominican Political Theory of John of Paris in Its Context," in Diana Wood, ed., *The Church and Sovereignty, c. 590-1918: Essays in Honour of Michael Wilks* (Oxford: Basil Blackwell, 1991), pp. 187-223.

79. Sturzo, *Church and State,* vol. 1, pp. 120-24; on Dante's political philosophy, see also Kantorowicz, *King's Two Bodies,* chap. 8.

hierocracy, but also the first counterargument for imperial/secular political monism and hierarchicalism, for the former lifting up the Franciscan model of the supreme poverty of Jesus (derived from Scripture, tradition, and ecclesial canon law) as normative for the church, and for the latter prioritizing natural law theory (reason) in the Aristotelian and Averroist vein over the divine law tradition;[80] and, later, the political philosopher Machiavelli (1469-1527), whose *Principe* (1532; *The Prince*) presumed, from scriptural, historical, and philosophical arguments, a royalist authority quite apart from any ecclesial support.[81] The articulation of this divine-right royalism culminated, arguably, in the rule of King James VI/I (1566-1625), whose *The Trew Law of Free Monarchies* (1598) defended — in terms of Scripture, reason, and history — an absolutism in which royal rule was unending, not based on any social contract but on divine appointment,[82] and in the political philosophy of Thomas Hobbes (1588-1679), whose *Leviathan* (originally, 1651) defended a sovereign whose rule extended over civil, military, judicial, and ecclesiastical spheres.[83]

Much is neglected and as much needs to be further unpacked in the preceding account. My intention, however, is not to be exhaustive. Instead, I wish to highlight three important elements of this overview of theologies of the political in the medieval period. First, the debates about the priority of the papacy or emperor or the independence of church and state only make sense assuming the political configuration of Christendom in which the rule of Constantine and the crowning of Charlemagne were the key events. Second, however, even in the context of Christendom, there were at least these three divergent views, and we have not even mentioned the emergence of the

---

80. Marsilius's *Defensor pacis* (1324) was not well received in ecclesial circles, was anathemized by John XXII in 1327, and was put on the "Index" in 1559 — not least because Marsilius also reinterpreted priestly oversight as being empowered only to declare, rather than to confer, absolution of sins, and as having only pedagogical rather than jurisdictional authority. But note also that Marsilius's royalism was not totalitarian since political authority was finally dependent upon the rule of the people. For further discussion, see Thomas Turley, "The Impact of Marsilius: Papalist Responses to the *Defensor Pacis*," in Gerson Moreno-Riaño, ed., *The World of Marsilius of Padua*, Disputatio 5 (Turnhout, Belgium: Brepols, 2006), pp. 47-64.

81. Niccolo Machiavelli, *The Prince,* trans. N. H. Thompson (Buffalo, NY: Prometheus Books, 1986).

82. King James VI and I, *Political Writings,* ed. Johann P. Sommerville (Cambridge: Cambridge University Press, 1994).

83. See Gerrit Manenschijn, "'Jesus is the Christ': The Political Theology of *Leviathan*," trans. John Vriend, *Journal of Religious Ethics* 25, no. 1 (1997): 35-64, and Alan Ryan, "Hobbes' Political Philosophy," in Tom Sorell, ed., *The Cambridge Companion to Hobbes* (Cambridge: Cambridge University Press, 1996), pp. 208-45.

conciliarist tradition in the fourteenth century.[84] Finally, note that the afore-mentioned overview remains primarily at the theoretical level; the political practices "on the ground" exhibit much more diversity than what we have described. In the following discussion of political theologies derived from Reformation traditions, a bit more attention will be paid to political practices in order to highlight the diversity of Christian views.

2.2.2. Luther's "Two Spheres" and His Descendants

The Reformer Martin Luther did not himself present a systematically articulated political theology.[85] In fact, his mind changed sharply not just over his lifetime but during the course of the tumultuous decade of the 1520s. Thus in the first part of the decade, when Luther found himself excommunicated from the Catholic Church and declared an outlaw by Emperor Charles V at the Diet of Worms (1521), to the point of living under the threat of death, emphasis was placed on *The Freedom of the Christian* (1520), on the importance of toleration, and on the church rather than the state as having the responsibility for dealing with heresy.[86] In the mid- to later 1520s, however, after the Peasant War and the demand by some of its leaders (like Thomas Müntzer) to pick up arms to further the cause of the Reformation beyond where Luther was willing to go,[87] Luther himself began to argue that the magistrate had responsibility to suppress social unrest forcefully and punish religious blasphemy, even if that required using capital punishment in some

84. On the conciliarism of the late medieval period, see Francis Oakley, *Council over Pope? Towards a Provisional Ecclesiology* (New York: Herder & Herder, 1969), esp. part 1.

85. Two major studies are W. D. J. Cargill Thompson, *The Political Thought of Martin Luther*, ed. Philip Broadhead (Sussex, UK: Harvester Press, and Totowa, NJ: Barnes & Noble, 1984), and Per Frostin, *Luther's Two Kingdoms Doctrine: A Critical Study*, Studia Theologica Lundensia 48 (Lund, Sweden: Lund University Press, 1994).

86. Luther wrote then: "Heresy can never be restrained by force. . . . Here God's word must do the fighting. . . . Heresy is a spiritual matter which you cannot hack to pieces with iron, consume with fire, or drown with water"; see Luther's *Temporal Authority: To What Extent It Should Be Obeyed* (orig., 1523), in Timothy F. Lull, ed., *Martin Luther's Basic Theological Writings* (Minneapolis: Fortress Press, 1989), pp. 655-703, quote from p. 688. All other citations of this translation in the following paragraph will be made parenthetically in the text by page number.

87. For some of the details, see Carter Lindberg, "Theology and Politics: Luther the Radical and Müntzer the Reactionary," *Encounter* 37, no. 4 (1976): 356-71. Lindberg argues, not implausibly, that Müntzer sought to re-establish the medieval framework of Christendom in the face of its unraveling, except that his emphasis was on the rule of the elect, while Luther rejected the medieval compromise and its sacralizing of the political.

cases.[88] Yet Luther felt his later position was a logical extension of the distinction between the law and the gospel: the latter governed the spiritual lives of believers according to the Word of God, while the former governed the public or political lives of all people, believers included, according to the laws of the temporal or secular authority.

It is in his *Temporal Authority: To What Extent It Should Be Obeyed* (1523) that Luther lays out the set of ideas that have since taken on a life of their own. In this treatise, Luther's focus is the government's use of the sword, and the possibility of using it "in a Christian manner" (p. 655). Four major points are argued. 1) There is a sound biblical (Rom. 13 and 1 Pet. 2:13-14 are cited) and theological basis for the government's wielding of the sword (p. 659). 2) The New Testament injunctions toward nonviolence, especially those in the Sermon on the Mount, are directed to all Christians in their spiritual relationships with one another, and are not to be interpreted literally especially with regard to the work of government in the secular sphere.[89] 3) While Christians or true believers "need no temporal law or sword . . . since [they] have in their heart the Holy Spirit" (p. 663), the lawless world, which includes Christians as fallen creatures, needs both (p. 664; citing 1 Tim. 1:9). Finally, 4) non-Christians are not only under the law but need to be restrained for peace to reign (p. 665). Toward this end, Christians have to use the sword not for themselves but for their weaker, sinful, fallen fellow humans (p. 669). If governments are divinely appointed servants (Rom. 13), then Christians serving in those capacities can and should take up the sword not on their own behalf, but on behalf of others, to take vengeance, achieve justice, protect and help the oppressed, etc. (p. 675). As Luther had earlier written, "since the temporal power is ordained of God to punish the wicked and protect the good, it should be free to perform its office in the whole body of Christendom without restriction and without respect to persons, whether it affects pope, bishops, priests, monks, nuns, or anyone else."[90]

88. See the discussion, along with references to Luther's writings, in Frostin, *Luther's Two Kingdoms Doctrine,* pp. 70-71.

89. Thus Luther opposed on the one hand the medieval and Roman tradition which applied the Sermon only to those seeking to go toward perfection, and, on the other hand, Anabaptist literal interpretations of this text vis-à-vis governmental duties and interactions with non-Christians. See Luther, *Commentary on the Sermon on the Mount,* trans. Charles A. Hay (Philadelphia: Lutheran Publication Society, 1892), pp. vi-viii; cf. Jaroslav Pelikan, ed., *Luther's Works,* vol. 21: *The Sermon on the Mount (Sermons) and the Magnificat* (St. Louis: Concordia, 1956), pp. 113-14.

90. Martin Luther, *To the Christian Nobility of the German Nation* (orig., 1520), in Luther, *Three Treatises,* rev. ed., trans. Charles M. Jacobs (Philadelphia: Fortress Press, 1970), pp. 1-112, quotation from p. 15.

In some respects, Luther's distinction between the spiritual and temporal authorities is an elaboration of the medieval doctrine of two powers or two swords, as well as an extension of the Augustinian notion of two cities.[91] The differences between Luther and Augustine, however, are important to note. Whereas the latter wrote the *City of God* under the shadow of the fall of Rome, the former's ideas on the two authorities/domains emerged out of the historical situation of Saxony (Germany) in which bishops were attempting to govern territories and secular authorities were attempting to root out papist heresies. More important, Augustine's two cities were ontologically and theologically distinct — divided between that of God and that of the devil — even if they were epistemologically blurred. Luther's two authorities in their respective spheres, however, were both divinely established, with God's presence and activity (against the devil) equally in both arenas.[92] Hence there is the possibility that Christians could be called to service in the secular sphere, and in that way fulfill their vocational duties before God.

The major developments in Luther's two authorities through the early twentieth century can be summarily discussed. Building on the work of the later Luther, Melanchthon opened the way for state churches among Lutherans in Europe. His notion of *opera externa* located authority in the state to maintain "the prescription of forms of worship, the education and appointment of clergymen, and the defense of the accepted orthodoxy."[93] From there, it was not until 1867 that Luther's distinction was retrieved to theorize the separation of the temporal/public from the spiritual/ecclesial sphere.[94] Ernst Troeltsch then took the next step to suggest a dualism between public (political) and private (sectarian) ethics in Luther with the former assigned to its own relatively autonomous area established by God and demanding, in effect, a paradoxical Christian obedience as an expression of faith.[95] Max Weber, on

---

91. John F. Johnson, "Augustine, Aquinas, and Ockham: The Two Kingdoms Doctrine in Medieval Theology," in John R. Stephenson, ed., *God and Caesar Revisited,* Luther Academy Conference Papers 1 (Shorewood, MN: Luther Academy, 1995), pp. 30-36.

92. See esp. Heinrich Bornkamm, *Luther's Doctrine of the Two Kingdoms in the Context of His Theology,* trans. Karl H. Hertz, 2nd rev. ed., Social Ethics Series 14 (Philadelphia: Fortress, 1966), p. 22.

93. Theodore G. Tappert, "The Doctrine of the Two Kingdoms after Luther in Europe and America," in Paul D. Opsahl and Marc H. Tanenbaum, eds., *Speaking of God Today: Jews and Lutherans in Conversation* (Philadelphia: Fortress Press, 1974), pp. 81-86, quote from p. 82.

94. For a brief discussion of developments in the late nineteenth century into the middle war years of the following century, see Frostin, *Luther's Two Kingdoms Doctrine,* pp. 2-7.

95. Ernst Troeltsch, *The Social Teachings of the Christian Churches,* 2 vols., trans. Olive Wyon (ET 1931; reprint, New York and Evanston, IL: Harper & Row and Harper Torchbooks, 1960), vol. 2, pp. 506-11.

the other hand, read this dualism in terms of Luther making space for an autonomous and coherent rationality in the various spheres or orders.[96] These ideas were then co-opted by the National Socialist Party so that the distinction between the violence and power of the secular realm and the interiority of the spiritual domain was emphasized for its own purposes.

In opposition to the Nazi ideology, Karl Barth and others congregated at Barmen (in 1934) challenged the notion, among others, regarding the autonomy of the state.[97] Lutheran theologians sought (in response) to either reunite the two spheres of Luther under the redemptive reality of Christ (Dietrich Bonhoeffer)[98] or open up space for Protestantism as a critical and even prophetic principle that can speak into any historical situation (Paul Tillich).[99] What bound the Reformed Barth together with these Lutheran thinkers was a distrust of all ideologies and political systems, and the belief that those which laid claim to being Christian could only do so as a result of an idolatrous stance.[100]

Partially in response to the debate, Harald Diem published his *Luthers Lehre von den zwei Reichen* in 1938,[101] and argued that Luther's two-authorities/orders distinction, now renamed the teaching of the Two Kingdoms, was related to the evangelical (Lutheran) doctrine of justification — thus raising the question: How do justified people interface with the world? Diem's response emphasized the distinction *(Unterscheidung)* but not separation *(Scheidung)* of the two domains, since Christ is still lord over both. This suggested, for Diem, the compatibility of such an interpretation of Luther's legacy with the theological declaration of Barmen.

96. Max Weber, *The Protestant Ethic and the Spirit of Capitalism*, trans. Talcott Parsons (New York: Charles Scribner's Sons, 1958), chap. 3.

97. See Arne Rasmusson, "Church and Nation-State: Karl Barth and German Public Theology in the Early 20th Century," *Ned Geref Teologiese Tydskrif* 46, nos. 3-4 (2005): 511-24, and "'Deprive Them of Their Pathos': Karl Barth and the Nazi Revolution Revisited," *Modern Theology* 23, no. 3 (2007): 369-91. For more on Barth's political theology, see George Hunsinger, ed., *Karl Barth and Radical Politics* (Philadelphia: Westminster, 1975), and, more recently, Timothy J. Gorringe, *Karl Barth: Against Hegemony* (Oxford: Oxford University Press, 1999), and Frank Jehle, *Ever Against the Stream: The Politics of Karl Barth, 1906-1968*, trans. Richard and Martha Burnett (Grand Rapids and Cambridge, UK: Eerdmans, 2002).

98. E.g., Dietrich Bonhoeffer, *Ethics,* ed. Eberhard Bethge, trans. Neville Horton Smith (1955; reprint, New York: Collier/Macmillan, 1986), pp. 196-207 and 332-53.

99. See Paul Tillich, *Political Expectation,* ed. James Luther Adams (New York: Harper & Row, 1971), esp. chap. 2. I return to discuss Tillich later (4.2.1).

100. René de Visme Williamson, *Politics and Protestant Theology: An Interpretation of Tillich, Barth, Bonhoeffer, and Brunner* (Baton Rouge: Louisiana State University Press, 1976), p. 149.

101. Harald Diem, *Luthers Lehre von den zwei Reichen* (München: C. Kaiser, 1938).

Since Diem, the Two Kingdoms doctrine has been reformulated variously in Lutheran circles.[102] The major questions being debated include: What is the relationship between Luther's own theology of the state — recalling that our own discussion focused only on one, albeit central, text of Luther's — and these more recent developments in the last century? Does the distinction between the law and the gospel carry over into a theology of the political and an ecclesiology, as sometimes suggested? Put alternatively, are recent articulations of the Two Kingdoms doctrine extrapolations of a Lutheran theology of creation (establishing the temporal or secular) and of redemption (related to the church)? Is there a separation or merely a distinction between the spiritual and the secular spheres (kingdoms) and if so, what does that consist of? Is God present and active differently in the two spheres — i.e., directly in the church and indirectly in the political?[103] And last but certainly not least, is the use of force and the sword justified by Christians serving in the secular realm? We will need to keep these questions in mind in the remainder of this book.

2.2.3. Reformed Theologies of the Political

The complexity of issues does not subside when we shift from the Lutheran to the Calvinistic side of the Reformation tradition. Calvin's political theology must be understood not only in terms of what he wrote, but also in terms of the reforms he instituted in transforming Geneva into a Protestant city. Under his guidance, Geneva came to be seen as a model theocracy, although it has been more rightly identified as a "clerocracy" — a government deeply informed by ecclesial leadership.[104]

The final edition of Calvin's *Institutes of the Christian Religion* (1559) reflects aspects of his political theology that had been tried and tested at

102. See Frostin, *Luther's Two Kingdoms Doctrine,* chap. 1, for a summary of the debate; cf. Ulrich Duchrow, ed., *Lutheran Churches — Salt or Mirror of Society? Case Studies on the Theory and Practice of the Two Kingdoms Doctrine,* trans. Dorothea Millwood (Geneva: Lutheran World Federation, 1977), and John R. Stumme and Robert W. Tuttle, eds., *Church and State: Lutheran Perspectives* (Minneapolis: Fortress, 2003).

103. These last few questions all converge on the issue of whether there is a substantive dualism between the two spheres or kingdoms in Luther; for further discussion of this worry, see Helmut Thielicke, *Theological Ethics,* 2 vols., ed. William H. Lazareth (Philadelphia: Fortress, 1966-1969), esp. vol. 1, chap. 18, on the two kingdoms, and vol. 2, chap. 31, on the church and politics.

104. John T. McNeill, *The History and Character of Calvinism* (1954; reprint, London: Oxford University Press, 1967), p. 185; for further discussion of Calvin at Geneva, see Harro Höpfl, *The Christian Polity of John Calvin* (Cambridge: Cambridge University Press, 1982), esp. chap. 6.

Geneva.[105] Within the two swords, two powers, and two authorities tradition, Calvin distinguished between spiritual/ecclesial and the civil governments and insisted on their not being antithetical but complementary (4.20.2). In line with Luther's later position on the role of government especially against the violence of the peasants, the primary task of the civil government is to prevent "idolatry, sacrilege against God's name, blasphemies against his truth, and other public offenses against religion from arising and spreading among the people" (4.20.3, 1488). Since the government is ordained by God, magistrates should be faithful as God's deputies and were authorized to use coercive power or force to check both civil and ecclesial lawlessness. By extension, the people owe obedience and deference even to unjust rulers, who may represent the judgment of God (4.20.27). The combined result was that whereas Luther secularized the state, Calvin clericalized it: "Church and State are united and inseparable. To the State belongs all coercive authority. The sword of the Church is the word of God."[106]

It is important to realize that Calvin's political theology and the reformation he directed at Geneva were part and parcel of his theological vision, which centered on the glory and sovereignty of God.[107] His work in Geneva reflected this God-centeredness: political leaders should rule according to divine law; the people should live upright, moral, and peaceful lives that reflect the justice, holiness, and peaceableness of God; and the church and its ministers should exemplify and propagate this vision of God for the benefit of the people and for the well-being of the community. And, ironically (at least as popularly considered), Calvin's doctrine of divine sovereignty and providence, far from resulting in a fatalism, provided the kind of assurance that instead grounded the human pursuit, both individually and collectively — i.e., politically — of the good, the true, and the beautiful.[108]

---

105. Book 4, chapter 20, is on "Civil Government"; see John Calvin, *Institutes of the Christian Religion,* 2 vols., ed. John T. McNeill, trans. Ford Lewis Battles (Philadelphia: Westminster Press, 1960), vol. 2, pp. 1485-1521. Citation from this chapter will be made parenthetically in the text following the standard convention of book, chapter, and section numbers; I will add the page number as well, to this McNeill/Battles translation, for direct quotes.

106. R. N. Carew Hunt, "Calvin's Theory of Church and State," in Richard C. Gamble, ed., *Calvin's Thought on Economic and Social Issues and the Relationship of Church and State,* Articles on Calvin and Calvinism 11 (New York and London: Garland, 1992), pp. 2-17, quote from p. 17; for further discussion, see William R. Stevenson, Jr., "Calvin and Political Issues," in Donald K. McKim, *The Cambridge Companion to John Calvin* (Cambridge: Cambridge University Press, 2004), pp. 173-87.

107. Ralph C. Hancock, *Calvin and the Foundations of Modern Politics* (Ithaca and London: Cornell University Press, 1989), p. 164.

108. Eric Fuchs, "Providence and Politics: A Reflection on the Contemporary Relevance

The result was the development of a Reformed political posture in (perhaps) unanticipated directions. I am referring here to Weber's thesis that in the next few generations and centuries after Calvin, the ongoing Reformed, especially Puritan, quest for certainty in the face of the questions regarding divine election (or reprobation) led to emergence of an entire cultural and ethical way of life emphasizing hard work, thrift, sobriety, prudence, honesty, etc., which converged with, if not causally contributed to, the economic system of modern capitalism.[109] Baptism initiates individuals into an elect community, and exemplification of the Christian virtues becomes an ongoing marker of individual election. After the Thirty Years War (1618-48) and the ensuing Peace of Westphalia (1648) not only introduced the modern concept of state sovereignty but also shifted the emphasis from religious beliefs (which were to be tolerated) to public practices (contributing to the common good), Calvinist sensibilities that the world was the theater for the expression of the glory of God remained a constant theme — except that the construction of a good society was now no longer directed from the top down, as it was in Calvin's Geneva, but emerged from the bottom up, as the Reformed faithful lived out their salvation and sanctification in their communities, their institutions, and the public sphere.

By the late nineteenth century, the political landscape of Europe had become increasingly pluralistic. In this context, the political theology of Abraham Kuyper (1837-1920) deserves some extended comment. Kuyper was not only a Reformed pastor and theologian (his doctoral dissertation was on John Calvin, and he pastored in Dutch Reformed churches from 1863 to 1874), but he also founded the Free University of Amsterdam (in 1880) and then was a public servant: first as a member of the Dutch Parliament from 1874 to 1877,

---

of the Political Ethics of John Calvin," in Richard C. Gamble, ed., *Calvin and Calvinism*, vol. 3: *Calvin's Work in Geneva* (New York and London: Garland, 1992), pp. 185-97.

109. Weber, *The Protestant Ethic and the Spirit of Capitalism*; a shorter version of the thesis, focused on the American scene, is Weber, "The Protestant Sects and the Spirit of Capitalism," in H. H. Gerth and C. Wright Mills, eds. and trans., *From Max Weber: Essays in Sociology* (1947; reprint, New York: Oxford University Press, 1970), pp. 302-22. Against Weber, see W. Stanford Reid, "John Calvin, Early Critic of Capitalism: An Alternative Interpretation," and "Jean Calvin: The Father of Capitalism?" both reprinted in Richard C. Gamble, ed., *Calvin's Thought on Economic and Social Issues and the Relationship of Church and State,* Articles on Calvin and Calvinism 11 (New York and London: Garland, 1992), pp. 158-70 and 199-205, respectively. A more updated and nuanced restatement of Weber's thesis, one that avoids the problems posed by seeing a mono-causal set of relations going from Puritanism and capitalism and that is informed by multidisciplinary perspectives, is Philip S. Gorski, *The Disciplinary Revolution: Calvinism and the Rise of the State in Early Modern Europe* (Chicago and London: University of Chicago Press, 2003).

then as chairman of the Anti-Revolutionary Party from 1879 to 1905, and finally as prime minister of The Netherlands from 1901 to 1905.[110] In short, Kuyper was no armchair political thinker, but, in the model established by Calvin himself, a practitioner as well, and it is against this background that we can appreciate the creativity of his theory of sphere sovereignty.

Kuyper first introduced the concept of sphere sovereignty in his inaugural address at the Free University of Amsterdam in 1880.[111] The central idea is that there are different spheres or domains of human life, each with their own authorities — i.e., the family, the economic, the religious (seen in the institution of the church), the socio-cultural (as represented in the arts), the educational (as manifest in the university), and the political (as organized in the government) — and hence not subject to the rule of other spheres. Yet the sovereignty of each sphere is secured theologically: precisely in each sphere's establishment by God in his divine sovereignty, and through each sphere's accountability to God.[112]

The Reformed theological framework within which Kuyper developed his ideas is what interests us here. Kuyper's *Lectures on Calvinism* given at Princeton Theological Seminary in 1898 locate the political theology of sphere sovereignty within an all-encompassing life-and-world-view.[113] Three points are worth noting. First, while Kuyper is squarely in the Reformed tradition in viewing the state and the magistrate as "an instrument of 'common grace,' to thwart all license and outrage and to shield the good against the evil in order that he may preserve the glorious work of God, in the creation of humanity, from total destruction" (pp. 82-83), he goes beyond Calvin to locate

110. The definitive biography so far is John Bolt, *A Free Church, a Holy Nation: Abraham Kuyper's American Public Theology* (Grand Rapids and Cambridge, UK: Eerdmans, 2001); also helpful is McKendree R. Langley, *The Practice of Political Spirituality: Episodes from the Public Career of Abraham Kuyper, 1879-1918* (Jordan Station, ON: Paideia Press, 1984).

111. It is reprinted in James D. Bratt, ed., *Abraham Kuyper: A Centennial Reader* (Grand Rapids and Cambridge, UK: Eerdmans, and Carlisle, UK: Paternoster, 1998), pp. 463-90.

112. Thus Kuyper's famous line: "Oh, no single piece of our mental world is to be hermetically sealed off from the rest, and there is not a square inch in the whole domain of our human existence over which Christ, who is Sovereign over *all,* does not cry: 'Mine!'" (in Bratt, ed., *Abraham Kuyper,* p. 488). See also Gordon Spykman, "Sphere-Sovereignty in Calvin and the Calvinist Tradition," in David E. Holwerda, ed., *Exploring the Heritage of John Calvin* (Grand Rapids: Baker, 1976), pp. 163-208, esp. pp. 166-67, and John P. Tiemstra, "Every Square Inch: Kuyperian Social Theory and Economics," in James M. Dean and A. M. C. Waterman, eds., *Religion and Economics: Normative Social Theory* (Boston: Kluwer Academic, 1999), pp. 85-98.

113. Abraham Kuyper, *Calvinism: Six Stone Foundation Lectures* (1931; reprint, Grand Rapids: Eerdmans, 1943). All quotations will be referenced by page number parenthetically in the text, and all italics are original to Kuyper unless otherwise noted.

the sphere of the political in the prelapsarian order of creation instead.[114] Even apart from the fall, there would have been one united "state" or a one-world theocracy, and political life would have evolved "from the life of the family" (p. 80).[115] Precisely because the political is its own divinely appointed sphere, it is sovereign in its own domain, answerable only to God.

But second, there are other spheres, also given to creation by God in the prelapsarian context, and therefore sovereign apart from the state: "1. In the social sphere, by personal superiority. 2. In the corporative sphere of universities, guilds, associations, etc. 3. In the domestic sphere of the family and of married life, and 4. In communal autonomy. In all these four spheres the State-government cannot impose its laws, but must reverence the innate law of life. God rules in these spheres, just as supremely and sovereignly through his chosen *virtuosi,* as He exercises dominion in the sphere of the State itself, through his chosen *magistrates*" (p. 96). The state can intervene only to resolve interspheric clashes, defend the weak against the abuse of power, or "coerce all together to bear *personal* and *financial* burdens for the maintenance of the natural unity of the State" (p. 97).

Finally, there is also the sphere of religion or, in the context of The Netherlands at the turn of the twentieth century, that of the church. Kuyper here realizes this to be an especially challenging issue given the traditional Calvinist position regarding the role of civil government "defending against and . . . extirpating every form of idolatry and false religion" (p. 99), especially as that had played out even in Geneva itself. The problem is the Constantinian and medieval notion of a visible united church-state. But in a post-Constantinian context, such state-interventionism is indefensible. Rather, the traditional Calvinist insistence on the freedom of conscience must be retrieved and defended, with the result that religion "may never be imposed by force upon other people" (p. 103). So if the church is to be sovereign in its own sphere, free from encroachment by the state or any other sphere, then so should the church not (be in a position to) impose its own vision outside of its domain.[116]

---

114. See Timothy Sherratt, "Rehabilitating the State in America: Abraham Kuyper's Overlooked Contribution," in Thomas W. Heilke and Ashley Woodiwiss, eds., *The Re-Enchantment of Political Science: Christian Scholars Engage Their Discipline* (Lanham, MD: Lexington Books, 2001), pp. 121-49.

115. This differs from Aristotle's notion of *homo sapiens* as a political animal, and from the political in Aquinas, which is part of the natural order, although oriented toward the supernatural.

116. As Bolt summarizes, "it was largely through Kuyper's initiative that the 1905 Synod of the Dutch *Gereformeerde Kerken* . . . excised from Article 36 of the Belgic Confession the trou-

I suggest that Kuyper's accomplishment has been to retrieve and reappropriate the Calvinist tradition for the modern world and its political complexities.[117] As Nicholas Wolterstorff has noted, the Kuyperian notion of "sphere" paralleled Weber's notion of social differentiation as a hallmark of modern societies.[118] Kuyper's major breakthrough was to recognize the need for a social ontology "formulated in conscious opposition to all monistic visions, whether they be church-controlled societies or state-controlled ones"; thus, his "very definition of liberty was linked to a *structurally pluralistic* social vision that encouraged flourishing *independent* spheres of society. Social spheres and institutions were truly free when, existing *directly* under the sovereign rule of God, they could develop *organically* in accord with their true nature, in accord with the *ordinances* of God's creation."[119] Hence there are not just two spheres, as debated about during the medieval and early Reformation traditions, but there are a plurality or diversity of spheres.[120] Might this conception of sphere pluralism and sovereignty inform or even correlate with the diversity of political theologies and practices already noted earlier in this chapter?[121]

---

bling passage about the magistrate's responsibility to protect and promote true worship, destroy the kingdom of anti-Christ and promote the kingdom of Christ" (*A Free Church, a Holy Nation*, pp. 321-22).

117. Luis E. Lugo, ed., *Religion, Pluralism, and Public Life: Abraham Kuyper's Legacy for the Twenty-First Century* (Grand Rapids: Eerdmans, 2000).

118. Nicholas P. Wolterstorff, "Abraham Kuyper (1837-1920): Commentary," in John Witte Jr. and Frank S. Alexander, eds., *The Teachings of Modern Protestantism on Law, Politics, and Human Nature* (New York: Columbia University Press, 2007), pp. 29-69, esp. p. 56.

119. Bolt, *A Free Church, a Holy Nation*, p. 308; italics in original.

120. We need to be concerned, however, about the potentiality of Kuyper's ontology underwriting an ideology of pluralism that could result in disastrous and destructive exclusivisms, as happened, for example, in the South African context; hence it is important that we articulate, finally, a pluralistic approach to the political not just for pluralism's sake, but one that yet speaks to the harmony-in-difference of the pentecostal outpouring of the Spirit — see 6.3.3 and 8.3.3, especially. For discussions of how Kuyper's ideas were adapted, contrary to the spirit of his philosophical and theological vision, by South African Calvinist theologians to legitimate the apartheid government and its policies, see Patrick Joseph Baskwell, "Kuyper and Apartheid: A Revisiting," *Hervormde teologiese studies* 62, no. 4 (2006): 1269-90, and Piet Naude, "From Pluralism to Ideology: The Roots of Apartheid Theology in Abraham Kuyper, Gustav Warneck and Theological Pietism," *Scriptura* 88 (2005): 161-73.

121. Kuyper's large book on the Holy Spirit — Abraham Kuyper, *The Work of the Holy Spirit*, trans. Henri de Vries (New York and London: Funk & Wagnalls, 1900) — did not say much about the political. More recently, Vincent E. Bacote, *The Spirit in Public Theology: Appropriating the Legacy of Abraham Kuyper* (Grand Rapids: Baker Academic, 2005), esp. chap. 3, has connected Kuyper's pneumatology and political theology via the Reformed doctrine of common grace. I will suggest a pentecostal reappropriation of Kuyper's ideas later.

2.3. Political Theology in the Twentieth Century

The discussion of Kuyper finally brings us into the twentieth century. In this last section, we turn to the beginnings, as it were, of political theology by looking at the work of Carl Schmitt, whose book *Politische Theologie* in 1922 provided the nomenclature for this field of inquiry. We then briefly survey developments since Schmitt before ending the chapter by laying out the contemporary state-of-the-question. As before, it is impossible to be exhaustive in what follows. Our goal is to get a sense of how the discussion has continued to unfold over the last hundred or so years in order to situate the constructive reflections of this book.

2.3.1. Carl Schmitt: Founding the Field of Political Theology

Carl Schmitt (1888-1985) was a jurist, legal scholar, political philosopher, and professor of law (at various universities and business schools in Germany), and a lifelong member of the Roman Catholic Church.[122] In a number of influential essays and books in the 1920s and 1930s,[123] Schmitt addressed what he saw were the primary challenges confronting postwar Germany: the incapable leadership of the *Deutsches Reich* (also known later as the Weimar Republic), the emergence of Communism especially on the Russian front, and the emergence of liberalism — as adopted from, or forced upon Germany by, the allied nations such as the United Kingdom, France, and the United States which defeated Germany in the war — that threatened to undermine the workings of the sovereign state by redefining the political in more or less economic terms.[124] Firmly com-

---

122. The standard scholarly biography in English is Joseph W. Bednersky, *Carl Schmitt: Theorist for the Reich* (Princeton: Princeton University Press, 1983). An excellent theological introduction is Michael Hollerich, "Carl Schmitt," in Peter Scott and William T. Cavanaugh, eds., *The Blackwell Companion to Political Theology* (2004; paperback ed., Malden, MA: Blackwell, 2007), pp. 107-22.

123. The most important for our purposes are his essay "Die Diktatur" (1921), and the following books [English translations in brackets, from which I will be citing]: *Politische Theologie: Vier Kapitel zur Lehre von der Souveränität* (1922) [*Political Theology: Four Chapters on the Concept of Sovereignty,* trans. George Schwab (Cambridge, MA, and London: MIT Press, 1985)]; *Römischer Katholizismus und politische Form* (1923) [*Roman Catholicism and Political Form,* trans. G. L. Ulmen, Global Perspectives in History and Politics: Contributions to Political Science 380 (Westport, CT, and London: Greenwood Press, 1996)]; and *Der Begriff des Politischen* (1932) [*The Concept of the Political,* trans. George Schwab (New Brunswick, NJ: Rutgers University Press, 1976)].

124. See, respectively, Ellen Kennedy, *Constitutional Failure: Carl Schmitt in Weimar* (Dur-

72

mitted to the German cause, Schmitt called consistently for a more resolved and courageous leadership, apart from which the country would continue to list at the hands of the allied nations.

Schmitt's political theories were sufficiently well received so that in 1933 he was both promoted to professor at the University of Berlin and, on May 1, appointed an official constitutional lawyer for the Nazi Party. Six months later he was selected as president of the *"Vereinigung nationalsozialistischer Juristen"* ("Union of National-Socialist Jurists"), and six months after that he rose to become chief editor of the *Deutsche Juristen-Zeitung* (German Jurists' Newspaper). Although at one point he had publicly come out in support of the movement to purge Germany of the "Jewish spirit," Schmitt was never invited into the inner circles of the Nazi Party and he increasingly came to see his own political thinking as not only distinct from but also in opposition to that of the Third Reich's. The disparities became more obvious soon enough, so that he was accused at the end of 1936 of being pretentious given his Catholic affiliation and previous criticisms of Nazi racial theories. After this, Schmitt fell out of favor with the Nazi leadership and ceased to play a major political role.

Because of the controversy surrounding Schmitt's work,[125] we will

ham, NC, and London: Duke University Press, 2004), and David Dyzenhaus, ed., *Law as Politics: Carl Schmitt's Critique of Liberalism* (Durham, NC, and London: Duke University Press, 1998).

125. The first and final chapters in Paul Edward Gottfried, *Carl Schmitt: Politics and Theory,* Global Perspectives in History and Politics: Contributions in Political Science 264 (New York: Greenwood Press, 1990), discuss the extremely critical post–World War II reception of Schmitt, read especially through the assumption that he was a Nazi ideologue. To be sure, Schmitt's predominantly traditionalist (Hobbesean) theory of the state was deployed by some in the Nazi regime for their own legitimation, even while Schmitt himself was not completely blameless given his own opportunistic (rather than ideological) alignment with the Nazi Party from 1933 to 1936. Yet the efforts to prosecute Schmitt as a war criminal were ultimately unsuccessful as no evidence could be presented that the regime's criminal activities could be traced to Schmitt; on Schmitt's interrogation as well as his response, see Joseph W. Bendersky, trans., "Interrogation of Carl Schmitt by Robert Kempner (I-III)," *Telos: A Quarterly of Critical Thought* 72 (1987): 97-107; Carl Schmitt, "On *Grossraum,* the Hitler Regime and Collaboration (I-III): Answers to Allegations," trans. Capers Rubin, in *Telos: A Quarterly of Critical Thought* 72 (1987): 107-29; and Joseph W. Bendersky, "Carl Schmitt's Path to Nuremberg: A Sixty-Year Reassessment," *Telos: A Quarterly of Critical Thought* 139 (2007): 6-34.

There is also the question of anti-Semitism at the root of Schmitt's thinking, as argued, e.g., by Raphael Gross, *Carl Schmitt and the Jews: The "Jewish Question," the Holocaust, and German Legal Theory,* trans. Joel Golb (Madison: University of Wisconsin Press, 2007). We will not be able to adjudicate this issue; in defense of my decision to discuss Schmitt here, let me only say that he is unavoidable in any substantive treatment of political theology. We will need to be careful, however, about the possible anti-Semitic leaven in political theology discourses; see further my discussion in 8.2.1.

need to be focused in our discussion. Most important for our purposes are the specifically theological aspects of Schmitt's political theory. While not trained specifically in theology, Schmitt insisted that modern politics was structured by the theological: "All significant concepts of the modern theory of the state are secularized theological concepts not only because of their historical development . . . but also because of their systematic nature, the recognition of which is necessary for a sociological consideration of these concepts."[126] Thus the secularization of the theological idea of creation out of nothing results in political decisionism — the political act that is infallible and cannot be repealed or contested; theology's omnipotent deity, the emperor's "divine right," and the Catholic Church's papacy all translate into the political monarch and lawgiver; and religion's miracle becomes the political exceptional case, a state of emergency that demands an authoritative judgment and resolution.[127]

Further, the theological contrast between God and the satan finds a political analogy in Schmitt's friend-foe distinction. Note here that Schmitt's decisionism, authoritarianism, and absolutism were forged amidst the perceived crises of the Weimar Republic. And crises were political precisely because they involved friends against enemies, and these "are to be understood in their concrete and existential sense, not as metaphors or symbols, not mixed or weakened by economic, moral, and other conceptions, least of all in a private-individualistic sense as a psychological expression of private emotions and tendencies."[128] To clarify how seriously he understood this notion, Schmitt wrote: "An enemy exists only when, at least potentially, one fighting collectivity of people confronts a similar collectivity,"[129] and "The friend, enemy, and combat concepts receive their real meaning precisely because they refer to the real possibility of physical killing. War follows from enmity. War is the existential negation of the enemy. It is the most extreme consequence of enmity. It does not have to be common, normal, something ideal, or desirable. But it must nevertheless remain a real possibility for as long as the concept of the enemy remains valid."[130] If at the beginning of his career the enemies of the *Deutsches Reich* were external (e.g., the Allies and communist Russia), then by the mid-1930s, the enemies were as much internal (e.g., Jews or the more liberal trajectories within the nation) as exter-

126. Schmitt, *Political Theology*, p. 36.
127. Thus, "The exception in jurisprudence is analogous to the miracle in theology" (Schmitt, *Political Theology*, p. 36).
128. Schmitt, *The Concept of the Political*, pp. 27-28.
129. Schmitt, *The Concept of the Political*, p. 28.
130. Schmitt, *The Concept of the Political*, p. 33.

nal.[131] But if some think the domain of the political is meant to resolve enemy-friend relations, for Schmitt, such a distinction was itself constitutive of the political. "A world in which the possibility of war is utterly eliminated, a completely pacified globe, would be a world without the distinction of friend and enemy and hence a world without politics."[132]

Hence the domain of the political featured threatening enemies, and such crisis contexts are exceptional situations demanding authoritative decisions and leadership. This leads to Schmitt's postulation of the sovereign:

> Sovereign is he who decides on the exception. . . . He decides whether there is an extreme emergency as well as what must be done to eliminate it. Although he stands outside the normally valid legal system, he nevertheless belongs to it, for it is he who must decide whether the constitutional needs to be suspended in its entirety. All tendencies of modern constitutional development point toward eliminating the sovereign in this sense. . . . But whether this extreme exception can be banished from the world is not a juristic question. Whether one has confidence and hope that it can be eliminated depends on philosophical, especially on philosophical-historical or metaphysical convictions.[133]

Clearly, the sovereign is grounded not only philosophically but also theologically.[134] If divine revelation divided the world into the elect and the non-elect, the us and them, the friends and their enemies, then the political required the naming of the enemy. That the world is constituted by friends and enemies is

131. Heinrich Meier, *Carl Schmitt and Leo Strauss: The Hidden Dialogue,* trans. J. Harvey Lomax (Chicago and London: University of Chicago Press, 1995), esp. pp. 17-28.

132. Schmitt, *The Concept of the Political,* p. 35. Later in the book, Schmitt writes, "A world state that embraces the entire globe and all of humanity cannot exist. The political world is a pluriverse, not a universe. In this sense every theory of state is pluralistic. . . . If the different states, religions, classes, and other human groupings on earth should be so unified that a conflict among them is impossible . . . , then the distinction of friend and enemy would also cease. What remains is neither politics nor state, but culture, civilization, economics, morality, law, art, entertainment, etc." (p. 53).

133. Schmitt, *Political Theology,* pp. 5 and 7. While Schmitt's exceptionalism might sound ominous, especially during the 1930s in Germany, Jean Bethke Elshtain reminds us that "the notion is venerable, trailing in its wake the dust of centuries" — back at least to Justinian in the sixth century, according to Elshtain's genealogy; see Elshtain, *Sovereignty: God, State, and Self* (New York: Basic Books, 2008), p. 32.

134. Thus does Heinrich Meier, *The Lesson of Carl Schmitt: Four Chapters on the Distinction between Political Theology and Political Philosophy,* trans. Marcus Brainard (Chicago and London: University of Chicago Press, 1998), argue that Schmitt is first a political theologian rather than a political philosopher.

an extension of the doctrine of the fall into original sin, and it takes a re-deemer — understood politically as the sovereign — to make the kinds of ex-ecutive decisions that will be salvific in exceptional situations.[135]

It should also now be clear why some of Schmitt's critics believed that the Nazis used his political philosophy (and theology) to provide the ideolog-ical legitimation for the kind of constitutional dictatorship aspired to by Hit-ler and thus declared his political theology to be heresy.[136] The German theo-logian Erik Peterson (1890-1960) argued that while the "one God" of the ancient world was not only religious, but derived from sacred law and hence already political, and although the earliest Christian liturgy, doxology, and hymnography were political expressions, yet this was not a politics of the world, but rather functioned as a counter-politics amidst the world.[137] Fur-ther, he argued that the Christian deity is neither monotheistic nor polytheis-tic, but trinitarian, and that such a conception is thus opposed to all monar-chic and polycratic forms of political rule, including that of Schmitt's sovereign.[138] Thus, in a deeply Augustinian manner, Peterson insisted that a "thoroughly eschatological view of the Church cannot look upon *any* existing

135. Schmitt's "mentors" in this regard include the political philosopher Hobbes — see Schmitt's *Der Leviathan in der Staatslehre des Thomas Hobbes* (1938) [*The Leviathan in the State Theory of Thomas Hobbes: Meaning and Failure in a Political Symbol*, trans. George Schwab and Erna Hilfstein, Contributions in Political Science 374 (Westport, CT, and London: Greenwood Press, 1996)] — and the French Catholic counter-revolutionary theologians Louis de Bonald (1754-1840) and Joseph de Maistre (1754-1821). On the latter two, see George F. Fitzgibbon, "De Bonald and De Maistre," *The American Catholic Sociological Review* 1, no. 3 (1940): 116-24. Graeme Garrard, "Joseph de Maistre and Carl Schmitt," in Richard A. Lebrun, ed., *Joseph de Maistre's Life, Thought, and Influence: Selected Studies* (Montreal: McGill-Queen's University Press, 2001), pp. 220-38, argues that Schmitt drew very selectively from de Maistre, so that it is not quite right to view Schmitt's project as an extension of de Maistre's.

136. Here I am following György Geréby, "Carl Schmitt and Erik Peterson on the Prob-lem of Political Theology: A Footnote to Kantorowicz," in Aziz Al-Azmeh and János M. Bak, eds., *Monotheistic Kingship: The Medieval Variants*, CEU Medievalia 6 (Budapest and New York: Central European University Department of Medieval Studies, 2004), pp. 31-61, esp. pp. 41-46.

137. Erik Peterson, *Heis Theos: Epigraphische, formgeschichtliche und religionsgeschicht-liche Untersuchungen*, Forschungen zur Religion und Literatur des Alten und Neuen Testa-ments, NF 24 (Göttingen: Vandenhoeck & Ruprecht, 1926), and *Der Monotheismus als Poli-tisches Problem: Ein Beitrag zur Geschichte der Politischen Theologie im Imperium Romanum* (Leipzig: Jakob Hegner, 1935).

138. Erik Peterson, "Göttliche Monarchie," *Theologische Quartalschrift* 112 (1931): 537-64; cf. D. Vincent Twomey, "The Political Implications of Faith in a Triune God: Erik Peterson Re-visited," in D. Vincent Twomey and Lewis Ayres, eds., *The Mystery of the Holy Trinity in the Fa-thers of the Church: The Proceedings of the Fourth Patristic Conference, Maynooth, 1999*, Irish Theological Quarterly Monograph Series 3 (Dublin, Ireland, and Portland, OR: Four Courts Press, 2007), pp. 118-30.

political order as the fulfillment of the promise of the heavenly Jerusalem and the *coming* kingdom of God."[139] Instead, any claim to establish or realize the divine monarchy on earth could only be that of the Antichrist's.[140]

In a belated response to Peterson,[141] Schmitt accused him of retrieving the Lutheran notion of two kingdoms, thus showing that he completely misunderstood the point about the church being an unavoidably political community. Schmitt could not comprehend, even later in his life under different circumstances, how the church might function as an alternative political option. Has the tradition of political theology formally launched by Schmitt come to see any differently?

2.3.2. Since Schmitt: Surveying Contemporary Options in Political Theology

In this section I quickly overview developments in the field of "political theology," first by highlighting trajectories that have consciously adopted that nomenclature, and then by surveying other trends at the interface of theology and politics, especially as these will feature in Part II of this volume. Whereas Schmitt wrote on political theology as a jurist and philosopher (rather than as a theologian), the following will focus chiefly on theologians who have written in the wake of Schmitt's legacy. As before, we will see an entire spectrum of options about how to think of the relationship between theology and politics in the twentieth century.[142]

Beginning with the left side of the spectrum, the work of German Roman Catholic theologian Johann Baptist Metz led the way in thinking about the interconnections between politics and theology in a post–Vatican II context.[143] Forging ahead in conscious resistance to Schmitt's legacy, Metz at-

139. Geréby, "Carl Schmitt and Erik Peterson," p. 46; italics original.

140. Peterson, "Göttliche Monarchie," p. 563. I should also add, as I read Schmitt, that the judgment regarding the friend-foe distinction is itself a political one — and thus susceptible to the will to power — rather than a moral, theological, or teleological one "dictated" by a transcendental principle.

141. Carl Schmitt, *Political Theology II: The Myth of the Closure of Any Political Theology*, trans. Michael Hoelzl and Graham Ward (Cambridge, UK, and Malden, MA: Polity Press, 2008).

142. The diversity and scope of political theology as of the mid-1970s can be seen in the anthologies of Alistair Kee, ed., *A Reader in Political Theology*, 2nd ed. (London: SCM Press, 1977), and Kee, ed., *The Scope of Political Theology* (London: SCM Press, 1978).

143. Metz's most pertinent book remains *Theology of the World*, trans. William Glen-Doepel (New York: Seabury Press, 1973); a more recent summary is "Theology in the New Para-

tempted to articulate a *new* political theology, one not linked to a state ideology but subjected to God.[144] Thus central to Metz's proposal were theological notions like the subversive memory of the church focused on Jesus Christ (which resists all political ideologies), the public (rather than private) character of Christian faith (which engages rather than leaves the domain of the secular to itself), and Jesus' preferential option for and solidarity with the poor. The latter notion linked Metz's political theology project with that of the emerging discourse of liberation theology.[145]

Even further "leftward" than Metz have been liberation theologians that have drawn intentionally and substantively on Marxist theory in articulating a political theology.[146] Thus Peruvian theologian Gustavo Gutiérrez, while in basic agreement with Metz, also goes beyond the latter in socio-economic analysis.[147] Gutiérrez's proposals are thus much more concretely focused on liberation not in the abstract but from conflicts between social classes (so that development genuinely alleviates poverty rather than devolves into developmentalism), on the economic formation and the emergence of a new society, and on Christ as liberator from sin, oppression, and injustice.

Metz's work as a Catholic has also found a counterpart among German Protestant theologians like Dorothee Sölle and Jürgen Moltmann. Sölle the political theologian cannot be understood apart from Sölle the feminist, liberationist, mystic, and activist.[148] Writing also in the wake of the "Death of God" movement of the 1960s, Sölle proposed a post-classical political theology emphasizing not divine interventionism amidst the tragedies of the

digm: Political Theology," in Hans Küng and David Tracy, eds., *Paradigm Change in Theology: A Symposium for the Future* (New York: Crossroad, 1991), pp. 355-66.

144. Derek Simon, "The *New* Political Theology of Metz: Confronting Schmitt's Decisionist Political Theology of Exclusion," *Horizons* 30, no. 2 (2003): 227-54, esp. p. 251.

145. Metz's work has drawn extensive analysis — e.g., Roger Dick Johns, *Man in the World: The Political Theology of Johannes Baptist Metz*, American Academy of Religion Dissertation Series 16 (Missoula, MT: Scholars Press, 1976); John K. Downey, ed., *Love's Strategy: The Political Theology of Johann Baptist Metz* (Harrisburg, PA: Trinity Press International, 1999); and Bruce T. Morrill, SJ, *Anamnesis as Dangerous Memory: Political and Liturgical Theology in Dialogue* (Collegeville, MN: Liturgical Press, 2000).

146. Joseph M. Petulla, *Christian Political Theology: A Marxian Guide* (Maryknoll, NY: Orbis, 1972); cf. later, John Joseph Marsden, *Marxian and Christian Utopianism: Toward a Socialist Political Theology* (New York: Monthly Review Press, 1991).

147. Gustavo Gutiérrez, *A Theology of Liberation: History, Politics and Salvation,* trans. and ed. Sister Caridad Inda and John Eagleson (Maryknoll, NY: Orbis, 1973).

148. See Dorothee Sölle, *Political Theology,* trans. John Shelley (Philadelphia: Fortress Press, 1974), and *The Window of Vulnerability: A Political Spirituality,* trans. Linda M. Maloney (Philadelphia: Fortress Press, 1990), among other writings; cf. Sarah K. Pinnock, ed., *The Theology of Dorothee Sölle* (Harrisburg, PA: Trinity Press International, 2003)

world, but the Crucified God who lives amidst and empowers the people of God to act transformatively in the world. Sölle's notion of the Crucified God derives (with acknowledgments) from Moltmann's now classic text,[149] yet Moltmann's major ideas have been developed within a political theology framework almost from the beginning of his career. Thus his books on Trinity, christology, pneumatology, and ecclesiology combine to present what might be said to be a systematic political theology of the cross, which now serves as the foundation and criticism not only of theology but also of political ideologies left and right. Interestingly, his two books devoted explicitly to political theology are actually collections of essays that illuminate how his more systematically developed ideas are applicable to political topics like the environment, human rights, Jewish-Christian relations, interreligious dialogue, the modern university, etc.[150]

The preceding developments on the Continent are all influenced, directly or indirectly, by the work of Schmitt.[151] Political theologies in North America, on the other hand, have been less concerned about Schmitt's legacy. On parallel tracks with Metz and Gutiérrez, for example, but informed instead by the history of racism and racial discrimination in the United States, is the work of black theologians like J. Deotis Roberts.[152] For Roberts, liberation theology is a theology of class-politics engaged by Latin American Catholics while black theology is a theology of race-politics that "emerges out of the crucible of black suffering and out of the dark night of the black soul's distress."[153] Along with others in his generation like James Cone and younger contemporaries like Cornel West and Robert Beckford (in the United Kingdom), Roberts has been instrumental in articulating a black political theology that is theologically informed but also politically relevant.[154]

---

149. Jürgen Moltmann, *The Crucified God: The Cross of Christ as the Foundation and Criticism of Christian Theology,* trans. R. A. Wilson and John Bowden (1974; reprint, San Francisco: HarperSanFrancisco, 1991).

150. See Jürgen Moltmann, *On Human Dignity: Political Theology and Ethics,* trans. M. Douglas Meeks (Philadelphia: Fortress Press, 1984), and *God for a Secular Society: The Public Relevance of Theology,* trans. Margaret Kohl (Minneapolis: Fortress Press, 1999).

151. Richard Higginson, "From Carl Schmitt to Dorothee Sölle: Has Political Theology Turned Full Circle?" *Churchman* 97, no. 2 (1983): 132-40.

152. J. Deotis Roberts, *A Black Political Theology* (Philadelphia: Westminster, 1974), *Liberation and Reconciliation: A Black Theology,* rev. ed. (Maryknoll, NY: Orbis, 1994), and *The Prophethood of Black Believers: An African American Political Theology for Ministry* (Louisville: Westminster/John Knox Press, 1994).

153. Roberts, *A Black Political Theology,* p. 204.

154. The legacy of Cone is assessed in Dwight N. Hopkins, ed., *Black Faith and Public Talk: Critical Essays on James H. Cone's Black Theology and Black Power* (Waco, TX: Baylor University

At about the same time that Roberts's work first came into prominence, there was also a move to identify the work of American public theologians of the stature of Reinhold Niebuhr in terms of political theology.[155] This followed the recognition that Niebuhr's earlier work on social ethics and theological anthropology opened up during and after World War II to writings on American history and international politics.[156] Niebuhr's accomplishment was to adapt St. Augustine's realism — specifically, the Augustinian doctrines of original sin and the fall, and his understanding of the earthly city as tension-filled, conflicted, competitive, and self-loving — to the complexities of political issues related to war, secularity, democracy, and empire. Here was a public intellectual who was also one of America's most profound and respected theologians, and hence deserving, in retrospect, the label of political theologian.[157]

A further development since the early 1970s has been the "political theology" of John Howard Yoder and others in the contemporary Anabaptist movements more specifically, and in the Free or Believers Church tradition more generally.[158] I put political theology in quotation marks because Yoder and those in this "camp" do not generally use the label,[159] and because what

---

Press, 2007). West's project is still very much unfinished, beginning with Cornel West, *Prophesy Deliverance: An Afro-American Revolutionary Christianity* (Philadelphia: Westminster, 1982), while Beckford's is just getting off the ground — e.g., Robert Beckford, *Dread and Pentecostal: A Political Theology for the Black Church in Britain* (London: SPCK, 2000), and *Jesus Is Dread: Theology and Black Culture in Britain* (1998; reprint, London: Darton, Longman & Todd, 2002).

155. See William R. Coats, *God in Public: Political Theology Beyond Niebuhr* (Grand Rapids: Eerdmans, 1974). I cite Coats's book not because he attempts to retrieve Niebuhr's proposals for the purposes of constructing a political theology — he does not; the book focuses instead on the "beyond" in his subtitle — but because this is the first title (book or journal article) that specifically categorizes Niebuhr as a political theologian.

156. E.g., Reinhold Niebuhr, *Christianity and Power Politics* (New York: Charles Scribner's Sons, 1940), *Christian Realism and Political Problems* (New York: Charles Scribner's Sons, 1953), and *The Structure of Nations and Empires* (New York: Charles Scribner's Sons, 1959).

157. Thus there has now been a range of re-assessments of Niebuhr as political theologian: Larry Rasmussen, ed., *Reinhold Niebuhr: Theological of Public Life* (Minneapolis: Fortress Press, 1991); Robert Thomas Cornelison, *The Christian Realism of Reinhold Niebuhr and the Political Theology of Jürgen Moltmann in Dialogue: The Realism of Hope* (San Francisco: Mellen Research University Press, 1992); and Charles C. Brown, *Niebuhr and His Age: Reinhold Niebuhr's Prophetic Role and Legacy,* new ed. (Harrisburg, PA: Trinity Press International, 2002).

158. As launched by Yoder's now classic text, *The Politics of Jesus* (Grand Rapids: Eerdmans, 1972).

159. See, e.g., Nathan E. Yoder and Carol A. Scheppard, eds., *Exiles in the Empire: Believers Church Perspectives on Politics,* Studies in the Believers Church Tradition 5 (Kitchener, ON: Pandora Press, 2006).

they propose may more accurately be called a political ecclesiology, viz., an understanding of the interrelationship of theology and politics in which the practices of the church as a community of believers play a central role. While rejecting those Radical Reformation movements that embraced violence as a means of furthering the cause of reform, contemporary Anabaptism remains committed to their forebears' disavowal of Constantinianism and persists in seeing the witness of the church as having not only spiritual but also social and political ramifications.[160]

Returning to the discussion as it has developed across the church catholic, we need to mention two other options in political theology: the more developed Roman Catholic tradition of social teaching and the more recent Radical Orthodoxy movement. With regard to the former, whereas Catholic theologians in the global south have by and large opted for some version of liberation theology, the Roman magisterium has now been articulating a social vision for over a hundred years that has unequivocally defended the rights of workers and the poor on the one hand but has also been critical of aspects of liberation theology on the other. For our purposes, however, the Catholic social teaching tradition is important less because of its specifically political proposals (there are very few of these that have been presented) but because it articulates a theological vision of social and economic justice that has broad political implications.[161]

Radical Orthodoxy is a fairly new theological program that joins an Anglo-Catholic theological and ecclesiological vision with a neo-Platonic metaphysics of participation and a socialist-democratic politics.[162] Its foremost proponents, including John Milbank, Graham Ward, and William Cavanaugh, have attempted to retrieve St. Augustine in the attempt to rethink the relationship between theology and the social sciences and to re-assert theology as the "queen of the sciences" (rather than perpetuate its subservience to the social sciences as has happened since the late nineteenth century), to reconfigure modern soteriologies of the state according to theological

160. In chapter 5 (below), I will return to discuss the work of Yoder as well as that of Stanley Hauerwas, who although not an Anabaptist, proposes a political ecclesiology very similar to that of Yoder's.

161. Francis P. McHugh and Samuel M. Natale, eds., *Things Old and New: Catholic Social Teaching Revisited* (Lanham, MD: University Press of America, 1993), and Robert A. Sirico, *Catholicism's Developing Social Teaching: Reflections on Rerum Novarum and Centesimus Annus*, expanded ed. (Grand Rapids: Acton Institute, 2002). We will return to engage with Catholic social teaching ideas in chapter 7.

162. For an introduction, see James K. A. Smith, *Introducing Radical Orthodoxy: Mapping a Post-Secular Theology* (Grand Rapids: Baker Academic, 2004).

soteriologies of the church, to reformulate a theology of culture and of religious pluralism relevant to our time that involves a theological interpretation of culture and the religions, and to re-envision a theology of desire vis-à-vis contemporary market consumerism. Central to the Radical Orthodoxy proposal, however, is a political ecclesiology, albeit one of the High Church (rather than the Yoderian Free Church) tradition, which thus emphasizes the social, economic, and political relevance of the church's liturgical practices.[163]

2.3.3. The State of the Discussion: Issues and Challenges

It remains for us to summarize the ground gained in this chapter, and to identify the unresolved questions that have emerged in the preceding discussion. There are three major concluding observations, with the third opening up to some of the thorniest issues in contemporary political philosophy and political theology.

First, if anything, this chapter has shown that even in the pages of the Bible, multiple political postures, structures, and models are presented, and that this leads, unsurprisingly, to the varied number of beliefs and practices regarding the political in the history of Christianity. Thus, there is no single normative political theological stance to be derived either from the biblical text or from the Christian tradition. Instead there are multiple political theological options, each perhaps more viable in some respects in some contexts, but then also less viable if not altogether impracticable in other respects in other contexts.[164] It now needs to be clearly stated that this does not constitute an advocacy for political and theological relativism, as if any option in political theology is just as good as any other at any time. Rather, Christian theological faithfulness and political engagement is a context-specific affair, albeit one guided by the discerning application of both theological and political norms. The constructive proposals I will make later constitute one such attempt to render discernment in this case of global pentecostalisms.

Second, the domain of the political is, as we have seen, rather encompassing. The politics of ancient Israel and of Jesus were inseparable from their economics, just as the theology of the Puritans was intricately intertwined

---

163. We will focus much more attention later (in chapter 6 below) on the ideas of Radical Orthodoxy.

164. So when Hent de Vries and Lawrence E. Sullivan, eds., *Political Theologies: Public Religions in a Post-Secular World* (New York: Fordham University Press, 2006), present a diversity of options in political theology, this lack of consensus is not a contemporary dilemma but one that reaches back to the origins of early Christianity as well as ancient Israel.

with their socio-economic way of life, and the Catholic tradition of social teaching is deeply informed by its tradition of moral theology. Put in contemporary terms, political theology is an expansive field of discourse, including within its domain not only the social and the economic, but also issues of gender (as Sölle's work reminds us), race (as seen in J. D. Roberts's proposals), ethnicity (e.g., related to proposals from the global south), and class (as will be seen playing out in the "debate" between Yoder's "low church" tradition and Radical Orthodoxy's "high church" theologians). This state of affairs recalls Kuyper's sphere sovereignty proposal and raises the question: Are there just two spheres — that of the political and that of the ecclesial/theological — or are there many (e.g., the political, the religious, the social, the economic, the cultural, the educational, the family) that need to be adjudicated? My own theological instincts, to be explicated further in the following chapter, are to follow Kuyper's lead and develop political theology in terms of multiple interacting spheres (along with their various authorities), albeit in terms of a pentecostal and pneumatological theology as complementary to rather than exclusive of Kuyper's Reformed theology of common grace.

Finally (setting Kuyper's pluralistic theology of sphere sovereignty aside for the moment), the major contemporary questions in political theology are the perennial ones concerning the relationship between theology and the political. We have seen the issues debated over the last seventeen hundred years — between Augustine and the Donatists, in the post-Gelasian period, between Gregory VII and Henry IV and their descendants in the High Middle Ages, between Luther and the Radical Reformers on the left and the Genevan theocracy on the right, in the Two Kingdoms debate among Lutheran theologians in the twentieth century, and so on — without any consensus. Let me explicate the unanswered questions along three lines.

1) As the "father of political theology," at least in terms of its nomenclature, Schmitt's decisionistic theology of the enemy raises the meta-theoretical question: What, if anything, is the role of theology for political philosophy in general and for political science as a practical discipline? Is his claim that all political concepts are theological a political one (so that politicians cannot avoid being theologians) or a theological one (that can safely be ignored by politicians)? Is it an interpretive explication of politics as Schmitt understood it, or is it a normative claim about all political philosophies, at least in the modern period, as he insisted? In other words, is there an unavoidable theological element in all politics? On the other side of this question, what, if anything, is the role of the political in theology? Are liberation and black theologians correct in depending on social scientific analyses as part of the theological task, or are the Radically Orthodox theologians right to insist on

theology as an interpreter of rather than a dialogue partner with the social sciences? It is not too difficult to see that how one answers one side of this question regarding the relationship between theology and the political will deeply inform how one responds to the inquiry as approached from the other side. My own preliminary reply, to be explicated in the following chapter and then defended at length in Part II, is to follow Kuyper's lead in seeing both the independence of the various spheres in some important respects but yet also their interdependence in other respects.

2) From the various standpoints of the public or political sphere, the question has perennially been that of identifying how the political reacts to the theological (or religious). In our democratic and late-modern context, the dominant model, heir to the two spheres tradition, is that of the separation of church and state, especially as that has played out in America. The questions here are how to understand the non-establishment of religion clause in the Constitution: Does that mean a) not favoring any religion (especially the majority religion), b) being neutral to and thus equal in treatment of all religions, or c) being equally opposed to the involvement of any religion in the public square? While from a historical perspective, disestablishment probably meant either a) or c),[165] a plausible contemporary explication would seem to be one that advocated b) the neutrality position (equal treatment of all religions) against the no-aid-to-religion interpretation.[166] Yet we have just lived through a lengthy period in which it was assumed that disestablishment meant c) the banning of religion from the public square. The argument is that all religious views are biased and, in a secular state, are not to be imposed on those not so religiously committed unless they can be presented and argued in "neutral" language that does not presume the truth or normativity of the religious tradition in question.[167] Against this view, there has been a more recent outcry that to prohibit the giving of religious reasons even in the public square is illegal (interpreting disestablishment in c] rather than a] or b] terms), impossible (because religious convictions cannot be arbitrarily bracketed off from our worldviews), and, impracticable (since the lines between religion and the political are blurred, at best).[168] In short, the efforts to keep re-

165. Thomas J. Curry, *Farewell to Christendom: The Future of Church and State in America* (Oxford: Oxford University Press, 2001), chap. 2, favors (c) rather than (a).

166. See Stephen V. Monsma, "Where Church and State Intersect," in David P. Gushee, ed., *Christians and Politics Beyond the Culture Wars: An Agenda for Engagement* (Grand Rapids: Baker Books, 2000), pp. 195-204.

167. As defended by, among others, John Rawls, *Political Liberalism* (New York: Columbia University Press, 1993), esp. chap. 6, "The Idea of Public Reason."

168. See, e.g., Stephen L. Carter, *The Culture of Disbelief: How American Law and Politics*

ligion out of the political, while somewhat successful in recent generations, appear now to have come to an end.

3) In a sense, we are now right back where this concluding section began: With the plurality of political theologies, how might people of faith — in this case, Christian theologians like myself — clarify the relationship between theology and the political if the standpoint of faith is assumed rather than either ignored or denied? More precisely, if we are not to presume what might be called the re-enchantment of the world and of the public sphere,[169] then how should we proceed in a religiously plural world? Do we adopt the Anglo-Catholic liturgical approach of Radical Orthodoxy, or the Believers Church ecclesiology of Yoder and his disciples? What about the political and liberation theologies of Metz, Sölle, Moltmann, Roberts, and others, or the neo-Augustinianism of Niebuhr, or the Catholic social teaching tradition? My theological intuitions tell me that there are essential insights to be gained from each of these proposals, as well as others. The task in Part II of this book will be to articulate a political theology that can incorporate the indispensable contributions from each of these proposals and traditions while yet integrating them into a coherent theological framework.

Trivialize Religious Devotion (New York: Basic Books, 1993), and Jeffrey Stout, *Democracy and Tradition* (Princeton: Princeton University Press, 2004).

169. As in the subtitle of James K. A. Smith, ed., *What Comes After Modernity? Secularity, Globalization, and the Re-enchantment of the World* (Waco, TX: Baylor University Press, 2008).

CHAPTER 3

Toward a Political Theology:
Pentecostal Trajectories

The first two chapters have provided surveys of both the political and public faces of global pentecostalism and the various developments in and schools of political theology in the Christian tradition. Part II (chapters 4 through 8) will attempt to articulate a distinctive proposal in political theology informed by pentecostal insights. In this chapter, however, we will have to directly confront the methodological question: How can we achieve anything like a normative theological account of the political by starting from a phenomenology of global pentecostalism?

My thesis to be presented in what follows is that there is a unique pentecostal theological approach that can be discerned from out of pentecostal piety, spirituality, and religious experience. The first two sections explicate this thesis methodologically and hermeneutically, before we turn in the final section to an overview of the constructive theological vision. My immediate goal is to lay the groundwork for the viability of a distinctive pentecostal contribution to the contemporary discussion in political theology.

At the same time, however, I wish to caution against any reading of this chapter as being about *merely* either theological method or theological hermeneutics. In a previous work, I have argued at length that both methodological and hermeneutical issues cannot be viewed only as theological prolegomena but are always already informed by and even emergent from out of substantive theological convictions.[1] If so, then theological content cannot be easily divorced from its forms of presentation even while various styles and genres of theological reflection have implications for and are implied by various theo-

---

1. Amos Yong, *Spirit-Word-Community: Theological Hermeneutics in Trinitarian Perspective* (Burlington, VT, and Aldershot, UK: Ashgate, and Eugene, OR: Wipf & Stock, 2002).

logical understandings. This interdependence between method and theology was assumed early in the Christian theological tradition in terms of the interconnection between ecclesial practices and the confessions of the church. The fifth-century theologian Prosper of Aquitaine (c. 390-465) viewed this in light of the relationship between the church's worship and its doctrines or confessions.[2] I am suggesting here that, when mapped onto the approach adopted so far in this book, there is (or should be) a correlation between the phenomenology of pentecostal political (public) practices (as outlined in chapter 1) and the ideas of Christian theologies of the political (as sketched in chapter 2 and to be elaborated on in the rest of this volume). In the following pages, I intend to further substantiate this claim about the interwoven nature of Christian practices and Christian beliefs, as well as instantiate how pentecostal praxis and theology are normatively intertwined in ways that may be illuminating for the ongoing discussion in political theology.

3.1. Method in (Political) Theology: A Pentecostal Framework

Up until fairly recently, pentecostalism has been viewed primarily in terms of its spirituality and its missionary emphasis, much less so as a distinctive theological tradition in its own right. There are many reasons for this, including the fact that theology was handed down primarily within an oral tradition for much of the first two generations of modern pentecostalism and the concomitant fact that the emergence of pentecostal theology in the academy has occurred only in the last two decades.[3] I would suggest, in addition, that the pluralism of global pentecostalism makes it difficult to articulate especially the ecclesial self-understanding of pentecostalism — at least within the predominant ecclesiological frameworks that have been bequeathed by the Christian tradition — and this further complicates the task of comprehend-

---

2. The aphorism *lex orandi, lex credendi* — or, "the rule of prayer equals the rule of doctrine" — has been attributed to Prosper; see Geoffrey Wainwright, *Doxology: The Praise of God in Worship, Doctrine and Life* (New York: Oxford University Press, 1980), pp. 225-27. For further reflections on "Prosper's rule," see W. Taylor Stevenson, "Lex Orandi — Lex Credendi," in Stephen Sykes, John Booty, and Jonathan Knight, eds., *The Study of Anglicanism* (London: SPCK, and Minneapolis: Fortress, 1988), pp. 187-202, and Michael Downey, "*Lex Orandi, Lex Credendi:* Taking It Seriously in Systematic Theology," in Michael Downey and Richard N. Fragomeni, eds., *A Promise of Presence: Studies in Honor of David N. Power, O.M.I.* (Washington, DC: Pastoral Press, 1992), pp. 3-26.

3. See my "Pentecostalism and the Theological Academy," *Theology Today* 64, no. 2 (2007): 244-50.

ing pentecostal theological identity and methodology. In this section, I wish to clarify the methodological issues confronting pentecostalism and then briefly sketch how there is embedded within pentecostal intuitions and sensibilities a distinctive set of theological (more specifically: pneumatological and christological) commitments that are capable of generating and then sustaining theological inquiry.

3.1.1. Pentecostalism and Theological Method: Challenges and Opportunities

Theological method has been a modern academic preoccupation concerned with the question of the sources and authorities of, and procedures involved in, theological reflection.[4] Its problematic can be traced to the confluence of interrelated trajectories in early modernity including the post-Reformation dissolution of ecclesial authority (especially after the Wars of Religion), the emergence of the post-Cartesian and post-Kantian subject as a locus of epistemology, and the ascendancy of Enlightenment rationality as a technical model of inquiry. In the late-modern West, the task of theological method sought to adjudicate the questions raised by each of these issues, and this inevitably converged in the debates over foundationalism.

Although we have neither the time nor the space to enter fully into the disputes regarding foundationalism,[5] suffice it to say that at a very basic level, the theological issue has to do with the starting points or grounding of any theological system. In order to highlight how difficult it is to locate pentecostalism in the existing theological landscape, I will simplify matters by distinguishing three major methodological responses developed in the modern period to the foundationalist question: the Reformation and post-Reformation *sola scriptura,* the liberal Protestant turn to experience, and the Orthodox and Catholic approach that sees Scripture as the book of the church and therefore in continuity with the church's teachings and traditions.

At one level, most pentecostals would unhesitatingly align themselves with the Reformation tradition of *sola scriptura.*[6] Pentecostals who are self-

---

4. Arguably, the high point of the discussion was Bernard Lonergan's magisterial *Method in Theology* (New York: Herder & Herder, 1972).

5. For those interested, I explore the terrain in *Spirit-Word-Community,* pp. 96-101. For a fuller discussion, see Stanley J. Grenz and John R. Franke, *Beyond Foundationalism: Shaping Theology in a Postmodern Context* (Louisville: Westminster/John Knox Press, 2001).

6. I cannot here provide any extensive discussion of this complicated idea. For recent articulations with which some classical pentecostals, especially in North America, would be sym-

identifying Protestants would affirm the normativity of the Bible for the church and its teachings,[7] even as many lay pentecostals would go even further and insist that the Bible alone is all that is needed for Christian faith and practice. Yet even as the postmodern discussion is illuminating how there is no direct approach to the biblical (or any other historical) text that is not mediated by the contemporary horizon,[8] so also have pentecostals discerned their own approach to Scripture to have been informed by their encounters with the living Spirit of God.[9] Theirs is not, in other words, a reliance only on the Bible in any simplistic sense; instead, their contemporary experiences of the Holy Spirit lead them to resonate with the biblical narratives, so that they utilize what might be called a "this is that!" hermeneutic which sees the "this" of the present connecting with the "that" of (especially) the apostolic life (as recorded in the book of Acts) and vice versa.[10] It is this experientially informed hermeneutic that most radically distinguishes pentecostals from their fundamentalist cousins, many of whom are cessationists regarding the charismata of the Spirit, since any possibility of the ongoing revelation of the Spirit would threaten the rule of "Scripture alone."[11]

Is pentecostal hermeneutics then experientially driven? In light of the preceding, the answer will have to be a nuanced "yes" and "no." Yes, in the sense that experience plays an undeniable role in the pentecostal reading and interpretation of the Bible, and that astute observers have noted the parallels here with the experientialism characteristic of the more liberal or mainstream Protestant theological traditions.[12] Of course, the major problem with relying on experience is that this can sometimes develop into an ideological agenda

---

pathetic, see Don Kistler, ed., *Sola Scriptura! The Protestant Position on the Bible* (Morgan, PA: Soli Deo Gloria Publications, 1995), and R. C. Sproul, *Scripture Alone: The Evangelical Doctrine* (Phillipsburg, NJ: P & R Publishing, 2005).

7. See John R. Riggins, "God's Inspired Word," in Stanley M. Horton, ed., *Systematic Theology,* rev. ed. (Springfield, MO: Gospel Publishing House, 1995), pp. 61-115.

8. As articulated most forcefully by Hans-Georg Gadamer, *Truth and Method,* 2nd rev. ed., trans. Joel Weinsheimer and Donald G. Marshall (New York: Continuum, 1994).

9. See William R. Menzies, "Synoptic Theology: An Essay in Pentecostal Hermeneutics," *Paraclete* 13, no. 1 (1979): 14-21.

10. I discuss the "this is that" approach to Scripture further in my "The 'Baptist Vision' of James William McClendon, Jr.: A Wesleyan-Pentecostal Response," *Wesleyan Theological Journal* 37, no. 2 (Fall 2002): 32-57, esp. pp. 33-34.

11. For a pentecostal response to the cessationism that drives many conservative Reformed theological traditions, see Jon Ruthven, *On the Cessation of the Charismata: The Protestant Polemic on Postbiblical Miracles* (Sheffield: Sheffield Academic Press, 1993).

12. As suggested by Harvey G. Cox, *Fire from Heaven: The Rise of Pentecostal Spirituality and the Reshaping of Religion in the Twenty-first Century* (Reading, MA: Addison-Wesley, 1995), esp. chap. 15.

that in turn reads Scripture selectively.[13] But pentecostals cannot be said to have adopted an experientialist hermeneutic in the sense that the Bible remains, in most cases,[14] authoritative and normative for pentecostal self-understanding and theological reflection. Philip Jenkins has recently provided a sketch of pentecostal Bible-reading habits in the global south and identified how, in a fundamental way, pentecostals remain a people of the Bible.[15] Yet, any consideration of the role of experience in pentecostal hermeneutic will be complicated by two additional factors: the unresolved question of what precisely is meant by experience, and the pluralism of pentecostalism "on the ground." The former question has been registered most forcefully by Donald Gelpi,[16] a theologian of the Roman Catholic charismatic renewal, and his work cautions us about too naïve an understanding of the notion of experience, particularly as that interfaces with issues of theological hermeneutics and methodology. The latter concerns the variety of pentecostal experience, especially in the global south.[17] My discussion in chapter 1 highlights pentecostal pluralism with regard to its interface with the public square; beyond these domains, pentecostalism is even more diverse and resistant to categorization. Hence any discussion of pentecostal experience has to be sensitive to the bewildering diversity of the movement, and this inevitably will defy efforts to homogenize the notion for hermeneutical or methodological purposes.

In light of the preceding, pentecostals have recently come to appreciate the

13. Thus David Martin, "The Political Oeconomy of the Holy Ghost," in David Martin and Peter Mullen, eds., *Strange Gifts? A Guide to Charismatic Renewal* (Oxford and New York: Basil Blackwell, 1984), pp. 54-71, esp. pp. 60-61, discusses how pentecostalism's experience of the Spirit can be hijacked, especially by charismatic leaders, to legitimate sectarian and parochial goals.

14. An exception might be the Friday Masowe apostolics of Zimbabwe — as documented by Matthew Engelke, *A Problem of Presence: Beyond Scripture in an African Church* (Berkeley: University of California Press, 2007) — who reject the printed Bible as representative of God's word, and operate instead with an understanding of the living word of God as mediated by the Holy Spirit's work in the congregation; however, a close reading of this book will reveal how the church is dependent on the scriptural witness even while publicly eschewing the materiality of the Bible in its own self-understanding.

15. See Philip Jenkins, *The New Faces of Christianity: Believing the Bible in the Global South* (Oxford: Oxford University Press, 2006), esp. chap. 2 and passim.

16. See Donald L. Gelpi, *The Turn to Experience in Contemporary Theology* (New York: Paulist, 1994), esp. the "Preface"; see also my discussion in "In Search of Foundations: The *Oeuvre* of Donald L. Gelpi, S.J., and Its Significance for Pentecostal Theology and Philosophy," *Journal of Pentecostal Theology* 11, no. 1 (2002): 3-26, esp. pp. 13-18.

17. An overview is provided by Walter J. Hollenweger, *The Pentecostals: The Charismatic Movement in the Churches* (Minneapolis: Augsburg, 1972); see also, more recently, Allan Anderson, *An Introduction to Pentecostalism: Global Charismatic Christianity* (Cambridge: Cambridge University Press, 2004).

important role of community and tradition in the theological task. Experience itself is not only pluriform, but is also open to a multiplicity of interpretations. A theological tradition, however, has to have some unifying features that hold the differences together. Orthodox and Roman Catholic traditions are unified in the early ecumenical councils and (for the latter) the church's teaching magisterium, and these provide a distinctive ecclesial identity even while staking out the hermeneutical and methodological parameters for theological reflection. The unavoidability of tradition has registered itself even among Protestant churches, so much so that many — e.g., Reformed, Anabaptist, Wesleyan, among others — have "founding fathers," authoritative confessions, and a range of canonical voices that shape and guide their ongoing self-understanding. Some pentecostals have therefore begun to identify a historical genealogy especially in the first generation of the movement for theological purposes,[18] and I am not unsympathetic with such a quest. However, one does not have to dig too much in order to discover that the pluralism of pentecostalism is not only a contemporary "problem," but one that is lodged even within the first generation itself.[19] Then there is the additional challenge of Oneness pentecostalism — which numbers up to one-fourth of the movement worldwide and therefore cannot be ignored — since its rejection of Nicene orthodoxy is a brutal reminder both that the notion of tradition remains problematic theologically and that the historic pluralism of pentecostal traditions will not be unifying anytime soon.

In short, pentecostals appear to be a hodgepodge in terms of theological method. They are, in turn, traditional Protestants regarding the authority of Scripture even while simultaneously being strange bedfellows with liberalism in terms of how experience functions to shape theological understanding. And, with the emergence of pentecostalism in the theological academy, there is now a quest to identify the contours of the pentecostal theological tradition. Whither then pentecostal hermeneutics and theological method?

3.1.2. *"Starting with the Spirit":*
Toward a Pentecostal Theological Method

I propose that internal to pentecostal spirituality is a distinctive theological impulse that not only values and preserves the diversity of pentecostal experi-

---

18. See especially Kenneth J. Archer, *A Pentecostal Hermeneutic for the Twenty-First Century: Spirit, Scripture, and Community* (London and New York: T. & T. Clark, 2004).

19. Thus Walter J. Hollenweger, *Pentecostalism: Origins and Developments Worldwide* (Peabody, MA: Hendrickson, 1997), identifies five roots of pentecostalism: black/African; Catholic; evangelical; critical/prophetic; and ecumenical.

ence but also opens up to an ecumenical methodology without undermining the centrality of Scripture in the theological task. My hypothesis is that starting with the Holy Spirit allows pentecostalism to enter into the debates in theological method on its own terms, even as it invites a specifically pentecostal contribution to the discussion. As I have elsewhere provided extended elaborations of this proposal,[20] let me very briefly summarize the key moves in what follows.

First, the pentecostal "this is that" presumes that the same Holy Spirit who was poured out upon the apostles remains present and active today, and that there is no Christian encounter with God that is not always and already a visitation from, with, and in the Spirit of God. From this, theology, as a second-order activity of reflecting on experience, is informed by life in the Spirit.[21] Having stated it thus, the claim that we begin with the Spirit, both experientially and methodologically, would seem uncontestable. Yet in the history of Christian thought, this insight has rarely been either articulated or its corollary theological project pursued. Part of the reason for this may be that the Spirit has, perennially, been neglected as the "shy" or "hidden" member of the Trinity.[22] I submit that the emergence of this insight came, not coincidentally, following the explosion of the pentecostal and charismatic movement in the twentieth century.[23]

20. The argument is laid out more abstractly in *Spirit-Word-Community*, while the method is clarified in *The Spirit Poured Out on All Flesh: Pentecostalism and the Possibility of Global Theology* (Grand Rapids: Baker Academic, 2005), esp. pp. 27-30, and then exemplified throughout that book.

21. See Yong, "On Divine Presence and Divine Agency: Toward a Foundational Pneumatology," *Asian Journal of Pentecostal Studies* 3, no. 2 (July 2000): 167-88, drawing especially from the work of D. Lyle Dabney, as developed in the following essays: "Otherwise Engaged in the Spirit: A First Theology for the Twenty-First Century," in Miroslav Volf, Carmen Krieg, and Thomas Kucharz, eds., *The Future of Theology: Essays in Honor of Jürgen Moltmann* (Grand Rapids: Eerdmans, 1996), pp. 154-63; "Starting with the Spirit: Why the Last Should Now Be First," in Gordon Preece and Stephen Pickard, eds., *Starting with the Spirit: Task of Theology Today II* (Adelaide: Australia Theological Forum, Inc., and Openbook Publishers, 2001), pp. 3-27; and "Why Should the Last Be First? The Priority of Pneumatology in Recent Theological Discussion," in Bradford E. Hinze and D. Lyle Dabney, eds., *Advents of the Spirit: An Introduction to the Current Study of Pneumatology* (Milwaukee: Marquette University Press, 2001), pp. 238-61.

22. See Frederick Dale Bruner and William Hordern, *The Holy Spirit: Shy Member of the Trinity* (Minneapolis: Augsburg, 1984).

23. For the correlation between pentecostalism and a pneumatological approach to theology, see Clark H. Pinnock, *Flame of Love: A Theology of the Holy Spirit* (Downers Grove, IL: InterVarsity Press, 1996), and Veli-Matti Kärkkäinen, *Toward a Pneumatological Theology: Pentecostal and Ecumenical Perspectives on Ecclesiology, Soteriology, and Theology of Mission*, ed. Amos Yong (Lanham, MD: University Press of America, 2002).

From a pentecostal and charismatic perspective, however, I submit that starting with the Spirit provides a specifically theological rationale for doing theology pluralistically. Let me explicate this claim at three levels: that of experience, that of community, and that of the canonical Scripture. From an experiential perspective, the Lukan account of the Day of Pentecost provides a narrative template that preserves the many languages that separately and together bear witness to the mighty deeds of God (Acts 2:4, 6, 7, 11). Peter's explanation, drawing from the prophet Joel, was that this was the Spirit's eschatological outpouring upon all flesh, equally upon men and women, young and old, slave and free (Acts 2:17-18). In other words, the experiences and voices of those previously marginalized and excluded were now central to the church's witness. The crucial late-modern insight applicable here is that there is a much more reciprocal and interconnected relationship between language, culture, and experience rather than any simplistic movement from the latter to the former.[24] The strong and perhaps unmistakable inference to be drawn is that the preservation of the many tongues of the Day of Pentecost is an indication that God values not only linguistic diversity but also cultural plurality.[25] In short, the Spirit was given on the Day of Pentecost without partiality to all (cf. Acts 10:34), and this in turn enabled each one to give testimony to the wondrous works of God in his or her own language and from out of his or her own cultural experience.

Yet the pentecostal outpouring not only warrants the diversity of experience at the individual level, but also at the corporate level. Here, we need to turn to St. Paul's reflections on the charismata to see that he observed how the one Spirit gave many gifts (1 Cor. 12:4), and baptized all — Jews and Greeks, slave and free — into one body (12:13); yet, the one body is constituted without remainder by many members (12:14-26), and such constitution is accomplished by the Spirit who distributes many gifts. Hence, he concludes, "Now you are the body of Christ and individually members of it" (12:27). I am less interested in how the many gifts of the Spirit reside within the church and function congregationally than I am in the ecumenical implications of Paul's theology of the Spirit's charisms. If the many members constitute one local congregation, then the many local congregations constitute one body of

---

24. This was one of the main arguments in George Lindbeck's influential *The Nature of Doctrine: Religion and Theology in a Postliberal Age* (Philadelphia: Westminster, 1984).

25. For a more extended argument, see also Frank D. Macchia, "The Tongues of Pentecost: A Pentecostal Perspective on the Promise and Challenge of Pentecostal/Roman Catholic Dialogue," *Journal of Ecumenical Studies* 35, no. 1 (1998): 1-18, and Samuel Solivan, *The Spirit, Pathos and Liberation: Toward an Hispanic Pentecostal Theology* (Sheffield: Sheffield Academic Press, 1998), pp. 112-18.

Christ. In this case, the many congregations each contribute something distinctive — derived from the contextual particularities of experience, language, culture, etc. — to the church universal by way of the Spirit's special presence and activity in each locale, and it is only when the many members are recognized and their gifts received that the whole body of Christ is healthy. In short, the many tongues and many gifts of the Spirit are particular expressions of the church universal, each with its own role in the wider church and indispensable regardless of how small or insignificant such may appear.[26]

Last for our purposes (but not least), starting with the Spirit allows us to appreciate the diversity of voices and perspectives that constitute the canonical Scripture. There are two related pneumatological claims here: that involving the pluralism of the scriptures themselves and that involving the plurality of interpretations of the scriptures. With regard to the former, I am referring here not only to the theological notion that all Scripture is God-breathed or Spirit-inspired (θεόπνευστος or *theopneustos* — 2 Tim. 3:16; cf. 2 Pet. 1:21), but also to fact that the earliest followers of Jesus also encountered the risen Christ and read the sacred Scripture in the Holy Spirit. In other words, the scriptures that record these pneumatic encounters and experiences themselves are products of the Spirit's inspiration, so that there are four Gospels, not one; there are multiple ecclesial/communal traditions within the pages of the New Testament — e.g., Matthean, Lukan, Johannine, Pauline, Petrine, and others — not one; and there are, even within one authorial corpus (like St. Paul's), a diversity of perspectives, not one. With regard to the latter, I only note how James's summary at the Jerusalem council (c. 49 C.E.) — that "For it has seemed good to the Holy Spirit and to us" (Acts 15:28) — points to how the Spirit brings forth new light from the sacred Scripture. In short, the Spirit both inspires the sacred text in all of its pluriformity and illuminates that same text to the many Christian readers and communities of faith across space and time.

I further suggest that given the centrality of the Pentecost narrative in the pentecostal theological imagination, there is a real sense in which pentecostalism is comfortable with the cacophony of the many tongues. What seems to others like drunkenness early in the morning (Acts 2:13-15) is but a sign of the multitudes that have been caught up in the work of the Spirit. In this case, the Pentecost account provides a theological rather than a merely politically correct rationale for methodological pluralism.

---

26. For elaboration, see Thomas Ryan, "Sharing Spiritual Gifts at the Dawn of the Third Millennium," *Ecumenism* 132 (December 1998): 8-12, and Raniero Cantalamessa, *Come, Creator Spirit: Meditations on the Veni Creator* (Collegeville, MN: Liturgical Press, 2003), esp. chap. 10.

Yet from a theological perspective, we cannot simply assert that mere pluralism makes sense without some indication of how there can be coherence amidst the many. More importantly, without further theological interpretation, mere pluralism is incapable of discerning the truth of the Holy Spirit from the falsity of many other spirits. So w(h)ither pentecostal pluralism and theological method?

3.1.3. *The Fivefold Gospel: A Pentecostal Theological Framework*

Let me suggest that the fivefold gospel can serve as a framework that, on the one hand, provides a distinctive and coherent pentecostal theological self-understanding and, on the other hand, honors the pluralistic impulses set in motion by starting with the Spirit. The following discussion will seek to defend both of these claims; before doing so, however, I briefly outline and define the fivefold gospel.

The fivefold gospel has recently been proposed by some pentecostal theologians as representing "the theological heart" of the movement.[27] It consists, in sum, of the good news of Jesus as savior, sanctifier, Spirit-baptizer, healer, and coming king. While we will use the fivefold framework and defend this decision in what follows, two important caveats need to be registered before proceeding. First, adopting the fivefold structure should not be interpreted as thinking there is a theological essence to pentecostalism. Not only is there is no universal agreement on the exact order or verbiage of the five elements apart from the starting point of salvation in Christ,[28] but our own focus on pentecostalism in the global south should alert us about imposing a western theological grid on the global movement. Second, while I am sympathetic with the desire (among some of my pentecostal colleagues) to locate the heart of pentecostalism in the first generation of the movement in the

27. John Christopher Thomas, "Pentecostal Theology in the Twenty-First Century," *PNEUMA: The Journal of the Society for Pentecostal Studies* 20, no. 1 (1998): 3-19, esp. p. 17; cf. Mark J. Cartledge, "The Early Pentecostal Theology of *Confidence* Magazine (1908-1926): A Version of the Five-Fold Gospel?" *The Journal of the European Pentecostal Theological Association* 28, no. 2 (2008): 117-30.

28. Thus another advocate for thinking theologically about pentecostalism using the fivefold gospel, Steve Land, outlines the full gospel in terms of justification in Christ, sanctification as a second work of grace, bodily healing as provided in the atonement, the premillennial return of Christ, and the baptism in the Holy Spirit with the evidence of tongues-speech; see Steven J. Land, *Pentecostal Spirituality: A Passion for the Kingdom* (Sheffield: Sheffield Academic Press, 1993), p. 18.

streams coming out of Azusa Street and spreading throughout North America, I also think that such a historiographical argument, while helpful in some respects, ultimately cannot be sustained since historical movements develop much more dynamically in multiple rather than unilateral directions. In short, I have chosen the fivefold gospel less for genealogical (historical) reasons than for heuristic ones: I simply think it provides us with a helpful framework for thinking theologically and pluralistically about the politics of global pentecostalism.

Still, some historical background will be helpful for us to see the promise of the fivefold approach to global pentecostal theology. It seems clear that the fivefold gospel represents a constellation of early modern pentecostal beliefs and practices that evolved out of a more primordial fourfold framework. The fourfold gospel was bequeathed to the earliest pentecostals by the holiness movement of the nineteenth century. A. B. Simpson (1843-1919), the founder of the Christian and Missionary Alliance movement (in 1887), published *The Four-Fold Gospel* originally in 1890,[29] and in it proclaimed Jesus as savior, sanctifier (resulting, in holiness parlance, in separation from sin and dedication to God), healer (against all forms of medical, metaphysical, magnetic, and spiritualist healing), and coming Lord. The early pentecostals who had been shaped by the holiness movement often just added the baptism in the Holy Spirit as a third work of grace (following after justification or salvation and sanctification), resulting in various renditions of the fivefold formula.

Yet there were other non-holiness pentecostals for whom the notion of sanctification as a second work of grace was problematic, either because of the assumption that it was included and incorporated into salvation (as in the Finished-Work pentecostal theology of William Durham)[30] or because of the view that sanctification was a process culminating in glorification rather than a distinct experience culminating at a moment in time (the more general Keswickian Reformed view that prevailed in pentecostal churches outside the American South). For these, the motif of Jesus as sanctifier was frequently replaced by that of Jesus as Spirit-baptizer, leaving the fourfold framework intact.[31] Scholars like Don Dayton argue that the fourfold model is more inclu-

29. A. B. Simpson, *The Four-Fold Gospel* (1890; reprint, Harrisburg, PA: Christian Alliance Publishing Co., 1925).

30. D. William Faupel, "William H. Durham and the Finished Work of Calvary," in J. A. B. Jongeneel, ed., *Pentecost, Mission and Ecumenism: Essays on Intercultural Theology — Festschrift in Honour of Professor Walter J. Hollenweger* (Frankfurt am Main: Peter Lang, 1992), pp. 85-95.

31. This is seen, for example, in the founding of the Foursquare Church in 1927. For the origins of the "foursquare" motif, see Matthew Avery Sutton, *Aimee Semple McPherson and the*

sive for understanding the heart of pentecostal theology since there were too many who did not embrace the holiness conviction about sanctification, and even for those who did, the notion of Jesus as baptizer in the Spirit that empowered Christian witness could be understood to include within it the holiness emphasis on purity as a prelude to power.[32]

I will opt instead to retain the fivefold gospel as an organizing motif for the specific reason that the notion of sanctification is too important to be assumed or subsumed under Spirit-baptism, and that there are few pentecostals who would today deny its importance. This reflects, in part, the fact that we are now far enough removed from the internecine polemics between two- and three-works of grace that were prevalent during the early pentecostal movement, and therefore can opt for the more comprehensive formulation without incurring the wrath of theological gatekeepers who were beholden to the theological streams of thought that flowed into and informed pentecostalism. Finally, I will also maintain that the doctrine of sanctification has important implications for the task of contributing a distinctively pentecostal perspective to the discussion of political theology.

We will say more about the specifics of the fivefold gospel throughout Part II of this book. For now, however, I need to return to my claim that the fivefold framework summarizes a distinctively pentecostal theological self-understanding and preserves the pluralism of the many tongues of Pentecost foregrounded by our starting with the Spirit. What is distinctive is not necessarily any of the five axioms taken by themselves, but the specific constellation that emerges when brought together. The fivefold pentecostal gospel is thus, as the proverbial saying goes, greater than the sum of its parts: together, they set pentecostalism apart as a distinct expression of Christian faith.

With regard to pneumatological and methodological pluralism, the fivefold framework presents a pluriform and polyphonic christology, pneumatology, and, by extension, soteriology. There is not just one view of Jesus as the anointed one of God, nor only one view of what Jesus has been anointed to accomplish. Hence the pluralism of pentecostalism on the ground — i.e., as it exists in the global south and around the world, and as I have documented already in the first chapter with regard to pentecostalism as it interfaces with the public sphere — can be said to reflect, even if only in-

---

Resurrection of Christian America (Cambridge, MA, and London: Harvard University Press, 2007), pp. 44-45; for doctrinal elaboration in McPherson's church, see Nathaniel M. Van Cleave, *The Vine and the Branches: A History of the International Church of the Foursquare Gospel* (Los Angeles: International Church of the Foursquare Gospel, 1992), pp. 75-76.

32. Donald W. Dayton, *Theological Roots of Pentecostalism* (Metuchen, NJ: Scarecrow Press, 1987; reprint, Peabody, MA: Hendrickson, 1991), pp. 19-22.

stinctively rather than intentionally, the pluralism inherent in the fivefold theological construct. In other words, the many tongues (and cultures, etc.) of the Spirit are suggestive of the many ways in which pentecostals experience the saving power of the anointed Jesus and have provided the theological intuitions and sensibilities that embraced the fourfold model and then developed it. The result is that pentecostal theology informed and structured by the fivefold formulation will itself be sensitive to the pluralism of the pentecostal experience on the one hand, while also being open to providing a distinctively pentecostal and pneumatological accent on the pluralism that exists in the theological academy on the other hand.

Finally, I note that the fivefold formulation is both Jesus-centered and christocentric, simultaneously. This reflects the Jesus-oriented spirituality and piety of the pentecostal movement (hence the appeal and even theologic of Oneness pentecostalism as a "Jesus-centered" movement). Yet at the same time, Jesus is also the Christ, the messiah anointed by the Holy Spirit. The theological paradox here is that Jesus becomes the Christ by the Spirit even while the ascended Christ pours out the gift of his Spirit upon all flesh (Acts 2:33). Thus, the Spirit of the Day of Pentecost (and of pentecostalism) is none other than the Spirit of Jesus the Christ. This central theological confession is what ensures that the pneumatological approach adopted in this volume is also both christological and trinitarian. In short, pentecostal theology that starts with the Spirit also begins with Jesus as Christ, even as pentecostal spirituality itself is simultaneously both pneuma- and christocentric — albeit in different respects (in the former case, as pointing to Jesus, and in the latter case, as denoting how the anointing of Christ is also available to all flesh) — and in this way resists and rejects any subordination in their trinitarian vision of God.[33]

---

33. Some might view such a robust trinitarian framework as exclusive of Oneness or apostolic pentecostals. Elsewhere, I have argued that the central issue separating these two streams of pentecostalism is a naïve Cartesian and post-Kantian definition of divine persons as individualized subjects (rather than either the Cappadocian or Thomistic notion that understands Father, Son, and Spirit as subsistent relations) and that once this is recognized and rejected, there is sufficient theological space cleared for Oneness and trinitarian pentecostal dialogue and even rapprochement. See Yong, "Oneness and the Trinity: The Theological and Ecumenical Implications of 'Creation *Ex Nihilo*' for an Intra-Pentecostal Dispute," *PNEUMA: The Journal of the Society for Pentecostal Studies* 19, no. 1 (Spring 1997): 81-107, and *Spirit Poured Out on All Flesh*, chap. 5.

3.2. The Hermeneutics of Political Theology:
Many Tongues and Practices in Luke-Acts

Besides the theological framework of the fivefold gospel, however, any pentecostal theological project will include moments of scriptural engagement — critical points where the Bible informs pentecostal theological reflection as befits their being a "people of the biblical book." In this section, I turn from the more general and abstract discussions of pentecostal theological method to the more concrete explorations of pentecostal biblical hermeneutics in order to tease out the parameters of a pentecostal-scriptural approach to political theology. In order to accomplish this task, I will focus — as pentecostals often do in their seeing contemporary encounters with the Spirit as being in continuity with that of the apostolic experience — on St. Luke's two volumes on the life of Christ and the Acts of the Apostles. Our goal is to understand the implications of Luke's own political perspectives for the task of political theology, especially as representative of the early church, so that we can consider how a distinctively pentecostal reading of Luke-Acts might generate a creative hermeneutical approach for contemporary Christian beliefs within and practices amidst the political.

3.2.1. Luke and the Political: An Overview

We have previously had the opportunity to survey scholarship on the New Testament read in political perspective (2.1.2). In the following, I wish to delve further into this issue by focusing on the two volumes of Luke and Acts.[34] What does Luke the evangelist have to tell us about Christianity and its relationship to the political?[35]

The person who initiated the most recent form of the debate in this area was Hans Conzelmann (1915-89).[36] For our purposes, Conzelmann's thesis can be summarized thus: that the problem was the delay of the Parousia (the return of Jesus), and that this led Luke to present two complementary arguments. For Christian readers of his two volumes, Luke's minor objective was

34. The days when Luke's two volumes were not read as theological works are long over; for a bibliographic survey of the theology of Luke, see François Bovon, *Luke the Theologian: Fifty-Five Years of Research (1950-2005)*, 2nd rev. ed. (Waco, TX: Baylor University Press, 2006).

35. I assume the scholarly consensus about Luke as the author of both volumes; see the discussion in any standard commentary.

36. Hans Conzelmann, *The Theology of St. Luke,* trans. Geoffrey Buswell (1961; reprint, Philadelphia: Fortress, 1982).

to convince them that in the long run of salvation history it would behoove them to render to Caesar what was Caesar's and view the state not as an opponent but as a guarantor of their freedom to missionize and evangelize (e.g., as in the case of St. Paul, who used his Roman citizenship to secure his rights as a minister of the gospel).[37] Regardless of whether or not one accepts Conzelmann's interpretation of Lukan eschatology,[38] more important for our purposes was his insight regarding Luke's recommendations for Roman officials: that Christians were law-abiding members of the empire and hence no threat to the stability of Roman rule, and that they were therefore a legitimate form of Judaism deserving of protection under imperial regulations. In short, for Conzelmann, Luke's writings were an *apologia pro ecclesia* directed to the state. In his view, Christians were politically quiescent and thus supportive of the status quo.

In response to Conzelmann, however, arguments about the politically revolutionary character of the early church emerged, the most widely discussed being that by the Mennonite theologian John Howard Yoder and the Roman Catholic scholar Richard Cassidy. Yoder's *The Politics of Jesus* argued that while Conzelmann was right to see early Christianity as being formally apolitical in terms of not seeking to be involved in the work of statecraft, he was wrong to therefore conclude that early Christian faith and practice did not have political consequences.[39] In fact, Jesus announced the arrival of the kingdom of God; he embodied a new form of human, social, and economic life and invited others to follow in his steps; he also proclaimed the Jubilee principle of the Old Testament, and his earliest followers enacted that way of life in a community that shared all they had so none were needy.[40] In short, while Jesus did not advocate a political revolution against the Romans, his life set in motion developments that in the long run could be potentially even more subversive of the political, social, and economic structures of Empire.

37. This *apologia pro imperio* directed to the early church is elaborated by Paul W. Walaskay, *"And So We Came to Rome": The Political Perspective of St. Luke* (Cambridge: Cambridge University Press, 1983).

38. For an overview of the debate in the generation after Conzelmann — some of which has called his thesis into question, others of which require a nuancing of his original argument — see James A. H. Reeves, "Apology, Threat, or a New 'Way': The Socio-Political Perspective of Luke-Acts," *Proceedings, Eastern Great Lakes and Midwest Biblical Societies* 10 (1990): 223-35.

39. John Howard Yoder, *The Politics of Jesus* (Grand Rapids: Eerdmans, 1972).

40. This thesis has also been elaborated by Philip Francis Esler, *Community and Gospel in Luke-Acts: The Social and Political Motivations of Lucan Theology* (Cambridge: Cambridge University Press, 1987).

Richard Cassidy, a Catholic priest and New Testament scholar, published three volumes on Luke-Acts in the fifteen years following Yoder's book, expanding on the basic thesis.[41] If Yoder's Anabaptist background leads him to understand the early church's political program in terms of non-violent resistance, Cassidy's graduate training during the post-Vatican II period featuring the emergence of liberation theology has shaped his own reading of Luke-Acts as a revolutionary document. In particular, class and socio-economic analyses of these texts suggest that Jesus initiated a movement that was threatening to Rome precisely because it garnered significant popular support for a new social order. Hence, Jesus' teachings and doings were potentially revolutionary vis-à-vis the empire, both at the direct level of confronting its political rulers and at the social, political, and economic levels in terms of the consequences of the implementation of his deeds and teachings. Cassidy does not use Luke-Acts to advocate a revolutionary politics, as might be expected from the application of a liberation hermeneutic to these texts. He does, however, provide a strong argument for why Conzelmann's view of Luke as being supportive of the political status quo is untenable, both from a historical perspective and from the normative and ethical stance regarding what the Scripture means for us today.

In 2006, two studies by East Asian scholars appeared that extended this discussion in opposite directions. Japanese scholar Kazuhiko Yamazaki-Ransom argued in his doctoral dissertation that, "For Luke, even Jewish political and religious authorities belonged to the Roman imperial system, which was in turn under demonic control."[42] Drawing from the role of the satan in the temptation narrative and other cues, especially in the Gospel of Luke, Yamazaki-Ransom suggests that the gentile and Roman officials "must be seen not only in the purely political context of the imperial administration but also in the cosmic context of the diabolic system of authority."[43] This proposal makes sense in light of the Pauline notion (Eph. 6:12) that our struggle against flesh and blood is actually against spiritual principalities and powers; in Yamazaki-Ransom's terms, the struggles of Jesus and the early Christians against the concrete challenges of imperial Rome thus unfold against the

---

41. Richard J. Cassidy, *Jesus, Politics, and Society: A Study of Luke's Gospel* (Maryknoll, NY: Orbis, 1978), and *Society and Politics in the Acts of the Apostles* (Maryknoll, NY: Orbis, 1987); see also Richard J. Cassidy and Philip J. Scharper, eds., *Political Issues in Luke-Acts* (Maryknoll, NY: Orbis, 1983).

42. Kazuhiko Yamazaki-Ransom, "God, People, and Empire: Anti-Imperial Theology of Luke-Acts in Light of Jewish Portrayals of Gentile Rulers" (Ph.D. diss., Trinity Evangelical Divinity School, 2006), p. 39.

43. Yamazaki-Ransom, "God, People, and Empire," p. 211.

spiritual and cosmic horizon of diabolical forces. In this framework, all political and national decisions — e.g., those of members of the Herodian dynasty, or of Roman provincial governors like Pilate, Herod, Sergius Paulus (the only one portrayed positively), Gallio, Felix, Porcius Festus, in Luke and Acts — are also spiritual ones, freighted with christological, ecclesiological, and theological significance.

In contrast, Korean scholar Yong-Sung Ahn argued in his published dissertation that "Luke is neither as pro-Roman as, for instance, the Romans 13 passage nor as anti-Roman as Revelation 13. Luke's narrative as a third way is not a simple middle path, but a complicated position that is characterized both by a counter-hegemonic discourse and as a colonial product."[44] On the one hand, Ahn embraces the conclusions of Yoder, Cassidy, and others, that the way of Jesus represents a counter-imperial socio-economic and political vision. On the other hand, Ahn's postcolonial hermeneutic opens up the conflicted trajectories of the Gospel account: the Jews, being those victimized at the hands of the Romans, are victimizers in relationship to Jesus and his followers, even while the early messianic believers sought, simultaneously, *both* alliances with the Romans in order to gain protection from the Jews *and* a retrieval of the Jewish socio-economic vision in resistance to the salvific offerings of the *Pax Romana*. In short, Luke's overall political message is ambiguous: being counter-hegemonic in some respects (and this has been highlighted in postcolonial readings of these texts[45]) while preserving of the status quo in other respects (and this plays out in the ways that, for example, South Korean readers of the New Testament have adopted an apolitical perspective as being most conducive to the mission of the church in a politically conflicted situation).

It should be clear by now that it will not be easy to determine in any definitive manner Luke's view of the political.[46] This has led to the judgment

44. Yong-Sung Ahn, *The Reign of God and Rome in Luke's Passion Narrative,* Biblical Interpretation Series 80 (Leiden and Boston: Brill, 2006), p. 2.

45. E.g., Gilberto J. Medina, "The Lukan Writings as Colonial Counter-Discourse: A Postcolonial Reading of Luke's Ideological Stance of Duplicity, Resistance, and Survival" (Ph.D. diss., Vanderbilt University, 2005); V. George Shillington, *An Introduction to the Study of Luke-Acts* (London and New York: T. & T. Clark, 2007), chap. 7; and Virginia Burrus, "Gospel of Luke and the Acts of the Apostles," in Fernando F. Segovia and R. S. Sugirtharajah, eds., *A Postcolonial Commentary on the New Testament Writings* (London: T. & T. Clark, 2007), pp. 133-55.

46. One might say that the argument of Oscar Cullmann, *Jesus and the Revolutionaries,* trans. Gareth Putnam (New York: Harper & Row, 1970), a generation ago continues to make sense: that there are texts supporting Jesus' political zealotry on the one hand and yet also his lack of a social and political agenda on the other; therefore, we should hold fast to the tension of Jesus' eschatological vision of instantiating an already-but-not-yet kingdom.

that "the political stance in Luke-Acts [is] a matter of political pragmatics,"[47] flexible enough to engage a wide range of political situations. I would add that this Lukan pragmatism is in part related to the author's realistic assessment of the *Realpolitik* of his day. I posit further that the multiplicity of interpretations of "Luke's political theology" is suggestive of the complexities of the early Christian political self-understanding. Much of this had to do, I think, with their conviction that the messiah was the one who would restore and renew Israel.

3.2.2. The Restoration of Israel: The Unfolding Story of the Church and the Political in Acts

It is undeniable that Luke's narrative unfolds amidst a heavily contested political field. The evangelist notes, for example, that Jesus was born in the days when Quirinius was governor of Syria and Emperor Augustus called for a census (Luke 2:1-2), and that Jesus' ministry was launched in "the fifteenth year of the reign of Emperor Tiberius, when Pontius Pilate was governor of Judea, and Herod was ruler of Galilee, and his brother Philip ruler of the region of Ituraea and Trachonitis, and Lysanias ruler of Abilene" (3:1). There is also no doubt that the titles Luke ascribes to Jesus — i.e., savior/σωτήρ and Lord/κύριος (2:11 and passim) — belonged to Caesar, whose cult celebrated the provision of health, protection, and material sustenance as belonging to the domain of the emperor. Further, the origins of the emperors often were traced to divine sources and heralded by auspicious events including the divine impregnation of human mothers. Jesus' conception by the Holy Spirit coming upon a virgin as well as his message announced as good news would have been heard by the first-century Judean audience as indicative of a divine presence and program of action competing against, if not directly challenging, the "gospel" of the imperial ideology, its nationalism, and its religious cult.[48]

That Jesus' ministry is presented as centrally focused on restoring Israel and heralding the impending kingdom of God probably did nothing to quell the suspicions of those who viewed his popularity as a threat to the *Pax*

47. Gerd Theissen, *Gospel Writing and Church Politics: A Socio-Rhetorical Approach,* Chuen King Lecture Series 3 (Hong Kong: Chung Chi College, 2001), pp. 95-96.

48. See Robert G. Reid, "'Savior' and 'Lord' in the Lukan Birth Narrative: A Challenge to Caesar?" *Pax Pneuma: The Journal of Pentecostals and Charismatics for Peace and Justice* 5, no. 1 (2009): 46-61, available at http://www.pcpj.org/images/paxpneuma/pcpj_pax_pneuma_spring _2009.pdf (last accessed 14 March 2009).

Romana. The birth narratives of Jesus are replete with anticipation that the time had come for the deliverance of Israel and the redemption of Jerusalem from the hands of her enemies, and this translated, positively put, into the realization of the long-awaited restoration of Israel, fulfillment of the Abrahamic covenant, and renewal of the Davidic kingdom (Luke 1:32-33, 54-55, 69-74; 2:38).[49] Jesus then announces, at the beginning of his public ministry, that

> The Spirit of the Lord is upon me,
>> because he has anointed me
>> to bring good news to the poor.
> He has sent me to proclaim release to the captives
>> and recovery of sight to the blind,
>> to let the oppressed go free,
> to proclaim the year of the Lord's favour.
>
> (4:18-19)

The rest of Jesus' words and deeds carried out this agenda under the power of the Spirit. Arguably, Jesus was eventually executed because he advocated a way of life that threatened the political, economic, social, and religious status quo.[50]

My goal at this juncture, however, is to follow the development of Jesus' vision of the kingdom as that unfolded in the beliefs and practices of the early church. During the interim period between his resurrection and ascension, after having spoken to the disciples extensively about the kingdom of God (Acts 1:3) — not to mention that he had spent three years with them teaching about and doing the works of the kingdom — the disciples were still led to query: "Lord, is this the time when you will restore the kingdom to Israel?" (1:6). The book of Acts shows how the earliest followers of Jesus struggled to reconcile their ethnocentric Jewish understanding about the restoration of Israel with God's more universal designs to redeem the world of the gentiles. Jesus' answer to the disciples' question signaled that the renewal of Israel would not be accomplished apart from extension of the message, enabled by the power of the Holy Spirit, "to the ends of the earth" (1:8).

49. David Ravens, *Luke and the Restoration of Israel,* Journal for the Study of the New Testament Supplement Series 119 (Sheffield: Sheffield Academic Press, 1995); for an overview, see Richard Bauckham, "The Restoration of Israel in Luke-Acts," in James M. Scott, ed., *Restoration: Old Testament, Jewish, and Christian Perspectives,* Supplements to the Journal for the Study of Judaism 72 (Leiden: Brill, 2001), pp. 435-87.

50. I have already (3.1.2) presented the broad outlines of this thesis drawing from the work of N. T. Wright.

The work of Max Turner is directly relevant to my argument here.[51] Turner suggests that whereas the Spirit anoints Jesus as Messiah in order to inaugurate the liberation and renewal of Israel in Luke, the exalted Messiah in turn pours out the Spirit from on high (cf. Luke 24:49 and Acts 2:33) in order to expand the redemption of Israel to include the world in Acts. If in Luke the anointed Jesus comes "to free Israel from her 'slave-poverty,' 'exile-captive' and 'blind' estate and to lead her along the wilderness 'way' towards restored Zion," in Acts, the anointed disciples experience the "new life, worship and joyful service to God in the messianic community of grace and peace, the brotherhood and New Exodus 'way' leading to ultimate salvation" for all.[52] In sum, the Spirit is "executive power" of the risen Jesus and ascended Christ who forms a community of reconciliation, worship, and service as a light to the nations.[53]

Now Turner's thesis regarding the role of the Spirit in the restoration of Israel is directed primarily into the scholarly debate regarding whether the Spirit in Luke initiates salvation or empowers believers for witness.[54] His response is to suggest that the salvific work of the Spirit focused on the liberation and renewal of Israel is accomplished through empowering the renewal community to bear witness to the ends of the earth about the imminent kingdom of God. Consistent with Turner's emphases but simultaneously building on them, I wish to highlight the political dimension of the Spirit as "the power of Israel's restoration, cleansing and purging . . . as the messianic people of God, through the variety of charismata afforded, and through the way they impact on the community and on the individual."[55] The result is that the church in Acts cannot be a merely sectarian community isolated from the public square; rather, as a people called to participate in the restoration of Israel precisely by being a light to the nations, the church becomes a political body whose "way of life as a community of reconciliation and unity, promoted and guarded by the Spirit, makes her a witness; and the Spirit also fills different individuals to articulate this witness with power to those outside the community."[56]

51. Max Turner, *Power from on High: The Spirit in Israel's Restoration and Witness in Luke-Acts*, Journal of Pentecostal Theology Supplement Series 9 (Sheffield: Sheffield Academic Press, 1996).

52. Turner, *Power from on High*, pp. 266 and 436.

53. Turner, *Power from on High*, pp. 306, 315, passim.

54. For a summary of the issues, see William Atkinson, "Pentecostal Responses to Dunn's *Baptism in the Holy Spirit*: Luke-Acts," *Journal of Pentecostal Theology* 6 (1995): 87-131.

55. Turner, *Power from on High*, p. 455.

56. Turner, *Power from on High*, p. 455.

What emerges in this picture is the public, even political, work of the Spirit.[57] The Spirit of salvation and prophecy (the two primary categories through which the Spirit has been understood in Luke-Acts) is also the Spirit of the political. In other words, the saving, sanctifying, and empowering works of the Spirit produce a new body politic, one in which socio-economic, class, ethnic, and gender differences are leveled out in a variety of ways.[58] Hence Jesus' mission to renew and restore Israel is continued in and through the church, except that the chasm between Jew and gentile has now been bridged by the outpouring of the Spirit on all flesh (Acts 2:17), with the result that the gentiles of the world have now been invited to participate in the redemption of Israel.

3.2.3. Pentecostal Hermeneutics: Toward a Lukan Political Theology

The preceding discussion has sought to demonstrate the promise of a distinctively Lukan approach to the topic of political theology. In the constructive portion of this book (Part II), I will continue to hedge my bets that the use of Lukan material, especially in the book of Acts, as a springboard into the wider biblical canon will be fruitful for theological reflection on the political. In the meantime, I will summarize the hermeneutical rationale developed thus far in three basic theses.

1) The book of Acts has been central to pentecostal beliefs and practices from the beginning of the movement in the early twentieth century. As already noted (1.3.1), pentecostalism can be understood as a restorationist movement, particularly with respect to the retrieval and reappropriation of the life of the early church as recorded particularly in the pages of the Acts of the Apostles. This pentecostal canon-within-a-canon has not generally resulted in a neglect of the remainder of the scriptural witness, but instead functions more like a hermeneutical lens through which pentecostals read and engage the rest of the Bible. For our purposes, however, I wish to challenge pentecostals to go beyond focusing on an individualistic framework for understanding the healings, the miraculous, and the charismatic manifesta-

57. See also Michael Welker, *God the Spirit*, trans. John Hoffmeyer (Minneapolis: Fortress, 1994); cf. W. B. Blakemore, "The Holy Spirit as Public and as Charismatic Institutions," *Encounter* 36, no. 3 (1975): 161-80.

58. This is the argument of Turner's student, Matthias Wenk, *Community-Forming Power: The Socio-Ethical Role of the Spirit in Luke-Acts*, Journal of Pentecostal Theology Supplemental Series 19 (Sheffield: Sheffield Academic Press, 2000); Wenk identifies how the perlocutionary effects of the Spirit's speech acts transform individuals and their communities.

tions of the Spirit in Acts and to see how these phenomena may also function as signs of the Spirit's work in the public — i.e., social, economic, and political — sphere. In other words, if pentecostals have devoted much of their theological and hermeneutical energy in times past to defending from the book of Acts their distinctive understanding of the Spirit's baptism in power for witness as evidenced by speaking in tongues,[59] I would like to expend as much if not more effort now on mining Acts as a biblical resource for a distinctive pentecostal theology of the political and the public square.

2) Yet as the work of Turner and others (3.2.2) has suggested, Acts is about the emergence of the Christian community as a work of the Spirit. There are two sides to this thesis: the pneumatological and the ecclesiological. The former aspect highlights that the heart of the pentecostal biblical imagination — which is deeply shaped by the Day of Pentecost narrative regarding the outpouring of the Holy Spirit on male and female, young and old, slave and free — opens up to an ecclesiological reading of Acts. This then further invites consideration of how the public and community-forming roles of the Spirit in Luke and especially Acts may be much more illuminating for the task of political theology than previously anticipated both within and even outside the pentecostal academy. If emphasis is placed (following St. Luke himself) on the restoration of Israel, not to mention the redemption of the world, then the political character of the Spirit's activities looms much larger. This is because the focus will no longer be only on what the Spirit accomplishes in the lives of individuals, but will be on the formation of community and the body politic instead. Further, if Acts is also read in light of Jesus' Spirit-empowered works of liberation in the Gospel of Luke,[60] then a liberative pentecostal theology of the political also becomes a possibility.[61] This is not to minimize the pentecostal

<hr/>

59. E.g., Guy P. Duffield and Nathaniel M. Van Cleave, *Foundations of Pentecostal Theology* (Los Angeles: LIFE Bible College, 1983), pp. 304-25; John R. Higgins, Michael L. Dusing, and Frank D. Tallman, *An Introduction to Theology: A Classical Pentecostal Perspective* (1993; reprint, Dubuque, IA: Kendall/Hunt, 1994), pp. 151-58; and William W. Menzies and Robert P. Menzies, *Spirit and Power: Foundations of Pentecostal Experience* (Grand Rapids: Zondervan, 2000), chap. 8.

60. E.g., Michael Prior, *Jesus the Liberator: Nazareth Liberation Theology (Luke 4:16-30)*, The Biblical Seminar 26 (Sheffield: Sheffield Academic Press, 1995).

61. The notion of the liberating Spirit has been explored by pentecostals such as Eldin Villafañe, *The Liberating Spirit: Toward an Hispanic American Pentecostal Social Ethic* (Grand Rapids: Eerdmans, 1993), and Samuel Solivan, *The Spirit, Pathos and Liberation: Toward an Hispanic Pentecostal Theology* (Sheffield: Sheffield Academic Press, 1998); for more on the idea of a political and pneumatological theology of liberation, see Mark Lewis Taylor, "Spirit," in Peter Scott and William T. Cavanaugh, eds., *The Blackwell Companion to Political Theology* (2004; paperback ed., Malden, MA: Blackwell, 2007), pp. 377-92, esp. pp. 388-90.

accent on transformed hearts and Spirit-empowered lives, but it is to locate such works of the Spirit within the wider corporate body called the church even while understanding the church's location within an even wider social, economic, and political context. A political rereading of Acts will thus be valuable also for how it might shape the church's self-understanding.[62] This will be important not only for pentecostals who have perennially been accused of having an underdeveloped ecclesiology,[63] but also for the ongoing ecumenical reflections of the church catholic.[64] Hence I am suggesting that when pentecostals expand their pneumatological lens and hermeneutic in order to focus on the political dimensions of the Luke-Acts narrative, heretofore unforeseen insights will ensue, not only about political theology but also about (pentecostal) pneumatology and ecclesiology.

3) Finally, I wish to reiterate how important Scripture is for the pentecostal theological task in general and for any pentecostal attempt to develop a theology of the political in particular. With regard to the former, we have already noted (3.1.2) the pluralistic impulses set in motion by starting theologically with the Spirit. Spirit-enthusiasms have often led in the history of Christianity to anarchic practices, not to mention heterodox beliefs. A christological focus and commitment to the Bible as a rule of faith and practice are necessary to discipline the pneumatological imagination of pentecostalism. On the other side, such a biblical orientation energizes rather than hinders the quest for a political theology. This is because, as Timothy Gorringe notes, it is practically impossible, given the shape of the biblical canon — not to mention Luke and Acts, as we have seen — for there to be a "non-political exegesis."[65] Rather, the private spheres of the lives of the earliest followers of the messiah as well as of our own were and are deeply intertwined with the public domains that are socially, economically, and politically constituted. Hence any reading of Scripture will bring together not only two generic horizons (that of the ancient world and that of the contemporary readers and their communities) but also

---

62. As Reinhard Hütter notes, "in a world of modernity that increasingly privatizes the Christian faith, the church's public character is reclaimed only and precisely by overcoming the internal splits and by (re-)creating a truly catholic and evangelical church and theology"; see Hütter, *Bound to Be Free: Evangelical Catholic Engagements in Ecclesiology, Ethics, and Ecumenism* (Grand Rapids: Eerdmans, 2004), p. 41.

63. See Veli-Matti Kärkkäinen, *An Introduction to Ecclesiology: Ecumenical, Historical, and Global Perspectives* (Grand Rapids: Baker Academic, 2002), pp. 72-74.

64. For an ecclesiological reading of Acts, see Anthony B. Robinson and Robert W. Wall, *Called to Be Church: The Book of Acts for a New Day* (Grand Rapids: Eerdmans, 2006).

65. Tim Gorringe, "Political Readings of Scripture," in John Barton, ed., *The Cambridge Companion to Biblical Interpretation* (Cambridge: Cambridge University Press, 1998), pp. 67-80, esp. pp. 75-76.

two political contexts and frames of references. Pentecostals take comfort, however, in the fact that the same Spirit who was at work in the lives of Jesus and his disciples remains at work today in those who attempt to follow in their footsteps.

In sum, I am proposing a distinctive pentecostal hermeneutic that begins with the narrative of the early church, and focuses on the work of the Spirit as empowering the early Christian encounter and engagement with the public domain. Such a pentecostal approach to Scripture will complement the pentecostal theological method of starting with the Spirit in terms of bringing the biblical narrative into dialogue with the contemporary pentecostal experience of the political in its various aspects.

3.3. Renewing Political Theology: A Pentecostal Assist

We are now almost ready to proceed to the political theology that constitutes Part II of this book. Before doing so, however, I will sketch the thesis to be prosecuted, summarize the form of the argument to be deployed, and locate the wider theological project that informs this volume. The following serves as a transition from the phenomenological, descriptive, and methodological tasks of Part I to the constructive task at hand.

3.3.1. *Sketching the Thesis: Many Tongues, Many Political Practices*

My hypothesis is that pentecostal reflections on political theology can be summarized with the motto, "many tongues, many political practices." There are three interlocking motifs that frame the thesis: the biblical, the pentecostal, and the political-theological.

Biblically, I posit that the dominant theme of the restoration of Israel and the renewal of the world in Luke-Acts opens up the people of God to a multiplicity of political stances, practices, and theologies.[66] The notion of the gospel going forth to the ends of the earth fulfills the Old Testament promise that through Abraham, all the nations of the earth would be blessed. At the same time, then, the multiplicity of political forms and structures in ancient

---

66. In a companion to this book, I provide an exegetical-political reading of Luke-Acts through a pentecostal and pneumatological lens; see Yong, *The Holy Spirit and the Public Square* [working title] (Brewster, MA: Paraclete Press, forthcoming). By contrast, my incursions into Luke and especially Acts throughout this volume will be primarily thematic.

Israel (2.1.1) anticipate the pluralism characteristic of "new Israel" in a predominantly gentile world. In this case, the many tongues of the Spirit that represent the many cultures of diaspora Judaism (in Acts 2) not only foreshadow the many tribes, peoples, and nations (in the Apocalypse) but also the many political structures amidst which the church fulfills her vocation in the present age. I will attempt to make the case in Part II of this book that this biblical insight belongs not only to pentecostalism or to pentecostal theology but also to all Christians as well as those in search of a viable political theology for our time.

From a pentecostal perspective, we have already seen that there is no one form of political, economic, or social engagement in global pentecostalism (chapter 1). Rather, there is a multiplicity of pentecostalisms in the global south, with distinct orientations toward the political, broadly construed. The preliminary biblical explorations provided in this chapter suggest that the many tongues of Pentecost, precisely because they represent a diversity of ethnic, linguistic, and cultural experiences, also imply the redemption of many political practices. If pentecostalism has been portable around the world because of its translatability — its capacity to be indigenized and vernacularized in local languages, customs, and experiences[67] — then any pentecostal approach to political theology will be similarly informed by the pluralism of the pentecostal body politic. In short, I suggest that pentecostals have intuitively correlated the "many tongues" motif central to their spirituality and piety with the complexity of their social, economic, and political lives. I will argue in the rest of this book that there are normative implications suggested in this pentecostal correlation for political theology.

Finally, then, from the standpoint of political theology itself, we have observed (chapter 2) that there is no one normative standard for how Christians should think about the political. Instead, there have always been a multiplicity of political structures in and through which the people of God have borne witness to the coming kingdom. Not without reason, we are beginning to see accounts that discuss political pluralism as if that itself were normative for Christian theology.[68] What I hope to provide in the remainder of this volume is a theological rationale for this pluralism in Christian political think-

---

67. E.g., Murray W. Dempster, Byron D. Klaus, and Douglas Petersen, eds., *The Globalization of Pentecostalism: A Religion Made to Travel* (Oxford, UK, and Irvine, CA: Regnum International, 1999).

68. E.g., Hent de Vries and Lawrence E. Sullivan, eds., *Political Theologies: Public Religions in a Post-Secular World* (New York: Fordham University Press, 2006), and J. Budziszewski et al., *Evangelicals in the Public Square: Four Formative Voices on Political Thought and Action* (Grand Rapids: Baker Academic, 2006).

ing. The task is to avoid either a relativism of political options or a politically correct legitimation that devolves into an ideology of the majority. Further, we must resist providing a merely pragmatic account that baptizes many theological beliefs derived from the diverse political contexts within which such beliefs are shaped.[69] Instead, if I am successful, my thesis will not only provide a theological justification for the diversity of Christian politics, but also empower the many different practices required to bear witness to the gospel in a politically pluralistic world.

In short, I am proposing that the many tongues of Pentecost and the many concomitant political practices may constitute a distinctive pentecostal contribution to the wider Christian discussion of political theology. One might read the following as a "pentecostal political theology," and that would be appropriate at one level. I'm more interested, however, in how pentecostal perspectives can shape a Christian political theology that is viable for the church catholic.

3.3.2. Summarizing the Argument: Pentecostalism and Political Theology

I will unfold the "many tongues, many political practices" thesis over the five chapters in Part II. Each chapter will be framed, successively, in terms of one element of the fivefold gospel of Jesus as savior/deliverer, sanctifier, Spirit baptizer, healer, and coming king (see 3.1.3). This scheme means that the fundamental theological categories will be christologically focused, but pentecostally delineated. In other words, one might certainly read the following as suggestive for a global pentecostal christology; my intent, however, is not first and foremost to write a pentecostal christology but to ensure a christomorphic shape for pentecostal reflections on political theology. Hence the christological ideas are subordinate to the overall agenda of this volume, even if they should not therefore be dismissed as being non-substantive.

Yet the fivefold gospel opens up, I propose, to five important angles on political theology. Jesus as savior is understood, especially across pentecostalism in the global south, in terms of deliverance from cosmic forces of evil; this invites consideration of how pentecostalism might think about the polit-

---

69. André Dumas, *Political Theology and the Life of the Church*, trans. John Bowden (Philadelphia: Westminster, 1978), pp. 20-22, almost suggests as much, that Christian thinking about the political is shaped by different political situations.

ical in terms of the biblical principalities and powers. Jesus as sanctifier shapes the pentecostal self-understanding of being a community that is set apart from the world, and this begs for theological reflection on the church as being an alternative *polis* to the dominant world order. Jesus as Spirit baptizer is at the heart of the pentecostal missiological thrust, and this demands reconsideration in a postcolonial, post-Western, and post-secular era of globalization. Jesus as healer has developed in holistic and non-dualistic directions to include Jesus as the one who blesses with material and financial abundance; this gospel of prosperity will be considered in terms of contemporary theologies of economics. Finally, Jesus as coming king invokes eschatological renditions of political theology, whether in terms of dispensationalistic Zionism or apocalyptic scenarios of the end of the world; these images and ideas require interrogation in light of alternative understandings of the coming kingdom and the renewal of the cosmos.

The five chapters in Part II thus explore these five venues for thinking pentecostally about political theology. The three sections of each chapter i) explicate how each of these christological themes interface with both pentecostalism and politics; ii) enter into a dialogue with another (non-pentecostal) tradition of or other perspectives on political theology; and iii) propose a constructive set of Christian practices and beliefs regarding the political. The movement is from the particularity of pentecostalism toward a more ecumenical frame of reference relevant to the church catholic and the wider theological academic discussion.

Let me say more about the dialogical approach of each chapter. This reflects my following through on the "many tongues" aspect of my thesis as a methodological guideline. Elsewhere I have defended the claim that starting with the Spirit opens up to an ecumenical conversation in which the many Christian (and even other religious) traditions will need to be represented and heard in any theological undertaking.[70] In this volume, I bring pentecostalism into dialogue with five sets of theological voices that have been recently prominent in the arena of political theology: those that have proposed thinking about the biblical principalities and powers in political perspectives (in the chapter on Jesus as savior and deliverer); the post-Christendom and post-Constantinian proposals of John Howard Yoder, Stanley Hauerwas, and members of the New Monasticism (in the chapter on Jesus as sanctifier); the alternative *civitas* formulations of political theology proffered by Radical Orthodoxy (in the chapter on Jesus as Spirit baptizer); the Catholic social teaching tradition (in the chapter on Jesus as healer); and a spectrum of voices ad-

---

70. Yong, *Spirit-Word-Community*, esp. chaps. 8-9.

vocating for a range of political theologies in eschatological perspective (in the chapter on Jesus as coming king). The answer to the question — Why these specific conversation partners? — is complex, but ultimately it is one that says: these are at present some of the most relevant contemporary voices and potentially the most conducive to interacting with the issues raised by pentecostal perspectives, commitments, and intuitions. Section 2 of each of the next five chapters will provide further rationale for engaging these dialogue partners and elucidate the various ways in which pentecostal interlocutions can be beneficial to an ecumenically relevant political theology.

The third and final section of each chapter in Part II will combine to present a constructive Christian political theology of "many tongues and many political practices" in three steps. There will be a biblical subsection that focuses on relevant passages in the book of Acts (and Luke), a practical subsection that proposes a range of political practices in light of the preceding pentecostal, dialogical, and biblical considerations, and an explicitly theological, pneumatological, and trinitarian revisioning of political theology along five trajectories:

> chapter 4 — a liturgical theology of cosmopolitical resistance
>
> chapter 5 — a sanctified politics of cultural redemption
>
> chapter 6 — a prophetic politics of civil society
>
> chapter 7 — a political economy of healing and shalom
>
> chapter 8 — an eschatological politics of hope

As will be clear, the argument winds around like a fivefold chord, emergent out of pentecostal sensibilities and intuitions (as framed by the theological categories of the fivefold gospel), strengthened by dialogical forays into at least five different traditions of political theology, informed by the ecclesiological considerations derived from Luke (especially the Acts of the Apostles), and directed toward a performative and trinitarian theo-political proposal (see Figure 1 on p. 114). The result, I anticipate, will be neither a systematically formulated political theology nor a merely pentecostal version of political theology, but a Christian political imagination that is informed by, albeit irreducible to, pentecostal sensibilities.

Figure 1. Overview of the constructive argument for chapters 4-8

	Chapter 4	Chapter 5	Chapter 6	Chapter 7	Chapter 8
Fivefold Gospel	Jesus as savior and deliverer	Jesus as sanctifier	Jesus as Spirit-baptizer	Jesus as healer	Jesus as coming king
Topic	Principalities, powers, politics	Theology of culture	Theology of civil society	Theology of economics	Theology of history
Dialogue partners	Political theologies of the demonic	Post-Christendom theologians	Radical Orthodoxy	Catholic social teaching	Jewish, liberation, and green theologies
Thesis	Many tongues, many spirits	Many tongues, many cultures	Many tongues, many witnesses	Many tongues, many economies	Many tongues, many histories
Acts narrative	Spirit of prayer, praise, and power	Spirit of cultural redemption	Spirit of civic boldness	Spirit of health and commonwealth	Spirit of the "last days"
Political praxis	Politics of worship	Perfectionist politics	Prophetic politics	Shalomic politics	Politics of hope
Theological imagination	Liturgical imagination	Sanctified imagination	Pneumatic imagination	Charismatic imagination	Eschatological imagination

3.3.3. Locating the Larger Project: Pentecostal Theology for the Twenty-First Century

In concluding this part of the book, some final comments will help to frame the considerations to come. Most immediately, note that my thesis of "many tongues and many political practices" is an adaptation and extension of a proposal, "many tongues, many practices," I presented in a preceding volume on theology and religious pluralism.[71] In that book, I argued that there are many forms of interreligious practices — e.g., evangelistic witness, dialogue, and social activism — by which we meet, greet, and relate to people of other faiths, sometimes as hosts, and other times as guests. The methodology adopted there, however, is very similar to the one driving this argument, with the difference being that the focus on Luke-Acts in that book was informed explicitly only by a pneumatological theology, while the approach being developed here is a specifically pentecostal one, within which the Lukan hermeneutic is situated. The goals in both volumes, however, are complementary:

71. Yong, *Hospitality and the Other: Pentecost, Christian Practices, and the Neighbor* (Maryknoll, NY: Orbis, 2008), esp. pp. 62-64.

there to argue that a Lukan and pneumatological theology of interreligious encounter should be open to a diversity of forms of Christian witness and here to develop a Lukan and pentecostal theology of the political that sustains Christian engagement with the pluralism in the public sphere.

An earlier precursor to this volume is my book *The Spirit Poured Out on All Flesh,* published in 2005 and subtitled *Pentecostalism and the Possibility of Global Theology.* In that volume I adopted a similar methodological approach by beginning with a phenomenology of pentecostalism in the global south, as well as deploying a Lukan hermeneutic as a springboard into the wider biblical canon. My objective there, however, was to sketch the contours of pentecostally conceived systematic theology, resulting, after the opening phenomenological chapter, in six essays on soteriology, ecclesiology, ecumenism, the doctrine of God, theology of culture, and theology of nature. The moves made in each of these essays parallel many of the moves that will be seen in the chapters in Part II of this book — i.e., bringing global pentecostal perspectives into dialogue with voices in the historical and ecumenical traditions of the church. However, the broad systematic aspirations of that volume meant that in-depth analyses could only be hinted at, leaving the discussion operating, in general, at a very programmatic level.

In the present book, I aim to burrow deeper into some of the issues opened up in that previous work. More precisely, I hope to supplement the earlier discussion of a pentecostal and pneumatological ecclesiology by thinking about a Christian doctrine of the church vis-à-vis the public square. Further, insisted upon but undeveloped in *The Spirit Poured Out on All Flesh* was the christological commitments that mark pentecostal piety. The five chapters to come will fill in some of the blanks left over from my past endeavors, particularly in terms of exploring the interconnections between christology and ecclesiology and vice versa.

More important, in my estimation, is the emergence in my thinking of soteriology as a, if not *the,* central pentecostal doctrine. In some ways, this was already signaled in *The Spirit Poured Out on All Flesh,* especially in that the doctrine of salvation was the first of the theological loci to be treated (in chapter 2 of that book). However, I have come to see even more clearly that the pentecostal doctrine of Spirit-baptism, while certainly distinctive to the movement, serves larger missiological and hence soteriological purposes.[72] In

---

72. I have been helped in this regard by the work of my good friend, Frank Macchia — e.g., his *Baptized in the Spirit: A Global Pentecostal Theology* (Grand Rapids: Zondervan, 2006), and *Justified in the Spirit: Creation, Redemption, and the Triune God* (Grand Rapids: Eerdmans, 2010).

this volume, my political theology is being formulated not only in a general theological manner, but more explicitly so in terms of the fivefold pentecostal soteriology. In that sense, the discussion to come expands on the pentecostal soteriology presented previously, but does so within a triadic christological-ecclesiological-and-pneumatological framework.

More specifically, however, my soteriological reflections will be undertaken not in theological abstraction but as rooted in the concrete material and social realities of pentecostal life in particular and Christian life in general, especially in the global south. In other words, the doctrine of salvation to be articulated in the rest of this book concerns neither the eschatological saving of the soul in the life to come nor the forensic justification of the heart in the present; rather, I will argue for a pentecostal and Christian soteriology that is robustly political, such that the Spirit's saving, sanctifying, empowering, healing, and eschatological work in Christ and through the body of Christ have palpable economic, social, and public consequences, implications, and applications.[73] In all of these ways, then, Part II of *Pentecostalism and Political Theology* thus tends to the ecclesiological, christological, and soteriological business unfinished in my earlier work.

Last but not least, the remainder of this book intends on contributing from the standpoint of political theology to two broad conversations with which I have been engaged since the beginning of my work as a systematic and comparative theologian: that of global pentecostalism and that of theology in global context.[74] With regard to the former, I continue to insist on rigorous interdisciplinary, phenomenological, and ethnographic portraits of pentecostalism worldwide in order to deconstruct stereotypes and to illuminate the complexity of this global movement; but as a theologian, however, I also insist on theological analyses that would inform these other approaches, even while drawing from the work of others in order to provide second-order and self-critical reflection as a pentecostal insider on theological issues of interest to the wider public. This effort at constructing a Christian political theology wagers

73. Put alternatively, this book can be read as an extended elaboration of global pentecostalism as a "multitude become disciples — historical agents engaged in historical projects that lead to new forms of community in their multitudinous splendor"; see Elaine Padilla and Dale T. Irvin, "Where Are the Pentecostals in an Age of Empire?" in Bruce Ellis Benson and Peter Goodwin Heltzel, eds., *Evangelicals and Empire: Christian Alternatives to the Political Status Quo* (Grand Rapids: Brazos Press, 2008), pp. 169-84, esp. p. 175.

74. I provide some additional perspective on these matters in my "Between the Local and the Global: Autobiographical Reflections on the Emergence of the Global Theological Mind," in Darren C. Marks, ed., *Shaping a Global Theological Mind* (Aldershot, UK: Ashgate, 2008), pp. 187-94.

that pentecostal perspectives on these matters will produce unique insights into an existing discussion even while illuminating the public (and political) challenges confronting pentecostalism as a global phenomenon.

With regard to the task of theology in global context,[75] it has now become trite to mention that the new face of Christianity in the twenty-first century is increasingly being refracted through what is occurring on the ground in Asian, African, and Latin American contexts. Christian theology, long dominated by Western discourses, categories, and approaches, will need to factor in voices from the global south in order to effectively engage the world as we know it in the twenty-first century. More than two decades ago, Harvey Cox opined that the theology of the future "will come not from the center but from the bottom and from the edge" of the world.[76] My own theological education has occurred in the West, but the pentecostal perspectives that I hope to represent are those from the margins of world Christianity, not to mention the theological academy. Let us see what kind of ferment is concocted when pentecostal Christianity meets the Western academy on the field of political theology.

---

75. See Yong and Peter G. Heltzel, "Robert Cummings Neville and Theology's Global Future," in Amos Yong and Peter Goodwin Heltzel, eds., *Theology in Global Context: Essays in Honor of Robert Cummings Neville* (New York and London: T. & T. Clark, 2004), pp. 29-42.

76. Harvey Cox, *Religion in the Secular City: Toward a Postmodern Theology* (New York: Simon & Schuster, 1984), p. 21.

PART II

Pentecostal Intersections with Political Theology: Enacting the Performance

CHAPTER 4

Pentecostal Salvation as Deliverance from the Powers: The Political Dimensions

This is the first of five constructive chapters on political theology as informed by pentecostal perspectives. Given the scope of the pentecostal fivefold gospel, we begin with the theme of Jesus as savior. The first section of this chapter will explore how the notion of Jesus as savior has included that of Jesus as deliverer from principalities, powers, and other spiritual forces, and how these soteriological motifs in pentecostalism have had political applications. Section 2 will then turn to a discussion of how various understandings of principalities, powers, and the demonic have played out in wider theological approaches to the political. This sets us up, in the concluding section of this chapter, to develop a cosmopolitical liturgics of resistance, whereby I sketch how Christian worship, including its distinctive pentecostal and charismatic variations, enables us to correlate a re-enchanted cosmology with a multi-leveled and multi-dimensional political praxis.

At one level, our efforts in this chapter do no more than lay out a robust soteriological and trinitarian framework for our considerations in the remainder of this book. At another level, however, this first of a five-step argument also goes to the heart of live issues not only in the field of political theology in particular but also in the discipline of Christian theology in general. I am referring here to questions concerning how we understand such historic Christian practices as exorcisms as well as such difficult (especially in the modern West) Christian beliefs regarding principalities, powers, and the demonic. More to the point, what is the relevance of these beliefs and practices for world Christianity in the public square of the twenty-first century?

I will argue in what follows that global pentecostalism forces us to re-engage these questions not merely as theological abstractions but as practical, existential, and even political realities. Our conclusions will need to be provisional and measured, but they cannot afford to be non-committed in light of the issues at stake. If the Christian doctrine of salvation has political consequences, then we will need to proceed carefully, strategically, and yet intentionally in order to engage with concerns at the heart of Christianity as a world religious tradition.

4.1. Jesus as Savior:
Pentecostal Salvation, Deliverance, and the Political

In a sense, that Jesus is savior is a non-controversial claim at the core of Christian faith. However, the twentieth-century pentecostal re-articulation of this confession, especially as it has developed in the global south, is retrieving and reappropriating the ancient Christian claim that Jesus has saved us precisely by redeeming us from the power of the evil one.[1] In this section, I will explore the political dimensions of this pentecostal soteriology in three steps: first by laying out the classical pentecostal theology of salvation understood as deliverance from the powers of darkness; second by explicating how the notion of pentecostal deliverance from the powers has functioned in the public sphere, especially in the arena of political economy; and third by exploring how popular pentecostal understandings of the powers have been translated into political praxis. Our goals are to identify both the problematic elements of pentecostal soteriology in our late-modern context and some potential resources for rethinking the interface of theology, cosmology, and politics in world context.

4.1.1. Classical Pentecostal Soteriology: Jesus as Savior and Deliverer

For pentecostals, fundamentally, salvation is to be found in Jesus and in his name, "for there is no other name under heaven given among mortals by which we must be saved" (Acts 4:12). In classical pentecostalism, this notion was formally articulated, with the help of late nineteenth-century conservative Protestant categories, to mean that human beings are guilty because of original sin and are unable to save themselves. But the life, death on a cross, resurrection, and ascension to heaven of Jesus Christ have made possible rec-

---

1. Thus the earliest Christian understanding of the doctrine of the atonement featured Jesus' life and death serving as a ransom that accomplished the redemption of humankind and the world from out of the clutches of the devil; for a now classic statement of this view, see Gustaf Aulén, *Christus Victor: An Historical Study of the Three Main Types of the Idea of the Atonement,* trans. A. G. Hebert (1931; reprint, London: SPCK, 1970), esp. chaps. 2-4.

onciliation between God and humankind. By repenting from their sin and placing faith in the person and work of Christ, human beings are regenerated by the power of the Holy Spirit, adopted as sons and daughters of God, and justified, sanctified, and, eschatologically, glorified. This, in gist, is what it means to confess Jesus as savior.[2]

From the beginning, however, pentecostals have experienced Jesus as saving them not only from their sins, but also from their sicknesses and diseases.[3] In the world pentecostal context, especially in the global south, this salvation includes a redemption from the powers of the devil and his demons since these are, ultimately, the causes of sickness (both physical and psychosomatic), poverty, and other material and socio-economic ills that keep human beings from experiencing the abundant life promised by God.[4] Especially in the global south, it is not unusual to find pentecostals blaming the demonic for the prostitution industry, the AIDS virus, medically inexplicable conditions, unemployment, political corruption, and other real-life challenges.[5] Given these assumptions, Jesus as savior is understood not only as healer but also as deliverer, and, in some cases, as exorcist,[6] and pentecostal evangelistic services thus include moments in the liturgy devoted to prayer for the sick as well as to rituals of deliverance and exorcism.[7] When understood in this manner, it is clear that pentecostalism in global context preaches a much more holistic as well as this-worldly gospel: Jesus saves not only human souls in the next life but also human bodies and lives in the present age.

To be sure, the salvation of individuals remained at the center of pentecostal soteriology: Jesus forgives *my* sins, heals *my* body, and delivers *me* from the powers of darkness.[8] At the same time, Jesus' salvific deliverance has

---

2. This summary is drawn from Daniel B. Pecota, "The Saving Work of Christ," in Stanley M. Horton, ed., *Systematic Theology,* rev. ed. (Springfield, MO: Logion Press, 1995), pp. 325-73.

3. See, e.g., F. F. Bosworth, *Christ the Healer* (1924; reprint, Grand Rapids: Fleming Revell, 1994); we will expand on this notion in chapter 7 below.

4. J. Kwabena Asamoah-Gyadu, *African Charismatics: Current Developments within Independent Indigenous Pentecostalism in Ghana,* Studies of Religion in Africa 27 (Leiden and Boston: Brill, 2005), esp. chaps. 5-6.

5. See Ayo Oritsejafor, "Dealing with the Demonic," in C. Peter Wagner and Joseph Thompson, eds., *Out of Africa* (Ventura, CA: Regal, 2004), pp. 78-99, esp. pp. 80-85.

6. E.g., Cheryl Bridges Johns, "Healing and Deliverance: A Pentecostal Perspective," in Jürgen Moltmann and Karl-Josef Kuschel, eds., *Pentecostal Movements as an Ecumenical Challenge* (London: SCM, and Maryknoll, NY: Orbis, 1996), pp. 45-51.

7. Aldwin Ragoonath, *Preach the Word: A Pentecostal Approach* (Winnipeg, MB: Agape Teaching Ministry of Canada, Inc., 2004), chap. 6.

8. Paul Gifford, *Ghana's New Christianity: Pentecostalism in a Globalizing African Econ-*

wider implications going far beyond the individual. In the remainder of this first section, we will discuss pentecostal salvation as deliverance unfolding in the economic and political arenas. To situate that discussion, however, we must understand how this distinctive soteriology of pentecostalism impacts family life as well as the larger community.

Central to the pentecostal notion of salvation, especially in the global south, is the idea of deliverance understood in socio-cultural terms. There are at least three aspects to this soteriological conception. First, the "curses" of the past are mediated through one's culture, especially when that culture is understood as being either subservient to or representative of a demonic agency. Most pentecostals accept the Old Testament idea that suggests the division of humanity into nations, people groups, and cultures was made "according to the number of the gods" or angels (Deut. 32:8; cf. Ps. 82).[9] The problem is that these "gods" are fallen angels, and hence their national and cultural forms, along with their religious beliefs and practices, are at best distortions of or at worst opposed to the goodness, truth, and beauty of God's intentions for humankind.[10] Hence Christian conversion involves a complete repudiation of one's cultural past[11] — and pentecostals have generally rejected celebrations like the trans-continental World Black and African Festival of Arts and Culture because it is seen as a means of perpetuating the demonic in the African heritage[12] — even as specifically pentecostal conversion includes a deliverance from the oppressive spirits (demons) derived from culture and a concomitant infilling of the Holy Spirit. Only in this way are the cultural curses broken and the intended blessings of God able to reach believers.

Yet pentecostals realize that we are socialized into our cultures from a very young age through our families. Much is made of the early Christian experience of the conversion and baptism of entire households (e.g., Acts 11:14,

---

omy (Bloomington and Indianapolis: Indiana University Press, 2004), p. 109, observes that such an overemphasis on the this-worldly dimension of salvation has resulted, in some parts of Africa, in a minimization of the notion of sin in pentecostal soteriology.

9. See E. Theodore Mullen, *The Divine Council in Canaanite and Early Hebrew Literature* (Chico, CA: Scholars Press, 1980).

10. See Gregory A. Boyd, *God at War: The Bible and Spiritual Conflict* (Downers Grove, IL: InterVarsity Press, 1997), esp. chaps. 4-5. A more accessible explication of this view, one that many pentecostals would recognize and even affirm, is Wilbur O'Donovan, *Biblical Christianity in African Perspective*, 2nd ed. (Carlisle: Paternoster Press, 1996), chap. 11.

11. See the arguably classic essay by Birgit Meyer, "'Make a Complete Break with the Past': Memory and Post-Colonial Modernity in Ghanaian Pentecostalist Discourse," *Journal of Religion in Africa* 28, no. 3 (1998): 316-49.

12. Matthews A. Ojo, *The End-Time Army: Charismatic Movements in Modern Nigeria* (Trenton, NJ, and Asmara, Eritrea: Africa World Press, 2006), pp. 107-8.

16:15, 16:34, 18:8), since in that case, the intra-family links between the cultural past and the Christian future are wholly severed. The issue is complicated, however, when individuals come to Christ but not their family members. In these cases, the curses handed down from generation to generation by ancestral practices remain active and potentially capable of following the believer insofar as he or she remains intimately associated with the family (according to pentecostal readings of biblical passages like Exod. 20:4-6, Ezek. 18:1-4, and Mal. 3:11-12).[13] The pentecostal rite of deliverance in this case involves the renunciation of the occultic beliefs and practices of the ancestors — as represented by burning the magical arts at Ephesus (Acts 19:19) — even while there is a struggle to honor and respect especially one's immediate elders (parents and grandparents) according to New Testament injunctions. In more extreme cases, Christians are expected to sever ties with non-Christian family members, particularly if it is thought that they might be conduits for or strongholds of demonic activity.[14] In this way, deliverance is accomplished from the generational curses that operate within the family, both "vertically" through the ancestors and "horizontally" through wider kin relationships.

This leads to the third aspect of socio-cultural deliverance: that involving protection from destructive curses and forces derived from the popular practices of witchcraft. By and large, pentecostals accept the cosmologies of indigenous traditions across the global south, and find confirmation for these worldviews from the biblical etiologies that variously link sickness, misfortune, tragedy, etc., to supernatural or demonic activity (for example, as in the case of Job, or of various pericopes in the gospel narratives). But if the practice of witchcraft in indigenous cultures includes the casting of curses carried by malevolent spirits, the erection of protective hedges in order to ward off negative outcomes, or the appeasement of restless (usually ancestral) spirits in order to redirect their destructive energy, pentecostal deliverance counteracts the destructive powers of witchcraft through rituals of exorcism and of baptism or possession by the Holy Spirit.[15] The result of pentecostal deliver-

---

13. J. Kwabena Asamoah-Gyadu, "Mission to 'Set the Captives Free': Healing, Deliverance, and Generational Curses in Ghanaian Pentecostalism," *International Review of Mission* 93, nos. 370-71 (2004): 389-406.

14. See Birgit Meyer, *Translating the Devil: Religion and Modernity among the Ewe in Ghana* (Edinburgh: Edinburgh University Press, and Trenton, NJ, and Asmara, Eritrea: Africa World Press, 1999), chap. 7, which studies the tensions introduced between the global pentecostal ideal of the nuclear family (imported mostly from the West) and the human need for familial belonging and (even extended) family life and networks.

15. Opoku Onyinah, "Deliverance as a Way of Confronting Witchcraft in Modern Africa: Ghana as a Case Study," *Asian Journal of Pentecostal Studies* 5, no. 1 (2002): 107-34.

ance is that new ecclesial relations replace cultural, ancestral, or wider kin networks through which spiritual beings might otherwise maintain destructive authority over unsuspecting individual believers.

4.1.2. The Spirit/s, Witchcraft, and the Public Sphere: Pentecostalism and Political Economy

I now want to explore how specific pentecostal soteriological beliefs (cosmology) and practices (e.g., exorcism and Spirit possession) have implications for our understanding of political economy (the unified field of study involving political science and economics). While we will return to discuss economics in more depth in chapter 7, here I intend to focus on how the pentecostal encounter with witchcraft is a performative one directed toward achieving deliverance from evil spirits and experiencing the salvation and abundant life for individual Christians. In other words, our discussion here will note how pentecostal deliverance has economic assumptions, implications, and consequences.

In the background of pentecostal soteriology is the conviction that the hardships confronting humankind are ultimately spiritual in nature. In the words of the apostle Paul, "our struggle is not against enemies of blood and flesh, but against the rulers, against the authorities, against the cosmic powers of this present darkness, against the spiritual forces of evil in the heavenly places" (Eph. 6:12). This means that economic challenges, business failures, unemployment, poverty, and even famine, etc., are works of the devil and his demons, all of whom have been sent "to steal and kill and destroy" (John 10:10). The fall of the satan has produced a chaos manifest now in the world's social and economic structures, and only pentecostal deliverance is equipped to engage and ward off the "demons of the system — daily injustices, poverty, isolation, and disenfranchisement."[16] The key to economic success therefore resides in the churches' properly engaging in spiritual warfare prayer (oftentimes involving fasting, laying on of hands, exorcisms, Spirit-filled worship, etc.) against the cosmic powers that beset believers and their communities.[17]

---

16. Jill DeTemple, "Chains of Liberation: Poverty and Social Action in the Universal Church of the Kingdom of God," in Gastón Espinosa, Virgilio P. Elizondo, and Jesse Miranda, eds., *Latino Religions and Civic Activism in the United States* (Oxford and New York: Oxford University Press, 2005), pp. 219-31, quote from p. 221; DeTemple references the work of the Universal Church of the Kingdom of God founder, Bishop Edir Macedo, *Nos Passos de Jesus* (Rio de Janiero: Editora Grafica Universal, 1986), which addresses these matters.

17. The popular literature on spiritual warfare is humongous, with the contrasting absence of serious academic engagement with this material quite stark. For some of the literature

As Ogbu Kalu notes, "To deal with the spirits of wickedness . . . , Pentecostals apply fasting, prayer retreats, researches on the dominant spirits possessing the gates of the communities, and prayer actions. These efforts may also involve prayer walking, traveling throughout the community, speaking and calling into being the good of the community."[18]

In chapter 1 (specifically, 1.2.2), we have already seen how global pentecostalism has been ideologically compatible if not correlative with the neoliberal market economy. There we focused on identifying how the logic of the market — with its emphases on individual choice, pluralism of supply and demand, and centrality of risk-taking entrepreneurship — has made it possible for those with pentecostal sensibilities to enter and survive in the global market. We also observed how the market structures of decentralization, privatization, and local enterprise were conducive to pentecostal intuitions and its work ethic. In the following, however, I want to further illuminate the role that pentecostal beliefs and practices regarding supernatural powers play in pentecostal encounters with the global economy. Three levels of analysis offer themselves: the practical, the theoretical, and the political.

At the practical level of production and consumption, pentecostal cosmology and spirituality play what might be called a purifying role in its economic life.[19] In the classical pentecostal mentality, excessive wealth and economic success were ploys of the devil to seduce true believers away from the faith. This missionary legacy has been tempered since the independence movements of the mid-twentieth century, however, as the postcolonial peoples have not been content to simply observe the "wealth of the nations" concentrated in the Anglo-European world. Yet the production of wealth inevitably requires, within the neoliberal political economy, the willingness to supply what the world demands and consume what the world produces. The

---

and further discussion of the socio-economic dimensions of pentecostal spiritual warfare, see Amos Yong and Samuel Zalanga, "What Empire, Which Multitude? Pentecostalism and Social Liberation in North America and Sub-Saharan Africa," in Bruce Ellis Benson and Peter Goodwin Heltzel, eds., *Evangelicals and Empire: Christian Alternatives to the Political Status Quo* (Grand Rapids: Brazos Press, 2008), pp. 237-51, esp. pp. 242-49.

18. Ogbu Kalu, *African Pentecostalism: An Introduction* (Oxford: Oxford University Press, 2008), p. 218.

19. Here I draw from the work of Birgit Meyer, "'Delivered from the Powers of Darkness': Confessions of Satanic Riches in Christian Ghana," *Africa* 65, no. 2 (1995): 236-55; "Commodities and the Power of Prayer: Pentecostalist Attitudes towards Consumption in Ghana," *Development and Change* 29 (1998): 751-76; and "'You Devil, Go Away from Me!' Pentecostalist African Christianity and the Powers of Good and Evil," in Paul Clough and Jon P. Mitchell, eds., *Powers of Good and Evil: Moralities, Commodities and Popular Belief* (New York and Oxford: Berghahn Books, 2001), pp. 104-34.

latter is problematic since, in the pentecostal framework, a commodity that comes from parts unknown and has been handled by a multitude of hands in production lines around the world may be a conduit for malevolent spiritual forces to enter the life of the believer. Here is where pentecostal spirituality, including its rites of purification — whether of homes, automobiles, or other smaller commodities — cleanses what is purchased out of the global market from occultic residue, thus making such commodities safe for pentecostal consumption.

At the theoretical level of explaining poverty and wealth, especially as that may characterize the lives of believers (i.e., Why are we not more prosperous?) and also unbelievers (i.e., Why are the unjust so affluent?), pentecostal cosmology provides an all-encompassing theological frame of reference for understanding the global economy. When banks and other economic institutions are unreliable, when the production of wealth is a mysterious process accessible only by a few, and when economic power seems always to reside elsewhere rather than in local hands, supernatural explanations become much more plausible. Thus have recent studies instructively traced the revival of witchcraft in the global south as most intense particularly in areas experiencing severe economic recession.[20] Witchcraft provides a theory about how the supernatural invisible realm impacts the material realms of human fortunes, and how dependence on such powers enables achievement of both economic wealth and political power. Pentecostals would not deny that consorting with demonic spirits can produce such results. They would insist instead that illicit accumulation is doomed to ultimate loss and failure, and that alliances with malevolent spirits will lead finally to destruction and tragedy. Instead, genuine reliance on the power of God and the Holy Spirit will ensure that temporary setbacks will eventually be overturned and that divinely ordained wealth will not only last but serve as a means for the blessing of others as well.

At the political level of economic agency, pentecostal cosmology and spirituality play what might be called an empowering role in its financial and monetary practices. In the pentecostal imagination, human actors are motivated, ultimately, by spiritual agents. One is empowered either by the Holy Spirit or by other lesser (evil) spirits. So if in indigenous cultures, the practices of witchcraft enable access to supernatural powers for the purpose of achiev-

20. Leading the way was Jean Comaroff and John Comaroff, *Modernity and Its Malcontents: Ritual and Power in Postcolonial Africa* (Chicago and London: University of Chicago Press, 1993); see also Henrietta L. Moore and Todd Sanders, eds., *Magical Interpretations, Material Realities: Modernity, Witchcraft and the Occult in Postcolonial Africa* (London and New York: Routledge, 2001).

ing financial success and economic affluence,[21] in pentecostalism, the practice of spiritual warfare resists the powers of darkness by the power of the Holy Spirit for similar purposes. As economic agents, pentecostal believers must be appropriately prepared not just for economic activity, but for spiritual warfare.

One of the critical questions that emerge at this juncture concerns the degree to which pentecostalism, especially in the global south, abets indigenous cosmological assumptions and thereby perpetuates existential fears derived from such views. Researchers have identified cases whereby pentecostal successes, linked in part to the embrace of the prosperity gospel on the global stage, have led to counter-accusations by jealous local competitors that such accomplishments are also complicit with satanic practices.[22] These observations have led some anthropologists to note: "the abilities to battle witchcraft, to heal witchcraft and to detect witchcraft partake of the same force as witchcraft itself."[23] So even when pentecostals deny such claims and condemn and denounce the practices of witchcraft (which they regularly do), their cosmological worldview and liturgical practices do not question the assumption that the divine powers that oppose the occultic powers are of the same, rather than of an entirely different, kind. In short, can pentecostal Christianity be said to have challenged such indigenous beliefs and practices, or is the result, in the end, simply another variation on a similar theme? And beyond this question of the potentially prophetic dimension of pentecostalism is the alethic question regarding the truth of the matter: Do pentecostal and indigenous cosmologies rightly portray the way things are regarding the principalities and powers?

4.1.3. Principalities, Powers, and Politics: Spiritual Warfare as Pentecostal Political Praxis

I now wish to focus explicitly on how pentecostal cosmological notions about the spiritual world have had political applications, explications, and implica-

---

21. This phenomenon has also been closely studied by anthropologists and sociologists like Peter Geschiere, *The Modernity of Witchcraft: Politics and the Occult in Postcolonial Africa*, trans. Peter Geschiere and Janet Roitman (Charlottesville, VA, and London: University Press of Virginia, 1997), and Stephen Ellis and Gerrie ter Haar, *Worlds of Power: Religious Thought and Political Practice in Africa* (New York: Oxford University Press, 2004).

22. Daniel Jordon Smith, "'The Arrow of God': Pentecostalism, Inequality, and the Supernatural in South-Eastern Nigeria," *Africa* 71, no. 4 (2001): 587-613.

23. Sasha Newell, "Pentecostal Witchcraft: Neoliberal Possession and Demonic Discourse in Ivoirian Pentecostal Churches," *Journal of Religion in Africa* 37 (2007): 461-90, quotation from p. 465.

tions. The biblical worldview that pentecostals claim informs their political theology and praxis is an elaboration of the previously referred-to conviction about the gods of the nations being equivalent, primordially, with fallen angels. Thus pentecostals conclude from the New Testament (e.g., 1 Cor. 8:4-6 and 10:19-21) that these national spiritual beings are actually either non-divine idols (at best) or demons opposed to the true God (at worst).[24] Last but certainly not least, scriptural references such as those regarding the "prince of the kingdom of Persia" or the "prince of Greece" (Dan. 10:12-13, 20-21) have further shaped the pentecostal political imagination about the existence of national spirits or territorial principalities and powers.

As a result, notions of spiritual warfare against territorial spirits have emerged across the spectrum of global pentecostalism.[25] By this is meant the concerted and focused activity of congregational or parachurch agencies that identifies the "spiritual strongholds" over specific geographic territories, cultural regions, or national governments or institutions, engages and/or resists the corporate sins and activities perpetuated by such spirits, and mobilizes sustained warfare prayer devoted to neutralizing, binding, and rendering impotent such spiritual realities. This kind of spiritual warfare prayer includes but goes beyond the New Testament injunctions to pray for leaders of governments (e.g., 1 Tim. 2:1-2) since there is a more proactive agenda of countering the political effects of alleged spiritual entities. Insofar as these spiritual strongholds "are possessed with both a defensive and an offensive character . . . , they will simultaneously resist light and export darkness" in reaction to the gospel's advance.[26] Hence the goal of such territorial warfare is to reclaim such strongholds from destructive cosmic forces for the sake of the gospel.[27]

---

24. Most pentecostals are unaware that this particular reading of the Bible owes much to the patristic church, including Justin Martyr and, as we have seen earlier, Augustine himself; see 2.1.3 and, on Justin, Elaine H. Pagels, "Christian Apologists and 'the Fall of the Angels': An Attack on Roman Imperial Power?" *Harvard Theological Review* 78, nos. 3-4 (1985): 301-25.

25. Leading the way has been the missiologist C. Peter Wagner, in a number of influential volumes — e.g., C. Peter Wagner and F. Douglas Pennoyer, eds., *Wrestling with Dark Angels: Toward a Deeper Understanding of the Supernatural Forces in Spiritual Warfare* (Ventura, CA: Regal, 1990); Wagner, *Engaging the Enemy: How to Fight and Defeat Territorial Spirits* (Ventura, CA: Regal, 1991); Wagner, *Warfare Prayer* (Ventura, CA: Regal, 1992); and Wagner, *What the Bible Says About Spiritual Warfare* (Ventura, CA: Regal, 2001).

26. George Otis Jr., ed., *Strongholds of the 10/40 Window: Intercessor's Guide to the World's Least Evangelized Nations* (Seattle: YWAM Publishing, 1995), p. 10. Note: The assumption of this volume is that the world's "least evangelized nations" (in the volume subtitle) are explicable in terms of their being strongholds of spiritual (perhaps demonic) activity.

27. Although, it should also be said, not all pentecostals embrace the practice of spiritual warfare engaging territorial spirits; some are concerned about these as going beyond the dic-

When successful, entire people groups and even nations are believed to be delivered from the powers of darkness and converted to Christ, and this will result in a divine visitation of forgiveness, healing, and blessing.[28]

In today's political climate, I want to call attention to three levels of how such territorial warfare approaches have translated into what might be considered as "politically incorrect" pentecostal political practices. Each level, it will be noted, involves a demonization of the political "enemy," whether understood in terms of social problems or in terms of the political opposition.

First, perhaps the most prevalent, is the demonization of all that contrasts with what pentecostals most value. Note, for example, the rhetoric of pentecostal candidates for public office in the Brazilian elections of the early to mid-1990s: "Demons must be expelled from social life in the name of the vote, justice, organisation and democracy by the power of the name of Jesus. . . . We desire a Brazil free from spiritual oppression such as hunger, misery, unemployment, inflation, corruption, organised crime. . . . No demon can resist our faith"; and "The social, political and economic chaos is due to spiritual curses lying on our country. . . . The transformation of Brazil will begin with spiritual restoration. . . . God is raising up men full of the Spirit to take over the positions of power."[29] More to the political point were the 1994 elections in Brazil, with the Assemblea de Dios saying, "This will be a battle between God's and the devil's candidates," and representatives of the Iglesia Universal del Reino de Dios going so far as to suggest, "that the candidate of the devil was Lula (Partido dos Trabalhadores) [a socialist], in opposition to Fernando Henrique Cardoso (curiously, a declared atheist)."[30] Clearly, the

---

tates of Scripture — e.g., Charles Harris, "Encountering Territorial Spirits," in Opal Reddin, ed., *Power Encounter: A Pentecostal Perspective*, rev. ed. (Springfield, MO: Central Bible College Press, 1999), pp. 240-86. For evangelical critiques, see Melvin Tinker, "The Phantom Menace: Territorial Spirits and SLSW," *Churchman* 114, no. 1 (2000): 71-81, and Chuck Lowe, *Territorial Spirits and World Evangelisation? A Biblical, Historical and Missiological Critique of Strategic-Level Spiritual Warfare* (1998; reprint, Ross-shire, UK: Mentor/Christian Focus, and Kent, UK: OMF, 2001). A more even-handed and balanced evangelical discussion is A. Scott Moreau, *Essentials of Spiritual Warfare* (Wheaton, IL: Harold Shaw, 1997).

28. Thus Matthews Ojo, *The End-Time Army,* pp. 204-9, notes that pentecostals consider national deliverance to involve the renunciation of the heritage of black Africa and the embrace of globalization, internationalization, and even consumerism, arguing this from 2 Chronicles 7:14 — "if my people who are called by my name humble themselves, pray, seek my face, and turn from their wicked ways, then I will hear from heaven, and will forgive their sin and heal their land."

29. Cited in Paul Freston, *Protestant Political Parties: A Global Survey* (Aldershot, UK, and Burlington, VT: Ashgate, 2004), p. 44.

30. Richard Shaull and Waldo Cesar, *Pentecostalism and the Future of the Christian Churches: Promises, Limitations, Challenges* (Grand Rapids and Cambridge, UK: Eerdmans,

demonization of candidates representing the other end of the political spectrum raised the spiritual stakes of what would otherwise be a mundane (this-worldly) political election. The more pentecostals view politics as a "spiritual battleground," the more likely they are to be politically belligerent.[31]

A second and certainly more potentially explosive level of pentecostal demonization occurs in religiously pluralistic environments. In such contexts, all too often, the opposition party or opposing candidate that is demonized is from the "other" religious tradition. Given the dualistic framework of the pentecostal cosmology, Jesus' words, "Whoever is not with me is against me" (Luke 11:23), lend themselves to the conclusion that the non-Christian option receives its mandate, empowerment, and agenda from the prince of darkness himself.[32] In Muslim contexts such as Nigeria, with a population almost evenly divided between Muslims and (a majority pentecostal) Christians, the rhetoric of demonization going in both directions is extremely volatile, with both sides jostling for political supremacy, economic control, land rights, and other social advantages.[33]

A third level of "politically incorrect" pentecostal political praxis represents perhaps the most inexcusable deployment of demonization rhetoric: that which provides a theological legitimation for egregious political and military activity. One example that stands out concerns the government of Ríos Montt in Guatemala in the early 1980s.[34] Montt, at that time, had testified of a pentecostal conversion, and submitted himself under the spiritual advisement of a neo-pentecostal church. In response to the accusations of human rights atrocities committed against the indigenous people of Guatemala by Montt's army, Verbo Church pastors said: "The Army doesn't massacre the Indians. It massacres demons, the Indians are demon possessed; they are

---

2000), p. 74. But note that within the span of eight years, the Universal Church had moved from demonizing Lula to an alliance with him! See Paul Freston, "Introduction: The Many Faces of Evangelical Politics in Latin America," in Paul Freston, ed., *Evangelical Christianity and Democracy in Latin America* (Oxford: Oxford University Press, 2008), pp. 3-36, esp. p. 33.

31. Emily Elspeth Mitchell, "Liberationist Pentecostalism: Politics as a Spiritual Battleground in Contemporary Latin America" (BA honors thesis, Whitman College, 2006), pp. 27-30.

32. Birgit Meyer, "The Power of Money: Politics, Occult Forces, and Pentecostalism in Ghana," *African Studies Review* 41, no. 3 (1998): 15-37, esp. pp. 32-33.

33. Kalu, *African Pentecostalism*, chap. 12, discusses the confrontation of pentecostal and Islamic rhetoric in West Africa; see also 1.1.2 above.

34. I present an overview of the issues in my *The Spirit Poured Out on All Flesh: Pentecostalism and the Possibility of Global Theology* (Grand Rapids: Baker Academic, 2005), pp. 35-37. Regretfully, I did not then come out forcefully against the crimes that Montt's government perpetrated against the indigenous people of Guatemala.

communists. We hold Brother Efraín Ríos Montt like King David of the Old Testament. He is the king of the New Testament."[35] At a broader level, as this quotation suggests, there is also the theological justification provided by the rhetoric of demonization for international military operations, whether that against the advance of socialism during the Cold War era or that of American-led forays into the Middle Eastern arena.[36] At this point the lines between American neo-pentecostalism and the wider evangelical and conservative Protestant "right" become blurred; unfortunately, pentecostals have, in general, supported such political agendas with their own distinctive theological rationales rather than prophetically protested against these developments.

In multi-religious contexts, pentecostals have often assumed that adherents of other traditions represent the "enemy" of Christian faith and are thus opposed to what pentecostalism represents. Such a viewpoint is what precipitates forecasts of an impending "clash of civilizations,"[37] in which aggressive Christian populations confront and collide with equally belligerent members of other faith traditions, resulting in a final conflagration (at least according to pentecostal interpretations of end-time apocalyptic scenarios).[38] Pentecostals must rethink some of their traditional theological notions, especially the tendency to demonize their political opponents, if they are going to engage the political and public sphere in a more responsible way in their second century of existence.

35. Sara Diamond, *Spiritual Warfare: The Politics of the Christian Right* (Boston: South End Press, 1989), p. 166, quoting from *Sectas y religiosidad en America Latina* (October 1984): 23. For a discussion of Guatemalan politics that shows a much more pluralistic pentecostal interface with the political than this brief discussion lets on, see C. Mathews Samson, "From War to Reconciliation: Guatemalan Evangelicals and the Transition to Democracy, 1982-2001," in Paul Freston, ed., *Evangelical Christianity and Democracy in Latin America* (Oxford: Oxford University Press, 2008), pp. 63-96.

36. At the popular level, few pentecostals would question this statement: "The U.S. military machine was God's way of defending the peace so that his message of salvation could be made known. Washington's adversaries around the world therefore continue to be God's adversaries, and evangelizing the world continued to hinge on U.S. power." See David Stoll, *Is Latin America Turning Protestant? The Politics of Evangelical Growth* (Berkeley: University of California Press, 1990), p. 67. For an account of the gradual transformation of the Assemblies of God in the USA from a pacifist denomination into one supporting militarization and an idolatrous form of nationalism, see Paul Alexander, *Peace to War: Shifting Allegiances in the Assemblies of God*, The C. Henry Smith Series 9 (Telford, PA: Cascadia Publishing House, 2009).

37. Samuel P. Huntington, *The Clash of Civilizations and the Remaking of World Order* (New York: Simon & Shuster, 1996); cf. Philip Jenkins, *God's Continent: Christianity, Islam, and Europe's Religious Crisis* (New York and Oxford: Oxford University Press, 2007).

38. I will return in chapter 8 to discuss how pentecostal eschatological ideas have shaped its view of history and how this has played out politically.

In other contexts, the demonized opponents of pentecostalism often include those in their own churches. Walter Hollenweger, commenting on developments in Guatemala mentioned above, portrays what happened as follows: that pentecostals who were part of Montt's political team

> meet in exclusive hotels for their prayer meetings and actively support police terror and torture. That means, in certain cases, torturing those of their own faith, the poor Pentecostals. The aim would appear to be freedom for big business and suppression of social protest through an authoritarian state. These self-interests, however, are biblically camouflaged as a fight of good against evil. That "the evil" can also be their brothers and sisters in the faith who happen to be on the other side of the social [and political] divide is a particularly cruel irony of this story.[39]

In short, the politics of pentecostal deliverance has been shown to be too easily hijacked by uncritical nationalistic aspirations. Pentecostal spirituality and piety, buttressed by a complex cosmology of spirits, principalities, and powers, has been applied dualistically in naïve ways, resulting not only in "politically incorrect" practices, but in theologically heretical ideas and practically dangerous political agendas. Can such pentecostal notions about salvation, deliverance, and the powers be redeemed for a viable political theology today?

4.2. Principalities and Powers in Political Theology

My answer to the previous question is: Yes! However, the road toward the redemption of these pentecostal notions will take us through similar considerations in dialogue with others who have thought about a theology of the political in terms of principalities and powers. In this section, we begin first by discussing the reappearance of a theology of the demonic in modern theological thinking about the political. Then, we shift to explore explicit proposals to think through a theology of the political utilizing the Pauline notion of the principalities and powers. Our final deliberations will return us back to St. Paul himself, in order to clarify what is at stake theologically in this discussion. My objective in the next few pages is to locate a broader theological landscape within which to reconsider, in dialogical fashion in the last part of

39. W. J. Hollenweger, "The Pentecostal Elites and the Pentecostal Poor: A Missed Dialogue?" in Karla Poewe, ed., *Charismatic Christianity as Global Culture* (Columbia: University of South Carolina Press, 1994), pp. 200-214, quotation from p. 203, drawing also on the work of Heinrich Schaeffer.

this chapter, how the pentecostal beliefs (cosmology) and practices (politics) in the preceding discussion may yet yield resources for a constructive theology and cosmology of the public square.

4.2.1. The Demonic and the Political: Modern Interpretations

In chapter 2, I briefly overviewed Augustine's understanding of demonology and angelology (2.1.3), and how these notions informed his portrayal of the relationship between the earthly and the heavenly cities. If the heavenly city had the worship of God as its telos, the earthly city was focused on the self's exaltation. Demons, as fallen angels, worked to seduce human beings to pursue their own distorted desires, and thus establish the creaturely realm as its own independent sphere apart from the grace of God. Luther's two spheres, authorities, or governments (2.2.2), we noted, differed from Augustine's two cities in that for the former both were ordained by God to accomplish divine purposes, whereas for the latter both were ontologically and theologically distinct, which the arrival of the eschatological kingdom of God would make plain. At the same time, the Augustinian and Lutheran notions were similar on at least the following two counts: that both recognized the political sphere to be a site contested between God and the devil, and that the latter was continuously at work even in and through the divinely appointed structures of the political, whether that be the law or even the state as a whole.[40] But for Luther, what was disconcerting was the murky line between God and the devil since the latter was manifest, often enough, as the "other" or "under" side of the divine, almost as the law was related to the gospel or as the wrath of God was related to divine holiness and love.[41]

In the twentieth century, we saw (2.3.1) the jurist and constitutional philosopher Carl Schmitt develop a political analogy from the theological contrast between God and the satan. Although a lifetime member of the Roman Catholic Church, Schmitt did not propose an explicitly theological argu-

---

40. See Gordon Rupp, "Luther against 'The Turk, the Pope, and the Devil,'" in Peter Newman Brooks, ed., *Seven-headed Luther: Essays in Commemoration of a Quincentenary, 1483-1983* (Oxford and New York: Clarendon Press, 1983), pp. 255-73; David P. Scaer, "The Concept of *Anfechtung* in Luther's Thought," *Concordia Theological Quarterly* 47, no. 1 (1983): 15-30; and John R. Stephenson, "The Two Governments and the Two Kingdoms in Luther's Thought," *Scottish Journal of Theology* 34, no. 4 (1981): 321-37.

41. Carter Lindberg, "Mask of God and Prince of Lies: Luther's Theology of the Demonic," in Alan M. Olson, ed., *Disguises of the Demonic: Contemporary Perspectives on the Power of Evil* (New York: Association Press, 1975), pp. 87-103.

ment in dialogue with the legacy of Augustine and Luther. Instead, from his supposition that all political notions were secularized theological concepts, the battle between God and the satan in the theological plane played out as the contest between friend and foe in the political domain. Apart from the enemy, we should recall, there is no political arena. But when the enemy presents itself, especially in terms registered on the international stage such that one people group comes to recognize it is opposed by another, then the political emerges and demands our deepest commitments, even the willingness to go to war if necessary, and certainly the readiness to slay the enemy or give up our own lives in the attempt to do so.

In a sense, the reappearance of the notion of the demonic in twentieth-century theologies of the political can be said to be expansions of these Augustinian, Lutheran, and Schmittian lines of thought. The first major theologian who retrieved and reinterpreted the idea of the demonic vis-à-vis the political arena was Paul Tillich (1886-1965). As the scope of Tillich's theological system is exceedingly broad, we will need to focus specifically on his understanding of the demonic as a historical, social, and political reality. After Tillich, it was once again possible for theologians to speculate about the demonic, although many are still hesitant to do so for various reasons.[42]

What then did Tillich say about the demonic? Similar to but extending Luther's view of the devil, Tillich understood the demonic to be the inverse side of salvation history. While the latter preserves the unity of the depth dimension of history, the former irrupts from deep within the being of history and disrupts, fractures, and absolutizes history, with destructive consequences. But Tillich rejected the Lutheran notion of the two spheres or authorities because he saw that this construct could be used (and had indeed been used, by German theologians of the inter-war years) to justify and legitimate the political status quo.[43] Instead, if the demonic seeks to absolutize any aspect of historical or finite being, then the "Protestant principle" was a necessary safeguard that resists the absolutization of anything while seeking to preserve the absoluteness only of God.[44] In other words, the genius of Protestantism is its

42. As Vernon R. Mallow, *The Demonic: A Selected Theological Study — An Examination into the Theology of Edwin Lewis, Karl Barth, and Paul Tillich* (Lanham, MD, and London: University Press of America, 1983), shows, however, the re-emergence of this theme occurred among other theologians in the first half of the twentieth century; but it was Tillich who envisioned the demonic within the political sphere, more so than other theologians.

43. See A. James Reimer, *Paul Tillich: Theologian of Nature, Culture and Politics,* Tillich-Studien 6 (Münster: LIT, 2004), pp. 49-56 and 76.

44. Paul Tillich, *Political Expectation,* ed. James Luther Adams (New York: Harper & Row, 1971), chap. 2.

adoption of a critical, transcendental, and eschatological horizon that views all of history as penultimate in light of the coming kingdom of God.

Tillich can thus be seen as standing squarely within the Augustinian tradition on this matter. For similar reasons, the demonic is an unavoidable aspect to any Tillichian-inspired theology of history.[45] History, Tillich noted, should be seen as "a battlefield of the divine and the demonic,"[46] and as a "continuous fight . . . between divine and demonic structures."[47] If this is so, then we should be able to discern irruptions of the demonic on the historical field. From his vantage point in the 1930s, Tillich identified two broad manifestations of demonic absolutizations: in the economic and political spheres.

Economically speaking, the demonic could be seen as having made its appearance in the capitalist system of production. What was it that Tillich objected to in the capitalism of his day? It was "the autonomy of the capitalistic economic system, with all its contradictions, and the mass disintegration and destruction of meaning in all spheres of historical existence which it produces"; more precisely: "the economic sphere, which has become autonomous, has brought all the other spheres of human historical life into subjection to itself and has deprived them of independent meaning; thus it has set in motion a great process of mass disintegration, the movement of which is subject to destructive laws."[48] Further, the effect of capitalism on society in general and on individuals that comprise society "takes the typical form of 'possession,' that is, of being 'possessed'; its character is demonic."[49] Capitalism, which presumed the competition of individuals and corporations against one another, produced a split consciousness: competition was necessary for the economic system, although it engendered and relied upon attempts to overcome the other — such is a characteristic feature of demonic systems. In its place, like Barth and other theologians in the 1930s, Tillich advocated a religious socialism guided by a vision of the kingdom of God.[50]

45. Thus Tillich's earliest forays into a theology of the demonic were in the context of developing a theology of history; see Paul Tillich, *The Interpretation of History,* trans. N. A. Rasetzki and Elsa L. Talmey (New York: Charles Scribner's Sons, 1936), pp. 77-95.

46. Paul Tillich, "The Kingdom of God and History," in H. G. Wood et al., *The Kingdom of God and History* (New York and Chicago: Willett, Clark & Co., 1938), pp. 105-41, quote from p. 117.

47. Paul Tillich, *The Protestant Era,* trans. James Luther Adams, abridged ed. (Chicago: University of Chicago Press, 1957), p. xvii.

48. Tillich, "The Kingdom of God and History," pp. 131-32.

49. Tillich, *Political Expectation,* p. 50.

50. See the essays on "Religious Socialism," "Basic Principles of Religious Socialism," and "Christianity and Marxism," all in Tillich's *Political Expectation,* as well as *The Protestant Era,* chap. 11.

Politically speaking, the demonic could be discerned both in nationalisms that absolutized their respective states as well as in the authoritarianisms with which some governments ruled. The latter included, for Tillich, the Bolshevism that he saw in Russia, especially its dictatorial and "unrestricted exercise of power [that] drives men into presumption towards God and to destruction of the human values which belong to the Kingdom of God: formal justice, truthfulness and freedom."[51] Thus was Hobbes's "Leviathan" a "demonic symbol, [signifying] the all-consuming might of the state."[52] The demonic manifestation of nationalism, on the other hand, involved the mistaken identification of finite nations as constituting "the supreme good to all who belong to it."[53] In the ancient world, "primitive Christianity challenged the Roman state as a demonic power having the ambiguity of the demonic to be creative and destructive at the same time, establishing order and compelling men to the worship of itself."[54] Other examples given later included the Germanic, British, Russian, and even American empires, each of which was a materialization, however ambiguous, of the demonic in its "self-elevating claim to ultimacy."[55]

It should not be forgotten, however, that the demonic remained for Tillich primarily a religious category. Hence, economic and political expressions of the demonic were fundamentally religious in character, which meant that even religious claims could become demonic. Thus Jesus is the Christ who defeats the powers of the demonic precisely because he avoided the self-grasping and self-elevating characteristic of the seductions of the demonic,[56] and relied instead upon the power of the Spirit. In this way, Christ as the New Being exposes all of history's false/demonic absolutes, and points forward toward the transcendental and eschatological absolute of divine justice. Simultaneously, the power of the Spirit — the Spiritual Presence, for Tillich — relativizes all of history in anticipation of the coming kingdom.

The preceding discussion is not meant to endorse all of Tillich's ideas about the demonic. His notion of demonic authoritarianism is illuminating,[57] while his demonization of capitalism will need to be critically assessed

51. Tillich, "The Kingdom of God and History," p. 135.

52. Tillich, *Political Expectation,* p. 100.

53. Tillich, "The Kingdom of God and History," p. 133.

54. Tillich, *The Protestant Era,* p. 168.

55. Paul Tillich, *Systematic Theology,* 3 vols. (Chicago: University of Chicago Press, 1951-63), vol. 3, p. 344.

56. Tillich, *Systematic Theology,* vol. 2, p. 126.

57. Tillich's theory helpfully clarifies why, for example, democratic forms of government in postcolonial Africa are problematic: because Africans continue to inhabit a sacralized notion

(see chapter 7 below).[58] My more immediate objective is to introduce Tillich's theology of the demonic within a political framework. We shall see the Tillichian influence in the following discussion, even if others may not always explicitly appeal to his insights.

4.2.2. *The Powers and the Political: Contemporary Options*

Whereas the demonic remained as a central category in Tillich's theology of the political, a shift occurred toward the language of principalities and powers with the translation of a book by the Dutch Reformed theologian, Hendrikus Berkhof (1914-95), into English.[59] Berkhof canvassed the broad scope of Paul's letters — discussing Romans 8:38-40; 1 Corinthians 2:8, 15:24-26; Ephesians 1:20-23, 2:1-3, 3:10, 6:12; Colossians 1:16, 2:15; and Galatians 4:1-11, among other texts, that include mention of the principalities and powers as well as of rulers, thrones, authorities, etc. — and posited not only that the powers are fallen, but, as primordial "structures of earthly existence,"[60] they are also creations of God, continue to serve the Creator's will in their preservation of the world, and hence are redeemed in some sense and can even be

---

of authority derived from the elders and ancestors, which in turn serves to legitimate the decisions of the "big man." Thus Kwame Bediako, "Unmasking the Powers: Christianity, Authority, and Desacralization in Modern African Politics," in John Witte, ed., *Christianity and Democracy in Global Context* (Boulder, CO: Westview Press, 1993), pp. 207-29, calls for a desacralization of African politics and its Christianization instead. I would concur in general, while being cautious, given the pentecostal examples, about baptizing an ideological perversion of government in the name of Christ.

58. In anticipation of that discussion, I simply note the work of Tillich's colleague at Union Theological Seminary, Reinhold Niebuhr. Building on his thesis about *Moral Man and Immoral Society* (New York and London: Scribner's, 1932), Niebuhr also drew on the Augustinian (and Lutheran) two cities (two kingdoms) motif in his *The Children of Light and the Children of Darkness: A Vindication of Democracy and a Critique of Its Traditional Defense* (New York: Charles Scribner's Sons, 1944). These two "children" he defined as follows: "the moral cynics, who know no law beyond their will and interest, with a scriptural designation of 'children of this world' or 'children of darkness.' Those who believe that self-interest should be brought under the discipline of a higher law could then be termed 'the children of light'" (p. 9). From this, Niebuhr went on to comment that both liberalism and capitalism are, at best, ignorant "children of light" in their failure to see how private or public property can become instruments "of particular interest against the general interest" (p. 106).

59. Hendrik Berkhof, *Christ and the Powers*, trans. John H. Yoder (1962; reprint, Scottdale, PA, and Kitchener, ON: Herald Press, 1977); Berkhof's *Christus en de Machten* appeared in Dutch originally in 1953.

60. Berkhof, *Christ and the Powers*, p. 23.

Christianized.[61] The notion that the political, economic, and other domains are creational structures were by now a staple in the Reformed tradition (see 2.2.3); what Berkhof added was the link between these creational spheres and the Pauline principalities and powers.[62] So yes, the powers are fallen, but nevertheless they continue to preserve the world according to God's creational mandate. Christ's triumph over the powers signifies more their dethroning than their destruction.[63] Of course, in anticipation of the eschatological victory, the powers have been conquered only in a sense, and are awaiting their full redemption at the end of the age.

John Howard Yoder (1927-97), the Mennonite theologian who translated Berkhof's volume, was motivated to expand these ideas into a more comprehensive theological ethics. While we will return later to a more extensive discussion of Yoder's proposals (see 5.2.1), for now we should note that Yoder followed Berkhof in understanding the powers to have been created good, but as being currently fallen and in need of redemption.[64] More precisely, the biblical and New Testament language of powers paints "an inclusive vision of religious structures . . . , intellectual structures ('ologies and 'isms), moral structures (codes and customs), [and] political structures (the tyrant, the market, the school, the courts, race, and nation)."[65] Yoder's distinctive Anabaptist perspective led him to suggest that the church's participation in this redemptive work would involve both a pietistic option focused on changing society by changing individual hearts, and an ecclesiological strategy whereby "the primary social structure through which the gospel works to change other structures is that of the Christian community."[66] For Yoder, Jesus' lordship, "a proclamation to which only individuals can respond, is nonetheless a social, political, and *structural* fact which constitutes a [non-violent] challenge to the Powers."[67]

---

61. In a later work, Berkhof referred to the Holy Spirit as the transformative power of the world's structural Christianization; see Berkhof, *The Doctrine of the Holy Spirit* (Richmond, VA: John Knox Press, 1964), pp. 100-104.

62. For a dissenting Reformed perspective on this linkage, see H. I. Lederle, "Better the Devil You Know? Seeking a Biblical Basis for the Societal Dimension of Evil and/or the Demonic in the Pauline Concept of the 'Powers,'" in Pieter De Villiers, ed., *Like a Roaring Lion: Essays on the Bible, the Church, and Demonic Powers* (Pretoria: C. B. Powell Bible Centre, University of South Africa, 1987), pp. 102-20. Lederle believes instead that the Pauline powers are more likely to refer to the political and religious traditions of human beings than to the political structures of society.

63. Berkhof, *Christ and the Powers*, p. 42.

64. John Howard Yoder, *The Politics of Jesus* (Grand Rapids: Eerdmans, 1972), esp. chap. 8.

65. Yoder, *The Politics of Jesus*, p. 145.

66. Yoder, *The Politics of Jesus*, p. 157.

67. Yoder, *The Politics of Jesus*, p. 161; italics Yoder's.

Meanwhile, on the European continent, the French social philosopher and theologian, Jacques Ellul (1912-94), was also developing a sociological understanding of the powers for the modern world.[68] In his earlier work, Ellul viewed the powers in more personal terms as spiritual beings that interfaced with the various domains of human existence: "Underneath the phenomena that we are able to see in the social, political, economic realms, there are some permanent forces of which the tracks are found in each of the phenomena considered, and which ensure its unity to our times beneath its chaotic and disorderly appearance."[69] Further reflection, however, led Ellul to think about the powers as human dispositions that constitute human trajectories rather than as objective realities that influence humans from without.[70] While unable to completely free himself from the idea that the powers are spiritual realities that exist independently of humanity on the one hand, he also said, on the other hand, that the powers "do not act simply from outside after the manner of Gnostic destiny or a *deus ex machina*"; rather, they "find expression in . . . human decision and action. To this extent, then, man does constitute them. It is the fact that they act on the level of the concrete reality of human life, and not just in the spiritual or moral sphere, which leads me to believe that the world of which the New Testament speaks is not just a spiritual and abstract reality but one which is identical with what man in general calls the world, i.e., society."[71]

Yet even though emergent through human subjectivity, the powers seem capable of taking on a life of their own. They are "able to transform a natural, social, intellectual, or economic reality into a force which man has no ability either to resist or to control,"[72] thus subjecting humankind to the systems of alienation they had constructed. Once unleashed, however, "the powers have objective reality and . . . act for themselves apart from the force that man gives them."[73] Ellul's work over the years on the technological,

68. For an introduction to Ellul's notion of the powers, see Marva J. Dawn, "The Biblical Concept of 'the Principalities and Powers': John Yoder Points to Jacques Ellul," in Stanley Hauerwas et al., eds., *The Wisdom of the Cross: Essays in Honor of John Howard Yoder* (Grand Rapids and Cambridge, UK: Eerdmans, 1999), pp. 168-86, which is a distillation of her "The Concept of 'the Principalities and Powers' in the Works of Jacques Ellul" (Ph.D. diss., University of Notre Dame, 1992).

69. Jacques Ellul, *Sources and Trajectories: Eight Early Articles by Jacques Ellul That Set the Stage,* trans. Marva J. Dawn (Grand Rapids and Cambridge, UK: Eerdmans, 1997), p. 42.

70. Jacques Ellul, *The Ethics of Freedom,* trans. Geoffrey W. Bromiley (London and Oxford: Mowbrays, and Grand Rapids: Eerdmans, 1976), pp. 144-51.

71. Ellul, *The Ethics of Freedom,* p. 152.

72. Ellul, *The Ethics of Freedom,* pp. 152-53.

73. Ellul, *The Ethics of Freedom,* p. 160.

monetary, and legal systems that now both engulfed and even, to a large degree, predetermined human life, had convinced him that the powers were much more destructive as forces of "anti-creation" and "chaos" than when imagined in personalistic terms.[74] So by the time of his later writings, then, Ellul had almost fully shifted toward a more depersonalized, functional, and structural understanding of the powers: "contrary to a tenacious belief, there can be no question of Lucifer, who is an invention of the end of the Romantic age, nor of detailed infernal powers. . . . [The] majority of people hold little interest for the devil. . . . The devil is not a person or individual but the reality of a fact, namely, division."[75] So the "new demons" of the modern world included not only political religions like Maoism, Hitlerism, and Stalinism, but all-encompassing systems like secularism, scientism, and technological determinism.[76]

More important for our purposes, however, is that Ellul rejected the "common theory that [the powers] are creations that conform to God's will (the state, law) but have been deflected from their true and valid purpose by the wicked action of Satan."[77] The corollary was also denied: that the powers were redeemable, transformable, or Christianize-able. In fact, the cross was Jesus' victory over the powers simply because he did not compete against them.[78] In his life, Jesus "refuses to be the liberator of Israel. He refuses to answer the question of whether he is for or against Caesar or whether taxes should be paid or not. Indeed, his rejection of the central problem that divided the Jews is not even grave and serious. He devaluates it by subjecting politics to a kind of ridicule."[79]

74. Ellul, *The Subversion of Christianity*, trans. Geoffrey W. Bromiley (Grand Rapids: Eerdmans, 1986), pp. 174, 176. Ellul wrote over forty books, many of them major analyses of modern life as dominated by technology, money, and law.

75. Ellul, *The Subversion of Christianity*, pp. 176-77 and 184.

76. Jacques Ellul, *The New Demons*, trans. C. Edward Hopkin (New York: Crossroad/Seabury, 1975). Hence Ellul's analyses have added sociological and historical weight to the claim, made without much argument, of church historian Gordon Rupp that the powers were "the giant and impersonal forces of history"; see E. Gordon Rupp, *Principalities and Powers: Studies in the Christian Conflict in History* (London: Epworth, 1952), p. 94.

77. Ellul, *The Subversion of Christianity*, p. 179.

78. Ellul argued: "The principalities and powers were themselves stripped of power because they encountered the one who did not compete with them but let himself be stripped. They did not meet a victor. They met a prisoner who gave himself up to them. The powers were thus stripped of the one thing they have, namely, their power to vanquish. They had nothing here to vanquish" (*The Ethics of Freedom*, p. 159). This Ellul-ean posture is consistent with Yoder's non-violent approach and explains why Yoder himself was attracted to Ellul as a resource for thinking about these matters (see Dawn, "The Biblical Concept," pp. 170-72).

79. Ellul, *The Ethics of Freedom*, p. 372.

Ellul thus argues that explicitly political projects were ultimately doomed illusions since they could only operate according to the fallen conditions of this world. Instead of trying to develop a Christian politics, we need to focus on a Christian and ecclesial way of life, and that would be a genuine subversion of Christianity, which has otherwise become allied and complicit with the powers of the age.[80] Such would embody a Christian realism that, following the example of Jesus, enables God to accomplish the divine will.[81] It would involve spiritual vigilance, disengagement from the powers (so that we do not participate in such systems), desacralization of the powers (which include identifying their limits and exposing their ideologies), and (on the most radical front) critique and confrontation of the powers.[82]

Walter Wink has reconnected Ellul's systemic notion of the powers with the biblical and especially Pauline language. Whereas Ellul spoke of the powers as all-determining forces that subjugate human life, Wink has shown how the powers have constituted, through their violent mechanisms, a "domination system" that perpetuates a fallen and anti-God world order. Developing Berkhof's idea of the redemptability of the powers and embracing Yoder's advocacy of a path of non-violent resistance against the powers, Wink believes that the present world-order can be redeemed and transformed into a "domination-free" system, and that this happens through the spiritual practices of loving and forgiving our enemies, praying for God's intervention, and

80. See Ellul, *The Ethics of Freedom,* pp. 374-75, and the overall argument of Ellul's *The Subversion of Christianity.*

81. This is the argument of Ellul's *The Politics of God and the Politics of Man,* trans. Geoffrey W. Bromiley (Grand Rapids: Eerdmans, 1972).

82. Such a prophetic stance was adopted by William Stringfellow (1928-85), who adapted Ellul's ideas to the American context. A lay theologian, ethicist, and social critic, Stringfellow identified the biblical principalities and powers with contemporary ideologies, institutions, and media and other images; thus the demonic powers are instantiated in and expressed through political regimes/administrations, their wider institutional systems, constitutions, and charters, and their ethnic, geographic, cultural, and ideational constellations. He repeatedly called attention to American nationalism as representative of an idolatrous and fallen spirit of the age, and proffered in its place a radical politics of biblical spirituality that resisted embracing the power structures of the world and lived out of the freedom of the gospel instead. Unlike Ellul (but like Berkhof), however, Stringfellow seems to hold out for the possibility of the redemption of the powers and their restoration in the divine orders of creation. For representative works, see William Stringfellow, *Free in Obedience* (New York: Seabury Press, 1964); *Conscience and Obedience: The Politics of Romans 13 and Revelation 13 in Light of the Second Coming* (Waco, TX: Word, 1977); and *The Politics of Spirituality* (Philadelphia: Westminster, 1984). An overview of Stringfellow's political theology is provided by Stanley Hauerwas, *Dispatches from the Front: Theological Engagements with the Secular* (Durham, NC, and London: Duke University Press, 1994), chap. 5.

doing the works of righteousness that bring about the healing of a divided world.[83]

As longtime professor of biblical interpretation at Auburn Theological Seminary, however, Wink's contributions to this discussion have been to present a systematic theology of the powers that includes both scriptural exegesis and social analysis.[84] In his assessment, the biblical principalities and powers refer to a wide range of realities, in some cases to human institutions, in others to cosmic elements, and in a third instance to personified structures like the law or even the event of death. In attempting to understand their contemporary relevance, Wink proposes to understand the powers as "inner aspects" of material, social, and institutional realities.[85] So if the biblical "angels" of churches identify the personality, vocation, or ministry of their congregations (e.g., Rev. 2–3), then the "demons" of anything are the inner personal or collective dimensions of outwardly destructive behaviors and manifestations. Yet this is not merely a demythologizing hermeneutic that reduces the principalities and powers to social conventions. Rather, the principalities and powers are

> the invisible, intangible interiority of collective enterprises, the invariant, determining forces of nature and society, or the archetypal images of the unconscious, all of which shape, nurture, and all too often cripple human existence. These mighty Powers are still with us. They are not "mere" symbols — that too is the language of the old worldview that is passing, for we now know that nothing is more powerful than a living symbol. As symbols they point to something real, something the worldview of materialism never learned to name and therefore never could confront.[86]

Wink's ideas have not gone unchallenged, even as they have also been a springboard for far-reaching theological discussions about the powers in various quarters.[87] My intentions are not to baptize Wink's articulations regarding

---

83. For an overview of Wink's proposals, see his *The Powers That Be: Theology for a New Millennium* (New York: Galilee/Doubleday, 1998), which summarizes his *The Powers* trilogy (see below).

84. Unfolded in three volumes: Walter Wink, *Naming the Powers: The Language of Power in the New Testament* (Philadelphia: Fortress, 1984); *Unmasking the Powers: The Invisible Forces That Determine Human Existence* (Philadelphia: Fortress, 1986); and *Engaging the Powers: Discernment and Resistance in a World of Domination* (Philadelphia: Fortress, 1992).

85. Wink, *Naming the Powers*, pp. 103-12.

86. Wink, *Unmasking the Powers*, p. 173.

87. There have been a wide range of elucidations, adaptations, and expansions of Wink's ideas. See, e.g., Robert C. Linthicum, *City of God, City of Satan: A Biblical Theology of the Urban*

"domination system" wholesale, but to clarify how the Pauline principalities and powers have been a catalyst for thinking about a theology of the political in the last half of the twentieth century. Yet this survey — from Berkhof through Yoder, Ellul, and Wink — raises the question: Are these legitimate interpretations of the biblical material for us in the twenty-first century?

4.2.3. Principalities and Powers: Biblical Reinterpretations and Theological Reconsiderations

More precisely, two questions demand further consideration in light of the preceding discussion: What do the biblical powers actually refer to, and are these powers redeemable? Put another way, we are seeking what might be called an ontology of the biblical powers on the one hand, and hoping to clarify if the powers are created good, have fallen, but are now restored (or are restorable) in Christ on the other.[88] We will seek responses to these queries by engaging specifically with Pauline scholarship focused on the principalities and powers.

There are basically three contemporary interpretations of the New Testament powers: a traditional (spiritualist) view, a demythologized (reductionist) model, and a dual-reference option. The first has been most forcefully defended recently by evangelical biblical scholar Clinton Arnold in a number of books.[89] Arnold argues that the first-century background beliefs in magic, divination, astrology, and pagan religious traditions combine to suggest that the Pauline principalities and powers were no less than cosmic forces but yet also personal demonic entities that were responsible for human inclinations

---

Church (Grand Rapids: Zondervan Academic, 1991); Max Stackhouse, "General Introduction," in Max L. Stackhouse and Peter J. Paris, eds., *God and Globalization,* vol. 1: *Religion and the Powers of the Common Life* (Harrisburg, PA: Trinity Press International, 2000), pp. 1-52; Timothy Gorringe, "The Principalities and Powers: A Framework for Thinking about Globalization," in Peter Heslam, ed., *Globalization and the Good* (Grand Rapids and Cambridge, UK: Eerdmans, 2004), pp. 79-95; and Ray Gingerich and Ted Grimsrud, eds., *Transforming the Powers: Peace, Justice, and the Domination System* (Minneapolis: Fortress, 2006).

88. These are my specific interests; for a broader discussion of the powers in contemporary theology, see Thomas H. McAlpine, *Facing the Powers: What Are the Options?* (1991; reprint, Eugene, OR: Wipf & Stock, 2003).

89. See Clinton E. Arnold, *Ephesians: Power and Magic — The Concept of Power in Ephesians in Light of Its Historical Setting* (Cambridge: Cambridge University Press, 1989); *Powers of Darkness: Principalities and Powers in Paul's Letters* (Downers Grove, IL: InterVarsity, 1992); and *The Colossian Syncretism: The Interface between Christianity and Folk Belief at Colossae* (Grand Rapids: Baker Books, 1996).

to evil, sicknesses and diseases, and hindrances to the gospel's expansion.[90] While operative at this level, Arnold grants also that the powers exert their influences even today through pagan cults, counterfeit religions, and political, economic, and social structures.[91] His emphasis, however, is on the spiritual and personal ontology of the powers, apart from their structural expressions, as well as on Christ's triumph over the powers initially in the cross, and eschatologically at the Parousia.

The project of demythologizing the powers has unfolded across the spectrum from Rudolf Bultmann's existentialist interpretation on the one side to Elaine Pagels's sociological construal on the other.[92] There are two main challenges confronted by efforts to interpret the Pauline powers in either psychological or sociological terms: exegetical and theological. An answer to the former challenge has been attempted most extensively by Wesley Carr, who argues that the more dualistic interpretations of the powers were later first-century and especially second-century developments influenced by the emergence of Gnosticism.[93] Hence the powers are not evil cosmic forces or entities, but refer to the angelic and heavenly hosts and their regulative functions. The Colossians text traditionally understood as referring to Christ's disarming and triumphing over evil powers (2:15) is thus reinterpreted in terms of Christ's leading the angelic hosts in triumphal procession and celebration. While Carr is correct to highlight the influence of Gnosticism in the Christian reception and understanding of this passage in the post-Apostolic period,[94] there are numerous problems with his thesis, in-

---

90. This complicated cosmological backdrop to Paul has long been recognized since Martin Dibelius's *Die Geisterwelt im Glauben des Paulus* (Göttingen: Vandenhoeck & Ruprecht, 1909); for an overview, see G. H. C. Macgregor, "Principalities and Powers: The Cosmic Background of Paul's Thought," *New Testament Studies* (September 1954), reprinted in Harvey K. McArthur, ed., *New Testament Sidelights: Essays in Honor of Alexander Converse Purdy* (Hartford, CT: Hartford Seminary Foundation Press, 1960), pp. 88-104, and for a recent restatement, see Jerome H. Neyrey, *Paul, in Other Words: A Cultural Reading of His Letters* (Louisville: Westminster/John Knox Press, 1990).

91. Arnold, *Powers of Darkness*, pp. 208-9; on this point, Arnold is joined by other evangelicals like Stephen F. Noll, *Angels of Light, Powers of Darkness: Thinking Biblically About Angels, Satan and Principalities* (Downers Grove, IL: InterVarsity, 1998).

92. For an overview, see Peter T. O'Brien, "Principalities and Powers: Opponents of the Church," in D. A. Carson, ed., *Biblical Interpretation and the Church: Text and Context* (Exeter, UK: Paternoster, 1984), pp. 110-50, esp. pp. 111-28. A recent sociological interpretation of the demonic is presented by Elaine Pagels, *The Origin of Satan* (New York: Random House, 1995).

93. Wesley Carr, *Angels and Principalities: The Background, Meaning and Development of the Pauline Phrase hai archai kai hai exousiai,* Society for New Testament Monograph Series 42 (Cambridge: Cambridge University Press, 1981).

94. One author agreeing with Carr's claim that a more cosmic interpretation of the pow-

cluding his lack of attention to other contemporary data (e.g., the Synoptic Gospels, Qumran, and other pagan traditions in Asia Minor in the first century) and his handling of texts resistant to his thesis. The most recalcitrant is Ephesians 6:12, and since Carr accepts Ephesians as belonging to the first century, this "problem" is dismissed as a later interpolation. Yet no manuscript evidence for this claim is produced or clarification provided as to why it is out of place within the broader scope of that epistle's emphasis on the defeat of evil powers.[95]

The theological opposition to any reductionistic view of the powers has been reinvigorated especially in the last few decades. This emboldened theological discourse has occurred amidst the shift from a modern to a postmodern climate in the wider academy.[96] This is not to say that contemporary theological readings of the powers simply take off where Arnold's exegetical studies leave off. Rather, whether in the process demonology of David Ray Griffin, the "hypercomplex" angelology of Michael Welker, or the "ornamental" angelology and demonology of Amy Plantinga Pauw,[97] many contemporary theologians are looking for a *via media* "between naïve credulity and arrogant dismissiveness."[98] As a result, even biblical scholars like

---

ers is a later development is Gottfried Nebe, "Christ, the Body of Christ and Cosmic Powers in Paul's Letters and the New Testament as a Whole," in Henning Graf Reventlow, Yair Hoffman, and Benjamin Uffenheimer, eds., *Politics and Theopolitics in the Bible and Postbiblical Literature*, Journal for the Study of the Old Testament Supplement Series 171 (Sheffield: Sheffield Academic Press, 1994), pp. 100-18.

95. Many reviewers question Carr's major thesis and constitutive arguments; for a summary of these and other issues, see Clinton E. Arnold, "The 'Exorcism' of Ephesians 6.12 in Recent Research: A Critique of Wesley Carr's View of the Role of Evil Powers in First-Century AD Belief," *Journal for the Study of New Testament* 30 (1987): 71-87.

96. The work of James Kallas in the previous generation represents the faltering attempt to rescue the New Testament powers from the obscurity with which they were cloaked during the modern era; see James G. Kallas, *The Satanward View: A Study in Pauline Theology* (Philadelphia: Westminster, 1966); *Jesus and the Power of Satan* (Philadelphia: Westminster, 1968); *Revelation: God and Satan in the Apocalypse* (Minneapolis: Augsburg, 1973); and *The Real Satan: From Biblical Times to the Present* (Minneapolis: Augsburg, 1975).

97. David Ray Griffin, "Divine Goodness and Demonic Evil," in William Cenkner, ed., *Evil and the Response of World Religion* (St. Paul, MN: Paragon House, 1997), pp. 223-40; Michel Welker, "Angels in the Biblical Traditions: An Impressive Logic and the Imposing Problem of Their Hypercomplex Reality," *Theology Today* 51, no. 3 (1994): 367-80; and Amy Plantinga Pauw, "Where Theologians Fear to Tread," *Modern Theology* 16, no. 1 (2000): 39-59. By "ornamental," Plantinga Pauw wishes to call attention to how the Christian understanding of both angels and demons may play important secondary roles in a theological system to the point of enhancing the major doctrines of the faith.

98. Plantinga Pauw, "Where Theologians Fear to Tread," p. 41.

Wink, who emphasizes the socio-structural aspects of the powers as an entire system of domination, deploys the language of "inner" and "outer" dimensions to avoid a thoroughgoing reduction of the Pauline notion to other, more scientific categories.

Wink's dual-dimensional approach to the Pauline powers actually has a lengthy and illustrious pedigree going back to the work of biblical scholars like Oscar Cullmann (1902-99) and G. B. Caird (1917-84). Cullmann argued that Paul's language of *exousia* (authorities or powers) refers to spiritual realities (e.g., Eph. 2:2, 3:10, 6:12) and human structures/institutions (e.g., Rom. 13:1-3); hence the Pauline principalities and powers denoted *both* empirical states and, behind them, angelic or personal spiritual entities.[99] Caird proposed not only that the Pauline powers had a double meaning, pointing to both invisible spiritual beings and human/social instruments and structures, but also that if in Jewish writings the powers were *behind* the state, for Paul the powers *included* the state.[100] The reigning consensus among those who have thought about the Pauline powers vis-à-vis the political seems to be either that the powers "more likely speak of both earthly and heavenly realities at the same time,"[101] or that while they may have their own objective realities apart from socio-political manifestations, such realities at the very least exist "in and through structures."[102]

99. Oscar Cullmann, *The State in the New Testament* (New York: Charles Scribner's Sons, 1956), pp. 108-14; cf. Clinton D. Morrison, *The Powers That Be: Earthly Rulers and Demonic Powers in Romans 13.1-7*, Studies in Biblical Theology 26 (London: SCM, 1960).

100. G. B. Caird, *Principalities and Powers: A Study in Pauline Theology* (Oxford: Clarendon Press, 1956).

101. Anthony J. Tambasco, "Principalities, Powers and Peace," in Anthony J. Tambasco, ed., *Blessed Are the Peacemakers: Biblical Perspectives on Peace and Its Social Foundations* (New York: Paulist, 1989), pp. 116-33, quote from p. 121; cf. P. T. O'Brien, "Principalities and Powers in Their Relationship to Structures," *The Reformed Theological Review* 40, no. 1 (1981): 1-10, and Andrew T. Lincoln, "Liberating from the Powers: Supernatural Spirits or Societal Structures?" in M. Daniel Carroll R., David J. A. Clines, and Philip R. Davies, eds., *The Bible in Human Society: Essays in Honour of John Rogerson,* Journal for the Study of the Old Testament Supplement Series 200 (Sheffield: Sheffield Academic Press, 1995), pp. 335-54, esp. p. 349.

102. Joseph Weber, "Christ's Victory over the Powers," in Thomas E. Clarke, ed., *Above Every Name: The Lordship of Christ and Social Systems* (New York: Paulist Press, 1980), pp. 66-82, quote from p. 69. So also does Willard Swartley write: "the power of Satan is ever ready to enter the people and systems, thus functioning as the causative force of the evil; people in the structures make decisions that operationalize Satan's sinister goals; and the structures as structures may become dominated by evil and thus become also structures of domination over human life, germinating and multiplying evil by nature of their impersonal, complex, and 'super-human' functional reality"; see Willard M. Swartley, *Covenant of Peace: The Missing Peace in New Testament Theology and Ethics* (Grand Rapids: Eerdmans, 2006), pp. 230-31.

I will adopt a slightly modified version of this dual-reference thesis in my own constructive reflections (4.3.3). Suffice it to say for now that the double-reference in Paul is also at work in the Lukan material. The powers and authorities Luke mentions are both spiritual (e.g., Luke 9:1; Acts 1:7, 8:19, 26:18) and socio-political (e.g., Luke 12:11, 20:20, 22:25; Acts 9:14, 26:10, 12). We will need to sort out the relationship between these two domains of power in the pages to come.

The question about the redemptability of the powers is less contentious once a clarification of terms is provided. Ellul's resistance to the idea that the powers are redeemable seems to me to be based more on ecclesiological and political considerations than on theological and exegetical ones. I am sympathetic with his proposals for a more subversive form of Christianity that is not collusive with the mechanisms of the (fallen) state. Yet a more complete response to Ellul would require analysis not only of the doctrine of redemption but also of creation. From a canonical-Pauline perspective,[103] it appears to me undeniable that the powers were both created by God for divinely ordained purposes, and have been and will be redeemed in the eschatological scheme of things. Here I am relying less on Romans 8:38-39 (as do others like Heinrich Schlier[104]) than on Colossians 1: "for in him all things in heaven and on earth were created, things visible and invisible, whether thrones or dominions or rulers or powers — all things have been created through him and for him. He himself is before all things, and in him all things hold together" (vv. 16-17). The clarity with which this text affirms the createdness of the powers enables a better appreciation for the apostle's insistence that "there is no authority [ἐξουσίαις] except from God, and those authorities [ἐξουσία] that exist have been instituted by God" (Rom. 13:1).

But even if the powers are created, are they also then to be redeemed? While most scholars will agree that the redemption of the fallen powers minimally involve their chastisement and correction in the present age (e.g., Col. 2:10, 15; 1 Pet. 3:22; and in the Gospel accounts), what is the fate of the powers in the eschaton? One response would be to see Christ's triumph over the powers in terms of their subjection in the present age and their destruction or an-

---

103. My use of "canonical-Pauline" is meant to include the disputed "deutero-Pauline" epistles of Ephesians and Colossians. There is nothing at stake in my argument to conclude one way or the other about the authorship of these letters.

104. The Romans text is cited by Heinrich Schlier, *Principalities and Powers in the New Testament* (Freiburg: Herder, and London: Burns & Oates, 1961), p. 38, as the basis for seeing the powers as divinely created. My problem here is that the "anything else in all creation" in verse 39 is not necessarily inclusive of the preceding list, which includes "death." In other words, this text is not definitive with regard to this question.

nihilation in the age to come. However, this line of thought is to be found only in one Pauline text — 1 Corinthians 15:24 — but even here, the powers that are to be destroyed are also said to be subjugated under Christ's feet (15:25) "so that God may be all in all" (15:28).[105] On the other hand, other canonical-Pauline texts suggest that the language of the subjection of the powers is not antithetical to their ultimate restoration. The Colossians 1 passage cited above continues: "For in him all the fullness of God was pleased to dwell, and through him God was pleased to reconcile to himself all things, whether on earth or in heaven, by making peace through the blood of his cross" (vv. 19-20). The "all things" here would necessarily include the aforesaid powers.[106] And in another parallel passage about the eschatological subjugation of the powers under the feet of Christ, there is not only no mention of their destruction but an explicit declaration of what could be understood as their restitution to their proper domain, under Christ and God: "God put this power to work in Christ when he raised him from the dead and seated him at his right hand in the heavenly places, far above all rule and authority and power and dominion, and above every name that is named, not only in this age but also in the age to come. And he has put all things under his feet and has made him the head over all things for the church" (Eph. 1:20-22).[107]

Broader theological considerations regarding the creational spheres (2.2.3) and their continued operation not only in the kingdom but also in the new heavens and the new earth lead me to embrace the notion that the redemption of the powers points to their judgment and ongoing purification in the present era and to their ultimate renovation in the time to come.[108] The

105. Thus exegetes have not been able to resolve the tension in this text, between the alleged annihilation of the powers on the one hand (15:24), and the redemption and renewal of all creation on the other (15:28); see, e.g., Gordon D. Fee, *The First Epistle to the Corinthians* (1987; reprinted, Grand Rapids: Eerdmans, 1993), pp. 754 and 760. Thanks to my graduate assistant, Timothy Lim, for help with this passage.

106. If the headship of Christ in Colossians 1:18 points to his supremacy, then the defeat of the powers "is their redemption, for they are restored to their proper creatureship"; see quote from Lorenzo Bautista, Hidalgo B. Garcia, and Sze-Kar Wan, "The Asian Way of Thinking in Theology," *Evangelical Review of Theology* 6, no. 1 (1982): 37-49, quote from p. 47.

107. That these powers are evil and hence will not be finally restored — e.g., Arnold, *Ephesians: Power and Magic*, pp. 51-56, and *Colossian Syncretism*, pp. 267-69 — seems an unwarranted conclusion to be drawn from these texts. Rather, the overcoming of the powers (evil in their fallen state) by Christ could mean no less than the re-establishment of divine and christological lordship over the powers, rather than their ultimate destruction.

108. Thus O'Brien, "Principalities and Powers," p. 135, notes that in the end, the autonomous rule of the powers will be terminated and "they must worship and serve the victor [Christ]."

following constructive reflections therefore assume the powers as created good, presently fallen and hence dysfunctional, judged in the Christ-event, and currently in the process of ultimate restoration according to God's providential plan for creation.

4.3. Many Tongues, Many Spirits: Toward a Cosmopolitical Liturgics of Resistance

So far in this chapter we have introduced the pentecostal doctrine of salvation understood in terms of deliverance from the powers and showed how this has had political implications and applications, and then discussed a range of broader theologies of the principalities and powers with an eye especially on their intersections with the political. In the remainder of this chapter, I present what may be called a pentecostal intervention on the conversation at the interface of the powers and the political, and do so by sketching an understanding of how the worship of the church can be understood as cosmopolitical praxis of resistance. We will proceed in three steps: biblically, via a select reading of relevant passages in the Acts of the Apostles; practically, in dialogue with contemporary liturgical theologies of the political; and theologically, in terms of the church as an alternative and even counter-cosmopolis.

4.3.1. Delivering All "Oppressed by the Devil": Prayer, Praise, and Power Politics in Early Christianity

I wish to make three interlocking sets of observations from the text of Acts that are relevant to the thesis to be argued here. These have to do with the practices of the church vis-à-vis the state, vis-à-vis its pagan environment, especially as that entwined with the domain of the political, and vis-à-vis the gods of the nations.[109] In the process, I present a cosmology of "many spirits" and show how the liturgical practices of the church enable a pluralism of political approaches that neither compromise ecclesial identity nor disrespect the principalities and powers.

We begin with the early Christian experience of persecution at the hands of the religious leaders and captain of the temple guard (Acts 4:1).[110]

---

109. I present more detailed readings of these passages in *The Holy Spirit and the Public Square* [working title] (Brewster, MA: Paraclete Press, forthcoming).

110. The captain of the temple was head over the temple police, with official and civil

After being imprisoned and threatened the apostles returned to the ecclesial community and "raised their voices together to God," saying (4:24):

> Sovereign Lord, who made the heaven and the earth, the sea, and everything in them, it is you who said by the Holy Spirit through our ancestor David, your servant:
> "Why did the Gentiles rage,
> and the peoples imagine vain things?
> The kings of the earth took their stand,
> and the rulers have gathered together
> against the Lord and against his Messiah" . . . [drawing from Ps. 2:1-2].[111]

Later in Acts, we see similar practices of the church praying for Peter while he was imprisoned by King Herod (12:3-5), and Paul and Silas in prayer and praise while in a Philippian jail thanks to the local magistrates (16:25). While noting that these are not the normal circumstances under which Christians encounter the state — indeed they are almost extreme cases in which the people of God are unjustly persecuted by the state — they are nevertheless instructive with regard to one's proper posture toward political authorities. All governments are ultimately subordinate to God's sovereignty (thus historically anticipating St. Paul's claim in Romans 13:1, even if Acts was written after the letter to the Romans), and the church's primary response is to engage in liturgically dense practices of prayer, praise, and worship directed to God. This is not to defend a merely sectarian stance toward the political, but rather to highlight that ecclesial worship is an authentic mode of political engagement whereby the church meets the principalities of the world in the power of the Holy Spirit.[112]

Let us observe, next, the church's response to its pagan environment. Acts 19 describes a large number of conversions at Ephesus in response to the failed exorcisms of the seven sons of Sceva, and this in turn led to a rite of

---

powers to imprison in cases where the peace of the precinct was disturbed; see Darrell L. Bock, *Baker Exegetical Commentary on the New Testament: Acts* (Grand Rapids: Baker Academic, 2007), p. 186.

111. The early Christian tendency to interpret the Psalms christologically, especially "Royal Psalms" such as this one, should be understood as having emerged from a long history of reading these ancient songs of Israel both messianically and eschatologically, especially during and after the exilic period brought to full realization the failure of the Davidic monarchy; for discussion, see Jamie A. Grant, "Singing the Cover Versions: Psalms, Reinterpretation and Biblical Theology in Acts 1–4," *Scottish Bulletin of Evangelical Theology* 25, no. 1 (2007): 27-49, esp. pp. 37-38.

112. See also Jean-Pierre Ruiz, "Praise and Politics in Revelation 19:1-10," in Steve Moysie, ed., *Studies in the Book of Revelation* (Edinburgh and New York: T. & T. Clark, 2001), pp. 69-84.

mass exorcism of the occult: "A number of those who practised magic collected their books and burned them publicly; when the value of these books was calculated, it was found to come to fifty thousand silver coins" (19:19). Part of the result of this event was the loss of business among Ephesian silversmiths due to the lack of demand for the shrines they manufactured (19:23-27). Similarly, the earlier deliverance of the slave girl at Philippi resulted in the upsetting of her owners' political economy (16:19), and landed Paul and Silas in jail. The difference was that whereas the Philippian exorcism conducted on an individual occurred in a non-liturgical setting, the Ephesian activity of book burning was a well-known public rite of social renunciation.[113] I would go further to argue that such a public ceremony directed toward explicitly religious ends and conducted by the early followers of Jesus amounts to a quasi-liturgical rite of socio-political purification.

There were, of course, many other exorcisms among the early Christians (e.g., 5:16; 8:7). One event that is not explicitly identifiable as an exorcism deserves further comment because of its politically charged environment. Thus Paul's earlier encounter with the Jewish magician on the island of Paphos (13:6-11) was dramatic enough that when the proconsul "saw what had happened, he believed" (13:12). This implies that the future of the proconsul's administration was conducted in reliance upon the Holy Spirit rather than on his shaman's spirit of divination.[114] Notice then three levels of political encounters with the "spirits" of pagan or occultic traditions: that involving signs and wonders resulting in the transformation and redemption of the political order (at Paphos); that involving "public" exorcisms conducted as an ecclesial rite of purification (at Ephesus); and that involving ritual exorcisms impacting in different ways a region's political economy (at Philippi and Ephesus).[115]

Before transitioning to contemporary applications, we need to also observe the early church's responses to the gods of the nations. While the preceding discussion illustrates the "power-encounter" dimension of the early Christian engagement with the pagan spirits of the ancient world, here I am

113. See Ben Witherington III, *The Acts of the Apostles: A Socio-Rhetorical Commentary* (Grand Rapids and Cambridge, UK: Eerdmans, 1998), p. 582.

114. On Barjesus, or Elymas, as a "shaman" or "holy man" who served as a diviner for his proconsul, see Bruce J. Malina and John J. Pilch, *Social Science Commentary on the Book of Acts* (Minneapolis: Fortress, 2008), pp. 90 and 211-13.

115. For further discussion of the political dimensions of spirit possession and, by extension, exorcisms, see Santiago Guijarro, "The Politics of Exorcism," in Wolfgang Stegemann, Bruce J. Malina, and Gerd Theissen, eds., *The Social Setting of Jesus and the Gospels* (Minneapolis: Fortress, 2002), pp. 159-74.

more concerned with how the first believers responded to the Greco-Roman religious traditions. There are at least three accounts in Acts: regarding Zeus and Hermes at Lystra (14:8-18), the religiosity of Athens (17:16-34), and Artemis of Ephesus (19:23-41).[116] A number of summary comments can be made from these narratives about how the early church responded in their encounter with the gods of nations. First, there is no doubt that there was a polemical edge in the interactions, as manifest in Paul and Barnabas' identification of Lystran religion as "worthless things" (14:15), in Paul's invitation to the Athenians to repent (17:30), and in Paul's indication that the shrines made by Demetrius and his colleagues were no gods at all (19:27). But it is also clear that however aggressive the evangelistic thrust of the gospel may have been, the Ephesian city clerk acknowledged that Paul and his compatriots were "neither temple-robbers nor blasphemers of our goddess" (19:37) — i.e., they were not overtly sacrilegious vis-à-vis Artemis of the Ephesians. So on the one hand there is emboldened Christian witness, but on the other hand there is also a non-provocative and even deferential posture in relating to people of other faiths.[117] The latter is also manifest in the sensitivity of Paul to the contextual assumptions of his pagan audiences so that he began where they where, adopting as it were a natural theological approach that was better able to connect with these co-religionists (see 14:17 and 17:24-28). In short, the early Christian encounters with the gods of the nations did not involve any concession of Christian convictions; but they also did not include any needlessly confrontational strategies that were offensive and inflammatory.

I realize the foregoing is exceedingly underdeveloped, and can only beg the reader's indulgence here while pointing ahead to other elaborations of this Lukan material in the next four chapters. Yet we can still draw two preliminary conclusions for our current purposes. First, nothing said above is intended to deny the thesis argued by Susan Garrett that "The struggle between Jesus (or the Holy Spirit) and Satan lies at the very heart of Luke's story."[118] I

116. See respectively, Marianne Fournier, *The Episode at Lystra: A Rhetorical and Semiotic Analysis of Acts 14:7-20a,* American University Studies VII, Theology and Religion 197 (New York: Peter Lang, 1997); Stephen G. Wilson, *The Gentiles and the Gentile Mission in Luke-Acts,* Society for New Testament Studies Monograph Series 23 (Cambridge: Cambridge University Press, 1973), chap. 8 (on Acts 17 and the Areopagus speech of Paul); and Rick Strelan, *Paul, Artemis, and the Jews in Ephesus,* Beifahte zur Zeitschrift für die neutestamentliche Wissenschaft und die Kunde der älteren Kirche 80 (Berlin and New York: Walter de Gruyter, 1996).

117. I develop a theology of interfaith encounter that has space for these diverse postures, attitudes, and practices in Yong, *Hospitality and the Other: Pentecost, Christian Practices, and the Neighbor* (Maryknoll, NY: Orbis, 2008), esp. chap. 5.

118. Susan R. Garrett, *The Demise of the Devil: Magic and the Demonic in Luke's Writings* (Minneapolis: Fortress, 1989), p. 58.

take it for granted that Luke's worldview includes not only the satan (Luke 4:1-13, 10:17-19) but a plethora of other spirits, and that part of the unfolding of the Lukan narrative details the liberating and redeeming power of the Holy Spirit who enabled Jesus to go about "doing good and healing all who were oppressed by the devil" (Acts 10:38). More precisely, part of the encounter between the Holy Spirit and other spirits involved exorcism and the "cleansing" of the public square. This leads to my second point: that exorcism understood as a public rite of purification may be a liturgical practice that can be beneficially adapted so that the church's worship includes not only prayer and praise but also deliverance as a mode of public engagement. If this is so, then spiritual warfare may be retrieved and reimagined as a viable form of political praxis so that the church can effectively exist amidst the principalities of the cosmos and the powers of the *polis* — in short, so that the church can be a viable and alternative *cosmopolis.*

4.3.2. Principalities, Powers, and the Spirit/s: Worship as Alternative Political Praxis

We began this chapter by observing instinctive pentecostal performances vis-à-vis the political, especially in terms of its practices of prayer, praise, and spiritual warfare. In light of the preceding discussion, particularly given the practices of the early church, I want to retrieve and reappropriate pentecostal political praxis for the purposes of articulating a liturgical politics of worship. In the process, I hope to accomplish two objectives: to illuminate for pentecostals how worship is a political rather than apolitical activity, and to contribute to the emerging discussion among those who have been developing liturgical theologies of the political.

Proposals for thinking about how liturgics can inform political theology are a relatively recent but growing phenomenon. A recent collection of exploratory essays provides a broad range of perspectives about how the liturgy functions as a mode of political praxis.[119] For starters, the prayers, songs, scriptural recitations, and sacramental modalities of the liturgy are formative of human habits, character, and agency.[120] In other words, the Christian lit-

---

119. Randi Rashkover and C. C. Pecknold, eds., *Liturgy, Time, and the Politics of Redemption* (Grand Rapids and Cambridge, UK: Eerdmans, 2006); the following summarizes the key insights of this volume.

120. Thus, for example, the Eucharist can be understood as "nothing less than a political act in which the communicants actualize and suffer the citizenship that has been bestowed on them by baptism"; see Bernd Wannenwetsch, "Liturgy," in Peter Scott and William T. Cavanaugh,

urgy shapes ethical and political agents. Further, liturgical performances are not only memorial (drawing from past ideals and events) but also anticipatory (enacting the promises of Scripture with regard to how the world should be). Christian worship helps followers of Christ identify the kingdom of God even as it unveils how the world falls short of that ideal. In that sense, liturgical practices might be understood as forms of repairing or redeeming the world.

Thus worship is not a private act accomplished by isolated religious persons, but a public celebration that is lived out as a communal form of life.[121] My claim is that such an interpretation of the Christian liturgy is helpful to understand pentecostal spirituality and political praxis.[122] Pentecostal worship, consisting of prayer, singing (including "singing in the Spirit"), praise, the testimony, interactive preaching, tarrying at the altar, and the operation of the charismatic gifts of the Spirit, etc.,[123] carves out political space and enables a new political identity to emerge over social space and social time among pentecostal communities.[124] In the global south, especially, observe how pentecostal liturgical practices dominate their weekly rhythms, in terms of putting believers in church five to seven nights (or days) a week; how weekly, monthly, or quarterly all-night prayer meetings and their concomitant seasons of fasting shape the pentecostal expectation of divine provision in a hostile *polis;* and how the intensity of pentecostal praise and worship is a public expression of an alternative community consisting of brothers and sisters in Christ through the Spirit. With these practices, pentecostals are not only engaging with God, but also with the spiritual realm of the principalities and powers — taking authority over the turmoil in their personal lives, the devastations of their economies, and the challenges in the public domain (many pentecostals live in regions of the world where they are persecuted for their faith).

---

eds., *The Blackwell Companion to Political Theology* (2004; paperback ed., Malden, MA: Blackwell, 2007), pp. 76-90, quote from p. 85.

121. This is the thesis of Bernd Wannenwetsch, *Political Worship: Ethics for Christian Citizens,* trans. Margaret Kohl (Oxford: Oxford University Press, 2004).

122. While pentecostalism accentuates the more spontaneous moments in its congregational gatherings, this does not mean that pentecostals lack liturgical structure in their worship practices; for a delineation of pentecostal liturgical forms, see Daniel E. Albrecht, *Rites in the Spirit: A Ritual Approach to Pentecostal/Charismatic Spirituality* (Sheffield: Sheffield Academic Press, 1999).

123. Cecil M. Robeck Jr., *The Azusa Street Mission and Revival: The Birth of the Global Pentecostal Movement* (Nashville: Nelson Reference, 2006), esp. chap. 4.

124. André Corten, *Pentecostalism in Brazil: Emotion of the Poor and Theological Romanticism,* trans. Arianne Dorval (London: Macmillan, and New York: St. Martin's Press, 1999), esp. chaps. 2 and 5.

In the following I would like to elaborate on the notion of worship as alternative political praxis by focusing on the theological and political aspects of praise, prayer, and exorcism. Praise is the distinctive liturgical moment where believers adore God, extol God's majesty, and glorify God's name. Political theologians have articulated a "politics of praise" whereby the naming of the divine is a means toward a paradoxical friendship with the divine.[125] Such friendship is paradoxical because, on the one hand, God reveals himself and invites us into a relationship with him that is, at least in part, sealed by praise, but also, on the other hand, God is really other to and than us, and not just another being or friend like ourselves. Pentecostal spirituality has long recognized this paradox of worship as exemplified in their singing and praising in tongues. But instead of viewing such tongues merely (or only) as the "language of angels" (1 Cor. 13:1) directed toward God, why not also see them as political? Inasmuch as such practice "disrupts and confounds the travesty of much that has been regularly said and done in churchly sanctuaries, it also exposes the scandal of emperors deemed divine, of principalities treated idolatrously, of national vanity displacing God, of death extolled."[126] In this light, all of Christian praise enthrones God above every other power. Simultaneously, praise de-absolutizes the historical, the national, and the mundane (Tillich); praise dethrones the powers, or at least identifies their creational status and place under the lordship of God (Wink et al.); and praise exposes the idols of our lives.

This leads us to reflect on the political dimensions of prayer. Here I am less concerned about the explicitly political prayers that we pray, whether for our governmental leaders or for the political affairs of our countries, as important as these are. Rather, I am more interested in the form and function of prayer, and how these are, by their very nature, political acts of subversion. What does prayer express? On the one hand, prayer reflects our casting aside our own schemes, plans, efforts, powers, etc., and our reliance upon the power of God; in other words, prayer acknowledges our weakness and dependence on God. But on the other hand, prayer recognizes that our opponents are, scandalously, not only other human beings and institutions, but the principalities and powers, and that therefore the most effective weapons, even in the domains of the social, economic, and political, are spiritual (Eph. 6:10-18). Perhaps more importantly, spiritual disciplines like prayer are

125. William W. Young III, *The Politics of Praise: Naming God and Friendship in Aquinas and Derrida* (Aldershot, UK, and Burlington, VT: Ashgate, 2007).

126. William Stringfellow, *An Ethic for Christians and Other Aliens in a Strange Land*, 2nd ed. (Waco, TX: Word, 1978), pp. 147-48.

speech acts that not only manifest personal piety but also reconstitute, even if in a counterintuitive manner, the public space that pray/ers inhabit and actively engage.[127] In other words, prayer reflects our engagement with the most important things in life, and is a performative dynamic that has the potential to transform the public square as inhabited by the church.

What about exorcism as a liturgical mode of political praxis? Here we need to tread carefully, and I propose to do so in three steps. First, while we realize that exorcism has not been a part of our liturgical experience — at least not recently — might it be possible to imagine things otherwise? For help, we can recall the sacrament of baptism and Christian initiation, at least as practiced historically in the church.[128] Throughout much of the first millennium of Christian faith, an explicit renunciation of the devil, and in some cases an elaborate rite of exorcism, was part of the liturgy of holy week through which people were initiated into the body of Christ.[129] This initiatory ejection of the demonic continues in many pentecostal contexts, albeit not specifically as part of the rite of baptism (since most pentecostals view baptism as an ordinance rather than a sacrament of initiation); instead, the tarrying or initial conversion experiences at the altar sometimes involve rites of deliverance, especially when conducted during an evangelistic service by those who think of Christian initiation in terms of a "born again" experience. My claim is that liturgical traditions that do not regularly involve exorcisms will not be sufficiently habituated to its capacity to shape Christian life, much less to inform Christian political praxis. At the same time, I am not suggesting that pentecostal exorcisms are unproblematic as they occur "on the ground."[130] I would concur with the

127. Here I am expanding on Gavin D'Costa's call to restore prayer as a central practice for the vocation of theology, even for theologians in the secular university context. In fact, it is precisely because of the privatization (at best) or altogether neglect (at worst) of prayer that theologians find themselves estranged from their vocation, even as theology itself is increasingly exiled as a viable form of (public) knowledge. See D'Costa, *Theology in the Public Square: Church, Academy and Nation* (Malden, MA: Blackwell, 2005), chap. 4.

128. See Kilian McDonnell, "Does the Theology and Practice of the Early Church Confirm the Classical Pentecostal Understanding of Baptism in the Holy Spirit?" *PNEUMA: The Journal of the Society for Pentecostal Studies* 21, no. 1 (1999): 115-33, esp. p. 120. The most extensive discussion is Henry Ansgar Kelly, *The Devil at Baptism: Ritual, Theology, and Drama* (Ithaca, NY, and London: Cornell University Press, 1985).

129. First mentioned in Hippolytus's early third-century *Apostolic Tradition* 21:7-10; see Hippolytus, *On the Apostolic Tradition,* trans. Alistair Stewart-Sykes (Crestwood, NY: St. Vladimir's Seminary Press, 2001), p. 111.

130. A helpful pentecostal perspective is Jacques Theron, "A Critical Overview of the Church's Ministry of Deliverance from Evil Spirits," *PNEUMA: The Journal of the Society for Pentecostal Studies* 18, no. 1 (1996): 79-92.

recommendation of Cardinal Léon-Joseph Suenens for the Catholic charismatic renewal that the goal is "to chart a safe course between two dangers: — that of underestimating the presence of the Spirit of Evil in the world; — and that of fighting against the Spirit of Evil without the indispensable discernment and safeguards of the Church."[131] I would simply point out that the current problem, especially in the Western churches, is the first danger referred to by the cardinal: a complete disregard of the important ritual function of banishing the powers of darkness.

How is this neglect rectified? One approach — this is step two, part one — is to rehabilitate our cosmological imagination, especially our angelology. Erik Peterson (whom we met above as a critic of Carl Schmitt; 2.3.1) has helpfully reminded us in this regard about the centrality of the hosts of angels in Christian worship.[132] More particularly, he argues — from the scene around the throne in Revelation chapters 4 and 5, as well as from existing liturgies, particularly the Liturgy of St. Mark which focuses on the Isaiah 6 passage — "All acts of worship would have to be seen, therefore, as a participation by the angels in earthly worship, or conversely, all the worship of the Church upon earth would have to be seen as a participation in that worship which is offered to God in heaven by the angels."[133] Peterson goes on to suggest that a liturgical imagination (my term) attuned to the presence of the angelic host in the midst of worship will experience the worshiping angels as part of the mystical life of the church, purifying the worship of the church, and drawing us human creatures into the many possibilities of enhancement and intensification of our very beings. In short, "the Church's worship is no merely human occasion. The angels and the entire universe take part in it. The songs of the Church are the counterparts of heavenly songs . . . and because the angels are related to the politico-religious world in heaven, they imbue the liturgy of the Church with a relation to the political realm."[134]

From here — this is step two, part two — I would suggest that a secondary "audience" of the church's worship might be the principalities and pow-

---

131. Cardinal Léon-Joseph Suenens, *Renewal and the Powers of Darkness: Malines Document IV*, trans. Olga Prendergast (London: Darton, Longman & Todd, 1983), p. xiii. Similarly, a more balanced approach, such as suggested by Graham H. Twelftree, *In the Name of Jesus: Exorcism among Early Christians* (Grand Rapids: Baker Academic, 2007), esp. pp. 293-94, would see exorcism as only one method of confronting the demonic, the other being the proclamation of the gospel of truth.

132. Eric Peterson, *The Angels and the Liturgy: The Status and Significance of the Holy Angels in Worship*, trans. Ronald Wells (London: Darton, Longman & Todd, 1964).

133. Peterson, *The Angels and the Liturgy*, p. xi.

134. Peterson, *The Angels and the Liturgy*, p. 50.

ers. St. Paul wrote to the Ephesians: "so that through the church the wisdom of God in its rich variety might now be made known to the rulers and authorities in the heavenly places" (3:10). Let me be clear that I am seeking neither to centralize the powers in any fashion nor to give them more "air time" than they deserve. More pointedly, I am not recommending, as Clinton Arnold warns against, that the church "serve notice" to the principalities and powers.[135] Instead, all I am suggesting here is that the principalities and powers are not absent from the liturgical life of the church; recognizing their "presence," however, is an important step toward forming liturgical practices of exorcism that have social and political significance.

If step one invites us to create ritual space and time for exorcism in the church's liturgical life, and step two invites us to imagine a much richer cosmology within which the worship of the church takes place/time, then step three suggests that there may be corporate rites of exorcism that could serve to purify the wider public square. Here I am taking my cues from the burning of pagan and occultic books at Ephesus that we saw earlier. I am also drawing from the work of theologians like Alexander Schmemann, whose Orthodox sensibilities see the personal renunciation of the devil at baptism and initiation to have implications for understanding the cosmic dimension of exorcism;[136] from Daniel Day Williams, who has called for religious rituals of resistance to the demonic powers and structures of society;[137] and from George McClain, whose social activism has been informed by what he calls rituals of social exorcism.[138] The latter's discussions draw from Jesus' cleansing of the temple (Luke 19:45-46 and par.), and are informed by examples of social exorcisms such as those conducted by the Catholic Worker Movement in inner-city Philadelphia in response to church and school closings, and by the New York and Northern New Jersey conferences of the United Methodist Church confronting the spirit(s) of Apartheid at the South African consulate in New York City.[139] McClain also suggests that any ritual of social exorcism should

135. Clinton E. Arnold, *3 Crucial Questions About Spiritual Warfare* (Grand Rapids: Baker Books, 1997), p. 167. Arnold's approach is sympathetic to but also cautious about and, in places, critical of spiritual warfare practices and notions of territorial spirits.

136. See discussion of "Alexander Schmemann: Baptism Is Death and Resurrection," which is chapter 1 in Russell Haitch, *From Exorcism to Ecstasy: Eight Views of Baptism* (Louisville and London: Westminster/John Knox Press, 2007), esp. pp. 10-13.

137. Daniel Day Williams, *The Demonic and the Divine*, ed. Stacy A. Evans (Minneapolis: Fortress Press, 1990), pp. 21-23.

138. George D. McClain, *Claiming All Things for God: Prayer, Discernment, and Ritual for Social Change* (Nashville: Abingdon, 1998).

139. For these and other examples, see McClain, *Claiming All Things for God*, chap. 12, and Bill Wylie Kellermann, *Seasons of Faith and Conscience: Kairos, Confession, Liturgy* (Mary-

include, minimally, the following liturgical components: invocation, the reading of Scripture, discerning of spirits/powers, confession of sins and their absolution, Holy Communion, words of deliverance, prayer for renewal of the institution's purpose, prayer for thanksgiving, and exhortation and benediction. Needless to say, any rite of social exorcism should be followed by the church's continuing witness for peace and justice.

4.3.3. The Liturgical Imagination: Toward a Re-enchantment of the Cosmopolitical

In this last part of this chapter, I want to summarize the gains made toward what I have called a cosmopolitical liturgics of resistance. There are three broad threads to this liturgically informed political theology: concerning the liturgical imagination; concerning the re-enchantment of the cosmopolitical; and concerning what I am calling an apophatic theology of the powers. The first two moments are constructive, the last cautionary.

The liturgical imagination: The direction of this chapter has been to argue for the centrality of the liturgy in engaging the principalities and powers of the political. I have argued that Christian worship nurtures the proper stance toward God, the powers, and the political. Worship is the activity of giving adoration due to God alone. Simultaneously, worship occurs in the presence of angels, and of the powers in the spiritual domain; hence worship would also enable the cultivation of a deferential posture toward the angelic hosts, as well as a proper respect for the principalities and powers (the epistle of Jude, vv. 8-9, warns against slandering celestial beings). Yet worship situates believers to respond appropriately to divine authority, and thereby to take proper human responsibility in the political domain.[140] This means, at

---

knoll, NY: Orbis, 1991), chaps. 5-6. Compare the liturgical politics of these accounts with those of C. Peter Wagner, ed., *Territorial Spirits: Insights on Strategic-Level Spiritual Warfare from Nineteen Christian Leaders* (Chichester, UK: Sovereign World Ltd., 1991), part 2; C. Peter Wagner, *Confronting the Powers: How the New Testament Church Experienced the Power of Strategic-Level Spiritual Warfare* (Ventura, CA: Regal, 1996), esp. chap. 4; and Jean DeBernardi, "Spiritual Warfare and Territorial Spirits: The Globalization and Localisation of a 'Practical Theology,'" *Religious Studies and Theology* 18, no. 2 (1999): 66-96. I think McClain's suggestions are the kinds of first steps that will enable the church to inhabit a form of Christian praxis in order to discern some of the more radical practices advocated by Wagner and others in the "spiritual warfare" movement.

140. Thus does Randi Rashkover, *Revelation and Theopolitics: Barth, Rosenzweig and the Politics of Praise* (London and New York: T. & T. Clark, 2005), insist that a politics of praise involves a practical testimony that is morally and ethically enacted in response to the encounter

least in part, that we respond in the political arena by following in the footsteps of Jesus, and even of Paul, both of whom embraced the "weakness" of powerlessness in order to resist, by the power of the Spirit, the worldly systems of domination corrupted by fallen principalities and powers.[141]

The re-enchantment of the cosmopolitical: But how then should we understand the previously raised question (4.2.3) regarding the ontology of the powers? And, in connection with that, how is the rite of exorcism related to the claim regarding the redemptability of the powers? If the powers are to be cast out, then in what sense are they to be redeemed? I will respond to this set of questions in three theses that flesh out how I conceived the re-enchantment of the cosmopolitical domain.

i) The powers are creations of God ordained for his purposes. The powers associated with the natural world are often personified as having spiritual agency and thus capable of glorifying God (as seen throughout the Psalter), while the powers presiding over the human realm were understood among the ancient Hebrews as members of the divine council, and by the early Christians as angels "sent to serve for the sake of those who are to inherit salvation" (Heb. 1:14). Kuyper used the language of "spheres" to denote the distinct domains of human life (2.2.3). I suggest that the biblical language of powers related to the public realm — e.g., the political, the economic, and the social — can be understood in terms of Kuyperian spheres. Because these are prelapsarian natural, human, and social realities, they are good as created by God.

ii) But the powers are fallen, and in their fallen condition are susceptible to demonic manifestations. This claim needs to be clarified in three subtheses: a) that the demonic has no ontological reality of its own but is rather a perversion of the goodness of the orders of creation — or, put alternatively, since the demonic is not created by God, it does not possess its own being;[142] b) that the demonic is, nevertheless, objective as an emergent reality, parasitic and dependent upon certain configurations of the material, institutional, and

---

with a transcendent and loving God. I agree, except to insist that an ethical witness is only one mode of confessional praise; glossolalic singing, for example, is just as deeply theological quite apart from any moral register.

141. Marva J. Dawn, *Powers, Weakness, and the Tabernacling of God* (Grand Rapids: Eerdmans, 2001).

142. This hints at the apophatic theology of the demonic that I will develop further below; for further discussion of the metaphysics I am presuming regarding the demonic, see my *Discerning the Spirit(s): A Pentecostal-Charismatic Contribution to Christian Theology of Religions,* Journal of Pentecostal Theology Supplement Series 20 (Sheffield: Sheffield Academic Press, 2000), pp. 127-32.

organizational structures of the powers, but yet irreducible to the sum of its constituent parts;[143] c) that once emergent, the demonic is manifest as a force of destruction wielded in and through the fallen and disordered powers, appearing in ways that suggest the powers have become transcendental realities, "larger" than what they are, certainly overreaching their authority, and seemingly personal and intentional in their destructive capacities.[144] When taken together, these three sub-theses suggest that in a fallen world, the powers of the political, while continuing to carry out the intentions of God in some respect, are also susceptible to the emergence of demonic trajectories. If and when this happens, governments become tyrannical, nations become anarchic, economic systems become unjust, and social systems foster death instead of life.

iii) But the powers can be redeemed! That is at the heart of the gospel of Jesus Christ and the triune God, who in the incarnation and at Pentecost have triumphed over the demonic character of the powers and whose economy of salvation has begun to restore to the powers their God-intended functions. Rites of social exorcism such as I have suggested above, then, cast out not the powers themselves, but rather oust the demonic distortions that have come to infest, infect, and infiltrate the various spheres of human life. The powers, understood primordially as the creational spheres, cannot be banished; what can be evicted and expelled are the emergent forces of destruction that have misdirected and deformed these structural domains.

The liturgical imagination therefore inhabits a re-enchanted cosmos, which correlates with, if not clarifies the pluralism of the human *polis*. In other words, the "gods of the nations" in the Hebraic imagination that

143. Elsewhere I have elaborated on a theory of emergence as a whole, and with regard to the human soul; for the former, see my *"Ruach,* the Primordial Waters, and the Breath of Life: Emergence Theory and the Creation Narratives in Pneumatological Perspective," in Michael Welker, ed., *The Work of the Spirit: Pneumatology and Pentecostalism* (Grand Rapids: Eerdmans, 2006), pp. 183-204, and for the latter, see my *Theology and Down Syndrome: Reimagining Disability in Late Modernity* (Waco, TX: Baylor University Press, 2007), pp. 170-72.

144. In a book focused on a theology of the political, I do not have time or space to clarify a full-blown ontology of the demonic in terms of spiritual beings with personalities. Minimally, my account recognizes the demonic as personal to the degree that its emergent "face" is manifest in destructiveness that touches the lives of human persons. For other preliminary reflections on these matters, see Yong, "Spirit Possession, the Living, and the Dead: A Review Essay and Response from a Pentecostal Perspective," in *Dharma Deepika: A South Asian Journal of Missiological Research* 8, no. 2 (2004): 77-88, and "The Demonic in Pentecostal-Charismatic Christianity and in the Religious Consciousness of Asia," in Allan Anderson and Edmond Tang, eds., *Asian and Pentecostal: The Charismatic Face of Christianity in Asia* (London: Regnum International, and Baguio City, Philippines: Asia Pacific Theological Seminary Press, 2005), pp. 93-127.

morphed into the angelology and demonology of the New Testament now inform the "many tongues, many spirits" of the human cosmopolis. Metaphorically, the many spirits represent potentialities for good or for evil, to be ritually exorcised when they are discerned to have materialized in the latter direction, or to be subjugated under the lordship of Christ if they are to be redeemed for the glory of God and for the accomplishment of the divine intention. Jesus is the savior and deliverer, the one who liberates humankind by the power of the Holy Spirit from demonic perversions and redeems the powers for God's good purposes.

An apophatic theology of the powers: Having said all this, we still must not claim to know too much about the powers. The liturgical imagination thus concludes that doxology is sustained amidst a field of apophatic confession.[145] We know who God is, we worship and adore God, and we render to God what is due to him; but we know enough about the demonic only to know what it is not. I hence conclude this chapter with three cautionary clarifications regarding the significance of the church's "confession" regarding the principalities and powers.

First, embracing a re-enchanted cosmopolis is an attempt to find a *via media* between the materialisms, naturalisms, and reductionisms of modernity on the one side and the fantastic cosmological anarchism of premodern worldviews on the other side. The created world is more than space and time, although it is less than a "pluriverse" without a center. Acceptance of St. Paul's principalities and powers is one way to complicate an otherwise one-dimensional universe without at the same time having to assume that we need to assign a Cartesian subjectivity to each principality and power that we think we might have identified.

Second, the Pauline principalities and powers also help us to avoid either a rigid dualism on the one hand or a polytheism on the other. Pentecostals are right to think that Christian conversion requires a "breaking away from the past" (see 4.1.1 above), although it is clear that such a strict dualism cannot account for the pluralism of the created orders. More importantly, so long as we understand that the work of Christ has indeed exposed the futility of the powers, we can then see how they have also been disciplined within an eschatological horizon that anticipates their ultimate redemption and subjection to God's rule and reign.

145. This apophatic moment in doxological theology was operative at the Council of Chalcedon, where the church fathers confessed the mystery of the incarnation in terms of what it was not; for explication of this apophatic approach and application toward a theology of divine providence, see my *Theology and Down Syndrome*, pp. 167-69.

Finally, the liturgical imagination is focused on the lordship of Christ and the majesty of God, not on the principalities and powers per se. In this theological framework, there is no room for absolutizing the "lesser" powers, and this means there is also no space for thinking that "we" are on God's side against "them" who are not. In other words, the liturgical imagination worships God and refuses to demonize the powers, especially people, as enemies of God. Should demonic materializations of the powers be discerned, then the weapons of resistance are spiritual and non-violent — thus removing any possibility of legitimating violence by utilizing the rhetoric of spiritual warfare

In short, a pentecostal contribution to political theology that begins with Jesus' victory over the powers will enable focus on the demonic not for its own sake but for the sake of constituting the church as an alternative cosmopolis amidst the many fallen principalities and powers, and will empower deployment of liturgical practices to engage in non-violent witness directed toward the redemption of the powers. But this first of five interventions is only the beginning of what there is to say.

CHAPTER 5

Pentecostal Holiness:
A Sanctified Theology of Culture

If salvation — Jesus as savior and deliverer — is considered the first work of grace in classical pentecostal theology, then Jesus' work of sanctification and Spirit-baptism are considered the second and third works of grace, respectively. This and the following chapter are devoted to exploring the political implications of these moments of the pentecostal *via salutis*. At the same time, while recognizing the distinctiveness of sanctification and Spirit-baptism as experiences subsequent to deliverance in the pentecostal theological scheme, we should also view these three "works of grace" as inseparably intertwined, dynamically fluid, and differentiated — more so heuristically for the sake of theological explication than because they are experientially discrete.[1]

The three sections of this chapter therefore will take up the following tasks: 1) explore how pentecostal theologies of sanctification have nurtured certain postures, dispositions, and practices toward the larger culture; 2) enter into a dialogue with a number of theologians in what might loosely be called a post-Constantinian theological tradition — e.g., John Howard Yoder, Stanley Hauerwas, and leading thinkers in the New Monasticism movement — focusing particularly on their ideas about the relationship between the church and culture and society; and 3) formulate, in a critical dialogue between pentecostal self-understandings and these post-Constantinian theologies, a sanctified politics and theology of culture. As in each of the constructive chapters in Part II of this book, we begin with distinctively pentecostal intuitions but seek to articulate a theological point of view that is applicable to the church ecumenical and the wider theological conversation.

---

1. I argue these points at length in *The Spirit Poured Out on All Flesh: Pentecostalism and the Possibility of Global Theology* (Grand Rapids: Baker Academic, 2005), chap. 2.

Thus our goal in this chapter is to provide some pentecostal perspective on a theology of culture and a theology of society, broadly speaking. This will be a challenge, as pentecostalism has largely neglected to make explicit or thematize its theological understandings of culture. We shall see, however, that there are resources in pentecostal spirituality and piety that will be helpful in rethinking a theology of culture and society, even as there will be aspects of that spirituality and piety that will need to be critiqued. In engaging the wider theological academy, however, including the Yoder-Hauerwas connection and related conversations, we shall see emergent a sanctified and aesthetic imagination that, rather than denying or rejecting the present age, is a catalyst for the renewal, reformation, and even redemption of the many cultures of the world. I will attempt to articulate over the course of this chapter a renewal theology of culture which is centrally informed by the Spirit's harmonizing of the many tongues of the world so that separately and together the diversity of human life can declare the glory of God.

5.1. Jesus the Sanctifier: Sanctified from What?

In this section, we shall see a range of pentecostal understandings of Jesus as sanctifier. By this I am referring both to formal articulations of the doctrine of sanctification and how these were lived out. I will argue that the pluralism of early pentecostal theologies of sanctification translated two overall orientations toward holiness — one focused on purification and the other on consecration directed toward a vocational calling — and these in turn have shaped the two dominant early classical (North American) pentecostal stances toward wider social and cultural realities. More recent developments have reappropriated these earlier pentecostal postures toward and amidst popular culture to produce new modalities of global cultural engagement, especially at the level of the media and electronic arts. The following examines these three aspects of pentecostal-holiness spirituality and piety — the doctrinal/classical, the practical/North American, and the aesthetic/global — in order.

5.1.1. Classical Pentecostal Theologies of Sanctification

Classical pentecostalism produced at least four types of theologies of sanctification.[2] The first to articulate a more or less systematic view of sanctification

2. There is no book-length study, to my knowledge, that analyzes this typology of views;

— keeping in mind that early pentecostals were not theologically trained and did not produce systematic theological works in the conventional sense — was the polemical pentecostal preacher, William H. Durham (1873-1912).[3] Durham was reacting to the dampened spiritual fervor he observed among especially the holiness churches with which he was associated, and diagnosed the problem as related, at least in part, to the Wesleyan teaching of sanctification as a second work of grace. The result, from Durham's perspective, was that this two-stage understanding of Christian perfection provided theological justification for those who had not yet received the second blessing to remain in their state of being less than committed to the pursuit of holy living.[4] Durham's response was to emphasize the reception of full salvation at conversion based on the finished work of Christ on the cross. The holiness of Christ was imputed to the believer once and for all, thus regenerating the soul and enabling a holy life (while rendering superfluous the need for a subsequent experience of sanctification).[5] To be sure, the baptism of the Holy Spirit made possible the further maturation of the believer, but this was not a second work of sanctification.

Durham's "finished work" soteriology sparked extensive reactions.[6] Besides the response of those in the pentecostal holiness tradition — which bore the brunt of Durham's critique, and to which we will return momentarily — two other interpretations of the theology of sanctification coming out of the debate adapted the main lines of Durham's lead. The Oneness tradition, which was launched within years after Durham's death, can be said to have completed what Durham began in terms of frontloading into conversion and initiation not only the experience of sanctification but also that of the baptism of the Holy Spirit. More widely known for their anti-trinitarian theology

---

a very brief historical survey is David Michel, "Revisiting the Methodist Legacy in American Pentecostalism: Nuances in the Early Pentecostal Understanding of 'Sanctification' (1896-1950)," *Methodist History* 41, no. 4 (2003): 196-205, albeit one focused on the pentecostal holiness tradition.

3. The definitive study on Durham to date remains unpublished: Thomas George Farkas, "William H. Durham and the Sanctification Controversy in Early American Pentecostalism, 1906-1916" (Ph.D. diss., Southern Baptist Theological Seminary, 1993).

4. For explication, see Douglas Jacobsen, *Thinking in the Spirit: Theologies of the Early Pentecostal Movement* (Bloomington: Indiana University Press, 2003), esp. pp. 142-45.

5. William H. Durham, from the *Pentecostal Testimony* (1907), reprinted in William K. Kay and Anne E. Dyer, eds., *Pentecostal and Charismatic Studies: A Reader* (London: SCM, 2004), pp. 132-34.

6. Some of this is discussed in Edith L. Blumhofer, "William H. Durham: Years of Creativity, Years of Dissent," in James R. Goff and Grant Wacker, eds., *Portraits of a Generation: Early Pentecostal leaders* (Fayetteville: University of Arkansas Press, 2002), pp. 123-42.

of the Godhead, the other no less central Oneness doctrinal tenet concerns their explication and extension of Durham's "finished work" thesis.[7] Durham did not go far enough, according to the Oneness perspective, because he allowed for a separation between conversion and Spirit-baptism which the Bible did not. In particular, Peter's response to the question asked on the Day of Pentecost, about what needed to be done in order to be saved, remains normative: "Repent, and be baptized every one of you in the name of Jesus Christ for the remission of sins, and ye shall receive the gift of the Holy Ghost" (Acts 2:38).[8] According to this view, conversion is initiated by repentance, involves in one package the regeneration of water baptism (in Jesus' name rather than according to the trinitarian formula), and culminates in the reception (baptism) of the Holy Spirit (evidenced with the sign of speaking in tongues, as the classical pentecostal argument otherwise usually goes).[9] Sanctification is thus part and parcel of salvation, properly considered, which means also that holiness is both the immediately expected fruit and the ongoing lifelong expression of the regenerating work of the Holy Spirit.

Other pentecostals who were sympathetic to Durham's proposals rejected both the Oneness doctrines of God and salvation even while adapting the "finished work" motif. Typical in this regard are classical pentecostal churches influenced by Keswick "higher Christian life" revivalism, like the Assemblies of God (AOG), which rejected, as did Durham, the idea of sanctification as a second work of grace, but revised Durham's soteriology in a more Reformed-evangelical theological direction.[10] The work of the Holy Spirit in this framework could be understood as unfolding in three logically differentiated phases: initial sanctification occurred at conversion, understood largely in terms compatible with Durham's notion of Christ's righteousness imputed to the believer; ongoing sanctification occurred over the course of the remainder of the believer's life, culminating at either death (glorification) or the eschaton (parousia); and the baptism of the Holy Spirit, which was subsequent to con-

---

7. The definitive study of Oneness theology is now David A. Reed, *"In Jesus' Name": The History and Beliefs of Oneness Pentecostals* (Blandford Forum, UK: Deo Publishing, 2008).

8. For elaboration, see David K. Bernard, *The New Birth* (Hazelwood, MO: Word Aflame, 1984).

9. A historical and critical analysis of this Oneness view is Thomas A. Fudge, *Christianity Without the Cross: A History of Salvation in Oneness Pentecostalism* (Parkland, FL: Universal Publications, 2003).

10. A historical survey is William W. Menzies, "The Reformed Roots of Pentecostalism," *Asian Journal of Pentecostal Studies* 9, no. 2 (2006): 260-82, esp. pp. 268-72; a doctrinal/theological overview is in Timothy P. Jenney, "The Holy Spirit and Sanctification," in Stanley M. Horton, ed., *Systematic Theology*, rev. ed. (Springfield, MO: Gospel Publishing House, 1995), pp. 397-422.

version but denoted a purified life empowered to bear witness to the gospel.[11] While holiness was not minimized, at least not in the first generation of classical pentecostal denominations shaped within the Keswickian stream, its detachment from a distinctive work of grace led, one could argue, to its eventual subordination to the experience of being filled with the Spirit. In these pentecostal circles, then, later generations unintentionally subordinated the emphasis on holiness to that of Spirit-baptism and the missionary task and mandate of the church (see chapter 6). The orientation here was much more outward-looking: holiness understood as consecration for the purpose of empowerment for evangelization to the ends of the earth, rather than concerned with maintaining a certain form of piety as a church or a movement.

Classical pentecostals with roots in the holiness movement were motivated to clarify and think through their own theologies of sanctification in part in response to Durham's criticisms. As Douglas Jacobsen notes, "no one did this better than Joseph H. King [1869-1945],"[12] a holiness preacher who came into the pentecostal experience of the Spirit in midlife, and then became a leader, bishop, and longtime general superintendent in the Pentecostal Holiness Church.[13] The distinctiveness of King's response, which has since come to be widely accepted in pentecostal holiness circles, can be summarized in three major points.[14] First, whereas Keswickian-influenced denominations like the AOG delineated between initial sanctification (occurring at conversion) and ongoing sanctification (culminating in glorification), pentecostal holiness churches talked about initial and full sanctification, with the difference that the latter — full sanctification and full salvation — was understood to occur in a distinct experience subsequent to conversion in this life whereby the sin nature would be fully suppressed or eradicated (pentecostal holiness groups disagreed about this specific issue).[15] Second, whereas most

11. For elaboration, see Harold D. Hunter, *Spirit-Baptism: A Pentecostal Alternative* (Lanham, MD: University Press of America, 1983), esp. chaps. 5-6.

12. Jacobsen, *Thinking in the Spirit*, p. 164.

13. David A. Alexander, "Bishop J. H. King and the Emergence of Holiness Pentecostalism," *PNEUMA: The Journal of the Society for Pentecostal Studies* 8, no. 2 (1986): 159-83. Note: I will capitalize "Pentecostal" and "Holiness" only when they are part of proper names — otherwise, both will be uncapitalized according to the convention I have adopted for this book; see the discussion in the Prologue.

14. The most comprehensive discussion is J. H. King, *From Passover to Pentecost,* 4th rev. and enlarged ed. (Franklin Springs, GA: Advocate Press, 1976).

15. Further comparisons between Keswickian and Wesleyan forms of early pentecostalism can be explored in Ian M. Randall, "Old Time Power: Relationships between Pentecostalism and Evangelical Spirituality in England," *PNEUMA: The Journal of the Society for Pentecostal Studies* 19, no. 1 (1997): 53-80.

pentecostal groups (except the Oneness organizations) followed Durham in identifying the baptism with the Holy Spirit as a separate experience of empowerment to witness, pentecostal holiness retained the Wesleyan doctrine of instantaneous and entire sanctification as a second work of grace and added to that the distinctively pentecostal doctrine of Spirit-baptism for spiritual consecration and empowerment to witness as a third work of grace. Third, if the emphasis on holiness diminished over time in pentecostal churches that did not understand sanctification as a subsequent work of the Spirit, then the pentecostal holiness movement as a whole was able to retain a much more vigorous commitment to personal holiness as a way of life given its affirmation of the possibility of full Christian perfection.[16] To be sure, what Christian perfection meant — i.e., whether that involved the obliteration of the sin nature or only repression of the desire to sin, or whether this happened at a moment in time or gradually, or whether perfection was a singular experience from which one could later fall away — has been and remains disputed at the levels of doctrine and experience. But it is also clear that pentecostal holiness churches and denominations debated these matters precisely because they were concerned not only about retaining the confession of holiness but also about nurturing the living form thereof.[17]

In short, at least four theologies of sanctification emerged in the first general phase of classical pentecostalism, amidst which two forms of holiness dispositions are discernible: the Keswickian strand which thought about holiness in terms of purity in relationship to the empowerment of the Spirit for mission and evangelism, and the pentecostal holiness tributary which emphasized the notion of holiness as cleansing from the impurities of the world. In the following, we will see that the latter shaped the early to mid-twentieth-century pentecostal engagement with culture while a re-emergence of the former especially more recently is also noticeable.

16. A powerful restatement of the notion of personal holiness has been provided recently by Cheryl Bridges Johns, "Transformed by Grace: The Beauty of Personal Holiness," in Kevin W. Mannoia and Don Thorsen, eds., *The Holiness Manifesto* (Grand Rapids: Eerdmans, 2008), pp. 152-65.

17. Historical perspective on (in contrast to my theological reading of) southern holiness pentecostalism can be found in Vinson Synan, *The Holiness-Pentecostal Movement in the United States* (Grand Rapids: Eerdmans, 1971), a by-now classic study, and Randall J. Stephens, *The Fire Spreads: Holiness and Pentecostalism in the American South* (Cambridge, MA, and London: Harvard University Press, 2008), more recently.

5.1.2. Pentecostal-Holiness Cultures: W(h)ither the Sanctified Church?

One way to explicate the history of North American pentecostal interaction with culture is to see how the two sides of holiness — that of purification *from* and that of consecration *toward* — played out amidst the public square. The debates regarding whether sanctification occurred as a second work of grace and about the relationship between purity (holiness) and power (Spirit-baptism and mission) can be understood as representative aspects of these twin themes. The former notion of holiness as purification wondered about the sin nature and the possibility of its eradication in this life. As the emphasis here was on how to rid the human soul from inbred and original sin, the practical outworkings of such a focus unfolded in varied forms of sectarian withdrawals from a fallen and sinful world.[18] The latter notion of holiness as consecration highlighted the links between the second and third works of grace — between purity and empowerment — and worked itself out in terms of holiness as vocation and way of being in the world. Pentecostals have always struggled with the tension of these two complementary, albeit also distinct, notions of holiness.

The sectarian trajectory, as we saw earlier (esp. 1.3.1-2), centered on abstaining from the lures, temptations, and contaminations of the world in light of the holiness of God. Seeing the biblical injunction to "come out from them, and be separate from them" (2 Cor. 6:17) as being applicable to their own lives, and taking seriously the Pauline insistence on the body as being the dwelling place of a holy God and his Holy Spirit (1 Cor. 3:17; 6:19), pentecostal holiness cultures in North America, especially in the first half of the twentieth century, rejected what they considered worldly practices, spaces, and symbols: alcohol (or even caffeine), gambling, tobacco, social dancing, mixed-bathing, card games, television, and the theater, among other socially accepted pastimes, not to mention makeup, ornamentation, jewelry, short hair, and pants for women.[19] On many of these issues, pentecostals lined up with their fundamentalist and conservative evangelical cousins and in doing so converged on a broader socio-cultural agenda dedicated to preserving traditionally articulated values in opposition to the "ways of the world."[20]

Simultaneously, however, pentecostals wrestled with living out what

18. As in 5.1.2, I am using "sectarian" here in a descriptive rather than pejorative sense.

19. Stanley M. Horton, "Pentecostal View," in Stanley N. Gundry, gen. ed., *Five Views on Sanctification* (Grand Rapids: Zondervan, 1987), pp. 103-35, esp. p. 111; see also David K. Bernard, *Essentials of Holiness* (1989; reprint, Hazelwood, MO: Word Aflame, 1995), pp. 31-33.

20. See Robert Mapes Anderson, *Vision of the Disinherited: The Making of American Pentecostalism* (1979; reprint, Peabody, MA: Hendrickson, 1992), chap. 11.

Grant Wacker calls the tension between marginality and respectability.[21] Because they came not just from the lowest rungs of the social ladder but also from the lower median and median levels of the American population, and because they did not shirk the American ideals of personal autonomy and individual responsibility, pentecostals have from the beginning "evinced a trajectory of insistent upward mobility and personal achievement."[22] Such a course was not only consistent with but also resonated theologically with the notion of holiness understood as vocational consecration. But ironically the outworking of such an ethic of holiness would inevitably bring pentecostalism into the mainstream of American society.

The life of Aimee Semple McPherson, founder of the Church of the Foursquare Gospel (see 3.1.3), provides an exemplary case study of how the complicated interrelations between purity and power played out in the second pentecostal generation.[23] McPherson by and large questioned neither the cultural taboos of most first-generation pentecostals nor the "old time faith" that marked the evangelical rhetoric of the earlier sectarianism. At the same time, she saw and took opportunities to "market" the gospel using cutting-edge technology and to make an impact in the wider American culture through a theological reinterpretation that brought patriotism together with pentecostal spirituality (especially during the years leading up to and including World War II). So alongside the ongoing defense of Prohibition, McPherson cautiously interacted with organized labor parties; championed the rights of the poor; campaigned against the "evils" of socialism, communism, and fascism; was concerned about public education as well as with the well-being of American institutions of higher education; mobilized her church and constituency in support of the war effort; and intentionally "linked religious revival to political and social reform."[24] As these were all

21. Grant Wacker, *Heaven Below: Early Pentecostals and American Culture* (Cambridge, MA, and London: Harvard University Press, 2001), p. 198.

22. Wacker, *Heaven Below*, 205. As discussed further in Grant Wacker, "Living with Signs and Wonders: Parents and Children in Early Pentecostal Culture," in Kate Cooper and Jeremy Gregory, eds., *Signs, Wonders, Miracles: Representations of Divine Power in the Life of the Church* (Suffolk, UK, and Rochester, NY: Ecclesiastical History Society and Boydell Press, 2005), pp. 423-42, pentecostal radicalism led to extraordinary commitments to world evangelization that included, in some cases, the abandonment of their children "for the sake of the gospel," even while pentecostal pragmatism led the vast majority to a this-worldly focus on the proper education and training of the younger generation so that they would not have to struggle with the challenges of their parents.

23. This is the thesis of Matthew Avery Sutton, *Aimee Semple McPherson and the Resurrection of Christian America* (Cambridge, MA, and London: Harvard University Press, 2007).

24. Sutton, *Aimee Semple McPherson*, p. 215.

conscientious efforts on her part to "Christianize" America,[25] they required a shift in emphasis from holiness understood as purification to that viewed as vocational — even evangelical and missionary — consecration. McPherson was on an intentional quest for what could be called a pentecostal politics of holiness.

McPherson's journey, and that of her church's, anticipated developments in the larger classical pentecostal movement. The Assemblies of God (AOG), for example, also experienced upward social mobility during its second and third generations. While one might view the church's increasing bureaucratization, routinization, and institutionalization as inevitable by-products of its transitions toward cultural respectability,[26] such developments can also be understood in terms of the movement's missionary adaptation to the middle-class demographics of the second half of the twentieth century.[27] Along with that, necessary adjustments to the various civil rights movements of the 1960s, the charismatic renewal of the 1970s, and the growing Hispanic and African American population within its ranks — all of these combined to lead the AOG to intentionally engage ecumenical and cultural trends in order to maintain an effective missionary and evangelistic presence. In short, the earlier, counter-cultural and individualistic ethic of holiness has morphed during the general movement of upward mobility and expanded into a more socially engaged and reformist politics of holiness.[28]

Against this backdrop, the fortunes of the African American pentecostal churches in North America can be seen, at least in part, as a search for a sanctified politics. The "sanctified church," as it has been called, refers to a dazzling array of Baptist, Methodist, holiness, and pentecostal churches as these have developed in the black church tradition.[29] Both the themes of holiness as cleansing and holiness as consecration are evidenced in the sanctified church as well.[30] The title of Cheryl Sanders's book on the sanctified church, *Saints in*

25. Sutton, *Aimee Semple McPherson*, p. 212.

26. Margaret M. Poloma, *The Assemblies of God at the Crossroads: Charisma and Institutional Dilemmas* (Knoxville: University of Tennessee Press, 1989).

27. Thus, Edith L. Blumhofer, *Restoring the Faith: The Assemblies of God, Pentecostalism, and American Culture* (Urbana and Chicago: University of Illinois Press, 1993), chap. 11.

28. Jane Harris, "Holiness and Pentecostal Traditions: Making the Spirit Count," in William D. Lindsey and Mark Silk, eds., *Religion and Public Life in the Southern Crossroads: Showdown States* (Walnut Creek, CA: AltaMira Press, 2005), pp. 79-102, esp. p. 97.

29. For an overview, see Zora Neale Hurston, *The Sanctified Church* (Berkeley, CA: Turtle Island, 1981).

30. For an overview of how the sanctified church has interfaced concretely with the political, see David D. Daniels III, "'Doing All the Good We Can': The Political Witness of African American Holiness and Pentecostal Churches in the Post–Civil Rights Era," in R. Drew Smith,

Exile, suggests that one way to consider the Afropentecostal tradition is as being in search of an exilic politics of holiness.[31]

In Sanders's account, pentecostalism emerged, under the leadership of the son of a slave, William J. Seymour, as an implicitly reformist movement resistant toward the racial, sexist, and classist barriers confronting southern holiness believers at the turn of the twentieth century. Hence the liturgy of the sanctified church has long encoded a discourse of counter-cultural resistance, rebellion, and reform, not only in terms of the songs that were sung, but also in terms of the musical styles that were adopted, the rhetorical tropes (of preaching) that were deployed, and the embodied forms that were enacted. As a result, however, the sanctified church can be understood as having existed outside the mainstream — even in exile — rejected not only by the dominant culture (because of race and class), but also by both sides of the ecclesial world within which it had one foot: the white churches, including white pentecostalism, because of race, and the black mainline churches, because of class.[32]

Interestingly, Sanders suggests that the future "homecoming" of the sanctified church may be intimated in the emerging forms of gospel music.[33] The gospel song is, for the sanctified church, a "future-giving memory" that binds the eschatological hope of redemption together with the past promises of the biblical narrative. This discussion ties in with Sanders's astute analyses of how gospel music in all its genres (the spirituals, the blues, jazz, soul music, rap, etc.) has both been a gift of the sanctified church (in its participation in the wider black church tradition) to the wider culture and a mode of cultural accommodation at the same time.[34] Arguably, the evolution of gospel music

---

ed., *New Day Begun: African American Churches and Civic Culture in Post–Civil Rights America* (Durham, NC, and London: Duke University Press, 2003), pp. 164-82.

31. Cheryl J. Sanders, *Saints in Exile: The Holiness-Pentecostal Experience in African American Religion and Culture* (New York and Oxford: Oxford University Press, 1996). I have previously discussed Sanders's work in my essay, "Justice Deprived, Justice Demanded: Afropentecostalisms and the Task of World Pentecostal Theology Today," *Journal of Pentecostal Theology* 15, no. 1 (2006): 127-47; cf. also Yong, *The Spirit Poured Out on All Flesh,* pp. 72-79.

32. See also David D. Daniels III, "Navigating the Territory: Early Afropentecostalism as a Movement within Black Civil Society," in Amos Yong and Estrelda Y. Alexander, eds., *Afropentecostalism : The Changing Discourses of Black Pentecostal and Charismatic Christianity* (New York: New York University Press, forthcoming).

33. Sanders, *Saints in Exile,* pp. 149-50.

34. See also Teresa L. Reed, *The Holy Profane: Religion in Black Popular Music* (Lexington: University Press of Kentucky, 2003), chap. 1; cf. Jerma Jackson, "Sister Rosetta Tharpe and the Evolution of Gospel Music," in Beth Barton Schweiger and Donald G. Mathews, eds., *Religion in the American South: Protestants and Others in History and Culture* (Chapel Hill and London: University of North Carolina Press, 2004), pp. 219-81, and Louis B. Gallien Jr., "Crossing Over

reflects the challenges encountered by sanctified churches when holiness is understood in terms of vocational consecration, and such commitments elicit a direct engagement with the wider culture.[35]

As important, however, is that the sanctified church's expression of gospel music also provides a window into what Sanders calls the sanctified aesthetic.[36] Worshiping the Lord "in the beauty of holiness" (Pss. 29:2; 96:9) involves not only the holy dance and shout, congregational affirmations of "Yes, Lord!" and call-and-response interactions between the preacher, the organist, and the congregation, but also the ecstatic forms of being possessed, slain, and filled with the Spirit, the active modes of tarrying in and for the Spirit, and the melodious and harmonious activities of singing in the Spirit. When we further observe that sanctified worship is offered (in the Sunday service context) in a specific style of sanctified (Sunday) dress,[37] we note that the sanctified aesthetic is embodied, kinesthetic, and participatory. In other words, Afropentecostal versions of "having Church" enabled congregational participation in the divine beauty as expressed in the church's worship, even as these activities sustained ongoing projects of resistance to the oppressiveness of the dominant culture as well as of engagements with the opportunities afforded by upward mobility in the world.[38]

In short, developments in the African American pentecostal tradition paralleled what was happening in the white pentecostal churches. In both movements, there was a sustained quest for personal holiness that was nurtured in their respective liturgies; but these quests were stretched as members found themselves crossing over into, confronting, or engaging the dominant culture. The question repeatedly posed was whether upward social mobility would come at the cost of cultural accommodation — in which case, would the sanctified politics of holiness pentecostalism be compromised by the *Realpolitik* of the world?[39]

Jordan: Navigating the Music of Heavenly Bliss and Earthly Desire in the Lives and Careers of Three 20th Century African American Holiness-Pentecostal 'Cross-over' Artists," in Yong and Alexander, eds., *Afropentecostalism*.

35. See also Anthea D. Butler, *Women in the Church of God in Christ: Making a Sanctified World* (Chapel Hill: University of North Carolina Press, 2007), esp. chap. 6, for an account of how sanctified women navigated the path from personal holiness focused on motherhood, the home, and the family to a more politically engaged holiness expressed in the civil society.

36. Sanders, *Saints in Exile*, chap. 3.

37. Butler, *Women in the Church of God in Christ*, pp. 77-86.

38. For further ethnographic description of such workings in the black church tradition, see Frances Kostarelos, *Feeling the Spirit: Faith and Hope in an Evangelical Black Storefront Church* (Columbia: University of South Carolina Press, 1995).

39. From here on, references to "holiness pentecostalism" are not limited to the specific

5.1.3. *Global Pentecostal Cultures: Consecration, Mission, and the Quest for a Sanctified Aesthetics*

When expanded onto the global stage, both tracks of holiness as purification and holiness as consecration have been registered in the pentecostal encounter with culture. I now want to focus primarily on the latter as that opens up more directly to questions regarding theology of culture. In what follows, we will see how holiness as consecration motivated pentecostal mission efforts in terms of indigenization and the use of communications technologies.

From the beginning of the pentecostal movement, Western pentecostal missionaries have struggled with the challenge of "translating" the pentecostal message into locales in the global south. While we will explore the various issues in greater depth in the following chapter (see 6.1.2-3), suffice it to say at this juncture that the results have been mixed: from the kinds of sectarian opposition to and rejection of indigenous cultures and especially religious traditions (cf. 1.3.1 and 4.1.1) on the one hand to a very cautious approach to contextualization on the other. Not surprisingly, more tentative steps toward contextualization are taken when missionaries remain in control as compared to when indigenous leaders take the reins. In some cases, local pentecostal leadership has not only infused a more intense form of pentecostal spirituality than was introduced by the missionaries, but also, as in the case of the 'Weenhayek pentecostals of southern Bolivia, has begun to use the Bible for nativist purposes, to defend cultural continuity and traditional Amerindian values against Western encroachments and the development projects threatening their indigenous ways of life.[40]

---

pentecostal holiness churches or denominations derived primarily from the American South, but are understood more inclusively to refer to pentecostalism understood as a subset of the holiness tradition; similarly, references henceforth to the "sanctified church" will not be limited to the specific Afropentecostal movement, but will be synonymous with pentecostalism as a whole, albeit highlighting its holiness dimensions.

40. Jan-Åke Alvarsson, "True Pentecostals or True Amerindians — or Both? Religious Identity among the 'Weenhayek Indians of Southern Bolivia," in Jan-Åke Alvarsson and Rita Laura Segato, eds., *Religions in Transition: Mobility, Merging and Globalization in the Emergence of Contemporary Religious Adhesions* (Uppsala: Acta Universitatis Upsaliensis, 2003), pp. 209-52; "The Ethnified Gospel — The Christian Message as Presented by 'Weenhayek Preachers," in Jan-Åke Alvarsson, ed., *The Missionary Process,* Studia Missionalia Svecana 49 (Uppsala: Swedish Institute of Mission Research, 2005), pp. 169-208; and "Traditional Amerindian Religion: In the Eyes of an Indigenous Pentecostal Church," in David Westerlund, ed., *Global Pentecostalism: Encounters with Other Religious Traditions,* Library of Modern Religion 14 (London and New York: I. B. Tauris, 2009), pp. 277-93.

One way to interpret such indigenous expressions of pentecostal embrace of culture is to see them as outworkings of the notion of holiness understood in terms of consecration for mission. Pentecostal spirituality is in no sense compromised; yet what is accomplished is the sense of rendering pentecostal piety compatible with indigenous forms of life. Such a view illuminates similar approaches to culture that have been documented among the Maya pentecostals in Guatemala.[41] While it would be going too far to say that Maya pentecostals have valorized their history and culture, their own agenda to evangelize their fellow Guatemalan and central American neighbors has been "predicated on the notion that God had a plan to redeem the nation's deep, historical suffering by pouring out his specific and unique blessings on Guatemala and its people per se."[42] So whereas non-pentecostal evangelicals had shunned indigenous practices and artifacts with religious significance, pentecostals began reinterpreting their newfound faith in terms of their indigenous worldview — "from Pentecostal *acciones de gracias,* prayer services held at the planting and harvest of corn, to the faith healing *(sanación)* that provides an analog to ancient shamanic practices associated with fertility, illness, and mental problems. Even the common phrase used by Maya Pentecostals, *camino cristiano,* while resonant with Christian imagery, is also rich with Mayan religious symbolism of journey, crossroads, and the divine 'white path' of the cosmos."[43]

Such local adaptation of pentecostal spirituality has long been a hallmark of the emerging global pentecostalism. If world cultures both homogenize local cultures but also introduce local particularities into global consciousness, then pentecostalism's concurrent affirmation of indigenous cultures (at least in some respects) and absorption of them into a more global frame of reference suggests that it also has emerged as one among other competing global cultures.[44] In Karla Poewe's terms, pentecostalism is now a global culture "because it transcends national, ethnic, racial, and class bound-

41. Virginia Garrard-Burnett, "'God Was Already Here When Columbus Arrived': Inculturation Theology and the Mayan Movement in Guatemala," in Edward L. Cleary and Timothy J. Steigenga, eds., *Resurgent Voices in Latin America: Indigenous Peoples, Political Mobilization, and Religious Change* (New Brunswick, NJ, and London: Rutgers University Press, 2004), pp. 125-53.

42. Garrard-Burnett, "'God Was Already Here When Columbus Arrived,'" p. 144.

43. Garrard-Burnett, "'God Was Already Here When Columbus Arrived,'" p. 145. For discussion of how the process of indigenization was negotiated by pentecostals in Puerto Rico, see Samuel Cruz, *Masked Africanisms: Puerto Rican Pentecostalisms* (Dubuque, IA: Kendall/Hunt, 2005).

44. Frank J. Lechner and John Boli, *World Culture: Origins and Consequences* (Malden, MA: Blackwell, 2005), esp. chap. 7.

aries"; but more than that, pentecostal-charismatic Christianity is a global culture "because it is experiential, idealistic, biblical, and oppositional. Being experiential, it is not tied to any specific doctrine nor denomination. Being idealistic, it embraces the whole person and the whole world. . . . Being biblical, it places the 'Word' above politician, government, or any other worldly authority. Being oppositional, it is always potentially in tension with the establishment, which includes church, government, university, ethnic, class, and racial structures."[45] I would add, further, that pentecostalism is global precisely because its understanding of holiness as consecration maps onto the Great Commission to make disciples of all nations and to take the gospel to the *ends* of the earth (Acts 1:8).[46]

Yet what is the means toward pentecostalism as global culture? Among other tools, pentecostals have perennially utilized new developments in media technologies to further the mission and expansion of the church. The earliest pentecostals were on the radio blanketing the airwaves with the gospel for the masses while refining a public face presentable to mass culture.[47] Then, while their "holiness as purification" cousins continued to reject television, the "holiness as consecration" pentecostals developed successively more sophisticated forms of TV ministries over time.[48] Gradually, pentecostals have also adopted the media of filmmaking and cinema,[49] no doubt in part now "sanctified" by the fact that an increasing number of pentecostals were congregating in abandoned theaters, redeeming these "corrupt" spaces for the sake of the gospel. All the while, local congregations in more conventional church buildings around the world continued to adapt, employing state-of-the-art sound equipment, video cameras, projection screens, and other new technologies. The result is the dynamic pentecostal worship characterized by the convergence of raw kinesthetic movements — e.g., singing, hand-clapping, dancing, swaying, etc. — and energy unleashed by the new electronic media that are "translatable" on every continent.[50]

45. Karla Poewe, ed., *Charismatic Christianity as a Global Culture* (Columbia: University of South Carolina Press, 1994), p. xii.

46. See Murray W. Dempster, Byron D. Klaus, and Douglas Petersen, eds., *The Globalization of Pentecostalism: A Religion Made to Travel* (Irvine, CA, and Oxford: Regnum, 1999).

47. Benjamin A. Wagner, "'Full Gospel' Radio: Revivaltime and the Pentecostal Uses of Mass Media, 1950-1979," *Fides et Historia* 35, no. 1 (2003): 107-22.

48. See David Edwin Harrell, "Pentecost at Prime Time: Early Religious TV Presented Huge Challenges, Which Pentecostals Met Better Than Most," *Christian History* 49 (1996): 52-54.

49. See Ben Armstrong, *The Electric Church* (Nashville: Thomas Nelson, 1979), chap. 7, and Bill J. Leonard, "The Electric Church: An Interpretive Essay," *Review and Expositor* 81, no. 1 (1984): 43-57.

50. Simon Coleman, *The Globalization of Charismatic Christianity: Spreading the Gospel*

These ventures with the various communications technologies represent pentecostal engagement with culture as a result of its self-understanding regarding a sanctified vocation. The results, developed over time, highlight three aspects of pentecostalism as global culture.[51] First, the globalization of pentecostalism remains at the same time its ongoing permutation as local cultures are absorbed; this is the process of "glocalization," whereby the global becomes local even as the local enriches the global, albeit in different respects. Second, culture is understood instrumentally, as a means toward an end — usually considered in terms of the evangelization of the world. In other words, the various communicative technologies are a medium for the carrying out of the Great Commission, and the sanctified church is now producing a material and media culture utilizing a dynamic aesthetics that is capable of registering across multiple sites of a globalizing world.[52] Finally, and most distinctively about pentecostalism as global culture, is the transmutation of pentecostal spirituality by the different communicative technologies. Thus the embodied, affective, and kinesthetic dimensions of pentecostal worship and piety are mediated now through the radio, TV, and cinematic instruments. What happens, though, is not just a "secularization" of the receiving or local environments but the "sacralization" of such spaces. The result is that the power of God remains present to save, to heal, and to transform lives, whether that involves touching the radio, kneeling before the TV set, or stretching forth one's hands toward the big screen during the "altar call" that appears at the end of the film. In short, the distinctive form of pentecostal sacramentality, with its locus primarily in the sanctified body,[53] is now mediated through the technological mechanisms adapted by a sanctified aesthetics.

Of course, none of the above is meant to either ignore or dismiss the valid criticisms that have been leveled against pentecostal appropriations of

---

of Prosperity, Cambridge Studies in Ideology and Religion 12 (Cambridge: Cambridge University Press, 2000), esp. chap. 7.

51. The following derives from, among other sources, J. Kwabena Asamoah-Gyadu, "Anointing through the Screen: Neo-Pentecostalism and Televised Christianity in Ghana," *Studies in World Christianity* 11, no. 1 (2005): 9-28; Rosalind I. J. Hackett, "Charismatic/Pentecostal Appropriation of Media Technologies in Nigeria and Ghana," *Journal of Religion in Africa* 28, no. 3 (1998): 258-77; and Manuel A. Vásquez and Marie Friedmann Marquardt, *Globalizing the Sacred: Religion across the Americas* (New Brunswick, NJ, and London: Rutgers University Press, 2003), chap. 8.

52. See the discussion of "Aesthetics: From Iconography to Architecture," in Coleman, *The Globalization of Charismatic Christianity,* chap. 6.

53. See Frank D. Macchia, "Tongues as a Sign: Towards a Sacramental Understanding of Pentecostal Experience," *PNEUMA: The Journal of the Society for Pentecostal Studies* 15, no. 1 (1993): 61-76.

the mass media.[54] There are not only concerns about the subtle ways in which Western ideologies and political agendas are communicated, but also criticisms that the medium has compromised the message and that in the global pentecostal context, these diverse media contribute to and perpetuate the consumerism of Western culture, particularly in the form of the prosperity gospel. We will return later to take up especially the challenges posed by prosperity theology (chapter 7), but meanwhile, the confrontation between holiness pentecostalism and the mass media raises profound theological questions for the movement. But part of the problem is that in many ways, pentecostal scholars and theologians may still not be ready to grapple deeply with the issues. So on the one hand, the emergence of global and even glocal pentecostalism can be said to be bringing about a cultural revolution, but on the other hand, pentecostals have not taken time to formulate a theology of culture. Further, global pentecostalism can be said to have, to a large degree, baptized the mass media for the stated purpose of world evangelization, but pentecostals have yet to develop either a theology of the communicative arts or a theology of the electronic media. Finally, pentecostals may be constructing larger and larger buildings as the number of their megachurches continues to increase, but their puritanical approach to images, architecture, and the arts — informed by their having inherited the iconoclastic legacy of the Protestant Reformers — means that they have so far not intentionally sought to think theologically about their aesthetic intuitions.[55]

In short, holiness pentecostals have been of two hearts and minds about culture: a sectarian side that claims to reject the world, and a mission-driven side that seeks to reform and transform society. This unique combination, however, has produced a sanctified church that has perennially been in quest of a sanctified politics and a viable theology of culture. Perhaps one way forward might be the exploration of a sanctified aesthetics, or theology of the arts, broadly conceived. To whom might pentecostals turn for dialogue about all of these matters?

54. The most sustained and critical analysis so far, even if ideologically tainted, is Pradip Ninan Thomas, *Strong Religion, Zealous Media: Christian Fundamentalism and Communication in India* (New Delhi, London, and Thousand Oaks, CA: SAGE, 2008).

55. These various elements are discussed in David Lehmann, *Struggle for the Spirit: Religious Transformation and Popular Culture in Brazil and Latin America* (Cambridge, UK: Polity Press, and Cambridge, MA: Blackwell, 1996), pp. 163-88.

5.2. Political Theologies Post-Christendom: Contemporary Models

I now wish to introduce into the discussion three perspectives on political theology and theology of culture that can be loosely categorized together under the label of "post-Constantinian theologies": John Howard Yoder, Stanley Hauerwas, and leading thinkers of the New Monasticism. Each of these, in its own way, has called for the church to adopt a post-Constantinian or post-Christendom identity, one that disavows any attempt to attain or retain political control of the public square. Simultaneously, however, each has also advocated for the church's engagement with the wider culture and society, albeit on the church's own terms as a sanctified community. In the following discussion, we will explore how Yoder, Hauerwas, and the New Monastic theologians all wrestle with the tension of being set apart from the world and yet making a difference to the world — of embracing both a holiness of purification and a holiness of consecration, to use pentecostal holiness terms — and what that has meant for their respective theologies of culture.

5.2.1. The Politics of Diaspora: The Radical Reformation in a Post-Constantinian World

We have already had the opportunity to mention aspects of John Howard Yoder's political ecclesiology (2.3.2, 4.2.2). As a Mennonite theologian, Yoder is located within the broader Anabaptist tradition with roots in the Radical Reformation. Central to Anabaptism from its beginnings has been the rejection of any collusion with the state.[56] Yoder and other theologians in this tradition have since come to characterize the dominant church-state model as it had existed from the fourth century through the early modern period as the "Constantinian captivity" of the church.[57] There are at least four aspects to

---

56. See Gerald Biesecker-Mast, "Critique and Subjection in Anabaptist Political Witness," in Nathan E. Yoder and Carol A. Scheppard, eds., *Exiles in the Empire: Believers Church Perspectives on Politics*, Studies in the Believers Church Tradition 5 (Kitchener, ON: Pandora Press, 2006), pp. 45-59.

57. John Howard Yoder, *The Priestly Kingdom: Social Ethics as Gospel* (Notre Dame: University of Notre Dame Press, 1984), chap. 7. For an overview, see also Thomas Heilke, "Yoder's Idea of Constantinianism: An Analytical Framework Toward Conversation," in Ben C. Ollenburger and Gayle Gerber Koontz, eds., *A Mind Patient and Untamed: Assessing John Howard Yoder's Contributions to Theology, Ethics, and Peacemaking* (Telford, PA: Cascadia, and Scottdale, PA: Herald Press, 2004), pp. 89-126.

this claim. Politically, the church was co-opted by the state so that even when the church was in control, its *modus operandi* was dictated by political exigencies rather than by the gospel. Socially, the church was relocated to the center of society rather than capable of speaking prophetically from the margins. Ethically, the church's way of life was accommodated to the mores and value system(s) of the dominant culture rather than living out the distinctive ways of Jesus. And, finally, theologically, the church's self-understanding was increasingly measured by the logic of the public square rather than by its own sources and practices. The result was a collapse of the distinction between the church and the world.

How should the church respond? Yoder has unceasingly defended the Anabaptist stance of insisting on a Free or Believers Church. The key here is not so much the emphasis on adult baptism (as opposed to infant baptism) but the understanding that the church is a voluntary society that depends on a conversion experience and a community of like-minded individuals who are committed to the distinctive ways of Jesus. This is precisely what allows the Free Church to be a contrast society to the dominant culture and to be a political force even without being engaged in the *Realpolitik* of the world. As Yoder spelled out in his now classic book, *The Politics of Jesus*,[58] the way of Christ did not lead to political quietism but rather to political radicalism, precisely in and through the church's living out the Jubilee economics of sharing and liberation, the nonviolent politics of forgiveness and reconciliation, and the prophetic mysticism of peace and justice. The way of Jesus was thus neither political, as conventionally construed, nor sectarian, as sociologically defined in terms of a withdrawal from the world; rather, the church was most politically radical when it did not ape the ways of the world but instead lived out of its innermost convictions as "an alternative social group."[59]

Yoder's Anabaptist hermeneutic led him to see the Free Church tradition as modeled after that of the Jewish experience in at least three ways.[60] First, the Jews were called by God to be his unique representatives and witnesses who were within but also set apart from the world; similarly, the Free Church's witness will remain uncompromised only when it is in but not of the world. Second, although the Jews continually apostatized in their empire-building en-

58. John Howard Yoder, *The Politics of Jesus* (Grand Rapids: Eerdmans, 1972).

59. Yoder, *The Politics of Jesus*, p. 111. As Craig Carter notes, when understood in this way, it is Constantinianism that is sectarian in terms of rejecting as "sects" all who did not buy in to the policies of empire; see Craig A. Carter, *The Politics of the Cross: The Theology and Ethics of John Howard Yoder* (Grand Rapids: Brazos Press, 2001), p. 175.

60. John Howard Yoder, *The Jewish-Christian Schism Revisited*, eds. Michael G. Cartwright and Peter Ochs (Grand Rapids and Cambridge, UK: Eerdmans, 2003).

deavors, God's continual response was to disperse them among the nations —
e.g., from the Tower of Babel, and through the Babylonian captivity — precisely in order that they might be liberated from the tentacles of centralized
power and free to witness to the truth from the margins; similarly, the Free
Church tradition can be understood as breaking from the Constantinian mold
in order to retrieve the early Christian practices that resisted the *Pax Romana*
of its time and to reappropriate them for life on the margins of the modern
world.[61] Finally, then, the Jews in exile were called to "seek the welfare of the
city where I have sent you into exile, and pray to the Lord on its behalf, for in
its welfare you will find your welfare" (Jer. 29:7); similarly, the Free Church is
called not to withdraw from the world but to work for the welfare of the world
through instantiation of the distinctive practices of Jesus.

From this, Yoder has developed what might be called a politics of diaspora or an exilic politics.[62] He identified diasporic existence not only as due
to divine graciousness — in not allowing for the people of God to settle into a
comfortable accommodation with the powers of the world — but also as normative for the life of the covenant people. Life in exile allows for the people of
God to maintain their true vocation: that of bearing witness to another way
of being in the world. Here, Yoder's discussion of the Jewish experience in
Babylon deserves to be quoted at length:

> When Jews in Babylon participated creatively, reliably, but not coercively
> in the welfare of that host culture, their contribution was more serious
> than "bricolage." There was no problem of shared meanings, since they
> had accepted their host culture and become fluent in it. Their own loyalty
> to their own culture (*kashrut*, anikonic monotheism, honouring parents,
> truth-telling, work ethic, circumcision) was not dependent on whether
> the Babylonians accepted it, yet much of it was not only transparent but
> attractive to Gentiles. . . . The surrounding Gentile culture had become
> their element. The polyglot Jews were more at home in any imperial capi-
> tal, more creative and more needed, than were the monolingual native
> peasants and proletarians (and priests and princes) in that same city.[63]

61. The essays in John Howard Yoder, *For the Nations: Essays Evangelical and Public*
(Grand Rapids and Cambridge, UK: Eerdmans, 1997), argue this point from different angles.
62. See Yoder, *For the Nations,* chap. 3, and *The Jewish-Christian Schism Revisited,* chap. 10.
63. Yoder, *The Jewish-Christian Schism Revisited,* p. 193. The mention of "bricolage" registers the concerns of those who think that postmodern "conversations" across cultures remain
on the surface due to the incommensurabilities between cultural-linguistic forms of life; Yoder
acknowledges the disparateness of the many cultures but thinks that genuine cross-cultural interactions are possible — I agree and will make my argument later in this chapter.

Hence the Jewish witness was most effective when the distinctiveness of their way of life was not compromised even while their commitments to promote the welfare of their host city were evident.[64]

Not surprisingly, then, Yoder rejected the classic fivefold model of Christ in relationship to culture as proposed by H. Richard Niebuhr.[65] The problem was that Niebuhr's proposal both took for granted the pre-existing disjunction of Christ *and* culture and presumed an individualistic framework for responding to this situation.[66] Instead, the church should be understood to function as its own sociological and cultural entity through which it bears witness to an alternative way of life. In this case, the church does not respond to the wider culture but is itself a cultural way of being.[67]

From a pentecostal holiness perspective, Yoder's politics of diaspora reflects both a sanctification *from* the ways of world but also a consecration *to* a vocational engagement with the world.[68] On the one hand, there is the insistence on remaining distinct and set apart from the world, even while on the other, there is a commitment to seek the welfare and peace of the earthly city from its margins. This position of marginality is important, especially since

64. For further explications of the shape of an exilic politics, see, in the Anabaptist tradition, Alain Epp Weaver, *States of Exile: Visions of Diaspora, Witness, and Return* (Waterloo, ON, and Scottdale, PA: Herald Press, 2008), and, in dialogue with Yoder, Nathan Kerr, *Christ, History and Apocalyptic: The Politics of Christian Missions,* Theopolitical Visions 2 (Eugene, OR: Cascade Books, 2009), chap. 6.

65. H. Richard Niebuhr, *Christ and Culture* (1951; reprint, New York: Harper & Brothers/ Torchlight, 1956), set forth five models: Christ against culture (an inadequate position seen in the colonial enterprise); Christ of culture (an accommodationist approach as found in the emergence of Christian Gnosticism in second century and the "culture-Protestantism" of the late nineteenth century); Christ above culture (the synthesis of Christendom); Christ and culture in paradox (a dualist position as seen in Paul, Marcion, Luther, etc.); and Christ transforming culture (which Niebuhr himself advocated following Augustine and F. D. Maurice). Niebuhr himself granted in conclusion that each of these positions was viable depending on different socio-historical situations.

66. See Yoder's "How H. Richard Niebuhr Reasoned: A Critique of *Christ and Culture,*" in Glen H. Stassen, D. M. Yeager, and John Howard Yoder, *Authentic Transformation: A New Vision of Christ and Culture* (Nashville: Abingdon, 1996), pp. 31-89.

67. In this case, the goal is not to find ways to relate Christ and culture, which are always already related, but to "follow faithfully Christ's example and be obedient to his will in the midst of their [our] cultural milieu"; Stephen B. Wilson, "Christ and Cult(ure): Some Preliminary Reflections on Liturgy and Life," *Liturgical Ministry* 12 (2003): 177-87, quote from p. 185.

68. Yoder's position is not immune to criticism — e.g., even from within his own Anabaptist tradition, as in A. James Reimer, "Mennonites, Christ, and Culture: The Yoder Legacy," *The Conrad Grebel Review* 16, no. 2 (1998): 5-14 — but my first and foremost goal is to draw from him into my project on pentecostalism and political theology. For this reason, mine is a charitable and sympathetic reading of Yoder rather than a critical one.

the Constantinian seduction would continually tempt Christians to aspire toward the power structures at the center, and this would result in a blurring of the lines between the church and society (as happened with the Christendom project). However, Christian communities needed to firmly resist "being in charge" so as not to compromise their distinctive witness.[69] Simultaneously, marginality does not mean sectarian withdrawal, but rather requires what might be called a sanctified mode of engaging the world. Thus for Yoder, the distinctive Christian practices like binding/loosing in prayer, breaking bread and sharing together, baptism (understood as the formation/creation of a new community), the relativizing of the priestly hierarchy, and the empowerment of all the people of God — all of these "can be translated into non-religious terms. The multiplicity of gifts is a model for the empowerment of the humble and for the end of hierarchy in social process. Dialogue under the Holy Spirit is the ground floor of the notion of democracy."[70] Thus it is possible to be set apart from the world, but yet to be engaged and in dialogue with, and servants of, those outside the community of faith.[71]

5.2.2. A Sectarian Politics? The Colony of Resident Aliens Post-Christendom

Yoder's work has served as a stimulus for Stanley Hauerwas's thinking, as Hauerwas himself has readily acknowledged.[72] Of course, there are differences between the two, such as Yoder being a member of a more marginal (Mennonite) Christian community and Hauerwas being part of the "mainline," which perhaps explains his more liturgical sensibilities. These ecclesial locations may also explain why Yoder thinks a pluralistic society opens up space for minority voices while Hauerwas thinks that pluralism leads to the illusion of modern liberalism's mantra regarding freedom of choice. Part of

69. Yoder, *The Jewish-Christian Schism Revisited*, chap. 9, titled, "On Not Being in Charge."

70. John Howard Yoder, *Body Politics: Five Practices of the Christian Community before the Watching World* (1992; reprint, Scottdale, PA: Herald Press, 2001), p. 72.

71. See also John Howard Yoder, *The Royal Priesthood: Essays Ecclesiological and Ecumenical,* ed. Michael G. Cartwright (1994; reprint, Scottdale, PA, and Waterloo, ON: Herald Press, 1998), pp. 242-61, for an argument for Yoder's Radical Reformation ad hoc approach to interfaith encounter.

72. One result of this indebtedness is the festschrift edited by Hauerwas with Harry J. Huebner and Chris K. Huebner, titled, *The Wisdom of the Cross: Essays in Honor of John Howard Yoder* (Grand Rapids: Eerdmans, 1999).

the result is that Yoder is more receptive of the idea of the "translatability" of Christian discourse into other "tongues," while Hauerwas tends to think more in terms of the incommensurability of discourses.[73]

It is impossible to adequately overview Hauerwas's vast and ever-increasing corpus, so what follows is a very selective reading of the Hauerwasian *oeuvre* focused on his idea of the church as colony, and what that means for a theology of culture. In two books jointly written with William Willimon, Hauerwas the theological ethicist has expanded Yoder's exilic politics and ecclesiology in the direction of thinking about the members of the church as "resident aliens" in the world.[74] For Hauerwas the church is a colony in the sense that "A colony is a beachhead, an outpost, an island of one culture in the middle of another, a place where the values of home are reiterated and passed on to the young, a place where the distinctive language and life-style of the resident aliens are lovingly nurtured and reinforced."[75] The church in this framework does not *have* a social strategy but *is* a social strategy, with its primary political task and responsibility being "to worship Christ in all things" and to "be odd."[76] Yet resident aliens are not sectarians — if such is defined sociologically as that form of religious life that evolves later on into a fully fledged church type — but specially trained to embody their stories and engage the world. Such engagement, however, occurs not on the world's terms, but as defined by exemplary saints. So where those in the world are surrounded by enemies and respond violently, resident aliens respond through loving, forgiving, and serving their enemies. These "alien" postures and practices have been formed by the normative Christian life of baptism, confession, eucharistic prayer, faithfulness, obedience, suffering, fasting, holiness, truth telling, worship, friendship, giving to the poor, homelessness, sexual fidelity, witness, and even martyrdom.

If Yoder the Anabaptist is reacting to the "Constantinian captivity" of the church, Hauerwas the ethicist is reacting also to modern liberalism's insis-

---

73. For further discussion of some of these comparisons and contrasts, see Craig R. Hovey, "The Public Ethics of John Howard Yoder and Stanley Hauerwas: Difference or Disagreement?" in Ben C. Ollenburger and Gayle Gerber Koontz, eds., *A Mind Patient and Untamed: Assessing John Howard Yoder's Contributions to Theology, Ethics, and Peacemaking* (Telford, PA: Cascadia, and Scottdale, PA: Herald Press, 2004), pp. 205-45.

74. Stanley Hauerwas and William H. Willimon, *Resident Aliens: Life in the Christian Colony* (Nashville: Abingdon, 1989), and Stanley Hauerwas and William H. Willimon, *Where Resident Aliens Live: Exercises for Christian Practice* (Nashville: Abingdon, 1996).

75. Hauerwas and Willimon, *Resident Aliens*, p. 12.

76. Hauerwas and Willimon, *Resident Aliens*, p. 45, and Hauerwas and Willimon, *Where Resident Aliens Live*, pp. 61-66.

tence on an objective, universal rationality to which all religious positions must finally submit, and to the modern church's assumption of this perspective as a leftover from the Christendom paradigm.[77] For Hauerwas, however, the result was both the privatization of the church in terms of its practices and convictions being reserved only for Christians, and the blurring of the lines between church and state so that Christian patriotism could only be demonstrated through the church's underwriting of the violence of the modern state.[78] The proper response should be to reject the foundationalist temptation as that will transform the church's resident aliens into being centrist citizens, and to reclaim instead the gospel narrative as that has been preserved in the practices of the church insofar as these have set the church apart from the world. In other words, the call to life in the Christian colony cannot be justified on universal grounds but rests on the attractiveness of resident-alien forms of life. As Hauerwas says, Christians are "required to be nothing less than a sanctified people of peace who can live the life of the forgiven. Their sanctification is not meant to sustain the judgment that they are 'better' than non-Christians, but rather that they are charged to be faithful to God's calling of them as foretaste of the kingdom. In this sense, sanctification is a life of service and sacrifice that the world cannot account for on its own grounds."[79]

From this it is clear that Hauerwas's vision of the Christian colony presumes the Christian doctrine of sanctification and promotes what might be called a politics of holiness.[80] Yet Hauerwas is no mere defender of a legalistic moralism, as he rejects any individualistic construal of holiness as incapable of warding off the heresy of Pelagianism (whereby good deeds are effectively understood as meritorious and holiness is seen as what human beings achieve instead of what God accomplishes). Instead, holiness is about being "made part of a body that makes it impossible for us to be anything other than disci-

77. This is a dominant theme running through a number of Hauerwas's collections of essays and books — e.g., Stanley Hauerwas, *After Christendom? How the Church Is to Behave If Freedom, Justice, and a Christian Nation Are Bad Ideas* (Nashville: Abingdon, 1991); *Dispatches from the Front: Theological Engagements with the Secular* (Durham, NC, and London: Duke University Press, 1994); and *With the Grain of the Universe: The Church's Witness and Natural Theology* (Grand Rapids: Brazos Press, 2001) — the last being his Gifford lectures given in 2000-2001.

78. Stanley Hauerwas, *Christian Existence Today: Essays on Church, World, and Living in Between* (1988; reprint, Grand Rapids: Brazos Press, 2001), pp. 180-84.

79. Stanley Hauerwas, *The Peaceable Kingdom: A Primer in Christian Ethics* (Notre Dame: University of Notre Dame Press, 1983), p. 60.

80. See Hans S. Reinders, "The Meaning of Sanctification: Stanley Hauerwas on Christian Identity and Moral Judgment," in Albert W. Musschenga, ed., *Does Religion Really Matter? The Critical Reappraisal of the Thesis of Morality's Independence from Religion* (Kampen, The Netherlands: Kok Pharos, 1995), pp. 141-67.

ples,"[81] and about the church as the sanctified body of Christ. In the latter framework, becoming holy is about following the examples of the saints and having one's life woven into the larger narrative of the church.[82]

As expected, Hauerwas has been charged with promoting a Christian sectarianism that tends toward withdrawal from the world and embraces a form of sociological tribalism as well as a tribal theology.[83] In response, Hauerwas has identified the sociological presumption that favors a Christendom notion of the church (and its alliances with the state) operative among his critics and insisted that, "rather than being a justification for tribalism, my emphasis on Jesus as the first form of the new age is, I believe, our best hope to stand against contemporary tribalism."[84] Going further, "The very idea that Christians can be at home, indeed can create a home, in this world is a mistake," so that, for example, an American "National Day of Prayer" in support of war efforts "is idolatrous and pagan, the same sort of prayer Caesar always prays to Mars before battle."[85] Instead, the church needs to be reminded of "how odd it is that we have made that strange entity called the USA into a tribe rather than recognizing that the church catholic, spread out across Caesar's artificial boundaries, is our true home."[86] On the other side of

81. Stanley Hauerwas, *Sanctify Them in the Truth: Holiness Exemplified* (Edinburgh: T. & T. Clark, and Nashville: Abingdon, 1998), p. 84.

82. So, as Michael Cartwright observes, Hauerwas "is resolutely committed to the *holiness* of the church but refuses to entangle himself in the standard Protestant debates about the experience or appropriation of holiness"; see Michael G. Cartwright, "Afterword: Stanley Hauerwas's Essays in Theological Ethics — A Reader's Guide," in Stanley Hauerwas, *The Hauerwas Reader*, eds. John Berkman and Michael Cartwright (Durham, NC, and London: Duke University Press, 2001), pp. 623-71, quotation from p. 657.

83. The initial salvo was fired by James Gustafson, "The Sectarian Temptation: Reflections on Theology, the Church, and the University," *CTSA Proceedings* 40 (1985): 83-94. See also Scott Holland, "The Problems and Prospects of a 'Sectarian Ethic': A Critique of Hauerwas' Reading of the Jesus Story," *The Conrad Grebel Review* 10 (1992): 157-68, and Nigel Biggar, "Is Stanley Hauerwas Sectarian?" in Mark Nation and Samuel Wells, eds., *Faithfulness and Fortitude: In Conversation with the Theological Ethics of Stanley Hauerwas* (Edinburgh: T. & T. Clark, 2000), pp. 142-60.

84. Hauerwas, *Christian Existence Today*, p. 18.

85. Stanley Hauerwas, *In Good Company: The Church as Polis* (1995; reprint, Notre Dame: University of Notre Dame Press, 2001), pp. 53 and 55; Hauerwas is referencing here President George H. W. Bush's declaration of 3 February 1991 as a National Day of Prayer in support for American efforts in the Gulf War.

86. Hauerwas, *In Good Company*, p. 59. Thus also Robert W. Brimlow, "Solomon's Porch: The Church as Sectarian Ghetto," in Michael L. Budde and Robert W. Brimlow, eds., *The Church as Counterculture* (Albany: State University of New York Press, 2000), pp. 105-25, argues that overdependence on secular society and its political order undermines the power of the gospel.

the argument, however, Hauerwas has also clarified that Christians do not have exclusive copyright or ownership of practices like forgiveness, reconciliation, and nonviolence, but that Christians have as their unique mission that task of reminding the world to re-enact or re-actualize such practices through peacemaking, worship, evangelism, moral purity, and friendship.[87] Hence the church is called to live as a colony of resident aliens on the one hand even while rubbing shoulders with the world on the other hand.

The pentecostal holiness quest for a sanctified politics will observe the built-in tension in Hauerwas, as with Yoder, between the call to purification from the world and the call to consecration for mission for the sake of the world. I would further suggest that global forms of pentecostalism provide myriad case studies for Hauerwas's proposals for a resident-alien ecclesiology. As a theological ethicist, Hauerwas's focus has been predominantly on the saints as exemplars of holiness, but there is still a need for congregational narratives that provide concrete patterns showing that the ecclesiological ideals of the colony of resident aliens can exist in a fallen world. In other words, while I agree that Hauerwas does not advocate a sectarian politics of withdrawal, we still need other instances of how the quest for holiness has produced a sanctified politics of cultural engagement and of being in the world.

5.2.3. The Politics of the New Monasticism: Seeking Perfectionism in Culture and Society

We do not have to look long to find that the tensions in holiness pentecostalism between a cleansing *from* and a consecration *for* the world have been played out among other perfectionist movements. Historically, for example, Christian asceticism and monasticism emerged initially during and after the fourth century in seeking to retain the significance of baptism understood as a dying to the world, since as a result of the formation of Christendom martyrdom no longer preserved that symbolism.[88] But later, with the fragmentation of the Roman Empire, the monks began to see that they could not simply avoid the world; there was an apostolic mandate to convert it.

---

87. Stanley Hauerwas, *A Better Hope: Resources for a Church Confronting Capitalism, Democracy, and Postmodernity* (Grand Rapids: Brazos Press, 2001), part 3.

88. That is a brief version; the reality is much more complex, involving how Christian ascetics provided a model not only for spirituality and a way of life but also for civic community after the Constantinian revolution; for details, see David Brakke, *Athanasius and the Politics of Asceticism* (Oxford: Clarendon Press, 1995).

Henceforth, "The saint was still someone who renounced the world (a monk) but the monk's duty was not only cenobitic ascesis but also the conversion of the people. . . . The saint was the person who brought God to history and proclaimed the Church as God's historical home."[89]

Closer to the modern pentecostal movement is the mid-nineteenth-century holiness quest for what Douglas Strong has called a "perfectionist politics."[90] Wesleyan, Methodist, and other holiness believers during this time were convinced that sanctification was not just a personal experience of the eradication of sin, but that it had a socio-political dimension. Hence sanctified saints had the responsibility of forming "sanctified organizations" and to work for the "sanctification of local institutions."[91] In a fallen world, even institutions "wander from holiness," and it was the task of the church to spread holiness across the land in order to "harmonize earth with heaven."[92] Holiness Christians thus worked for the revival and purification of their churches (they urged a dismantling of denominationalism because of its divisiveness, and a formation of "unionist" churches bound together by the experience of sanctification), a transformation of their society (they were the leading activists in support of the abolition of slavery and for the equal rights of all people, and they established cooperative networks of abolitionist schools, periodicals, and conventions), and a reformation of their political system (they formed the Liberty Party to achieve their socio-political goals).

These projects were essential, these holiness Christians believed, for the fulfillment of God's plan for "a perfect state of society."[93] Thus the earliest Wesleyans "stressed specific reform activities as normative for one's entire sanctification," even as they "criticized holiness preachers who thought that entire sanctification was 'too spiritually minded to plead the cause of the op-

89. Claudio Leonardi, "From 'Monastic' Holiness to 'Political' Holiness," trans. Dinah Livingstone, in Christian Duquoc and Casiano Floristán, eds., *Models of Holiness* (New York: Seabury, 1979), pp. 46-55, quotations on pp. 49 and 50.

90. Douglas M. Strong, *Perfectionist Politics: Abolitionism and the Religious Tensions of American Democracy* (Syracuse, NY: Syracuse University Press, 1999). For an earlier but still valuable discussion, see Timothy L. Smith, *Revivalism and Social Reform in Mid-Nineteenth-Century America* (New York and Nashville: Abingdon, 1957).

91. Strong, *Perfectionist Politics,* p. 164.

92. Strong, *Perfectionist Politics,* pp. 165 and 169; the former quotation draws from the *Christian Investigator* 6 (June 1848): 507-8.

93. Douglas M. Strong, "The Application of Perfectionism to Politics: Political and Ecclesiastical Abolitionism in the Burned-Over District," *Wesleyan Theological Journal* 25, no. 1 (1990): 21-41, quotation from p. 21, citing Jonathan Blanchard's commencement address at Oberlin College, 3 September 18939, published as *A Perfect State of Society* (Oberlin: James Steele, 1839).

pressed.'"[94] So while the heyday of perfectionist politics in the early 1840s thus brought together Methodists, Baptists, Presbyterians, and Lutherans around the common cause of socio-political transformation, their underlying theological commitments to an experiential — i.e., personal and social — holiness should not be underestimated as a merely dependent variable. By the 1850s, however, internal fragmentation of the Unionist churches, the abolitionist movement, and the Liberty Party, among other factors, brought about a tempering of this quest for a sanctified society.[95]

I propose that the quest for a sanctified politics exemplified in early Christian monasticism and nineteenth-century holiness perfectionism can be seen in a different guise in the New Monasticism of the present time.[96] These are new Christian communities predominantly in urban settings — e.g., Shane Claiborne's Potter Street New Monastic (formerly: Simple Way) Community in Philadelphia, Chris Haw's new environmentalism (informed by Willow Creek spirituality) at Camden House in Camden, New Jersey, and Jonathan Wilson-Hartgrove's Rutba House in the Walltown area of Duke University in Durham, North Carolina, among many others[97] — that are revitalizing evangelicalism through adoption of simple lifestyles even while be-

94. Strong, "The Application of Perfectionism to Politics," pp. 26-27, with the latter quotation citing from William Goodell, "Entire Sanctification" (manuscript sermon from 1850 in Berea College Archives, Berea, Kentucky), pp. 10-11. Richard George Eli, "Social Holiness: The Politics of Wesleyan Theology" (Ph.D. diss., Duke University, 1990), esp. chaps. 2-3, has argued that this extension of sanctification to the public sphere is intrinsic to the theological project of the founders of Methodism, John and Charles Wesley.

95. Still, holiness projects of social work did not disappear; see Norris A. Magnuson, *Salvation in the Slums: Evangelical Social Work, 1865-1920* (Metuchen, NJ: Scarecrow Press, 1977). It should be noted that one of the dangers of drawing from this well of Wesleyan perfectionism is the tendency, in the wrong hands, toward a triumphalist and elitist political theology and theology of culture — as if the advocates of such perfectionist proposals may have thought that they had arrived at the final solution for a perfect society. I call attention in turn to the Wesleyan emphasis on the *via salutis* — the way of salvation — that emphasizes seeing the achievements in and of this world as a process anticipating the final salvation to come.

96. Another model of what I am calling a sanctified politics is the "politics of holiness" presented by Jon Sobrino — especially *Spirituality of Liberation: Toward Political Holiness*, trans. Robert R. Barr (Maryknoll, NY: Orbis, 1988), esp. chap. 4 — that takes off from the model of Jesus as liberator in order to present a spirituality of liberation; I return to discuss aspects of liberation theology in chapters 7 and 8.

97. A preliminary list of communities can be found in Shane Claiborne, *The Irresistible Revolution: Living as an Ordinary Radical* (Grand Rapids: Zondervan, 2006), pp. 359-62. The New Monasticism can be considered an international movement in terms of its having networks around the world; see Paul R. Dekar, *Community of the Transfiguration: The Journey of a New Monastic Community* (Eugene, OR: Cascade Books, 2008).

ing committed to projects of social transformation.[98] Members of these communities understand themselves as "new friars" committed to holy living (i.e., celibacy or monogamous marriage), working with the poor, the outcast, and the homeless, nurturing a local and communal economy, and fostering peacemaking and reconciliation. Their goals include the "remonking of the church" via resistance against pervasive consumerism and individualism, and the embodiment of self-sacrificial modes of holistic spirituality.

While the architects of the New Monasticism have sought to be informed by the various monastic streams of the Christian tradition, in the main the contemporary movement is Protestant in its overall ethos, albeit often linking (paradoxically) Free Church proclivities with ecumenical sensibilities. So on the one hand, the commitment to the way of Jesus, especially as reflected in the New Testament in general and in the Gospel accounts in particular, is plainly evident. Thus New Monastic theologians like Shane Claiborne resonate with Yoder's *Politics of Jesus* because it highlights a Jesus who has not been domesticated by Constantinian or modern preoccupations.[99] This is a Jesus not of the creeds but of the heart, of the feet, and of the hands, a real-life figure who can be emulated in his interactions with sinners and the world, not just worshiped. For the New Monasticism, then, holiness is not a doctrine but an all-encompassing way of life — of social, political, economic, and cultural life — the way of Jesus.

On the other hand, the New Monasticism is unlike earlier generations of evangelicals who were often forgetful about the rich historical legacy of the church, at least of the life of the church between the times of the apostles and the Reformation. Thus these New Monastics think of themselves as "new ascetics," similar to the ascetics of the fourth century in their rejection of the emerging Constantinianism, albeit generally avoiding the austere practices of self-mortification prevalent among the desert fathers.[100] Intending to be more deeply rooted in the historic practices of the church, they have drawn from the wellsprings of Orthodox and Catholic traditions of asceticism. By doing so, they have bypassed the fundamentalist, holiness, and conservative evangelical traditions that have devolved legalistic approaches especially over the course of the twentieth century, and instead have retrieved and reappropriated established contemplative traditions for the pres-

98. Rob Moll, "The New Monasticism," *Christianity Today* (September 2005): 39-46.

99. Acknowledgments of the influences of not only Yoder's *Politics of Jesus* but also Hauerwas and Willimon's *Resident Aliens* are made in Shane Claiborne and Chris Haw, *Jesus for President: Politics for Ordinary Radicals* (Grand Rapids: Zondervan, 2008).

100. Jonathan Wilson-Hartgrove, *New Monasticism: What It Has to Say to Today's Church* (Grand Rapids: Brazos Press, 2008), chap. 3.

ent.[101] Hence the contemporary engagement with culture is shaped by drawing deeply from the wellsprings of the Christian tradition. This is not novelty for newness' sake, but rather a contextual creativity whereby the treasures from the past are relevant precisely because they contrast with the mundane world of the present.

For the New Monasticism, then, holiness is less a set of rules to be followed than a set of marks to be improvised.[102] Contemplation is less about rigorously focusing the mind than it is on cultivating a posture and life of prayer. Sanctification is considered in terms not only of purification but of bearing witness to the peculiarity of Jesus' way of being in the world. In a sense, the New Monastics are "ordinary radicals,"[103] as they like to call themselves: ordinary when compared to previous generations of monastics, perfectionists, and even holiness Christians, but radical when compared to both contemporary Christendom and the wider culture of our time. Yet the wider culture is never to be merely looked or talked down on; rather, it is faithfulness in the way of Jesus that already acts as a redemptive leaven that reveals the irregularity and atypicality of life in the body of Christ. Hence with the New Monasticism, "perfectionist" and holiness politics has found an ancient but yet also fresh resource for living in, embracing (at least in some respects), and yet subverting the cultural habits of our time.

5.3. Many Tongues, Many Cultures: The Politics of Holiness for the Sanctification of the World

The preceding has demonstrated the interconnections between Christian beliefs about sanctification and holiness and Christian practices related to interactions with society and the wider culture, with regard to pentecostalism and the New Monasticism as well as their predecessor holiness and Anabaptist movements. In the rest of this chapter, I continue the constructive task of this volume — the presentation of a pentecostally informed but yet ecumenical Christian political theology — by elaborating here on how a sanctified politics shapes a theology of culture in general and a theology of aesthetics in particular. As before, we proceed in three steps: biblically, via a rereading of the early

101. Thus, e.g., the primary dialogue partner for Jon Stock, Tim Otto, and Jonathan Wilson-Hartgrove, *Inhabiting the Church: Biblical Wisdom for a New Monasticism* (Eugene, OR: Cascade Books, 2007), is St. Benedict, and his vows of conversion, obedience, and stability.

102. See the Rutba House, ed., *School(s) for Conversion: 12 Marks of a New Monasticism* (Eugene, OR: Cascade Books, 2005).

103. This is in the subtitle of Claiborne's *Irresistible Revolution*.

church's handling of the holiness code in Acts and the Gospel of Luke; practically, with regard to contemporary articulations of a politics of holiness and its redemptive theology of culture; and theologically, in terms of a pneumatological and trinitarian approach to aesthetics. Our goal is the formulation of a politics of holiness that insists on a purging of the world's social conventions and yet also advocates a commitment to redeeming culture as enabled by the outpouring of the Spirit of the triune God on all flesh.

5.3.1. "God Shows No Partiality": Redeeming (Saving) Languages, Reforming (Sanctifying) Cultures

My thesis is that a sanctified politics involves simultaneously the rejection and redemption of culture, in different respects. The working out of this dual stance requires, ironically, what I am calling, following Luke the evangelist, a radically sectarian and even "heretical" politics. Building on but also going behind Yoder and the New Monastic theologians, I am referring here to the fact that the earliest followers of Jesus as Messiah were called a Nazarene sect, especially by opposing Jewish leaders (Acts 24:5, 14; 28:22). The word translated "sect," αἵρεσεως/αιρεσιν — literally, "heresy" (especially when used by outsiders) — is descriptive of a coalition or school that rivals with or competes against other parties within a larger movement.[104] At the same time, it is also used with reference to a sub-group of Pharisees (15:5; 26:5), highlighting not only their moral rigorism and zealousness for the law but also their commitments to purity as linked to their believing in and following Jesus as Messiah (cf. Acts 15:22).[105] Hence, the early Christians were seen as separatists, at least from the point of view of the Jewish leadership who felt threatened by the expanding messianic movement.

But why did the Jews consider the early Christians to be sectarian heretics? The answer, contextually understood, is that the growing numbers of God-fearing followers of the Nazarene led to a gradual rejection of Jewish religious and cultural commitments, especially in gentile-dominated ecclesial communities. As the Christian mission expanded from Judea into Samaria and around the Mediterranean world, the original group of disciples was led to reconsider their relationship with those outside their community of faith.

104. James D. G. Dunn, *The Acts of the Apostles* (Peterborough, UK: Epworth, 1996), p. 326.

105. This point is emphasized by David B. Gowler, *Host, Guest, Enemy, and Friend: Portraits of the Pharisees in Luke and Acts*, Emory Studies in Early Christianity 2 (New York: Peter Lang, 1991), esp. pp. 300-305, passim.

Peter, one of the leading apostles in Jerusalem, had a vision in which he was told three times to prepare a meal from animals declared impure for consumption by the Mosaic Law. This prepared him for his visit to the home of the gentile centurion, Cornelius, at which he confessed initially, "You yourselves know that it is unlawful for a Jew to associate with or to visit a Gentile; but God has shown me that I should not call anyone profane or unclean" (Acts 10:28), and later, "I truly understand that God shows no partiality, but in every nation anyone who fears him [including gentiles like Cornelius thought to be unclean in light of Jewish law] and does what is right is acceptable to him" (10:34-35).[106]

The apostolic leadership continued to wrestle with this matter, as the account of the Jerusalem council clarifies. On the one hand, the questions concerned what the gentiles had to do to be saved, and, if saved, to what degree gentiles were beholden to the laws of Moses. On the other hand, however, the salvation of the gentiles also raised questions about Jewish self-understanding: What about the covenant promises to Israel, and what about the status of Israel's election by Yahweh? On this latter set of issues, James's response was that the restoration of Israel included the salvation of the gentiles as well (15:14-18).[107] Yet this did not mean a relaxation of the law for the Jews; instead, it meant that while Israel remained the people of God and retained the sign of circumcision (as part of the holiness code), the gentiles were included among this new people of God apart from circumcision and the keeping of the Mosaic law (with the exception of those aspects of the law that, in gentile interactions with Jews, would compromise the purity of the latter).

In this light we can see how the apostle Paul both kept the law (as an observant Jew) and yet also accepted the gentiles (as one called to evangelize those outside the community of Israel) as part of the new people of God who were made holy in their hearts by faith.[108] Thus Paul circumcised Timothy (who had a Jewish mother) "because of the Jews who were in those places" (16:3), "had his hair cut [at Cenchrea], for he was under a vow" (18:18), and undertook a rite of purification with four others at Jerusalem in order to

---

106. See Mikael C. Parsons, *Luke: Storyteller, Interpreter, Evangelist* (Peabody, MA: Hendrickson, 2007), chap. 7; cf. J. Julius Scott, "The Cornelius Incident in the Light of Its Jewish Setting," *Journal of the Evangelical Theological Society* 34, no. 4 (1991): 475-84.

107. On this point, see Royce Dickinson, "The Theology of the Jerusalem Conference: Acts 15:1-35," *Restoration Quarterly* 32, no. 2 (1990): 65-83, esp. pp. 71-81.

108. See Robert W. Wall, "Reading Paul with Acts: The Canonical Shaping of a Holy Church," in Kent E. Brower and Andy Johnson, eds., *Holiness and Ecclesiology in the New Testament* (Grand Rapids: Eerdmans, 2007), pp. 129-47.

demonstrate his Jewish commitments to the thousands of believers who were "zealous for the law" (21:20). At the same time, Paul did not hesitate to interact with gentiles on their own turf — i.e., at the Areopagus in Athens or the lecture hall of Tyrannus in Ephesus (19:9) — as well as fellowship and eat with them (at the home of the Philippian jailer, with the pagans who were shipwrecked on the sea voyage to Rome, and on the island of Malta), all without expectation that gentiles maintain the Jewish holiness code. So on the one hand, Paul abided by the letter of the law and defended its ongoing legitimacy for Jewish life and practice, even while on the other, he did not hesitate to "transgress" the law in his dealings with gentiles.[109]

However, I see Paul, in committing these transgressions, as merely following in the footsteps of Jesus.[110] Whereas the Jewish quest for holiness in the post-exilic period led those who were the most zealous for things of the law to expect that the messiah would restore the Temple to Jewish administration, cleanse the land from gentile contaminants, return governance over the region of Palestine to the Jews, and re-establish Torah observance for the people of God, Jesus not only challenged these understandings of holiness but invited the Jews to exchange them for an alternative vision of divine holiness that was inclusive of sinners and tax collectors. Jesus not only ate with sinners and others considered unclean (Luke 5:29-30; 14:13, 21; 15:2; 19:5-7), but also contravened the ritual washing/cleaning of hands (11:38), de-emphasized the tithe (18:9-14), "worked" on the Sabbath, touched the ritually impure (7:14), and advocated the love of enemies (6:27) and acceptance of the despised Samaritans (17:11-19). If the Jews had taken Torah observance in ritually exclusive directions, Jesus translated Torah as enabling the merciful embrace of "outsiders" so that the lines between "us" and "them" were overcome. Now the unclean were holy because their sins were graciously forgiven in the Day of the Lord announced by Jesus in the power of the Spirit; the Sabbath

---

109. Thus Vladimir Wozniuk, "In Pursuit of a Politics of Holiness: Reconciling Hellenic and Hebraic Political Wisdom in the Acts of the Apostles," *Journal of Church and State* 45, no. 2 (2003): 283-304, argues that the emerging church challenged Roman civil religion in light of Hebraic theological commitments even while expanding Jewish political understandings in light of Hellenistic conventions.

110. In what follows, I rely primarily on Marcus J. Borg, *Conflict, Holiness and Politics in the Teachings of Jesus*, Studies in the Bible and Early Christianity 5 (New York and Toronto: Edwin Mellen Press, 1984); cf. also Hisao Kayama, "Christianity as Table Fellowship: Meals as a Symbol of the Universalism in Luke-Acts," in Daniel J. Adams, ed., *From East to West: Essays in Honor of Donald G. Bloesch* (Lanham, MD: University Press of America, 1997), pp. 51-62, and Richard P. Thompson, "Gathered at the Table: Holiness and Ecclesiology in the Gospel of Luke," in Kent E. Brower and Andy Johnson, eds., *Holiness and Ecclesiology in the New Testament* (Grand Rapids: Eerdmans, 2007), pp. 76-94.

was holy because it was a day for works of compassion; and the Temple was holy because it would be restored as the house of prayer for all people (indeed, for all nations; cf. Mark 11:17 and Isa. 56:7). The outcome of these heretical acts — heretical to those who continued to advocate a strict observance of the letter of the Mosaic law — was a new politics of holiness that restored and renewed Israel not by eliminating the impure from the land, but by announcing the good news regarding the Day of the Lord's graciousness and favor on the poor, the outcast, and the marginalized.[111]

The same Holy Spirit who anointed Jesus to proclaim good news and freedom to the poor and oppressed was then poured out on all flesh by the ascended Christ on the Day of Pentecost (Acts 2:17, 33). Although initially given primarily to the Jews of the diaspora — but note there were also gentiles in Jerusalem and among those who received the Spirit, even if these were proselytes to Judaism (2:10) — this initial outpouring was a foreshadowing of God's intention not only that the gospel would be taken to the ends of the earth but that it would be made available and received by the Samaritans and the gentiles (1:8; cf. Luke 2:32). Yet the Pentecost event signaled that the gospel's universality did not involve a homogeneous people of God; quite the contrary, the many tongues from around the Mediterranean diaspora were not muted but rather preserved and even accentuated (Acts 2:6-8).[112]

When set in canonical context, the many tongues of Pentecost represent the down-payment of the Spirit (cf. 2 Cor. 1:22; 5:5; Eph. 1:13-14) anticipating the divine intention to achieve the full restoration of Israel and the eschatological redemption of the world. Yet the salvation of the world would not be

111. Having said all this, it should also be noted that Jesus did not merely intend to be a lawbreaker. In fact, as William R. G. Loader, *Jesus' Attitude Towards the Law,* Wissenschaftliche Untersuchungen zum Neuen Testament 2. Reihe 97 (Tübingen: Mohr Siebeck, 1997), chap. 3, notes, Luke's portrayal, by and large, is of Jesus as a law-observant Jew, even if (as we shall see) gentiles were not bound to the Mosaic code. On the other hand, from a conservative first-century Jewish perspective, aspects of Jesus' behavior were threatening enough so that there may have arisen the fear that wide acceptance of his teachings would lead to a gradual blurring of the lines between Jews and gentiles, even an assimilation of the former to the latter; on this point, see Alan Watson, *Jesus and the Law* (Athens, GA, and London: University of Georgia Press, 1996), p. 133.

112. In this regard, Luke arguably "christianizes" the Roman social policy of "receiving all nations" into the *Pax Romana* — perhaps as "John" adapted the Hellenistic philosophy of the Logos for his own purposes — in order to articulate an inclusive vision of what it meant to be the people of God for the early church; see David L. Balch, "The Cultural Origins of 'Receiving All Nations' in Luke-Acts: Alexander the Great or Roman Social Policy?" in John T. Fitzgerald, Thomas H. Olbricht, and L. Michael White, eds., *Early Christianity and Classical Culture: Comparative Studies in Honor of Abraham J. Malherbe,* Supplements to Novum Testamentum 110 (Leiden and Boston: Brill, 2003), pp. 483-500.

accomplished in the abstract but would include the languages, cultures, and nations of the world.[113] If before, God had merely established the boundaries of the nations (Acts 17:26) and allowed them to follow their own ways (14:16), at Pentecost God had gathered representatives from every nation (2:5) in anticipation "that repentance and forgiveness of sins is to be proclaimed in his name to all nations" (Luke 24:47). Hence the many languages "speaking about God's deeds of power" (Acts 2:11) at Pentecost prefigure the eschatological healing of the nations (Rev. 22:2) and their glory and honor being brought into the New Jerusalem (21:26).[114]

In short, the restoration and sanctification of the people of God include not only its cleansing but also its consecration for witness, and this in turn involves the redemption of the world. The early Christians recognized that "in every nation anyone who fears him and does what is right is acceptable to him" (Acts 10:35) because they were witnesses to the fact that "God, who knows the human heart, testified to them [the gentiles] by giving them the Holy Spirit, just as he did to us; and in cleansing their hearts by faith he has made no distinction between them and us" (15:8-9). Hence the heretofore unclean gentiles were now sanctified by the Spirit, and their redemption meant that their languages could now glorify God, their cultural accomplishments could bear witness to God (17:28), and their hospitality could be received in gratitude (28:2, 7-10). So if the Christian politics of holiness required abstention from gentile idolatry, sexual immorality, and unhygienic meats (15:20) on the one hand, the Christian politics of heresy enabled the reception of gentile languages and cultural attainments on the other. What might this mean for a pentecostally informed theology of culture in the twenty-first century?

5.3.2. The Spirit of Holiness: Perfectionist Politics as Redemptive Cultural Praxis

The discussion in theology of culture has come a long way since the publication of Niebuhr's *Christ and Culture* (see 5.2.1 above). While some continue to

---

113. For further elaboration, see Yong, *The Spirit Poured Out on All Flesh*, chap. 4; cf. Craig S. Keener, "Why Does Luke Use Tongues as a Sign of the Spirit's Empowerment?" *Journal of Pentecostal Theology* 15, no. 2 (2007): 177-84.

114. This does not, of course, conclude toward a straightforward universalistic soteriology; see Ronald Herms, *An Apocalypse for the Church and for the World: The Narrative Function of Universal Language in the Book of Revelation*, Zeitschrift für die neutestamentliche Wissenschaft und die Kunde der älteren Kirche 143 (Berlin and New York: Walter de Gruyter, 2006).

adapt Niebuhr's proposals and others have attempted to revise them in light of the biblical metanarratives,[115] I agree with Yoder and others who argue that Niebuhr's categories fail because they presume a dualism between Christ and culture. Thus it is now difficult to appreciate Niebuhr's achievements given our post-Christendom assumptions about the inextricable cultural dimensions of human identity, even for the theological event Christians call the incarnation. I would go further and say, however, that while the proper response is to continue to explore the contours of what might be called a post-Christendom theology of culture, another way of reading Niebuhr is precisely as a quest for such a theological posture. After all, *Christ and Culture* seeks to affirm, above all, the Christ as transformer of culture model, and this parallels Niebuhr's own search for a viable response to the questions raised by what was being recognized as the gradual dissolution of the Christendom project.

I find Yoder's exilic politics of diaspora replete with possibilities for reimagining a post-Christendom theology of culture. I especially appreciate his attempt to hold together the following two commitments: to remain social and political guests — i.e., of "not being in charge" — and thus continuing to embrace the social and cultural margins as normative for followers of Jesus, and to nevertheless "seek the welfare of the city" wherever believers find themselves. For Yoder, the Jewish model of interacting with the dominant culture from out of the specificity and particularity of their experience of Jewishness remains to be emulated today.

This was also the example of Jesus, so that the acknowledgment that Jesus was the Christ not apart from but in and through his cultural Jewishness does not mean that the task of cultural engagement no longer pertains. Rather, as always, the challenge is "to find incarnational ways to live and articulate a vision of life that discerns how to be appropriately influential and transformational."[116] More specifically, Jesus' own pursuit of an inclusive politics of holiness remains our task today. To embrace the vision of Jesus is itself to be grasped by "a new sense of faith and mission" that brings the quest for holiness into the sphere of the political.[117] This is especially important if we are to avoid, as under the Christendom project, collapsing the distinction be-

115. For the former, see Angus J. L. Menuge, ed., *Christ and Culture in Dialogue: Constructive Themes and Practical Applications* (St. Louis: Concordia Academic Press, 1999), while the latter approach is best exemplified in D. A. Carson, *Christ and Culture Revisited* (Grand Rapids and Cambridge, UK: Eerdmans, 2008).

116. Bruce L. Guenther, "The 'Enduring Problem' of Christ and Culture," *Direction* 34, no. 2 (2005): 215-27, quotation from p. 223.

117. Daniel H. Levine, "Holiness, Faith, Power, Politics," *Journal for the Scientific Study of Religion* 26, no. 4 (1987): 551-61.

tween the church and the wider culture. What is needed, then, is a politics of holiness that preserves Christian marginality on the one hand (Yoder's insistence on marginal or exilic life, Hauerwas's colony of resident aliens, as well as the New Monastic communities) but also inspires a Christian leavening, if not explicit cultural engagement, on the other.[118]

Yet whereas Yoder relies hermeneutically on the Gospel of Luke and the broad scope of the First Testament narrative regarding the exilic fortunes of ancient Israel,[119] I wish to insert volume two of the Lukan corpus into the discussion in order to develop further what may be called a pneumatological (and ecclesiological) theology of culture. The turn to pneumatology is helpful for at least the following three reasons. First, it provides a transcendent and theological legitimation of Jesus' normativity so that we can recognize both his cultural embeddedness as a first-century Mediterranean Jew and his announcing and bringing about the kingdom under the power of the Spirit. Second, the gift of the Spirit preserves the diversity of tongues (languages) in a way that undermines any attempt to reconstruct or re-establish Christendom; rather, the many tongues signify the many centers that those on the margins need to heed and respect, rather than replace.[120] But finally, in eschatological perspective, the Spirit nevertheless inspires the many tongues to give glory to God, each in their own distinctive language; in this way, the Pentecost narrative signifies not only the preservation of the many tongues but also anticipates the final redemption of the many languages and cultures of the world.

A politics of holiness inspired by the Pentecost narrative and the broad storyline of the early church as recorded in the book of Acts therefore both invites a purification from the world and inspires a vocational mandate directed for its redemption. How this works itself out historically, however, is much more complicated. In order to tease out the complexities involved in any local situation, I will draw briefly from the work of Birgit Meyer on pentecostal filmmaking and video-production in Ghana.[121] In the last twenty

---

118. In this regard, Peter Hinchliff's *Holiness and Politics* (1982; reprint, Grand Rapids: Eerdmans, 1983), is a disappointment since it focuses primarily on Christian perspectives on moral theory amid the public square rather than articulating either a political theology or a theology of culture.

119. With which I am very sympathetic, as argued in Yong, *Hospitality and the Other: Pentecost, Christian Practices, and the Neighbor* (Maryknoll, NY: Orbis, 2008), pp. 108-17.

120. Thus the church can embrace "difference as a gift of the Spirit," and can be "committed to difference"; see T. J. Gorringe, *Furthering Humanity: A Theology of Culture* (Aldershot, UK, and Burlington, VT: Ashgate, 2004), p. 261.

121. Meyer has been publishing on this topic for almost the last ten years, and is an engag-

plus years, coinciding with the period in which pentecostal growth in Ghana has been exponential,[122] and also with the deregulation of the film industry since the 1970s, an increasing number of locally produced films and videos have catered to a pentecostal audience and included themes drawn from or reflecting on pentecostal spirituality. My interest lies in showing how the Ghanaian pentecostal encounter with culture involves a rejection and resistance of culture on the one hand and a reappropriation and renewal on the other hand. The complication lies, however, in that both aspects of this interchange occur at the local and global levels.[123]

Pentecostal holiness understood in terms of purification from the world, for example, is clearly communicated in films and videos that not only reject but also present exposés of African culture, heritage, and traditions.[124] This is consistent with the classical pentecostal scheme that demonizes indigenous traditions, not only metaphorically as representing the superstitions of premodern cultures but also literally as mediating access to the wiles and

---

ing read for theologians because of her capacity to combine ethnographic and anthropological detail (her field) with sophisticated theoretical analyses. The most recent overviews are Birgit Meyer, *Religious Sensations: Why Media, Aesthetics and Power Matter in the Study of Contemporary Religion* (Amsterdam: Vrije Universiteit, 2006); "Images of Evil in Popular Ghanaian Christianity," in Nelly van Doorn-Harder and Lourens Minnema, eds., *Coping with Evil in Religion and Culture: Case Studies,* Currents of Encounter 35 (Amsterdam and New York: Rodopi, 2008), pp. 9-23; and "Powerful Pictures: Popular Christian Aesthetics in Southern Ghana," *Journal of the American Academy of Religion* 76, no. 1 (2008): 82-110. I will cite other essays below — hopefully a full book-length study from Meyer will be forthcoming on this fascinating topic.

122. I touched briefly on Ghanaian pentecostalism above (1.2.2). We have neither time nor space to explore the various contours of this rapidly changing phenomenon; for an overview, see E. Kingsley Larbi, *Pentecostalism: The Eddies of Ghanaian Christianity* (Dansoman-Accra, Ghana: Centre for Pentecostal and Charismatic Studies, 2001).

123. A similar assessment has been made regarding Nigerian pentecostalism — Asonzeh F.-K. Ukah, "Advertising God: Nigerian Christian Video-Films and the Power of Consumer Culture," *Journal of Religion in Africa* 33, no. 2 (2003): 203-31. Although I will remain within the Ghanaian context in my analysis, it is interesting to compare what is happening in the Ghanaian context with what is transpiring in the Nigerian one, especially since travel and migration between the two nations has resulted in cross-media influences. For a discussion of how Nigerian developments have impacted Ghanaian film-production and marketing, see Birgit Meyer, "Prayers, Guns and Ritual Murder: Power and the Occult in Ghanaian Popular Cinema," in Jim Kiernan, ed., *The Power of the Occult in Africa: Continuity and Innovation in the Renewal of African Cosmologies,* Modernity and Belonging 4 (Berlin: LIT Verlag, 2006), pp. 182-205, esp. pp. 191-201.

124. Birgit Meyer, "Popular Ghanaian Cinema and 'African Heritage'," *Africa Today* 46, no. 2 (1999): 93-114, and "Mediating Tradition: Pentecostal Pastors, African Priests, and Chiefs in Ghanaian Popular Films," in Toyin Falola, ed., *Christianity and Social Change in Africa: Essays in Honor of J. D. Y. Peel* (Durham: North Carolina Academic Press, 2005), pp. 275-306.

clutches of the devil (see 1.3.2 above). Yet while the African heritage is resisted, its symbolism is retrieved and reinterpreted within the dualistic cosmological framework of pentecostal spirituality. Thus, witches, Mami Water spirits, and other demonic spiritual forces, beings, and powers are central to the plots of many films, as is the message about the power of Jesus' name and of the Holy Spirit in overcoming the forces of darkness. As film producers go to great lengths to present the world of the occult realistically, the production of these films is fraught with tensions since original materials, especially concerning the demonic world, are eschewed. But even if fake representations have to be utilized, this in itself is a dangerous task: as "there is no clear-cut boundary between reality and fiction, in the process of shooting a film simulation always entails the risk of mimesis, thereby affecting those who seek to represent 'the spiritual' for the sake of revelation."[125] In short, there are clearly elements of African culture that are discarded, even as there are other elements that are reappropriated, albeit with a sense of trepidation. Pentecostals hereby have to negotiate the challenges involved in the Yoderian task of seeking the peace of the city within which they are found.

Similarly, Ghanaian films and videos represent pentecostalism as struggling with globalization not only at the religious but also at the economic level. Whereas modernity tends to be reductionistic regarding religion and spirituality, Ghanaian media accentuate the possibility of divine revelation through dreams and visions. If modernism and consumerism are uncritically equated, these films view the global capitalist economy with a great deal of ambiguity: on the one hand, consumer goods are a sign of blessing but on the other, they are a danger for the soul, so "born-again Christians are called to sanctify all the commodities they buy through prayer, and to abstain altogether from buying particular goods such as rasta-hair, fashionable jewelry, and shining materials."[126] Likewise, the quintessential icon of modernity, the city, is treated with ambivalence. Comparable to the global market, the city symbolizes moral corruptions, temptations, and seductions; yet middle- to upper-middle-class urban lifestyles — rather than life in the village — are depicted as normative signs of divine blessing so that the city is not condemned without qualification but invites instead a discerning mode of engagement. Thus, "most currently produced Ghanaian video-films affirm the need to adopt Pentecostal religion

125. Birgit Meyer, "Impossible Representations: Pentecostalism, Vision, and Video Technology in Ghana," in Birgit Meyer and Annelies Moors, eds., *Religion, Media, and the Public Square* (Bloomington and Indianapolis: Indiana University Press, 2006), pp. 290-312, quotation from p. 307.

126. Birgit Meyer, "Visions of Blood, Sex and Money: Fantasy Spaces in Popular Ghanaian Cinema," *Visual Anthropology* 16, no. 1 (2003): 15-41, quote from p. 29.

[and *not* the Christianity of non-pentecostalism, I might add!] in order to engage with modernity in a safe and disciplined way."[127]

The result of these crisscrossing trajectories of Ghanaian filmmaking is the emergence of a distinctively Ghanaian pentecostal aesthetic and culture. Along with the production of films and videos come their advertising (wall posters, bumper stickers), music CDs and DVDs, and other popular expressions (including paintings, various kinds of literature). Yet these external cultural markers are complemented by an emerging video culture that "consumes" such media products in a distinctively pentecostal manner. So, for example, the viewing of these video-films at home is a more socially engaging affair than watching them at the cinema (where it is more of an individualistic exercise). Often small groups gather in private residences or youth leaders have a movie night, and these engender discussion of various aspects of the plot, the styles, and the moral points portrayed. Like the preacher-congregation exchanges during the sermon, the audiences interact with the unfolding story, yelling out warnings to characters when threatened by evil, participating in exorcisms in Jesus' name, applauding when decisions for the good, the truth, and Christ are made, clapping and cheering for heroes, scolding villains, etc.[128] Thus the modernist split between representation and reality is overcome so that the power of images is affective and effective in mediating access to the spiritual domain.[129]

A politics of holiness inspired by the Pentecost narrative therefore enables both a separation from the world and yet commitment to work for its welfare and redemption, albeit in distinctive respects. In the case of Ghanaian pentecostalism, the medium of film is enabling the emergence of a sanctified culture that distances itself from some elements of the world on the one hand even while redeeming other aspects on the other. Perhaps this ambivalence reflects in part the Ghanaian quest for participation in the global economy that has been gradual and halting, even forty years after independence (see also 7.1.3). In the meantime, since it is impossible to completely separate the medium from the message, the latter is always vulnerable to being trans-

127. Birgit Meyer, "Pentecostalism, Prosperity, and Popular Cinema in Ghana," in S. Brent Plate, ed., *Representing Religion in World Cinema: Filmmaking, Mythmaking, Culture Making* (New York: Palgrave Macmillan, 2003), pp. 121-43, quote from p. 133.

128. Meyer, "Pentecostalism, Prosperity, and Popular Cinema in Ghana," p. 134.

129. For a discussion of television viewing as formative of pentecostal identity and as providing one mode of engaging the world and the spiritual domain, see the insightful thesis, being revised for publication at the time of this writing, of Martijn Oosterbaan, "Divine Mediations: Pentecostalism, Politics and Mass Media in a Favela in Rio de Janeiro" (Ph.D. diss., Free University of Amsterdam, 2006), esp. chap. 7.

formed by the former, even as it is intended by its consumers to be a transformative antidote to the dangers of modernity.[130] Here Hauerwas's warnings are apropos about how the wider cultural hazards are a menace to the colony of resident aliens.

Yet, as the New Monasticism reflects, the proper response can never be merely a withdrawal from culture. If the incarnation suggests the possibility of redeeming the cultural, then Pentecost suggests this will occur in and through the many tongues that are sanctified for such purposes. In such cases, the sanctifying power of the Spirit on the margins brings about a purification of the center even as it works to accomplish the transformation of the center into new sites of marginality.[131]

5.3.3. The Sanctified Imagination: The Beauty of Holiness and a Renewal of Aesthetics

To be sure, not all aspects of culture are equal, nor are they therefore equally susceptible to the redemptive power of the Spirit. In the following chapter, I take a more critical stance toward the public sphere in discussing the possibility of a prophetic politics. Here in this last section, however, I conclude our present discussion about the possibility of cultural redemption via a politics of holiness by elaborating on the issue of cultural discernment. My thesis so far in this chapter has been that the sanctifying Spirit of the triune God is poured out upon all flesh in order to accomplish the redemption of the world. More precisely, such a redemptive salvation is to be understood not necessarily with regard to the eschatological salvation of every person but as involving the potential renewal of the many cultures of the world as a means of revealing and glorifying God. In this case, the redemption of the many tongues at Pentecost hopes for and also prefigures the "universal restoration" that is to come (Acts 3:21; cf. 9.3.1).

---

130. Similarly, projects begun with the intention of missionizing secular society have to be vigilant that society's influences do not undermine the missionary mandate; for a discussion of how one parachurch project negotiated — in some ways successfully, in other ways not — these issues, see Paul Bagshaw, "Sheffield Industrial Mission: The Politics of Holiness," in John W. Rogerson, ed., *The Industrial Mission in a Changing World: Papers from the Jubilee Conference of the Sheffield Industrial Mission* (Sheffield: Sheffield Academic Press, 1996), pp. 18-31.

131. As Cheryl Johns notes, at its core pentecostalism's "being filled with the Spirit" is deconstructive and reconstructive of the status quo; see Cheryl Bridges Johns, "Partners in Scandal: Wesleyan and Pentecostal Scholarship," *Wesleyan Theological Journal* 34, no. 1 (1999): 7-23, esp. pp. 16-21.

Yet the renewal and redemption of culture requires theological norms by which to determine how culture can be purified (or else why it should be rejected) and rendered pleasing and acceptable to God (when sanctified by the Spirit). One norm to consider is aesthetic in nature: What aspects of culture are both constitutive of the wholeness (holiness) that fulfills human aspirations (the criterion of harmony) and open to reflecting the splendor of divine holiness (the criterion of trinitarian beauty)? In pursuing this line of questioning I am joining in the discussion initiated by Cheryl Sanders's analyses of the sanctified church in terms of a sanctified worship and a sanctified aesthetic. My contribution is to expand on a sanctified aesthetic that can play a role in understanding the Spirit's redemption of culture. For this task, I extrapolate Sanders's sanctified aesthetic in two complementary directions: an anthropological modality focused on human embodiment and reflective of human creativity as an embodied activity, and a theological dimension focused on the gift of the Spirit that makes possible the production of cultural beauty.

We have already seen (5.1.2) that sanctified worship and sanctified aesthetic are embodied, kinesthetic, and participatory. The gift of the one Spirit that cleanses and renews the many tongues at Pentecost now also makes available many gifts in and through the many members of the body of Christ (1 Cor. 12). Three points are noteworthy in the Pauline explication: 1) that no gift from any member of the body is of lesser value than any other; 2) that each gift and member is essential to the functioning of the full body; and 3) that the whole body suffers/rejoices if any member suffers and that the whole body is edified by the contributions of each of the members. The central features of a sanctified aesthetic can now be more clearly delineated from the saints' worshiping in the beauty of holiness.[132] There is a diversity of ritual modalities featuring different ritual actors: singing/praising, prayer, shout, devotional, testimony, sermon, etc. There is a range of physical gestures including the waving/clapping/lifting of hands, dancing, running, prostrating, bodily and facial gestures, etc. There are also within the various components of the worship service a wide range of musical productions: "Other forms of ritual play such as improvisation, and experimentation may also incorporate various literary devices such as rhyme, onomatopoeia, meter, rhythm, metaphor, or personal narrative as a means of creating dramatic exchanges between pulpit, congregation, and musicians."[133] In short, the wor-

132. The following derives from Thomasina Neely-Chandler, "Modes of Ritual Performance in African-American Pentecostalism," in Daniel Kodzo Avorgbedor, ed., *The Interrelatedness of Music, Religion, and Ritual in African Performance Practice,* African Studies 68 (Lewiston, NY: Edwin Mellen Press, 2003), pp. 313-45.

133. Neely-Chandler, "Modes of Ritual Performance," p. 324

ship of the sanctified church is beautiful because the Spirit orchestrates a harmonization out of the many ritual moments, embodied movements, genres of activities, functional roles, and media instruments that interrelate when the saints are gathered together in Jesus' name.

But we can go further and suggest that the sanctified church has adapted specific African aesthetic principles in the production of what might be called a sanctified culture. Arguably, a central feature of African aesthetics is its non-mimetic character.[134] So if Western aesthetics has often sought to represent nature, Africans have by and large rejected mimesis in their philosophy of art, and have chosen instead to accentuate spontaneity and allow for human creativity that taps into the abstract and mystical dimensions of the human psyche. In sanctified worship, such a non-mimetic approach emphasizes "individual expression, audience input, musical elaboration, emphasis on contrastive timbres, percussive sound, asymmetrical and nonlinear structures, polyrhythm, allusion, irony, etc."[135] Similarly, in Ghanaian pentecostalism, visions, dreams, and the invisible realm of the "supernatural" (rather than that of the mundane) are illuminated in a relational and participatory mode of cultural production that includes film and video producers, directors, and actors, pastoral models and leaders who provide the theological content and spiritual authorization, and engaged audiences (5.3.2). Rather than being a mere or bland syncretism of gospel and culture, these adaptations of African aesthetics may be seen instead as examples of what Walter Hollenweger calls a "theologically responsible syncretism" that looks for signs of the Spirit's redemption of the many tongues and cultures of the world.[136] The results are the edification of the saints, an ironic outcome in which the many tongues or many different parts yet harmonize in mediating the sanctifying presence and activity of God in the cultural domain. Somehow, in a sanctified aesthetics, the cacophony of difference does not degenerate into chaos but rather glorifies the creativity of the living God.[137]

But more than this, a sanctified aesthetics of participation and difference edifies by producing a liminal form of "communitas" that enables the

134. Stephen J. Casmier and Donald H. Matthews, "Why Scatting Is Like Speaking in Tongues: Post-Modern Reflections on Jazz, Pentecostalism, and 'Africomysticism'," *Literature and Theology* 13, no. 2 (1999): 166-76.

135. Neely-Chandler, "Modes of Ritual Performance," p. 345n.5.

136. Walter J. Hollenweger, *Pentecostalism: Origins and Developments Worldwide* (Peabody, MA: Hendrickson, 1997), chap. 11.

137. See also David D. Daniels III, "'Gotta Moan Sometime': A Sonic Exploration of Earwitnesses to Early Pentecostal Sound in North America," *PNEUMA: The Journal of the Society for Pentecostal Studies* 30, no. 1 (2008): 5-32.

many members of the body to suspend their mundane social identities and adopt instead a counter-cultural posture toward the world.[138] From this perspective, there is what Hauerwas would call a culturally subversive dimension to sanctified worship and its politics of holiness that liberates the saints from pressures to conform to society's conventions. Hence the sanctified church understands the many tongues of the Spirit (glossolalia) not just as manifestations of the tongues of angels (1 Cor. 13:1) but as a counter-ideological and counter-hegemonic defiance of the socio-cultural and political status quo.[139] As noted by Willie Jennings (a colleague of Hauerwas), "Jesus' disciples speak in tongues and ethnic boundaries get disrupted. The place of disruption is in their very bodies. . . . It signifies a fundamental confusion of ethnic identities. . . . Pentecost is about one people who will allow the power of the Spirit to change their alliances and their allegiances. . . . At Pentecost, biracial existence announced by the gift of tongues means that Jesus' disciples might now live 'in-between' the nations and their classificatory schemas, their hopes and plans, and their desires."[140] In short, a sanctified aesthetics redeems culture in part by challenging its unholy elements insofar as these are resistant and not conformable to the harmony and beauty of the trinitarian God.

In the end, the Spirit of holiness is also the Spirit of beauty and the Spirit who enables human perception of the beauty of Christ and the holiness of God. There is a venerable theological tradition going all the way back to some of the earliest strata of the Old Testament (e.g., Exod. 31:2-5 and 35:30-35) of the divine spirit as the source of cultural productivity and artistic design — what might be called the sanctified imagination.[141] Not only does the

138. See Bobby C. Alexander, "Pentecostal Ritual Reconsidered: Anti-structural Dimensions of Possession," *Journal of Ritual Studies* 3, no. 1 (1989): 109-28, and "Correcting Misinterpretations of Turner's Theory: An African-American Pentecostal Illustration," *Journal for the Scientific Study of Religion* 30, no. 1 (1991): 26-44.

139. Robert Beckford argues this point in his analysis of pentecostalism against the background of Afro-Caribbean culture; see his *Jesus Dub: Theology, Music, and Social Change* (New York and London: Routledge, 2006).

140. Willie James Jennings, "Speaking in Tongues: Language, Nationalism, and the Formation of Church Life," in Todd H. Speidell, ed., *On Being Christian . . . and Human: Essays in Celebration of Ray S. Anderson* (Eugene, OR: Wipf & Stock, 2002), pp. 224-35, quotation derived from pp. 230, 234, and 235. Thus also Casmier and Matthews, "Why Scatting Is Like Speaking in Tongues," pp. 174-75, suggest that "scatting and speaking in tongues are not the only outbursts of the rebellious, transforming, liberating spirit that imbues these speaking events. Rejecting conventional sounds and words to say something that is normally unspeakable or ineffable is commonplace in most African American secular and religious music."

141. Patrick Sherry, *Spirit and Beauty: An Introduction to Theological Aesthetics* (Oxford: Clarendon Press, 1992).

Spirit enable the re-production of earthly beauty (the mimetic dimension), but the Spirit also inspires creative genius (the non-mimetic aspect) that anticipates the divine glory which humans have yet to perceive because such remains hidden in the incarnation, humiliation, and ascension of Christ. The Spirit's creation of the beautiful in and through human agents is an eschatological work that sanctifies, transfigures, fulfills, and perfects all things, even in their fallenness, in order to renew the world in the glorious beauty of the triune God.[142]

Because of the gift of the Spirit at Pentecost and the accompanying tongues and gifts, not only Christian art but human creation in general can be potentially sacred and revelatory of the beauty and holiness of God. Not only art but music, sculpture, architecture, poetry, and drama can be redemptive in mediating the present and eschatological salvation of God.[143] There must be many modes of artistic production and many means of aesthetic representation of the divine glory because of the diverse modes of human perception; while there are the five "normal" senses (seeing, hearing, touching, tasting, and feeling), one of these may be dominant for some, while one or more of these may be lacking in part or altogether for others.[144] The sanctified imagination is thereby animated by the many tongues of Pentecost in anticipating the new creation when the many tribes, peoples, and nations (Rev. 5:9) will worship the trinitarian God in the beauty of holiness. Then will the redemption of the many tongues and cultures of the world be complete, when the brokenness of the world is finally and fully reconciled to God and the creations of humankind reflect the light of the Son in the glory of the Father.

142. This pneumato-eschatological aesthetic is beautifully portrayed in Sherry, *Spirit and Beauty,* chap. 7.

143. Robert Faricy, "Art as a Charism in the Church," *Thought* 57 (1982): 94-99, esp. p. 96. Thus Faricy also writes: "Art as revelation has an apocalyptic dimension. The Spirit that inspires art is the eschatological Spirit, the Holy Spirit who breaks into the present from God's promised future. . . . The Holy Spirit renews us toward the future. Partly, the Spirit renews through inspired art"; from Faricy, "Art and the Holy Spirit," *Theological Renewal* 16 (1980): 27-32, quote from p. 30. In response, Peter D. Ashton, "The Holy Spirit and the Gifts of Art," *Theological Renewal* 21 (1982): 12-22, urges less emphasis on the sacramental, eschatological, and redemptive nature of art than on its creational aspects as manifesting the creativity of the human imagination made in the *imago Dei.* I am unsure that there is as much of a dualism between creation and redemption in this regard as Ashton might suggest.

144. I thus explore how the many tongues of Pentecost invite consideration of modes of perception vis-à-vis a theology of disability in my 2009 presidential address to the Society for Pentecostal Studies, published as "Many Tongues, Many Senses: Pentecost, the Body Politic, and the Redemption of Disability," *PNEUMA: The Journal of the Society for Pentecostal Studies* 30, no. 2 (2009): 167-88. See also chapter 3 in my forthcoming book *The Bible, the Church, and Disability* (Grand Rapids: Eerdmans).

I close this chapter with three statements that might be said to contribute to an *apophatic theology of culture*. After all that is said above, we must still not claim to know too much about God's ways of redeeming the world. Hence, first, a theology of culture informed by the sanctified imagination cannot on this side of the eschaton pronounce the accomplished redemption of culture; rather, it can only make the much more modest claim about the redeemability of culture according to the salvific and sanctifying power of the Holy Spirit. Second, a politics of holiness informed by a pneumatological theology of sanctification cannot provide a once-for-all template that dictates how to negotiate the fine line between withdrawing from and engaging with culture; rather, the call toward purification *from* or vocational consecration *for the sake of* the world must be continually discerned as the Spirit leads the community of faith in its various contexts. Finally, a sanctified aesthetic cannot present an objective criterion that exhaustibly demarcates the domain of the beauty of holiness. Rather, true worship in the Spirit is a communally- and praxis-shaped (per Hauerwas) eschatological orientation toward the Father whose glory has only yet been partially revealed in the Son, and thus requires an ongoing renewal of the heart and mind of the worshiper. The remainder of this book will both elaborate on and in some respects qualify the theology of culture proposed here.

CHAPTER 6

Pentecostal Power:
A Prophetic Politics of Civil Society

The theology of culture sketched in the preceding chapter was derived from a politics of holiness rooted in the pentecostal theology of sanctification. The two sides of such a theology — being *not of* while remaining *in* the world — invite both a posture that challenges the world and one that hopes and works for its redemption. My thesis there of "many tongues and many cultures" argued for the possibility of the latter as shaped by a Pentecostal, pneumatological, and sanctified imagination. In this chapter, however, we now turn to explicate the prophetic witness that should also characterize the Christian encounter with the public square.

Whereas I have commended that Jesus the sanctifier invites us to consider a redemptive theology of many cultures, I now propose that the third element of the pentecostal fivefold gospel, Jesus the Spirit-baptizer, is suggestive of what might be called a politico-prophetic theology of mission and socio-cultural evangelization. The argument in this chapter thus proceeds — as before — in three steps (corresponding to the following three sections): an explication of the pentecostal theology of Spirit-baptism as empowerment for witness and how such a theological posture has unfolded missionally, socially, and politically; a dialogue with the post-secular theology of Radical Orthodoxy, particularly as focused on its attempts to provide what might be called a prophetic and counter-hegemonic theology of the social, the market, the state, and culture; and a constructive sketch of what I call a prophetic and missionary politics of civil society in a post-secular but yet not anti-secular mode. If the foregoing politics of holiness argued for the possibility of the redemption of the many cultures of the world, the present politics of mission is motivated by a prophetic posture to achieve an evangelization of civil society and a re-evangelization of the secular domain in the Euro-American West.[1]

Our quest in what follows focuses therefore on what it means to bear Christian witness in civil society, especially in our postmodern and post-secular situation. On the one hand, this motif enables us to articulate a political theology of civil society; on the other hand, it will also allow us to highlight a Christian mode of engaging civil society in terms of counter-cultural resistance (rather than one of cultural redemption) so that the prophetic dimension of the Christian witness would complement our previous articulation (in chapter 4) of a political theology of principalities and powers and open up further space for reflecting on how the structures and spheres of creation might be delivered from their fallen condition and liberated for the glory of God. In short, we will mine the pentecostal theology of Jesus as Spirit-baptizer for resources to think about a prophetic politics and theology of missionary witness specifically as enacted in a post-secular civil society.

6.1. Jesus as Spirit-Baptizer: Baptized in and for What?

The doctrine of Jesus as baptizer in the Holy Spirit has been called the "crown jewel" as well as the "distinctive testimony" of pentecostalism.[2] I will delineate the main lines of the classical pentecostal theology of Spirit-baptism understood as empowerment for mission and evangelism, explore its developments and expansions in a global — especially South Korean — context, and then refocus on how its theology of empowerment has had political applications in response to the secularization of the West. Two features of the pentecostal doctrine will emerge in what follows: its underwriting of a bold public witness and its motivation to replace the stereotypically apolitical posture of pentecostalism with a form of direct political engagement. Our objective over the scope of this chapter will be to find ways to accentuate both aspects to-

---

1. The notion of "prophetic" in this chapter refers less to the foretelling of future events than to the forth-telling of the word of God; we will return in our final chapter to discuss the former aspect of prophecy.

2. See Frank D. Macchia, *Baptized in the Spirit: A Global Pentecostal Theology* (Grand Rapids: Eerdmans, 2006), pp. 20-27, and David Petts, "The Baptism in the Holy Spirit: The Theological Distinctive," in Keith Warrington, ed., *Pentecostal Perspectives* (Carlisle: Paternoster Press, 1998), pp. 98-119. For a contrary perspective, see Henry Lederle, "An Ecumenical Investigation into the Proprium or Distinctive Element of Pentecostal Theology," *Theologia Evangelica* 21 (1988): 34-41.

ward a prophetic politics of mission while negotiating the pitfalls that inevitably accompany the latter.

6.1.1. Classical Pentecostal Theologies of Spirit-Baptism: Empowerment for World Evangelization

The origins of the doctrine of Jesus as baptizer in the Holy Spirit are also rooted in the nineteenth-century holiness movement in North America, particularly in the holiness linkage of the doctrine of sanctification with the baptism of the Holy Spirit.[3] By the end of the century, holiness preachers and evangelists in certain circles had also adopted the nomenclature of the baptism with the Holy Ghost and with fire, and revival movements connected salvation by faith to sanctification, healing, and the enduement with the power of the Spirit. Many of these trends converged in the theology of Charles Fox Parham (1873-1929), the holiness preacher who more than anyone else forged the distinctive theology of classical pentecostalism.

Four distinct biblical motifs were woven together in Parham's theology of the baptism of the Holy Spirit.[4] First, the prophetic reference to God's "abundant rain, the early and the later rain" (Joel 2:23), was read within a premillennialist hermeneutical framework and thought to foreshadow the "last days" outpouring of the Spirit (Acts 2:17). Second, this "promise of the Father" (Acts 1:4) would counter the distressing skepticism of the end times (cf. 2 Tim. 3:1 and 2 Pet. 3:3) with the power of the Holy Spirit, who would embolden believers to bear witness to the gospel to the ends of the earth (Acts 1:8). Third, the Spirit's empowerment would be for the purpose of world evangelization just before the parousia: "this good news of the kingdom will be proclaimed throughout the world, as a testimony to all the nations; and then the end will come" (Matt. 24:14). Finally, according to the Acts narrative, the indisputable sign of the baptism of the Spirit was the gift of speaking in other tongues or languages — the apostles knew "that the gift of the Holy Spirit had been poured out even on the Gentiles, *for* they heard them speak-

---

3. See, e.g., the holiness writings of Phoebe Palmer, *Promise of the Father; or, A Neglected Specialty of the Last Days* (Boston: H. V. Degen, 1859), and published together, Charles Grandison Finney, *Enduement with Power,* and Asa Mahan, *The Baptism of the Holy Ghost* (London: E. Stock, 1876). For an overview of nineteenth-century developments, see Donald Dayton, *Theological Roots of Pentecostalism* (1987; reprint, Peabody, MA: Hendrickson, 1991), chap. 3.

4. The most comprehensive account of Parham's life and thought is James R. Goff Jr., *Fields White unto Harvest: Charles F. Parham and the Missionary Origins of Pentecostalism* (Fayetteville and London: University of Arkansas Press, 1988).

ing in tongues and extolling God" (Acts 10:45-46, italics added; cf. 19:1-6). The importance of the evidential sign of the Spirit, for Parham, was that it equipped believers not only with the boldness to evangelize the nations but also with the means of doing so — in the tongues of native speakers, so that missionaries could communicate the gospel without having to spend months or years learning foreign languages.

Even if these early pentecostal missionaries arrived on their mission fields abroad only to discover that their gift of tongues did not allow them to circumvent language training,[5] the expectation and boldness with which they approached their missionary vocation were more than sufficient motivations for most to stay the course. Missionaries from Azusa Street went almost immediately to Asia, Africa, and Latin America, while others from these continents visited the Los Angeles mission and took the pentecostal message back to their countries of origin.[6] Although there is a contemporary debate about the precise role of the Azusa Street missionary movement in the origins of pentecostalism in what we now call the global south — i.e., whether pentecostalism in the global south began as a result of the ministry of Western missionaries or whether there were indigenous revivals of pentecostalism before the missionaries arrived — it cannot be denied that Azusa Street became a central node in a global pentecostal network devoted to the evangelization of the world.[7] The work of countless missionaries connected to, informed by, and even tangentially related with this network has established pentecostalism as *the* missionary movement of the twentieth century.

In time, however, the early pentecostal conviction that the gospel would be preached in the last days in the native languages of the many tribes and people of the world was transformed, by pentecostal missiologists, into what they called the "indigenous principle." In dialogue with proposals of Roland Allen (1868-1947) regarding the development of self-supporting, self-governing, and self-propagating mission churches,[8] Assemblies of God missiologist Melvin Hodges argued for the importance of the "indigenous church" for the pente-

---

5. See D. William Faupel, "Glossolalia as Foreign Language: An Investigation of the Early Twentieth-Century Pentecostal Claim," *Wesleyan Theological Journal* 31 (1996): 95-109.

6. Walter J. Hollenweger, *The Pentecostals: The Charismatic Movement in the Churches*, trans. R. A. Wilson (Minneapolis: Augsburg, 1972), esp. chap. 5 and following.

7. See Allan Anderson, *Spreading Fires: The Missionary Nature of Early Pentecostalism* (London: SCM, 2007).

8. Allen was a missionary to China with the Anglican Society for the Propagation of the Gospel; see David M. Paton and Charles H. Long, eds., *The Compulsion of the Spirit: A Roland Allen Reader* (Grand Rapids: Eerdmans, and Cincinnati: Forward Movement Publications, 1983).

costal missionary enterprise.[9] Hodges's pentecostal experience led him to take his missiological cues from the book of Acts. From this he discerned not only that the church is God's missionary agency to the ends of the earth, but also that the Spirit empowers the church for the ministries of the gospel in various contexts. At the level of the individual, all persons, including nominal Christians, are to be brought into an experiential knowledge of the gospel and "into the fellowship of the life in the Holy Spirit."[10] At the corporate level, the Christian mission is to establish self-propagating, self-governing, and self-supporting local congregations and ministries. These would be the dominant features of what Hodges calls "the indigenous church": established, overseen, and developed by local (i.e., "native") leadership with (Western) missionaries serving only the role of consultants. The concept of the "indigenous church," of course, opposes the entire colonial enterprise and attempts to empower local leaders in their various contexts. To be sure, local leadership experienced significant resistance from the missionaries (including pentecostal missionaries) when it came to asserting their local initiative and vision. However, the point is that theologically and missiologically, at least, Hodges's call for an indigenous church helped pentecostal mission agencies to take the important first steps away from the colonial paradigm.

Although Hodges's definition of the indigenous church is congruent with the pentecostal narrative of the diversity of tongues that gave testimony to the mighty works of God on the Day of Pentecost, he nowhere makes the explicit connection, nor does he fully develop the ecclesiological and missiological implications of this pentecostal perspective. Next steps toward this end, however, have been taken by the next generation of pentecostal missiologists. Former Assemblies of God missionary Paul Pomerville, for example, has combined Allen's three-self model and nascent pneumatological insights with Hodges's indigenous church vision in attempting to articulate a more consistently integrated and systematically developed pentecostal theology of mission.[11] Pomerville's key move is to correct what he calls the "pneumatological deficit" in mission theology, and he does so by formulating what he calls a trinitarian and pneumatological missiology.[12] The central elements of his proposal in-

9. E.g., Melvin L. Hodges, *The Indigenous Church and the Missionary* (South Pasadena, CA: William Carey Library, 1978).

10. Melvin Hodges, *A Theology of the Church and Its Mission: A Pentecostal Perspective* (Springfield, MO: Gospel Publishing House, 1977), p. 95.

11. Note that Allen published *The Ministry of the Spirit* (Grand Rapids: Eerdmans, 1960); see also Allen, *The Compulsion of the Spirit.*

12. See Paul A. Pomerville, *The Third Force in Missions: A Pentecostal Contribution to Contemporary Mission Theology* (Peabody, MA: Hendrickson, 1985).

clude a recognition of the diversity of the global pentecostal and charismatic renewal movement (which simply replicates the diversity of God's intentions in salvation history and corrects the distortions of theology and mission theory as they have been developed in the West); a connection between the work of the Spirit and the arrival of the coming kingdom; and an explication of the shape of the kingdom according to the trinitarian revelation of God.

Over the course of the last century, pentecostal missions and commitment to world evangelization have not abated. There has been an increasing realization that earlier approaches fostered a triumphalism based on the ideas that only pentecostals were concerned about global evangelism (in contrast to the liberal Protestant focus on the Social Gospel) and that only pentecostals were equipped with the means to accomplish this task (since the non-pentecostal churches lacked the empowerment of the Holy Spirit).[13] Helpful in tempering this elitism has been the emergence of missiological voices that are sympathetic with even if neither denominationally affiliated with pentecostalism nor otherwise committed to classical pentecostal perspectives.[14] Thus Anglican charismatic missiologist Andrew Lord has presented a pneumatological theology of mission in dialogue with pentecostal sources that simultaneously affirms the importance of an experiential, contextual, communal, and holistic ministry in the global context.[15] As classical pentecostal missiologists interact with these and other voices, there will be a moderation of self-understanding even as the dedication to world evangelization remains a top priority.[16]

6.1.2. South Korean Pentecostal Missions: A Vision for Personal and Social Evangelization

We have already had the opportunity to introduce South Korean pentecostalism in an earlier discussion of pentecostal conservatism (1.3.2). While South Korean pentecostal conservatism mirrors and reflects that of classical North American pentecostalism in many respects, more recent growth has catapulted the former onto the world stage, particularly with regard to its becoming a representative leader of a pentecostal way of being and doing

13. Gary B. McGee, "Pentecostal Missiology: Moving Beyond Triumphalism to Face the Issues," *PNEUMA: The Journal of the Society for Pentecostal Studies* 16, no. 2 (1994): 275-81.

14. E.g., J. A. B. Jongeneel, ed., *Pentecost, Mission, and Ecumenism: Essays on Intercultural Theology* (Frankfurt am Main and New York: Peter Lang, 1992).

15. Andrew Lord, *Spirit-Shaped Mission: A Holistic Charismatic Missiology* (Waynesboro, GA, and Milton Keynes, UK: Paternoster, 2005).

16. Thus John V. York, *Missions in the Age of the Spirit* (Springfield, MO: Logion Press, 2000).

church. The following discussion examines in more detail how the pentecostal doctrine of Spirit-baptism understood in terms of empowerment for witness has played out in the South Korean context. We will look specifically at Yoido Full Gospel Church's (YFGC) home cell group strategy, social ministries, and international vision as expressions of Reverend Yonggi Cho's pneumatological theology of mission and evangelism.

Cho tells us that his church started its explosive growth after he learned to delegate pastoral roles to others rather than attempt to pastor each of his church members directly.[17] The central idea of the home cell group ministry was to release the people themselves to do the work of pastoral ministry. A hierarchical pyramid of trained leaders emerged over time, each working with between a dozen and fifteen leaders or members, with the final level of lay-trained leadership overseeing a small home group of up to fifteen families. When a group expanded above that number of families, it would be divided and two home groups would appear instead. Cho came upon this template for house churches by observing what happened in the book of Acts.[18] The results, since the late 1960s, have been the emergence of YFGC as the largest congregation (of congregations) in the world, with over 700,000 members.

The driving force behind Cho's visionary ministry from the beginning, however, has been theological — i.e., the work of the Holy Spirit to save souls and empower the growth of the church to the ends of the earth.[19] A tripartite theological anthropology (the human being as constituted by spirit/soul, body, and environment) and a correlative tripartite theology of the Fall (spiritual separation from God, bodily death, and the curse of the land) anticipate Cho's "threefold blessing" soteriology: the work of Christ as securing first the salvation of the soul (the forgiveness of sins), then the healing of the body, and finally the material, circumstantial, and social prosperity of the people of God.[20] It is the work of the Spirit to lead people to Christ, to distribute gifts of healing, and to lead believers to accept and live out divinely intended principles (i.e., ho-

17. David Yonggi Cho, with Harold Hostetler, *Successful Home Cell Groups* (Seoul: Seoul Logos Co., 1997), chaps. 1-2.

18. Cho, with Hostetler, *Successful Home Cell Groups*, pp. 17-18.

19. David Yonggi Cho, *The Holy Spirit, My Senior Partner: Understanding the Holy Spirit and His Gifts* (Lake Mary, FL: Charisma House, 1989).

20. David Yonggi Cho, *Salvation, Health, and Prosperity: Our Threefold Blessings in Christ* (1987; reprint, Altamonte Springs, FL: Creation House, 1990). For a brief explication of the interrelationship between Cho's theological anthropology, the doctrine of the fall, and soteriology, see Jun Hee Cha, "The Anthropology of Rev. Yonggi Cho's Threefold Blessing Theology: In the Light of the Old Testament," in Young San Theological Institute, ed., *Dr. Yonggi Cho's Ministry and Theology*, 2 vols. (Gunpo, Korea: Hansei University Logos, 2008), vol. 1, pp. 129-56.

liness, tithing, a work ethic) that bring about abundant life. Home cell groups are sites where individuals are healed and Christian community is shaped in ways that allow for the realization of the prosperity promised by God.

Cho's concept of prosperity is thus a complex blend of East Asian ideas of blessing, the Western "prosperity gospel" teachings, and a wide range of biblical notions.[21] In part for this reason, charges of syncretism have surfaced, insinuating that Korean pentecostalism is more akin to indigenous shamanism than authentically Christian.[22] Cho's defenders have suggested that his achievements should be understood not only against the shamanic background of the South Korean context but also of the poverty, pain, and collective suffering *(han)* of the people up through the 1950s and 1960s.[23] As Cho insists, the poor are "needy people," and part of the proclamation of the good news of Jesus Christ is to meet the needs of the people.[24]

A further analysis would note that while not going as far as the Minjung theologians in advocating socio-political activity, Cho's theology of blessing is sufficiently broad as to encompass social welfare and ministry. More precisely, there has been a complementarity between what Minjung theologians from the more progressive Protestant churches in South Korea are advocating and what YFGC has been doing: the former have championed social reformation while the latter has worked for social integration.[25] Thus YFGC's social ministries have included at least the following components:[26]

21. Gwi Sam Cho, "The Missional Contextualization of *Bok* (Blessings) in Korean Religious Mentality on Cases of Yoido Full Gospel Church," in Young San Theological Institute, ed., *Dr. Yonggi Cho's Ministry and Theology,* 2 vols. (Gunpo, Korea: Hansei University Logos, 2008), vol. 1, pp. 215-34.

22. Initially raised by Yoo Boo-Woong, "Response to Korean Shamanism by the Pentecostal Church," *International Review of Mission* 75, no. 297 (1986): 70-74; cf. Harvey G. Cox, *Fire from Heaven: The Rise of Pentecostal Spirituality and the Reshaping of Religion in the Twenty-First Century* (Reading, MA.: Addison-Wesley, 1995), chap. 11.

23. Allan Anderson, "The Contribution of David Yonggi Cho to a Contextual Theology in Korea," *Journal of Pentecostal Theology* 12, no. 1 (2003): 85-105, and "The Contextual Pentecostal Theology of David Yonggi Cho," *Asian Journal of Pentecostal Studies* 7, no. 1 (2004): 101-23; cf. Veli-Matti Kärkkäinen, "'March Forward to Hope': Yonggi Cho's Pentecostal Theology of Hope," *PNEUMA: The Journal of the Society for Pentecostal Studies* 28, no. 2 (2006): 253-63.

24. Yonggi Cho, *My Church Growth Stories* (Seoul: Seoul Logos Co., 2006), chap. 5.

25. Hyeon Sung Bae, "Full Gospel Theology and a Korean Pentecostal Identity," in Allan Anderson and Edmond Tang, eds., *Asian and Pentecostal: The Charismatic Face of Christianity in Asia* (Oxford: Regnum Books International, and Baguio City, Philippines: APTS Press, 2005), pp. 527-49, esp. pp. 531-32; cf. Lee Hong Jung, "*Minjung* and Pentecostal Movements in Korea," in Allan Anderson and Walter J. Hollenweger, eds., *Pentecostals after a Century: Global Perspectives on a Movement in Transition* (Sheffield: Sheffield Academic Press, 1999), pp. 138-60.

26. Young-gi Hong, "Social Leadership and Church Growth," in Wonsuk Ma, William W.

- social welfare and relief activities as seen in the Elim Welfare Town initiative
- leadership development (especially in the many women trained in the home cell group context, a breakthrough given the Confucian and patriarchal heritage of East Asian societies like South Korea)
- building of schools and establishment of educational programs including institutions of higher education
- publication of the *Kookmin Daily News* to inform and influence public opinion
- subsidizing of heart disease medical operations (for over 3,000 people from 1984 through 2003)
- collaboration with the Green Seoul Citizen Association to address environmental and ecological issues.[27]

Each of these is understood to be part and parcel of the Spirit's work of "redemption and lift." As Cho has proclaimed, "What our own nation, Korea, requires today is Spirit-filled businessmen, Spirit-filled politicians, and Spirit-filled citizens. . . . When we as Christians recognize the Holy Spirit, welcome Him, rely on Him, and always communicate and work in unity with Him, the new Korea will begin to blossom."[28]

Yet Cho's vision for social ministry is not parochially limited to South Korea. Through establishment of the non-governmental organization, Good People World Family, YFGC's humanitarian relief has been expanded to focus on the poor in the global village. Its services include assistance to refugees, career training, food and clothing provision, medical assistance, family and personal counseling, prevention and treatment of AIDS, and emergency/disaster relief.[29] To be sure, such socially engaging activities are not

Menzies, and Hyeon-sung Bae, eds., *David Yonggi Cho: A Close Look at His Theology and Ministry* (Goonpo, Korea: Hansei University Press, and Baguio City, Philippines: APTS Press, 2004), pp. 221-51.

27. On this point, Cho writes: "[T]he redemption of Jesus Christ is holistic in that it embraces social redemption that eradicates social depravity and environmental redemption for the sake of the whole groaning creation (Rom 8:22), not only spiritual redemption of men. By means of the grace of God's salvation, all the wickedness, injustice and disjointedness must be transformed; also the abuse of nature must be stopped to restore nature, bring it to life and bless it"; see Cho's *Soteriology for the 21st Century,* ed. International Theological Institute (Seoul: Logos, 2005), pp. 4-5, cited in Jun Hee Cha, "The Anthropology of Rev. Yonggi Cho's Threefold Blessing Theology," p. 155n.81.

28. David (Paul) Yonggi Cho, *Great Businessmen* (Seoul: Seoul Logos Co., 1995), p. 74.

29. See Young-gi Hong, "The Influence of His Church Growth on Korean Society," in

stand-alone projects but are part and parcel of Cho's and the YFGC's vision for world evangelization.

YFGC is undertaking the task of world mission in a variety of ways. Not only are Cho's books being translated into many languages, but his church is attracting international visitors who are not only implementing but also revising and adapting his church growth and home cell group evangelism principles in their own contexts.[30] There are also, of course, the more traditional forms of missionary sending, but this time, from South Korea to the rest of the world, including the western hemisphere.[31] Even if many of these South Korean missionaries in the West are ministering first and foremost to South Korean emigrants, others are launching out new initiatives to local peoples, especially across the global south. In short, the vision for world evangelization involves not only traditional forms of missionizing and proselytizing, but also new efforts of re-evangelization, especially in the Western world.[32]

It should be noted that Cho writes not as a formally trained theologian but always as a pastor, preacher, and evangelist. He is animated by the call to preach the gospel of Christ through the power of the Holy Spirit. For this reason, social ministries are important, but always subordinate to the higher priority of proclaiming the good news of the forgiveness of sins, and of grace, peace, and joy in Jesus Christ. For similar reasons, Cho has always been hesitant to step more formally into the domain of the political.[33]

Sung-Hoon Myung and Young-Gi Hong, eds., *Charis and Charisma: David Yonggi Cho and the Growth of Yoido Full Gospel Church* (Waynesboro, GA, and Milton Keynes, UK: Paternoster, 2003), pp. 197-217, esp. pp. 209-14.

30. See Kevin Hrebik and Adrienne S. Gaines, "Church-Growth Strategy Goes Global," *Charisma Magazine* (September 2003), available at http://www.charismamag.com/articles/index.php?id=7978 (last accessed 9 January 2009); cf. Phil Wingeier-Rayo, "The Transculturalization and the Transnationalization of the Government of 12: From Seoul to Bogota to Charlotte, North Carolina," unpublished paper presented to the American Academy of Religion, Chicago, Illinois, 1 November 2008 (my thanks to Wingeier-Rayo for sharing his research with me).

31. See Ig-Jin Kim, *History and Theology of Korean Pentecostalism: Sunbogeum (Pure Gospel) Pentecostalism,* Mission Series 35 (Zoetermeer, The Netherlands: Uitgeverij Boekencentrum, 2003), pp. 187-90.

32. In this regard, South Korean missionaries are part of a much larger movement of re-evangelization from the "rest" to the "West"; see Larry D. Pate, "Pentecostal Missions from the Two-Thirds World," in Murray W. Dempster, Byron D. Klaus, and Douglas Petersen, eds., *Called and Empowered: Global Mission in Pentecostal Perspective* (Peabody, MA: Hendrickson, 1991), pp. 242-58.

33. At best, prayer remains the ever-present socio-political "weapon" of choice: "Bible school students of the Yongmoon Prayer Mountain attempted more than once to march to the north across the heavily fortified demilitarized zone for national reunification. The Yongmoon

6.1.3. Neo-Pentecostalism's Re-Christianizing the Secular: A Case Study of Political Evangelization

If Cho remains reluctant to become more politically engaged, M. G. "Pat" Robertson has been much more explicitly political in North America. He burst onto the public scene in the mid-1980s when as a religious broadcaster he went on to challenge George H. W. Bush for the Republication nomination to the 1988 U.S. presidential election.[34] Although unsuccessful then, Robertson has been actively involved since as founder of the grassroots Christian Coalition organization and has mobilized evangelicals and other conservative Protestants as a voting bloc to make a difference in local, state, and national elections over the last two decades.[35] Because of his influence and his political agenda, his opponents — inevitably those on the political left — have gone so far as to label him "the most dangerous man in America"![36] I suggest, however, that Robertson is first and foremost a pentecostal evangelist, a minister of the gospel whose political platform is best understood as an attempt to re-evangelize a secular culture of decadence.

To be sure, Robertson was raised in political circles, the son of United States senator A. Willis Robertson (1887-1971), had served in the Korean War as a member of the Marine Corps, and completed a law degree from Yale University Law School (1955). However, his years at the Biblical Seminary in New York City (renamed New York Theological Seminary in 1965), from 1956 to 1959, were much more formative since it was during this time that he came into the pentecostal experience of Spirit-baptism with the evidence of speaking in other tongues.[37] Although by the late 1970s he had subordinated his pentecos-

---

Prayer Mountain also started a 24-hour prayer altar for national security, and many prayer mountain churches followed this and began similar programs"; see Won Suk Ma, "David Yonggi Cho's Theology of Blessing: A New Theological Base and Direction," in Young San Theological Institute, ed., *Dr. Yonggi Cho's Ministry and Theology,* 2 vols. (Gunpo, Korea: Hansei University Logos, 2008), vol. 1, pp. 179-200, quote from p. 191.

34. For an overview of Robertson's rise to political prominence, see Jeffrey K. Hadden and Anson Shupe, *Televangelism: Power and Politics on God's Frontier* (New York: Henry Holt, 1988).

35. See Justin Watson, *The Christian Coalition: Dreams of Restoration, Demands for Recognition* (New York: St. Martin's Press, 1997).

36. See Richard Boston, *The Most Dangerous Man in America? Pat Robertson and the Rise of the Christian Coalition* (Amherst, NY: Prometheus Books, 1996). A similar critique from within Christian circles is articulated in Norman R. Gulley, "The Christian Coalition and the End Game," *Journal of the Adventist Theological Society* 8, nos. 1-2 (1997): 120-36.

37. For Robertson's own account of his quest for the pentecostal baptism, see Pat Robertson, with Jamie Buckingham, *Shout It from the Housetops* (Plainfield, NJ: Logos, 1972), chaps. 4-5.

tal or charismatic self-identification in favor of the "evangelical label,"[38] he has neither denied its significance for his personal life and vocational calling nor rejected the pentecostal theological understanding of the phenomenon. Thus even in a fairly recent book, Robertson has not only defended the veracity of the gift of tongues as well as other spiritual gifts (such as healing and miracles), he has also continued to accept the almost unique role of tongues in validating a Spirit-filled and Spirit-empowered life.[39] In other words, Robertson remains a practicing pentecostal Christian, even if his political ventures have led him to emphasize his evangelical credentials instead.

Yet it is precisely Robertson's pentecostal self-understanding that has motivated his endeavors in the public square. For Robertson, as for all pentecostals, the pentecostal gift of the baptism of the Holy Spirit empowers believers with boldness to bear witness to the gospel, to accomplish the impossible, and to resist the powers of darkness. Thus he viewed his calling as a religious broadcaster to take the gospel to the ends of the earth, and he made his first foray outside of the continental U.S. by the end of the 1960s when he purchased a radio station in Bogota, Colombia.[40] In the last forty years, Robertson's Christian Broadcasting Network (CBN) has continued to expand, and is now a presence worldwide. Yet throughout, the goal has been not only the evangelization of souls but also the transformation of culture itself. CBN contests the reigning values of the times and promotes instead biblical morality, traditional family values, and a Christian way of life.[41] In short, Robertson the religious broadcaster is motivated by a vocational commitment to make a difference not only by preaching the gospel but also by revealing its power to transform the world.[42]

My thesis is that Robertson's felt "divine call" into the political arena

38. Garry Wills, *Under God: Religion and American Politics* (New York: Simon & Schuster, 1990), p. 172.

39. Pat Robertson, *Bring It On: Tough Questions, Candid Answers* (Nashville: W Publishing, 2003), pp. 225-26; chaps. 8-9 of this book defend tongues, miracles, and other spiritual gifts as relevant for contemporary Christian faith.

40. Robertson, with Buckingham, *Shout It from the Housetops,* chaps. 22-23.

41. See Stewart M. Hoover, "The Meaning of Religious Television: The '700 Club' in the Lives of Its Viewers," in Quentin J. Schultz, ed., *American Evangelicals and the Mass Media* (Grand Rapids: Zondervan Academic, 1990), pp. 231-49, and Razelle Frankl, "Transformation of Televangelism: Repackaging Christian Family Values," in Linda Kintz and Julia Lesage, eds., *Media, Culture, and the Religious Right* (Minneapolis and London: University of Minnesota Press, 1998), pp. 163-89.

42. Thus John B. Donovan, *Pat Robertson: The Authorized Biography* (New York: Macmillan, and London: Collier, 1988), p. 123, correctly emphasizes the role that a theological notion of vocation plays in Robertson's self-understanding.

should be understood at least in part as a Spirit-led and Spirit-empowered response to make a prophetic difference in a world gone awry. Like other cultural conservatives reacting to trends in the 1950s, 60s, and 70s, Robertson was concerned about the Cold War, communism, feminism, liberalism, *Roe v. Wade*, the Vietnam War, etc.[43] But more than anything, he was deeply troubled that America was moving far away from the biblical roots established by the Founding Fathers. Robertson's political platform consisted, in effect, of a vision of restoring Christian America, as one nation under God. The problem was, to put it bluntly, godlessness, albeit manifest in many forms: ideologically in terms of secularism (instead of religious values), humanism (instead of theism), relativism and skepticism (about truth), and naturalism and materialism (in worldview);[44] morally and socially in terms of the undermining of the traditional family by sex education in the public schools, feminism, homosexuality, pornography, abortion rights, drug abuse, and rampant crime; legally in terms of liberal justices with constructivist views of the law undermining not only the Constitution but also the biblical principles of the nation: prayer and Bible reading in public schools, the dignity of life, and the centrality of the Ten Commandments as a symbol of the nation's morals and values;[45] and internationally in terms of a foreign policy that emphasized a strong military to withstand expansion of non-theistic forms of government (i.e., communism) and to support and defend the nation of Israel against its enemies. The problem was exacerbated by the fact that evangelical views on these matters were laughed out of (at best) or not even allowed in (at worst) the public square by the liberal and secular elite. The solution was that Christians needed to be mobilized to restore what had been forgotten, to renew the American covenant (and its "Manifest Destiny"), to re-evangelize the (religiously naked) public square, and to re-establish Christian values across and dominion over the nation, if not the world.[46]

43. See Robertson, *America's Dates with Destiny* (Nashville: Thomas Nelson, 1986), part 2, for his views of some of the ills plaguing American society.

44. These are matters that many conservative evangelicals would agree are threatening post-Christian, postmodern, and multicultural America; see also Herbert Schlossberg, *Idols for Destruction: The Conflict of Christian Faith and American Culture* (1990; reprint, Wheaton, IL: Crossway, 1993).

45. See Pat Robertson, *Courting Disaster: How the Supreme Court Is Usurping the Power of Congress and the People* (Nashville: Integrity, 2004), and *The Ten Offenses: Reclaim the Blessings of the Ten Commandments* (Nashville: Integrity, 2004).

46. Robertson has long been intrigued by aspects of Dominion Theology (or Reconstructionism), which calls for Christians to take social and political responsibility, although he shies away from a full embrace of Reconstructionist retrievals of the Old Testament and from its explicit commitments to a postmillennial eschatology. See Pat Robertson, with Bob Slosser, *The*

Robertson's popularity is an indication that his message resonates with many evangelical (not to mention pentecostal and charismatic) Christians in North America.[47] The difference is that while others may be complaining that the secularization of the public square has effectively excluded and discriminated against (only) conservative Christian presence and activity therein, Robertson has actually attempted to do something politically about it. I propose that this difference can be understood as a reflection of what happens when pentecostal faith in the empowering courage of the Spirit of God converges with other elements. In Robertson's case, pentecostal audacity was mixed with media savvy and an evangelical and wider/popular cultural restlessness to produce an arguably prophetic form of pentecostal politics vis-à-vis the reigning liberal ideologies of the last generation.[48]

To be sure, Robertson has had his fair share of critics, both left and right.[49] The secular media, however, does not understand that he is first and foremost a pentecostal preacher and evangelist rather than a politician. Thus Robertson's first political act is also the deeply pentecostal one of prayer,[50] and from out of such time of private prayer and even fasting, he believes he hears from God. Pentecostals believe that God continues to speak, but Robertson's distinctiveness is that he thinks God reveals matters of political (pub-

---

Secret Kingdom (Nashville: Thomas Nelson, 1982), chap. 14; cf. William Martin, *With God on Our Side: The Rise of the Religious Right in America* (New York: Broadway, 1996), esp. chaps. 12-13.

47. For a brief ethnography of the congregation Robertson has attended, which is representative of a broad swath of evangelical churches that would be sympathetic to his views, see Daniel Vaca, "Saving America's Soul: Religion and Politics at Pat Robertson's Church, Kempsville Presbyterian Church, Virginia Beach, Virginia, March 23, 2003," *Anglican and Episcopal History* 74, no. 1 (2005): 137-42.

48. See Allen D. Hertzke, *Echoes of Discontent: Jesse Jackson, Pat Robertson, and the Resurgence of Populism* (Washington, DC: Congressional Quarterly Press, 1993), for the thesis that Robertson answered the call of the masses for leadership against the policies of the leftist elite; see also James M. Penning, "Pat Robertson and the GOP: 1988 and Beyond," *Sociology of Religion* 55, no. 3 (1994): 327-44. On the other hand, not all conservative Protestants or evangelicals supported Robertson, which should go without saying since these are not homogeneous groups; see Stephen D. Johnson, Joseph B. Tamney, and Ronald Burton, "Pat Robertson: Who Supported His Candidacy for President?" *Journal for the Scientific Study of Religion* 28, no. 4 (1989): 387-99.

49. An informative volume that registers the major criticisms is David John Marley, *Pat Robertson: An American Life* (Lanham, MD: Rowman & Littlefield, 2007). A somewhat dated but still scholarly and even-handed treatment is David Edwin Harrell Jr., *Pat Robertson: A Personal, Religious, and Political Portrait* (San Francisco: Harper & Row, 1987).

50. In his book on *Courting Disaster,* for example, there is the repeated call for evangelical Christians to pray that God will intervene in history so that the course of the Supreme Court can be corrected and redeemed.

lic) import to him personally — matters he then publicizes (even if he admits that he may not always hear God rightly). In the contemporary political arena, of course, such a mode of operation is incomprehensible, just as we recall that the prophets of ancient Israel were rejected and stoned for their proclamations. But Robertson is driven by the conviction that there is a "secret kingdom" that is God's way of doing things, that this is revealed in the Bible, and that it remains for believers to seek first the kingdom of God and its righteousness, and then to live that out in following Christ by the power of the Spirit.[51] Sometimes, this may mean a call to public office, even if it will always include the call to public service.[52]

Even if some will disagree with Robertson's political views, there is no gainsaying his spiritual, religious, and theological convictions. Is this an illegitimate mixing of religion and politics? There is a good deal of talk about the biblical (and ancient Hebraic) view that does not compartmentalize these domains; yet there is inevitably an outcry when preachers step into the political realm. Is Cho's more ecclesially driven approach to mission and evangelism and ecclesially oriented strategy of social engagement more palatable for contemporary ecumenical theologies of the public square than Robertson's more confrontational interaction with the political? Or might it be instead that Cho and Robertson are both living out the pentecostal theology Spirit-baptism as endowing believers with the daring needed to bear witness to the gospel in a fallen world, but are doing so in different contexts — a Korean one in which Cho sees the need for an initial Christianization and a secularized American one in need of re-evangelization?

6.2. Post-Secularism in the Western World: A Radically Orthodox Theopolitics

If Robertson and large segments of North American conservative evangelicalism and pentecostalism have identified the enemy as secular humanism, the

---

51. See Robertson, with Slosser, *The Secret Kingdom*, along with the sequel to this volume — Pat Robertson, *The New World Order* (Dallas: Word, 1991), esp. chaps. 11-12.

52. As we have seen, other pentecostals have turned to more explicit political engagement for other reasons (1.1.2). In the Nigerian case, for example, pentecostals have revised their theology in order to legitimate political involvement directed to resisting the felt threat of Muslim Islamization, especially in the northern states. For discussion, see Cyril Imo, "Evangelicals, Muslims, and Democracy: With Particular Reference to the Declaration of Sharia in Northern Nigeria," in Terence O. Ranger, ed., *Evangelical Christianity and Democracy in Africa* (Oxford: Oxford University Press, 2008), pp. 37-66, esp. pp. 59-64.

new theological movement Radical Orthodoxy can be understood as no less than a "frontal attack on . . . an enemy: secular liberalism."[53] More broadly, if pentecostalism is committed to taking the gospel to the ends of the earth, Radical Orthodoxy is committed to a re-establishing the priority of theology across the theological academy. In view of the bold and comprehensive visions that animate both pentecostalism and Radical Orthodoxy, the line of conversation opened up recently by James K. A. Smith between the two may be a fruitful one for further exploration.[54] I am betting that the encounter between pentecostalism and Radical Orthodoxy will be helpful not only for pentecostals seeking to clarify their own stances regarding the public square, but also for sharpening the issues at stake for contemporary political theology broadly construed. The following therefore explicates, in order, Radical Orthodoxy's post-secular theology (focused on the work of John Milbank), its theology of the market and the state (with the interlocutors here being D. Stephen Long and William Cavanaugh, respectively), and its theology of the city and of culture (in dialogue with Graham Ward). Throughout we will anticipate the question: How might a pentecostal dialogue with Radical Orthodoxy stimulate further thinking about a prophetic politics of mission?

6.2.1. What Is Radical Orthodoxy?
A Post-Secular Theology of the Social

Radical Orthodoxy formally arrived on the theological scene with the publication of a volume under that title in 1999.[55] Yet its "founding father," one of the editors of the volume that inaugurated the book series in its train,[56] had announced and prosecuted at least part of the project ten years before that

---

53. Graham Ward, "On Being Radical and Hopefully Orthodox," in Darren C. Marks, ed., *Shaping a Global Theological Mind* (Burlington, VT, and Aldershot, UK: Ashgate, 2008), pp. 177-86, quote from pp. 183-84.

54. See James K. A. Smith, "What hath Cambridge to do with Azusa Street? Radical Orthodoxy and Pentecostal Theology in Conversation," *PNEUMA: The Journal of the Society for Pentecostal Studies* 25, no. 1 (2003): 97-114. In the same issue, see also the response of one of the central figures in the Radical Orthodoxy camp: Graham Ward, "In the Economy of the Divine: A Response to James K. A. Smith," *PNEUMA: The Journal of the Society for Pentecostal Studies* 25, no. 1 (2003): 115-20.

55. John Milbank, Catherine Pickstock, and Graham Ward, eds., *Radical Orthodoxy: A New Theology* (London and New York: Routledge, 1999). An overview essay is D. Stephen Long's "Radical Orthodoxy," in Kevin Vanhoozer, ed., *The Cambridge Companion to Postmodern Theology* (Cambridge: Cambridge University Press, 2003), pp. 126-45.

56. At least a dozen volumes from 2000 to 2007, published by Routledge.

with the publication of his *Theology and Social Theory: Beyond Secular Reason*.[57] The following does not attempt any exhaustive presentation or evaluation of Milbank's corpus of writings, but focuses on the major arguments in *Theology and Social Theory* in order to grasp the main thrusts of the Radical Orthodoxy project.

In a nutshell, Milbank's quest was to overcome the subservience of theology to modern canons of rationality established by the secular public square. In Milbank's genealogy, the story of modern theology's eclipse is the flip side of the story of the rise to prominence of social scientific disciplines. The field of sociology, for example, exerted its authority against theology in at least two ways: by reducing the domain of the religious and the theological to sociological categories and explanations (Durkheim), and then by clearly demarcating the social (concerned with the public realm) from the religious (rendered to the private domain) (Weber).[58] The result was that theological reason concerned the subjective sphere of personal and religious faith, while sociological reason participated in the wider Enlightenment rationality that was public and universal. If theology sought to make public claims to truth, they had to be validated according to (anti-theological) sociological and Enlightenment modes of rationality. With this emergence of "secular reason," then, "all twentieth-century sociology of religion can be exposed as a secular policing of the sublime."[59]

In our late-modern and even postmodern context, however, the illusory universality of sociology and the Enlightenment paradigms are plainly evident. Secular reason rests on nothing more than its own narrative that has attempted to subsume theology within its framework. But it has now become clear that the myth of secular reason is nihilistic (with the unraveling of the modern project), malign (with its ontology of violence that not only works according to the invisible hand of the market [Adam Smith], the survival of the fittest [Darwin], and the will to power [Nietzsche], but also valorizes the exploitative mechanisms of economic, biosocial, and political power), and hedonistic and materialistic (with its being tied in with the excesses of modern capitalism). In short, "The secular *episteme* is a post-Christian paganism, something in the last analysis that can only be defined, negatively, as a refusal of Christianity and the invention of an 'Anti-Christianity.'"[60] With this,

---

57. John Milbank, *Theology and Social Theory: Beyond Secular Reason* (Malden, MA: Blackwell, 1990), 2nd ed. (Malden, MA: Blackwell, 2006); I will be citing the 2nd edition in what follows, as the major revisions of the text will not bear on the issues important for our purposes.

58. Milbank, *Theology and Social Theory*, chaps. 3-4.

59. Milbank, *Theology and Social Theory*, p. 106.

60. Milbank, *Theology and Social Theory*, p. 280.

Milbank succeeds in rendering an internal or immanent critique of secularism, one that goes to the core of secularism in order to reveal its theological agenda and to unmask the implausibility of its ideological vision.

So rather than engage in a Christian apologetic on the basis of ground rules established by secularism with its assumptions about universal rationality that has already privatized religious and theological reason, Milbank reasserts the explanatory power of the Christian story amidst the increasingly post-secular space that has opened up within late modernity. The goal is to continue to expose the secular assumption that there is a real world encountered on terms universally accessible to all reasonable creatures. What is masked, however, is that such a "universal rationality" is a construct of a particularly modern project that has already defined what is and is not publicly real (the secular, versus the religious). Instead, Milbank proposes a realism that reads the world not "out there" on its own awaiting encounter with Christians, but rather always/already engaged through Christian modes of understanding and habitation: "Like everyone else we assume that our constant revisions of our language are evidence that it is indeed *reality* we are dealing with, but either the *entire* Christian narrative tells us how things truly are, or it does not. If it does, we have no other access to how things truly are, nor any additional means of determining the question."[61] The goal, then, is to restore theology's voice, and to do so by out-narrating competing rhetorical and mythological accounts.

Radical Orthodoxy thus calls for a restoration of Christian orthodoxy. This means a retrieval of the Christian story that provides a counter-history, counter-ethics, and counter-ontology to that of the myth of secularism. But more, the orthodoxy being reintroduced is no mere retelling of the Christian narrative; instead its radicality consists of the insistence that the power of the Christian mythos as a counter-metanarrative rests in its being embodied in a community of faith. Hence the role of the church and its practices is central to the Radical Orthodoxy project. And in contrast to modernity's ontology of violence (which legitimizes the wars of nation-states, the exploitation of the capitalist laborer, and marginalization of the "unfit" to the underside of history), the church manifests and proclaims an alternative — for Milbank, primarily Augustinian — ontology of peace. So, "Instead of a peace 'achieved' through the abandonment of the losers, the subordination of potential rivals and resis-

---

61. John Milbank, *The Word Made Strange: Theology, Language, Culture* (Oxford and Cambridge, MA: Blackwell, 1997), p. 250, italics original. Thus Milbank assumes there is no naked and uninterpreted experience of the world but that all human experience is shaped by a pre-understanding; in this, he is in broad agreement with the post-Barthian school of narrative theology.

tance to enemies, the Church provides a genuine peace by its memory of all the victims, its equal concern for all its citizens and its self-exposed offering of reconciliation to enemies."[62] By nurturing the central practices of charity, the forgiveness of sins, and reconciliation, then, the church becomes a redemptive community, a "city of God" that contrasts with the practices of earthly cities.[63]

Yet make no mistake about it: amidst the quest for an ontology of peace, Milbank is no one-dimensionally conciliatory theologian. Rather, the radicality of his vision translates into a hard-hitting, confrontational, even prophetic, theological style of discourse that calls theology to re-assert itself in a post-secular world. In the Milbankian corpus, then, there is an intensity to the arguments, even a (frequent and predictable) hyperbolic exaggeration that *only* the Christian story is plausible and viable in the face of competing accounts and practices as well as a (repeated) insistence that there is *no other* path forward to a post-secular Christian faith than that proposed by Radical Orthodoxy. But Milbank's theological confidence, even hubris, is not just a rhetorical ploy; Radical Orthodoxy also makes bold pronouncements about the Christian mythos vis-à-vis the pluralism of the public square. Thus Milbank straightforwardly proclaims that "Christianity's universalist claim that incorporation into the Church is indispensable for salvation assumes that other religions and social groupings, however virtuous-seeming, were, in their own terms alone, finally on the path of damnation."[64]

Put in pentecostal terms, Milbank easily qualifies as an evangelist in and to the theological academy. Precisely in part for this reason, however, the Radical Orthodoxy project in general and the work of Milbank in particular have provoked strong reactions.[65] Even sympathetic voices have noted that Milbank's project to out-narrate or out-persuade other narratives are actions of privilege and power that do not follow from his ontology of peace, and that a theological discourse founded upon the latter should embrace a more dialogical mode of interaction instead.[66] Yet my claim is that it is the purpose

---

62. Milbank, *Theology and Social Theory*, p. 394.

63. Augustine is rife throughout Milbank's work; for the latter's discussion of the former's "two cities," see *Theology and Social Theory*, pp. 391-95 and passim.

64. Milbank, *Theology and Social Theory*, p. 390.

65. Many of the most critical voices have been collected in two volumes: Wayne J. Hankey and Douglas Hedley, eds., *Deconstructing Radical Orthodoxy: Postmodern Theology, Rhetoric and Truth* (Burlington, VT, and Aldershot, UK: Ashgate, 2005), and Rosemary Radford Ruether and Marion Grau, eds., *Interpreting the Postmodern: Responses to "Radical Orthodoxy"* (New York and London: T. & T. Clark, 2006); see also Steven Shakespeare, *Radical Orthodoxy: A Critical Introduction* (London: SPCK, 2007).

66. See Oliver Davies, "Revelation and the Politics of Culture: A Critical Assessment of

of a prophetic posture to incite, aggravate, and (when necessary) inflame rather than mollify. After all, Milbank's project is not to make peace with the secular, but to overthrow its pretensions and overcome its strictures in order to accomplish a radical restoration of Christian orthodoxy to the theological academy.

6.2.2. Church, Market, State: Radically Orthodox Alternatives

It should be clear by now that part of the radicality of Milbank's vision consists in returning to the roots of the Christian tradition, in particular reaching behind the Enlightenment project to the premodern strands running from Augustine through Aquinas. Following the medieval theologians, then, the Radical Orthodoxy proposals have also insisted that, in view of the Christian account of creation and redemption, the logic of Christian theology is as "a *metadiscourse* that positions all other discourses within its own narrative order."[67] In the modern world, however, such a theological hegemony will inevitably be resisted by the other sciences. When this happens, yes, "[s]uch conflict should be remedied, but it will *not* be so by theology abdicating its role as the 'queen of the sciences.'"[68] In other words, Radical Orthodoxy boldly insists that theology should make its stand not as just one more epistemology within the social sciences, but as an overarching orientation that impacts every academic endeavor, even in the modern secular university.

Thus D. Stephen Long insists on theology being the "queen of the sciences" specifically with regard to the discipline of modern economics. If for Milbank the social sciences have illegitimately usurped a theological role in providing a metanarrative for human social understanding, for Long the market has illicitly seized a practical sovereignty over human life in our late-modern context, and in the process, the global economy has presumed to displace the providential hand of God with the invisible hand of the market.[69] The problems of the capitalist economy that are rehearsed by Long (and

---

the Theology of John Milbank," in Laurence Paul Hemming, ed., *Radical Orthodoxy? — A Catholic Inquiry* (Aldershot, UK, and Burlington, VT: Ashgate, 2000), pp. 112-25, esp. p. 116.

67. D. Stephen Long, *The Goodness of God: Theology, the Church, and Social Order* (Grand Rapids: Brazos, 2001), p. 228.

68. D. Stephen Long, *Divine Economy: Theology and the Market* (London and New York: Routledge, 2000), p. 270; emphasis added.

69. At least in this minimal sense, Long argues, "Capitalist economics is based on the death of God. This is no secret revelation; some of the key architects of capitalist economics fully understood this and stated it publicly" (*Goodness of God*, p. 249).

many others) — i.e., its underlying mechanism that presumes a certain amount of human greed, its contractual basis that proceeds from a minimalist understanding of justice, and its propensity to marginalize the "have nots," etc.[70] — need not be repeated here. What is important for Long is that the global market misdirects human desires and thereby offers a false sense of satisfaction, a false salvation, and a false catholicity.[71] More precisely, the neoliberal economy has deeply shaped the desires of our hearts in ways that have escaped our attention so that it is the market's commodities which are presumed to be finally satisfying and salvific. And insofar as globalization now means that nations, regions, and peoples "outside" the market are in effect non-existent, not only economically but also socially and politically, to that same degree there is a market "ecumenism" that has displaced the catholicity of the church, and now claims authority over all who worship at its altars of consumption. Long concludes: "[T]he global market is not a sign of the rule of God; it is a competing salvific institution whose spokespersons claim it can offer what the church cannot. When we accept this rhetoric, we are held captive to an idol."[72]

The field of economics therefore needs to be disciplined theologically. In other words, the desires distorted by market economics need to be reordered toward that which will finally be satisfying, and the false goods offered by the market need to be critiqued by theological notions of what is transcendentally good, true, and beautiful. But, as Milbank has insisted, theology's claims are only as good as the community of the faithful that embodies its prophetic message. Hence, theology can rule as queen over the science of economics only insofar as the church provides an alternative economic model that effectively exposes the pretensions of the market. The task of the church, thus, "is to produce countless alternatives to the marginalist domination of rationality by interests. The theological task is the proliferation of a complex space. Such a space will resist the questions posed by the search for a univocal catholic economy."[73]

The complex space Long refers to connects with a central theme in the wider Radical Orthodoxy corpus wherein modernist and universalist homog-

---

70. E.g., Daniel Bell, *The Cultural Contradictions of Capitalism*, paperback ed. (New York: Basic Books, 1978); Franz J. Hinkelammert, *The Ideological Weapons of Death: A Theological Critique of Capitalism*, trans. Phillip Berryman (Maryknoll, NY: Orbis, 1986); and Ronald H. Preston, *Religion and the Ambiguities of Capitalism* (Cleveland: Pilgrim, 1993). We will return to further discuss the shape of contemporary capitalism later (7.2.2).

71. Long, *Divine Economy*, p. 173.

72. Long, *Goodness of God*, p. 258.

73. Long, *Divine Economy*, p. 269.

enization is countered by local processes and initiatives. For Milbank and other Radical Orthodoxy theologians, the medieval Christian *polis*, with its guilds, hospitals, trading associations, universities, and monastic orders, etc., reflects a complex space free from or at least resistant to dominating organizational structures. The problem with the global market is that local desires are shaped by global forces, and such impersonalism does nothing to foster compassion or motivate just transactions. Hence what is needed are local economic productions that can overcome the alienation between workers and their products, restore the personal connections between buyers and sellers, and thereby finally reshape human hearts in accordance with the justice demanded by face-to-face relations.

Long is now careful to insist he is not suggesting that the church is or provides an alternative economy to that of the market except in analogical terms.[74] But if on the one hand there is no place or way for Christians to withdraw from the economy (there being no possibility of a sectarian Christian economy), there is also no purely secular and theologically free economy either. The key then is for Christians to engage the global market with discernment, to be vigilant against its anti-Christian vices, and to seek to embody the Christian virtues in their economic practices. And the church does all of this by being the church: worshiping God, nurturing families, ordering households, loving neighbors, sharing goods, etc.[75] By being faithful in each of these ways, the church nurtures newly ordered desires, embodies the goodness of God, and reforms the market economy toward other than hedonistic, materialistic, and consumeristic ends.[76]

Roman Catholic theologian William Cavanaugh has also addressed the challenges of late-modern consumer culture and the failings of the market economy.[77] But while also proposing, like Long, a robust ecclesial response,

74. D. Stephen Long and Nancy Ruth Fox with Tripp York, *Calculated Futures: Theology, Ethics, and Economics* (Waco, TX: Baylor University Press, 2007), p. 4; I will return later (7.3.2) to the question regarding the possibility of an alternative Christian political economy.

75. The details are explicated in Long, *Goodness of God*, part 2.

76. Milbank's response is to advocate much more explicitly and forcefully for a Christian socialism. See Milbank, *The Future of Love: Essays in Political Theology* (Cascade, OR: Cascade, 2009), part 2; cf. Trevor Hogan, "With and Beyond Barth? John Milbank's Postmodern Christian Socialism as an Alternative Modernity," in Geoff Thompson and Christiaan Mostert, eds., *Karl Barth: A Future for Postmodern Theology?* (Hindmarsh, Australia: Australian Theological Forum, 2000), pp. 253-75.

77. The Radical Orthodoxy group is comprised primarily of Anglican and Roman Catholic scholars, although Long as an evangelical Methodist theologian is representative of the much wider appeal of the movement's ideas. In view of the diversity of positions represented within the Radical Orthodoxy circle, it may be better considered a theological sensibility rather

Cavanaugh has in addition insisted on the centrality of the church's liturgical practices for combating the forces of globalization. The Eucharist, for instance, not only enables recollection of Jesus and celebration of his life and death, but also teaches us how to consume rightly and fosters in us the desires proper to the kingdom.[78] Thus rather than "being consumed" by the world's commodities, we might be more intentional and discerning about how to produce materials for consumption locally so that our work is not tainted by the global market and so that we can appreciate how we nourish one another.

Cavanaugh's liturgical emphasis was honed in earlier reflections on a theology of the modern state. In line with Milbank's analysis of the social and Long's of the economy, the problem is that the modern secular state evolved from out of a triadic myth — Locke's private property, Rousseau's social contract, and Hobbes's *Leviathan* — into an alternative soteriology.[79] With the ensuing privatization of religion, then, there emerges a new religion of the state that binds individuals not to the body of Christ but to the sovereign. Nationalism becomes a false ideology not only because it presumes that the modern state deserves our allegiance but also because it legitimates the violence of the state in the interests of self-defense. And the problem is exacerbated as the church has internalized these secular and naturalistic constraints, removing religion from the public square.[80]

Yet the premise of Radical Orthodoxy is that "first, there is no separate history of politics apart from the history of salvation; and second, the church is indispensable to the history of salvation."[81] Hence what is needed is a new ecclesial self-understanding capable of empowering and enacting a peaceful body politic through which the church becomes a resistance movement that

than a formally organized school of thinking; see James K. A. Smith, *Introducing Radical Orthodoxy: Mapping a Post-Secular Theology* (Grand Rapids: Baker Academic, and Milton Keynes, UK: Paternoster, 2004), p. 67.

78. See William T. Cavanaugh, *Being Consumed: Economics and Christian Desire* (Grand Rapids and Cambridge, UK: Eerdmans, 2008), esp. pp. 53-59.

79. William T. Cavanaugh, "The City: Beyond Secular Parodies," in John Milbank, Catherine Pickstock, and Graham Ward, eds., *Radical Orthodoxy: A New Theology* (London and New York: Routledge, 1999), pp. 182-200.

80. William T. Cavanaugh, *Torture and Eucharist: Theology, Politics and the Body of Christ* (Oxford, UK, and Malden, MA: Blackwell, 1998), part 2, argues that in the Catholic context, the church's self-definition as a "mystical body" effectively left the political sphere to the oversight of the state and undermined the church's authority in the public square.

81. William T. Cavanaugh, "Church," in Peter Scott and William T. Cavanaugh, eds., *The Blackwell Companion to Political Theology* (2004; paperback ed., Malden, MA: Blackwell, 2007), pp. 393-406, quotation from p. 393.

"challenges the false order of the state."[82] More precisely, the distinctive practices of such a body politic are concretely liturgical, specifically baptism and Eucharist. Reflecting on the history of the Catholic Church in Chile during the military dictatorship of Agosto Pinochet (1915-2006), including his brutal suppression of opposition perspectives and torture of church officials during the 1970s and 1980s, Cavanaugh formulates what may be called a eucharistic politics of prophetic resistance. In the Chilean context, the eucharistic rite unleashed a range of ecclesial counter-practices — e.g., the excommunication of torturers, the Vicariate of Solidarity, and the Sebastián Acevedo Movement Against Torture — through which the church defied the mechanisms of the state. So against the state's liturgy of torture that attempted to silence the church and cause it to either disappear or remain invisible, the Eucharist "create[d] martyrs out of victims by calling the church to acts of self-sacrifice and remembrance, honoring in Jesus' sacrifice the countless witnesses to the conflict between the powers of life and the powers of death."[83]

If in Catholic teaching the whole (universal/ecumenical) church is present in every local breaking of bread, the Eucharist then becomes a cosmic story whose performance amidst pilgrimage occurs in time/space but is not tied to any particular times or places, and enables universal human participation in the redemptive work of God.[84] In contrast to the false freedoms promised by the secular state — i.e., the national freedoms of the sovereign state, the personal freedoms of civil society, and the economic freedoms of the politically organized (violently imposed) free market — the eucharistic community that emerges is the only truly free alternative space (of embodied communities) and time (with dangerous memories and anticipations). Liturgical and eucharistic practices thus anticipate the new "cities of God" in a post-Christian, post-Western, and post-secular world.

6.2.3. Christ and Culture: Reclamations of/for the Cities of God

With Graham Ward, we have a Radically Orthodox approach that complements and yet also contrasts with that of Milbank's in at least two ways: in terms of a focus on theology of culture and in terms of a more dialogical

82. Cavanaugh, "The City," p. 194.

83. Cavanaugh, *Torture and Eucharist*, p. 281.

84. William T. Cavanaugh, *Theopolitical Imagination* (London and New York: T. & T. Clark, 2002), pp. 112-16. For more on Radical Orthodoxy's theology of the liturgical, see Catherine Pickstock, *After Writing: On the Liturgical Consummation of Philosophy* (Malden, MA, and Oxford: Blackwell, 1998).

method. Although Ward has more recently turned his attention explicitly to engage issues in political theology,[85] I want to focus here on his work as a theologian of culture, especially those of his proposals that are suggestive for the transformation and redemption of cultural media. For our purposes, Ward's contributions in this vein have been threefold.

First, while acknowledging the centrality of the liturgy in general and of the Eucharist in particular for a viable post-secular theology, Ward's interests lie in how eucharistic praxis informs the Christian understanding of the doctrine of christology and what this means for a theology of the incarnation.[86] If in the Anglo-Catholic framework Christ is consumed in the eucharistic meal, then the "body of Jesus Christ, the body of God, is permeable, trans-corporeal, transpositional."[87] More precisely, the body of Jesus is constituted by a radical porosity: transfigured on the mount, de-formed and per-formed at the Passover Meal, broken on the cross, dis-appeared from the tomb, dis-located with the ascension, and now dis-posed and deferred in the ecclesial body. Ward thus argues that "the body of Jesus Christ is continually being displaced so that the figuration of the body is always transposing its identity. That logic of displacement is now taken up in the limbs and tissue of his body as the Church."[88]

There are two further implications to be drawn from this theology of the incarnation: that regarding a theology of human embodiment and that regarding a theology of cultural materialism. Regarding the former, Ward is led to explore how "What happens at the ascension, theologically, constitutes a critical moment in a series of displacements or assumptions of the male body of Jesus Christ such that the body of Christ, and the salvation it both seeks and works out (Paul's *katergomai*) becomes multi-gendered."[89] Resisting the gnostic and docetic applications of a theology of incarnation, Ward seeks instead to follow out the logic of Jesus' own embodiment to think about the salvation of all human beings in their bodily "pain, tiredness, or-

---

85. E.g., Michael Hoelzl and Graham Ward, eds., *Religion and Political Thought* (London and New York: Continuum, 2006), and Carl Schmitt, *Political Theology II: The Myth of the Closure of Any Political Theology*, trans. Michael Hoelzl and Graham Ward (Cambridge, UK, and Malden, MA: Polity Press, 2008).

86. Ward's interest in a theology of incarnation can be traced back to his first book, in which his quest for the language of theology led him to a theology of the Word; see Graham Ward, *Barth, Derrida and the Language of Theology* (Cambridge: Cambridge University Press, 1995).

87. Graham Ward, *Cities of God* (London and New York: Routledge, 2000), p. 113.

88. Ward, *Cities of God*, p. 112.

89. Ward, *Cities of God*, p. 97.

gasms, aches, delights, coughs, tearings, hiccups and itchings."[90] More point-edly, salvation in Christ suggests not only that there is neither male nor fe-male (both are equally saved), but that there is also neither a monolithic nor dualistic notion of genderedness (human beings are thus equally saved as gendered beings, regardless of their sexual identity or orientation).[91] And if there are is neither male nor female in heaven, but all are like angels, this speaks to the overcoming of all binary identities — nature/culture, matter/spirit, male/female, and even homosexual/heterosexual, etc. Angelic bodies are thus anticipated by angelic discourses (the ruminations of Radical Ortho-doxy): indeterminable and unstable hybrids signaling the shape of the com-ing kingdom.[92] If the postmodern cities of our time are hubs of many tongues and practices, then the liturgical practices of our churches (or at least the parishes Ward serves) are events constituted by a multiplicity of gendered, linguistic, and cultural bodies.[93]

Beyond a theology of embodiment, Jesus' incarnational body also in-vites reflection on a theology of materialism.[94] For those who have embraced the Radically Orthodox sensibility, the human participation in the incarna-tional reality of God is a divine gift made possible because the material cre-ation has been suspended from the transcendent or spiritual world.[95] Ward identifies this as an "analogical worldview" that retrieves Augustine's theory of signs/symbolism to articulate a relational metaphysics of space, time, and materiality toward a postmodern notion of embodiment and participation. Given such a relational and participatory metaphysics, the (Lutheran) two-kingdoms approach (2.2.2) is unhelpful not only for pragmatic and sociologi-cal reasons (because we live in human cities) but also for specifically theologi-cal and christological ones (because of the doctrine of the incarnation).[96] Hence not only does the materiality of human embodiment participate in the being of God, so also does the materiality of human cultural achievement re-flect the creativity of God.

90. Ward, *Cities of God*, p. 115.

91. Ward, *Cities of God*, chaps. 5-7.

92. Ward, *Cities of God*, chap. 8.

93. Further argument is provided in Graham Ward, *Christ and Culture* (Malden, MA, and Oxford, UK: Blackwell, 2005).

94. Thus also Phillip Blond, "The Politics of the Eye: Toward a Theological Materialism," in Creston Davis, John Milbank, and Slavoj Žižek, eds., *Theology and the Political: The New Debate* (Durham, NC, and London: Duke University Press, 2005), pp. 439-62.

95. John Milbank, *The Suspended Middle: Henri de Lubac and the Debate Concerning the Supernatural* (Grand Rapids: Eerdmans, 2005).

96. Ward, *Cities of God*, p. 69.

Yet this Radically Orthodox participatory metaphysics has implications for the doctrines of creation and redemption. While Milbank would put it more in terms of grace supervening upon or supernaturalizing nature (in contrast to the transcendental neo-Thomistic move of naturalizing the supernatural),[97] Ward prefers to use the language of economies of redemption.[98] So if the Gospel narratives are invitations to participation in the soteriological work of Christ, and if the church is the historical and material community that mediates the saving love of God, then the wider culture is a field upon which the economy of salvation is played out. In this wider field, human cultural productions — literature, the arts, media, etc. — both reflect human participation in the divine creativity and provide analogies anticipating the redemptive works of God.[99] Similarly, Christian liturgical acts are no more than cultural constructions on the one hand, but also no less than culturally redemptive signs on the other. Thus, "we might characterize Christian acting as a *praxis* that participates in a divine *poiēsis* that has soteriological and eschatological import. It is a *technē*, a crafting, a production — of redemption."[100] In short, insofar as the goodness, symbols, and beauty of culture and its forms participate in the transcendental good, true, and beautiful, to that same degree they anticipate the final reclamation of human cities and their sanctification and transformation as cities of God.

Christians can therefore not only embrace the materiality of their embodiment and their cultural production but also expect these will serve as points of contact that witness to the gospel of Christ. Perhaps in part for these reasons, Ward's approach is distinct from Milbank's. Although both insist on reading the world through the Christian narrative and its theological frame of reference, Milbank's rhetoric is more confrontational and his posture wary about the encroachment of the secular into the domain of theology, while Ward is more dialogical in his approach to the realm of culture. If, as we have seen, Milbank is generally more exclusivistic with regard to other religions (even if there are moments when he sounds otherwise), Ward advocates suspending judgment on other faiths.[101] In a sense, the one is con-

97. Milbank, *Theology and Social Theory*, chap. 8.

98. Ward, *Christ and Culture*, part 3.

99. Graham Ward, *True Religion* (Oxford and Malden, MA: Blackwell, 2003).

100. Graham Ward, "A Christian Act: Politics and Liturgical Practice," in Randi Rashkover and C. C. Pecknold, eds., *Liturgy, Time, and the Politics of Redemption* (Grand Rapids and Cambridge, UK: Eerdmans, 2006), pp. 29-49, quote from p. 49 (italics orig.); see also Ward, "Radical Orthodoxy and/as Cultural Politics," in Laurence Paul Hemming, ed., *Radical Orthodoxy? — A Catholic Inquiry* (Aldershot, UK, and Burlington, VT: Ashgate, 2000), pp. 97-111.

101. Ward, *Cities of God*, p. 257.

cerned to put the secular in its place (Milbank), while the other is more optimistic about reclaiming the secular as a sign of the redemption of the cities of God (Ward).

Elsewhere I have suggested that Radical Orthodoxy's christological and incarnational emphases beg for pneumatological elucidation.[102] In particular, I will suggest later in this chapter that while the Anglo-Catholic sensibilities of Milbank et al. are well equipped to engage with the presumptions of the Western world and to articulate a post-secular theological vision, Radical Orthodoxy's critique of the secular is less effective across the postcolonial landscape of the global south. In this global context the many tongues of Pentecost that inform a prophetic theology of the political may supplement the Radical Orthodoxy witness, and vice versa.

6.3. Many Tongues, Many Civilian Practices: Toward a Prophetic Theology of Civil Society

Our goal in this chapter is to tease a political-theological posture and disposition out of the pentecostal doctrine of Spirit-baptism understood in terms of empowerment for witness. The preceding dialogue with Radical Orthodoxy has illuminated what a bold and counter-hegemonic but yet also incarnational and redemptive theology looks like. Might it be that the convergence of pentecostal and Radically Orthodox sensibilities provides a formula for a prophetic politics of mission in a post-secular but yet not anti-secular world? If the theopolitics of Radical Orthodoxy can be said to seek a re-evangelization of the Euro-American cultures and post-secular societies of the western hemisphere, the pneumato-politics of a pentecostally informed Christian orthodoxy seeks to bear a prophetic but yet also redemptive witness to the world. More to the point, drawing together insights from Cho's cell group model of ministry and evangelization and Radical Orthodoxy's notion of complex space, I suggest that one way forward for a politics of mission is to articulate a prophetic theology of civil society. I develop such a stance by examining the prophetic yet civic politics of the early Christians (in Acts), revisiting the dialogue between pentecostalism and Radical Orthodoxy in search of a prophetic politics of witness amidst civil society, and exploring how such a prophetic

102. Yong, "Radical, Reformed, and Pentecostal: Rethinking the Intersection of Post/Modernity and the Religions in Conversation with James K. A. Smith," *Journal of Pentecostal Theology* 15, no. 2 (2007): 233-50, esp. pp. 246-50; see Smith's reply, "The Spirit, Religions, and the World as Sacrament: A Response to Amos Yong's Pneumatological Assist," *Journal of Pentecostal Theology* 15, no. 2 (2007): 251-61.

imagination might be suggestive for understanding secular civil society and the redemptive nature of the triune God.

6.3.1. The Apostolic Subversion of Civil Society: Prophetic Politics in Acts

Pentecostal scholar Roger Stronstad has argued that when Luke is read on his own terms rather than through other lenses (i.e., in light of Paul or other Reformational paradigms), then we can more easily see how the Holy Spirit not only empowers Jesus as a mighty eschatological prophet in the Gospel but also how the Spirit raises up a community — even nation — of charismatic prophets to bear witness to the ends of the earth in Acts (thus transforming the Reformational "priesthood of all believers" into the pentecostal "prophethood of all believers").[103] While the thesis that all believers are prophets can be sustained only in the sense that all are empowered with the potential to witness to the messiah in some respect (Acts 1:8),[104] a canonical understanding of prophecy would recognize that there are also occasions of the Spirit's anointing — which Paul, for instance, identifies as gifts — that empower particular prophetic words and deeds for specific situations. My claim in this chapter is that the many tongues of Pentecost also empower various forms of prophetic witnesses in the many public situations within which Christians find themselves.

A perusal of the fortunes of the earliest Christians unveils at least three forms of what is recognizable as prophetic politics. First, a prophetic politics recognizes and announces that allegiances to the state are secondary to allegiances to God. This means that when commanded not to bear witness in word or deed, the proper response is that given by Peter and John: "Whether it is right in God's sight to listen to you rather than to God, you must judge; for we cannot keep from speaking about what we have seen and heard" (Acts

103. Roger Stronstad, *The Prophethood of All Believers: A Study in Luke's Charismatic Theology* (Sheffield: Sheffield Academic Press, 1999).

104. So while I agree that the answer to the question in the title of Max Turner's "Does Luke Believe Reception of the 'Spirit of Prophecy' Makes All 'Prophets'? Inviting Dialogue with Roger Stronstad," *Journal of the European Pentecostal Theological Association* 20 (2000): 3-24, is no, I also think that both Turner and Stronstad define "prophets" in static ways. I propose to view the prophethood of all believers subjunctively, so that people act prophetically if and when the Spirit comes upon them and inspires a prophetic act or message. Such a dynamic notion of prophecy as a verb is sensitive to the contingencies of the Spirit's moving and avoids having to ask the original question.

4:19-20). It also means there is a recognition that no matter how the state conspires against, threatens, and even harms the community of believers, the prophets in the community pronounce that the state can do no more than what God "had predestined to take place" (4:28). Here the Holy Spirit who has inspired the psalmist's recognition that the nations of the world remained under the providence of God and his anointed one (4:25-26) is the same Spirit who emboldens the prophetic ministry of the apostles in response to the threats of the state.

Even more to the point, the prophets will boldly proclaim that whenever the state claims divine status for itself, it risks being judged by the God of the nations. So, when Herod (Agrippa I), the nephew of Herod Antipas (whose reign he displaced), not only persecuted the church and put to death James the brother of John in an attempt to please the Jews (12:3),[105] but also presumed to receive the accolades of the people as if offered to the deity (12:21-22) and failed to deflect their worship and praise unlike the servants of the Most High God (10:25-26 and 14:11-15), the prophets of the community forthrightly declared: "And immediately, because he had not given the glory to God, an angel of the Lord struck him down, and he was eaten by worms and died" (12:23). While historians and biblical scholars remain unclear about what motivated Herod's persecution of the church,[106] in the larger scheme of Luke's narrative, Herod's

105. External evidence indicates that Herod Agrippa's popularity was achieved in large measure because he, along with his son, Herod Agrippa II who succeeded him, albeit both client-kings of Rome, consciously worked on behalf of local Jewish interests — and this in contrast to the tyrannical rule of Agrippa I's uncle, Herod Antipas, who also had John the Baptist beheaded; see B. W. Bacon, "Pharisees and Herodians in Mark," *Journal of Biblical Literature* 39, nos. 3-4 (1920): 102-12, esp. pp. 107-9.

106. Even a scholar as renowned as Joseph A. Fitzmyer, *The Acts of the Apostles*, The Anchor Bible (New York: Doubleday, 1998), p. 487, says no more than that Herod's persecution of the apostles and murder of James were capricious actions. I surmise that as a client-king of Rome, Herod was an agent of the *Pax Romana*, but as a descendant of the Hasmonean royal family, he also sought "the good of the Jewish nation" and earned the favor of the people (M. Stern, "The Reign of Herod and the Herodian Dynasty," in S. Safrai and M. Stern, eds., *The Jewish People in the First Century*, vol. 1 [Assen, The Netherlands: Van Gorcum, and Philadelphia: Fortress, 1974], pp. 216-307, quote from p. 291; cf. pp. 288-300). In the process, however, he suppressed minority Jewish factions, especially those he considered as disruptive of the religious status quo. Thus Herod may have been motivated by the sense that the message of the messianists about the coming kingdom of Jesus and their deeds — which were subversive not only regarding Jewish life within the confines of the *Pax Romana* but also with regard to his own authority over Palestine — combined to threaten the fragile Judean climate (which had heretofore been a scene of repeated rebellions and insurrections). For more discussion, see Yong, *The Holy Spirit and the Public Square* [working title] (Brewster, MA: Paraclete Press, forthcoming), chap. 12 and passim.

demise confirmed the principle of divine retribution included in Mary's response to the Spirit's enunciation (Luke 1:41-45) that the mighty would be debased and the proud would be humbled (1:51-52).[107] It is important to note that even in this situation of persecution, however, the church resisted not violently but through communal prayer (Acts 12:5).

Second, a prophetic politics will challenge the state to do what it is supposed to do: uphold the law. If the state has the responsibility of ensuring justice within its borders — i.e., of commending the righteous and punishing wrongdoers (Rom. 13:3-5) — then there needs to be some means of calling the ruling authorities to accountability in the cases where they fail to do their duty. Internal assessments can be established by the state for such a task or, in a democracy (broadly understood), the people either become whistleblowers or replace unjust rulers through their vote. From a theological perspective, God can also raise up prophetic voices either to act as the conscience for the state, or to demand proper or remedial measures. St. Paul's informing the Roman authorities before the Jerusalem mob that a Roman citizen should not be flogged prior to being found guilty (Acts 22:25) is an example of a prophetic warning about the illegality of the state's actions and their consequences. His previous experience at Philippi is more puzzling, as it appears he may not have mentioned his citizenship until the day after he was beaten with rods and imprisoned (16:22-24).[108] However, emboldened by God's miraculous deliverance — for all of the prisoners,[109] not just for him and Silas — Paul now refuses to leave town in silence: "They have beaten us in public, uncondemned, men who are Roman citizens, and have thrown us into prison; and now are they going to discharge us in secret? Certainly not! Let them come and take us out themselves" (16:37). In this case, the prophetic witness of the saints held the Philippian magistrates accountable for their actions under Roman law.[110]

---

107. O. Wesley Allen, Jr., *The Death of Herod: The Narrative and Theological Function of Retribution in Luke-Acts,* SBL Dissertation Series 158 (Atlanta: Scholars Press, 1998), esp. pp. 116-17; cf. John O. York, *The Last Shall Be First: The Rhetoric of Reversal in Luke,* Journal of the Study of the New Testament Supplement Series 46 (Sheffield: JSOT Press, 1991).

108. Maybe the ruckus caused by the Philippian mob either drowned out the protests of Paul and Silas or overwhelmed the intentions of the magistrates, or maybe Paul was more motivated in Jerusalem to avoid being flogged with a scourge, "a more frightful instrument than the lictors' rod" he received in Philippi — see F. F. Bruce, *A Commentary on the Book of the Acts of the Apostles,* New International Commentary on the New Testament (Grand Rapids: Eerdmans, 1979), p. 340n.61, cf. p. 445.

109. This is noted by Stephen H. Phelps, "Acts 16:16-40," *Interpretation* 61, no. 2 (2007): 206-8, at p. 208.

110. Boyd Reese, "The Apostle Paul's Exercise of His Rights as a Roman Citizen as Recorded in the Book of Acts," *Evangelical Quarterly* 47 (1975): 138-45, esp. at p. 144.

Third, the prophetic politics of Spirit-empowered believers includes an explicit witness in the public square. Here I am referring not only to Paul's public apologies — given before the inhabitants of Jerusalem, before the religious leaders, and before the Roman authorities (Felix and his wife Drusilla, Festus, and King Agrippa II and his wife Bernice) — but also to Paul's private interactions with the political leadership representing the rule of Caesar. Before Felix the procurator of Judea, for example, Paul gave testimony to Christ but also "discussed justice, self-control, and the coming judgement" (24:25). Felix was a politician, negatively understood, in at least two senses: in his willingness to accept bribes (24:26), and in his seeking to please and do favors for his constituency (24:27). Paul interacted with Felix on various occasions over the course of two years, and Felix, while a competent and effective ruler,[111] appeared also to have been convicted, fearing the consequences of his unrighteousness. Regardless, Paul, although in chains, did not cease to proclaim a politically relevant gospel, a gospel of righteousness with implications for and applications to the public square and its servants.

Beyond these more explicit forms of prophetic political witness, however, I suggest there are other less explicit, but no less prophetic political postures and practices discernible among the apostolic Christians. I am referring here to the subversive political roles embraced by the early church that functioned prophetically to illuminate the shape of an alternative way of life in contrast to that of the world. How might the preceding discussions of Cho's cell group ministries and Radical Orthodoxy's call for a proliferation of complex spaces enable identification of Lukan motifs that can stir up the pneumatological imagination about how to live out a prophetic politics of mission?

First, I want to briefly mention the earliest Christian community of mutuality and generosity wherein its members broke bread daily from house to house, those who were more affluent shared with the more needy, and the apostles ensured a just distribution among the community. We will return later to discuss the specifically economic dimensions of this apostolic community (7.3.1), but I here note its prophetic embodiment of the gospel against the unjust practices of the world. Further, although the provisions for the widows in the community eventually encountered severe challenges (Acts 6:1), such measures initially presented a prophetic social contrast on at least two levels: that emphasizing the provision for one of the most vulnerable population groups in society (recall the special concern for widows in Luke's

---

111. Filippo Canali de Rossi, "The 'Notorious' Felix, Procurator of Judaea, and His Many Wives (Acts 23–24)," *Biblica* 82, no. 3 (2001): 410-17, at p. 413.

Gospel — i.e., Anna, the widow of Nain, the persistent woman, and the poor widow),[112] and that regarding the possibility of intercultural friendship and mutuality.

Second, note the plausibility of understanding Paul's church-establishment activities as both following in the path of Jesus' itinerant ministry and of extending the apostolic community beyond the confines of Jerusalem and the countryside of Judea. In other words, Paul the missionary and house-church planter can also be seen as a community organizer. Arguably, the house churches Paul founded were based on organizational forms of Roman civil life.[113] The difference is that Paul was seeking not just to accomplish civic goals in support of the *Pax Romana* — although he did not seem to work intentionally to undermine such — but rather to build up a people who would embody the life of Jesus as mediated through the apostolic community.

Last but not least, I suggest viewing Paul as a subversive agent of civil society in his daily lecturing in the Ephesian hall of Tyrannus for two years (Acts 19:9). Certainly here is a form of leadership development and, arguably, community mobilization, "so that all the residents of Asia, both Jews and Greeks, heard the word of the Lord" (19:10). Unsurprisingly, then, many converted and relinquished their occultic practices (19:18-20). The economic recession that followed for the craftsmen of Ephesus provoked an uproar that involved provincial officials as well (19:31). My point is that here we find Paul the teacher bearing kerygmatic witness in a manner that founded, nurtured, and mobilized a new community of faith, and inevitably had both economic and political repercussions for the wider society.

To be sure, neither Acts in particular nor the rest of the New Testament as a whole provide a systematically formulated prophetic politics, and there are other passages that indicate the early Christians were collusive with the political status quo.[114] My claim, however, is that the outpouring of the Spirit on the Day of Pentecost empowered the apostles to bear witness in the many tongues of the gospel in a variety of political contexts. More precisely, such

112. F. Scott Spencer, "Neglected Widows in Acts 6:1-7," *Catholic Biblical Quarterly* 56, no. 4 (1994): 715-33, rightly points out how the Acts 6 narrative reflects on the apostolic leadership in ambiguous light, especially given the authoritative model of Jesus reflecting the importance of caring for widows.

113. Eugene Brewer, "Roman Citizenship and Its Bearing on the Book of Acts," *Restoration Quarterly* 4, no. 4 (1960): 205-19, esp. p. 218.

114. Succinctly presented by Virginia Burrus, "The Gospel of Luke and the Acts of the Apostles," in Fernando F. Segovia and R. S. Sugirtharajah, eds., *A Postcolonial Commentary on the New Testament Writings*, The Bible and Postcolonialism 13 (London and New York: T. & T. Clark, 2007), pp. 133-55.

forms of prophetic and missionary politics can be seen as functioning both explicitly and more subtly among the apostolic Christians. From this, one could legitimately conclude toward at least two forms of prophetic political witness: one that stands against the political status quo in any context, and one that works more subversively within civil society. The former is best exemplified perhaps by the Barmen Declaration in 1934, when the confessing church in Germany condemned the Nazi ideology as being incompatible with the gospel. The latter, I suggest, can be seen in pentecostalism's home cell groups on the one hand, and in Radical Orthodoxy's complex spaces on the other. A Yoido Full Gospel Church and Radical Orthodoxy dialogue thus invites further consideration about how a prophetic politics of the local church and a post-secular theopolitics can mutually shape a missionary theology and praxis of civil society for our time.

6.3.2. The Empowering Spirit: Post-Secularity and the Redemption of Civil Society

In the following, I elaborate a prophetic theology of civil society in three broad steps: by summarizing the gains made so far in the juxtapositioning of pentecostalism and Radical Orthodoxy; by elaborating on how a post-secular theology of civil society requires a kind of prophetic political witness; and by outlining the basic features of such a prophetic theology of civil society. My goal is to advocate neither for pentecostalism nor Radical Orthodoxy, but to craft a prophetic politics in dialogue with both sets of voices. I will argue that the many tongues of the Spirit empower many prophetic practices for a post-secular civil society.

A pentecostal-Radical Orthodoxy dialogue: The preceding encounter renders salient issues of contextual location informing any stance in political theology. A number of considerations need to be explicated:

- pentecostalism's global presence and scope of vision, with its most vital sectors being located in the global south, in contrast to Radical Orthodoxy's primary identity as an academic movement (or sensibility) located in the Western world
- pentecostalism's concerns both with Christianization and development (e.g., with Cho) on the one hand, and with evangelization and re-evangelization (e.g., with Robertson) on the other, compared with Radical Orthodoxy's concerns to redeem secularized social and academic spaces

- pentecostal politics as grassroots efforts engineered by pastors and evangelists, as distinct from Radical Orthodoxy's scholarly projects promulgated by intellectuals.

Given these comparisons, my claim is that there must be a range of prophetic politics relevant to these various social contexts. St. Paul's model of conversing about righteousness will look differently in the West versus the global south. Thus Radical Orthodoxy's immanent critique of secularism will be less relevant to underdeveloped regions of the world that are only now beginning to come to grips with modernity and the Enlightenment project; on the other side, global Christianity should reckon with the fact that world evangelization will not look the same everywhere. In other words, we need a multiplicity of prophetic discourses — some socially engaged, others more dialogical, and still others more unapologetically kerygmatic and even prophetic, etc. — in order to respond to the diverse political contexts within which we find ourselves.[115]

Such a plurality of prophetic-political discourses and postures inevitably translates into an assortment of political practices. Thus the platform on which Pat Robertson ran for the 1988 presidential nomination can be compared and contrasted with respect to both Cho and the Yoido Full Gospel Church (YFGC) approach and with Radical Orthodoxy. On the one hand, Robertson and his Christian Coalition adopted a more direct mode of political engagement than did Cho and the YFGC. But if the former can be said to have utilized the political process in an attempt to turn back the tide of secularism in the United States, the latter can also be said to have been no less public even if less explicitly political in their efforts to transform the social and cultural landscape of South Korea through very intentionally developed social services, civic networks, and grassroots organizations. On the other hand, Robertson's strategy of arguing for a restoration of the Judeo-Christian vision of the founding fathers in some respects parallels Radical Orthodoxy's exposé of the secular as masking an ultimate theological agenda, and its retrieval of the primordial theological politics of Christian faith. Robertson's prophetic stance is thus directed against the liberal/secular political establishment, even while Radical Orthodoxy's prophetic theology is designed to overturn the metanarrative of secularism promulgated by those who have bought into the Enlightenment and modern project.

A further comparison between Cho and the YFGC and Radical Ortho-

---

115. I argue this point at much greater length in my *Hospitality and the Other: Pentecost, Christian Practices, and the Neighbor* (Maryknoll, NY: Orbis, 2008), esp. chap. 5.

doxy is also illuminating. The former is hesitant to adopt an explicitly political posture, preferring instead a more ecclesially based response to and within civil society. Radical Orthodoxy also insists on the priority of the church as a body politic, and from that foundation explores how the church subsists (at least analogously) as a set of complex spaces that provide an alternative *polis*, market/economics, and culture. In some respects, Cho's home cell groups in South Korea are more comparable to New Monastic movements in the West (see 5.2.3), even if the latter have in many ways adopted a more straightforwardly political rhetoric. In other respects, Cho's social strategy, including YFGC's publication of a daily newspaper intended to influence public opinion, is comparable to Radical Orthodoxy's attempts to renew and revitalize the civic domain, especially in terms of Graham Ward's critique and appropriation of mass culture: both seek to influence civil society by adopting and adapting social and cultural resources while being guided in these efforts by explicitly religious ideologies. Ward, along with his fellow Radically Orthodox colleagues, have used the printed word to provide immanent criticisms of the ideology of secularism; perhaps Cho and YFGC's daily may also be emboldened to bear prophetic witness in the public square. The reluctance to do so more frequently can be traced to the overriding tendency among pentecostals worldwide not to formally criticize or interface with the government, especially in order to protect the movement's right to engage in proselytizing activities. Yet precisely for this reason, pentecostalism can nevertheless engage peacefully and less controversially, even if no less effectively, with matters in the public square by way of influencing and shaping civil society.[116]

Theology of civil society in search of a prophetic politics: The preceding discussion illuminates how the church functions politically in civil society — commonly identified as that sphere and "network of institutions that exists between private individuals and the state"[117] — and thus invites more explicit

---

116. It may be that so long as pentecostals remain as a minority in the *polis*, their approaches will tend neither to be abrasive or aggressive nor to contest the status quo. Instead, a more peaceful socio-political conservatism can help create the more favorable public face and space for otherwise embattled minorities. See also the discussion of the east and south European Roma in David Thurfjell, "Pentecostalism and the Roman: Cultural Compatibility and Ethno-Genesis," in David Westerlund, ed., *Global Pentecostalism: Encounters with Other Religious Traditions*, Library of Modern Religion 14 (London and New York: I. B. Tauris, 2009), pp. 179-91.

117. I borrow this basic definition from Albert G. Miller, *Elevating the Race: Theophilus G. Steward, Black Theology, and the Making of an African American Civil Society, 1865-1924* (Knoxville: University of Tennessee Press, 2003), p. xvii. This historical study of Miller's (a pentecostal scholar) illuminates how African Americans (like Steward) have traditionally engaged with the

consideration of its prophetic witness in that domain.[118] The major concerns are that the church is either co-opted by civil society and the state (hence muting its prophetic voice), or that the church is either fragmented or locked within civil society (so that its prophetic element is denied as having any political relevance). These challenges can be historically delineated.

The early modern notions of civil society sought to construct a rationale for civil exchange given the natural "brutish" condition of the human race highlighted by the Wars of Religion.[119] In this conception, citizens needed to be reshaped to be more tolerant of the diversity that existed within modern nation-states. Classical political economists like Adam Smith then saw how the civil sphere could also foster social cohesion with the result of increasing economic productivity and international commerce. By the nineteenth century, civic and market pluralism were firmly lodged in the Anglo-American West, operating in many respects as a major antidote against all forms of state intrusion and totalitarianism. "The dominant theme . . . was the value of voluntary associations in curbing the power of centralizing institutions, protecting pluralism and nurturing constructive social norms, especially 'generalized trust and cooperation.'"[120]

For liberal Catholics like de Tocqueville, American civil society was precisely the right mix of secularized religion that could support and sustain a democratic politics.[121] On the one hand, the role of religion in shaping the public square was profound indeed, and no society could last for long without widespread religious belief; on the other hand, however, the Christian religiosity that had emerged on American soil was a reasonable rather than rigid orthodoxy that supported individual freedoms (in the religious, economic, and political domains). But now the problem was that American Christianity had morphed into a kind of bland civic religiousness, one that was disempowered to critically confront the nation's moral conscience.[122] In-

---

dominant society from the political margins — through transformation of the civic sphere — precisely what I am proposing from a pentecostal perspective in this chapter.

118. For a preliminary articulation of a theology of civil society, see Francis Sullivan and Sue Leppert, eds., *Church and Civil Society: A Theology of Engagement* (Adelaide, Australia: ATF Press, 2004).

119. My summary comments derive from Michael Edwards, *Civil Society* (Cambridge: Polity, 2004), chap. 1.

120. Edwards, *Civil Society,* p. 7.

121. See Sanford Kessler, *Tocqueville's Civil Religion: American Christianity and the Prospects for Freedom* (Albany: State University of New York Press, 1994), esp. chaps. 2-4.

122. See Russell E. Richey and Donald G. Jones, eds., *American Civil Religion* (New York: Harper & Row, 1974).

stead, in this vein, it was possible that civil society and its religiosity — i.e., civic religion — would devolve into becoming an accomplice to the state to the point of lending legitimization to the state's exploitation and manipulation of the *polis* through its cultural, religious, and educational institutions.

A reaction to the public and political relevance of civic religion, however, may be the twin thrusts of modernist universalism and religious sectarianism. The combination of these two trajectories involves both the privatization of religion (by modernity) and the withdrawal of religion from the public domain (by religious communities). The result here is what some have called the "naked public square" — the absence of religion from both the political and the civic arena.[123] So whereas civil religion is incapable of speaking prophetically against the state, in the cases of modernity's sacralization (synonymous with privatization) of religion, religion by definition concerns the non-political domain and hence cannot enact a prophetic politics. Here again, the hegemony of the state is unrestrained.[124]

Rather than simply attempt to regain political control over the public square through electoral politicking or other mechanisms, perhaps there is a more subversive strategy of working for the transformation of civil society. In fact, a prophetic politics, as we have seen in this chapter, is public and political precisely through its civic connections and interactions.[125] This can be seen along at least the following three lines: a) if civil society includes a wide range of civic institutions and schools, clinics/hospitals, labor unions, business associations, community centers, radio and TV stations, self-help groups, social movements, development and relief organizations, etc., then the church can be seen both as a civic institution on the one hand and yet with a role to play as the conscience of the civil domain on the other; b) if civil society's institutions are designed, at least in part, to influence personal morality, to nurture civic responsibility, to work for the alleviation of poverty, to promote education, to advocate for peace and justice, to develop leadership, to assist with community organization, etc., then the church as a

123. E.g., Richard John Neuhaus, *The Naked Public Square: Religion and Democracy in America* (Grand Rapids: Eerdmans, 1984).

124. See Daniel M. Bell Jr., "State and Civil Society," in Peter Scott and William T. Cavanaugh, eds., *The Blackwell Companion to Political Theology* (2004; paperback ed., Malden, MA: Blackwell, 2007), pp. 423-38.

125. For an empirical case study of religion's interface with civil society, see Alison Brysk, "From Civil Society to Collective Action: The Politics of Religion in Ecuador," in Edward L. Cleary and Timothy J. Steigenga, eds., *Resurgent Voices in Latin America: Indigenous Peoples, Political Mobilization, and Religious Change* (New Brunswick, NJ, and London: Rutgers University Press, 2004), pp. 25-42.

participant in the civil sphere can (and does) contribute to each of these social tasks both materially and ideologically; c) if civil society is to contribute to the establishment of democratic forms of life (through the nurturing of civil processes, social integrity, political trust, and interpersonal relations), to provide socio-political space for the development of solidarity, to foster and cultivate participation in and leadership within the public square, to shape socio-political identities, etc., then the church can be selectively involved in these projects as a leaven within the whole in terms of providing a subversive model according to the values of the gospel.[126] At each level — the institutional, the teleological, and the functional — the church finds itself embedded within but yet also not wholly subsumed under the domain of civil society.

But if on the one side civil religion can be marshaled in support of the ideology of the state (whether by fascism on the left or caste-ism on the right, etc.), on the other side civic fragmentation can also result in the hegemony of the state. If civic pluralism degenerates into too many conflicting voices and agendas that either cannot or refuse to be coordinated, then it will be rendered impotent against the machinery of the state. So herein lies the tension for the church's prophetic politics: that it challenges the domination of the state through empowering the many voices in the civic sphere but at the same time also avoids becoming just one more ideology within the cacophony of voices that constitute civil society. What is needed, hence, is a prophetic politics of civil society, one that promotes the pluralism of the civic domain while yet harnessing its energies in ways that resist totalitarianism and injustice in all its forms.

Elements of a prophetic theology of civil society in a post-secular world: I suggest that the gospel of Jesus as the baptizer of the Spirit provides a transcendental and critical principle that can orient the many voices in the civic square in ways that avoid legitimizing the ideology of any state.[127] What I mean is that the many tongues of the Spirit of Jesus bear witness to Jesus' incarnational love for justice, and that this in turns serves as a formal critical stance against any and all political ideologies. More precisely, the many tongues of the Spirit empower many forms of prophetic practices in the

126. Some of the preceding is developed in Scott R. Paeth, *Exodus Church and Civil Society: Public Theology and Social Theory in the Work of Jürgen Moltmann* (Aldershot, UK, and Burlington, VT: Ashgate, 2008), esp. part 3.

127. Calling also for a critical organizational principle is A. Pushparajan, "Mission in Civil Society," in Thomas Malipurathu and L. Stanislaus, eds., *The Church in Mission: Universal Mandate and Local Concerns* (Anand, India: Gujarat Sahitya Prakash, 2002), pp. 265-80, esp. p. 272.

civic sphere. These prophetic practices can be elucidated at least at three levels.

First, the church serves as a forum for the raising up of prophets. In the sense articulated by Roger Stronstad (see 6.3.1 above), the outpouring of the Spirit on all flesh potentially empowers every believer to exercise the gift of prophecy, and even to embrace the vocation of a prophet. What I mean is that the church provides a site wherein Spirit-filled believers are emboldened to bear prophetic witness, and learn how to live prophetically in the Spirit. Thus the gathering of the saints allows for, encourages, and embraces the prophetic word (cf. 1 Cor. 14:29), which in turn nurtures the confidence of believers to speak, debate, and engage in matters of (first and foremost) ecclesial concern. Local leadership is cultivated and developed in the process, and believers are simultaneously conscientized vis-à-vis their role in the church.[128]

Beyond this level of developing a prophethood of believers internally, however, there is the second level of prophetically engaging the world external to the church. If Robertson's grassroots Christian Coalition movement is a more explicit form of prophetic engagement with the world, Cho's home cell groups are a more implicit, but precisely for that reason, more potentially subversive mode of prophetic interface. Here also Radical Orthodoxy's notion of the church existing as and amidst a complex public space is also helpful for considering the many ways the church interacts with the orders, guilds, networks, and organizations that constitute the civil and public square. Yet in and through these arenas, it is precisely as the church embodies the ecclesial way of Jesus that it provides a prophetic alternative to the world's conventions of corruption, patronage, and oligarchy.[129] What emerges is instead a pro-

---

128. As Frances Kostarelos notes, the church can potentially function as "a community-based organization that embodies the capacity to mobilize moral consciousness and inspire public support to create opportunities for inner-city" inhabitants; see Kostarelos, *Feeling the Spirit: Faith and Hope in an Evangelical Black Storefront Church* (Columbia: University of South Carolina Press, 1995), p. 124.

129. In addition to Cho's cell groups and Radical Orthodoxy's complex spatial forms of life, pentecostal churches and Roman Catholic base communities are further examples of effective ecclesial modes of civil interaction. For comparative discussion, see Charles E. Self, "Conscientization, Conversion, and Convergence: Reflections on Base Communities and Emerging Pentecostalism in Latin America," *PNEUMA: The Journal of the Society for Pentecostal Studies* 14, no. 1 (1992): 59-72; Carol Ann Drogus, "Private Power or Public Power: Pentecostalism, Base Communities, and Gender," in Edward L. Cleary and Hannah W. Stewart-Gambino, eds., *Power, Politics, and Pentecostals in Latin America* (Boulder, CO: Westview, 1997), pp. 55-575; and Philip Wingeier-Rayo, "The Early Methodist Revival, Base Christian Communities and Pentecostalism in Latin America: A Comparison of Ecclesiology," *Apuntes* 21, no. 4 (2001): 132-47.

phetic politics of charity, a practical form of social action constituted by charitable works — as opposed to the *Realpolitik* of the world — a politics that is simultaneously sensitive to larger socio-structural projects and tasks.[130]

But a prophetic politics of civil society not only trains disciples of Christ for the prophetic task and empowers the church to exist as a leaven in the civic sphere, but also emboldens confrontation with the principalities and powers when necessary. In the end, if civil society is not to disintegrate into a plurality of ideologies, the critical organizing principle of the gospel — the just and peaceable life of Jesus and the accompanying fellowship constituted by all who have been baptized in and by his Spirit[131] — must also be lived out in the civic and public square. The Radical Orthodoxy theologians are right to point out that in a post-secular world, there is no *polis* that is not already theologically inhabited. The question is not *whether* theology, but *what kind* of theology. My proposal is that many civil practices are required, but only if these are finally normed by the life of the Nazarene anointed by the Spirit of God, who himself extended the prophetic ministry of the prophets of ancient Israel in their call for peace, justice, and shalom to reign across the land (see also 7.3 below).

Hence for a prophetic politics of civil society, the issue is not *whether* but *how* to go about fulfilling the commission of Jesus to make disciples from many nations (Matt. 28:20). My claim, however, is that the pentecostal doctrine of Spirit-baptism is much more politically relevant than heretofore considered. As David Martin notes,

> To be baptized in the spirit . . . is quite different from orthodox baptism, because priestly mediation gives you a "name" embedded in a community of continuing time and settled place, whereas a new name in the spirit is the choice of those whose times and seasonal rotations have been ruptured and who have been disembedded from the ties of place, for example the fiesta or ancestor veneration. Their brothers and sisters are now a supportive community of those born in the spirit not the biological flesh. Their notion of a people in exodus and *en route* runs parallel to

130. I get the notion of a politics of charity from Marjo de Theije, "Charismatic Renewal and Base Communities: The Religious Participation of Women in a Brazilian Parish," in Barbara Boudewijnse, André Droogers, and Frans Kamsteeg, eds., *More Than Opium: An Anthropological Approach to Latin American and Caribbean Praxis* (Lanham, MD: Scarecrow, 1998), pp. 225-48, esp. pp. 240-43.

131. See Joan Lockwood O'Donovan, "A Timely Conversation with *The Desire of the Nations* on Civil Society, Nation and State," in Craig Bartholomew, Jonathan Chaplin, Robert Song, and Al Walters, eds., *A Royal Priesthood? The Use of the Bible Ethically and Politically — A Dialogue with Oliver O'Donovan*, Scripture & Hermeneutics Series 3 (Carlisle: Paternoster, 2002), pp. 377-94, esp. pp. 385-86.

and fuses with the great trek to the modern city. . . . So, what is that [Pentecostal] story? It is that tens of millions on the move know themselves to be released from ascribed categories and indelible markers into a dangerous and bewildering open-endedness which has been made meaningful and purposeful by a discipline that offers a destination.[132]

I would only emphasize that the Pentecost narrative also offers *many routes* to that "one" destination. From the perspective of theology of civil society, then, this translates into many prophetic tongues, postures, and practices. At the very least, a prophetic politics will conduct an immanent critique of the existing status quo, not only in terms of reminding the authorities to uphold the law whenever and wherever injustice remains, but also in terms of the Spirit-empowered church interfacing in a multitude of ways with civil society — augmenting, leavening, challenging, and provoking the world as the Spirit leads. Simultaneously, a prophetic posture is also dialogical, adjudicating conflicting notions of righteousness in the public square. On occasion, however, the prophetic witness extends, as did the apostolic experience, into a testimony given through martyrdom. Not only is the Spirit-empowered witness considered a martyr in Acts 1:8 (and later in the death of Stephen),[133] but the witness of the Spirit has often called forth unpopular stances resisted by the world. This raises the question about whether or not a prophetic politics can ever galvanize a majority vote or succeed at the level of electoral politics. On this point, the intuitions of the Anabaptist tradition seem more pneumatologically realistic: that the Spirit's empowerment will often draw forth opposition and persecution that relegates the prophet to the margins, rather than resulting in any kind of a civic popularity.[134]

6.3.3. The Pneumatological Imagination: Difference, Harmony, and Communities of the Spirit

But if this is the case, whither a post-secular political theology and wherein lies the possibility of the redemption of the secular and of civil society? In the

132. David Martin, *Pentecostalism: The World Their Parish* (Oxford, UK, and Cambridge, MA: Blackwell, 2002), p. 168.

133. See Charles H. Talbert, "Martyrdom in Luke-Acts and the Lukan Social Ethic," in Richard J. Cassidy and Philip J. Scharper, eds., *Political Issues in Luke-Acts* (Maryknoll, NY: Orbis, 1983), pp. 99-110.

134. Tripp York, *The Purple Crown: The Politics of Martyrdom* (Scottdale, PA, and Waterloo, ON: Herald, 2007).

remainder of this chapter I will seek to respond to these two related questions in view of the foregoing dialogue between pentecostalism and Radical Orthodoxy. In particular, a robustly pneumatological imagination is capable both of sustaining a post-secular but yet not anti-secular theology of civil society and of grounding the ontology of peace required for witness to and redemption of the public square.

Any response to the initial question — whither a post-secular theology of civil society? — needs to articulate a theological definition of the secular. The "dictionary" definition usually views the secular as the realm distinct from the domain of the religious. The problem, as Milbank rightly points out, is that the late-modern understanding of the secular has come about as a result of an anti-theological and anti-religious ideology. Milbank's response, as well as Radical Orthodoxy's in general, is to make explicit the genealogy of this ideological secularism and provide a counter-hegemonic account — specifically, the orthodox Christian metanarrative. The pentecostal response has been to ignore the ideology of the secular so long as its efforts of proselytization are unhindered; but given the proper political context and motivation, pentecostals have inevitably been tempted to subscribe to a version of salvation history that includes the "manifest destinies" of national localities (whether of America, South Korea, or other nations),[135] and these have more often than not brought with them a distinctively pentecostal triumphalism regarding its sacred recounting of "secular" histories. In most pentecostal cases, however, part of the underlying assumption is that the secular is a postlapsarian phenomenon in need of a kind of exorcism so that the day of the Lord may be hastened.

But what if the secular were not merely a postlapsarian problem to be eliminated but had its own creational integrity and even autonomy? What if the foundations of the secular were not the modern split between the public domain of the political and the private realm of the religious, but the various and distinctive orders of creation in all its diversity? What if Augustine were right not only in asserting as an ideal the eschatological peace of the City of God (Milbank) but also in articulating a theological justification of the many cities as having their own legitimacy and autonomy during this dispensation that anticipates the eschatological kingdom?[136] In other words, what if

---

135. Or of various regions of Africa, given the important roles certain African nations have played in the pentecostal evangelist Reinhard Bonnke's "Africa for Jesus" campaigns; see Gary Lease, "Reinhard Bonnke: German Missionary in a Strange Land — An Introduction to Contemporary Evangelization in Africa," *Journal for the Study of Religion* 8, no. 2 (1995): 59-73.

136. This is the argument of Robert A. Markus, *Christianity and the Secular* (Notre Dame: University of Notre Dame Press, 2006), esp. chap. 4.

Kuyper and others in the Dutch Reformed tradition (see 2.3.3) were correct in insisting both that the various spheres of the political, economic, social, etc. were part and parcel of the created domain and that God has therefore endowed each sphere with its own realm of influence and responsibility, and has intended that social goods are most easily produced through free, collaborative, and even covenantal associations within and across the various spheres?[137]

This particular reading of the Augustinian and Kuyperian traditions is even more compelling if we think about the secular, as we have done in this chapter, also in terms of civil society. The civic sphere is certainly also theologically funded — incarnational, to use the Radically Orthodox metaphor — in its suspension from the life of God; but yet the civic sphere is also a pluralistic domain within which the diversity of God's peoples, all created in the divine image, live, move, and have their being. Not only did the theocracy of Israel make space for the alien and the stranger, but later exilic Israel was invited both to sojourn in and to seek the prosperity of an alien and strange land. Such a prophetic and yet exilic politics thus suggests that a post-secular theology of the political would resist the illicit anti-theology of modern secularism but yet not reject the legitimately secular and civic sphere, whose harmony-in-difference (and vice versa) propels the world toward its eschatological fulfillment.

What emerges would be a social ontology that would resist any artificial hegemony of theology and any political triumphalism of a mass religious movement. In terms of theology as an academic discipline, it means neither that theology is the queen of the sciences in any simplistic sense nor that theology is unrelated to other disciplines; rather, theology informs other disciplinary endeavors, and vice versa, in ways that always have to be freshly discerned. Similarly, in terms of a theology of the secular, it means neither that theology dominates the political sphere nor that theology comes alongside to provide legitimation for any pre-existing ideology (i.e., any version of the "manifest destiny" idea); instead theology needs to provide a discursive, critical, and prophetic perspective on any national or political ideology in light of the gospel. In short, there is a need to recognize the foundational character of theology on the one hand without denying the relative autonomy and integrity of other disciplines, spheres, and domains — such as that of the secular and of civil society on the other hand.

---

137. Jonathan Chaplin, "Suspended Communities or Covenanted Communities? Reformed Reflections on the Social Thought of Radical Orthodoxy," in James K. A. Smith and James H. Olthuis, eds., *Radical Orthodoxy and the Reformed Tradition: Creation, Covenant, and Participation* (Grand Rapids: Baker Academic, 2005), pp. 151-82.

In part for this reason I am in basic agreement with Radical Orthodoxy's metaphysics of participation that attempts to supernaturalize the natural, since there is within this scheme space to acknowledge the secular without separating it off completely from the religious dimension. But from a pentecostal perspective that sometimes overlooks the materiality, creatureliness, and finitude of nature (not to mention the secular), I think that a parallel strategy of naturalizing the supernatural is also helpful. In order to preserve both trajectories, I suggest that a pneumatological imagination informed by the Genesis narratives insists that nature dances to the Spirit's hovering over the face of the deep on the one hand, even while it recognizes that the Spirit's outpouring into creation allows for nature's rhythms to produce its own distinctive tunes on the other. In other words, while on some days and for some aspects of creation God commands or makes and things appear, on other days for other aspects of the world, God invites the earth and waters to bring forth and produce, and things emerge from out of the primeval waters.[138]

The Pentecost narrative also preserves both aspects of divine activity and human response, with the latter being unleashed so as to manifest the scope and depth of human creativity (as symbolized in language) rather than constrained by any predetermined divine template.[139] The result is that such a pneumatological ontology liberates the many voices of creation to sing their own tunes, authorizes the many orders of creation to do their own thing, and commissions the many civic spheres to organize their own domains — yet somehow (supernaturally!) harmonizes the many voices, orders, and spheres so that God is glorified precisely in and through these varied creaturely activities. If Radical Orthodoxy's incarnational ontology provides a theological explication of nature's, creation's, and civil society's participation in the transcendental goodness, truth, and beauty of the triune God, then the proposed pneumatological imagination encourages us to register and even preserve the particularity, plurality, and differentiatedness of God's creation within this metaphysical vision.

This leads us to the second question regarding the possibility of the redemption of the sphere of the secular in general and of civil society in particular. Pentecostalism's response is to preach Jesus as the prince of peace, while

---

138. See the extended argument in Yong, "*Ruach,* the Primordial Waters, and the Breath of Life: Emergence Theory and the Creation Narratives in Pneumatological Perspective," in Michael Welker, ed., *The Work of the Spirit: Pneumatology and Pentecostalism* (Grand Rapids: Eerdmans, 2006), pp. 183-204.

139. Here I am summarizing the pneumatological ontology and metaphysics developed in *Spirit-Word-Community: Theological Hermeneutics in Trinitarian Perspective* (Aldershot, UK, and Burlington, VT: Ashgate, and Eugene, OR: Wipf & Stock, 2002), chap. 3.

Radical Orthodoxy proffers the broken but yet reconciling body of Christ as a harbinger of the eschatological peace of the triune God. So while Radical Orthodoxy rightly intuits the importance of the body of Christ for an ontology of peace, such a move can be further grounded and enriched by the pneumatological imagination's capacity to register the non-homogeneity within the ecclesial body. More expansively, the diversity internal to the Lord's body is matched by the pluralism without, and the latter is required in order to register the distinctiveness of the former in this present dispensation.[140] Apart from such a pentecostally and pneumatologically constituted ecclesial body, the voices from the margins — even the many pockets of civil society — will be silenced, and the totalizing, colonializing, and imperializing centers of power will presume to speak to, for, and even sometimes against the interests of the many. These tendencies toward Christendom can be countered only when the many tongues of the Spirit are seen to reflect not the monotheistic God but the trinitarian life of Father, Son, and Spirit.

More importantly, the unleashing of the pneumatological imagination will also empower the many tongues to speak prophetically and redemptively of the glory of God. The prophetic dimension will confront and, where necessary, exorcize the anti-theistic elements that have infected the creational, political, and civic spheres, while the redemptive modalities will reclaim, retrieve, and reappropriate what was originally created good in anticipation of the coming kingdom. But simultaneously, a pneumatological ontology will resist any theological hegemony that refuses to register the diversity of the political/secular sphere; instead, the many tongues of Pentecost foreshadow the harmonious pluralism of the eschatological peace of the Holy Spirit. This dual approach thus accounts for both sides of the Christian doctrine of sanctification — that requiring purification and that emphasizing vocational mission — which we have developed in this and the previous chapter. Taken together, the sanctified and pneumatological imaginations both resist the fallen powers (of creation, the political, and the public square) and also discipline them according to the gospel of peace.

140. Nicholas M. Healy, *Church, World and the Christian Life: Practical-Prophetic Ecclesiology* (Cambridge: Cambridge University Press, 2000), esp. chap. 6.

CHAPTER 7

Pentecostal Health and Wealth:
A Theology of Economics

In this chapter we turn to confront head on an issue that has already registered its importance at various places so far throughout this book: the economic dimension of a theology of the public square. Not only have we defined the political in sufficiently broad terms so as to include the economic
domain (see chapter 1 above), but we have also seen that the theopolitics of
Radical Orthodoxy includes explicit proposals for a post-secular political
economy wherein alternative Christian practices serve as critiques of the existing civil society and the economic status quo (6.2.2). In the following, then,
we hope to do no more than sketch the broad contours of a theology of economics in order to explore the implications of the Christian "way" for a contemporary theology of the political.

My thesis is that a pneumatological and even trinitarian approach to
economics — one informed by pentecostal perspectives — invites us to think
not about one normative economic paradigm but about a multiplicity of economic models and modes of exchanges, each potentially making a distinct
contribution to the kind of economy of shalom that our world needs. We will
begin, as with each of the other arguments in Part II of this book, with the
pentecostal fivefold gospel, in particular with the doctrine of Jesus as healer,
in order trace out how there are internal to pentecostalism theological motifs
regarding salvific health that have over the course of the last century empowered the pentecostal quest for prosperity amidst the global market. In section
2 we will trace a similar development within the Roman Catholic Church, especially its tradition of social teaching, which has also enabled the Church to
engage the various challenges of the modern economy. Section 3 will then explore, in light of the comparisons and contrasts between pentecostalism and
Catholicism, an economic theology of many tongues and many economic

practices through which the healing of the world might be accomplished in anticipation of the coming kingdom. An underlying thread throughout the chapter concerns the correlation between individual healing/health and socio-economic peace and justice (shalom): that neither is ultimately secure without the other.[1]

We need to keep in mind throughout this chapter our overarching task and correlative constraints. Regarding the former, we should not be deterred from articulating in this volume a political theology, broadly considered. This means that our foray into the realm of economics is neither for its own sake nor for the sake of formulating a full-blown theology of economics; instead, we hope to supplement our quest for a political theology by exploring the interface between the political and the economic as well as by understanding how a theology of economics informs a more comprehensive theology of the public square. In terms of constraints, of course, I am a theologian, not an economist, so I am ill-equipped to wax eloquent on debated issues in economic theory or the complexities of the discipline of political economy. Still, this will not prevent me from moving forward with this chapter, even if it should motivate my readers to proceed critically and cautiously.

7.1. Jesus as Healer: Pentecostal Health, Wealth, and Economics

How do we get from Jesus as healer to Jesus as wealth-provider, and what does this shift mean for pentecostalism and political economy? These are the questions that this section is designed to answer. We will trace out the basic line of development from classical pentecostalism through the charismatic renewal movement, then delineate the distinctive features of the health-to-wealth motif as it has unfolded in the African American pentecostal and charismatic church tradition, and finally broaden the scope of our vision to include the global south, especially the transmutations of this theme in the Ghanaian context. Along the way, we will certainly observe the liberating elements of pentecostalism's theology of health/wealth even as we confront its problematic aspects. More important for our purposes, however, is to note how this doctrine functions in different pentecostal contexts, thus providing clues to

1. We will develop the notion of shalom in more detail later (7.3.2); for now, I am simply using the term to encapsulate what the Hebrew prophets foretold about the Day of YHWH when peace, justice, and righteousness would reign in the land — see Walter Brueggemann, *Living Toward a Vision: Biblical Reflections on Shalom,* 2nd ed. (New York: United Church Press, 1982), esp. part 1.

how the many tongues of Pentecost may be suggestive of the many contextual theologies of healing and shalom that mediate God's redemptive purposes.

7.1.1. Classical Pentecostal Health — and the Evolution of Wealth

The belief in Jesus as healer was one of the fourfold holiness doctrines adopted by classical pentecostals into their fivefold scheme (see 3.1.3). To be sure, the divine healing movement in nineteenth-century America was much wider than the holiness movement,[2] but the pentecostals drew more from their holiness ancestors and contemporaries than they did from Christian Science, New Thought, or other metaphysical movements. In particular, the christocentric and soteriological aspects of the holiness confession of Jesus as healer stand out. Thus pentecostals embraced Jesus' healing ministry as intimately connected with his saving work, and concluded from biblical texts such as Isaiah 53:4 and its citation in 1 Peter 2:24 that bodily healing was included in the atonement.[3] If the work of Christ reversed the effects of the fall with regard to the nature of sin, then it did so also with regard to the nature of sickness and disease.

For pentecostals, then, healing was not an appendage to Christian life, not a historically accidental event that may or may not happen for believers who were sick or ill; rather, Jesus came to save and did so in part through healing all whom he encountered, and the same Spirit who healed through Jesus continues to work the healing touch of God for the followers of Christ today. Well-known pentecostal ministers such as F. F. Bosworth thus preached that healing was available for all who would receive it; that believers should confess their healing according to the covenantal promises of the Bible; and that the gift of salvation included a victorious Christian life accomplished by the work of Christ and the dispensing grace of the Holy Spirit.[4] In short, early pentecostal conceptions of healing were deeply christocentric and soterio-

---

2. Nancy Hardesty, *Faith Cure: Divine Healing in the Holiness and Pentecostal Movements* (Peabody, MA: Hendrickson, 2003), and Heather D. Curtis, *Faith in the Great Physician: Suffering and Divine Healing in American Culture, 1860-1900* (Baltimore: Johns Hopkins University Press, 2007).

3. Kimberly Ervin Alexander, *Pentecostal Healing: Models in Theology and Practice* (Blandford Forum, UK: Deo, 2006), esp. pp. 36-54; cf. John R. Higgins, Michael L. Dusing, and Frank D. Tallman, *An Introduction to Theology: A Classical Pentecostal Perspective* (1993; reprint, Dubuque, IA: Kendall/Hunt, 1994), pp. 200-207.

4. These themes are replete in the collection of sermons in F. F. Bosworth, *Christ the Healer* (1924; reprint, Grand Rapids: Fleming Revell, 1994).

logical: experiencing the wholeness of the body was what it meant to receive the full salvation wrought by Christ.[5]

The mid-twentieth-century Latter Rain revival reinvigorated pentecostal healing in a number of ways.[6] Believing in multiple fulfillments of the prophecy of Joel which foretold of the Pentecost outpouring, the Latter Rain pentecostals distinguished between the "early rain" as referring to the Azusa Street revival and the "later rain" as referring to the final revitalization in their own generation in expectation of the parousia of Christ (Joel 2:23).[7] In this case, then, there was also an expectation that the miraculous signs of healing promised to accompany the proclamation of the gospel to all the world (Mark 16:18) would be manifest in abundance.[8] These biblical considerations led to the inclusion of healing as a prominent feature of Latter Rain revival services and crusades, as was manifest in the ministry of William Branham.[9]

5. A hundred years later, pentecostals are re-examining these theological conclusions. Keith Warrington, for example, argues that Jesus' ministry of healing is not necessarily paradigmatic for the church; there are distinctions between the two that must not be conflated. Warrington is motivated in part by the fact that not as many are healed in the church's healing ministry, so pentecostal theology must account for this and enable the coping with sickness, illness, disease, suffering, and death (rather than just deny such as being the result of a "lack of faith," etc.). See Keith Warrington, "The Role of Jesus as Presented in the Healing Praxis and Teaching of British Pentecostalism: A Re-examination," *PNEUMA: The Journal of the Society for Pentecostal Studies* 25, no. 1 (2003): 66-92. For further discussion of this issue in contemporary pentecostal theology, see Warrington, "Acts and the Healing Narratives: Why?" *Journal of Pentecostal Theology* 14, no. 2 (2006): 189-217; James B. Shelton, "'Not Like It Used to Be?' Jesus, Miracles, and Today," *Journal of Pentecostal Theology* 14, no. 2 (2006): 219-27; and Warrington, "A Response to James Shelton concerning Jesus and Healing: Yesterday and Today," *Journal of Pentecostal Theology* 15, no. 2 (2007): 185-93. In effect, the remainder of the argument in this chapter will suggest a theology of healing and wholeness that does not depend on adjudicating the christological question Warrington raises.

6. For an overview, see Richard M. Riss, *A Survey of 20th-Century Revival Movements in North America* (Peabody, MA: Hendrickson, 1988), chap. 5.

7. See the brief explication of the pentecostal concept in Vinson Synan, *In the Latter Days: The Outpouring of the Holy Spirit in the Twentieth Century* (Ann Arbor, MI: Servant Books, 1984), chap. 1.

8. Up until recently, pentecostals have not paid much attention to the historical-critical consensus regarding 16:9-20 as an addendum to the Gospel of Mark, and certainly pentecostals reading their King James Bible throughout the twentieth century would not have thought to question the authenticity of this passage. From a canonical perspective, however, there are reasons not to dismiss this text, even if it is a later redaction. For an insightful pentecostal reconsideration of this issue, see John Christopher Thomas and Kimberly Ervin Alexander, "'And the Signs Are Following': Mark 16.9-20 — A Journey into Pentecostal Hermeneutics," *Journal of Pentecostal Theology* 11, no. 2 (2003): 147-70.

9. For discussion of Branham, see C. Douglas Weaver, *The Healer-Prophet, William*

For many of these Latter Rain evangelists, healing was not only christological and soteriological but also an eschatological sign: it provided a foretaste of the wholeness of the coming kingdom.[10]

The charismatic renewal in the mainline denominations and the Catholic Church emerged almost on the heels of the Latter Rain revival. The major difference for the transmutation of the emphasis on healing may be demographically charted. In contrast to the lower-class population of classical pentecostal and Latter Rain adherents (at least up through the 1960s), members of the established denominations and churches derived mostly from the middle classes. Thus the nature of Jesus as healer expanded in the charismatic movement beyond that of bodily healing to include psychosomatic healing and the healing of the emotions. These "middle-class afflictions" (as I call them) highlighted the importance of having a multifaceted theology of healing — i.e., healing as a result of receiving the forgiveness of sins, healing of the body, deliverance/exorcism, and healing of the inner person, memories (often suppressed), or hurt emotions.[11] In charismatic prayer settings, the Spirit accomplishes inner healing in the name of Jesus by bringing to light root causes of psychic and emotional pain and enabling the individual to make peace with them through God's grace. In some charismatic circles, inner healing prayer involves leading the wounded person to visualize the traumatic experience along with Jesus' redemptive presence.[12]

The appearance of the charismatic renewal therefore brought about a more holistic understanding of healing. Not only were illnesses and diseases now understood to be psychosomatic conditions, but there were also emotional, mental, and even spiritual dimensions of human lives that were in need of the healing power of God. Human wholeness, in other words, included but was not reducible to physical well-being. The leaven of the charismatic renewal led pentecostals to revise their own understanding of healing in a more holistic direction. Of course, there were already resources in the

Marrion Branham: A Study of the Prophetic in American Pentecostalism (Macon, GA: Mercer University Press, 1987).

10. Systematic theological articulation of this idea came much later — e.g., Howard M. Ervin, *Healing: Sign of the Kingdom* (Peabody, MA: Hendrickson, 2002).

11. This fourfold typology of healing is elaborated in Francis MacNutt, *Healing* (Notre Dame: Ave Maria Press, 1974), part 3.

12. For an explication of the practice of visualization in the pursuit of inner healing in Protestant and Catholic circles respectively, see Charles E. Hummel, *Fire in the Fireplace: Charismatic Renewal in the Nineties* (Downers Grove, IL: InterVarsity, 1993), chap. 10, and Thomas J. Csordas, *The Sacred Self: A Cultural Phenomenology of Charismatic Healing* (Berkeley: University of California Press, 1994), chaps. 5-6.

pentecostal tradition for a reconsideration of these matters. Although on the boundaries of the early pentecostal movement, writers like E. W. Kenyon (1867-1948) were widely read in pentecostal circles and had already suggested that Jesus as healer not only destroyed the works of the devil but also accomplished mental and spiritual healing for believers who would lay claim to the full salvation (healing included) of God by faith.[13] By the 1950s and 1960s, pentecostal evangelists were fusing together the various streams of pentecostal teachings of and practices regarding healing — e.g., those of Bosworth, Kenyon, and Branham — while slowly competing with the claims of the charismatic renewal.[14] Those on the vanguard of healing evangelism during this time developed a holistic theology of healing that included the physical, emotional, mental, spiritual, and socio-material domains.

Leading the way here were evangelists like Kenneth Hagin, Kenneth Copeland, and Oral Roberts, among others.[15] Each emphasized to some degree the responsibility of the believer to claim his or her healing and material blessings by faith, in the name of Jesus, based on the promises of the Bible.[16] Scriptural texts such as 3 John 2 and John 10:10 — "Beloved, I wish above all things that thou mayest prosper and be in health, even as thy soul prospereth" and "I am come that they might have life, and that they might have it more abundantly" (as printed in the King James Version that was widely used in pentecostal circles) — alongside many other biblical passages highlighting the importance of faith in realizing the healing and blessings of God (e.g., Matt. 17:20; Mark 11:22-24) were read together toward the formulation of what has since come to be known as a "word-faith" theology. The principle of

13. See E. W. Kenyon, *Jesus the Healer*, 17th ed. (Lynnwood, WA: Kenyon Gospel Publishing Society, 1968). It is Douglas Jacobsen, ed., *A Reader in Pentecostal Theology: Voices from the First Generation* (Bloomington and Indianapolis: Indiana University Press, 2006), p. 123, who calls Kenyon a "borderline figure" within early pentecostalism, while noting his many friends within the movement and the popularity of his writings in pentecostal circles. The latter fact leads Dale H. Simmons, *E. W. Kenyon and the Postbellum Pursuit of Peace, Power, and Plenty*, Studies in Evangelicalism 13 (Lanham, MD, and London: Scarecrow Press, 1997), p. ix, to write: "Although Kenyon himself was never a Pentecostal, his influence on this segment of Christendom is extensive."

14. Some with "crossover" appeal such as Kathryn Kuhlman drew from both pentecostal and charismatic constituencies; see Wayne E. Warner, *Kathryn Kuhlman: The Woman Behind the Miracles* (Ann Arbor, MI: Vine/Servant, 1993).

15. David Edwin Harrell, Jr., *All Things Are Possible: The Healing and Charismatic Revivals in Modern America* (Bloomington: Indiana University Press, 1975).

16. See Keith Warrington, "The Use of the Name (of Jesus) in Healing and Exorcism with Special Reference to the Teachings of Kenneth Hagin," *Journal of the European Pentecostal Theological Association* 17 (1997): 16-36.

giving — not only the tithe (usually 10 percent of one's income) but also offerings beyond the tithe — was a means of "sowing seeds of faith" that God would then bless and return a hundredfold (or more) to the believer. In these circles, bodily healing was but one dimension of the abundance promised to believers, and the salvation of God formerly realized in the present only in the healing of the body was now seen to be realized across the various domains of human social, economic, and material life.

With these developments, the transition from pentecostal healing through holistic health and finally to pentecostal wealth (prosperity) was complete. To be sure, in pentecostal circles, this always stopped short of a more explicitly articulated theology of society and thus never explicitly engaged the challenges of either a theology of economics or of a theology of peace and justice (shalom). Yet we are getting ahead of ourselves.

Before proceeding, it is imperative to note the widespread censure of the prosperity gospel, even within pentecostal circles.[17] In brief, the major criticisms are that its central doctrines are burdened with the theologically aberrant if not heterodox ideas of Kenyon and the metaphysical cultic traditions from which he drew (the historical critique); its gnostic hermeneutic skews the biblical metanarrative to produce an individualist worldview (the biblical critique); and its emphases on healing and prosperity seduce its advocates to proclaim a "name it and claim it" gospel that benefits themselves at the expense of their followers and renders adherents susceptible to tragic outcomes in the many cases where healing does not occur or material success is not realized (the ethical and pragmatic critique).[18] These three strikes — the cultic origins, heretical doctrines, and questionable practices — leave the movement suspect in the minds of many observers.

7.1.2. Pentecostal Wealth: Prosperity in White and Black

Now let me be clear that it is impossible to defend the scandal caused by some in the prosperity movement who have exploited the vulnerable, commercial-

17. There is no space here to list the many more popular critiques brought by those who oppose pentecostalism and the charismatic renewal. An even-handed critique is provided in Bruce Barron, *The Health and Wealth Gospel* (Downers Grove, IL: InterVarsity, 1987). For a reasoned pentecostal assessment by a recognized biblical scholar, see Gordon D. Fee, *The Disease of the Health and Wealth Gospels* (Beverly, MA: Frontline, 1985). See also the Assemblies of God criticism in its position paper, "The Believer and Positive Confession," available at http://www.ag.org/top/Beliefs/Position_Papers/index.cfm (last accessed 15 January 2009).

18. See D. R. McConnell, *A Different Gospel: A Historical and Biblical Analysis of the Modern Faith Movement* (Peabody, MA: Hendrickson, 1988).

ized the gospel, and taken advantage of their tax-exempt status to raise money on TV and in person and pocket millions.[19] In these cases, the gospel of health, wealth, and prosperity has devolved into nothing less than the anti-gospel of greed, and the only responsible theological response would be a form of prophetic denunciation such as that defended in the previous chapter. Having said that, there are other historical and theological perspectives that do not necessarily provide an apologetic for the phenomenon of pentecostal prosperity,[20] but may yet shed some light on it. For example, a historical rebuttal to the critics of the prosperity gospel would interrogate the "guilty by association" charge connecting prosperity theology with the metaphysical occult via Kenyon,[21] while a theological rejoinder could move in the direction of Cho's theology of blessing instead (see 6.1.2).[22] Both lines of response suggest that we need to examine the socio-historical and material conditions under which the movement has flourished and within which the criticisms of the movement originate. For example, how might an understanding of the socio-economic conditions of Kenyon and his audience, as well as of Cho and contemporary pentecostalism in South Korea, illuminate the function of the prosperity theology in these different contexts, and how might a socio-rhetorical analysis of the criticisms of pentecostal prosperity clarify the wider socio-cultural contexts behind these polemics?

My claim is that when historically, socially, and (even) racially contextualized, the prosperity gospel is not necessarily defensible as an overall theo-

19. See the discussion of David Pilgrim, "Egoism or Altruism: A Social Psychological Critique of the Prosperity Gospel of Televangelist Robert Tilton," *Journal of Religious Studies* 18, no. 1-2 (1992): 1-11.

20. Taken together and in general, I would agree that Word of Faith teachings tend to be theologically aberrant and sub-orthodox; see Robert M. Bowman Jr., *The Word-Faith Controversy: Understanding the Health and Wealth Gospel* (Grand Rapids: Baker, 2001), pp. 221-28.

21. This has been attempted, with a fair degree of success (I think), by Geir Lie, "E. W. Kenyon: Cult Founder or Evangelical Minister?" *Journal of the European Pentecostal Theological Association* 16 (1996): 71-86. In a later essay — Lie, "The Theology of E. W. Kenyon: Plain Heresy or within the Boundaries of Pentecostal-Charismatic 'Orthodoxy'?" *PNEUMA: The Journal of the Society for Pentecostal Studies* 22, no. 1 (2000): 85-114 — a theological defense of Kenyon's ideas has been mounted. In view of Lie's work, I would be more amenable to identifying Kenyon as "on the margins" of pentecostal-charismatic orthodoxy, rather than "within its boundaries."

22. It should now be clear that Cho's tripartite anthropology and its correlative holistic soteriology — e.g., humankind as constituted by body, soul/spirit, and environment, which redemption from the effects of the fall translates into bodily healing, the forgiveness of sins, and social/material blessings — has linkages to theological developments in the North American scene. But while Cho certainly learned from his North American counterparts (through their missionaries and other venues), his efforts to translate what he gained into the South Korean context required some creative reordering and rethinking on his part that we should not minimize.

logical scheme, but is understandable as one aspect of a broader public theology plausible in specific milieus. To clarify this thesis, I want to consider the transmutations of the prosperity message within contemporary African American pentecostal and charismatic Christianity. In some respects, the tributaries flowing into the current Afropentecostal televangelism and megachurch phenomenon include some of the aforementioned movements and players (Latter Rain, charismatic renewal, Kenneth Hagin, Kenneth Copeland, Oral Roberts, etc.). The difference is at least twofold.[23] On the one hand, the primary intermediaries have remained African American pastors and preachers; so the healing and prosperity themes of Hagin, Copeland, and Roberts, et al. were embraced by Afropentecostals like Frederick K. C. Price, Carlton Pearson, and others, who have disseminated them within the wider black pentecostal and black church communities. On the other hand, there has also been a pre-existing stream of black religious life carrying the legacies of previous generations of African Americans who pursued both spiritual and material success — e.g., Sweet Daddy Grace, Father Divine, Marcus Garvey, Johnnie Coleman, and others — that also informs the present permutation. What binds these diverse strands into the commonality known as the black church is the historic experience of slavery, Jim Crow, racial oppression, and the possibilities promised — but in few cases realized — by the civil rights movement.

The contemporary black pentecostal and charismatic embrace and adaptation of the prosperity gospel must be understood against this broader quest for equality, legitimacy, and social status. The emergence of Thomas Dexter Jakes as megachurch pastor, entrepreneur, and "America's new preacher" is best comprehended in this context.[24] Jakes was a small-town apostolic (Black Oneness) preacher from the hills of West Virginia who was introduced into the mainstream of the black pentecostal-charismatic church by Carlton Pearson in the early 1990s. His message of personal empowerment addressed to black women — launched initially by his "Woman, Thou Art Loosed!" conferences and books — was so well received that by 2000, he had landed a seven-figure book contract with Putnam Publishing. Along the way, Jakes relocated to the south Dallas area and established The Potter's House, a congregation that now includes over 30,000 congregants and has become the institutional home of both T. D. Jakes Ministries (non-profit) and TDJ Enterprises (for profit).

23. See Stephanie Y. Mitchem, *Name It and Claim It? Prosperity Preaching in the Black Church* (Cleveland: Pilgrim Press, 2007), esp. chaps. 4-5.

24. Thus Shayne Lee, *T. D. Jakes: America's New Preacher* (New York and London: New York University Press, 2005), notes that Jakes is poised to assume the role vacated by the aging Billy Graham as America's most visible and recognized preacher. The details in the remainder of this paragraph and the next are extrapolated from Lee's fine biography.

Jakes the businessman and CEO wears fancy suits, drives expensive cars, and lives in a $1.7 million mansion. His business savvy has led him to produce and even star in films for the many books he's written that have ended up on both the religious and secular bestseller lists. Dexterity Records produces his music and other brand merchandise. He embodies the principle of profitability he preaches, which challenges his audiences to take advantage of the opportunities that come their way and/or to make the necessary changes that will allow them to move ahead with their lives.[25] The result has been spectacular, as Jakes has been well received in the black church both within and outside of pentecostal and charismatic circles, as well as in the wider religious and secular spheres.

To be sure, Jakes has had his critics as well. What is happening at The Potter's House is a far cry from what continues to happen in the sanctified church tradition around the country (see 5.1.2). In addition, evangelicals and others concerned about theological orthodoxy have raised questions about Jakes's theology of the Godhead (typically modalistic, as is much of the apostolic and Oneness traditions of pentecostalism).[26] More challenging, however, have been the criticisms formerly launched against Hagin and others in his train that are now leveled against Jakes: "promoting middle-class consumerism rather than offering a developed sense of biblical justice."[27] Joining in this chorus of critics, however, are others in the black church tradition, in particular those who have seen themselves as upholding the legacy of Martin Luther King Jr. and his fight for civil rights, political liberation, and social justice, as well as feminists and womanists who see Jakes as sending out "a conflicting message to women that empowers and impairs, humanizes and objectifies, one that often looses and yet sometimes binds."[28] Jakes's response,

25. This is the central message of one of Jakes's latest books (at the time of writing): T. D. Jakes, *Reposition Yourself: Living Life Without Limits* (New York: Atria, 2007). Note, however, that Jakes's principle of profitability is not necessarily equivalent to the prosperity gospel; Jonathan L. Walton, "A Cultural Analysis of the Black Electronic Church Phenomenon" (Ph.D. diss., Princeton Theological Seminary, 2006), pp. 167-70, helpfully shows the distinction, at least as Jakes himself understands it. The published version of Walton's dissertation, *Watch This! The Ethics and Aesthetics of Black Televangelism* (New York: New York University Press, 2009), came across my desk too late for me to take advantage of this much more substantive discussion of Jakes.

26. In response, Jakes has begun to baptize according to the trinitarian formula when in trinitarian contexts; see the discussion in Douglas LeBlanc, "Apologetics Journal Criticizes Jakes," in *Christianity Today* (7 February 2000): 58.

27. Shayne Lee, "Prosperity Theology: T. D. Jakes and the Gospel of the Almighty Dollar," *Crosscurrents* 52, no. 7 (2007): 227-36, from p. 232.

28. Lee, *T. D. Jakes,* p. 139.

typically, has been to emphasize that his interpersonal approach, seeking to build bridges amidst the political, is needed alongside more public and prophetic confrontations with the powers, that his emphasis on personal betterment complements rather than dispenses with socio-political activism, and that without both, the African American community will be neither situated/prepared nor motivated/mobilized to take advantage of the opportunities afforded by affirmative action and other politically attained initiatives.[29]

For the rest, Jakes's actions may speak louder than his words (even book publications!). Critics should note that his projects demonstrate that personal and economic betterment is only a starting point rather than a goal in itself for his vision of transforming the black community. In addition to establishing a school (regular and GED completion programs), a residential center (for the elderly as well as for family units), and the usual social ministries delivered by megachurches (i.e., the City of Refuge that includes a ministry for literacy programs, tutoring, youth activities, domestic violence counseling and assistance, AIDS outreach; a prison ministry that includes training of thousands of prison chaplains across the country to engage with black men who may not be open to white ministers; and the Raven's Refuge that ministers to pregnant teens and assists prostitutes who wish to leave their trade[30]), Jakes has also prosecuted a vision for the economic and cultural development of the south Dallas area. Estimating that huge sums of money were flowing to the north, suburban side of the city, the non-profit Metroplex Economic Development Corporation was developed in 1998 and "devoted to alleviating poverty in southwest Dallas through real estate development, cooperative programs, and regional planning."[31] The result has been an intergenerational community center, shopping center, independent living center, golf course, and a performing arts center (for plays, concerts, orchestras, symphonies, etc.). Jakes's assistant Nat Tate summarizes this vision: "South Dallas needs that kind of exposure to culture . . . the ballet needs to come here. . . . We are

29. Jonathan L. Walton, "Empowered: The Entrepreneurial Ministry of T. D. Jakes," *Christian Century* (10 July 2007): 25-28, esp. p. 27. Put alternatively, if the civil rights movement made possible black upward mobility, Jakes and others have taken the initiative to realize these as actualities; see Scott Billingsley, *It's a New Day: Race and Gender in the Modern Charismatic Movement* (Tuscaloosa: University of Alabama Press, 2008), p. 104.

30. So while "politically charged topics like same-sex marriage and abortion are not big issues at the Potter's House," ministries to homosexuals and to teens and single women who are pregnant are major ministerial initiatives; see Sridhar Pappu, "The Preacher," *Atlantic Monthly* 297, no. 2 (2006): 92-103, esp. p. 101.

31. Hubert Morken, "Bishop T. D. Jakes: A Ministry for Empowerment," in Jo Renée Formicola and Hubert Morken, eds., *Religious Leaders and Faith-Based Politics: Ten Profiles* (Lanham, MD: Rowman & Littlefield, 2001), pp. 25-52, quote from p. 40.

firm believers that those who have the wealth aren't going to give it up. We have to develop our own wealth."[32]

In short, Jakes is not only a preacher-therapist/counselor, but he also fulfills the traditional role of the black church minister as a community representative and agent of cultural lift.[33] My claim is that it is precisely through such a role that Jakes has transmuted the traditional pentecostal notions of bodily healing and material prosperity into a larger vision that also seeks to complete the promise of the civil rights movement. In a word, the same power of the Holy Spirit to heal bodies (in pentecostalism) and to enable the socio-political upheaval of American society (in the 1960s) continues today to empower black Christians in particular as well as all believers in general to better their lot in life and contribute to a more prosperous society. In that case, both individual healing and social activism are necessary though insufficient conditions for the kind of social peace, prosperity, and justice in the African American community that would serve to herald the shalom of the coming kingdom.

My goal here is not to defend Jakes — any humanly conceived program can be criticized — but to understand his achievements within the larger matrix of changes that have taken place in the black church tradition in general and black pentecostalism in particular over the last generation. On the one hand, we might see the faith message as being appropriated by the black megachurches in order to sanctify the attainment of prosperity, but on the other hand, their rhetoric of economic empowerment could also be heard as a justification for redistributing wealth from sinners to born-agains.[34] How one chooses to evaluate Afropentecostal prosperity might well depend on where one is located on the socio-economic spectrum.

7.1.3. Pentecostal Holistic Soteriology:
Global Economics and Local Markets

It is undeniable that part of the reason for the explosive growth of pentecostalism in the global south has been its ministry of healing in underdevel-

---

32. Cited in Morken, "Bishop T. D. Jakes," pp. 58-59.

33. Not to mention the mission projects of The Potter's House that include million-dollar development initiatives in Africa, especially Kenya (Pappu, "The Preacher," pp. 102-3).

34. Thus Milmon Harrison, *Righteous Riches: The Word of Faith Movement in Contemporary African American Religion* (Oxford: Oxford University Press, 2005), p. 159, rightly notes that the prosperity gospel is an ideology of transition that "gives [religious and theological] meaning to socioeconomic mobility."

oped regions of the world.[35] The message of Jesus as healer resonates with those attempting to crawl out from the underside of history, and it makes a life-saving difference for those who otherwise have no access to medical or health care. But if pentecostals in the West have had to overcome the traditional bifurcations between 1) the this-worldly and otherworldly dimensions and 2) the material versus spiritual aspects of salvation, as well as its usual privileging of the latter in both cases, pentecostalism in the global south is deeply informed by indigenous traditions that typically accentuate the former either to the neglect or even dismissal of the latter. In other words, if the first wave of pentecostal expansion in the global south was driven by signs, wonders, and miraculous healings, the latest revivals attract new converts in part due to a promise of an abundant, prosperous, and successful life. The pentecostal churches experiencing the most spectacular growth invariably are those whose gospel of prosperity is gradually displacing the previous generation's gospel of asceticism and thereby providing hope for their members confronting unemployment, economic recession, a crisis of healthcare provision, massive individual and national debt (not to mention corruption), and other socio-economic challenges.[36]

The Redeemed Christian Church of God (RCCG) in Nigeria is a prime example of a church that has successfully shifted from a holiness emphasis to the prosperity message.[37] The entrepreneurial range of the RCCG is unsurpassed in Africa and, as the church expands along the routes of the current West African diaspora, around the world. There are RCCG business ventures (e.g., truck and securities companies, gas stations, hotels and villas, restaurants, management and consultant firms); RCCG bank partnerships (e.g., the City Express Bank);[38] the Redeemer Business Academy (a

35. See the theme, "Divine Healing, Pentecostalism and Mission," in *International Review of Mission* 93, nos. 370-71 (2004); this entire issue of ten articles discusses healing related to the spread of pentecostalism in Latin America and Africa.

36. Robert Mbe Akoko, *"Ask and You Shall Be Given": Pentecostalism and the Economic Crisis in Cameroon* (Leiden: African Studies Center, 2007). See also the report on pentecostalism in South Africa written by Lawrence Schlemmer, "Dormant Capital: The Pentecostal Movement in South Africa and Its Potential, Social and Economic Role" (Johannesburg, South Africa: The Centre for Development and Enterprise, 2008), available at http://www.cde.org.za/article .php?a_id=276 (last accessed 26 January 2009).

37. Asonzeh F.-K. Ukah, *A New Paradigm of Pentecostal Power: A Study of the Redeemed Christian Church of God in Nigeria* (Trenton, NJ, and Asmara, Eritrea: Africa World Press, 2008).

38. Ukah, *New Paradigm of Pentecostal Power*, p. 267, notes: "City Express Bank (CEB) . . . has put forward a range of 'mission products', which include Church Remittance Account Scheme (CREMAS), Church, Cheques, and Cash Collections (4cs), Church Assets Acquisition and

training and networking initiative); and the Cloud 7 Cruises (weeklong vacations advertised as times of spiritual renewal). Unsurprisingly, given these various programs, "Today, about forty per cent of RCCG members are in the professional, administrative and managerial occupations; more than eighty percent of its clergy are drawn from this pool of graduates of tertiary institutions."[39]

Of course, besides these commercial endeavors, there is also the production and marketing of RCCG sermons and teachings via audio- and videocassettes. The central message is the twelve laws of prosperity promulgated by the RCCG founder Enoch Adeboye: God's sovereignty; humans must be willing to prosper; humans must be in God's will; giving is the key to prosperity; sowing monetary seeds to one's pastor is related to the law of the harvest; giving the first fruits or the tithe is central; hard work is essential; prayer is imperative; preparing for spiritual warfare is part of prosperity; praising God always is important; and prosperity involves connecting with God through Jesus Christ.[40] This is a message of empowerment that Nigerians in particular and West Africans are responding to. But note that Adeboye and the RCCG continue to prosper in part because, while other African nations "are explicit about groups preparing annual accounts of [their] income and expenditure as well as other activities, groups in Nigeria are free from such legal requirements."[41]

To be sure, as The Potter's House is engaged in projects directed toward social transformation, so is the RCCG. Yes, its message empowers Christian business owners to make a difference in the local economy, but in addition, the megachurch has launched the Jubilee Development Foundation (whose objectives are the eradication of poverty in Nigeria, promotion of success and enabling of continual prosperity among Nigerians in general and church members in particular, and development of capital for church and national

---

Development Scheme (CAADs), and Church Planting and Missions Account (CHURPMAS). The bank claims to be a partner with the church in fulfilling its missionary dream and expanding its missionary work, which is to spread the gospel of Jesus Christ for the benefit of humankind."

39. Asonzeh F.-K. Ukah, "'Those Who Trade with God Never Lose': The Economics of Pentecostal Activism in Nigeria," in Toyin Falola, ed., *Christianity and Society Change in Africa: Essays in Honor of J. D. Y. Peel* (Durham: North Carolina Academic Press, 2005), pp. 253-74, quote from p. 262.

40. The twelve laws are summarized by Ukah, *New Paradigm of Pentecostal Power*, pp. 183-95.

41. A. Ukah, "Piety and Profit: Accounting for Money in West African Pentecostalism (Parts 1 and 2)," *Nederduitse Gereformeerde Teologiese Tydskrif* 48, nos. 3-4 (2007): 621-48, quotation from p. 631.

projects), and has established the Redeemed AIDS Program Action Committee.[42] Further, the RCCG is increasingly becoming an alternative social network in terms of its schools, businesses, and even water supply and energy-generating unit. Given the failure and corruption of the Nigerian government since the late 1980s, the church's accomplishments can be better appreciated. As Adeboye says, "[T]he problem of NEPA [National Electric Power Authority] . . . the escalating cost of *garri* [granulated cassava flour] and other foodstuffs . . . cannot be solved by human wisdom, not by legislation, except we go back to God. . . . God, who made the mouth of a fish a bank, can heal our economy."[43] So, "though the government has failed the Nigerian people, the church will help the faithful succeed."[44]

As elsewhere, the RCCG and the many other prosperity ministries in Africa have also come under heavy criticism.[45] They have been chided for illegitimately mixing ministry with economics/business, "prophesying" for economic gain, promising "hundredfold returns" in order to motivate giving, concentrating wealth in the hands of capitalist preachers, being driven by egocentricity and greed, embracing consumerism and materialism, deploying fallacious exegetical and hermeneutical principles to undergird the prosperity message, and producing swindlers, among other charges. Critics have thus moaned that in a region of the world struggling to adapt to a postcolonial but yet globalized economy and saddled with poverty and high unemployment rates, the uncritical adoption of free market capitalism has fed consumerism, made luxury clothes and cars normative, transformed churches into purveyors of video cameras and public announcement systems, and compromised authentic worship with professionalized musical productions. Discerning observers have noted that the African prosperity

42. Afe Adogame, "'A Walk for Africa': Combating the Demon of HIV/AIDS in an African Pentecostal Church — the Case of the Redeemed Christian Church of God," *Scriptura* 89 (2005): 396-405.

43. E. A. Adeboye, "What Obasanjo Must Do to Succeed," *Redemption Light* 6, no. 5 (2001): 5, cited in Asonzeh F.-K. Ukah, "Roadside Pentecostalism: Religious Advertising in Nigeria and the Marketing of Charisma," *Critical Interventions* 2 (2008): 125-41, at p. 136 (brackets in Ukah's text).

44. Ukah, "Roadside Pentecostalism," p. 138. See also George O. Folarin, "The Prosperity Gospel in Nigeria: A Re-Examination of the Concept, Its Impact, and an Evaluation," *Cyberjournal for Pentecostal-Charismatic Research* 16 (2007) [http://pctii.org/cyberj/cyber16.html].

45. Deji Isaac Ayegboyin, "A Rethinking of Prosperity Teaching in the New Pentecostal Churches in Nigeria," *Black Theology: An International Journal* 4, no. 1 (2006): 70-86; cf. Kwabena Asamoah-Gyadu, *African Charismatics: Current Developments within Independent Indigenous Pentecostalism in Ghana,* Studies of Religion in Africa 27 (Leiden and Boston: Brill, 2005), pp. 215-32.

message supports market consumption, but has thus far not developed a theology to motivate market production.[46]

The anomaly in the African context may be the Ghanaian pentecostal statesman Mensa Otabil, pastor of the 6000-member International Central Gospel Church (ICGC) in Accra.[47] In a small developing country that has nevertheless sprouted a large number of prosperity megachurches,[48] Otabil faces stiff competition. Yet as an ethnographic study of his weekly primetime telecast, *Living Word,* reveals, Otabil presents a message designed to attract not just those who want to be rich, but those who wish to learn how to succeed; not just those who want to feel prosperous, but those who are willing to work toward success; not just those who want to be beneficiaries of a prosperous economy, but those who are willing to be motivated to contribute to the forging of such an economy.[49] Thus, Otabil presents himself first and foremost as a teacher (not just preacher), reasoning with and educating his listeners (rather than only moving them rhetorically or emotionally), and challenging his audience to be learners and agents of cultural change (instead of being passive recipients of the achievements of others). As we have already noted how the film and video industry is creating a pentecostal economy and subculture in the Ghanaian context (see 1.2.3 and 5.3.2), it only needs to be noted here that Otabil's weekly program is designed to mobilize a nation of those who not only admire his message but are motivated to adopt his vision and emulate his way of life.

Hence Otabil breaks with the status quo of the Ghanaian/African version of the prosperity gospel in at least two respects. First, as hinted at above, whereas most prosperity ministries proclaim the believer's right to consumption, Otabil emphasizes the importance of production. Starting with the creational mandate to subdue and have dominion over the earth (Gen. 1:28), Otabil acutely notes:

> If you are a consumer, and most people consume what the flesh desires, then you are not a producer. You cannot have dominion. That is one of the reasons most of the third world countries are not productive and able

---

46. Akosua K. Darkwah, "Aid or Hindrance? Faith Gospel Theology and Ghana's Incorporation into the Global Economy," *Ghana Studies* 4 (2001): 7-29, esp. pp. 23-24.

47. Christian van Gorder, "Beyond the Rivers of Africa: The Afrocentric Pentecostalism of Mensa Otabil," *PNEUMA: The Journal of the Society for Pentecostal Studies* 30, no. 1 (2008): 33-54.

48. Paul Gifford, *Ghana's New Christianity: Pentecostalism in a Globalizing African Economy* (Bloomington and Indianapolis: Indiana University Press, 2004), chap. 2, overviews five other major prosperity churches.

49. Marleen de Witte, "Altar Media's *Living Word:* Televised Charismatic Christianity in Ghana," *Journal of Religion in Africa* 33, no. 2 (2003): 172-202.

to subdue the land God has given them. Most of them are consuming, not producing. They are receiving the end result of someone else's productivity. If you want dominion, you must be fruitful, multiply, and replenish your area. You must then subdue all of that, including yourself, in order to walk in full dominion. *Dominion* simply means "authority." If you do not subdue the flesh, it will have dominion over you. If you do not subdue a love of money, it will have dominion over you.[50]

Notice that Otabil is not only talking about the accumulation of wealth, but about having control over it. Rather than blaming the devil (as other deliverance-prosperity ministries tend to do), he urges personal responsibility. Thus, he writes:

When an organization or an individual operates with the paradigm that does not process its resources to generate greater benefit, they are happy and pride themselves in the raw materials they produce. They never stop to think that, they later buy the processed finished products made out of their raw materials at a higher price. Many third world nations are trapped in this kind of economy. They work so hard to produce items such as gold, only to export them in their raw state to the industrialized nations who process the raw materials into finished products which they in turn sell back to the third world nations at a higher cost. A nation becomes "third world" if it does not have the capacity to manage its resources from the raw primary product stage to the sophisticated processed stage. Such a nation will always struggle to catch up on its current deficits with its competitor nations who possess the capacity to process products to their varied refined stages.[51]

Otabil's message of prosperity is subtle and nuanced, directed toward the prosperity of the nation over the long haul, rather than seeking any quick fix. Individual prosperity, then, is intertwined with the prosperity of the nation.[52]

50. Mensa Otabil, *Four Laws of Productivity* (Tulsa, OK: Vincom, 1991), p. 115.

51. Mensa Otabil, *Buy the Future: Learning to Negotiate for a Future Better Than Your Present* (Lanham, MD: Pneuma Life Publishing, 2002), pp. 62-63.

52. Otabil preached: "Your personal breakthrough must be linked up with the total breakthrough of the nation. The nation must prosper and when it prospers, automatically you will prosper"; see Otabil's tape, "Independence Anniversary Message," delivered in 1996, cited in Joram D. Oudshoorn, "But Otabil Told You! The Message of a Ghanaian Neo-Pentecostal Africanist" (Doctoraalscriptie, Universiteit Utrecht, 2006), p. 74. Oudshoorn's unpublished thesis is the most in-depth scholarly discussion of Otabil so far, and I am grateful to him for sharing an electronic copy with me. My discussion in this section is more nuanced as a result.

This leads to the second way in which his gospel of production and dominion differs from those of other African prosperity preachers — wherein Otabil explicitly advocates what might be called a pro-African message.

Otabil's *Beyond the Rivers of Ethiopia* attempts to retrieve and redeem the black race in the Bible in order to argue that God views blacks as equal rather than inferior to whites.[53] This low personal and collective self-esteem must be replaced with human dignity and self-confidence. Thus Otabil urges his fellow Africans to rediscover their inheritance and take control of their lives and their destinies so that Africa may in the future be a blessing to others. To be sure, Otabil is unafraid to name and identify traditions that have kept Africans from achieving their God-intended dominion.[54] At the same time, African culture itself is to be redeemed so it can take its place on the world stage.[55] Herein the message of prosperity, dominion, and production interfaces with a vision for a revitalized African economy, one that allows the nations of Africa to participate in and contribute to the global market rather than be a dependent recipient of first world aid. Undoubtedly, Otabil provides what may be the first (and so far only) "evangelical-Pentecostal liberation theology which emphasises [how] the self-hood of the African, human development, critical thinking, and cultural renewal are a unique innovation in Pentecostal theological self-understanding."[56]

The local embeddedness of Otabil's message is undeniable, as the "Otabil factor" is less effective in the broader Ghanaian diaspora.[57] But it is precisely in the local Ghanaian and West African context that this prosperity message is displacing the older pentecostal asceticism. Of course, how convenient it was for the previous generations of African pentecostal missionaries who preached a theology of "simplicity-as-a-sign-of-divine-blessing" that

53. Mensa Otabil, *Beyond the Rivers of Ethiopia* (Bakersfield, CA: Pneuma Life Publishing, and Accra-North, Ghana: International Central Gospel Church, 1993).

54. Thus Otabil insisted, "Many of the societal ills ravaging our national life, such as corruption, nepotism, dictatorship and cronyism, have their origins rooted in old traditional values which are not well adapted to our present political and economic realities" (from Otabil's first Ofori-Atta lecture, 17 October 2000, cited in Gifford, *Ghana's New Christianity*, p. 134).

55. Oudshoorn, "But Otabil Told You!" p. 116, insightfully notes, however, that given his decrying at least of African traditional religions, Otabil is unclear about what specifically about African culture is to be retrieved for the African and common human good.

56. Emmanuel Kingsley Larbi, *Pentecostalism: The Eddies of Ghanaian Christianity* (Accra: Centre for Pentecostal and Charismatic Studies, 2001), p. 315.

57. Rijk van Dijk, "'Beyond the Rivers of Ethiopia': Pentecostal Pan-Africanism and Ghanaian Identities in the Transnational Domain," in Wim van Binsbergen and Rijk van Dijk, eds., *Situating Globality: African Agency in the Appropriation of Global Culture*, African Dynamics 3 (Leiden and Boston: Brill, 2004), pp. 163-89.

they themselves lived in relative abundance and were commodity-rich when they returned home on missionary furlough.[58] In other words, the message of simplicity and poverty was imposed on the African, and it has been on this basis that the African embrace of the prosperity message was critiqued. As with Afropentecostalism in North America, then, I am simply urging that any assessments of the health and wealth motif be sensitive to the historical, class, and race factors in the background.

When set in local Ghanaian and broader African context, however, Otabil's Afrocentrism is a theology of hope — of health, wholeness, empowerment, and prosperity — that has individual, social, national, and even continental aspirations. African pentecostals have in this case embraced a vision of the kingdom they believe is promised in the Bible, a message of vindication from their oppressors, and a gospel of shalom — of peace, justice, prosperity. The promise to ancient Israel, about the promised outpouring of the Spirit, is thus claimed as being fulfilled in this time:

> until a spirit from on high is poured out on us,
>   and the wilderness becomes a fruitful field,
>   and the fruitful field is deemed a forest.
> Then justice will dwell in the wilderness,
>   and righteousness abide in the fruitful field.
> The effect of righteousness will be peace,
>   and the result of righteousness, quietness and trust for ever.
>
> (Isa. 32:15-17)

7.2. The Economy, the Common Good, and the Catholic Social Teaching Tradition

Some might wonder why we now turn to the Roman Catholic tradition to further the discussion. One reason is that the teaching office of the Church has produced a series of statements either touching on or substantively engaging issues relevant to the modern economy. Further, the Catholic Church has also been deeply touched by the charismatic renewal movement,[59] and in

---

58. Rijk van Dijk, "The Pentecostal Gift: Ghanaian Charismatic Churches and the Moral Innocence of the Global Economy," in Richard Fardon, Wim van Binsbergen, and Rijk van Dijk, eds., *Modernity on a Shoestring: Dimensions of Globalization, Consumption and Development in Africa and Beyond* (Leiden and London: EIDOS, 1999), pp. 71-89, esp. p. 80.

59. See Kilian McDonnell, *Toward a New Pentecost, for a New Evangelization* (Collegeville, MN: Liturgical Press, 1993), and Paul Josef Cordes, *Call to Holiness: Reflections on the Catholic Charismatic Renewal* (Collegeville, MN: Liturgical Press, 1997).

that sense, perhaps some of its theological intuitions regarding economics may resonate with charismatic sensibilities if not perhaps be deepened by the following considerations. Finally, precisely because of the breadth and depth of the charismatic renewal in the Catholic Church, there have already been a series of formal dialogues between the Church and scholars and theologians representing a broad spectrum of the pentecostal tradition.[60] I am hopeful this exercise will provide another occasion to reflect on the Roman Catholic–pentecostal encounter, or at least stimulate further discussion about their theological convergences and differences. We will proceed with an overview of the Catholic social teaching tradition (CST), focusing on its economic ideas and proposals; then highlight interpretations of CST especially across the spectrum of North American Catholicism; and conclude by exploring central themes in CST that may not only be suggestive for carving a *via media* between Catholics on the "left" and the "right" but may also provide bridges for a constructive theology of economics. Even more crucial, thinking with CST will help ensure that the resultant theology of economics will include both individual and social dimensions — i.e., both a theology of healing and a theology of shalom — and clarify their interrelationship.

7.2.1. On Healing as Economic Justice: The Scope of Catholic Social Teaching

Besides the reasons provided in the preceding paragraph, I turn now to CST because it consists of papal encyclicals written over the last century and there-

60. There have been five previous quadrennial dialogues, the final reports of which have been published in both Catholic and pentecostal venues: "Final Report of the International Roman Catholic/Pentecostal Dialogue (1972-1976)," *PNEUMA: The Journal of the Society for Pentecostal Studies* 12, no. 2 (1990): 85-95; "Final Report of the International Roman Catholic/Pentecostal Dialogue (1977-1982)," *PNEUMA: The Journal of the Society for Pentecostal Studies* 12, no. 2 (1990): 97-115; "*Perspectives on Koinonia*: Final Report of the International Roman Catholic/Pentecostal Dialogue (1985-1989)," *PNEUMA: The Journal of the Society for Pentecostal Studies* 12, no. 2 (1990): 117-42; "Evangelization, Proselytism and Common Witness: The Report from the Fourth Phase of the International Dialogue (1990-1997) between the Roman Catholic Church and Some Classical Pentecostal Churches and Leaders," *PNEUMA: The Journal of the Society for Pentecostal Studies* 21, no. 1 (1999): 11-51 [cf. "Evangelization, Proselytism and Common Witness: The Report from the Fourth Phase of the International Dialogue 1990-1997 between the Roman Catholic Church and Some Classical Pentecostal Churches and Leaders," *One in Christ* 35, no. 2 (1999): 158-90]; and "On Becoming a Christian: Insights from Scripture and the Patristic Writings with Some Contemporary Reflections," Report of the Fifth Phase of the International Dialogue between Some Classical Pentecostal Churches and Leaders and the Catholic Church (1998-2006), *Cyberjournal for Pentecostal-Charismatic Research* 18 (2009) [http://pctii.org/cyberj/cyber18.html].

fore represents if not a coherent tradition of thinking then at least an attempt to consider newly developing situations in light of the previous papal reflections on society and the economy in particular and the entire scope of the church's authoritative teachings in general.[61] Because there are at least ten major encyclicals that are a part of the CST, because the scope of these encyclicals includes much more than the economy, and because of the unmanageable amount of secondary literature that has emerged in response, we must be very selective in our treatment.[62] I will focus on the CST's economic proposals and on the central theological themes that contribute perspective on these pronouncements.[63]

While general summary statements regarding CST that span one hundred years should be alert to the many qualifications that can be found even within the same documents, it is fair to say that the first of the two modern encyclicals on society were wary of socialism, understood in terms of the Marxist presumption of class warfare and advocacy of the collective means of production (*RN* 11-12; *QA* 111-26), and defended private property, free enterprise, and both the social and individual character of labor (*RN* 4-5, 35; *QA* 44-48, 69; cf. *CA* 41). At one level, the socialism that was rejected, at least in

61. The relative coherence of CST is better grasped when read against the long and variegated history of Christian social thought in general; see George W. Forell, *Christian Social Teachings: A Reader in Christian Social Ethics from the Bible to the Present* (1966; reprint, Minneapolis: Augsburg, 1971).

62. When referring to the following major papal documents, I will provide in-text parenthetical citations identifying the paragraph numbers, using the following set of abbreviations:

RN	*Rerum Novarum* by Leo XIII (1891)	
QA	*Quadragesimo Anno* by Pius XI (1931)	
MM	*Mater et Magistra* by John XXIII (1961)	
PT	*Pacem in Terris* by John XXIII (1963)	
PP	*Populorum Progressio* by Paul VI (1967)	
LE	*Laborem Exercens* by John Paul II (1981)	
SRS	*Sollicitudo Rei Socialis* by John Paul II (1987)	
CA	*Centesimus Annus* by John Paul II (1991)	

Footnotes will point to the page numbers of direct quotations from David J. O'Brien and Thomas A. Shannon, eds., *Catholic Social Thought: The Documentary Heritage* (Maryknoll, NY: Orbis, 1992).

63. For a helpful overview of CST in light of our concerns, see Albino Barrera, *Modern Catholic Social Documents and Political Economy* (Washington, DC: Georgetown University Press, 2001). A more systematic and theoretical analysis can be found in Charles E. Curran, *Catholic Social Teaching, 1891-Present: A Historical, Theological, and Ethical Analysis* (Washington, DC: Georgetown University Press, 2002), while a broader discussion in global context is provided by Judith A. Merkle, *From the Heart of the Church: The Catholic Social Tradition* (Collegeville, MN: Liturgical/Michael Glazier, 2004).

Quadragesimo Anno, was of the Stalinist, fascist, and "Bolshevik" variety (*QA* 122) — which had emerged in the intervening years since Leo XIII — and arguably in large part motivated by its atheistic philosophy which was seen as a threat to the Church's moral, spiritual, and cultural authority and as a counter-ideology to the Church's theistic-communitarian vision.[64] Yet we should also be clear that neither these nor later CST documents adopted wholesale a capitalist framework for the modern economy. Rather, there has been a repeated insistence on the priority of labor (and the laborer) over capital (*LE* 12) and consistent calls for workers' rights, just wages, fair distribution of profits, and workers' associations to ensure safe working conditions and fair worker-employer relations (*RN* 31-41; *QA* 53-69; *MM* 68-72; *LE* 16-20). Thus in response to the explicit question about whether or not CST advocated the embrace of the modern capitalist economy, Pope John Paul II wrote:

> If by "capitalism" is meant an economic system which recognizes the fundamental and positive role of business, the market, private property and the resulting responsibility for the means of production, as well as free human creativity in the economic sector, then the answer is certainly in the affirmative, even though it would perhaps be more appropriate to speak of a "business economy," "market economy" or simply "free economy." But if by "capitalism" is meant a system in which freedom in the economic sector is not circumscribed within a strong juridical framework which places it at the service of human freedom in its totality, and which sees it as a particular aspect of that freedom, the core of which is ethical and religious, then the reply is certainly negative (*CA* 42).[65]

John Paul II's statement would be incomprehensible apart from an awareness of the major theological commitments in the CST. Three interlocking theological doctrines are pertinent for our purposes: the emphasis on the dignity of the human person; the centrality of the church for the promotion of human well-being; and a vision of the common good as the proper goal of human and economic life. The notion of human dignity underlying the CST's theology of work — i.e., that the work done by people must not undermine the integrity and sanctity of their personhood as made in the image

---

64. Michael J. Schuck, *That They May Be One: The Social Teaching of the Papal Encyclicals 1740-1989* (Washington, DC: Georgetown University Press, 1991), has shown that the legacy of Pope Leo XIII was consistent with the hierarchical and communitarian emphases with which his predecessors resisted the Enlightenment and Revolutionary ideologies of their times.

65. O'Brien and Shannon, eds., *Catholic Social Thought*, p. 471.

of God (*RN* 20-21; *MM* 82-83; *LE* 9, 21) — is the basis for the CST's defense of not only religious freedom but human liberty and initiative in the economic sphere of life (*MM* 51), and is undergirded by the personalist theological anthropology prominent in the wider Catholic theological tradition (*LE* 15).[66] Embracing the dignity of all human persons, based in part on the biblical revelation and in part on natural law, ensures that their rights will be protected, that their initiative will be valued, and that their creativity will be encouraged. These are essential to human wholeness and health, both at the level of the individual and of the communal.

It is the Church's responsibility to not only preach the gospel and evangelize the world but also to proclaim the doctrine about human dignity and other theological truths and ensure their implementation across the various domains of life (*RN* 13; *QA* 17-24). In fact, "the Church's *social teaching* is itself a valid *instrument of evangelization*" (*CE* 54, italics in the original).[67] This is the Church's vocation: to participate in the healing and redemption of the world. In this bigger scheme of things, then, the purpose of CST is to provide guidance to the church and its members in their work for the common good, based on the common bond of all humankind (*QA* 84; *MM* 78-80; *PT* 53-59, 139). Private property and material achievements are not first and foremost for personal gain but have a "universal destination" (*CA* 30ff. [§4]) in that they are gifts of grace provided for the well-being of others. Included in the compass of the common good are such ideals as the fair and just distribution of wealth, the relief of poverty, the closure if not elimination of the gap between the rich and the poor, and even the subordination of the right to private property to the right to common use (*LE* 14). At each level, however — that of the individual, the church, and the social — the underlying principles are explicitly theological. In other words, CST understands the healing and wholeness of individuals to be integrally related to the wider community — whether of the Church or of the social sphere.[68]

Hence CST is a theological tradition focused on wholeness and redemption — the Hebraic notion of shalom, in its broad sense — rather than merely a set of guidelines for social life or political economy. Thus, reflecting on the broad scope of the CST, John Paul II noted:

66. For a discussion of the influence of the neo-Thomist philosophy of personalism in twentieth-century Catholic theology, see Bernard V. Brady, *Essential Catholic Social Thought* (Maryknoll, NY: Orbis, 2008), chap. 2.

67. This is also the main thrust of Pope Paul VI's encyclical, *Evangelii Nuntiandi* (1975).

68. The redemptive message of the papal teachings is evident: *QA* 130-35; *MM* 178-84; *PT* 146-73; *LE* 24-27; and *SRS* 48.

The Church's social doctrine is not a "third way" between liberal capital-ism and Marxist collectivism, nor even a possible alternative to other so-lutions less radically opposed to one another: rather, it constitutes a cate-gory of its own. Nor is it an ideology, but rather the accurate formulation of the results of a careful reflection on the complex realities of human ex-istence, in society and in the international order, in the light of faith and of the Church's tradition. Its main aim is to interpret these realities, deter-mining their conformity with or divergence from the lines of the Gospel teaching on man and his vocation, a vocation which is at once earthly and transcendent; its aim is thus to guide Christian behavior. It therefore be-longs to the field, not of ideology, but of theology and particularly of moral theology (*SRS* 41).[69]

In other words, CST provides a *theology* of sociality and of economics, rather than serves as a handbook of social or economic theory. Such a vision of a just and equitable society includes both a theological anthropology of human beings as created in the *imago dei* and the call toward peace and justice char-acteristic of the coming kingdom.

From one perspective, the CST's explicitly theological orientation would appear to leave little to argue about in the world of *Realpolitik* or on Wall Street. From another angle, however, the spiritual and moral authority of the papal magisterium remains sufficiently palpable in our time so that its social vision continues to influence and impact the lives of Catholics who conscientiously attempt to live out their faith in various local and global contexts of a fallen social and economic world. Here, where the mag-isterial rubber hits the laity's road, so to speak, the generality of the major-ity of the CST's socio-economic prescriptions has resulted in a wide range of interpretations and applications. In the following I will limit my discus-sion to the recent reception of CST primarily among North American Ro-man Catholics, in part because many of the salient issues can be observed within this framework and in part because the challenges related to the global economy about which they are engaging are driven by American mechanisms. We will see the amenability of CST to both leftward-leaning communitarian-liberationist interpretations and rightward-leaning per-sonalistic elucidations, even when confined to the North American Catho-

---

69. O'Brien and Shannon, eds., *Catholic Social Thought*, p. 425. That CST is best under-stood as a tradition of moral theology resonates with the proposals of Edward Hadas, *Human Goods, Economic Evils: A Moral Approach to the Dismal Science* (Wilmington, DE: ISI Books, 2007); cf. also Chuck Collins and Mary Wright, *The Moral Measure of the Economy* (Maryknoll, NY: Orbis, 2007).

lic context.[70] Along the way, the major theological issues for political economy, political theology, and a theology of health, wealth, and prosperity will also emerge.

7.2.2. Between Institutional Interventionism and Individual Initiative: American Catholic Interpretations

In 1986, the United States Catholic Bishops published a pastoral letter, *Economic Justice for All (EJA)*, wherein they interpreted and applied CST specifically to economic challenges that had emerged during the Reagan years.[71] This document has itself engendered a substantive response, and there remain many contested issues that we will not be able to adjudicate. My own reading, however, suggests that *EJA* represents the predominant authoritarian, hierarchical, and centrist mode of engagement characteristic of the historic Catholic Church and thereby provides economic recommendations consistent not only with such a philosophical presupposition but also with a more communitarian interpretation of the CST.[72] The result is a more traditional proposal for social organization that emphasizes structural, interventionist, and top-down approaches to modern economic challenges that can be more readily guided by the Church's magisterium.

The bishops' traditionalist mentality is seen in the various "Guidelines for Action" counseled on select economic issues. Regarding unemployment, the call is for "a careful mix of general economic policies and targeted employment programs" (*EJA* 155). The alleviation of poverty requires "funda-

---

70. That CST is characterized by a "personalistic communitarianism" is noted by David Hollenbach, "The Market and Catholic Social Teaching," in Dietmar Mieth and Marciano Vidal, eds., *Outside the Market No Salvation?* (Maryknoll, NY: Orbis, and London: SCM, 1997), pp. 67-76, esp. p. 71. A little further below, the identification of the other end of CST as reflecting a communitarian personalism is my own.

71. National Conference of Catholic Bishops, *Economic Justice for All: Pastoral Letter on Catholic Social Teaching and the U.S. Economy* (Washington, DC: U.S. Catholic Conference, 1986); all references to this document will include the paragraph number(s) and be provided parenthetically in the text.

72. I am influenced here by Bernard Laurent, "Catholicism and Liberalism: Two Ideologies in Confrontation," *Theological Studies* 68 (2007): 808-38, although I should also say that Laurent seems motivated much more to emphasize the Church's anti-modernist stance, while my reading notes instead the Church's efforts to retain ecclesial authority in a modern and pluralistic world. At the same time, however, I will suggest later (7.2.3) that there is another way to read and maybe even retrieve, the *EJA*, which highlights not its centrism and authoritarianism but emphasizes instead its presumption of solidarity up and down the ecclesial hierarchy.

mental changes in social and economic structures that perpetuate glaring inequalities and cut off millions of citizens from full participation in the economic and social life of the nation." The document suggests the need for "working collectively through government to establish just and effective public policies" (*EJA* 187, 189). Concrete proposals include an increase in welfare entitlements, a raising of the minimum wage, and a national jobs program. The global economy requires similar internationally negotiated strategies that address trade, foreign policies, finance, assistance, and development laws and initiatives (*EJA* 261-87; *PP* 58-59). In and of themselves, these recommendations may be argued for or against on their own terms. What I find striking, however, is that the primary channels of intercession are governmental, organizational, and programmatic, rather than ecclesiological.[73] The Yoderian contrast community, the Hauerwasian colony of aliens, and the Radically Orthodox notion of the church as an alternative site of economic practices — these Protestant proposals turn out to be much more ecclesially based and oriented than the bishops' ecclesiastical letter.

My goal here is not to criticize the *EJA* (as will be shown, I am very sympathetic to many of its fundamental proposals), but to observe the influence on the North American bishops of what William Murnion calls the ideology of liberation that has become prevalent in much of the Catholic world of the global south since Vatican II.[74] In some respects, then, the liberation theology emphasis on the centrality of social analysis for the theological task underlies the *EJA* socio-political proposals for responding to the economy.[75] Yet the

73. And it is precisely by traveling down this road that, as Michael Warner, *Changing Witness: Catholic Bishops and Public Policy, 1917-1994* (Grand Rapids and Cambridge, UK: Eerdmans, and Washington, DC: Ethics and Public Policy Center, 1995), points out, the bishops risked muting their specifically theological and Catholic contributions to the public square. My response would be to persist in the public arena while being vigilant about retaining the integrity of one's distinctive theological commitments; more on this later.

74. William E. Murnion, "The 'Preferential Option for the Poor' in *Economic Justice for All*: Theology or Ideology," in Bernard P. Prusak, ed., *Raising the Torch of Good News: Catholic Authority and Dialogue with the World*, Annual Publication of the College Theology Society 32 (Lanham, MD: University Press of America, 1988), pp. 203-37, suggests especially that the *EJA*'s reapplication of the preferential option doctrine in the U.S. with neither the corresponding interrogation of the socio-economic system recommended by the Latin American formulators of the idea nor any serious challenge to the North American "way of life" results in the devolution of the notion into a functional ideology that ultimately serves the interests of the status quo. I think this judgment may be unduly harsh since it seems to ignore that the bishops' retrieval of the doctrine was in part an attempt to stand in solidarity with their Catholic counterparts in the global south. Yet the critique highlights the challenges involved in the global context of the theological task today.

75. Thus even from the beginning of the drafting process, there have been more conser-

sway of liberation theology is also explicitly registered in the *EJA*'s champion-ing the "preferential option for the poor" (*EJA* 52, 86, 90, 260, 267). But the preferential option for the poor requires not so much a personal as a social transformation. As defenders of the *EJA* have noted, neoliberal market eco-nomic institutions "are incapable of realizing liberal values, for they are con-tradictory; self-realization within a community cannot be accomplished amid market competition, self-interest, and a materialist culture."[76] Hence, personal empowerment is secondary to socio-political change, and capitalist emphases on individual initiative are subordinate to socialist proposals for governmental interventions. Now let me be clear that I am suggesting neither that the preferential option for the poor is to be summarily dismissed nor that the *EJA* is wholly dependent on liberationist ideas.[77] I am only noting that the *EJA* consistently minimizes the personal or individual dimensions of economic analysis in favor of concentrating on social and structural factors.

To be fair, Catholic bishops in America and elsewhere are right to be concerned about various structural factors that raise questions about the neoliberal market economy, and their doing so is in line with various strands of CST. In particular, one of the major questions has to do not just with the inequality of wealth between developed and under- as well as undeveloped regions, but also with the suspicion that neoliberal capitalism almost requires the perpetuation of such a disparity. As political economist Michael Budde argues:

> Fundamental to the capitalist world economy is the division of the world
> into core and periphery regions, with the prosperity of the former de-

---

vative voices that have been wary of these left-leaning features of what became the *EJA*. Two "lay letters" were drafted in the attempt to sway the bishops: Lay Commission on Catholic Social Teaching and the U.S. Economy, *Toward the Future: Catholic Social Thought and the U.S. Econ-omy — A Lay Letter* (New York: Lay Commission on Catholic Social Teaching, 1984), and Cath-olic Lay Commission, *Challenge and Response: Critiques of the Catholic Bishops' Draft Letter on the U.S. Economy* (Washington, DC: Ethics and Public Policy Center, 1985). For discussion of the debates and negotiations, see Camilla J. Kari, *Public Witness: The Pastoral Letters of the American Catholic Bishops* (Collegeville, MN: Michael Glazier/Liturgical Press, 2004), chap. 4.

76. George E. McCarthy and Royal W. Rhodes, *Eclipse of Justice: Ethics, Economics, and the Lost Traditions of American Catholicism* (Maryknoll, NY: Orbis, 1992), p. 123.

77. Note that the *EJA* does not condemn capitalism tout court as liberation theologians from the global south are more likely to do, and that the latter also tend to overlook government corruption, which also plays a role in the increased poverty in the global south; on these matters, see Rembert G. Weakland, OSB, "The Economic Pastoral Letter Revisited," in John A. Coleman, ed., *One Hundred Years of Catholic Social Thought: Celebration and Challenge* (Maryknoll, NY: Orbis, 1991), pp. 201-11. I will discuss other aspects of liberation theology later (see 8.2.2).

pendent on the exploitation of the latter. The core-periphery division (with an intermediate semi-periphery status) is a constitutive feature of the world-economy; it has endured from the sixteenth century to the present and will disappear only with the demise of the capitalist world-system. . . . By its nature, the capitalist world economy cannot benefit all people equally; reformist state-level action cannot compensate for the structural imbalances that reserve prosperity for a minority.[78]

The question Budde raises is whether or not such a core-periphery distinction is intrinsic or accidental to the capitalist system. Budde's notion of "semi-periphery" regions suggests that ongoing development in the global south could possibly result in the "have nots" becoming "haves." At the same time, given the ongoing transformation of the "core" regions from being industrial nations (driven by manufacture, etc.) to post-industrial societies (dominated by the emergence of information technologies),[79] I am inclined to think that the core-periphery division will continue, at least for the foreseeable future, even if the terms of what characterizes "core" and "periphery" change. Budde's response is to call for a more informed critique of capitalism by Catholic leaders, theologians, and ideologues in the "core" regions. For him, even the *EJA* is too weak as it "provides nothing to offend or alienate the Church's middle-class membership, thus acting to sustain the Church's presently constituted social base."[80]

Rather than looking even further leftward, however, consider how American Catholics on the right side of the ideological spectrum have received and interpreted the CST. For this exercise, I briefly examine the work of Michael Novak, a moral philosopher and theologian, and longtime associate of the conservative public policy think-tank, the American Enterprise Institute. Novak's output is too vast to adequately summarize or critique here, but I am intrigued that this 1960s radical and longtime member of the Democratic Party came to embrace and then defend the capitalist enterprise.[81] If the bishops' vision of the economy "places more stress on sharing than cre-

---

78. Michael L. Budde, *The Two Churches: Catholicism and Capitalism in the World-System* (Durham, NC, and London: Duke University Press, 1992), p. 40.

79. Daniel Bell, *The Coming of Post-Industrial Society: A Venture in Social Forecasting*, 2nd ed. (New York: Basic Books, 1976).

80. Budde, *The Two Churches*, p. 99.

81. For an overview of Novak's life, see Derek Cross and Brian Anderson, eds., *Awakening from Nihilism: The 1994 Templeton Prize Awarded to Michael Novak* (N.p.: Crisis Books and Orestes Brownson Society, 1995), pp. 59-65. For insight into Novak the radical, see, in his own words, Michael Novak, *A Theology for Radical Politics* (New York: Herder & Herder, 1969).

ation, on redistribution than production,"[82] Novak's focus is on the latter in each pair. Novak's defense of a free economy, however, is less surprising when it is understood against the backdrop of his personalist reading of the CST.[83]

I am referring here to Novak's vigorous advocacy of the free market system as the one most conducive for encouraging and supporting personal responsibility, initiative, and creativity. If the freedom of religion, thought, and conscience are rights to be strenuously defended, then so is the idea of freedom in economic matters.[84] Capitalism is the most successful system of wealth generation known to humankind because at its root — from the Latin *caput*, or head — lies an emphasis on human ingenuity, discovery, innovation, and entrepreneurship.[85] Nature is transformed into a resource and then wealth only through the application of the human intellect.[86] Capitalism provides the social context within which voluntary associations are formed, flexible thought patterns are generated, and inventive creativity is nurtured (even if through competition). In a free market, human beings are motivated by the fact that others are working creatively to better their condition; at the same time, the market requires that self-interest and greed be tempered by recognition of what others want/need. Thus there is already, within the market system, a built-in dynamic that prevents it from collapsing. While it will be clear that Novak does not believe in an unbridled market, it is also evident that his emphasis on individual initiative builds on the doctrine of human dignity at the center of the CST.[87]

82. Mark R. Amstutz, "The Bishops and Third World Poverty," in Charles R. Strain, ed., *Prophetic Visions and Economic Realities: Protestants, Jews, and Catholics Confront the Bishops' Letter on the Economy* (Grand Rapids: Eerdmans, 1989), pp. 61-74, quote from p. 65.

83. Novak interacts with CST throughout his published work; the most substantive commentary can be found in the first two parts of his *The Catholic Ethic and the Spirit of Capitalism* (New York: Free Press, 1993). See also Michael Novak, *Three in One: Essays on Democratic Capitalism, 1976-2000*, ed. Edward W. Younkins (Lanham, MD: Rowman & Littlefield, 2001), chap. 28.

84. Novak has repeatedly defended the interdependence of freedom in the religious, political, and economic domains; see Michael Novak, *Will It Liberate? Questions About Liberation Theology* (New York and Mahwah, NJ: Paulist, 1986), 228; *The Catholic Ethic and the Spirit of Capitalism*, book 2; *The Universal Hunger for Liberty: Why the Clash of Civilizations Is Not Inevitable* (New York: Basic Books, 2004); and Michael Novak, William Brailsford, and Cornelis Heesters, eds., *A Free Society Reader: Principles for a New Millennium* (Lanham, MD: Lexington Books, 2000), among other places. For the encyclical basis for these interconnections, see *MM* 8-27.

85. Michael Novak, "The Person in Community," in Michael Novak and Ronald Preston, *Christian Capitalism or Christian Socialism?* (London: IEA Health and Welfare Unit, 1994), pp. 1-21.

86. Michael Novak, "Democratic Capitalism," *Transformation* 2, no. 1 (1985): 18-23.

87. Which is not to deny the tensions between Novak's democratic capitalism and that of the CST; see Todd David Whitmore, "John Paul II, Michael Novak, and the Differences between

As expected, any philosophy of individualism is rejected. Instead, Novak founds his valuation of individual initiative within a wider religious, moral, and communal-democratic framework.[88] Representative of such a philosophical vision is his theology and philosophy of the corporation.[89] Corporations in a free market are voluntary associations that focus individual initiative in a wide range of communal contexts. Hence corporations nurture creativity,[90] generate wealth (being even more adaptable than the factory to a post-industrial age, I would add), and even stimulate the civil sector through job creation, its reliance on networking and other forms of collaborative enterprise, and provision of goods/services. In fact, the modern corporation is only the most recent incarnation of what in the medieval period were guilds, hospitals, monasteries, and even whole religious orders. Yes, some corporations can become too large or powerful, but most corporations are smaller than our universities and all are subject to national and international laws of restraint. So the question should not be whether to allow or encourage the development of corporations, but how to hold them to the best of the moral-cultural ideals of any society. Hence the emphasis is not on private property for the sake of ownership or on individual inventiveness for the sake of fame and fortune, but on a democratic framework within which people can think together, pool resources, take risks, and share in the outcomes (gains or losses) of common ventures.[91] In the Novakian scheme of things,

Them," *Annual of the Society of Christian Ethics* 21 (2001): 215-32, and John Sniegocki, "The Social Ethics of Pope John Paul II: A Critique of Neoconservative Interpretations," *Horizons: The Journal of the College Theology Society* 33, no. 1 (2006): 7-32.

88. See Michael Novak, *The Spirit of Democratic Capitalism* (New York: American Enterprise Institute, and Simon & Schuster, 1982). For a succinct statement of Novak's religious ethic, see his essay, "Wealth and Virtue: The Development of Christian Economic Teaching," in Peter L. Berger, ed., *The Capitalist Spirit: Toward a Religious Ethic of Wealth Creation* (San Francisco: Institute for Contemporary Studies, 1990), pp. 51-80.

89. Novak has done more than most to think through this topic — see his *Toward a Theology of the Corporation* (Washington and London: American Enterprise Institute for Public Policy Research, 1981); *The Future of the Corporation* (Washington, DC: American Enterprise Institute Press, 1996); *The Fire of Invention: Civil Society and the Future of the Corporation* (Lanham, MD: Rowman & Littlefield, 1997); and Novak, *Three in One*, part 4. For further discussions in theology of corporation, see Stephen N. Bretsen, "The Creation, the Kingdom of God, and a Theory of the Faithful Corporation," *Christian Scholar's Review* 38, no. 1 (2008): 115-54.

90. Novak thus notes that corporations "add greatly to the diversity of sources of public imagination, initiative, and experimentation" (*Future of the Corporation*, p. 18).

91. In contrast, a social democracy "dampens ambition, imagination, personal independence, individual risk taking, and economic creativity; it nourishes a society of clients, suppliants, and demanders of rewards; and it aspires to a relative uniformity of condition among those whose stakeholding amounts to . . . serfdom" (*Future of the Corporation*, p. 21).

then, the corporation is (what CST called) a voluntary worker's association that, ideally, protects the dignity of the worker even while contributing to the wider common (communal) good.

Novak is not blind to the problems of neoliberal capitalism. He recognizes the paradox that capitalist progress is driven by competition and desire, and thus has consistently decried the hedonism, materialism, and consumerism that threaten the viability of a sound and democratically managed capitalism. Further, he is perennially wary of the rise of autocratic and greedy leaders, concerned about the possibility of the worker's alienation from his or her labor, vigilant against profit-making dominating the system, on guard against monopolies, and sensitive to the issue of income inequalities.[92] Yet he and other American Catholic conservatives remain convinced that poverty is best attacked through the capitalist economy even as economic freedom, like political and religious freedoms, should be protected from the machinery of big governments.[93] So even while he values the moral ideals contributed by socialist traditions,[94] he was also convinced, long before the fall of communism, that the most viable forms of socialism were those that were essentially democratic and capitalistic.[95] Thus he has continued to defend the liberty, initiative, and creativity of the human subject over socialist models.

This is not to say that there are no tensions in Novak's apology for democratic capitalism. On the one hand, he consistently defends the freedom of the individual against governmental intrusions. On the other hand, however, because Novak tends to minimize the implementation of democratic proce-

92. These are the main criticisms of capitalism as an economic system overviewed in Ronald H. Preston, *Religion and the Ambiguities of Capitalism* (Cleveland: Pilgrim, 1993), chap. 3.

93. Michael Novak, *In Praise of the Free Economy*, trans. Samuel Gregg (Smithfield, NSW, Australia: Center for Independent Studies, 1999), pp. 74-75, summarizes the ten moral advantages of capitalism: it breaks dependency mentality; it connects the poor with the wider world; it diminishes war; it facilitates a cross-fertilization of peoples, nations, etc.; it challenges social class divisions and helps overcome class barriers; it augments "human capital"; it teaches civility; it nurtures sympathy; it develops an orientation toward the future; and it tempers envy while motivating human ventures. See also Novak, "A Philosophy of Economics," in James W. Henderson and John Pisciotta, eds., *Faithful Economics: The Moral Worlds of a Neutral Science* (Waco, TX: Baylor University Press, 2005), pp. 73-88; cf. Peter L. Berger, *The Capitalist Revolution: Fifty Propositions About Prosperity, Equality, and Liberty*, 2nd ed. (New York: Basic Books, 1991), and Victor V. Claar and Robin J. Klay, *Economics in Christian Perspective: Theory, Policy and Life Choices* (Downers Grove, IL: InterVarsity Academic, 2007).

94. See Michael Novak, "Seven Theological Facets," in Michael Novak, ed., *Capitalism and Socialism: A Theological Inquiry* (Washington, DC: American Enterprise Institute for Public Policy Research, 1979), pp. 109-28 esp. pp. 110-12.

95. Thus Novak wrote in 1986 that "most democratic socialists are, in principle, democratic capitalists" (*Will It Liberate?*, p. 176).

dures in the corporation, the initiative and creativity of the individual are threatened in this domain.[96] To be more consistent, the Novakian corporation needs to be accountable to the workers in some respect, especially given the assumptions elsewhere embraced in Novak's philosophical and theological system. So my sense is that while some of the details of Novak's proposals (rightly) have been criticized,[97] the broad scope of his philosophical and theological project can be read as consistent with CST, especially when extrapolated in the personalist trajectories of that tradition.[98]

The preceding discussion reveals that the CST emphasis on economic justice can be interpreted in at least two ways: as motivating political or other strategies to transform the social structures that inhibit a more just economy (the *EJA* document as representative of a more communitarian perspective), or as seeking to clear socio-political "space" for private initiatives to expand in a free market (Novak and the neoconservative strategy emphasizing a more personalist approach). The mistake, however, would be to think that we have to choose between these. This means that even while seeking not only to protect free enterprise but also to nurture personal initiative, the role of the wider community — of faith, of civil society, and the *polis* as well — is not secondary but equally central. Hence there is no possibility of any naïve defense of capitalism without also an equally vigorous argument for a viable moral, religious, and socio-political framework for its operation.[99] The

96. See Novak, *Spirit of Democratic Capitalism,* p. 178, and *Three in One,* p. 84; cf. John Sniegocki, "The Social Ethics of Pope Paul II: A Critique of Neoconservative Interpretations," *Horizons* 33, no. 1 (2006): 7-32, esp. pp. 14-15, for more on this point.

97. E.g., Richard Roberts, "The Spirit of Democratic Capitalism: A Critique of Michael Novak," in Jon Davies, ed., *God and the Marketplace: Essays on the Morality of Wealth Creation* (London: IEA Health and Welfare Unit, 1993), pp. 64-81.

98. John Sniegocki argues that there is a much deeper chasm between CST and Novak than my reading suggests, including disagreements on economic rights, redistribution of wealth, stronger regulatory roles of state and international bodies, emphases on structural injustice, and deeper links between capitalism and the "evils of consumerism," all of which CST affirms and neoconservatives reject (see Sniegocki's "The Social Ethics of Pope Paul II"). While I can agree with the main thrust of Sniegocki's work — including his positive proposals articulated in "Neoliberal Globalization: Critiques and Alternatives," *Theological Studies* 69 (2008): 321-39, and "Implementing Catholic Social Teaching," in William R. Collinge, ed., *Faith in Public Life,* The Annual Publication of the College Theology Society 53 (Maryknoll, NY: Orbis, 2008), pp. 39-61 — my strategy is to neither accentuate nor minimize the contrasts but attempt to find a way forward between "leftist" and "rightist" interpretations of CST in order to boost pentecostal thinking about economics later in this chapter.

99. In other words, private enterprise and entrepreneurship cannot exist on its own; see Craig M. Gay, "Is Entrepreneurial Activity Necessarily Pleasing to God?" *Journal of Markets & Morality* 5, no. 1 (2002): 127-34.

personalistic communitarianism of the bishops needs the communitarian personalism of Novak and other neoconservatives precisely because both the theological themes of human dignity and of peace/justice are important, and neither can be or should be subordinated to the other.[100] The healing and wholeness of the individual is intricately tied in with the socio-economic health and prosperity of a people, a region, even society and a nation. Might it be that such a platform can bring both Catholic conservatives and progressives together?

7.2.3. Subsidiarity and Solidarity: Catholic Social Principles for the Common Good

It is at this point that I want to retrieve two central notions — that of subsidiarity and solidarity — from CST in order to chart a way forward for our discussion in the last part of this chapter. Together, these Catholic social themes protect and promote local initiative while not neglecting the broader ecumenical and political networks of accountability and responsibility. In other words, subsidiarity and solidarity are key theological motifs that can conjoin a theology of health and healing with a theological vision for a prosperous but yet just and peaceful society.

The principle of subsidiarity, while already present in *Rerum Novarum*, was first explicitly articulated by Pius XI:

> The supreme authority of the State ought, therefore, to let subordinate groups handle matters and concerns of lesser importance, which would otherwise dissipate its efforts greatly. Thereby the State will more freely, powerfully, and effectively do all those things that belong to it alone because it alone can do them: directing, watching, urging, restraining, as occasion requires and necessity demands. Therefore, those in power should

100. Thus conservative Richard John Neuhaus, *Doing Well and Doing Good: The Challenge to the Christian Capitalist* (New York: Doubleday, 1992), pp. 168 and 184, writes: "Catholic social teaching opposes the kind of liberalism that would leave everything to the dynamics of the market," but also notes: "the free economy is the economic corollary of a Christian understanding of human nature and destiny." On the other side, critical theorist and theologian Gregory Baum, *Essays in Critical Theology* (Kansas City: Sheed & Ward, 1994), p. 196, suggests: "If capitalism is understood as a system guided by the ideology of the [mechanistically blind] free market, it is unacceptable. But if it is understood as a market system regulated by public authority, constrained by the labour movement, and guided by a culture of solidarity, then capitalism or — as the Pope [John Paul II] prefers — 'the market economy' could become an economic system that serves the common good."

be sure that the more perfectly a graduated order is kept among the various associations, in observance of the principle of "subsidiary function," the stronger social authority and effectiveness will be the happier and more prosperous the condition of the State (QA 80; cf. MM 53).[101]

Three aspects of the preceding principle deserve further comment.

First, the state functions best when "subordinate groups" and "various associations," etc., are allowed to govern themselves. In CST framework, this may involve the ownership of private property and the privatization of at least some of the means of production (cf. LE 14). Beyond this, however, it also calls attention to the autonomy of the family, of civic society, and of voluntary social fraternities. To be sure, at one level, CST's affirmation of the subsidiarity principle might be read as a re-assertion of the authority of the Church against totalitarian, fascist, or autocratic states.[102] At another level, however, the notion of subsidiarity simply respects the various levels of autonomy, including those belonging to the state and, by implication and explication, even other international bodies, which are the only bodies that could do the work at those levels (i.e., of the global economy or with regard to the environment). What subsidiarity presumes is the late-medieval notion of a "harmonious concord," manifest most patently in the federalist quest for a *via media* between absolutism and particularism.[103] From this historical perspective, Pius XI's teaching can also be seen to articulate a doctrine of principled or institutional pluralism that situates the Church in a modern and pluralistic world (EJA 100). On the one hand, this effort preserves political autonomy at various levels of organization, comparable to what was asserted in the Dutch Reformed doctrine of sphere sovereignty (2.2.3). On the other hand, the subsidiarity function is a clearly Catholic conception since it also recognizes a hierarchical structure that proceeds from the person to the family to the community (or other civic associations) to the joint authorities of the state and the Church at the top (reminiscent of the two authorities of the medieval conception; see 2.2.1), in contrast to the Reformed idea that considers the var-

---

101. O'Brien and Shannon, eds., *Catholic Social Thought*, p. 60.

102. Russell Hittinger, "Introduction to Modern Catholicism," in John Witte Jr. and Frank S. Alexander, eds., *The Teachings of Modern Roman Catholicism on Law, Politics, and Human Nature* (New York: Columbia University Press, 2007), pp. 1-38, esp. pp. 16-21.

103. Franz H. Mueller, "The Principle of Subsidiarity in the Christian Tradition," *The American Catholic Sociological Review* 4, no. 3 (1943): 144-57. For more historical perspective, see George Higgins, *Subsidiarity in the Catholic Social Tradition: Yesterday, Today, and Tomorrow*, The Albert Cardinal Meyer Lectures (Mundelein, IL: Mundelein Seminary/University of St. Mary of the Lake, 1994), chap. 1.

ious spheres, including that of religion or the church, as linked organically, as coordinatively related, and as equally autonomous under the sovereignty of God. Yet when considered together, perhaps a viable communitarian pluralism emerges in which, "first, there exists a diversity of essential, divinely created, human purposes each of which needs to be concretely pursued within a corresponding community with a distinctive character appropriate to that purpose; second, each of these communities must be enabled by the state (and indeed by everyone) to pursue its particular purposes in responsible freedom and security."[104]

Second, and building on the first, the doctrine of subsidiarity's principled pluralism favors local autonomy and initiative instead of collectivism and bureaucratization.[105] Since the state is confronted with "problems which, because of their extreme gravity, vastness and urgency, must be considered too difficult for the rulers of individual States to solve with any degree of success," the principle of subsidiarity suggests that the state should see its essential purpose in the following objective: "to create world conditions in which the public authorities of each nation, its citizens and intermediate groups, can carry out their tasks, fullfill [sic] their duties and claim their rights with greater security" (*PT* 140-41).[106] From a philosophical perspective, the subsidiarity principle presupposes that "the nature of human personhood and human community demand a social multiplicity of expressions. Diversity of belief, idea and life-style is therefore good."[107] Beyond this more abstract conviction, subsidiarity also preserves human dignity at the existential level, even as it charges local associations and organizations with the tasks of production, distribution, and decision-making central to the viability of local economies.[108] Its decentralized form of socio-political organization thus re-

104. Jonathan Chaplin, "Subsidiarity and Sphere Sovereignty: Catholic and Reformed Conceptions of the Role of the State," in Francis P. McHugh and Samuel M. Natale, eds., *Things Old and New: Catholic Social Teaching Revisited* (Lanham, MD: University Press of America, 1993), pp. 175-202, quote from pp. 196-97. For a complementary attempt to forge common ground between the Reformed and Catholic traditions along these lines, see David H. McIlroy, "Subsidiarity and Sphere Sovereignty: Christian Reflections on the Size, Shape and Scope of Government," *Journal of Church and State* 45, no. 4 (2003): 739-63.

105. David A. Bosnich, "The Principle of Subsidiarity," *Religion and Liberty: A Publication of the Acton Institute for the Study of Religion and Liberty* 6, no. 4 (July and August 1996): 9-10.

106. O'Brien and Shannon, eds., *Catholic Social Thought*, pp. 153-54.

107. Bruno V. Manno, "Subsidiarity and Pluralism: A Social Philosophical Perspective," in David Tracy, Johann B. Metz, and Hans Küng, eds., *Toward Vatican III: The Work That Needs to Be Done* (New York: Concilium/Seabury Press, 1978), pp. 319-33, quotation from p. 322.

108. For some perspective on how the subsidiarity principle can be translated into a model that empowers local economies, see Ulrich Duchrow, *Alternatives to Global Capitalism:*

quires democratic participation: "Subsidiarity stands out as a practical work-ing hypothesis for effective policy design in fostering [bottom-up] develop-ment, understood as a non-mechanical process, as a concrete path to be traced and trekked at the same time by real people"; in effect, subsidiarity be-comes a form of "social justice [that] is essentially social participation."[109]

But third, the doctrine of subsidiarity has internal safeguards to prevent anarchism. Derived from the Latin *subsidium,* which means to help or aid, the subsidiarity principle insists on the role of the state (as well as the church) as enabling, intervening, and empowering local projects whenever and wherever necessary. Thus the communitarian dimension of CST prevents its personal-ism from devolving into a mere individualism. As David Hollenbach argues: "The principle of subsidiarity calls for the resolution of social problems at the level close to those affected by them. . . . Subsidiarity is thus a fundamentally anti-totalitarian principle. It is not, however, an anti-state principle that maintains that the government which governs least governs best"; instead, "The principle of subsidiarity demands that government be limited, but it is neither a libertarian principle nor an endorsement of the sort of neo-liberalism that is being newly discussed today."[110]

But what prevents state intervention from becoming despotic? Herein another venerable CST theme is helpful: that of solidarity. While the theme is replete throughout the CST, John Paul II has also helpfully defined solidarity not only as a Christian virtue (*SRS* 40) but as a kind of empathy that "helps us to see the 'other' — whether a person, people or nation — not just as some kind of instrument, with a work capacity and physical strength to be exploited at low cost and then discarded when no longer useful, but as our 'neighbor,' a 'helper' (cf. Gen 2:18-20), to be made a sharer, on a par with ourselves, in the banquet of life to which all are equally invited by God" (*SRS* 39).[111] Solidarity thus crosses multiple divides that keep human beings apart from and antago-nistic toward others. Solidarity is the call to love our fellow human beings (*PT* 98-100; *EJA* 64-67), regardless of their race, ethnicity, nationality, class, or ca-pacity, in order to work toward the common good at both local and global lev-els. Solidarity also enables workers to overcome the alienation that can devalue their labor (*MM* 146; *LE* 8). When bound together in solidarity, human beings

---

Drawn from Biblical History, Designed for Political Action, trans. Elizabeth Hicks et al. (Utrecht: International Books, and Heidelberg: Kairos Europa, 1995).

109. Simona Beretta, "Wealth Creation and Distribution in the Global Economy: Human Labor, Development and Subsidiarity," *Communio: International Catholic Review* 27, no. 3 (2000): 474-89, quotations from pp. 488 and 485, respectively.

110. Hollenbach, "The Market and Catholic Social Teaching," pp. 73 and 75.

111. O'Brien and Shannon, eds., *Catholic Social Thought,* p. 422.

work for the well-being of others, and this includes the protection of those who are incapable, for whatever reason, of caring for themselves.

When subsidiarity and solidarity are brought together, they presuppose and complement one another.[112] From a political perspective, the state should preserve the social, economic, and even political autonomy of local authorities even while looking out for the well-being of those who are incapable of caring for themselves.[113] From an economic perspective, the two principles preserve local freedom and initiative, while dispensing neither with structural, legal, or other forms of social restraints nor with participatory forms of communal decision-making.[114] Last but not least, from a theological perspective, subsidiarity and solidarity reflect the trinitarian themes of participation, reciprocity, and egalitarianism. As Dennis McCann notes, secular social and economic theory "is methodologically atheistic, and subsidiarity is emphatically theocentric — in fact, classically Trinitarian," and so if the former is individualistic and based on competition and self-interest, CST is essentially solidaristic.[115]

But if subsidiarity and solidarity can adjudicate between the bishops and neoconservatives like Novak, they still do not address the issues of self-interest, greed, cutthroat competition, and corruption that drive much of the

112. Ad Leys, *Ecclesiological Impacts of the Principle of Subsidiarity,* Kerk en Theologie in Context — Church and Theology in Context 28 (Kampen: Uitgeverij Kok, 1995), p. 85; Leys also argues that these principles are central aspects of the communion ecclesiology that marked the thinking of the Catholic Church's self-understanding during the middle of the twentieth century.

113. In the words of the American Catholic bishops: "The State must contribute to the achievement of these goals [the common good] both directly and indirectly. Indirectly and according to the *principle of subsidiarity,* by creating favorable conditions for the free exercise of economic activity, which will lead to abundant opportunities for employment and sources of wealth. Directly and according to the *principle of solidarity,* by defending the weakest, by placing certain limits on the autonomy of the parties who determine working conditions, and by ensuring in every case the necessary minimum support for the unemployed worker" (*CA* 15; O'Brien and Shannon, eds., *Catholic Social Thought,* pp. 450-51).

114. We are reminded that "the social encyclicals also postulate that the evolution of a just and fair market economy — as the guarantor of freedom, human dignity, and justice — cannot be left to chance but needs to be consciously guided"; see Siegfried G. Karsten, "Social Encyclicals and Social-Market Economics," in Thomas O. Nitsch, Joseph M. Phillips Jr., and Edward L. Fitzsimmons, eds., *On the Condition of Labor and the Social Question One Hundred Years Later: Commemorating the 100th Anniversary of Rerum Novarum, and the 50th Anniversary of the Association for Social Economics,* Toronto Studies in Theology 69 (Lewiston, NY: Edwin Mellen Press, 1994), pp. 427-46, quotation from p. 427.

115. Dennis P. McCann, "Business Corporations and the Principle of Subsidiarity," in S. A. Cortright and Michael J. Naughton, eds., *Rethinking the Purpose of Business: Interdisciplinary Essays from the Catholic Social Tradition* (Notre Dame: University of Notre Dame Press, 2002), pp. 169-89, from p. 185.

neoliberal global market.[116] The issue here has to do in part with the distinction between consumption and consumerism. If human creatures cannot avoid the former, the latter nevertheless is its hedonistic and excessive counterpart. Colin Campbell has thus insightfully argued that consumption is also an imaginative enterprise that can either lapse into hedonism when improperly motivated or can be productive and creative when properly nurtured.[117] So the challenge in a free market that preserves human initiative and motivates intellectual creativity is to nurture proper forms of consumption and ward off consumerism. Thus Peter Sedgwick notes: "I do not believe that the consumer society can be wished away, or condemned outright. If anything is pure fantasy, that is it. What is needed is attention to the theological issues of identity, desire, self-transcendence, creativity and education. This task of posing a creative alternative to consumerism, through the creation of a different community which expresses its longing through the symbols of freedom and love, will enable human identity to find a new vocation different both from the vocation of consumption and the old work ethic."[118]

Sedgwick's proposal, however, raises the question about how the desires of private individuals can be morally and spiritually formed in a free market economy. If the market economy provides the only framework for analysis, then selfish desire, greed, consumerism, and hedonism will inevitably shape not only our economic interactions but also our theological reflections. In the end, then, the problem is not the market *per se*, but the sinfulness and selfishness that characterize a consumer-driven economy. If the market economy is to be redeemed, then the church has to provide an alternative *telos* — another set of desires — that can contribute to the healing of the world.

Subsidiarity and solidarity help us see how human beings are both persons-in-community and communally formed persons, and these are first steps toward developing a theology of desire that is ecclesially shaped. What we need, in other words, is a vision of the church as a people of God who live *in* a free market economy but are not *of* such an economy. Such a set of alter-

---

116. For insightful theological analysis of the modern economy, see James M. Childs Jr., *Greed: Economics and Ethics in Conflict* (Minneapolis: Fortress, 2000), esp. chaps. 1-5; Miriam Defensor Santiago, *Christianity versus Corruption: Political Theology for the Third World* (Quezon City, Philippines: Worldview Publications, 2001); and Osvaldo Schenone and Samuel Gregg, *A Theory of Corruption: A Theology and Economics of Sin,* Christian Social Thought Series 7 (Grand Rapids: Acton Institute, 2003).

117. Colin Campbell, *The Romantic Ethic and the Spirit of Modern Consumerism* (Oxford and New York: Basil Blackwell, 1987).

118. Peter H. Sedgwick, *The Market Economy and Christian Ethics* (Cambridge: Cambridge University Press, 1999), pp. 149-50.

native economics will provide models for how to develop, nurture, and sustain a counter-consumerist way of life that alone provides for ultimate health, wholeness, and prosperity. Instead of an egocentric theology of healing, self-help, and economic empowerment, what will emerge is a trinitarian theology of desire, formed by the practices of the church, sensitive to the particularities and needs of each person as created in the image of God, and yet heralding the ultimate shalom — of wholeness, prosperity, peace, justice, and righteousness — that dawns with the coming kingdom.

7.3. Many Tongues, Many Economies: Toward a Charismatic Politics of Healing and Shalom

Informed both by pentecostal theologies of healing and prosperity and by CST as well as Catholic theologies of the economy, the last part of this chapter has the ambitious agenda of articulating a political theology of shalom that combines a theology of healing and wholeness with a theology of economic justice. As with the preceding chapters in Part II of this book, we proceed here in three steps: a biblical exploration of healing and economics in the Lukan corpus, especially in Acts, which highlights the communal nature of healing and retrieves Luke's vision of the role of poverty and wealth in his alternative (ecclesial) economy; a practical extrapolation of a range of local and informal economies that exist within and even alongside the global economy and are shaped by the practices of the church understood as the fellowship of the gift-giving Spirit; and a theological reflection on trinitarian desire as the product of the Spirit's gracious interface with the world that not only heals human lives but also shapes just and peaceful communities that anticipate the kingdom of God. If in the preceding chapter we sought to articulate a prophetic politics via consideration of a theology of civil society, in this chapter we will seek to formulate a political economy via exploration of a charismatic theology of the informal economy. Along the way, we shall see that ecclesial enfleshment of CST notions of subsidiarity and solidarity will be central to realizing the biblical shalom proclaimed by the prophets of old.

7.3.1. Healing and "Having All Things in Common": Poverty and Prosperity on the Way of Jesus

Luke can be understood to have provided his own succinct summary of his "life of Jesus" with a statement found on the lips of Peter in Acts about "how

295

God anointed Jesus of Nazareth with the Holy Spirit and with power; how he went about doing good and healing all who were oppressed by the devil, for God was with him" (Acts 10:38). Elsewhere, I have argued that the work of the Spirit through the life of Jesus in Luke can be seen as anticipating the accomplishments of the Spirit through the lives of the earliest followers of Jesus in Acts. In the following, we will look at the healings and economics of the earliest Christians and attempt to understand them as fulfillments of promises by the Hebrew prophets regarding the wholeness, peace, and righteousness that would characterize the restoration of Israel and the Day of YHWH.

We begin with the miraculous healings in Acts, and note that in the majority of cases, healing is not an end in itself but the means toward something more important: the proclamation of the gospel, the production of faith, and the expansion of the Word of God.[119] Thus there is a link between belief in the Lord, the growth of the church, and healing in Solomon's Portico (5:12-16), among the Samaritans (8:5-8), and in Lydda (9:32-35).[120] This connection between healing and evangelism suggests that the contemporary explosion of Christianity in the global south that is often a response to healing is not necessarily to be decried, even if the church should then be sensitive about discipling the lives of those who convert because of such an experience.

Aside from this evangelistic connection, however, I suggest that the healing of bodies has a social dimension beyond the cure of individuals.[121] In some cases, we almost need to read between the lines of the text in order to observe this social aspect, as when the healing of the man at the Beautiful Gate allowed him to enter the Temple with the apostles (3:8). More precisely, here was a man whose disability was both a legal and physical hindrance to

119. Surprisingly, there are few substantive discussions of healing in Luke-Acts. Audrey Dawson, *Healing, Weakness and Power: Perspectives on Healing in the Writings of Mark, Luke and Paul* (Milton Keynes, UK: Paternoster, 2008), approaches this material primarily from the perspective of one whose first career was a physician. I will mention a few other relevant studies as we proceed.

120. Not all healings, however, engender explicit faith — e.g., the healing in Lystra almost cost Paul his life, and the healing on Malta did not appear to be accompanied by verbal proclamation of the gospel.

121. I have argued this thesis elsewhere with regard to disability — see Yong, *Theology and Down Syndrome: Reimagining Disability in Late Modernity* (Waco, TX: Baylor University Press, 2007), chap. 8 — but focus the discussion here on the relevance of this idea to a theology of the public square. For a social framing of healing in Luke-Acts, see John Pilch, "Sickness and Healing in Luke-Acts," in Jerome H. Neyrey, ed., *The Social World of Luke-Acts: Models for Interpretation* (Peabody, MA: Hendrickson, 1991), pp. 182-209, revised in John J. Pilch, *Healing in the New Testament: Insights from Medical and Mediterranean Anthropology* (Minneapolis: Fortress, 2000), chap. 6.

his full participation in the Temple, and his first response was not only walking and leaping but also praising God in the sanctuary. My claim is that such a view of healing locates the cure of the body within the broader social environment and allows us to see how abundant life includes not just the removal of a physical impediment but the reincorporation of the individual into the wider community. This aspect of the lame man's healing is consistent with the Spirit-empowered healings of Jesus in Luke. The healing of Peter's mother-in-law enables her to resume her role in the family (Luke 4:38-39); the cleansing of lepers (5:12-14 and 17:11-14), including touching them, signals their acceptance and allows for their return to their communities, along with reconciliation across otherwise hostile ethnic groups (Jews and Samaritans); the curing of the hemorrhaging woman cleansed her from her ritual impurity and enabled her re-entry into Jewish society (8:43-48); exorcisms of demoniacs allowed for their communal reintegration (8:35 and 9:42); the healing of the crippled and bent-over woman involved her social exaltation and the downgrading of the synagogue ruler (13:10-17); the healing of the man with dropsy confirmed bodily curing as part of the wholeness of the Sabbath rest (14:1-6); and even the raising of the dead — in this case, the widow of Nain's only son — provided for her socio-economic well-being, so that the miracle here was as much the empowering of an otherwise abandoned woman as a biological reversal (7:11-17).[122] In short, bodily curing is never only an individualistic phenomenon, but is part and parcel of the restoration of wholeness (including body, mind, and soul) precisely through re-assimilation into the larger community (of faith).

I now turn to a related claim: that the earliest followers of the Messiah forged an alternative economy and way of life in the midst of the *Pax Romana* and by doing so intended to realize the shalom of the full restoration of Israel

---

122. For further discussion of the social dimension of healing in these pericopes, see Hans Dieter Betz, "The Cleansing of the Ten Lepers (Luke 17:11-19)," *Journal of Biblical Literature* 90, no. 3 (1971): 314-28; Musimbi Kanyoro, "Daughter, Arise," in Mercy Amba Oduyoye and Musimbi Kanyoro, eds., *Talitha, qumi! Proceedings of the Convocation of African Women Theologians, Trinity College, Legon — Accra, September 24-October 2, 1989* (Ibadan, Nigeria: Daystar Press, 1990), pp. 54-62; Frederick J. Gaiser, "'Your Faith Has Made You Well': Healing and Salvation in Luke 17:12-19," *Word and World* 16, no. 3 (1996): 291-301; John J. Kilgallen, "Animadversiones: The Obligation to Heal (Luke 13,10-17)," *Biblica* 82, no. 3 (2001): 402-9; Annette Weissenrieder, "The Plague of Uncleanness? The Ancient Illness Construct 'Issue of Blood' in Luke 8:43-48," in Wolfgang Stegemann, Bruce J. Malina, and Gerd Theissen, eds., *The Social Setting of Jesus and the Gospels* (Minneapolis: Fortress, 2002), pp. 207-22; Heidi Torgeson, "The Healing of the Bent Woman: A Narrative Interpretation of Luke 13:10-17," *Currents in Theology and Mission* 32, no. 3 (2005): 176-86; and Lindsey P. Pherigo, *The Great Physician — Luke: The Healing Stories*, rev. and expanded (Nashville: Abingdon, 1991), chap. 10.

proclaimed by Jesus. There are three components to my discussion: the economic configurations of the early church; their basis in Jesus' teachings about the year of YHWH; and their being understood as alternatives to the imperial economy and anticipations of the coming kingdom. We will discuss each in order.

Economies of sharing, mutuality, and the gift in the early church: Luke describes early Christian communism in the following terms: "All who believed were together and had all things in common; they would sell their possessions and goods and distribute the proceeds to all, as any had need. Day by day, as they spent much time together in the temple, they broke bread at home and ate their food with glad and generous hearts" (Acts 2:44-46), and "Now the whole group of those who believed were of one heart and soul, and no one claimed private ownership of any possessions, but everything they owned was held in common. . . . There was not a needy person among them, for as many as owned lands or houses sold them and brought the proceeds of what was sold. They laid it at the apostles' feet, and it was distributed to each as any had need" (4:32, 34-35). Four comments are pertinent in this regard. First, the central motif here is not the intention to form an alternative economy; rather, an alternative way of life with economic features emerges out of the fellowship of those gathered in the name of Jesus. Second, within the community of faith, the needs of the "have nots" are met through a mutual sharing. Third, former allegiances and patronage relations are replaced in the new community of faith; the apostles are not the new patrons, but are servants rather than lords, according to their master's injunctions. Finally, yes, there were some in the new community who were affluent, and whose generosity provided more substantively for the needs of the community; at the same time, there is also clear indication that the social demographics of the early Jesus movement were drawn principally from the majority peasant underclass, and thus the mutuality and sharing was embraced chiefly among needy equals.[123]

Why did the communistic experiment of the early church not last? The reasons for its demise can be traced to at least three interrelated factors: 1) the impossibility of keeping up with a fast-growing movement (a comparison of Acts 2:41 and 4:4 indicates that the movement had doubled in a very short span of time, involving thousands from Jerusalem, Judea, and the surrounding regions); 2) the challenges involved in maintaining economic co-

---

123. Thus Gerd Theissen, *Gospel Writing and Church Politics: A Socio-Rhetorical Approach,* Chuen King Lecture Series 3 (Hong Kong: Chung Chi College, 2001), pp. 109-14, argues that the earliest Christians practiced a form of "horizontal solidarity and reciprocity" wherein commoners practiced charity with one another.

hesion involving a diverse socio-cultural group of local and diaspora Jews, as well as proselytes and other Hellenistic groups;[124] and 3) the ensuing persecution that scattered the church (8:1). Regardless, however, my point is not to insist on a restoration of "biblical" communism as the normative economic paradigm. Instead, I am highlighting not so much the form but the principles of local sharing and mutuality that allowed for the (temporary) "prosperity" of the early Christians. Further, we should note that even after the dispersion of Messianists amid the persecution, they continue to meet and gather in homes (12:12; 16:15, 40; 18:7; 20:7-8, 20). This is indicative of the communal and relational nature of the early Messianic way of life. Yet the local Messianic communities looked out not only for themselves but also for others in need. Hence collections were taken, and gifts were given to aid those dealing with famine and other economic distresses (11:28-30). In short, the economic principle, "It is more blessed to give than to receive" (20:35), was manifest in a variety of ways: through local sharing, special charities, and mutuality as a way of life.

Jesus' teachings regarding poverty and wealth: While there has on occasion been the argument that Jesus himself derived from the Judean "upper class,"[125] the consensus is both that he came from the agrarian and peasant class and that he also chose a life of simplicity.[126] There is also no debate that of the four Gospels, Luke is most interested about Jesus' teachings regarding economic matters.[127] Central to the Lukan *evangelion*, in fact, is Jesus' announcement in the Nazarene synagogue that:

124. The dispute between Hebraic and Grecian widows in Acts 6 provides some perspective on how difficult it was to maintain ecclesial unity in a multicultural and multilingual situation. Some of the relevant issues are discussed in Reta Halteman Finger, *Of Widows and Meals: Communal Meals in the Book of Acts* (Grand Rapids and Cambridge, UK: Eerdmans, 2007). See also Yong, *The Holy Spirit and the Public Square* [working title] (Brewster, MA: Paraclete Press, forthcoming), chap. 14.

125. George Wesley Buchanan, "Jesus and the Upper Class," *Novum Testamentum* 7 (1964): 193-209.

126. Douglas E. Oakman, *Jesus and the Economic Questions of His Day,* Studies in the Bible and Early Christianity 8 (Lewiston, NY: Edwin Mellen Press, 1986), and Walter E. Pilgrim, *Good News to the Poor: Wealth and Poverty in Luke-Acts* (Minneapolis: Augsburg, 1981), chap. 2.

127. There is a growing literature — e.g., Luke Timothy Johnson, *The Literary Function of Possessions in Luke-Acts,* SBL Dissertation Series 39 (Missoula, MT: Scholars Press, 1977), and *Sharing Possessions: Mandate and Symbol of Faith* (Minneapolis: Fortress, 1981); Thomas E. Schmidt, *Hostility to Wealth in the Synoptic Gospels,* Journal for the Study of the New Testament Supplement Series 15 (Sheffield: JSOT Press, 1987); John Gillman, *Possessions and the Life of Faith: A Reading of Luke-Acts* (Collegeville, MN: Liturgical/Michael Glazier, 1991); and Thomas E. Phillips, *Reading Issues of Wealth and Poverty in Luke-Acts,* Studies in the Bible and Early Christianity 48 (Lewiston, NY: Edwin Mellen Press, 2001).

The Spirit of the Lord is upon me,
   because he has anointed me
   to bring good news to the poor.
He has sent me to proclaim release to the captives
   and recovery of sight to the blind,
   to let the oppressed go free,
to proclaim the year of the Lord's favour.

(Luke 4:18-19)

Citing from the prophet Isaiah (61:1-2), the reference to the Jubilee year of the Mosaic Torah is unmistakable.[128] Its central features include the cancellation of debts, liberation of servants, return of land to its original owners (or heirs), and celebration of the year according to the principles of Sabbath rest (Lev. 25 and Deut. 15). To be sure, while mandated, the Jubilee requirements had never formally been kept, so there was recognition that only the arrival of the Messiah would make its enaction possible.

Jesus' ministry seems to confirm that he understood part of the good news as announcing the Jubilee year of the Lord. He not only called for a cancellation of debts (Luke 16:1-9, 19:1-10) but also repeatedly forgave the debts of sinners.[129] He pronounced judgment on the rich and insisted that they sell what they had in order to provide for the poor (6:24, 12:13-2, 16:19-29, 18:18-30).[130]

---

128. Michael Prior, *Jesus the Liberator: Nazareth Liberation Theology (Luke 4:16-30)*, The Biblical Seminar 26 (Sheffield: Sheffield Academic Press, 1995), chap. 5, discusses Luke's (and Jesus') use of Isaiah.

129. There is some evidence that in Luke's hands, Jesus' insistence on debt relief is muted so that Zaccheus "refunds" over-collections rather than works toward the abolishment of the unjust system of taxation, and that the emphasis is placed on voluntary giving rather than structural adjustments directed toward collective ownership as seen in Acts 2 and 4. So, "while Luke has preserved much of the countryside in the early Jesus tradition for us, he has to some extent revised the original intention of the Jesus movement. For Jesus, the kingdom of God was world reconstruction, especially beneficial for a rural populace oppressed by debt and without secure subsistence. For Luke, political expediency [perhaps because of the wealthy among his audience] demands that the world restructuring be limited to alleviating the harshest aspects of political economy within the local Christian community"; see Douglas E. Oakman, *Jesus and the Peasants* (Eugene, OR: Cascade, 2008), p. 162.

130. I think, with Birchfield Charlesworth Preston Aymer, "A Socioreligious Revolution: A Sociological Exegesis of 'Poor' and 'Rich' in Luke-Acts" (Ph.D. diss., Boston University; Ann Arbor, MI: University Microfilms, 1987), that the notions "rich" and "poor" were used by Jesus both spiritually and socio-economically. At the same time, I am mindful of the caution that any naïve equation of contemporary notions of the "poor" with that of Luke may be anachronistic; see Justo L. González, *Faith and Wealth: A History of Early Christian Ideas on the Origin, Significance, and Use of Money* (San Francisco: Harper & Row, 1990), p. xiv, and Martin Hengel, *Property and Riches in Early Christianity*, trans. John Bowden (Philadelphia: Fortress, 1974)

And he also fed the hungry (9:10-17) and elevated the poor (21:1-4), thereby fulfilling that portion of the Magnificat about the Lord God having "filled the hungry with good things, and sent the rich away empty" (1:53). On the one hand, Jesus envisioned "the dissolution of personal wealth, a redistribution of land and resources, and a reduction in consumption levels";[131] on the other hand, Jesus' Jubilee vision could be understood as instituting, in a sense, the kind of preferential option for the poor that we have already noted (7.2.2). In other words, the arrival of Jubilee was good news for the poor, but bad news to those who wanted to hold on to their riches.[132]

Kingdom economics against the imperial economy: My claim is that as the earliest followers of the Way instinctively embraced the principles of Jubilee economics, the religious leaders and imperial authorities were also threatened by this growing movement. The imperial economy of the *Pax Romana*, after all, was undeniably oppressive toward the Palestinian masses. Exorbitant taxation (along with legally enforced debt collection), unjust rental and lease agreements, additional imperial and Temple tributes, exploitative servitude, and the outright theft of land — each of these were real challenges confronting local Judeans in their fight for survival. The hierarchical patronage system further ensured that each level was subservient to their benefactors at the higher level,[133] so that corruption, bribery, and favoritism were the rule rather than the exception. Against this unjust system, Jesus' alternative "represents a return to a simpler form for social organization, based on the solidarity of the village community and upon a rejection of the patronage system controlled by the rich elite."[134] His was the announcement of the good news of the kingdom, the arrival of the Jubilee year, the restoration and redemption of Israel as a people and new household of God.[135]

131. James A. Metzger, *Consumption and Wealth in Luke's Travel Narrative*, Biblical Interpretation Series 88 (Leiden and Boston: Brill, 2007), pp. 198-99.

132. Thus Sharon H. Ringe, *Jesus, Liberation, and the Biblical Jubilee: Images for Ethics and Christology* (Philadelphia: Fortress, 1985), p. 90, writes, "The Jubilee message is thus good news to those who know themselves to be dependent on God's grace and not on their own powers, and a word of judgment to those unable or unwilling to share in its rhythms of release and liberation"; cf. Ched Myers, *The Biblical Vision of Sabbath Economics* (Washington, DC: The Church of the Savior, 2001), chap. 3.

133. K. C. Hanson and Douglas E. Oakman, *Palestine in the Time of Jesus: Social Structures and Social Conflicts* (Minneapolis: Fortress, 1998), esp. chaps. 3-4.

134. Halvor Moxnes, *The Economy of the Kingdom: Social Conflict and Economic Relations in Luke's Gospel* (Philadelphia: Fortress Press, 1988), p. 159.

135. Halvor Moxnes, *Putting Jesus in His Place: A Radical Vision of Household and Kingdom* (Louisville and London: Westminster/John Knox Press, 2003), p. 123, writes: "we may characterize the images of the kingdom of God as a household as countercultural. The images broke

The early Messianic alternative community thus instantiated a range of alternative economies that were *in* but not *of* the imperial economy. For them, "God's rule overthrows the dominant political economy in favor of a fictive family. Political economy is to be transformed into domestic economy, a vision consonant with the traditions of Israel (Deut 15:2; Lev 25:35-46; Neh 5:6-13)."[136] So against an economy of patrons and clients, the Messianists began with an economy of kinship and friendship (of brothers and sisters in the new family of God); amidst a hierarchical and imperial economy, they adopted and developed instead an egalitarian one with God (the father of Jesus) as the prime, if only, benefactor; and in opposition to an economy that exploited the poor in favor of the rich, theirs was a shared economy of generosity (in which gifts were bestowed without any expectation of return). For followers of Jesus, the proclamation of the good news of the kingdom for the poor brought with it a rearrangement and redefinition of the "we" and the "they," or the "rich" and the "poor," of the able-bodied and the disabled, and of the elite and the outcast.

I suggest that we see the emergence of the church as a temporary expression of the preliminary restoration of Israel but also as anticipating the eschatological arrival of the Jubilee day of YHWH. As bodily healings are not merely miraculous events but soteriological signs of the kingdom,[137] so also is it possible that the Holy Spirit has and will continue to form local ecclesial communities and their alternative economies that provide a foretaste of the abundant life in the coming age. The Spirit's inspiration of various local economies of equality, mutuality, and generosity forms the church as a contrast-society that renounces domination and instantiates familial love in order to point toward a redeemed humanity.[138] In these ways, the church is, however partially and fragmentarily, a manifestation of the healing, reconciliation, peace, and justice included in the redeeming work of God. Such an ecclesial framework allows us

---

not only with expectations of God as king, but also with the traditional picture of a house-holder. The image of the father who provided for his children was emphasized, while the role of the patriarch was downplayed."

136. Oakman, *Jesus and the Peasants*, p. 105.

137. For development of the argument linking faith in the miraculous and healing power of God and faith in the salvific power of God, see Maureen W. Yeung, *Faith in Jesus and Paul: A Comparison with Special Reference to 'Faith That Can Move Mountains' and 'Your Faith Has Healed/Saved You,'* Wissenschaftliche Untersuchungen zum Neuen Testament 2.147 (Tübingen: Mohr Siebeck, 2002).

138. Gerhard Lohfink, *Jesus and Community: The Society Dimension of Christian Faith*, trans. John P. Galvin (Philadelphia: Fortress, and New York/Ramsey, NJ: Paulist Press, 1984), chap. 3.

to see health and wholeness, prosperity and peace, as indicators of the divine shalom intended for the healing of the world.

Let us recapitulate what we have covered in this already protracted chapter (easily the longest in this book) in order to reset our sights on the goals to be achieved. We began with an exploration of pentecostal healing, reviewed how the theme of prosperity developed from that basis, and learned that critical assessments of pentecostal "health and wealth" needed to be sensitive to the local historical, socio-economic, and political factors in any given region. We then turned to the Catholic social teaching tradition, noted its personalist-communitarian emphasis with its preferential option for the poor on the one hand and its communitarian-personalist strand that emphasizes human dignity, creativity, and freedom on the other, and we concluded with suggestions about how the CST's notions of subsidiarity and solidarity might be helpful for thinking about an economic theology of peace and justice. In the immediately preceding discussion, then, we reviewed early Christian beliefs and practices regarding healing, poverty, and wealth and observed the church instantiating, even if for all too short a period, the Hebrew Jubilee ideal as a sign and herald of the divine economy to come. I now present a model of the church as the matrix of a variety of alternative economic enterprises, one that exists within but is not bound to the present global economy of exchange, yet is simultaneously empowering local projects and initiatives that make an economic difference and are also capable of speaking to structural economic realities.[139] If in the previous chapters (4-6) we have attempted to sketch an understanding of the church as an alternative *polis*, a counter-culture, and a post-secular social praxis, consider the following as a thought experiment of the church as inspiring a distinctively ecclesial set of economic practices that look back to the Jubilee doctrine and yet anticipate the future economy of the kingdom, even while working as a leaven within the present market system.

---

139. The local church is central to my proposal, because it engages global issues from the ground up, albeit without neglecting working in the other direction. For other proposals favoring a grassroots and local economy approach, see Chris Baker, "Entry to Enterprise: Constructing Local Political Economies in Manchester," in John Atherton and Hannah Skinner, eds., *Through the Eye of a Needle: Theological Conversations over Political Economy* (Peterborough, UK: Epworth, 2007), pp. 191-206, and Wendell Berry, "The Idea of a Local Economy," in Stephen R. Kellert and Timothy J. Farnham, eds., *The Good in Nature and Humanity: Connecting Science, Religion, and Spirituality with the Natural World* (Washington, DC, and London: Island Press, 2002), pp. 199-211.

7.3.2. The Gift-Giving Spirit in the Church:
Shalom beyond the Political Economy of Exchange

I propose that one way to conceive the church as both *in* but yet not *of* the world's economy is to understand at least part of its economic agency in terms of what economists call the "informal sector." By definition, the informal economy exists outside the regulated (and legislated) economy.[140] An extremely heteronomous domain, the informal economy includes street vendors, rickshaw/cart pullers, shared transportation, recyclers, petty traders/hawkers, small item producers, (very) small business owners (often at street corners rather than in their own rented or owned buildings), casual living arrangements, home-workers (garment and shoe makers, embroiderers, assemblers, etc.), piece-rate workers, sub- and sub-sub-contractors, offsite data processors, farm and agricultural workers, unregistered/undeclared workers, cooperative partners, and part-time, temporary, and self-employed workers, among many other forms. While there is some overlap between informal economic transactions and premodern economies, the former is now acknowledged to be a more or less permanent feature of the market economy.[141] Of course, informal economic activity is prevalent both in regions (and nations) working to enter the global economy and during periods of economic crisis and recession in developed nations. But there is also enough of a continuum between the formal and informal economies — rather than a strict demarcation between them — that even in industrialized environments, upwards of one-fourth of all economic activity occurs in the informal sector.[142] In fact, there are even calls among economists to go beyond any rigid conceptual dichotomy between the formal and informal economy.[143] Certainly the thrust of

---

140. A classic analysis of the informal economy is Hernando de Soto, *The Other Path: The Invisible Revolution in the Third World,* trans. June Abbott (New York: Harper & Row, 1989). My one gripe with de Soto's work is that he focuses on the formalizing of property ownership as the almost "magical" resolution of global poverty to the neglect of cultural and religious analyses. How cultural-religious systems understand ownership is an equally important question for economic theory and developmental proposals. Yet de Soto's phenomenology of the informal economy is both engaging and clear for our purposes.

141. See Alejandro Portes, Manuel Castells, and Lauren A. Benton, eds., *The Informal Economy: Studies in Advanced and Less Developed Countries* (Baltimore: Johns Hopkins University Press, 1989).

142. See "Women and Men in the Informal Economy: A Statistical Picture" (International Labour Organization, 2002), available at http://www.ilo.org/public/english/employment/gems/download/women.pdf (last accessed 27 January 2009).

143. See Basudeb Guha-Khasnobis, S. M. Ravi Kanbur, and Elinor Ostrom, eds., *Linking the Formal and Informal Economy: Concepts and Policies* (Oxford and New York: Oxford University Press, 2006).

the most active theoreticians working in this area is to find ways to formalize in-formal economic activities in order to unleash the potential of these assets as a means of engaging the otherwise poor with the global economy.[144]

How else then might the informal economy be described or understood? Thus on the one hand, the existence of the informal sector "can be viewed as a constructed response on the part of civil society to unwanted state interfer-ence."[145] On the other hand, however, it is also fair to say that the explosion of informality has occurred in reaction to the mercantilism and state bureaucra-cies that hinder effective formalization of economic activity at the grassroots. As instinctive responses of the masses to poverty, underdevelopment, and the inefficiencies of the legal-political system, the informal economy exhibits a good deal of energy, spirit, entrepreneurship, ingenuity, productivity, persis-tence, and just plain hard work. By its nature, then, the businesses of the infor-mal economy are unregistered, their transactions not computed (nor comput-able) in gross national products, and their incomes untaxed (and oftentimes untaxable). Yet while the informal economy certainly includes semi-legal and even unlawful activity (about which we will say more momentarily), it is more accurate to understand this global phenomenon in terms of extra-legality.[146] But herein lie also the challenges: extra-legal operations in the informal sector result in unprotected employment (workers are without benefits of any sort), impinge on the capacity of informals to grow, develop, and expand their trade (at least in the formal/legal sector), and leave them vulnerable to theft, vio-lence, and extortion.

My proposal is that thinking with and through the informal economy might also shed new light on the interface between ecclesia and economics,

144. E.g., Ahmed M. Soliman, *A Possible Way Out? Formalizing Housing Informality in Egyptian Cities* (Dallas: University Press of America, 2004).

145. Alejandro Portes, "The Informal Economy and Its Paradoxes," in Neil J. Smelser and Richard Swedberg, eds., *The Handbook of Economic Sociology* (Princeton: Princeton University Press, and New York: Russell Sage Foundation, 1994), pp. 426-49; quote from p. 444. This article also clarifies the differences between what happens in the informal sector and in criminal or un-derground activities. For an early study of the blurred lines between lawful and unlawful inter-actions in this domain, see George Jenkins, "An Informal Political Economy," in Jeffrey Butler and A. A. Castagno, eds., *Boston University Papers on Africa: Transition in African Politics* (1967; reprint, New York: Frederick A. Praeger, 1968), pp. 166-94.

146. See de Soto, *The Other Path*, pp. 13-14. As de Soto suggests elsewhere, whereas many think of the informal economy as being on the margins of the world economic system, in some respects, "In fact it is legality that is marginal; extralegality has become the norm. The poor have already taken control of vast quantities of real estate and production"; see Hernando de Soto, *The Mystery of Capital: Why Capitalism Triumphs in the West and Fails Everywhere Else* (New York: Perseus, 2000), p. 30.

especially about how the church functions at least in part through providing an alternative set of economic practices. If the values and goals of the formal economy are based on competition, balancing the supply-and-demand market, the achievement of surplus/profit, and the principle of reinvestment of such for the further generation of wealth, the minimal goal of the informal economy appears to be that of achieving subsistence. Without access to the formal sector, informals necessarily work in (non-formalized) subsidiary organizations and often find solidarity with one another as they seek common cause. I suggest that the preceding discussion of the practices of the earliest followers of the Messiah can thus be seen as an ecclesial expression of informal economics (8.3.1). Similarly, today, if pentecostal independent congregations, come-outers, and restorationist house churches operate informally in reaction to established denominations,[147] might we not also be able to see the various forms of mutuality, reciprocity, sharing, and solidarity in ecclesial communities as providing a range of informal economic services both within congregational and communal life and to those outside in missionary and evangelistic witness?

It is in this sense that analysis of the practices of the church from the perspective of the informal economy unveils how ecclesial solidarity as a way of life provides an alternative set of economic values to that propounded by the formal capitalist economy. Thus Peter's saying to the lame man at the Beautiful Gate, "I have no silver or gold, but what I have I give you; in the name of Jesus Christ of Nazareth, stand up and walk" (Acts 3:6), suggests that the church operates not necessarily only within the formal economy (I would say that TDJ Enterprises is not specifically an ecclesial endeavor) but more so by mobilizing the generosity of the faithful and empowering the weak in their midst in the name of Jesus (what T. D. Jakes Ministries attempts to accomplish). Here the practices of the earliest Christians serve as a model for the kinds of economic arrangements that emphasize mutuality and sharing as well as local accountability and initiative.[148] Rather than being dominated by the economy of exchange and its supply-and-demand transactions, the church is guided by a pneumatological economy of grace that highlights charity (giving without anticipation of return), forgiveness

---

147. Andrew Walker, *Restoring the Kingdom: The Radical Christianity of the House Church Movement* (London: Hodder & Stoughton, 1985); cf. William K. Kay, *Apostolic Networks in Britain* (Milton Keynes, UK, and Waynesboro, GA: Paternoster, 2007).

148. For concrete expansion, see Lee Hong Jung, "*Minjung* and Pentecostal Movements in Korea," in Allan Anderson and Walter J. Hollenweger, eds., *Pentecostals after a Century: Global Perspectives on a Movement in Transition* (Sheffield: Sheffield Academic Press, 1999), pp. 138-60, esp. pp. 158-59.

(not only of sins but also of debts), and solidaristic fellowship (nurtured through interpersonal relations, common meals, and daily interactions). The largely impersonal features of the global market are tempered by ecclesially shaped relations that draw from, enrich, and network with local enterprises, communal associations and cooperatives, and kinship, extended household, and other domestic economic ventures.[149] Whereas the global economy is driven by speculative finance, credit extensions, and the flexibility of money as *the* medium of economic exchange, the church serves God rather than mammon and nurtures relationship while providing (especially voluntary) services that enable a more discerning engagement with the capitalist regime.[150]

In one respect, I would go beyond what political economists define as the margins of the informal economy and include the sphere of reproduction and care. The church that privileges the poor also prioritizes widows, orphans, children, the aged, the infirm, people with disabilities, and those otherwise vulnerable, so that their care is registered as most important from the standpoint of the economy of grace. In this framework, various forms of what we may call collective entrepreneurship emerge that on the one hand sustain vulnerable members who are on the margins if not the underside of history, even while they on the other hand nurture creativity not only for survival's sake but also for the wider communal good.[151]

Three clarifications are in order. First, note that such a consideration of the church from the perspective of the informal economy does not remove

149. The communal nature of such development initiatives in political economy is key; see Gregory Baum, "Beyond the Market: The Growth of the Informal Economy," in Dietmar Mieth and Marciano Vidal, eds., *Outside the Market No Salvation?* (Maryknoll, NY: Orbis, and London: SCM, 1997), pp. 26-32, and Douglas Petersen, "Towards a Latin American Pentecostal Political Praxis," in David Emmanuel Singh and Bernard C. Farr, eds., *Christianity and Cultures: Shaping Christian Thinking in Context* (Carlisle, UK, and Waynesboro, GA: Regnum, 2008), pp. 188-95, at p. 192 (cf. 1.2.3).

150. On this note, I recommend Philip Goodchild, *Theology of Money* (London: SCM, 2007), for the not faint-of-heart who are interested in rethinking the theological dimensions of money. Goodchild's major constructive proposal is to develop banks of evaluative credit that can provide religious and moral guidance for the assessment and investment of money in the market economy. My suggestion simply insists on the equal importance of ecclesial practices that embody the values of the Spirit, since apart from such concrete relations we will in due course cease to be able to develop viable criteria for the evaluation of money itself. Cf. also Goodchild's earlier *Capitalism and Religion: The Price of Piety* (London and New York: Routledge, 2002).

151. Thus Peter Sedgwick notes, "The Spirit can empower human creativity, but it can also lead communities into relationships which do not simply depend on wealth, consumerism or paid employment" (*The Market Economy and Christian Ethics*, p. 272).

the church either from the world or from the global market.[152] This is neither a call for the overthrow of capitalism nor the establishment of another form of socialism or communism, but rather a reminder about how the church, when going about its business of communal edification, automatically orders an economic way of life that follows in the footsteps of Christ by the power of the Spirit. Second, I am simply wishing to highlight how participation in the informal economy serves as a protest against the self-interested greed, consumerist materialism, and rampant hedonism that perennially threaten to undermine the market economy. Communal solidarity, private initiative directed toward the public good, and local and interpersonal relations, exchanges, and accountability — all of these combine to ameliorate the debilitating effects of the Fall on the free market. Finally, my assessment of the church as operating in effect within the informal sector is not intended to naïvely affirm all that transpires in that domain. The church should not legitimate the distribution of contraband (i.e., drugs, music, and other goods), condone tax evasion, bribery, kickbacks, and other forms of unlawful activity, or wink at the delivery of illegal services (i.e., prostitution and slave-trafficking). The church must also not think that a functional informal sector is a means of pacifying the poor or thereby alleviating its responsibility to speak prophetically regarding justice.

This raises the question of what the church should do to address the many injustices that are perpetuated by the informal economy. The fact is that the informal economy is dominated by the poor, who are exploited by both criminals (through illegal activities) and the rich (i.e., who put the poor to work in sweatshops, or for unjust wages), besides having to negotiate the challenges of otherwise unjust political, social, and economic systems. Desiring neither to idealize poverty nor sentimentalize the poor, I suggest that a pneumatological economy of grace according the Jesus' Jubilee paradigm will be sensitive to global factors that impinge on unjust economies but will also be focused on local projects and initiatives, especially at the congregational and parish levels. In other words, Jesus' meeting the needs of the poor in various aspects invites the contemporary church to be alert to the multiple levels

---

152. Sometimes, Mennonite intellectuals are more predisposed to withdrawing from the capitalist order and forming an alternative economics based on local community and advocating moral and environmental critiques of the current order from the Mennonite margins. I am sympathetic to the theological motivations behind such concerns but do not think that a withdrawal from the market is either feasible or the best way forward. See Jim Halteman, "Mennonites and Market Capitalism," in Calvin Redekop, Victor A. Krahn, and Samuel J. Steiner, eds., *Anabaptist/Mennonite Faith and Economics* (Lanham, MD: University Press of America, 1994), pp. 321-31.

of poverty that afflict people today. Individual healing is therefore incomplete without the provision of basic material necessities, friendships, and spiritual care, access to social, educational, political, economic, medical, and civil resources, and attention toward an environmentally and ecologically sustainable way of life.[153] Solidarity with the poor thus requires formation of subsidiary organizations that include those outside ecclesial communities in order to identify and redress the causes of poverty at each level, and in order that feedback from lower levels can also trigger revision, reform, and reorganization at the higher levels.[154] Socio-structural inequalities related to gender, race, class, and physical, intellectual, and sensory disabilities must be engaged both at the grassroots where particular challenges are involved, and the political levels where more general and abstract policies can be formulated in order to forge a more just society.[155] In the latter domain, the church must be a prophetic voice (perhaps much like CST or the *EJA*) that calls attention to the biblical vision of shalom but yet also provides instantiations of such shalomic practices in order to point toward a better way.[156]

These last recommendations also remind us that besides operating at or "within" this informal domain, the church nevertheless also remains active in the formal economy at many levels. The preceding proposals should not be taken to suggest that the church ceases formal operations as an economic agent. In fact, the church in its various local forms and even global shape can and should be understood as corporations of various types (cf. 7.2.2 above), and should be subject to the different political, social, and legal strictures within that formal domain. To some degree, much of the church's contributions to political reform, social justice, and economic development

153. Such a multi-leveled discussion of poverty is found in Bryant L. Myers, *Walking with the Poor: Principles and Practices of Transformational Development* (Maryknoll, NY: Orbis and World Vision, 1999), chap. 3.

154. Otherwise, as Anthony Campolo notes, we remain subservient to the powers that have gained control at the higher levels; see Campolo, "Politics and Principalities and Powers," in Charles P. De Santo, Calvin Redekop, and William L. Smith-Hinds, eds., *A Reader in Sociology: Christian Perspectives* (1980; reprint, Eugene, OR: Wipf & Stock, 2001), pp. 491-503, esp. pp. 499-500.

155. Andrew Hartropp, *What Is Economic Justice? Biblical and Secular Perspectives Contrasted* (Milton Keynes, UK: Paternoster, 2007), chap. 2.

156. At this level, proposals for a pneumatologically inspired economy of grace will find important conversation partners even among Christian socialists such as some in the Radical Orthodoxy camp; for a moderate version of Christian socialism shaped by the Anglican vision, see Timothy J. Gorringe, *Capital and Kingdom: Theological Ethics and Economic Order* (Maryknoll, NY: Orbis, and London: SPCK, 1994), and *Fair Shares: Ethics and the Global Economy* (London: Thames & Hudson, 1999).

projects should be properly formalized. My suggestion that viewing the church through the lens of the informal economy as providing a set of counter-economic practices should be seen neither as a denial nor a rejection of the fact that the church also functions variously, and rightly, in the formal sector.

Yet I am also proposing that the church's economic witness is not exhausted in its formal transactions. In fact, the distinctiveness of the church's economic witness occurs, I suggest, in the diversity of its informal economic activities. From a theological perspective, these alternative ecclesiological economies can be seen as retrieving and channeling the pneumatological economy of grace unleashed on the Day of Pentecost. They manifest an ecclesially shaped version of local autonomy and participation, propagate an ecclesially inspired form of creativity and initiative, and evoke an ecclesially rich sense of appreciation for diversity and particularity. Herein, the many tongues of the Spirit are anticipations of the many gifts that are expressed in the economic sphere. Further, such ecclesiological alternatives honor all members, especially the weak, so that all are available to come to the aid of those who are suffering, even as each potentially contributes his or her own peculiar gift for the edification of the whole. Finally, these many economies of the Spirit may also function as prophetic parables that challenge the corruption, injustice, hedonism, and environmental degradation characteristic of an unrestrained capitalism.

The result will not be *the* shalom of the coming kingdom, but will be intimations of the peace, justice, and righteousness that will be established on that day of the Lord. For the ancient prophets, the Hebrew shalom referred to the wholeness, completeness, security, friendship, well-being, and even salvation of the people both individually and collectively.[157] More than the absence of conflict, disability, or material deprivation, then, the Hebraic shalom "has in essence to do with the quality of a person's life and quality of their relationship with God, with one another, and with the rest of creation."[158] Herein will the sick find their healing, perhaps not necessarily in bodily cures but certainly in and through their integration in reconciling, caring, and welcoming communities. Herein also will the gospel of prosperity find its penultimate fulfillment, perhaps not necessarily in affluence and material wealth but certainly in and through the sufficiency of mutual, sharing, and generous

157. E.g., Malinda Berry, "Mission of God: Message of *Shalom*," in Dale Schrag and James Juhnke, eds., *Anabaptist Visions for the New Millennium* (Kitchener, ON: Pandora Press; Scottdale, PA, and Waterloo, ON: Herald Press, 2000), pp. 167-73.

158. John Swinton, *From Bedlam to Shalom: Towards a Practical Theology of Human Nature, Interpersonal Relationships, and Mental Health Care* (New York: Peter Lang, 2000), p. 58.

communities of faith.[159] Such a Spirit-inspired people of God will serve as an alternative healthcare even without boycotting the deliverances of modern medicine; will enact an alternative economics even without opting out of the market economy; will form an alternative way of life even without a radically separatistic mentality; and will engage actively in the civic domain without necessarily adopting a partisan political stance or supporting a formal economic ideology. Instead, the fellowship of the Spirit that binds the diversity of the ecclesial body together around the name of Jesus will graciously generate health, wealth, and shalom beyond the economy of exchange.

7.3.3. The Charismatic Imagination: Grace, Desire, and the Healing of the World

I have argued so far in this chapter that at least part of the answer to the human quest for healing and shalom are the many economic practices of the Spirit that are at work in the church (what political economists call the informal sector). There is one final step for our present reflections on economics — the explicitly theological one in which we think through how the preceding is theologically illuminating — i.e., what its implications are for the nature and even doctrine of God. There are three components to consider: how the preceding pneumatological economy of grace opens up to a charismatic doctrine of God; how such a charismatic theology and praxis reorient the human so as to desire the finding of rest in a gracious God; and how such a charismatic vision empowers the Christian mission for the redemption and healing of the world. Thus follows a sketch of how a pentecostal springboard into the political can inform and shape an ecumenical and Christian approach to political economy for our time.

From a charismatic church to the God of the charisms: The major thesis of this book rests on the premise that a pentecostal starting point on the political can shed new light for a Christian political theology. In this chapter, I have argued that pentecostalism invites us to rethink what it means to be the church amidst the present political economy of globalization, and suggested that part of this involves going beyond the usual either-ors of socialism v. capitalism, liberation v. empowerment, or formal v. informal, toward re-

159. This could be what Robert Beckford calls the emancipatory option for the Christian commonwealth, in opposition to focusing on the materialism of the prosperity gospel, popularly considered; see Beckford, *Jesus Dub: Theology, Music, and Social Change* (New York and London: Routledge, 2006), chap. 9.

imagining the ecclesial community as an informal "agency" within — but not completely subjected to — the world's economic dictates. In particular, I suggest that the many tongues of the Spirit are, in part, faint echoes of the many economic modes of existence in the informal sector, and that therefore the church can more explicitly articulate and embody a more shalomic way of being in the world.

In more explicitly pneumatological terms, M. Douglas Meeks has said, "The work of the Holy Spirit is about *access* to God's economy. The Holy Spirit is God working economically so that God's creatures and the whole creation may live and live abundantly. This is the reason the Holy Spirit is identified with God's righteousness, which appears paradigmatically in God's raising of Jesus from the dead (Rom. 1:4) and is called the 'spirit that gives life' (1 Cor. 15:45). God the Holy Spirit makes present God's righteousness, which is God's power for life against death."[160] My claim is that this mode of the Spirit's work, in which the church participates, reflects also the very trinitarian life of God. Hence as the church receives from and dispenses the gifts of the Spirit, so also does the church partake in the generosity of a gift-giving God. Further, however, God bestows not merely gifts but himself — in Christ and in the Spirit; hence also the church confers to the world not just spiritual gifts but the lives of Spirit-filled believers as "a living sacrifice, holy and acceptable to God, which is [its] spiritual worship" (Rom. 12:1). In short, a pneumatological theology of political economy emphasizes the human reception of gracious sustenance within the life and work of an interrelational, generous, and self-giving God. This is a God who not only grants charisms (grace and gifts) but *is* charismatic (gracious, "existing" perpetually as gracious gift to O[o]thers), and the Gift(s) of the Spirit reflect unlimited trinitarian giving, mutual life-giving love, and the free (non-necessitated) expression of divinely inspired creativity and novelty.

Reorienting desire for the charismatic God: This means that a pneumatological economy of grace, mediated through the life of the church as an expression of the body of Christ and the fellowship of the Spirit, redirects humanity toward what Augustine identified as the transcendental norms of all desire — that of the good, the true, and the beautiful, in effect, God himself (2.1.3). According to the world's political economy, however — which is presently dominated by the neoliberal capitalist system — what makes the world go around are human desires for the self, for profit, and for more. The market of supply and demand is therefore shaped less by an "invisible" hand than by

---

160. M. Douglas Meeks, *God the Economist: The Doctrine of God and Political Economy* (Minneapolis: Fortress Press, 1989), p. 171.

capitalist forces in charge of our systems of advertisement.[161] The market thus simply disorders human desire — for things, feelings, or even desire in itself[162] — and there is a need to discipline what is out of whack.

But how is such reordering of corrupt desires accomplished? One might be drawn toward Plato's oligarchic republic or even wish to temper that with some Aristotelian leaven that seeks after a broader consensus.[163] I would agree that we should not entrust the formation of our desires to oligarchs or, in our free market system, to capitalist advertisers, but insist instead that our desires ought to be communally and, more importantly, ecclesially shaped. For sacramental traditions — including some in the Radical Orthodoxy movement — the weekly celebration of the Eucharist is a means of forming the soul so as to direct the human heart toward the transcendental and theological domain. The eucharistic rite thus instantiates an economy of sharing rather than one of greed; inculcates a reverence for creation's provisions rather than exploitation of the environment; calls attention to an economy of debt remission rather than debt collection; and rejects the politics of power in favor of the politics of egalitarianism.[164] But for those in low-church traditions, on the other hand (which includes most pentecostals), the living with one another from day to day — as did the early Christians and as do many on the underside of (economic) history in the informal sector — also has the potential to shape human hearts in a distinctively trinitarian and kingdom-oriented direction. In these modes of existence, the self is subordinated to being in solidarity with the community; competition is replaced by bearing one another's burdens; and profits are understood instead as communal sharing, achievements, and investments.[165] In short, living with others, precisely what

---

161. See Jung Mo Sung, *Desire, Market and Religion* (London: SCM, 2007), esp. chaps. 2-3, and Diarmuid O'Murchu, *The Transformation of Desire* (Maryknoll, NY: Orbis, 2007), chaps. 9 and 11.

162. Note the example, that an advertisement about driving a BMW is certainly attempting to sway the viewer to purchase such a vehicle, but it also portrays a certain kind of life that is lived on the consumerist highway — the feeling of driving with the top down with the wind blowing through one's hair is its own desire, quite apart from owning a BMW; for this example, I am indebted to Bernd Wannenwetsch, "The Desire of Desire: Commandment and Idolatry in Late Capitalist Societies," in Stephen C. Barton, ed., *Idolatry: False Worship in the Bible, Early Judaism and Christianity* (New York and London: T. & T. Clark, 2007), pp. 315-30, esp. pp. 319-20.

163. As proposed by Martha Nussbaum, *Plato's Republic: The Good Society and the Deformation of Desire* (Washington, DC: Library of Congress, 1998).

164. T. J. Gorringe, *The Education of Desire: Towards a Technology of the Senses* (Harrisburg, PA: Trinity Press International, 2001), chap. 5, esp. pp. 107-22.

165. William T. Cavanaugh, *Being Consumed: Economics and Christian Desire* (Grand Rapids and Cambridge, UK: Eerdmans, 2008).

occurs amidst the fellowship of the Spirit, transmutes the capitalist desire into an explicitly theological key.

The charismatic gifts and the healing of the political: In the end, the many tongues, gifts, and works of the Spirit are for ecclesial (in particular) and human (in general) edification. What in the end is more edifying than the nurturing of faith, the instilling of hope, and the foretaste of the love that will remain forever? Human reception of the Spirit's gifts thus not only points beyond ourselves to the God who grants these gifts, but also provides a conduit for the generosity of God to be heaped on others. In this pneumatological economy of grace, mutuality, and sharing, the generosity not only exceeds but redeems the world's economy of barter and exchange, and the salvation of God is made available to a world otherwise sick, impoverished, and dying. If in a capitalist economy, the many tongues of the Spirit shape a mentality of creativity and a posture of saving and investment, and if in a socialist economy the many works of the Spirit nurture the praxis of justice and solidarity, then in the informal economy of the church the many gifts of the Spirit form the new household economy of the divine shalom.[166]

By way of transitioning to our final chapter, I close with three articulations of what might be called an apophatic theology of shalom that provides parameters for orienting further thinking about the three major themes in this chapter — health, wealth, and economics — beginning with the last.

1) A pneumatological theology of shalom neither affirms nor rejects capitalism, socialism, or any other economic -ism. Formal economic systems are all potentially redeemable according to the providential ways of God, and often such redemptive and life-giving forms of peace, justice, and righteousness are interlaced with what occurs in the informal sector of the church. But this therefore also means that no economic system in and of itself is divinely mandated. Rather, as already noted within the Kuyperian notion of sphere

---

166. Part of what I say here is inspired by Douglas Davies, "The Charismatic Ethic and the Spirit of Post-Industrialism," in David Martin and Peter Mullen, eds., *Strange Gifts? A Guide to Charismatic Renewal* (Oxford and New York: Basil Blackwell, 1984), pp. 143-44: "If Max Weber's Protestant ethic was grounded in worldly activism under the influence of predestination and the inscrutability of the divine will in a pragmatically and rationally organised world of a mechanistic type, then the contemporary charismatic ethic is rooted in a personal fulfilment in supporting relationships in this life within a potentially alienating and atomising world of partial personal relations within the service industries. . . . Tongues and fruitful group relationships replace economic success [the Puritan ethic] as a sign of the divine approval. . . . The charismatic response is . . . an act of re-enchantment of the individual domain involving family, leisure and corporate life outside politics related to work in the service industries." As should be clear from my formulation, I think there is a corporate (ecclesial) dimension to the charismatic experience beyond what Davis grants.

sovereignty, the economic domain is a creaturely realm, currently fallen from grace, but nevertheless to be eschatologically renewed by the Spirit for the glory of God.

2) A pneumatological theology of shalom neither idealizes poverty nor uncritically embraces a theology of prosperity. Neither poverty nor riches for their own sake are the will of God, although both poverty and riches are redeemable within the scope of God's redemptive work in the world. Shalom requires neither the absence of poverty nor the presence of wealth — only the presence of the Spirit even in the absence of the Father, who makes all things new. Proclamation of both the preferential option (for the poor) and the "Triple Blessing" (Yonggi Cho) are important, even if emphasizing one over the other is unhealthy in certain circumstances. The Spirit's redemption of poverty is not necessarily the production of wealth, although the healing of the world will involve, finally, the provision of what is more than sufficient for all.

3) A pneumatological theology of shalom neither valorizes sickness, disease, illness, or suffering for its own sake nor presumes that bodily health is an unambiguous sign of divine favor. Just as a theology of glory can only emerge from out of a theology of the cross, so also a theology of healing will finally come out of the ashes of Golgotha. The final eschatological healing of our bodies will involve both continuity and discontinuity with the present (albeit in unfathomable and unlikely ways), even as it must require the Spirit's final healing and sanctification of our communities, societies, and economies, as well as the public square.

More can be denied, even as more can also be affirmed, but within the scope of this chapter and in anticipation of the following, suffice to say we can only dimly perceive the eschatological resolutions to come for the healing and prosperity of the world.

CHAPTER 8

Pentecostal Hope:
A Political Theology of History and the Eschaton

This culminating chapter takes off from the fifth element of the pentecostal fivefold gospel, that of Jesus as the coming king. It is in one sense more ambitious than the other four chapters of Part II in that it seeks to argue three interrelated theses rather than one, although from another angle it might also be said that insofar as the entire book points in the eschatological direction explicated here, these three theses are different aspects that culminate the foregoing discussion. In brief, the three theses are that 1) many of the eschatological ideas popular in pentecostal circles actually do not fit well with central pentecostal commitments; 2) the pentecostal confession of Jesus the Christ who is the coming king invites a reconsideration of theology of history and eschatology in pneumatological terms; and 3) such a pneumatological interpretation opens up to a performative eschatological politics of hope, and this in turn can be retroactively seen to transfigure and transvalue the overall argument in the preceding four chapters of this book.

We will proceed, as usual, in three sections. The first unfolds the political implications and explications of classical pentecostal eschatological thinking, especially in terms of its dispensationalist politics of Zionism, its millennialist and futurist sensibilities focused on the end of history, and its apocalyptic worldview. Section 2 will take up each of these themes but now with the goal of bringing various theological interlocutors — i.e., a Jewish political theology, a Radically Orthodox liberation theology, and a political theology of the environment — into conversation with some more progressive pentecostal perspectives in quest for a pneumatological eschatology. The final section builds on the two movements in the chapter in order to complete the threefold theses summarized in the preceding paragraph. Because of the nature of the topic (eschatology, usually viewed as ungrounded speculations of the yet-to-occur future), I will be intentional about addressing the performative dimensions that show how Christian beliefs about the end have practical — and political — consequences in the here-and-now.

As this is the book's final chapter, the stakes are high. Part of the challenge is that whereas the preceding four chapters have focused on one major issue each, pentecostal perspectives regarding the eschatological motif in this chapter open up to three distinct challenges in political theology — the Christian-Jewish question, a theology of history, and a theology of the environment. Hence what might otherwise have been tackled in three separate chapters (not to mention three books!) is packed into one. If the following is read as a programmatic rather than an exhaustive treatment, then its sketchiness may be more palatable. I would also argue that insofar as the major task of this book is to explore pentecostal contributions to political theology, all three are important elements not only for pentecostalism but also for Christian thinking about the political. My final rationale for daring to cover such broad and disputed territory is that the entire flow of the book so far begs for what I am calling an eschatological theology of the political. If this is right (and the reader will in the end be the judge), then look at the following not merely as discrete treatments of aspects of political theology but as case studies of how a pentecostally, pneumatologically, and eschatologically shaped political theology is integrative of the theologies of culture, missions, and economics that have been previously discussed.

8.1. Jesus the Coming King: Coming for What?

The topic of eschatology is a maze of contested, complicated, and even fantastic propositions across the various Christian traditions. Concerned as it is with correlating the prophetic texts of the Bible with what has not yet happened, it is understandable that many different eschatological scenarios have been proffered over time.[1] This is certainly the case also across the pentecostal spectrum, so that it is impossible either to discuss the topic exhaustively or to proceed by way of making more than a few careful generalizations. I have therefore chosen to discuss three aspects of pentecostal eschatology: its dispensationalist views regarding the end times (wherein Jesus returns to re-inaugurate a dispensation centered on the nation of Israel), its escapist and futurist tendencies (wherein Jesus returns to remove the church from an in-

---

1. Hence here we focus on the futurist or fore-telling aspects of biblical prophecy compared to the forth-telling type we discussed in chapter 6.

creasingly wicked world), and its apocalyptic mentality (wherein Jesus returns to purify the world as we know it through its destruction). Throughout, we will focus on the political aspects of these eschatological beliefs and dispositions. I will argue in this section that while some of these eschatological ideas can be retrieved and redeemed for contemporary theological purposes, others are uncritically borrowed from other Christian traditions, are inconsistent with the ethos, intuitions, and sensibilities of pentecostalism, and should be either rejected or severely revised.[2]

8.1.1. Pentecostal Premillennialism
and the Politics of Dispensationalism

At one level, the tribulationism, futurism, and apocalypticism that I will discuss here are interrelated aspects of the dispensationalist eschatology that persists in some respect or other across global pentecostalism. Dispensationalism as an eschatological system and hermeneutic was developed in the nineteenth century by John Nelson Darby (1800-1882), one of the founders of the separatistic (from the Church of Ireland) Plymouth Brethren movement in the 1830s.[3] It spread to North America through the network of Bible prophecy conferences organized across the Anglo-American world in the second half of the nineteenth century,[4] was widely adopted in the Wesleyan holiness circles that gave rise to pentecostalism,[5] and was popularized — even in pentecostal circles — by the publication of the bestselling Scofield Reference Bible in 1909. During their first generation, pentecostals by and large adopted

---

2. In this chapter, my discussion and analysis is devoted primarily to pentecostal appropriations of dispensationalism rather than intended to counteract dispensationalism itself. This is not the place for a direct engagement with dispensationalism. For the beginnings of such a critical pentecostal assessment, see Peter E. Prosser, *Dispensational Eschatology and Its Influence on American and British Religious Movements,* Texts and Studies in Religion 82 (Lewiston, NY: Edwin Mellen, 1999), esp. chap. 10. A more hard-hitting critique is Ben Witherington III, *The Problem with Evangelical Theology: Testing the Exegetical Foundations of Calvinism, Dispensationalism, and Wesleyanism* (Waco, TX: Baylor University Press, 2005), chaps. 5-7.

3. See Larry V. Crutchfield, *The Origins of Dispensationalism: The Darby Factor* (Lanham, MD: University Press of America, 1992).

4. See Ernest Robert Sandeen, *The Roots of Fundamentalism: British and American Millenarianism, 1800-1930* (Chicago: University of Chicago Press, 1970), chap. 6.

5. Steven L. Ware, *Restorationism in the Holiness Movement in the Late Nineteenth and Early Twentieth Centuries,* Studies in American Religion 80 (Lewiston, NY: Edwin Mellen, 2004), esp. pp. 55-64; cf. Edith L. Blumhofer, *Restoring the Faith: The Assemblies of God, Pentecostalism, and American Culture* (Urbana and Chicago: University of Illinois Press, 1993), chap. 1.

the dispensationalist framework even if they adapted various elements so that it would be more conducive to the outworkings of pentecostal spirituality.[6]

In brief, dispensationalism as a theological system and eschatological scheme can be summarized in the following major tenets:[7]

- that God relates to the world in chronologically successive dispensations (periods of time), each with different covenantal or governmental features (here, there is often disagreement about exactly how many dispensations the Bible reveals or discusses)[8]
- that the present age of the church is an interlude between two dispensations featuring the centrality of Israel, and that Israel (comprised of the Jews) and the church (constituted primarily of gentiles) are related but quite distinct expressions of the elect people of God[9]
- that the transition to the next dispensation will be marked by the removal of the church (according to 1 Thess. 4:17), which event will inaugurate a seven-year period of worldwide woe and suffering known as the Great Tribulation (from the various references to seven years in the book of Revelation)[10]

6. The standard account of early pentecostal eschatology is D. William Faupel, *The Everlasting Gospel: The Significance of Eschatology in the Development of Pentecostal Thought* (Sheffield: Sheffield Academic Press, 1996).

7. A widely used text — until recently, even in pentecostal circles — on dispensational eschatology is J. Dwight Pentecost, *Things to Come: A Study in Biblical Eschatology* (1958; reprint, Grand Rapids: Academic Books/Zondervan, 1964).

8. The classical study of dispensationalism is Charles C. Ryrie, *Dispensationalism Today* (Chicago: Moody Press, 1965). For more recent restatements that have deeply reformed the dispensationalist tradition, see Craig A. Blaising and Darrell C. Bock, *Progressive Dispensationalism* (Wheaton, IL: Bridgepoint, 1993), and Ron J. Bigalke, Jr., *Progressive Dispensationalism: An Analysis of the Movement and Defense of Traditional Dispensationalism* (Lanham, MD: University Press of America, 2005). There is much to commend in these developments, and if there could be any attractive versions of dispensationalism, they would be found in these revisionist trajectories. To advocate for such, however, lies beyond the scope of this book.

9. Arguably, this and the following tenets are what set apart dispensationalism as a theological system and hermeneutics from dispensationalism as a theological doctrine; the latter has found many articulations in the history of Christian thought without the eschatological thinking accompanying the former. Here and in the remainder of this chapter, my use of "dispensationalism" refers, unless otherwise noted, to the more traditional rather than progressivist notions identified in the previous footnote.

10. A minority of dispensationalists hold that the rapture of the saints will occur during the middle of the Tribulation while an even smaller minority think it happens at the end of the seven-year period; see Richard R. Reiter, ed., *The Rapture: Pre-, Mid-, or Post-Tribulational?* (Grand Rapids: Academic Books, 1984).

- that at the end of the Tribulation period, Christ will return (with the church) to judge the world and establish his 1000-year reign (according to Rev. 20:4) on the earth.[11]

While dispensationalists debate about the finer points of each doctrine, the preceding provides an adequate framework for understanding pentecostal appropriations. In fact, insofar as they have given any formal thought to eschatology as a specific theological locus, classical pentecostal churches and denominations especially in the Anglo-American world have by and large adopted much of the dispensationalist theology and hermeneutic.[12]

I now turn to a discussion of how the dispensational distinction between Israel and the church has influenced pentecostal politics. We have already seen some preliminary hints of such an apocalyptic and eschatological politics in our previous discussion of Pat Robertson's views regarding international relations (6.1.3). In particular, I am referring to interfaces between dispensational eschatology and the broad spectrum of Zionist ideologies prevalent in the current Middle East arena.[13]

In the dispensationalist framework, the transition from the church age to the period of the Great Tribulation will be foreshadowed by certain signs (Matt. 24:3). Although disputed with regard to the details, there is general agreement that the following world events have been prophesied by the biblical writers as coming to pass in the time leading up to the seven-year Tribulation: 1) the re-establishment of Israel as a nation (preliminarily established in 1917, with formal independence declared in 1948); 2) increasing hostilities in the Middle

11. Most if not all dispensationalists are premillennialists — that is, they believe that Christ must return precisely in order to establish the millennial kingdom. Outside dispensational circles, however, others hold to postmillennialism (the idea that Christ returns at the end of the millennium in order to receive the kingdom established by the church through the Holy Spirit) or a-millennialism (the view that the 1000-year reference is strictly metaphorical rather than literal). See Darrell L. Bock, ed., *Three Views on the Millennium and Beyond* (Grand Rapids: Zondervan, 1999), and Stanley J. Grenz, *The Millennial Maze: Sorting Out Evangelical Options* (Downers Grove, IL: InterVarsity Press, 1992).

12. The Assemblies of God's Statement of Fundamental Truths includes two propositions about the rapture of the church (with the pre-tribulational view implicit) and the premillennial return of Christ. For further exposition, see Stanley M. Horton, "The Last Things," in Stanley M. Horton, ed., *Systematic Theology*, rev. ed. (Springfield, MO: Gospel Publishing House, 1995), pp. 597-638. See also the widely used textbook in pentecostal and charismatic circles: J. Rodman Williams, *Renewal Theology: Systematic Theology from a Charismatic Perspective*, 3 vols. (Grand Rapids: Zondervan, 1988-1992), vol. 3, part 2.

13. For an overview, see Timothy P. Weber, *On the Road to Armageddon: How Evangelicals Became Israel's Best Friend* (Grand Rapids: Baker Academic, 2004).

Eastern world (in anticipation of the final battle of Armageddon where Israel is vindicated before her enemies; see Rev. 16:14-16); 3) the emergence of a global system of governance (which some dispensationalists equate with the United Nations, others with the European Union, and still others with various international organizations), commerce, and finance representing the worldly system set in opposition to the things of God; and 4) the rebuilding of the Temple (still anticipated). Dispensationalists not only attempt to correlate biblical prophecies with signs of the times but also inevitably support international agendas and foreign policies that they think will assist with (rather than directly bring about) the fulfillment of the scriptural claims. For their part, pentecostals have found rather fascinating if not uncritically absorbed much of the dispensationalist hermeneutic, conclusions, and even political points of view.[14]

Inevitably, then, pentecostals like Robertson and many others not only at the academic but especially at the lay and congregational levels have been supporters of the nation of Israel.[15] Ironically, of course, in this case pentecostals love Israel first and foremost because of her role in the providential plan of God for the last days rather than because of her status as the current people of God since, in the dispensationalist scheme of things, the church has presently been grafted in as the elect people of God in place of disobedient Jews.[16] Further and even more problematic is that given the dualistic cosmology of most pentecostals, Israel's enemies are uncritically understood also to be God's enemies, and this means that Palestinians, Arabs, and others allied with Palestinian and Arab interests are at best absent from consideration and at worst framed in negative theological light.[17] The situation is exacerbated

14. See Frank M. Boyd, *Ages and Dispensations* (Springfield, MO: Gospel Publishing House, 1955); Ralph M. Riggs, *Dispensational Studies* (Springfield, MO: Gospel Publishing House, 1977); and Dwight Wilson, *Armageddon Now! The Premillenarian Response to Russia and Israel since 1917* (Grand Rapids: Baker, 1977).

15. See Mark G. Toulouse, "Pat Robertson: Apocalyptic Theology and American Foreign Policy," *Journal of Church and State* 31, no. 1 (1989): 73-99. For an ethnographic study of how support for Israel is manifest at congregational and denominational levels, see Kristina Helgesson, *"Walking in the Spirit": The Complexity of Belonging in Two Pentecostal Churches in Durban, South Africa* (Uppsala: Department of Cultural Anthropology and Ethnology, Uppsala University, 2006), chap. 8.

16. See Eric Gormly, "Evangelical Solidarity with the Jews: A Veiled Agenda? A Qualitative Content Analysis of Pat Robertson's 700 Club Program," *Review of Religious Research* 46, no. 3 (2005): 255-68.

17. Dan Cohn-Sherbok, *The Politics of Apocalypse: The History and Influence of Christian Zionism* (Oxford: Oneworld, 2006), chap. 15, discusses evangelical and pentecostal convergences with the ideology of the various strains of Zionism, both Christian and Jewish, against other agendas.

by the growing fears regarding Islamic emergence across the Arab world. Thus few pentecostals have been capable of developing empathy for the plight of Palestinians throughout this conflict,[18] while most have tended to support international agendas in general and Middle Eastern policies in particular according to the criterion of whether such were pro-Israel or anti-Palestinian/Arab. Finally, pentecostals have not questioned the dispensationalist view of the enemies of Israel as including alongside the Palestinian-Arab coalition also a northern bloc of nations commonly associated with Russia (the former Soviet Union) and her communist allies. The result, at least during the Cold War era, was the fierce pentecostal opposition to communism around the world, since to be arrayed with the forces of good is to be set against the powers of darkness represented by the communist ideology.[19]

In one respect, dispensational eschatology fits well within the pentecostal "this is that" hermeneutic (see 3.1.1). What I mean is that insofar as pentecostals have read the book of Acts in particular and the Bible in general as a narrative within which they can locate their own contemporary experiences, to that same degree the politics of dispensationalism invites a similar correlation between the apocalyptic genres of Scripture and contemporary events. Millenarian movements throughout the history of the church have read the Apocalypse and other like biblical texts as applicable to their own situation,[20]

18. One exception is Eric Nelson Newberg, "The Pentecostal Mission to Palestine, 1906-1948: A Postcolonial Assessment of Pentecostal Zionism" (Ph.D. diss., Regent University School of Divinity, 2008), esp. chap. 9, who honestly recounts pentecostal missionary attitudes toward Palestinians, even when such were not laudable. See also Melani McAlister, "Prophecy, Politics, and the Popular: The *Left Behind* Series and Christian Evangelicalism's New World Order," in Rebecca L. Stein and Ted Swedenborg, eds., *Palestine, Israel, and the Politics of Popular Culture* (Durham, NC, and London: Duke University Press, 2005), pp. 288-312, for a broader discussion.

19. Thus Calvin L. Smith, "Revolutionaries and Revivalists: Pentecostal Eschatology, Politics, and the Nicaraguan Revolution," *PNEUMA: The Journal of the Society for Pentecostal Studies* 30, no. 1 (2008): 55-82, notes how pentecostalism's politics of dispensationalism led to a resistance to the Sandinistas because of its Soviet connections. Ironically, the result was, often, brutal repression of pentecostals by Sandinistas, which some pentecostals interpreted according to their own apocalyptic worldview as a manifestation or representation of their martyrdom at the hands of the forces of evil. See also Sara Diamond, *Spiritual Warfare: The Politics of the Christian Right* (Boston: South End Press, 1989), chap. 6; cf. 4.1.3.

20. See John M. Court, *Approaching the Apocalypse: A Short History of Christian Millenarianism* (London and New York: I. B. Tauris, 2008); cf. Christopher Rowland, "The Apocalypse in History: The Place of the Book of Revelation in Christian Theology and Life," in Christopher Rowland and John Barton, eds., *Apocalyptic in History and Tradition*, Journal for the Study of the Pseudepigrapha Supplement Series 43 (London and New York: Sheffield Academic Press, 2002), pp. 151-71. For a pentecostal reappropriation of biblical prophecy and its application to a politics of the land in the Mexican American Borderlands of the mid-twentieth cen-

and the success of the contemporary *Left Behind* fictional book series reflects the ongoing explanatory power of prophetic narratives to invite a peculiar reading of the world, especially when the text in question is one that has been invested with sacred authority.[21] Contemporary narrative theologians might suggest that such an approach to the biblical materials is less an application of the Bible to current events — which seems to presume a dualism between the horizon of the text and that of the world to begin with — than it is a living out of the resources, assumptions, and story lines of the scriptural narratives, or an absorbing of the contemporary world into the biblical horizon of symbolism, plot, and meaning.[22] The specific pentecostal twist to such a narrative approach to the apocalyptic and eschatological materials of the Bible might be to emphasize Luke's distinctive perspective on the work of the Spirit in bringing about the kingdom of God "in the last days" (Acts 2:17).

8.1.2. Pentecostal Futurism and the End of History

As we shall see in the remainder of this book, however, such a distinctive pentecostal approach to eschatological matters runs in the opposite direction from the dispensationalist interpretation. In order to make this case, however, we must now turn to a discussion of the futurist emphasis in dispensationalism. In particular we shall see that such a focus not only promotes a mentality of escapism from the world but also contributes toward an ahistorical orientation to the political.

There are at least four hermeneutical approaches historically to the

---

tury, see Rudy V. Busto, *King Tiger: The Religious Vision of Reies López Tijerína* (Albuquerque: University of Mexico Press, 2005).

21. For an astute narratological discussion of the *Left Behind* books' dispensationalist politics, see Amy Frykholm, "What Social and Political Messages Appear in the Left Behind Books? A Literary Discussion of Millenarian Fiction," in Bruce David Forbes and Jeanne Halgren Kilde, eds., *Rapture, Revelation, and the End Times: Exploring the Left Behind Series* (New York: Palgrave Macmillan, 2004), pp. 167-95; cf. Glenn W. Shuck, *Marks of the Beast: The Left Behind Novels and the Struggle for Evangelical Identity* (New York: New York University Press, 2005), chaps. 2 and 6, and Gordon L. Isaac, *Left Behind or Left Befuddled: The Subtle Dangers of Popularizing the End Times* (Collegeville, MN: Liturgical Press, 2008).

22. The issues here are complex, including the question of how such an absorption occurs, or even if the biblical narratives are sufficiently transparent to enable contemporary readers to frame the world in a scriptural way; for a discussion of some of the challenges involved in this view, see Bruce Marshall, "Absorbing the World: Christianity and the Universe of Truths," in Bruce D. Marshall, ed., *Theology and Dialogue: Essays in Conversation with George Lindbeck* (Notre Dame: University of Notre Dame Press, 1990), pp. 69-102.

book of Revelation: a preterist perspective that posits much of the book was fulfilled in the first century; a historical view that looks for a general unfolding of the book from the first century to the end of the world; an idealist, spiritual, symbolic interpretation that is cautious about literal fulfillments of the Apocalypse, preferring instead to see the book illuminating the history of the world; and a futurist approach that insists that everything after Revelation chapter 3 is not only ahead of the author of the book but also of readers in the modern world.[23] Not surprisingly, dispensationalism unapologetically defends the futurist hermeneutic and insists on a predominantly forward-looking model of understanding the prophetic genres of the Bible. Along the way, however, such an eschatological orientation focused on the "end times" and the "last days" has spawned, at least in pentecostal circles, two misguided notions.

First, dispensationalism's identification of a future secret rapture of the church prior to the Great Tribulation, based primarily on 1 Thessalonians 4:16-17, invites an escapist mentality. When combined with the doctrine of the final apostasy in the last days (cf. Matt. 24:12 and 2 Tim. 3:1-9), there is little hope for the world as we know it. The rapture of the church is thus likened to the provision of the ark to Noah, which saved him and his family from the destruction of the wicked all around them. Thus, pentecostals sing the hymn, "This world is not my home, I'm just a passin' through. . . ."

Second, the dispensationalist focus on the future rapture, Tribulation, Parousia, and millennial reign of Christ minimizes the salvific work of God in the present. When set within the restorationist framework of pentecostalism (1.3.1), however, dispensational futurism exacerbates the already thin view of God's historical presence and activity. What I mean is that if the restorationist impulse already devalues the history of the church as apostate vis-à-vis the apostolic heritage — at least that is how the Free Church tradition has tended to view Christendom in the post-Constantinian period — then the dispensationalist leaven perpetuates the apostasy of not only the church but also of humankind in general in "these last days" and on until the end of time. So whereas pentecostal restorationism apart from dispensationalism at least viewed the modern pentecostal revival as a latter rain outpouring of the Spirit in anticipation of the coming kingdom (7.1.1), such restorationism combined with dispensationalism minimizes not only ecclesial history in general but also the pentecostal experience in particular by looking ahead to the "end-time events" as providing God's response to a dying world.

23. Steve Gregg, ed., *Revelation: Four Views — a Parallel Commentary* (Nashville: Thomas Nelson, 1997).

When combined, these pentecostally interpreted dispensational motifs lead to a focus on the end of history in at least two ways. On the one hand, the literal end of history is imminent, with the beginning of the end to be set in motion by the rapture of the church. On the other hand, the end of history is metaphorically but no less really promulgated in the dismissal of the historic period that dispensationalists call the age of the church, so that the history of the church is itself diminished as being inconsequential not only with regard to the apostate character of the church (the restorationist reading) but also with regard to the temporal and soon-to-be-over nature of the body of Christ (the dispensationalist distinction between the church and Israel).[24] Now when political theology is understood in part to refer to the Christian understanding of history and the public square, then what emerges in such a dispensationalistically informed pentecostal eschatology is an anemic ecclesiology and a deficient theology of history, and these combine theologically to undermine any quest for a viable theology of the political.[25]

I want to suggest, however, that even if they have sought to remain true to the Scripture as "Bible-believing Christians," pentecostals have been misguided by the dispensationalist framework, as such a system either assumes fundamental theological presuppositions or leads to certain theological conclusions that are counterintuitive to pentecostal spirituality.[26] More particularly, I will also argue that a dispensational eschatology seduces pentecostals

24. So my hesitation is not so much with regard to the notion of the "catching up" of the elect but to the dispensationalist scheme of interpreting such a rapture. In fact, Luke himself may have believed in the doctrine of the rapture of the elect, albeit without making such a hard-and-fast distinction between Israel and the church. Cf. Luke 17:34-37 and Steven L. Bridge, *"Where the Eagles Are Gathered": The Deliverance of the Elect in Lukan Eschatology,* Journal for the Study of the New Testament Supplement Series 240 (Sheffield: Sheffield Academic Press, 2003).

25. The problem of an anemic ecclesiology is being addressed in this book. On the lack of a theology of history, while pentecostals in the past generation have been hard at work on a distinctively pentecostal historiography, the discussion has by and large focused on internecine debates about the origins of pentecostalism and its genealogies. My call, however, is for pentecostal scholars to articulate a more robust theology and ontology of history, and I will sketch a pneumatological perspective below. See also my *Spirit-Word-Community: Theological Hermeneutics in Trinitarian Perspective* (Burlington, VT, and Aldershot, UK: Ashgate, and Eugene, OR: Wipf & Stock, 2002), chap. 8.3.

26. Gerald T. Sheppard, "Pentecostalism and the Hermeneutics of Dispensationalism: Anatomy of an Uneasy Relationship," *PNEUMA: The Journal of the Society for Pentecostal Studies* 6, no. 2 (1984): 5-34. In the main, I follow Sheppard's reading of the "uneasy relationship" between pentecostalism and dispensationalism. See also Peter Althouse, *Spirit of the Last Days: Pentecostal Eschatology in Conversation with Jürgen Moltmann* (London and New York: T. & T. Clark, 2003), for a similar argument to the one I am making here.

into embracing certain historical and political attitudes and positions that are theologically problematic. In order to clear the ground for the articulation of a distinctively pentecostal eschatological stance, let me raise the following questions and concerns about the pentecostal appropriation of dispensationalism, particularly with regard to its eschatological proposals.

First, dispensational futurism does not do justice to the embodied character of pentecostal spirituality. While pentecostalism is an experientialist pietism interested in what God is doing in every dimension of the human experience — the embodied, affective, and material domains, minimally — of the here-and-now, dispensationalism tends to be a propositionalist eschatology focused almost solely on what will happen in the then-and-there. Further, dispensationalism has divided the church age into two distinct periods: a primordial one during which signs, wonders, and the charismatic gifts were in operation in order to validate the apostolic ministry, and a post-apostolic one featuring the closure of the biblical canon and cessation of the charismata. While some pentecostals have taken the cessationist thesis to task,[27] most have not bothered to interrogate either the consistency of the dispensationalist system vis-à-vis this point or its overall compatibility with pentecostal spirituality.

Second, dispensationalism's sharp wedge between Israel and the church needs to be critically assessed. While on one reading it appears that by the time of the end of the book of Acts the Jews have been "replaced" by the gentiles because of the former's resistance to the gospel and the latter's acceptance of it, this reading accounts neither for the major theme throughout Luke-Acts regarding the present restoration of Israel nor for the Pentecost event, which signaled the outpouring of the Spirit upon Jewish diaspora. Such a revisioning will have implications not only for the articulation of a theology of history, but also for contemporary political practices in the Middle Eastern arena. I am persuaded that a close pentecostal rereading of the Lukan narratives will disabuse them of this seemingly innocuous dispensationalist ecclesiological view. The result, I anticipate, will be a more vigorous theology of the church and of history that is more conducive to pentecostal spirituality.

Finally, while the biblical literalism of dispensationalism was originally embraced by pentecostals against the liberal-modernist threat, on further thought its application to the prophetic texts and genres of the Bible raises questions for pentecostal hermeneutics. The attractiveness of pentecostal

---

27. I.e., Jon Ruthven, *On the Cessation of the Charismata: The Protestant Polemic on Postbiblical Miracles* (Sheffield: Sheffield Academic Press, 1993).

spirituality has been its insistence that the biblical reports about what the Spirit did among the apostles remain to be experienced today. Such a literalism, however, seems misguided when applied to apocalyptic texts. It is one thing to claim that people are healed and that the Spirit saves souls, heals the sick, and enables one to speak in strange tongues; it is quite another matter altogether to see references in the highly symbolic and metaphorical language of biblical apocalyptic to contemporary Russia, Egypt, or Iran. If pentecostals are pragmatists rather than speculative eschatologists,[28] they are more interested in how the Holy Spirit continues to save, sanctify, and redeem human life in the present age than in the esoteric aspects of biblical prophecy seen through the dispensationalist grid. Thus, my claim is that pentecostalism would be better advised to develop the implicit theology of history embedded in its spirituality than to continue pursuing tangents in dispensationalist eschatology that are alien to their piety.

In short, I think there are resources from within the pentecostal experience to articulate a counter-eschatology to the one that they have inherited from dispensationalism. Such a pentecostal theology of history and the eschaton will allow pentecostals to enter the biblical narratives so as to "read the world" in ways that bypass the problems bequeathed by the hermeneutics of dispensationalism. Before turning our attention toward such a constructive proposal, however, we need to confront one more of the unintended consequences of the pentecostal politics of dispensationalism.

8.1.3. Pentecostal Apocalypticism: The End of the World or the Arrival of the Spirit?

My reference to pentecostal apocalypticism describes a basic eschatological mood assumed by many in a movement deeply informed by the dispensationalist worldview. There are arguably three theological presuppositions of this outlook. First, pentecostals believe in a cosmic dualism that pits the power of God against the powers of evil (see chapter 4), and within this scheme view history as the battlefield between good and evil. Conversely eschatology is about the triumph of good over evil, and is often seen as culminating in a great and final conflict that destroys the devil, his minions, and all unbelievers (cf. Rev. 19:19-21 and 20:7-10). Second, given the ongoing cosmic

---

28. The pragmatism of early pentecostalism is argued by Grant Wacker, *Heaven Below: Early Pentecostals and American Culture* (Cambridge, MA, and London: Harvard University Press, 2001).

battle, it is expected that the powers of darkness will make increasingly intensified efforts to undermine the providential outworking of history. As it is expected that things will only get worse (the apostasy of the last days) before it gets better, only the personal return of Christ can overcome the work of evil, vindicate the righteous, punish evildoers, and establish the reign of God. Finally, in the end, God's judgment will be definitively pronounced on a fallen and wicked world (2 Pet. 3:7). This present dispensation is a sign of God's patience and graciousness since it allows for the repentance of many before it is too late. But be warned: "the day of the Lord will come like a thief, and then the heavens will pass away with a loud noise, and the elements will be dissolved with fire, and the earth and everything that is done on it will be disclosed . . . [and] the heavens will be set ablaze and dissolved, and the elements will melt with fire" (2 Pet. 3:10, 12). In this final cosmic inferno, the world itself will be purified and rendered a hospitable abode for the righteous people of God.[29]

I now wish to call attention to the wider political implications of this worldview.[30] More specifically, I suggest that pentecostal apocalypticism has induced an otherworldliness that is not only inconsistent with its spirituality but is also potentially perilous for the long-term economic and environmental sustainability of the world.[31] The precariousness of such an apocalyptic

29. To be sure, pentecostals across the spectrum hold these views with greater or lesser intensity. Felicitas D. Goodman, *Maya Apocalypse: Seventeen Years with the Women of a Yucatan Village* (Bloomington and Indianapolis: Indiana University Press, 2001), and Joel Robbins, *Becoming Sinners: Christianity and Moral Torment in a Papua New Guinea Society* (Berkeley: University of California Press, 2004), provide rich accounts of pentecostal apocalypticism lived out in the global south. For an ethnographic discussion sensitive to the many ways in which pentecostals in more upwardly mobile social contexts temper their apocalyptic eschatology, see Damian Thompson, *Waiting for Antichrist: Charisma and Apocalypse in a Pentecostal Church* (Oxford: Oxford University Press, 2005); cf. Stephen J. Hunt, "Forty Years of Millenarian Thought in the Charismatic Movement," in Kenneth G. C. Newport and Crawford Gribben, eds., *Expecting the End: Millennialism in Social and Historical Context* (Waco, TX: Baylor University Press, 2006), pp. 193-211.

30. Huibert Zegwaart, "Apocalyptic Eschatology and Pentecostalism: The Relevance of John's Millennium for Today," *PNEUMA: The Journal of the Society for Pentecostal Studies* 10, no. 1 (1988): 3-25, esp. pp. 23-25, argues that apocalypticism is not merely a speculative issue but has this-worldly consequences. In what follows, I extend Zegwaart's insights in the direction of an ecological politics.

31. Here I am following the lead of others who have recently taken up the call for a pentecostal theology of the environment — e.g., Steven M. Studebaker, "The Spirit in Creation: A Unified Theology of Grace and Creation Care," *Zygon: Journal of Religion and Science* 43, no. 4 (2008): 943-60, and Shane Clifton, "Preaching the 'Full Gospel' in the Context of Global Environmental Crises," and Matthew Tallman, "Pentecostal Ecology: A Theological Paradigm for

mentality is that it leads to the neglect of environmental issues in view of the transient nature of the present cosmos. Worse, environmental and ecological initiatives are at best a waste of time and at worst counter-productive to God's ultimate intentions for the world given the impending eschatological confla-gration. In the popular pentecostal mentality, the final destruction of the world demands concentrated efforts to save what can be saved (human souls) rather than misguided attempts to salvage either our bodies or our natural environments. What emerges is an implicit anthropocentrism that subordi-nates other animal species as well as the wider ecological habitat to human spiritual needs and concerns.

But such an apocalyptic orientation is itself at odds with the deepest in-tuitions of the pentecostal imagination: its understanding of healing, theol-ogy of embodiment, and holistic soteriology. What I mean is that the apoca-lyptic insistence on the obliteration of the world in the end is not only incompatible with a theology of a new heavens and a new earth, rightly un-derstood, but that it also undermines central pentecostal convictions about the theological value of the body, the materiality of the human condition, and the social dimensions of salvation. If there is one thing we have seen through-out this book, it is that there is also an incontrovertible this-worldliness to pentecostal spirituality that is focused on the present redemption of human life in all of its domains. To be sure, it sits alongside an equally palpable orien-tation toward the coming kingdom, but is no less deniable for all that.

In short, I suggest that pentecostal spirituality can and should be redi-rected away from an apocalyptic eschatology to a political theology of the en-vironment instead. After prayers for healing are delivered, after worship is of-fered, after local community projects are organized, etc., pentecostal convictions about the presence and activity of God's Spirit in the world invite the articulation of an ecological theology and an outworking of an environ-mentally liberating praxis. This is because there is an urgent need for socio-political action to clean up environmental waste, to change policies for han-dling toxic materials, to halt deforestation, and to engage in other initiatives in political economy that interface with the environment.[32] There is only so much the informal economy can do, so while that should not be neglected, neither should formal matters of political economy, society, and the ecology

---

Pentecostal Environmentalism," both in Amos Yong, ed., *The Spirit Renews the Face of the Earth: Pentecostal Forays in Science and Theology of Creation* (Eugene, OR: Pickwick Press, 2009), pp. 117-34 and 135-54, respectively.

32. An insightful essay here is Kelly Sharp, "Voices in the Space between: Economy, Ecol-ogy, and Pentecostalism on the US/Mexico Border," *Ecotheology* 11, no. 4 (2006): 415-30.

be ignored. And clearly, any attempt to develop pentecostal perspectives toward a political theology of the environment will need to be forged amidst a more wholesale rethinking of the dispensationalist framework of popular pentecostal eschatology.

What many pentecostals are concerned about in an eschatological revisioning, however, is a numbing of the posture of anticipation and a heightening of the skepticism voiced long ago about the delay of the Parousia (2 Pet. 3:3-4).[33] I would argue, however, that the doctrine of imminence so central to pentecostal piety and spirituality can continue to emphasize the possibility of Jesus' return at any time and the prospects of the believer's ultimate reunion with Christ without recourse to the dispensationalist scheme of things.[34] In fact, the dispensationalist eschatology undercuts the imminent expectation of believers simply because there are so many signs of the times and events that must be fulfilled before the next important thing can happen.[35] More problematically, if pentecostals spend too much time trying to discern the signs of the times — which, following Acts 1:6-7, none can know — this futuristic preoccupation will hinder their taking up the work of the kingdom.

What we need is to replace the futuristic apocalypticism of dispensationalism with another eschatological sensibility more congenial to pentecostal and charismatic piety. If dispensationalistic apocalypticism emphasizes the future devastation, disaster, and doom that will overtake the earth, the etymology of "apocalyptic" also includes the sense of a revelatory unveiling of what was previously hidden. I urge shifting away from a futuristic apocalypticism of destruction toward the pneumatological apocalypticism of the earliest followers of the Messiah, preserved by Luke, in which the last days' "portents in the heaven above and signs on the earth below" (Acts 2:19) are not signs of the final desolation but rather nature's reactions to the outpouring of the Spirit on all flesh.

33. Thus the Assemblies of God identify the teaching of the post-Tribulational rapture of the church as an eschatological error because it undermines the doctrine of the imminence of Christ's return; see the Assemblies of God Constitution and Bylaws (2007), Article XI.B.3.c.

34. Thus the Assemblies of God Statement of Fundamental Truths 13 is titled, "The Blessed Hope," and reads: "The resurrection of those who have fallen asleep in Christ and their translation together with those who are alive and remain unto the coming of the Lord is the imminent and blessed hope of the church"; see http://ag.org/top/Beliefs/Statement_of_Fundamental_Truths/sft_full.cfm#13 (last accessed 2 February 2009). For a defense of the imminence doctrine in Luke, see A. J. Mattill Jr., *Luke and the Last Things: A Perspective for the Understanding of Lukan Thought* (Dillsboro: Western North Carolina Press, 1979), esp. chaps. 4-6.

35. For discussion, see Benjamin L. Merke, "Could Jesus Return at Any Moment? Rethinking the Imminence of the Second Coming," *Trinity Journal* NS 26, no. 2 (2005): 279-92.

In anticipation of such a pneumatological rendition of apocalyptic eschatology, I turn briefly to the work of pentecostal theologian Steven Land.[36] For Land, pentecostal spirituality can be understood as apocalyptic in terms of its central feature that acknowledges the in-breaking work of the Spirit "in the last days" (Acts 2:17). Yet these "last days" are not only futuristically understood but refer to the present "dispensation" between the first and the second coming of Christ. During this period, the church is — and has always been — an end-time missionary fellowship that by the power of the Spirit participates in the redemptive work of God, passionately longing for the manifestation of the kingdom through affective gratitude, compassion, and courage, and hastening through worship, prayer, and witness the presence of the kingdom. In other words, the apocalyptic affections of pentecostal spirituality are indicative both of its pietistic passions that are wholly responsive to the outpouring of the Spirit and of the ensuing missionary commitments that are motivated for the sake of the world and in the hopes of the world's reconciliation to God.[37]

But further than Land, I would argue also that the apocalyptic revelation of the Spirit manifests and anticipates not just the *time* of the kingdom but redeems the many *places* of the world in anticipation of the kingdom. This is because when Luke says that the outpouring of the Spirit will not only empower evangelism to the ends of the earth (Acts 1:8) but also bring about "salvation to the ends of the earth" (13:47), in both cases the "ends of the earth" is ἐσχάτου τῆς γῆς *(eschatou tēs gēs)*, which suggests that the present time of the Spirit and of the kingdom involves also the world's geographies, spaces, and places.[38] So not only does Luke say that the time of the last days has begun with the coming of the Spirit, but he also says that the place of the kingdom is now being redeemed by the Spirit.

Such a pentecostal and pneumatological apocalypticism emphasizes not only the already-not-yet and "in between" character but also the geographical and topographical redemptability of the human condition. It also rejects the escapism and otherworldliness of a futuristic dispensationalism in favor of an incarnational and pneumatological spirituality. If the incarnation

36. Steven J. Land, *Pentecostal Spirituality: A Passion for the Kingdom* (Sheffield: Sheffield Academic Press, 1993).

37. Thus, as Fred O. Francis, "Eschatology and History in Luke-Acts," *Journal of the American Academy of Religion* 37, no. 1 (1969): 49-63, esp. p. 62, notes, "The substance of [Luke's] eschatological reality is the gift of the Holy Spirit."

38. Here I am following Vítor Westhelle, "Liberation Theology: A Latitudinal Perspective," in Jerry L. Walls, *The Oxford Handbook of Eschatology* (Oxford: Oxford University Press, 2008), pp. 311-27, esp. pp. 320-23.

is the in-breaking of the person of God in the human flesh of the historic Jesus of Nazareth and if Pentecost is the in-breaking of the Spirit of God to constitute the church as the historically concrete people of God, then these last days are not merely temporary moments in anticipation of the true salvation to come but are themselves the outworking of the salvific intentions of God in the history of the world. In other words, such a charismatic and pneumatological apocalypticism looks not merely for the future salvation of the world but for the present salvation of all flesh by the power of the in-breaking Spirit.[39]

8.2. Whither Political Eschatologies?
"In the Last Days . . . I Will Pour Out My Spirit . . ."

If the previous section was ground-clearing in terms of identifying how pentecostal embrace of dispensationalism has actually undermined rather than enabled the full flowering of pentecostal spirituality, in this section, we will draw pentecostal and pneumatological resources into a broader ecumenical and even interreligious arena in order to discern possible ways forward to what I am calling an eschatological politics of hope. Using the Day of Pentecost narrative as the central pivot upon which the following constructive reflections turn, I will suggest a revised theology of Israel and the church in dialogue with the Jewish political theology of Daniel Boyarin; outline a theology of history in dialogue with the Radically Orthodox theology of liberation proposed by Methodist theologian Daniel Bell; and sketch a pneumatological theology of the environment in dialogue with the political theology of nature developed by Anglican theologian Peter Scott. In each case, I seek to recalibrate pentecostal eschatological sensibilities away from its dispensationalist cast and in quest of the pneumatological and apocalyptic politics of the "last days" that is more in line with its charismatic spirituality and practices.[40]

39. My proposal preserves the central commitment to the imminent return of Christ — what is most important in pentecostal circles — and attempts to find a *via media* between a futuristic and a fully realized eschatology without insisting exclusively on any millennialist position. In other words, I think the revised pneumatological and apocalyptic of the last days being developed here could be consistent with any of the millennial visions, and that is one of the strengths of this eschatological view. Hence, I will say little more about millennialism in the remainder of this chapter.

40. I am aware that there is some dispute about the "last days" (ἐσχάταις ἡμέραις) being a later redaction — e.g., Richard I. Pervo, *Acts: A Commentary,* Hermeneia — A Critical and Historical Commentary on the Bible (Minneapolis: Fortress, 2009), pp. 76-79. However, since

8.2.1. ". . . On Jews and Proselytes": The Restoration of Israel, the Salvation of the Gentiles, and "Last Days" Politics

The dispensational understanding of the differences between Israel and the church and pentecostalism's uncritical internalization of such a theology of Israel and ecclesiology involve a number of major questions for political theology. These include, but are not limited to, the nature of Jewish particularity, especially its status as the elect people of God, the historic tragedy of Christian anti-Semitism and supersessionism with regard to Judaism, and the present and future role of Israel in the providential designs of history.[41] There is no possibility within the space of the following discussion to resolve all of these issues. Our goals must be much more limited, and these inevitably will revolve around the articulation of a Christian theology of Israel that can ameliorate rather than aggravate contemporary expressions of the politics of dispensationalism.

One way forward is to understand the "end times" in terms of Israel's restoration as initiated in the outpouring of the Spirit on both Jews and proselytes from around the Mediterranean diaspora (Acts 2:5-11). By way of bringing forward the earlier discussion (see 3.2.2) for our present purposes, the following three aspects of this view should be kept in mind. First, the restoration of Israel began for Luke with the life, death, and resurrection of Jesus, continued in the ministry of the earliest followers of the Messiah, and remains yet to be fully accomplished by the end of Acts. Second, the restoration of Israel includes, by the Spirit, the redemption of the known world of the Jewish diaspora so that the blessings promised to Israel are now also made available to the entirety of gentile humanity; hence now there is in effect, two aspects to the people of God: Jews and gentiles. Finally, however, this universal salvation (as distinct from universalism, I shall argue later) does not revoke the distinctiveness of Israel's role and place in God's providential history and even in the eschatological consummation, since the one salvation does not annul but preserves the many tongues of the human cultural-linguistic experience. My

---

the "last days" phrase is in the main lines of the received textual tradition, its eschatological reference is consistent with the thrust of the Joel passage and its context, and it aligns with the wider apocalyptic and eschatological thrust of the New Testament, I believe we are on solid ground to proceed in the direction I am proposing.

41. For recent attempts to rethink these matters that chart promising ways forward, see Hans Küng, *Judaism: Between Yesterday and Tomorrow*, trans. John Bowden (New York: Crossroad, 1992); R. Kendall Soulen, *The God of Israel and Christian Theology* (Minneapolis: Fortress Press, 1996); and Calvin L. Smith, ed., *The Jews, Modern Israel and the New Supersessionism: Resources for Christians* (Lampeter, UK: Kings Evangelical Press, 2009).

suggestion is that this Lukan vision of the salvific role of Israel within the wider Greco-Roman and Hellenistic context of the first century may be helpful for crafting a contemporary theology of Israel as well as for revisioning an eschatological politics in our presently shrinking global context.[42]

I have found a congenial dialogue partner on this matter in the Jewish postmodern culture critic and Talmudist scholar, Daniel Boyarin.[43] Boyarin resorts to Paul precisely because he sees Paul's primordial question as one of the perennial questions for Jewish identity since the axial period: how to interpret the Jewish self-understanding as the elect people of God in a wider Mediterranean context.[44] If Boyarin wrestles with this question in the contemporary global situation, then Paul struggled with the same question as a Hellenistic and diaspora Jew aware of the much wider Greco-Roman forging of the *Pax Romana.*

There are at least two interpretive moves Boyarin makes in his rereading of Paul. First, his textual basis is Galatians 3:28 — "There is no longer Jew or Greek, there is no longer slave or free, there is no longer male and female; for all of you are one in Christ Jesus." Hence neither Jewishness nor Greekness (gentile-ness) is of primary importance, but the one universal body of Christ. Second, his philosophical basis is Middle Platonism's dualism of flesh and spirit, which Paul retrieved for his own purposes. Thus, "the letter kills, but the Spirit gives life" (2 Cor. 3:6) is understood as justifying the subordination of the fleshliness of circumcision, the law, and of Jewish particularity to the universality of Jewish and gentile humanity in the spiritual church. In the hands of Paul's allegorizing hermeneutic (with the *locus classicus* being Gal. 4:21-31), then, Jewish particularity is not superseded but nevertheless relativized in favor of a more universal self-understanding. What motivates Paul, in Boyarin's assessment, is the need to reinterpret Jewish specificity in a predominantly gentile world.

Boyarin's appraisal of Paul is much more complex than the above sum-

---

42. For further elaboration of these matters, see Yong, *The Holy Spirit and the Public Square* [working title] (Brewster, MA: Paraclete Press, forthcoming), esp. chaps. 17, 23, 24, and 27.

43. I was first pointed in the Boyarin direction by Alain Epp Weaver, *States of Exile: Visions of Diaspora, Witness, and Return* (Waterloo, ON, and Scottdale, PA: Herald Press, 2008), chap. 3, and then reminded of the potential of Boyarin as an interlocutor in P. Travis Kroeker, "Whither Messianic Ethics? Paul as Political Theorist," *Journal of the Society of Christian Ethics* 25, no. 2 (2005): 37-58, esp. pp. 41-42. Note that Weaver as a Mennonite theologian was himself inspired by the political and exilic theology of John Howard Yoder.

44. Daniel Boyarin, *A Radical Jew: Paul and the Politics of Identity* (Berkeley: University of California Press, 1994).

mary lets on. My focus, however, is on the contemporary political implications of such a Pauline construal of Jewish identity. For Boyarin, here is where Paul is only half right. Paul the universalizing theorist (and theologian) is correct to insist on a rethinking of Jewishness in a global context that goes beyond its parochialism. On the other hand, if Paul is *not* anti-Semitic,[45] then his universalizing impulse is prone to neglecting the embodied, social, and material dimensions of Jewish uniqueness and is thus "inimical to Jewish difference, indeed to all difference as such."[46] For the latter, Boyarin the Talmudist turns to the rabbinic tradition, and, holding the Pauline and rabbinic proposals together, suggests a contemporary theology of "radical Jewishness."[47] This involves a diasporizing identity that preserves differences within a wider cultural milieu and "disrupts the very categories of identity, because it is not national, not genealogical, not religious, but all of these, in dialectical tension with one another."[48] In concrete political terms, this invites a reconsideration of a "deterritorializing Jewishness" — a multicultural nation rather than (single) Jewish state that is "devoid of exclusivist and dominating power" precisely because it is "founded on common memory of shared space and on the hope for such a shared space in an infinitely deferred future."[49] The result, for Boyarin, is the retention of the particularity of ethnic identities (like Jewishness) alongside universal solidarity while avoiding racism and ethnocentrism on the one side and bland indifference and homogeneity on the other.[50]

I find Boyarin's reinterpretation of Paul to be complementary to my own retrieval of Luke. If Paul was concerned about articulating a Jewish self-understanding in a Hellenistic context, Luke can be seen as seeking to understand the salvation of the world in light of the particular history of Israel. If Paul's "neither Jew nor Greek" is an attempt to overcome the disjunction between the two and Boyarin's diasporized identity is an effort to preserve particularity and universality in dialectical tension, then Luke's many Jewish and proselytic tongues that declare the wonders of God preserve differences within a wider harmony and do so precisely by identifying the harmony as

45. Boyarin, *A Radical Jew*, chap. 6.
46. Boyarin, *A Radical Jew*, p. 156.
47. Boyarin, *A Radical Jew*, chap. 10.
48. Boyarin, *A Radical Jew*, p. 244.
49. Boyarin, *A Radical Jew*, pp. 259 and 243.
50. Another postmodern Jewish theologian who arrives at a very similar theory of Jewish identity (without necessarily sharing Boyarin's political theology of Israel) is Peter Ochs, "Abrahamic Theo-politics: A Jewish View," in Peter Scott and William T. Cavanaugh, eds., *The Blackwell Companion to Political* Theology (2004; paperback ed., Malden, MA: Blackwell, 2007), pp. 519-34.

being constituted by such diversity. So whereas Paul's resolution to the problem of Jewish identity in a Greco-Roman setting was the spiritual body of Christ, and while Boyarin's answer to the existing challenge of Jewishness in global context involves a diasporic and deterritorialized identity, a Lukan response, then and now, is both pneumatological and eschatological: that the Spirit's outpouring on Jews and proselytes in the last days preserves the multiplicity of diasporic Jewish identity, with each difference enriching the whole.

This reading does not resolve the perennial debates regarding Luke's theology of the Jews.[51] It does, however, 1) recognize the priority of the Jews, even in a post-Pentecost age (e.g., the witness of Paul and others was always directed first toward the synagogue); 2) affirm that the fulfillment of the Mosaic Law in Christ and the Spirit does not involve its abrogation, at least for Jews (e.g., note Timothy's circumcision as well as Paul's adherence to the purification laws on at least two occasions in Acts 18:18 and 21:23-26); and 3) leave open the details regarding the full restoration of Israel (promised in Luke 1–2) and its relationship to the full salvation of the gentiles. In fact, Luke is consistent in recording warnings inviting the Jews to repentance so that they might more fully realize the restoring and redeeming hand of YHWH (even the closing of Acts includes the reminder that God's intention is to heal them — Acts 28:27), and be more intentional participants in the messianic movement. That the ongoing drama of history includes both the fulfillment of Israel's restoration and the apprehension of Jewish involvement in the ongoing redemption of the world leaves no room for either anti-Semitism or supersessionism.[52] My point is both that (for Luke) Jewish identity is multiple (in the many tongues) and eschatological (awaiting ongoing formation), and that it is God's saving work in and through the particularity of the Jewish people that lays the basis for the salvation of the gentiles (see 5.3.1).

Such an eschatological reading of Israel's identity in these "last days" (Acts 2:17) leads to the following proposals in place of (Zionist understandings of) dispensationalism. First, the "last days" is not merely to be understood futuristically (here against dispensationalism) but should be embraced as the entire period wherein God's salvific plan for Israel and the world is being accomplished at least in part in the here-and-now by the providential

51. For an overview of the disputed theories, see Joseph B. Tyson, *Luke, Judaism, and the Scholars: Critical Approaches to Luke-Acts* (Columbia: University of South Carolina Press, 1999).

52. See Craig C. Hill, "Restoring the Kingdom to Israel: Luke-Acts and Christian Supersessionism," in Tod Linafelt, ed., *A Shadow of Glory: Reading the New Testament after the Holocaust* (New York and London: Routledge, 2002), pp. 185-200; compare my reading of Israel's final restoration here and in 8.3.1 below.

workings of the Spirit.[53] This invites a rereading of the prophetic genres of Scripture in ecclesiological perspective, albeit one that includes rather than excludes Israel as part of the one people of God.

But second, the pneumatological preservation of the diasporic and complex nature of Jewish identity and thus its persistence to the present time also signals the impossibility of any dualistic eschatological scheme that pits Israel against the rest of the world. In fact, inasmuch as the original outpouring of the Spirit on Jews and proselytes also included those from Crete and the Arab world (Acts 2:11), to that degree the destinies of Jews and Arabs can also be understood as intertwined in the economy of the Spirit. Hence any theology of Israel requires also a theology of Palestine — and of Palestinians[54] — not to mention a theology of the wider Arabic and even Muslim world.[55]

Finally, a multifarious and ecclesiological approach to eschatology that includes both a complex Israel and the pluralistic lot of gentiles will reject any politics of Armageddon that sees Americans and Russians or any other world or national superpowers as being uniquely placed to bring about the culmination of history. If Boyarin's diasporized identity accurately defines the character of Jewishness as the elect people of God, then Yoder's exilic ecclesiology (5.2.1) also rightly describes the nature of the church as an eschatological community that includes both Jews and gentiles. In this case, no particular nation can displace the role of the church, and any exaltation of a nation as more elect than others in the contemporary political landscape is in danger of idolizing a state rather than acknowledging the supremacy and lordship of Christ and YHWH. Hence what counts is not the work of nation-states but the eschatological work of the Spirit. In sum, an ecclesiological eschatology will affirm a pneumatological and apocalyptic politics that sees the Spirit's pentecostal outpouring as a harbinger of the future but impending salvation of God that will finally make ready the many-ness of the world for the Parousia and usher in the full and final harmonious rule of the kingdom.

53. See Dale C. Allison Jr., "Jesus and the Victory of Apocalyptic," in Carey C. Newman, ed., *Jesus and the Restoration of Israel: A Critical Assessment of N. T. Wright's Jesus and the Victory of God* (Downers Grove, IL: InterVarsity, 1999), pp. 126-41.

54. E.g., Mitri Raheb, *I Am a Palestinian Christian*, trans. Ruth L. Gritsch (Minneapolis: Fortress, 1995), and Naim Stifan Ateek, *A Palestinian Christian Cry for Reconciliation* (Maryknoll, NY: Orbis Books, 2008).

55. The Muslim-Christian-Jewish discussion is barely under way. For starters, I would point to my previous work in theology of religions — i.e., *Hospitality and the Other: Pentecost, Christian Practices, and the Neighbor* (Maryknoll, NY: Orbis Books, 2008).

8.2.2. ". . . On . . . Every Nation under Heaven": Liberation, Forgiveness, and the Redemption of History

But if the outpouring of the Spirit inaugurates the "last days" and we currently live in this eschatological period, then the futurist emphasis of dispensationalism must be tempered not only with regard to the Jews, but also with regard to gentiles. This means that the "not yet" of the salvation history of the gentiles also includes a paradoxical "already" with regard to the Spirit's liberative activity in times and places of the world. My claim, however, is that the redemption of the gentiles should be understood similarly as with the restoration of Israel: both are made possible by the outpouring of the Spirit in the last days but yet both are only partially actualized, await final achievement, and depend, at least in part, on human repentance in response to the gift(s) of the Spirit. In other words, while the outpouring of the Spirit upon Jews and proselytes from every nation under heaven anticipates the inclusion of the gentiles in the restoration of Israel, such realization involves an embrace of the Spirit's calling toward the ends (chronologically and geographically — i.e., eschatologically — conceived) of the earth.

Similarly, then, I argue that the redemption of history has been inaugurated with the pentecostal outpouring even if the actualization of such a final salvation depends on what recipients of the Spirit do and how they respond. Hence a pentecostal and pneumatological reading of salvation history in this sense contrasts starkly with both restorationist ahistoricism and dispensationalist futurism. If these orientations minimize the present age either because of its apostate and temporary character or for other reasons, the Lukan declarations that Christ has been anointed by the Spirit "to proclaim the year of the Lord's favor" (Luke 4:19) and that the Spirit has been poured out upon all flesh in the last days for the same reasons insist instead that these present times somehow constitute the restoration of Israel and the redemption of the world. Hence the dispensationalist and futurist "end of history" is redeemed precisely because these last days of history are not merely apocalyptic expectations portending the world's desolation but are the stage upon which the salvific power of the Spirit is being and will be manifest.

But once this turn is made, then an overly realized eschatology looms. The Christian confession of Jesus as coming king, however, cannot merely collapse the future horizon into either the existential or historical present. Hence what is needed is what I have called a charismatic and pneumatological apocalypticism that affirms the Spirit's past, present, and future breaking into and redemption of history's times and places. A recent book published in Routledge's Radical Orthodoxy series, *Liberation Theology After the*

End of History: The Refusal to Cease Suffering, helps us to clarify the contours of such an already-but-not-yet as well as concretely specify theology of history's redemption.[56]

Space constraints prevent any lengthy explication of Daniel Bell's thesis, so I focus on the three major elements encapsulated in his book's title. Bell's starting point is Francis Fukuyama's claim that with the emergence of the secular, liberal, and free market democracy on the world stage, the "end of history" has arrived.[57] Fukuyama argued his point both philosophically in dialogue with the Hegelian view about the emergence of absolute freedom as the culmination of history and empirically against the Marxist claim that class warfare would drive the pages of history until the founding of a socialist utopia. But if Fukuyama asserts that the emergence and triumph of the global free market economy has brought about the end of economic striving quite apart from the establishment of socialism, Bell is concerned — consistent with the Radical Orthodoxy concerns of Steve Long and William Cavanaugh (6.2.2) — that global capitalism's promises to generate wealth indefinitely, eliminate poverty, and satisfy human desires threaten to displace the Christian faith with an alternative but false soteriology. In fact, the problem itself is that capitalism promotes, insidiously, its own materialist, consumerist, and hedonist desires so that the desires of the church are co-opted and disoriented by the capitalist regime (see 7.3.3). Thus Bell affirms liberation theology's resistance to the capitalist ethos, especially to the "savage capitalism" that proceeds unfettered by concerns for the poor.[58] But the problem with the proposals of liberation theology are twofold: a) its theory of justice understood in terms of rights pits individuals and groups against one another and perpetuates the Marxist theory of class conflict, and b) its socio-political strategies require the church to engage in statecraft on the world's terms rather than reflect or instantiate a counter-politics and counter-economy as the people of God.

The solution for Bell (and Radical Orthodoxy) is a revitalization of the practices of the church, in particular its liturgies, that can contest the technol-

---

56. Daniel M. Bell Jr., *Liberation Theology after the End of History: The Refusal to Cease Suffering* (London and New York: Routledge, 2001).

57. Francis Fukuyama, *The End of History and the Last Man* (New York: Free Press, 1992). Fukuyama's thesis stirred a humongous response from the left and the right, but he has also adjusted and qualified his claims in the last twenty years. My own theological response, as will be clear, is eschatological, emphasizing both the now and the not-yet aspects of the redemption of history.

58. Bell, *Liberation Theology after the End of History,* pp. 10-12, drawing here from the work of German theologian Franz Hinkelammert.

ogies of selfish desires formed by capitalism, and its practices of forgiveness that can overcome the aggravation of conflict inherent in modern theories of justice considered in terms of rights. Thus the "refusal to cease suffering" in the subtitle of Bell's book points to the ecclesial practices of peacemaking, penance (reparations), and graciousness, all of which are concrete and historically enacted/enfleshed risks bound up with forgiveness but nevertheless are also wagers that God will vindicate the oppressed, reconcile oppressors and their victims, generate solidarity between enemies, and overcome the violence instigated by sin. So rather than being disempowering, "Ultimately, forgiveness is an act of hope that denies the destructiveness of injustice the final word."[59]

Bell's proposals have been hotly disputed.[60] Rather than either countering his critics or defending Bell, let me propose instead what might be called a Lukan intervention that reads *Liberation Theology After the End of History* as an ecclesiological eschatology. What I mean here is that Bell's insistence on the church being the church serves to combat the false eschatologies of both capitalism and socialism. Capitalism may be the end of history but only in that in its savage sense, it represents the nadir rather than the culmination of the historical process, and socialism also provides a false utopian ideal since justice considered as receiving what one is due induces the terror of punishment instead. Forgiveness, however, inserts the healing presence and activity of God into the palpable realities of history. Thus in order to bring to completion the restoration of Israel and the redemption of the world, the Spirit-empowered disciples proclaimed the forgiveness of sins instead (Acts 2:38; 5:31; 10:43; 13:38; 26:18; etc.).

But what does all of this mean for a theology of history and for the redemption of history? Recall that part of the rationale given for the turn to Bell's work was to ask about how to avoid the pitfalls of either a futurist or realized eschatology. I suggest that Bell's dialogue with liberation theology invites a consideration of how liberation theology and pentecostalism complement one another in their witness to God as redeemer of the world. As Miroslav Volf had put it initially, liberationism's emphasis on social salvation understood in terms of political and economic justice is required along with

59. Bell, *Liberation Theology after the End of History,* pp. 152-53.

60. E.g., Lisa Isherwood, "Embodying and Emboldening Our Desires," in Rosemary Radford Ruether and Marion Grau, eds., *Interpreting the Postmodern: Responses to "Radical Orthodoxy"* (New York and London: T. & T. Clark, 2006), pp. 161-74. See also the exchange between Miroslav Volf and Bell: Volf, "Liberation Theology after the End of History: An Exchange"; Bell, "What Gift Is Given? A Response to Volf"; and Volf, "Against a Pretentious Church: A Rejoinder to Bell's Response" — all in *Modern Theology* 19, no. 2 (2003): 261-69, 271-80, and 281-85, respectively.

pentecostalism's insistence on personal salvation and bodily healing.[61] Beyond this, however, Bell's emphasis on the practice of forgiveness requires the charismatic presence and activity of the eschatological Spirit for its implementation, performance, and achievement.

What I mean is best captured in the colloquialism, "to err is human, to forgive is divine." The full manifestation of forgiveness involves the reconciliation of victims and oppressors. Beyond the interpersonal level, forgiveness can be granted and received intergenerationally, intercommunally, even internationally, and so on.[62] For these more social expressions of forgiveness to happen, however, there must be, among other developments, an understanding and recognition of the wrongs that have been committed, the ability to empathize with others (even in their absence), the willingness to seek after the truth, the right to represent victims and the capacity to communicate the willingness to overlook fault, a means of acknowledging the social participation in fault, the fortitude to pursue after justice, and a means of giving and receiving reparations, to the degree that each of these is possible.[63] None of this can occur apart from the communication across communities, cultures, and even languages. But if the Spirit has been poured out on all flesh, thus bringing the future of the kingdom into the present, so also has the Spirit's outpouring made possible the present redemption of the ends of the earth, including its inhabitants regardless of where they are to be found, what language they speak, what spaces or places they populate, or what barriers keep them from being reconciled to others. In short, because of the Spirit's outpouring and the gift of many tongues, forgiveness can be elicited not only in human hearts but also in human history.

Hence the outpouring of the Spirit — upon Jews, proselytes, those far

---

61. Miroslav Volf, "Materiality of Salvation: An Investigation in the Soteriologies of Liberation and Pentecostal Theologies," *Journal of Ecumenical Studies* 26, no. 3 (1989): 447-67; see also 1.3.3 above.

62. A succinct but yet suggestive discussion of the political dimensions of forgiveness is Rodney L. Petersen, "Forgiveness and Reconciliation in Christian Theology: A Public Role for the Church in Civil Society," in Emmanuel Clapsis, ed., *The Orthodox Churches in a Pluralistic World: An Ecumenical Conversation* (Brookline, MA: Holy Cross Orthodox Press, and Geneva: WCC Publications, 2004), pp. 110-29.

63. Two recent and evocative volumes on this topic are F. LeRon Shults and Steven Sandage, *The Faces of Forgiveness: Searching for Wholeness and Salvation* (Grand Rapids: Baker Academic, 2003), and Miroslav Volf, *Free of Charge: Giving and Forgiving in a Culture Stripped of Grace* (Grand Rapids: Zondervan, 2005). See also Volf's award-winning *Exclusion and Embrace: A Theological Exploration of Identity, Otherness, and Reconciliation* (Nashville: Abingdon Press, 1996), esp. pp. 119-25, for a discussion of forgiveness within the broader context of ethnic hostilities, one kind of cross-communal and social forgiveness that I'm focused on here.

away at the ends of the earth, and "everyone whom the Lord our God calls" (Acts 2:39) — means that the people of God are enabled to refuse to cease suffering and to forgive because they follow in the footsteps of the suffering Servant who did not withhold forgiveness from his persecutors.[64] The good news that he declared by the Spirit's power regarding freedom from oppression was also enacted in his forgiving sinners, including those who sinned against him. By extension, the message of the gospel that the church declares also cannot be enacted or lived out apart from the Spirit's power. And forgiveness is possible because the Spirit enables the speaking and understanding — indeed, confession — of many tongues.[65]

Hence this miracle of the Day of Pentecost is what allows for the redemption of history in a mode that avoids both the Scylla of a dispensationalist futurism or the Charybdis of a liberationist-Marxist-socialist utopianism. The outpouring of the Spirit upon those from every nation under heaven produces the apocalyptic affection of the Spirit that binds people, even enemies, together and makes forgiveness possible.[66] It is this good news of forgiveness of sins that facilitates reconciliation of all in enmity and strife, fosters solidarity across peoples, tribes, and nations, and brings about the harmony of many otherwise opposing voices for the glory of God. The result is not the end but the redemption of history; not an escape from the world's (coming) tribulations but an empowered perseverance in view of its eschatological

64. So, "When empowered by the Spirit, the life of a witness becomes continuous with the mission and suffering of Jesus"; see Martin William Mittelstadt, *The Spirit and Suffering in Luke-Acts: Implications for a Pentecostal Pneumatology,* Journal of Pentecostal Theology Supplement Series 26 (London and New York: T. & T. Clark, 2004), p. vii.

65. Lamin Sanneh calls this the translatability — or vernacularizability (my own neologism, adapted from Sanneh's work) — of the Christian message. See Sanneh, *Translating the Message: The Missionary Impact on Culture* (Maryknoll, NY: Orbis Books, 1989); cf. Sanneh, *Disciples of All Nations: Pillars of World Christianity* (Oxford and New York: Oxford University Press, 2008).

66. What does this mean for the politics of war? It suggests that the peace of the Spirit and of the Prince of Peace should resist embracing any form of nationalism that would involve the endorsement of militarism or the waging of war in the name of God. It also suggests that there is a distinctively pentecostal form of pacifism that may have been prominent in the past, but has since been, by and large, overtaken in the social and upward mobility of pentecostals in the Anglo-American West. For openings to such discussions — which we will need to return to on another occasion and in another book — see Jay Beaman, *Pentecostal Pacifism: The Origin, Development, and Rejection of Pacific Belief among Pentecostals* (Hillsboro, KS: Center for Mennonite Brethren Studies, 1989), and Paul Alexander, *Peace to War: Shifting Allegiances in the Assemblies of God,* The C. Henry Smith Series 9 (Telford, PA: Cascadia, and Scottdale, PA: Herald Press, 2009). See also the work of the Pentecostal Charismatic Peace Fellowship (http://www.pcpf.org/).

transformation; not a temporary human accomplishment in the present but the opportunity to participate in the apocalyptic (revelatory) in-breaking of the Spirit from the (heretofore hidden) divine future.

8.2.3. ". . . On All Flesh": Green Theologies and the Renewal of the Cosmos

So far I have attempted to steer away from the futuristic apocalypse of cataclysm toward a pneumatological apocalypse of revelation and hope. My argument so far is that the outpouring of the Spirit in the last days, beginning on the Day of Pentecost, inaugurates the time of the restoration of Israel and of the redemption of the gentiles. Elsewhere, I have also argued that the Spirit's outpouring on all flesh signals not only the salvation of Jews and gentiles, but also heralds the renewal of the cosmos — the topographical and geographical *ends* of the earth itself (see 8.1.3).[67] Peter's citation (in Luke's account) of Joel's prophecy refers to "portents in the heaven above, and signs on the earth below," includes "blood, and fire, and smoky mist," and indicates "[t]he sun shall be turned to darkness and the moon to blood" (Acts 2:19-20).

In the context of Joel's prophecy, these are apocalyptic phenomena most immediately related to the judgment of God especially against Israel's enemies (Joel 3). As such they are "principally concerned with the sociopolitical upheaval in that day: the blood and fire referring to warfare . . . and the rising smoke to gutted cities . . . though God's activity in the natural world may also play a part."[68] On the other hand, the fortunes of Israel in the prophecy of Joel were intertwined with the plague of locusts, and the outpouring of the Spirit was in part God's final response to renew the land and redeem the years that had been lost to the plague (Joel 2:18-27). This is consistent with other texts that connect the deluge of the Spirit of God (Ps. 104:30) with the renewal of the earth, its creatures, and its various forms of life (Ps. 104 passim). For the prophet Isaiah, when the Spirit is poured out from on

---

67. See Yong, *The Spirit Poured Out on All Flesh: Pentecostalism and the Possibility of Global Theology* (Grand Rapids: Baker Academic, 2005), chap. 7, and note also the literature cited therein; cf. Steve Walton, "'The Heavens Opened': Cosmological and Theological Transformation in Luke and Acts," in Jonathan T. Pennington and Sean M. McDonough, eds., *Cosmology and New Testament Theology*, Library of New Testament Studies 355 (London and New York: T. & T. Clark, 2008), pp. 60-73.

68. Richard D. Patterson, "Joel," in Frank E. Gaebelein, gen. ed., *The Expositor's Bible Commentary*, 12 vols. (Grand Rapids: Regency Reference Library/Zondervan, 1985), vol. 7, pp. 227-56, quotation from p. 256.

high, then "the wilderness becomes a fruitful field, and the fruitful field is deemed a forest" (Isa. 32:15), and for the prophet Ezekiel, the gift of the Spirit will replace the famine with the grain harvest, the abundance of the field, and the fertility of the land (Ezek. 36:26-30 and 37:14).[69] Thus, even if the pentecostal outpouring provides the occasion for repentance from sin before the judgment of the day of YHWH, it also inaugurates God's final plan to restore and renew the earth itself and all its creatures therein.

I propose that such a pentecostal perspective can inspire a specifically pneumatological theology of the environment.[70] Initially broached in the early 1980s,[71] the discussion has gradually intensified over the decades. On the one hand, we observe something like the cosmic pneumatology of Dennis Edwards and the liberation eco-theology of Sigurd Bergmann, both of whom retrieve patristic theologians for a social-relational, trinitarian, and redemptive theology of nature.[72] On the other hand, we find the postmodernist, post-metaphysical, and immanentist proposals of theologians like Mark Wallace, whose ruminations result in a new vision of a spirit-enlivened earth, albeit perhaps at the price of an orthodox conception of the Spirit.[73] In the middle are theologians like Jürgen Moltmann, whose universal "Spirit of life" is accused from the left of being too present-focused and immanentist and from the right of being too hope- and future-oriented and transcendentalist.[74] All, however, are responding at least in part to the ecological crisis and

69. Thus Mark Wallace is right to note that "the four traditional elements of natural, embodied life — *earth, air, water*, and *fire* — are constitutive of the Spirit's biblical reality as an enfleshed being who ministers to the whole creation God has made for the refreshment and joy of all beings"; see Mark I. Wallace, "God Is Underfoot: Pneumatology after Derrida," in John D. Caputo, ed., *The Religious* (Malden, MA, and Oxford: Blackwell, 2002), pp. 197-211, quotation from p. 207 (italics original).

70. The spectrum of religiously informed environmentalism is broad; for an introductory discussion, see Roger S. Gottlieb, *A Greener Faith: Religious Environmentalism and Our Planet's Future* (Oxford: Oxford University Press, 2006).

71. See the pneumatological connections in part 2 of George Hendry, *Theology of Nature* (Philadelphia: Westminster Press, 1980), esp. chaps. 7-9.

72. See Dennis Edwards, *Breath of Life: A Theology of the Creator Spirit* (Maryknoll, NY: Orbis, 2004), and Sigurd Bergmann, *Creation Set Free: The Spirit as Liberator of Nature*, trans. Douglas Scott (Grand Rapids and Cambridge, UK: Eerdmans, 2005).

73. Mark I. Wallace, *Fragments of the Spirit: Nature, Violence, and the Renewal of Creation* (Harrisburg, PA: Trinity Press International, 2002), and *Finding God in the Singing River: Christianity, Spirit, Nature* (Minneapolis: Fortress, 2005).

74. Jürgen Moltmann, *God in Creation: A New Theology of Creation and the Spirit of God*, trans. Margaret Kohl (San Francisco: Harper & Row, 1985); *The Spirit of Life: A Universal Affirmation*, trans. Margaret Kohl (Minneapolis: Fortress, 1997); and *The Source of Life: The Holy Spirit and the Theology of Life*, trans. Margaret Kohl (Minneapolis: Fortress, 1997).

have realized the need to construct adequate theological frameworks that can contribute to a more holistic view of human embeddedness in the cosmos and generate greater solidarity between humankind, the environment, and the many forms of life on earth.

In this connection, the pneumatological and trinitarian contributions toward a political theology of nature articulated by Peter Scott are deserving of consideration.[75] After exploring various contemporary proposals for a green politics such as deep ecology (a philosophical posture that views humankind not only as integral to nature but perhaps no more than equal to if not subordinate in value to other forms of life), ecofeminism (a reaction to patriarchal and androcentric approaches to nature via the emphasis on the reproductive powers of the environment), social ecology (which links ecological problems with social problems and advocates a radically democratic and egalitarian solution in both domains), and socialist ecology (which sees global capitalism as the root cause of environmental degradation and proposes a Marxist socialism of the commons in its place), Scott turns to a specifically theological consideration. His overarching framework is the trinitarian nature of God, within which the three major interlocking theses are: 1) an incarnational theology that provides for a cosmic and holistic view of God in relationship to the world; 2) a pneumatology of fellowship that emphasizes the sociality and solidarity of humanity within its wider environment; and 3) a trinitarian eschatology that understands human nature ultimately as neither natural (i.e., dependent wholly on nature) nor unnatural (independent of nature) but rather interlaced with the God of the crucified and resurrected Jesus Christ.[76] In short, paradoxically, nature is both central (now) but yet dispensable (eschatologically) for theological anthropology and political theology.

My interests, however, lie specifically in the pneumatological threads of Scott's political theology. An ecological pneumatology suggests, for Scott, that social relations are ecologically embedded. Thus the communion that is of the Holy Spirit (2 Cor. 13:13) invites re-envisioning a fellowship of all flesh in a way that binds humankind with all forms of creaturely and environmental life. Thus emerges a theological (specifically: pneumatological) justification for a "democracy of the commons" that values diversity within the common "space" that is the ecosphere, and that recognizes different forms of "agency" exercised within the biosphere that must be respected and properly

---

75. Peter Scott, *A Political Theology of Nature* (Cambridge: Cambridge University Press, 2003).

76. These three theses are argued in the last three chapters (part 3) of Scott's *Political Theology of Nature*.

negotiated by human beings.[77] Practically, such a political theology questions the stewardship model because of its tendency toward a domination and managerial approach to the environment. Theologically, however, Scott notes that "the Spirit's actions are eschatological actions," and as such they "renew the varied and variable social relations between humanity and nature and enable their fuller openness" to God's future.[78] In other words, the world considered as the fellowship of all flesh and as a democracy of the commons invites the revaluation of all things as having particular and unique contributions to make toward a shalomic environment of the coming kingdom.

Scott's project is motivated by the conviction that the Christian contribution to addressing the current ecological crisis can be accomplished only by a worldview transformation that rethinks nature in a theological key. Only then can we liberate ourselves from the dis-grace-ful habits and dispositions vis-à-vis our natural environment. In other words, the problem is not scientific but social and, more specifically, theological. Thus a theological revisioning is required in order to overcome the alienation not only between God and the world but also between humanity and its cosmic environment.

Elsewhere I have called attention to charismatic movements in the global south that are leading the way toward a liberative ecological praxis.[79] I am thinking here of what might be called the "green pentecostalism" of African independent charismatic churches like those included in the Association of African Earthkeeping Churches (AAECs) partnership.[80] These AAECs have implemented eucharistic liturgies that acknowledge the interconnections of human life with the natural resources of the biosphere; have developed tree-planting ceremonies to combat the deforestation and desertification of their environments; and have sought out alliances with NGOs and other environmentally conscious groups to address pressing issues of wildlife conservation and protection of water resources.[81] More precisely, there is the

77. Scott, *A Political Theology of Nature*, pp. 222-25.

78. Scott, *A Political Theology of Nature*, pp. 204-5.

79. See Yong, *The Spirit Poured Out on All Flesh*, pp. 61-64, and the literature cited there.

80. Other grassroots environmental movements in the global south are described by Stephen B. Scharper, *Redeeming the Time: A Political Theology of the Environment* (New York: Continuum, 1997), chap. 6.

81. For details, see M. L. Daneel, "African Independent Church Pneumatology and the Salvation of All Creation," *International Review of Mission* 82, no. 326 (1993): 143-66, reprinted in Harold D. Hunter and Peter D. Hocken, eds., *All Together in One Place: Theological Papers from the Brighton Conference on World Evangelization* (Sheffield: Sheffield Academic Press, 1993), pp. 96-126.

recognition that the Spirit who hovered over the primordial creation is the same Spirit who preserves and renews the face of the earth and will bring the world to its consummation. In short, the AAECs provide a practicable model for thinking about a pneumatological theology of the environment that avoids both the otherworldliness of dispensationalism and the (mere) this-worldliness of some green and Gaia eco-philosophies.

What I am proposing, in other words, is a pneumatological eschatology that emphasizes the apocalyptic revelation of the Spirit rather than demolition of the world. The outpouring of the Spirit in these last days is thus at least in part a response to the groanings of creation and its creatures, even at the very ends of the earth. More precisely, it is the Spirit who groans within us, enabling what is otherwise our incapacity to pray and hope for the final redemption of our bodies, and who works within and through us, empowering what is otherwise our inability to participate in the eschatological liberation of all creation that has been cursed by the Fall (Rom. 8:19-27). In this final renewal, a pneumatological and apocalyptic theology of the environment would speak of the revelatory and redemptive work of the Spirit not only in culture, society, and the economy — each of which interfaces with human activities and policies that concern the environment — but also vis-à-vis the principalities and powers that have to do with the various orders of creation.

8.3. Many Tongues Anticipating the Final Consummation: Living an Eschatological Politics of Hope

This final section will pursue a slightly different course than the concluding sections of the previous four chapters. Whereas the others have focused on sketching a biblical, practical, and theological framework for addressing the topic of that chapter, the following seeks to provide a pneumatological eschatology within which to address not only the political issues raised in this chapter but also those that have emerged throughout the volume. We will still begin with some exegetical considerations from the book of Acts, but then turn to explicate how such eschatological considerations have performative implications for Christian engagements with the political, and conclude with an overview of how such an eschatological imagination compares and contrasts with other parallel proposals. Our driving question in the rest of this book, however, is what difference being an eschatological people of the Spirit makes for political theology and Christian praxis in the public square.

8.3.1. "Times of Refreshing" from the Lord:
A Lukan Glimpse of the Universal Restoration

The Petrine (and Lukan) claim that the Spirit has been poured out on all flesh in the last days denotes that the time for the restoration of Israel is at hand, and that "everyone who calls on the name of the Lord shall be saved" (Acts 2:21). So far, I have presumed that such a Lukan eschatology is both Jewish and ecclesial, both present and future, and both now/already and not-yet — but I have not done much to defend this assumption. More comment is needed especially in light of Hans Conzelmann's effectively taking the study of Lukan theology to another whole level a generation ago precisely by arguing that the Lukan account was a salvation history narrative intended to address the disappointments regarding the delay of the Parousia.[82] If Conzelmann's resolution was to read Luke as re-directing belief in the imminent return of Christ to the hope for a future resurrection,[83] the alternative responses might either insist that Luke promulgated a realized eschatology of some sort or that there remains a future dimension of judgment and resurrection, with both proleptically anticipated in Jesus.[84]

I would think instead that a proper response would reject the available disjunctions — either realized or not, either eschatology or salvation history — and emphasize instead that with Jesus, in the Lukan view, "the end time, new age of salvation had broken into this world."[85] This allows not merely for the maintenance of the already-but-not-yet tension, but also invites a living out of an eschatological faith in a way that links the gospel's "eschatological claims with one's present manner of life."[86] Such a reading is more faithful to

82. Hans Conzelmann, *The Theology of St. Luke,* trans. Geoffrey Buswell (1961; reprint, Philadelphia: Fortress, 1982), esp. pp. 131-32.

83. On this interpretation, fairly widespread among Lukan scholars at the time that Conzelmann wrote, Luke "is required by practical conditions to correct the over-expectant attitude by emphasizing the delay that was to be expected"; see Henry J. Cadbury, "Acts and Eschatology," in W. D. Davies and D. Daube, eds., *The Background of the New Testament and Its Eschatology: In Honour of Charles Harold Dodd* (Cambridge: Cambridge University Press, 1964), pp. 300-321, at p. 320.

84. F. F. Bruce, "Eschatology in Acts," in W. Hulitt Gloer, ed., *Eschatology and the New Testament: Essays in Honor of George Raymond Beasley-Murray* (Peabody, MA: Hendrickson, 1988), pp. 51-63.

85. J. Bradley Chance, *Jerusalem, the Temple, and the New Age in Luke-Acts* (Macon, GA: Mercer University Press, 1988), pp. 3-4. I should note that Chance sees much more of a role for both Jerusalem and the Temple in the future dimension of Luke's eschatology than might be suggested, for example, in Acts 7:44-50; cf. my *The Holy Spirit and the Public Square* [working title] (Brewster, MA: Paraclete Press, forthcoming), chap. 16.

86. John T. Carroll, *Response to the End of History: Eschatology and Situation in Luke-Acts,* SBL Dissertation Series 92 (Atlanta: Scholars Press, 1988), p. 167.

the Lukan vision, which rejects any speculation about Parousia and the final redemption (Acts 1:6-7) while simultaneously exhorting its hearers and readers to respond to the present moment when and where past history and the coming future are interrelated.[87] It is in such a framework that I approach Peter's proclamation: "Repent therefore, and turn to God so that your sins may be wiped out, so that times of refreshing may come from the presence of the Lord, and that he may send the Messiah appointed for you, that is, Jesus, who must remain in heaven until the time of cosmic restoration that God announced long ago through his holy prophets" (3:19-21).

This declaration occurs in Peter's sermon following the healing of the lame man at the Beautiful Gate (7.3.1). In the following, I elucidate the eschatological elements of this text at four levels: that of the healing of the body, that of the restoration of Israel, that of the renewal of the Jubilee economy, and that of the redemption of the world and of all things. First, the context of this assertion is Peter's sermon in response to the crowd that was "filled with wonder and amazement at what had happened" to the lame man (3:10). Peter said "the faith that is through Jesus has given him this perfect health in the presence of all of you" (3:16). As Jesus' healings of the sick by the power of the Spirit were signs of the coming kingdom (7.3.1), so also the Spirit's healing of the lame man through Peter and John's mediation of the name of Jesus was a sign of the "last days." It turned out that the (formerly) lame man stayed with Peter and John even through the night in prison,[88] but this did not deter the apostles from insisting the next day that the man who remained in their midst provided an indubitable witness to the healing and saving power of Jesus' name (4:9-12). In short, the healing of the man crippled from birth was a sign that the power of the Spirit was present and that the beginning of the end of the age had dawned.

Second, the healing of the lame man occurred at the Temple and at a time of prayer (3:1),[89] and Peter's post-healing sermon was given in Solomon's Portico and address to his fellow Israelites (3:11-12). The sermon fur-

---

87. Anders E. Nielsen, *Until It Is Fulfilled: Lukan Eschatology according to Luke 22 and Acts 20*, Wissenschaftliche Untersuchungen zum Neuen Testament 2.126 (Tübingen: Mohr Siebeck, 2000), 280; see also Nielsen's discussion in chap. 6.

88. See Norm Mundhenk, "The Invisible Man (Acts 4.9-10)," *The Bible Translator* 57, no. 4 (2006): 203-6.

89. I should note that Chance, *Jerusalem, the Temple, and the New Age in Luke-Acts,* sees much more of a role for both Jerusalem and the Temple in the future dimension of Luke's eschatology than might be suggested, for example, in Acts 7:44-50. My reading is that the eschatological rebuilding of the Temple itself is not as significant for Luke's theology of Israel's final restoration. See Yong, *The Holy Spirit and the Public Square,* chap. 16.

ther includes references to the "God of Abraham, the God of Isaac, and the God of Jacob, the God of our ancestors" (3:13), links the miraculous healing and prophetic ministry of Jesus with that of Moses (3:22), warns that "everyone who does not listen to that prophet will be utterly rooted out from the people" (3:23), and specifically invites the repentance of the audience in order that they might experience the full restoration promised by the ancient prophets. There is no reason to bifurcate Israel from the church (as does dispensationalism) in this scenario, to think that the invitation extended to Israel's repentance has been withdrawn, or to read this only as applying to the specific historical circumstances surrounding the healing of the lame man. Instead, there is every reason in the pentecostal this-is-that hermeneutic (3.1.1) to view this call to repentance as an open-ended one extended to Israel in celebration of the healing of the crippled man and in anticipation of the nation's full restoration. As Dennis Hamm suggests, "Luke's paraenetic point is: repent and enter the times of refreshment already come upon us, for that is the view of the remainder of Acts regarding the opportunity of the Jews."[90]

Third, however, note that the promised "times of refreshing" are connected with the forgiveness of sins (3:19), which in the immediate context has to do not only with the individual sins of the audience but with the corporate sins of Israel for its role in putting Jesus to death (3:14-15).[91] But the forgiveness of sins had earlier been linked with baptism — now understandable as an eschatological sacrament — and the gift of the Holy Spirit (2:38), and we already know that the last-days outpouring of the Spirit had begun to usher in "the Lord's great and glorious day" (2:20), and that, in turn, was a sign of the arrival of the "year of the Lord's favor" (Luke 4:19) and of the age of Jubilee (7.3.1). Another clue that invites an equation of the times of Jubilee with the healing of the crippled man is that while Peter and John have neither silver nor gold (Acts 3:6) they are conduits of the eschatological power of the Spirit to "proclaim release to the captives and . . . let the oppressed go free" (Luke 4:18). Finally, the reference to the healed man "walking and leaping and praising God" (3:8) alludes to the messianic promises of the coming age when "the lame shall leap like a deer, and the tongue of the speechless sing for joy" (Isa. 35:6).[92] I would thus agree with Göran Lennartsson that the promised

90. Dennis Hamm, "Acts 3:12-26: Peter's Speech and the Healing of the Man Born Lame," *Perspectives in Religious Studies* 11, no. 3 (1984): 199-217, quote from p. 208.

91. C. K. Barrett, "Faith and Eschatology in Acts 3," in Erich Grässer and Otto Merk, eds., *Glaube und Eschatologie: Festschrift für Werner Georg Kümmel zum 80. Geburtstag* (Tübingen: J. C. B. Mohr, 1985), pp. 1-17, esp. p. 10.

92. See further Dennis Hamm, "Acts 3,1-10: The Healing of the Temple Beggar as Lucan Theology," *Biblica* 67, no. 3 (1986): 305-19.

restoration is the messianic era that can be "viewed both as an 'extended Sabbath', and the release of Jubilee."[93] In other words, the pneumatological apocalyptic (unveiling) amidst these winds of refreshing bring about not the end-times economic upheaval and devastation anticipated in dispensationalism, but the eschatological shalom of the people of God.

Finally, then, I suggest that Peter's invitation to repentance is not limited to Israel. Rather, the promised "times of refreshing" are interconnected with the "time of universal restoration" that will envelop both the gentiles and the creation as a whole. The latter cosmic restoration is what I am primarily interested in here. The Isaiah passage alluded to regarding the leaping man refers not only to the lame leaping like deer but also to the revitalization of creation itself:

> For waters shall break forth in the wilderness,
>   and streams in the desert;
> the burning sand shall become a pool,
>   and the thirsty ground springs of water;
> the haunt of jackals shall become a swamp,
>   the grass shall become reeds and rushes.
>
> (Isa. 35:6b-7)[94]

In other words, the "universal restoration" will involve the renewal of all creation, including (as I have already suggested — 4.3.1) its principalities and powers. The Spirit who now groans in and through the creation for relief and redemption will then be given to bring about the refreshment and rest of the messianic age.[95]

Such a universal restoration does not, however, result in any simplistic doctrine of universalism. Rather, these eschatological contentions are best considered subjunctively, with their fulfillment hinging upon the response of free creatures. Thus, the Petrine call to repentance establishes one of the primary contingencies related to the universalistic hope. But if from the perspective of stubborn and hard-hearted humanity there is no hope for either the restoration of Israel or for the redemption of the world, then from the view of the miraculous (even if subjunctively understood) outpouring of the

---

93. Göran Lennartsson, *Refreshing and Restoration: Two Eschatological Motifs in Acts 3:19-21* (Lund: Lund University Centre for Theology and Religious Studies, 2007), p. 226.

94. The context is the messianic restoration of Israel from exile; see Geoffrey W. Grogan, "Isaiah," in Frank E. Gaebelein, gen. ed., *The Expositor's Bible Commentary*, 12 vols. (Grand Rapids: Regency Reference Library/Zondervan, 1985), vol. 6, pp. 1-354, at p. 221.

95. W. Robert Shade III, "The Restoration of Israel in Acts 3:12-26 and Lukan Eschatology" (Ph.D. diss., Trinity Evangelical Divinity School, 1994), pp. 153-57.

Spirit upon all flesh, "What is impossible for mortals is possible for God" (Luke 18:27).

8.3.2. Performing Political Eschatologies: Theology and the Public Square between Now and Not Yet

But while political *theology* affirms God's power to save, *political* theology insists that human beings take responsibility for their lives in the public square. Thus Christians can be hopeful about what the "God who is at work in [them]" can and will do to redeem the political arena, but yet also recognize they must "work out [their] own salvation with fear and trembling" in the public domain (Phil. 2:12). Thus Peter's response to the incident at the Beautiful Gate confirms that it is the power of God in the person and name of Jesus Christ that is responsible for the healing of the man; but simultaneously, the healing inspires a sermon that functions illocutionarily as an invitation to repentance. Thus there is a performative dimension to this narrative at least at three levels: 1) theologically, the healing is a work of the Holy Spirit that demonstrates the lordship of Christ; 2) apostolically, the healing confirms the leadership of Peter and John as representatives of Christ who can neither refrain doing what they have been empowered to do nor "keep from speaking about what [they] have seen and heard" (Acts 4:20); and 3) in terms of Christian discipleship, the healing and its sermon are invitations to repent for the forgiveness of sins and to receive the Holy Spirit and the times of refreshing from the presence of God.[96]

From this, I want to insist that eschatological doctrines are not merely beliefs about what will happen in the future, but are also orientations for Christian practice in the present.[97] If people really believed that God has promised times of refreshing and that a time of universal and cosmic restoration is coming, then they will live appropriately, with repentant hearts, out of Christ-like obedience, and in docility to the Spirit whose outpouring on all flesh signals the beginning of these last days. This means doing the things that Jesus did, not out of ordinary human effort but, as he did, in the power of the

96. What I am calling the performative aspect of this passage is explicated by Donald H. Juel, "Hearing Peter's Speech in Acts 3: Meaning and Truth in Interpretation," *Word and World* 12 (1992): 43-50, in terms that explore the contemporary meaning and application of the ancient text.

97. For more discussion of the performative dimension of eschatological assertions, see my *Theology and Down Syndrome: Reimagining Disability in Late Modernity* (Waco, TX: Baylor University Press, 2007), chap. 9

Spirit, in order to proclaim and herald the coming kingdom. The Christian hope, in other words, is not merely about a future restoration, but about the present gift of the Spirit who draws us into the history of Jesus wherein we meet the God who is to come.

To temper the various tendencies of a dispensationalistically influenced worldview that has been imbibed not only in pentecostal circles but across a large swath of contemporary global Christianity, let me propose the following aspects of an apophatic eschatology for performative consideration. With regard to the interpretation of Revelation, I prefer neither a preterist reading that limits the significance of the book to the first century nor a futurist rendition that locates its relevance in a dispensationalist scheme of things; this apophaticism opens up a "middle space" or "betwixt-and-between temporality" that allows the letter to the Seven Churches to be understood as formative for Christian faith amidst a world that is both passing away and yet in the process of being sanctified and redeemed by the apocalyptic Spirit. With regard to the eschatological this-worldly or otherworldly disjunction, I reject either a fully realized stance or an escapist mentality; further, I also refuse both terms of the dilemma, favoring instead the paradoxical tension of living on the one hand as if "the kingdom of God is among [us]" (Luke 17:21) and on the other hand awaiting Jesus "who must remain in heaven until the time of universal restoration" (Acts 3:21). Finally, with regard to the good-versus-evil dualism and apocalypticism that pits "us" against "them" in the last days, I insist that 1) "No one is good but God alone" (Luke 18:19); 2) that none of us can presume to bring about "the times or periods that the Father has set by his own authority" (Acts 1:7); and 3) that it is not for us to determine either who is the "them" that are the enemies of God, or how "they" are to be opposed with our earthly weapons, often of mass destruction (see 4.3.3). Instead, the famous quote of the comic-strip character, Pogo, "We have met the enemy and he is us,"[98] can be seen as anticipated theologically in St. Paul's saying, "all have sinned and fall short of the glory of God" (Rom. 3:23), so any further division between "us" and "them" is both politically and theologically incorrect.

In light of these apophatic guideposts, what then can we affirm about the performance of our theologies in the public square in our present time, which is between the times of incarnation/Pentecost and the cosmic restoration? In one respect, the "answer" to this question has already been given at various junctures in the preceding chapters. The gift of the Spirit means that

98. See Walt Kelly, *Pogo: We Have Met the Enemy and He Is Us* (New York: Simon & Schuster, 1972).

the Day of Pentecost inaugurated an eschatological people of God consisting of Jews and gentiles, and that this new people embodies an alternative *polis,* enacts a counter-cultural way of life, is constituted by contrasting social values and practices, and lives out of the shalomic generosity of sharing and mutuality. Thus the church's liturgical imagination enables its eschatological performance in the public square as a people of prayer, praise, worship, sacraments, and even exorcism — all of which combine to bear witness to the powers of the way of the cross in anticipation of cosmic restoration and rehabilitation to come. Further, the church's sanctified and pneumatological imaginations empower a vocational mission to the world, prophetically resisting its fallen tendencies and boldly witnessing to the redemptive possibilities available to human culture and civic and social life. Finally, the church's charismatic imagination seeks to participate in the gracious hospitality of God so that the many gifts of the Spirit can unleash an economy of shalom that yearns and works for the reconciliation of all, seeks a just, common, and environmentally sustainable way of life, and anticipates the renewal of the ends of the earth, all of creation, perhaps even the cosmos itself. In each of these ways, the church is already living out a pneumatologically inspired eschatological imagination in the public square, patiently enduring the challenges of this time betwixt-and-between, but also urgently hastening the blessed hope of Jesus, the Messiah, whose coming from heaven will restore and renew the world.

8.3.3. The Eschatological Imagination: Toward a Political Theology of Suffering and Hope

In effect, the eschatological imagination with which we are concluding is an ancient notion, not only in the Lukan sense, but also in its Augustinian rendition. Recall that many chapters ago, we looked at St. Augustine's *City of God* for clues to how the church negotiated its new public character after the onset of Christendom (see 2.1.3). The two cities conception alerted us to the role of demonology in relationship to the earthly city as well as highlighted the role of the church as the eschatologically present and yet future *polis* in God's providential scheme of things. While we then took (in chapter 4) the demonological notions in a somewhat different trajectory than did the Bishop of Hippo, the rest of our constructive argument in Part II has basically adopted the Augustinian insight regarding the church as an instantiation and yet foreshadowing of a divine politics in the present course of history. As an eschatological reality, the church lives out a specific desire, one directed toward union with the triune God, which shapes the ecclesial city along the way of Jesus. In these final pages, I want to return to this Augustinian notion in dialogue with two contemporary readers and interpreters of this patristic theologian of the political.

Kristen Johnson has recently reminded us of the Augustinian resources that can be brought to bear on the difficult challenges in contemporary political theology regarding tolerance, difference, and peace.[99] In a fallen world, differences seem inevitably to perpetuate antagonistic conflict, polarizations, and binary oppositions. Liberal democracies, on the other hand, have insisted on the need for toleration, but these in turn have either turned out to be bland accommodations or resulted in further sectarian formulations of identity politics. It is in this context that Johnson — in a move reminiscent of and also explicitly in dialogue with the Radically Orthodox theologian John Milbank (6.2.1) at various places — retrieves Augustine, especially his contrasting of the Earthly and Heavenly cities, and his emphasis on the Heavenly City as alone capable of ushering in the peace that preserves difference amidst harmony. As this is the kingdom of peace, hope, and love based on the reign of God in Christ, the Earthly City can anticipate the true justice, peace, order, and harmony of the kingdom only via a reordering of lives "through participation in God through Jesus Christ and Christ's body, the Church."[100]

What does this Augustinian recovery mean for contemporary political theology? It means first the recognition that the present "political realm is . . . a providential provision for life in a fallen, divided world," and that therefore the goal is a minimalist one of "recovering a hope that our pluralist society can be marked by an ethos of rich, hospitable, and loving interaction among its differences."[101] What emerges, then, is a political theology of dialogue and conversation, but Johnson wants to move beyond mere toleration toward humble persuasion and even conversion. Yet theologically speaking, such a conversational posture cannot be nurtured apart from the Augustinian conviction regarding the temporal character of political engagement. Such a theological stance, then, has the role of "reminding the earthly city to limit its ambitions and be realistic about its aspirations."[102]

The dynamic and eschatological horizon that informs Johnson's theology of public dialogue is to be commended. Yet, Johnson does not directly address the question raised by Kuyper (2.2.3) about the prelapsarian, and there-

---

99. Kristen Deede Johnson, *Theology, Political Theory, and Pluralism: Beyond Tolerance and Difference* (Cambridge: Cambridge University Press, 2007).

100. Johnson, *Theology, Political Theory, and Pluralism*, p. 172.

101. Johnson, *Theology, Political Theory, and Pluralism*, pp. 26-27.

102. Johnson, *Theology, Political Theory, and Pluralism*, p. 185.

fore also eschatological, nature of the political dimension, nor does she press the question about whether the provisional nature of the political pertains solely to its current (fallen) form or to the nature of a public mode of being as a whole (which Kuyper argued would persist, in its redeemed version, even in the world to come). More pertinent for our purposes, however, is that while Johnson's goal of moving beyond a bland and undiscriminating toleration toward a more vigorous but yet civil dialogical engagement is to be endorsed, her recuperation of Augustine's ecclesiology is rather thin, resulting in a less comprehensive vision of the church as *polis*. Complementing and even extending Johnson's reclamation of Augustine along these lines is the work of Charles Mathewes.

Mathewes's focus is on a theology of public life more broadly conceived than a political theology of statecraft or of dialogue.[103] In dialogue with Augustine throughout, Mathewes argues for a theology of public engagement that "includes a more concrete ascetical spirituality and ecclesiology of public life, which are manifest in and reinforced by a set of concrete practices, 'spiritual' and otherwise. Such a theology is well described as a normative ethnography of religious practices. . . . Endurance is the crux of this proposal; it embodies the overall practice, the ascesis, that anchors this 'theology of public life.'"[104] The ecclesiological and eschatological dimensions of Mathewes's proposal are noteworthy. His politics of endurance, for example, presumes that selves are fundamentally *sufferers*, more passive recipients of the gifts of others, than active agents;[105] in this anthropological framework, the ecclesial and public domains both include, albeit in different respects, the plenitude and gifts of divine love that shape human persons from the beginning so that they are formed through participation. Ecclesial life, more specifically, is "proleptic communion" that forms us for public engagement precisely through enabling us to glimpse and participate, "through Christ in the divine *perichōrēsis* that is our ultimate destiny."[106]

Such an ecclesially and eschatologically shaped life prepares us for public citizenship that avoids agonistic conflict, in part through recognition of the provisionality rather than ultimacy of public life. But Mathewes goes further than Johnson on this point by arguing, following Augustine, that political life is "endless" in the sense that it has no historical goal (otherwise it becomes idolatrous), and seeks none. The result is that such an Augustinian

---

103. Charles T. Mathewes, *A Theology of Public Life* (Cambridge: Cambridge University Press, 2007).

104. Mathewes, *A Theology of Public Life*, p. 10.

105. See Mathewes, *A Theology of Public Life*, p. 75.

106. Mathewes, *A Theology of Public Life*, p. 129.

notion of public citizenship "makes politics proleptic play" through which "faith is revealed to be a matter of enduring; and faith engaged in public is a particularly pronounced site for such endurance."[107] Instead of a heaven-oriented eschatology translating into an escapist apocalypticism, Mathewes writes of how "a vision of life that is so fundamentally eschatological can also be so profoundly pro-creation as to shape a distinctive and powerful form of public engagement — yet a form of caring about the world that might not make 'the world' fully comfortable."[108] What this means is that the church engages the public domain not by accommodating to its ways and habits, but by living in a way so that "the public sphere itself becomes the forum for an ascetical inquiry that it cannot itself, in this dispensation, comprehend."[109]

What is missing in Augustine, Johnson, and Mathewes is a more robustly pneumatological articulation of the church as an eschatological body politic. On this point, Reinhard Hütter, whom Mathewes cites only once (with regard to Hütter's critique of Milbank instead), has provided a pneumatological ecclesiology that could deepen the specifically theological dimensions of Mathewes's politics of endurance. Hütter emphasizes the poetic and artistic agency of the Holy Spirit in forming and shaping an eschatological people of God, and views such a people as *pathically constituted* through participation in the charismatic gifts of the Spirit as mediated through the life and practices of the church.[110] Such a pneumatological conception, I suggest, is more eminently capable of highlighting the character of divine agency even in the public domain as well as preserving the eschatological nature of Johnson's theology of public conversation and Mathewes's theology of public citizenship amidst the signs of the "last days," thus anticipating the full payment of the Spirit that is to come.

It is such a pneumatological theology, I proffer, that provides not only an eschatological politics to redress the politics of dispensationalism, Zionism, and apocalypticism prevalent in the Christian world, but also to supplement and even structure the political theology, theology of culture and society, and theology of economics that we have unfolded in the previous chapters. Intuiting from the Petrine claim that the Spirit has been poured out on all flesh in the last days allows us to go beyond fundamentalist and dispensational eschatology to focus on the church's proleptic anticipation of the in-

---

107. Mathewes, *A Theology of Public Life*, pp. 192 and 213.

108. Mathewes, *A Theology of Public Life*, p. 309.

109. Mathewes, *A Theology of Public Life*, p. 260.

110. See Reinhard Hütter, *Suffering Divine Things: Theology as Church Practice*, trans. Doug Stott (Grand Rapids, and Cambridge, UK: Eerdmans, 2000). For my own interaction with Hütter's ideas, see Yong, *Hospitality and the Other*, pp. 59-61.

breaking kingdom of the Spirit.[111] History and the cosmos now become the site and even field of the Spirit's eschatological activity, and those upon whom the Spirit has been given now cry out for the kingdom and pathically live out a political theology of suffering and hope.

111. This is the argument also of pentecostal theologian Peter Althouse, "'Left Behind' — Fact or Fiction: Ecumenical Dilemmas of the Fundamentalist Millenarian Tensions within Pentecostalism," *Journal of Pentecostal Theology* 13, no. 2 (2005): 187-207.

Epilogue

I began this book with a testimony of how I came onto the topic. The preceding discussion provides a glimpse of how I have wrestled with the intersection of pentecostalism and political theology over the last two years. And while my original goals in writing this book were threefold — to contest stereotypes of apolitical pentecostalism for both insiders and those outside the pentecostal movement; to urge my fellow pentecostal colleagues and readers to think further about the political; and to contribute to the broader ecumenical and academic discussion of political theology — the writing process itself has enlarged my theological vision. Thus I have proposed a pentecostal and ecumenical ecclesiology, soteriology, and christology, albeit each interpreted in a political (public) key. We have covered much ground, and all along I have felt that part of my task was to be an interpreter of many tongues — the many tongues of pentecostalism and the many other tongues of political theology — across a divide that so far has seen few bridges or crossings.[1] I can only hope that these interpretations are also followed by "cross-cultural" understanding, as the discourses of pentecostalism and of political theology may indeed be thought of as strange tongues to the uninitiated. Perhaps others will come along and further interpret the various discourses in order to correct, supplement, and expand what has been offered here.

Yet I must also say that at this juncture, I have concluded that pentecostalism is much more political than I would have ever imagined —

---

1. Elsewhere, I have further developed this notion of interdisciplinarity using the "many tongues" metaphor of Luke; see Yong, "Academic Glossolalia? Pentecostal Scholarship, Multi-Disciplinarity, and the Science-Religion Conversation," *Journal of Pentecostal Theology* 14, no. 1 (2005): 63-82.

actually in terms of the many interfaces between pentecostalism and the political that we have covered, and potentially in terms of the kind of political impact that global pentecostalism can have, if such were intentionally sought. I do think that given the "state of the discussion" in political theology about the central role of the church as an alternative *polis,* pentecostalism at its best highlights such an ecclesial counter-politics in action around the world; but I also now know that all too often, pentecostalism does not live up to but instead betrays the ideals of the gospel in a complicated political world. Yet these triumphs and failures are not unique to pentecostalism either.

What I mean is that, when we look at the history of Christianity and the public square, we see cyclical replays of similar tendencies and developments. The earliest followers of the Way were neither political nor apolitical, even if collusive in some respects with the status quo while challenging the conventions of their time in other respects; these latter traits, however, invite assessment of the "political theology" of the early church in terms of its being an alternative *polis.* Yet the later emergence of Christendom also brought forth multiple interpretations, ranging across the spectrum from the church being compromised by the seductions of empire (Yoder et al.) to the church valiantly wrestling with the proper means to carry out its missionary mandate amidst changing socio-cultural-religious and demographic circumstances (O'Donovan) (see 2.1.3). Monastic and revival movements across the centuries have experienced similar trajectories of development: beginning by modeling an alternative form of life in contrast to the prevailing options of their age but oftentimes, after having institutionalized or "come of age" socially and culturally, eventually blending in to the broader Christian tradition. Similarly, early pentecostalism embraced a primitivist "this-is-that" hermeneutic and modeled itself after the apostolic experience, in the process being labeled as sectarian and fundamentalistic in its disavowal of taking responsibility for life in the public square. The later and more recent explosion of pentecostalism as the dominant form of world Christianity, however, has brought forth other criticisms: that it has been co-opted by a conservative political ideology or that it has uncritically embraced the mechanisms of the neoliberal market economy, etc.

Warts and all, then, pentecostalism's alleged apolitical posture may represent its halting efforts to be the church, to live as faithful witnesses to the risen Christ, and to engage the public square in some senses on its own Christian terms rather than on terms set by the "world." I hope it is clear from the above that I am far from presenting pentecostalism as irreproachable (what historical instantiation of Christian faith is spotless and without blame?); but at the same time, I am also suggesting that the concrete politics and public presence and activity of pentecostalism have much to contribute to the church ecumenical in terms not only of beliefs but also of practices. Of course, any dialogue goes in two directions: I think it is also clear from the preceding that I expect (and hope) pentecostals to be open to receiving the gifts of the church ecumenical — and this not limited to post-Constantinian theological movements, Radical Orthodoxy, or the Catholic Social Teaching tradition, etc. — since we need all the help we can get to make our way through the complex maze that is the field wherein Christianity and the public square overlap. The challenge, arguably, is for pentecostal Christianity in particular and for the church ecumenical in general to somehow retain, over the course of the twists-and-turns that mark the processes of growth, expansion, and institutionalization, the counter-political, counter-cultural, and counter-economic posture of the founding communities so as to be capable of not only speaking prophetically to the world but also of modeling a viable and alternative form of life in the footsteps of the Messiah, as empowered by the Holy Spirit.

How then do we summarize the gains of this "dialogue" between pentecostalism and the broader Christian tradition of political theology as we look toward the future? Theologically, I suggest that the diversity of political theologies is fundamentally shaped by the resources of the primordial Christian tradition, which is capable of funding a plurality of interpretations. The pentecostal fivefold gospel thus encapsulates a multifaceted christology correlated with a multi-stranded soteriology and ecclesiology — all of which, I have argued, are viable expressions of the many tongues of the Spirit given on the Day of Pentecost. Generalized from but yet remaining deeply informed by this pentecostal hermeneutical matrix, then, I have proposed an equally versatile political theology for the contemporary Christian engagement with the public square featuring a multiplicity of imaginative stances or postures:

- a liturgical imagination that lives out of the resources of the worshiping community before God and his angels and in deference to the principalities and powers, but yet simultaneously not merely acquiescing to the political mechanisms of the latter but rather participating in the redemption of the re-enchanted cosmopolis as enacted by the salvation-history events of the triune God
- a sanctified imagination that embodies the counter-cultural, exilic, and diasporic way of Jesus the Messiah that desires and longs for the beauty of divine holiness, but yet concurrently, as resident aliens in the earthly city, anticipates and works for the redemption of languages, the reformation of cultures, and the renewal of the world

- a pneumatological imagination that bears prophetic and contextually sensitive witness to the many faces of Jesus the Christ through many Spirit-inspired and -empowered speech acts, but nevertheless in the process reveals to civil society the possibility of a flourishing mode of interaction that reflects the diversity and harmony of God's primordial creation of all things and of the Spirit's redemptive outpouring upon all flesh and every sphere of human life between the individual and the state
- a charismatic imagination that unleashes the many gift(s) of the Spirit designed for the edification of the body of Christ and the people of God so that they might accomplish the saving and healing work of God through the formation of various levels of subsidiary communities of solidarity, peace, and justice that work jointly through the Spirit's orchestration for the good of the commonwealth of creation in anticipation of the shalom of the coming kingdom
- an eschatological imagination that suffers (passively) joyfully the down-payment of the Spirit's in-breaking from the future that pours out the refreshing reign of God in the present, but yet works (actively) energetically to participate in the Spirit's work for the universal restoration of Jews, for the redemption of gentiles, and for the renewal of the various orders of creation.

As should be clear, none of these are frontal "assaults" or approaches to the political; rather they are tactically indirect, engaging the public square through spiritual, cultural, civic, economic, and socio-historical modalities of being church. Yet, as I have argued throughout, the impact of these strategies may be more profound than most explicit interactions with the state. But even at the end of this long book, the proposals presented here are surely no more than programmatic hints for further thinking about a pneumatological theology of the political, of culture, of civil society, of economics, and of history. My hope is that the preceding pages signal the potential of a political theology whose central thesis is that the Spirit poured out on all flesh enables the thriving of many political practices, each animated by one of the many tongues of the Spirit in order to bear witness to the wondrous redemption of God in the many nations, tribes, peoples, and cities of the world.

But I also must insist in these transitional reflections that the thesis of many tongues and many political practices is not relativistic in the nihilistic sense. This is not relativism as a functional or pragmatic approach to political pluralism, but is instead a deeply contextual approach that requires discerning the presence and activity of the Spirit in the public square according to the normative image of Jesus as revealing the shalom of God. This means that pentecostalism in particular and the church ecumenical in general must be discerning about the forces of empire — in their political, cultural, civic-societal, economic, historical, and environmental dimensions — to determine when they promote and when they oppose the way of Jesus' shalom. Not all political mechanisms are conducive to the arrival of the kingdom, and hence not all activities in the public square are to be embraced: some will need to be prophetically denounced and actively resisted. What is especially problematic is when the church becomes assimilated to the dominant society because of numeric growth, demographic adaptation, or other reasons, since then she will need to be even more vigilant about discerning when she has been co-opted by the world versus when she is truly participating in the establishment of a more shalomic way of life. In all cases, the principles of solidarity and subsidiarity (7.2.3) impress upon us to think locally in a global world, to act concretely with awareness of wider effects, and to work for the redemption of the particular and to empower the expression of the diversity of tongues in their various contexts. This means that, as Yoder and his Anabaptist colleagues have forcefully reminded us, the church should never get too comfortable with the world, but must instead intentionally seek to live marginally — exilically and diasporically — *within* but not *of* the earthly city. The Wesleyan adage, "get all you can, save all you can, and give all you can,"[2] remains valuable for the purposes of political theology: grow all we can but also divide and reproduce all we can — maybe in the form of Yoido Full Gospel Church's home cell groups (6.1.2) — so that we do not become too big, too impersonal, and too irrelevant to the concrete struggles for healing, reconciliation, wholeness, peace, and justice. Otherwise, the risks of political, cultural, civic, social, and economic accommodation are great, to that point where, like the frog in a boiling pot of water, the church may not awaken to its compromises until it is too late. Even in such cases, however, God may call forth those who will pray for a fresh outpouring of the Spirit of God upon all flesh to renew parched lands and to begin again to restore and redeem the world.

In the end, of course, all theological discourse, whether pentecostal or political, or their combination, is in one sense confessional in terms of bearing witness of what one believes God has done and revealed, and in another

2. More precisely, "Having, First, gained all you can, and, Secondly saved all you can, Then give all you can"; see Wesley's Sermon 50, "The Use of Money," in Albert Cook Outler and Richard P. Heitzenrater, eds., *John Wesley's Sermons: An Anthology* (1984; reprint, Nashville: Abingdon, 1991), pp. 347-57.

sense eschatological in terms of anticipating the day when we shall no longer see through the glass as dimly as we do now (1 Cor. 13:12). Eschatological language thus should be characterized by humility, given that it is never exhaustive or complete; rather, it is partial, provisional, and subject to revision. Yet eschatological language is also a confession of hope — in this case, the hope for the reconciliation of all who have been at odds in the public square, the hope for the redemption of the principalities and powers, and the hope for the universal restoration when Christ returns to receive the world purified by the Spirit's fire. As such, the eschatological language of political theology is stumbling and faltering in its efforts to bear witness to the life in Christ and the power of the Spirit as it ought to be and as it is to come in the kingdom of the Father. Then, the political will be redeemed and the shalom of the triune God will provide the public forum in which all creatures will bear witness in the particularity and peculiarity of their own tongues, to the goodness, truth, and beauty of their Creator. In that day, the kingdom of peace will be among the creatures of God, and each will flourish in relation to the other, in the fellowship of the Spirit, as the body of many tongues, tribes, peoples, and nations constituting the new *polis* amidst the new heavens and earth. In this vein, the last words belong to St. Augustine:

> The important thing is that the seventh will be our Sabbath, whose end will not be an evening, but the Lord's Day, an eighth day, as it were, which is to last for ever, a day consecrated by the resurrection of Christ, foreshadowing the eternal rest not only of the spirit but of the body also. There we shall be still and see; we shall see and we shall love; we shall love and we shall praise. Behold what will be, in the end, without end! For what is our end but to reach that kingdom which has no end?[3]

---

3. St. Augustine, *City of God*, trans. Henry Bettenson, with a new intro. by G. R. Evans (1972; reprint, London and New York: Penguin, 2003), Book XXII, chap. 30, at p. 1091.

Index of Names

Adeboye, Enoch, 270-71
Alexander, Kimberly Ervin, 259n.3, 260n.8
Alexander, Paul, 133n.36, 342n.66
Alighieri, Dante, 60
Allen, Roland, 214-15
Althouse, Peter, 325n.26, 358n.111
Alvarsson, Jan-Åke, 177n.40
Anderson, Allan, 5n.4, 214n.7, 218n.23
Anderson, Robert Mapes, 6n.6, 172n.20
Aquinas, Thomas, 59, 70n.115
Archer, Kenneth J., 91n.18
Aristotle, 51-52, 59, 70n.115
Arnold, Clinton, 145-46, 150, 160
Asamoah-Gyadu, J. Kwabena, 125n.13, 271n.45
Augustine, 52-55, 59, 64, 80, 130n.24, 135, 354, 356-57, 364
Aulén, Gustaf, 122n.1

Bacote, Vincent E., 71n.121
Barker, Isabelle V., 20n.46, 21n.48
Barth, Karl, 65, 137
Bauckham, Richard, 42n.8, 47n.24, 104n.49
Baum, Gregory, 289n.100
Beckford, Robert, 79, 208n.139, 311n.159
Bediako, Kwame, 139n.57
Bell, Daniel M., 231n.70, 248n.124, 284n.79, 339-41

Benedict, St., 194n.101
Berger, Peter L., 21n.48, 287n.93
Bergmann, Sigurd, 344
Berkhof, Hendrikus, 139-40, 143
Bernard, David K., 169n.8
Blumhofer, Edith L., 27n.66, 168n.6, 174n.27, 318n.5
Boniface VII, 58-60
Borg, Marcus J., 197n.110
Bornkamm, Heinrich, 64n.92
Bosworth, F. F., 259, 262
Boyarin, Daniel, 334-37
Boyd, Gregory A., 124n.10
Brady, Bernard V., 279n.66
Branham, William, 260, 262
Bruce, F. F., 241n.108
Brueggemann, Walter, 42, 258n.1
Budde, Michael, 283-84
Bultmann, Rudolf, 146
Butler, Anthea D., 176nn.35, 37

Caird, G. B., 148
Calvin, John, 66-67
Campbell, Colin, 294
Carr, Wesley, 146
Carson, D. A., 200n.115
Carter, A. Craig, 183n.59
Carter, Warren, 44
Cartledge, Mark J., 95n.27
Cassidy, Richard J., 44n.16, 100-101

Index of Subjects

Index of Scripture References

Printed in Great Britain
by Amazon

24955377R00229